DYLAN

a biography

Also by Bob Spitz

THE MAKING OF SUPERSTARS
BAREFOOT IN BABYLON

BOB SPITZ

DYLAN

a biography

With a discography by
Jeff Friedman

W. W. Norton & Company
New York · London

First published as a Norton paperback 1991.

ISBN 0-393-30769-7
ISBN 978-0-393-30769-6

Library of Congress Cataloging-in-Publication Data

Spitz, Bob.
Dylan : a biography / by Bob Spitz.
p. cm.
Includes index.
1. Dylan, Bob, 1941– 2. Singers—United States—Biography.
I. Title.
ML420.D9886 1989
784'.092'4—dc19
[B] 88-12912
CIP
MN

W. W. Norton & Company, Inc.
500 Fifth Avenue, New York, N.Y. 10110
www.wwnorton.com

W. W. Norton & Company Ltd.
Castle House, 75/76 Wells Street, London W1T 3QT

7 8 9 10

For
Reid Boates
who presented the challenge,
and
Jenny Canick
who gave me the love and
encouragement to see it through

CONTENTS

"The worst tragedy for a poet is to be admired through being misunderstood."

—Jean Cocteau
Le Rappel a l'Ordre

"No, 18,000 people yelling isn't that much of a thing. It's nothing new. See, I used to sit in the dark and dream about it."

—Bob Dylan
1974

AUTHOR'S NOTE AND ACKNOWLEDGMENTS

The problem confronting any biographer of Bob Dylan is not merely one of reconstructing his life but also of demythifying it. For, in fact, such a book is not about one man, but many—the Bob Dylan who wrote brilliant songs and revolutionized our culture by making it conform to his abstract imagination; and the panoply of alter egos he created in order to become that pop phenomenon. In the process, Dylan constructed a persona based on paradox and mystery, illusion and misdirection, fantasy and exaggeration. The invention of "Bob Dylan" is his essence, and therein lies the hitch: to profile such a man accurately requires that one consider all the ambiguities and contradictions of the character Bob created as being true to life. "Fact and fiction," Graham Greene wrote, "—they are not always easy to distinguish."

That distinction has proved elusive to many of my predecessors, not because of any incapacity on their part, but rather owing to Dylan's genius for subtle deception. When it suited him, he could push secrecy to a fine art. His public, ritualistic life was a mask, and in a recent TV interview he repeated what he has always insisted from the time he first burst on the scene as a reluctant folk hero: "No matter what people think, they don't know *anything* about Bob Dylan."

Bob Dylan, the character to whom he was referring in the third person, has remained a mystery out of choice. He varnished his image with so many coats of romance and masquerade that, after a period, it became historical fact, told and retold like lore. Like the ancient court historians, Bob's biographers obediently wrote the story he put in front of them. Otherwise responsible journalists, dazzled by an audience with him, failed to question or examine the accuracy of his statements; incredibly enough, they just printed what he said verbatim. Leafing through the thousands of pages of articles and transcripts about Bob—from Nat Hentoff's *New Yorker* profile in 1964 to the most recent *Rolling Stone* interview—one is struck by the sheer number of untruths and epic exaggerations that have found their way into print. Few performers have been more protected by literary sycophants—critics and reputable journalists who either participated unwittingly or have allowed their own fortunes to be so intimately intertwined with Bob Dylan that the work they produced serves primarily as a library of memoir and self-promotion.

No wonder he remains profoundly ambivalent about such writings. Although the myth sharpened and expanded, Bob obviously recognized the hollow victory he had won. The press, like everything else, could be seduced and later manipulated so that its members would write affirmation and apology, connected with an umbilical dependency that supported their ambitions. So that despite Bob's ability to shape and control the Dylan image, he no doubt despised it as well.

Needless to say, this creates extraordinary difficulty for a biographer. The vast writings that constitute a loosely assembled Dylan archives provide a scant factual foundation upon which to build. Not surprisingly, many journalists refused to lend assistance to this work, fearful that either their past willingness to collude with Bob would be exposed or their cooperation with me would bring recrimination. In the same respect, no effort was made to speak with Bob Dylan himself, as it was not my purpose to embroider or become part of the legend. (Later, however, after this book was in its final stages, I was offered access to Bob as well as permission to explore certain resources under his tight control and to quote from his lyrics in exchange for an agreement allowing him to examine and amend the finished manuscript. Similarly, there were photographers to whose work I was denied access until I submitted to this demand. Not wishing to provide yet another literary whitewashing, I refused.)

My intention had always been to depend on the sweeping circle of Bob's family, friends, lovers, musicians, and associates to provide me with an eyewitness account of his life. I interviewed hundreds of people over the four years it took to complete this manuscript, compiling a Dylan archive of my own. Beginning in Hibbing, Minnesota, I traced the history of the Mesabi Range, its people and its idiosyncracies, under the guidance of Mrs. Patricia Mestek and the Hibbing Historical Society. Bob's family and boyhood friends filled in the facts documenting his formative years: Mrs. Marian Zimmerman Kenner, Max Edelstein, Sylvia Edelstein Goldberg, Ethel Edelstein Crystal, Melvin Bennett Rutstein, Charles Edelstein, Barbara Edelstein Fisher, Jean Edelstein Shore, Sue Storms, Robert J. Karon, Roy Karon, Ben Overman, George Berman, William Rocklin, Kopple Hallock, Sanford Margolis, Winifred Roth, Marilyn Walters, Martha Helstrom, Echo Helstrom Fernandez, John Bucklen, Larry Fabbro, Monte Edwardson, Leroy Hoikkala, Dale Botang, Rose Matonich, Tom Strick, Dee Dee Lockhart Paolo, Ben Orlando, Bud Crippa, Greg Rochester, Gary Stark and the staff of the Hibbing Memorial Building, Postmaster John Carlson, Frank "Gatemouth" Page, Stan Lewis, Lenny Lewis, Linda Fidler Wendell, the staff of the Iron Range Interpretive Center, and various Rangers and Duluth refugees who wish to remain anonymous. I am also indebted to Jeff Syme and the *Hibbing Daily Tribune* for providing me with unlimited access to the paper's morgue, as well as to Mike Richtarich, William Law, Charles Miller, and several unsung administrators at Hibbing Sr. High School who treated me to a glimpse of Dylan's school records and his life beyond the Jacket Jamboree.

In Minneapolis, I wish to thank Lorna Sullivan, Bruce Rubinstein, John Koerner, Hugh Brown, Stanley Gottleib, Judy Rubin Shaffer, David Lee, David Morton, Melvin McKosh, Red Nelson, Paul Davies, Dave Methany, Clark Batho, Mike Poznick, Wayne Freeman, Karen Tessler Katz, Rabbi Richard Rocklin, Paul Ravitch, Gretel Whitaker Pelto, David Whitaker, Michael Baker, Anne Marsden, the University of Minnesota, the *Minneapolis Star and Tribune,* and the Minnesota Department of Motor Vehicles.

Walter Conley and Dave Hamil recalled in fine detail Bob's disastrous experience in Denver, Colorado. His Chicago tenure, as well as background on the Gate of Horn and Albert Grossman's early years, were provided by Samuel D. Freifeld, Bob Gibson, Les Brown, Jones Alk, Robert Murphy, Tina Vessini and her staff at the Chicago Housing Authority, and Seymour Goldstein.

In New York: Steve Allen, George Auerbach, Lillian Bailey, Victoria Balfour, Sari Becker, Madeline Beckman, Theo Bikel, Nick Casey, John Cooke, John Court, Sis Cunningham, Bob Drew, Nora Ephron, Mimi Fariña, Bob Fass, Chet Flippo, Rob Fraboni, Gordon Freisen, David Gahr, Bob Gleason, Sid Gleason, Cynthia Gooding, Irwin Gooen, Arthur Gorson, Sue Zuckerman Green, Manny Greenhill, John Herald, Jeri Hertzenberg, Jac Holzman, Sam Hood, Robert L. Jones, Danny Kalb, David Kapralik, Peter Karman, Janet Reynolds Kerr, Barry Kornfeld, Bruce Langhorne, Harold Leventhal, Tommy Makem, Brice Marden, Melanie Margolis, Mary Martin, Toni Mendel, Bob Miles, John Mitchell, Mort Nasatir, Miriam Novall, Michael Ochs, Sonny Ochs, Donn Pennebaker, Fraser Pennebaker, Bob Precht, Quentin Raines, Rita Ticknor Randell, Al Romm, Ethel Romm, Len Rosenfeld, Paul Rothchild, Charlie Rothschild, Carla Rotolo, Mary Rotolo, Susan Rotolo, Tony Scaduto, Joe Schick, Betsy Siggens Schmidt, Jerry Schoenbaum, Lorrie Sebastian, Greg Shucker, Lena Spencer, Andrea Stern, Terri Thal, Edith Tiger and the Emergency Civil Liberties Committee, Stan Tonkel, Jane Traum, Bob Van Dyke, Steve Wilson, and Robbie Wolliver.

Michael Watts, Roy Burchell, the staff at *Melody Maker*, Fred Perry, and others filled in the facts surrounding Bob's escapades in Great Britain.

And, of course, the musicians and producers: Harvey Brooks, Paul Butterfield, Kenny Buttrey, Rick Danko, John Hammond, Sr., Carolyn Hester, Bob Johnston, Charlie McCoy, Roger McGuinn, Paul Martinson, Maria Muldaur, Kevin Odegard, Odetta, Tom Paxton, David Peel, Fritz Richmond, Tom Rush, Mark Spoelstra, Noel Stookey, Rob Stoner, Tiny Tim, Happy Traum, Mary Travers, Eric Von Schmidt, and Eric Weisberg.

Certain individuals deserve special thanks for their part in shaping the final manuscript. I am indebted to Dave Van Ronk, who made the Village scene come alive for me through his wonderful insights and recollections and took me on an extraordinary behind-the-scenes tour of the 1960s New York folk community. Faris Bouhafa also cut through the legend and laid out Bob's return to the Village at a time when its glamour had begun to fade. Bill Pagel provided a meticulously documented chronology of Bob Dylan's career, and Jonathan Black came through in a pinch. John Bauldie and the *Wanted Man* staff supplied literature and support material beyond my wildest imagination.

Many friends provided remarkable advice and showed faith in me throughout the long haul, namely: Reid Boates, Jennifer Rockwell,

Albert Goldman, Lanie Goodman, Diane Hailey, Leslie Horvitz, Bob Hofler, Bryan Lurie, Adam Taylor, Artie at the Strand, Gina Frantz, and the folks at David Wachsman Associates, not to mention my parents and sister, whose encouragement, as always, proved invaluable. And, above all, to Jenny Canick—to whom this book is gratefully dedicated—for her wonderful book cover, her support and love, and her boundless inspiration.

I wish also to thank Lois Wallace, my agent, who supported me through very, very thin days and kept this project afloat; Susan Adler, who conducted initial research; my editor, Lisa Frost, for her imaginative and insightful help in drawing out the narrative as well as for her efforts, using everything short of Ivory soap, to clean up my language; Marshall Sanderford; Ann Craig; Albert da Silva, for his generous advice; and to Alan Brooke, my editor at Michael Joseph Books in London, who, over four years, never once asked when I intended to deliver the manuscript, then acted delighted when he finally got it.

In the four-and-a-half years it took to research and write this book I have had the cooperation of hundreds of other people who contributed generously to filling out Bob Dylan's life—up to this point. And while the facts remain theirs, the interpretation is solely my own. I hope that I have at least captured some part of his unique personality and the essence of his art.

Finally, I wish to extend my gratitude to Jeff Friedman for providing me with literally hundreds of hours of tapes—concerts, outtakes, conversations, rehearsals, you name it; if something came out of Dylan's mouth, chances are Jeff's got it filed on one of the thousands of reels of tape in his archives. His friendship, as well as his generosity and true appreciation for the Dylan songbook, imbued this project with the spirit it sorely needed. In those moments when the pages seemed most difficult to fill, when the task appeared impossibly bleak, all I had to do was hear that *voice* and those magical lyrics to make me realize how the power of Bob Dylan's extraordinary music inspires our own delicate dreams.

Bob Spitz
New York City
May 1988

Prologue

Tel Aviv, Israel
September 5, 1987

Damn that Arab sun! It was worse than hot—it was a *curse!* All morning long the shop owners on Dizengoff fanned themselves with an almost stubborn perversity. "Egypt's revenge," they gibbered to a clientele of mostly geriatric browsers, ". . . for the Ten Plagues." But their humor was deflated by the miserable conditions. The metallic drone of air conditioners, pressed into twenty-four-hour service, thrummed a subtropical fugue motif. Outside, ribbons of steam danced off the molten streets, and every hour or so a truck stopped long enough to help free disgruntled pedestrians who wriggled in the viscous tar like flies on a no-pest strip.

By noon, the city sagged under the roiling heat. The only signs of life were low-flying Phantoms and F-16s, back from hourly reconaissance missions over the Negev. And the steady procession of teenagers who, like their ancestors en route to Canaan, inched wearily past the boutiques toward Hayarkon Park—at the north end of the city.

Was this any way for the Chosen People to live? Especially after waiting all this time for the Messiah? For twenty-five years they'd expected Him—*twenty-five years!* And all the time they remained faithful, undoubting, singing his praise. Then, when he finally decides to show up—

—Damn that heat!

In fact, he'd shown up much later than expected, on, of all things, a sightseeing bus from Cairo. Looking olive-tan and Sephardic, with a bosky growth of beard clinging to his chin, hair out like Struwelpeter, Bob Dylan arrived in Israel resembling an extra in a Charlton Heston epic. He'd been scheduled to fly in directly from Brussels, but a flight of fancy had diverted him to Egypt's Nile delta, near Luxor, in search of the biblical prison where Joseph was held and the site where Abraham took Sarah before the Pharoah.

Dylan had never played in Israel before, although his popularity there was enormous. In Israel, he was a true folk hero, a living legend celebrated under two different names: *Dylan,* the elusive superstar, and *Zimmerman,* the elusive Jew. "Robert Zimmerman—" one of the newspapers gushed with anticipation, "the people of Israel, your countrymen, welcome you!" After more than twenty-five years, Bob Dylan had come to perform. He'd agreed to play a pair of concerts in Israel, and the events were cause for celebration.

A good part of the commotion stemmed from Dylan's peerage. The Sixties cachet was strong among the ranks of Israel's teenagers who had come to romanticize a past that was alive in their present. The war in Lebanon had revived the familiar symbols of internal struggle: "PEACE—NOT WAR" signs were plastered on adobe-colored office buildings and schools; students trained to be conscientious objectors and plotted against "the establishment"; and all the movement's old anthems were strummed and hummed to protest what Israelis had begun referring to as "our Vietnam." Bob Dylan's sudden appearance was interpreted as a public gesture of support for the country and its struggle for survival.

In that spirit, Dylan was accorded the type of reception normally reserved for visiting heads of state. Foreign Minister Shimon Peres, up to his *yarmulke* in war plans, put aside an hour to meet with him. Mayor Shlomo Lahat prepared to personally guide him around Tel Aviv. City officials arranged a visit to the wailing wall in Bob's honor. And the administration planned for him to attend a traditional Shabbas dinner with prominent leaders. Israel hadn't witnessed such an extravaganza since...well, since Barbra Streisand's visit in the early 1970s.

Except...who in his right mind would expect Bob Dylan to respond? How could they think he'd conform to the whim of politicians or allow himself to be paraded around for people to gawk at, like a trained seal? He never gave a thought to what was *expected* of him—never. Whenever he sensed contentment, whenever he began to observe a staleness about his work, or perhaps even a lapse into self-parody, chaos followed. He'd hook a U-turn and race madly toward some distant beacon, some Circean inner voice that beckoned him, without regard for approval or hostile criticism.

At the age of forty-six, Bob Dylan could already claim more phases to his career than most people twice his age, always conquering each before discarding them like an old toy. He had transformed folk music from a square, suffocating dirge into a frothing torrent of new ideas. He had reinvented rock 'n roll, exploding teenagers' puerile fantasies, the bullshit moon-and-June, yeah-yeah-yeah utopianism it thrived on, and geezed them with the hip, acid-tongued abstractions of a paranoid world. He had converted to Christianity and became one of the most controversial apostles of fundamentalist cant. Persistent rumors of wanton drug-taking, sadism, a fake death-defying accident, adulterous affairs, wild ambition, and the spontaneous, go-go tempo of superstardom only added a delicious dash of mystery to his legend and made him seem all the more controversial—Dylanesque!

Reevaluating his kaleidoscopic career, *Time* had written in 1985: "There was hardly a beat for transition, just an amphetamine rush of allusive imagery and electric boogie fused by will and some dark unknowable divining spirit. Bob Dylan not only lived on the margin, he was the margin."

The margin. It seems almost too narrow an appraisal of a man who, for years, pushed music and life to epic levels of imagination. Bob Dylan's whole life has transcended margins and constraints in an attempt to move beyond the ruled lines of consciousness into the bohemian fringe of fantasy and illusion. For some other rock star, playing the Holy Land might have been a climax. But for Dylan, it was just another gig.

To thousands of fans, however, the impending concert was a spiritual event. Not even bad press—the news articles deploring Bob's manners—had cast a pall over the celebration. His refusal to meet with Shimon Peres, his failure to attend the local functions, had insulted

Israeli officials, and the papers were full of condemnation. But the fans themselves were forgiving. After all, Bob Dylan *was* the original rebel. He'd practically created the counterculture, epitomizing the American antihero who struggled to break free from almost every value he'd been bred to accept. Fuck the Prime Minister! The fact that Bob had come to Israel to perform was enough to placate their fierce national pride.

By six p.m., the streets around northern Tel Aviv looked like a reenactment of the Exodus. Hundreds, thousands of people in bleached Jordache jeans, Gali sneakers on practically every foot schlepped along on foot or hopped out of double-parked Suburus, Citröens, Peugeots, Volvos, and Mercedes. Every five minutes the red-and-white Egged buses groaned to the corner, depositing more people into the park. Security police frisked potential terrorists for weapons—not the least of which were the Jaffa oranges that had been used a month earlier to pommel Rod Stewart.

Inside the park, vendors competed like pushy garment salesmen for the crowd's spare shekels. Teenagers waved silk-screened T-shirts in everyone's face, shouting "Dee-lon! Bobe Dee-lon!" Stands selling hummus, falafel, and shwarma did a brisk trade. And drug dealers—whose fist-sized chunks of hash were discounted due to the invasion of Lebanon—worked the shadows like fireflies.

Hayarkon Park glowed like a jewel in the twilight that had settled over Tel Aviv. The flowers blushed brilliantly; the planted gardens threw musky blasts across the lawns sloped downward toward the stage. And at last the heat had dissipated, cooled by breezes blowing off the Golan Heights. So that when the spots finally came on, the audience responded passionately, jumping to its feet, so touched, so moved, so overwhelmed by the promise of Bob Dylan in Israel that the chorus of hands, the whistles and screams, could be heard almost to Jaffa.

It was shaping up to be a perfect night—until Roger McGuinn wandered out onto stage. *McGuinn?*—the crowd checked their programs for his name. What the hell was this clown doing in Tel Aviv? Talking about Ronald Reagan and peace and freedom? And arrogant enough to sing "My Back Pages" and "Mr. Tambourine Man"! What *was* this bullshit? Where was Bobe Dee-lon?

It wasn't until past ten o'clock that Dylan finally appeared. Dressed in a snakeskin-pattern smock and wearing a soft Rasta cap on the back of his head, Bob seemed self-absorbed, brooding, and nervous as he cued his bandleader, Tom Petty, over the peals of wild applause. Before anyone realized what happened—BAM!—"Maggie's Farm" thundered out across the desert amphitheater. A flash from the past—pre-Newport Dylan, the Sixties, *Bringing It All Back Home.* Instant memories. Far-fuckin'-out!

Out front, the fans were on fire. They were burning with twenty-five years of anticipation. Dancing, hugging, eyes moist, with the SIGNIFICANCE of it all, they interpreted the lyric symbolically: none of them—natives or *aliyah*—intended to work on Maggie's Farm anymore. Tremors of *Never Again!* swirled in the song's undertone, fanning the flames.

Then, suddenly, inexplicably, Bob segued into a dozy version of "I'll Be Your Baby Tonight" and the excitement screeched to a halt. The song was a cute, hummable little ditty—a lightweight on the Dylanometer, a throwaway. But—*hey!*—he's just warming up, they thought. Then, as the polite applause between songs subsided, Bob turned to Tom Petty's band and spit out the one bewildering word that ultimately sealed his fate: "Señor."

"Señor"!

A leaden, funereal dirge from *Street Legal*. It was just like throwing ice water on the audience. You could actually see their enthusiasm disappear. The energy died. No one swayed or bopped their heads in time with the tune—mainly because there was nothing to bop their heads in time to, no lilt or syncopation. "Highway 61" followed, a slurred monotonous riff song, then "I and I," which was equally dismissable. By "Watching the River Flow," most of the 35,000 fans were lost in conversation.

They'd waited long enough for their old favorites—"Don't Think Twice," "The Times They Are A-Changin'," "It Ain't Me Babe," "Just Like a Woman." What happened to "Like a Rolling Stone," rock's national anthem? Or "Lay Lady Lay"? Nothing doing. Dylan force-fed them things like "In the Garden" and "I'll Remember You" and the rarely performed "Joey," his tribute to a homicidal sociopath who was rubbed out in a New York mob war. This guy was pulling songs out of his ass! He was mocking them.

"Boo!" A ripple of discontent punctured the nightscape. *"Sssss!"*

Slowly, steadily, people stood up to leave. "Where's Dylan?" someone shouted in Hebrew, in the flabby wake of "Tangled Up in Blue." Others silently rushed the exits, without looking back. Even the eagerly awaited "Blowin' in the Wind," the second-to-last song on the short program proved anticlimactic to those who remained. And the encore—"Go Down Moses," of all things—thank God the P.A. system blew out after the second chorus! A vendor dubbed the electrical malfunction a terrorist act, but in the end only the show was a bomb.

Outside Hayarkon Park, the Israeli press corps grabbed a scattering of teenagers to help write the Dylan obituary. Gripes and bewilderment sifted through their disappointment, but one young woman's question struck a particularly melancholy resonance. "I don't *understand* him," she lamented, practically in tears. "Why does he have to confuse us this way? What's his *story?* . . ."

Part 1

Zimmy

Come gather 'round, people...

1

The North Country

History has taught us that no matter how we change the environment it is impossible to change the man. And yet the two collaborate, like derelict alchemists, on the contrivances of human nature. "After all, anybody is as their land and air is," Gertrude Stein wrote. "It is that which makes them and the arts they make and the work they do and the way they eat and the way they drink and the way they learn and everything."

If that is so, it is no wonder that Bob Dylan became such a luminous amalgam of showmanship and aloofness, spirituality and desolation, eloquence and exaggeration, individuality and schizophrenia. These seesawing extremes, among others, are indigenous to the historical landscape of northern Minnesota.

This composite is complicated by the fact that Dylan descends not merely from a town or city, but from a region. The Mesabi Range is an amorphous stretch of land fanning from tiny Grand Rapids to the lower tributaries of the Vermillion Lake region, in what was once regarded as the most productive county in the Midwest. Flaunting an illusory wealth of natural resources, these plains attracted an influx of disenfranchised Europeans who sought in the terra cotta soil and secluded wilderness their notion of the American Dream and its promise of peace and prosperity. These sturdy corn-fed laborers imported a hodgepodge of customs and folkways more suited to the temperate climes of their homelands than to the dolorous wasteland they found. That, and a nagging reluctance to assimilate, protracted a constant struggle against the tide in the Rangers' pursuit of a provincial, insular community. In that respect, they are similar in character to the Amish, who tilled the verdant fairways of eastern Pennsylvania. But unlike the productive Dutchmen, they inherited a shard of the country's least nourishing terrain, a patch of scabrous tundra cloistered by rock-ribbed prairies and mottled lakeland and battered by Canada's boreal winds.

Hibbing, where Dylan spent most of his youth, became, by accident of nature, the nerve center of the Mesabi Range. There, in 1893, a German prospector named Frank Dietrich Von Ahlen tapped the largest vein of merchantable ore in the nation. Pockets of civilization immediately sprang up around the mouth of the vast mine and were named after politicians or in honor of the pit bosses, who, like the gods of Olympus, had to be stroked to preserve peace and harmony. Von Ahlen, perhaps desiring a more melodious legacy, changed his name to Hibbing, beginning a somewhat circumspect practice that would coincidentally link the city's founding father to its favorite poet-son.

Hibbing became a lusty frontier town that catered to the fancies of every philistine and desperado drawn to the mines. Not surprisingly, "blind pig" saloons became the town's second leading industry. By 1895, over a hundred new test pits pockmarked the terrain. Speculators, acting on behalf of the major eastern iron concerns, sunk huge, gaping holes across the Iron Range as swiftly as the ravenous lumber companies could cut away the white pine blocking their paths. Together, they eviscerated the landscape, until every negotiable settlement was being worked to capacity.

By 1900, representatives of Hibbing's largest mining companies were forced to go abroad in order to recruit enough able-bodied men to sustain their teeming campsites. Promises of "good living, nice land, and ample pay" made easy prey of disgruntled peasants seeking an opportunity in America. A good many sought to escape the tyranny of religious persecution. But the labor drive also attracted its share of miscreants and draft dodgers from countries with mandatory military service.

The first wave to arrive in Hibbing came from Denmark, Finland, and Italy; later, Irish and Slavic immigrants swarmed in in such numbers that local hotel owners displayed signs declaring "NO MORE STIFFS WANTED" to discourage squatters.

In a relatively short period of time, Hibbing was overrun by a babel of migrant humanity—a dizzying forty-three nationalities. Unlike newcomers elsewhere in the country, the Rangers wanted no part of Americanization. They chose to preserve their separate European identities, and though most of them worked side by side in the mines, little was spoken of their mutual plight. Instead, they returned home each night and, in effect, stepped back into the past, depriving themselves of a common identity. If character, as Thomas Mann argued, is determined by the aggregate of one's contemporaries, then Hibbing emerged as a faceless body, without a compatible personality.

Be that as it may, it is somewhat misleading to say that the Rangers had no discernible personality. One might look for the obvious traits associated with people devoted to the land, expecting to find a community of earthy, passionate, hospitable individuals, but you wouldn't find them among those who settled the Mesabi Range. If anything, their self-imposed segregation laid a bedrock of suspicion and skepticism, obstinacy and narrow-mindedness that became as singular to the region as any idiosyncrasy or landmark. Couple this with their strict commitment to religious dogma, and you have the makings of one of the most repressed personalities north of the Mason-Dixon line.

Dylan would later claim that growing up in Hibbing imbued him with a sense of simplicity. He was most likely contrasting his perception of the Rangers' life with the trappings of celebrity: their unadorned homes, conservative dress, ethnic foods, and plain speech, the informalness of country living itself helped to create his misconception. But by no stretch of the imagination could life on the Range be construed as *simple.* Parochial, perhaps—but in a way that forged ideologies out of the Rangers' boldfaced limitations. So that ultimately they became a people doomed to looking at the rest of the world with wonder and amazement, without the courage to venture among it themselves.

Just as strongly as they shunned outsiders and their ideas, the Rangers placed great importance on strengthening their families. This actually served a dual purpose: one being to carry over a strong ancestry to America; the other—more maternal—was to keep the kids close to home. They were so successful at both that generations of Rangers grew up around one another, so that today many of Hibbing's youngsters have fond memories of their great- and great-great-grandparents.

Imagine, then, how it must have raised Ranger eyebrows when, in 1961, critic Robert Shelton wrote in *The New York Times,* "Mr. Dylan is vague about his antecedents." Saying that Dylan is vague about his antecedents is like saying Don Corleone was ignorant of the criminal activities of his so-called business associates.

Like many Rangers, Dylan enjoyed a close relationship with the first in his line to touch American soil. B'chezer Edelstein sailed into the port of Halifax, Nova Scotia, sometime around the end of 1902, having fled the pogroms that were ravaging his homeland. A blacksmith from Covina, Lithuania, B.H. (as he was called after the anglicized Benjamin Harold) probably thought nothing of settling his wife and three children in the bone-cold sweep of North America. The climate was similar to what he'd experienced in Eastern Europe. What's more, he had a built-in clientele for the cast-iron stoves that were wrought in his forge.

The long, bitter winters were obviously good for business, as B.H.'s business thrived in the budding community of North Hibbing, but they had an even more salutary effect on the old blacksmith's libido: B.H. and his wife, Lyba, produced another seven children in rapid succession. Their oldest daughter, Florence, born in 1896, was Bob Dylan's grandmother. B.H. reigned as the family patriarch until his death, in 1961, at the age of ninety-one.

B.H., even more than most immigrants, was an outsider knocking at the door to prosperity. The mines had transformed Hibbing from an outpost into a miniature boomtown, and its work force was drawn gradually into the mongrel culture. Merchants, however, were a breed apart. And if you also happened to be a Jew—*oy gevalt!* What trouble! There was a lot of antipathy toward the few Jews on the Range. According to one observer, "If you were unlucky enough to be there *and* be Jewish, you learned very quickly to fend for yourself."

For B.H., that meant an austerity toward his family and his God. He was a slight, teetery man whose imperious manner offset what he lacked in physical stature.

"My grandfather was a man of few words," recalls Melvin Bennett Rutstein, Bob's uncle, who grew up a few miles from the Edelstein homestead in neighboring Brooklyn, "but whatever he said was law. He was also a very stubborn and opinionated man who did exactly as he pleased." And what pleased him, in a way that his famous great-grandson would parallel, was keeping a low profile. To that end, B.H. spent a good part of each day in prayer or huddled over the Talmud. "Religion was my father's guiding force," says B.H.'s youngest daughter, Ethel Crystal, who now resides in Minneapolis. "He was very strict about it, and it provided him—and all of us—with a certain inner strength." According to Ethel, B.H. questioned his existence fiercely, but always seemed to find an answer in God. This, of course, is what Bob Dylan has exhibited throughout his professional career.

Looking further, B.H. also seems to be Dylan's ancestral link to show business. Sometime around the early 1920s, B.H. began phasing out his trade. Just how much this had to do with rumors that the mines were in trouble, no one knows. Nevertheless, the Edelstein family providentially made a transition into the theater business, opening their first two houses—the Victory on First Avenue and the Garden on Howard Street—in a suburb called Alice. Even when the mines suffered, people managed to sock away a few pennies for the movies. As such, the theaters were usually packed, and B.H. assigned each of his tribe to shifts in order to keep a tight rein on the family business. Only Florence, the oldest daughter, was excused from working there.

Florence was the distaff éminence grise of the Edelstein family, but like her famous grandson, she was out of the house by the time she was nineteen. An early bloomer in every respect, Florence had married a Russian intellectual named Ben Stone and moved into his house in nearby Stevenson, where they ran a dry goods concern called The Sample Shop. Whereas the other girls resembled Lyba, Florence was B.H.'s spit and image. She was on the plump side, unconventionally pretty, with dark hair worn loosely to the side and somber, ebony eyes that, on first glance, seemed to reflect B.H.'s striking intensity.

But Florence was "a very warmhearted, very loving person," recalls her sister, Sylvia Goldberg, who was still a child when Florence moved out of the house. "She possessed the kind of compassion the rest of us longed for, and after Lyba died, Florence was primarily responsible for keeping the family together."

Beatrice, Bob's mother, born in 1915, inherited Florence and Ben Stone's most appealing qualities. The embodiment of her mother's good nature and Ben's dry, authoritarian wit, Beatty, as she was called, developed into an aggressively outgoing, almost manically enthusiastic young woman.

"If you asked her a question, you had to be prepared to listen for the answer," says Beatty's cousin, Melvin Bennett Rutstein, who knew Beatty in her teens. "She'd go on for quite a bit about anything in the world that interested her. She had the gift of gab and a way of putting words together that left most people speechless"—a trait she no doubt handed down to her son Bob.

Loving, charitable, profound, witty, family-oriented—these are a few of the phrases friends and acquaintances use to describe the Stones. On the other hand, the Zimmermans, who lived about seventy miles east of Hibbing, were pragmatic, guarded, thick-skinned, undemonstrative, and businesslike people. Shuffle them together, and you have a fairly accurate portrait of the man Bob Dylan became.

Incongruously, the two families share similarities of origin. Like Beatty's family, the Zimmermans were from White Russia and sailed across the Atlantic, docking at Ellis Island sometime around the turn of the century. Zigmar Zimmerman, Bob's grandfather, settled with his wife, Amy, and their five children, in Duluth, on the rocky bluffs overlooking Lake Superior. Their sixth and last child was Abram H. Zimmerman, Bob's father, who came into the world on October 19, 1911. Abe's sister, Marian Kenner, remembers him as "a rambunctious little boy who could also turn unusually quiet and observant. He kept pretty much to himself," she says. "You hardly knew he was around."

With four older, more dynamic brothers, and an "older father" who still struggled with the English language, it is not surprising that classmates at Central High School remember Abe as withdrawn and introverted. Just as friends would later say about Bob, one never knew what Abe was thinking, only that he was thinking all the time. "Abe had an uncanny way of sizing up a situation, without really commenting on it," says a childhood friend from Duluth. "You just knew he had formed an opinion about you that wasn't necessarily going to be shared. It had a very unsettling effect on the person to whom it was directed. I think it was his way of remaining distant, even a bit superior to the rest of us."

As Bob Dylan would come most to life on a stage, Abe Zimmerman's personality was apparently roused on the playground. Robert Karon, who walked to school with him, claims Abe had the most confounding underhanded fast-pitch he'd ever seen. And another friend says Abe beat him regularly during their thrice-weekly handball games. Thus it must have been especially devastating for Abe when, in his early twenties, he suddenly contracted polio.

"He took it very hard, both physically and emotionally," recalls another handball partner, Ben Overman, who still resides in Duluth. "I think it stirred a great deal of bitterness in him."

George Berman, who remained close to Abe until the latter's death, remembers his friend as being a meticulously slow man. "He moved very cautiously, with a pronounced limp, and was tormented by the polio," he recalls.

On occasion, Berman was recruited to drape Abe over his back and carry him up to the Zimmerman's second-floor apartment on North Third Avenue. "Abe had difficulty making that long flight of stairs, but he never once complained about it," Berman says. "He internalized all the pain he was obviously going through. The only outward show of it was the two habitual aspirins he took every night before going to bed."

Undaunted, Abe participated in Duluth's lively social scene. The discovery of iron on the Mesabi Range had transformed Duluth into the chief ore-shipping port for the nation's steel mills, and a strong symbiosis developed between the neighboring municipalities of Hibbing and Duluth. The communities were interdependent socially, as well—especially the scattershot of Jewish families dispersed across northern Minnesota. Clearly, Hibbing held no future for them. Catholics made up ninety-two percent of the town's population; the rest were mostly Protestant or Unitarian. "You could name the few Jewish families there," says one observer—too few, even, to warrant the presence of a full-time rabbi. The likelihood of marriage within the faith was ridiculous. "We knew that all the worthwhile Jewish boys were in Duluth," says Beatty's aunt, Ethel Crystal, who schlepped her comely niece along to mixers in nearby towns. "To us, Duluth was a great big beautiful city with a large Jewish population, three or four synagogues to depend on, and plenty of people like us there to meet."

Each weekend Ethel, Beatty, and a battery of friends would travel by bus to Duluth—a caravan of wide-eyed *yiddelahs* en route to the Promised Land—where they'd be entertained by the local Jewish fraternities. One such group was AZA (American Zionist Association), to which Abe Zimmerman belonged.

Ethel Crystal says, "I met Abe, then introduced him to Beatty and told her: 'This is the right boy for you. Hang onto him!'"

Apparently, Beatty jumped on her aunt's advice. Legend has it that as soon as she made up her mind, Abe didn't stand a chance. Not exactly love at first sight, but the next best thing. "They balanced things in each other," says Ethel, probably referring to the oceanic gulf that divided their personalities.

An owl-eyed *bücher* boy, Abe must have been smitten by Beatty's spunk and chirpy spirit. At nineteen, one niece fondly recalls, "Beatty could take control of a room just by walking into it." Abe, on the other hand, seemed to shrink from such vitality. "I remember family gatherings where Beatty would take over the conversation and Abe would just disappear into the wallpaper," the same niece says.

There were other distinctions between them as well. Beatty possessed a great wit; Abe was all business. Beatty was loud and lusty; Abe, ever the perfect gentleman. More important, Beatty was the kind of woman who allowed her imagination to run wild, whereas Abe was bridled by practical-mindedness, choosing to see the world in black and white. By all accounts, stranger bedfellows would be hard to find.

Still, their marriage on June 10, 1934, was a joyous occasion. Beatty had originally planned a large June wedding, but at the last minute changed her mind in favor of a small family gathering to witness the vows; that way, they'd be able to hold the reception at her parents' home. Abe was twenty-two; Beatty, at twenty, was only a year older than Florence had been when she tied the knot.

Afterward, the young couple returned to Duluth, where Abe worked as a manager in the stock department of Standard Oil. They took a small place a few blocks from Abe's parents, in an unremarkable, working-class neighborhood—the upstairs flat of a cream-colored, two-family house on North Third Avenue. Beatty got a job selling clothing at a schlocky women's haberdashery called Mangol's. But she made no bones about her future calling; above all, Beatty wanted to be a mother.

It took her more than seven years to achieve that goal. Finally, on the night of May 24, 1941, at 9:05 p.m., Dr. James Manley strode into the smoke-filled waiting room of St. Mary's Hospital, where Abe had been doing figure-eights around the Bermans, to tell them the good news: Beatty had given birth to a son. Named Robert Allen Zimmerman, he was a hefty seven pounds thirteen ounces and, despite a delicate breech birth, appeared to be in excellent health. Abe heaved a sigh of relief and managed his best smile, causing George Berman's wife to remark years later: "It was the most emotional I'd ever seen Abe... then or since."

That is probably the most factual account ever given of Bob Dylan's birth. In the years to come, he would varnish it many times over with various fantasies, half-truths, and outright lies. That Dylan was his mother's name. Or that he was an orphan from Chicago. Or Oklahoma. Or New Mexico. Contrary to one claim, there were no Sioux Indians on either side of the family. Nor uncles who dealt blackjack in Las Vegas. Nor, for that matter, was he the illegitimate offspring of carnies out of Cheyenne, Wyoming. That night, he was merely a Zimmerman from Duluth in that hospital crib. It would be another nineteen years before those claims materialized into the sort of elaborate covers usually found in dime-store spy novels and Bob Dylan was born.

2

Back Home on the Range

Ask anybody who lives in Duluth today and they'll will tell you it's probably the last place on earth you'd want to raise a kid. It's become a no-man's land that was flat-out decked by the recession and never managed to recover. Its economy in relation to that of other cities of comparable size and potential is shot to hell. Companies with national identities avoid it like the plague, choosing instead to locate in St. Paul or Minneapolis or even Cincinnati. No expansion has taken place there in years. Downtown Duluth looks like someone was working on a scale model for a city planning commission, got bored, and simply walked away, leaving it rather like downtown Dresden after the war.

During the Forties, however, Duluth was on the move. The whole city was jacuzzed-up on overtime supplying ore for America's slack-jawed war machine. Its future appeared solid, bolstered by the kind of false economy that stalks middle-class opportunism. But the bottom fell out at almost the split second Germany surrendered, and Duluth, destined to take its place alongside Cleveland and Pittsburgh as the butt of toastmasters' bad jokes, has been struggling ever since to save face.

Characteristically, Abe Zimmerman had made contingency plans to ensure his family's well-being. His brothers Maurice and Paul had gone west to seek their fortunes but, as was the Zimmerman wont, west was a cautious seventy miles into the jerkwater lap of Hibbing.

Maurice was a refrigeration engineer, working for a man named Ed Micka, who ran an all-purpose appliance shop on Fifth Street. Paul joined his brother there, operating the retail end, and when Old Man Micka died, they asked Abe to "move west" and buy into the business with them. Why with Maurie's know-how, Paul's soft sell, and Abe's dollars-and-sensibility, perhaps the Zimmerman brothers could do with toasters and lawn sprinklers what the Hunts would eventually do with silver. Not exactly Manny, Moe, and Jack, mind you, but in Hibbing this was as close to big business as one got.

For Beatty, the move back home must have been a mixed blessing. She'd gladly have bolted Hibbing for a chance at life in what could be described at the time as a more sophisticated city. On the other hand, she had family back there. Bobby and David (her second son, born in 1945) would have tons of cousins to play with and one of the best school systems in the country. Abe would be in business for himself. Then, again, there was Hibbing itself to contend with. The city was now being called "The World's Largest Open Pit." Nevertheless, Abe and Beatty decided to take advantage of the opportunity in Hibbing, which had momentarily reclaimed its reputation, thanks to frenetic wartime production, as one of the most prosperous towns on the Great Plains.

The 1947 version of Hibbing was much the same as the one Beatty had left behind: backward and depressing. The only change was that there was seemingly less of it, a wide crater having formed around the outskirts of town where once-fertile earth had been dredged out by the mines. Only two years before, Truman had ordered the bomb dropped on Hiroshima; an aerial view of Hibbing provided an almost identical picture of reckless abandon: mounds of reddish-brown soil piled high atop the lips of abandoned pits, branchless trees and charred brush growing out of the overburden, a glaring absence of wildlife in the vicinity. The landscape was an environmentalist's nightmare, the handiwork of devoted outdoorsmen, fishermen, and backyard gardeners who looked the other way in order to preserve the soaring economy. This was the prosperity to which the Zimmermans returned. This was the aesthetic from which their sons would glean their own point of view. This was the Hibbing which eventually armed Bob Dylan with the kind of acid-tipped ammunition necessary to blast away at such hypocrisy.

Back in Hibbing, the Zimmerman family took an apartment in the style to which they were accustomed: a shabby but respectable little building next to the Alice School, only a few blocks from Abe's new digs at Micka Electric. It was a quiet, cheerful street, with overhanging shade trees. A playground next door attracted the kids. There was no traffic to speak of. Beatty went to work on the warren of tiny rooms, filling them imaginatively with used furniture and brightly-colored *chatzkas,* until the place was deemed comfortable. Granted, it wasn't the ideal place to quarter a growing family, but they wouldn't be there forever. Just long enough to get settled and to look around for a house.

Less than a year later, the Zimmermans bought a place at 2425 Seventh Avenue, on the corner of Twenty-Fifth Street. The area was a typical suburban development lined with modest ranch-style houses, small checkerboard lawns, and one or two trees placed identically in each yard to give the community that dreary balance for which the environmentalists were clamoring. By comparison, the beige stucco house stuck out like a sore thumb. Built in 1939—a good ten years after the others in the area—it was perfectly square and squat, as if the original structure had been put through a compactor and dropped mistakenly onto a vacant lot. The neighbors must have regarded it as an eyesore, what with its imitation hacienda facade. Whereas Ward and June Cleaver might have lived anywhere on the block, this house could have been occupied by the Munsters.

Bob lived in this house from the time he entered grade school until he graduated in 1959. During that time, he stuck pretty close to home and did not, as some accounts contend, run away repeatedly or hop freight trains or participate in any of those childish fairy tales that crept into his record-company biographies. Those stories were concocted much later, when the truth paled against the legendary exploits of Dylan's contemporary folk heroes. Did he ride the rails and befriend grizzled hoboes like his mentor, Woody Guthrie? Did he "survey a lot of farmland on the backside of a mule," as Hank Williams, his first idol, boasted? Did he even put in time as a teenager in something as unglamorous as the Merchant Marines, as did his pal Dave Van Ronk? Of course not. For the most part, Bobby Zimmerman suffered through a fairly normal, bourgeois adolescence.

"Bobby was just a very ordinary kid," his cousin Barbara Fisher recently told me, "except that he was more spoiled than most of us. The way I remember it, Bobby had more material possessions at a younger age than any of the other people I knew. He was very well taken care of."

A self-promoter, Bobby reputedly wheedled things out of friends and family more smoothly than an accomplished pickpocket. Abe and Beatty found it difficult to deny their son anything his little heart desired. A trip to his bedroom told an observer everything he needed to know. Bobby had his very own radio, a spindletop record player, and a collection of obscure 45s to rival the local record store. Down in the living room, he had a piano to bang on, and in the basement, enough toys and athletic equipment to outfit a moderately sized school. Such extravagance was unknown to the area's youngsters, who were weaned on the basic values. Very basic. In fact, wealth was considered anathema in Hibbing, and Rangers who had money often took great pains to conceal it. Abe and Beatty weren't wealthy by any stretch of the imagination, but between them they made enough to live quite comfortably in the early 1950s. And Bobby benefited handsomely. Think, for a moment, how people must have viewed the Jewish merchant's son, always immaculately dressed, well-groomed, excused from having to eat that *tref* they served in the school cafeteria, packed off to summer camp in the lake country, and indulged with musical instruments. In most cowtowns it was enough to warrant your ass being kicked whenever the local toughs got the urge. But in Hibbing, you were simply ignored.

And not just by your peers. One of the reasons Bobby turned into such an unusual kid was simply that he was lonely. All day long Abe would be working at Micka Electric and Beatty would be off at Feldman's Department Store, where she had a part-time job selling clothing, or at one of her Hadassah meetings. Bobby would come home from school (this is before his grandmother moved in with them) and find no one there to talk to him. No wonder he'd skip up to his room, close the door, daydream, and listen endlessly to his radio. To some extent, the radio became Bobby's best friend—a friend he could depend on to entertain him. He'd invariably sprawl on one of the twin beds against the wall, prop his chin on his hands, and stare, hypnotized, out the window while some disc jockey in Duluth or Minneapolis or Chicago jabbered like a magpie with the usual radio patter. To a boy of ten or twelve whose mind was on fire, their barrage of minutiae provided a fanciful picture of life beyond the Iron Range. "You can have some amazing hallucinogenic experiences doing nothing but looking out your window," he told an interviewer in 1978. And that vision, no matter how abstract or cosmic, created in Bobby an insatiable yearning to see what was out there.

Dylan spent his entire youth begging for any tidbit of information that fed his imagination. Like the time word got back to him that some Borscht Belt has-been was scheduled to perform at the Moose Lodge on Howard Street. *SRO!* All the yokels crammed into the upstairs paneled community room where they ordinarily held church dinners and drank beer out of gigantic glass pitchers. That night it was set for a full-scale extravaganza. You'd think Jerry Lewis himself was making an appearance.

Bobby was obsessed with talking to this guy. He paced outside the Moose Lodge until the show was over and he could sneak inside. And there he found his messiah—some sweaty lounge act in a loud, threadbare sports jacket and shiny pants packing up his gear. True to form, Bobby talked the guy into playing the piano for him. He even crawled up next to him on the bench while the man inveigled his young admirer with an off-colored ditty. "*Oh the maiden's face was taut, while the salesman pinched and caught his little dingy on the blah, blah, blah. . . .*" They sat around all night like that, Bobby pumping the guy about show business. Music. Life on the road. *The road!* What an aphrodisiac. It had a magical sound to it, much like the unbounded world of radio. And the song-and-dance man, finally feeling appreciated as the truly great entertainer he imagined himself to be, shared his long-time professional secrets with Bobby. Like: "Always leave 'em clamoring for more. Finish school, you'll be a better performer for it." All the old chestnuts. "Who knows, maybe someday *I'll* be opening for *you*. Heh-heh!" Bobby couldn't get enough.

This hunger for knowledge, coupled with a tremendous untapped creative drive, must have been torture for a kid stuck in postwar Hibbing. The town's inspirational coffers were barren, its intellectual climate almost as cold and unyielding as the dreaded nine-month winters that isolated Hibbing from neighboring cities. What's more, the Rangers scorned the kind of curiosity and free thinking that was apt to lure young minds across the city line. Undoubtedly, Bobby was forced to fight down these impulses for want of encouragement, although at that age he probably couldn't have explained the inner rumblings even if he tried. All he knew was that he was plugged into a battery of exciting, thought-provoking things going on everywhere about him—everywhere, that is, except in Hibbing. So that from a very early age Bobby recognized that his only chance to keep that sensitive part of him alive was to escape the brain-dead confines of the Range.

The irony here is that in our everyday usage the word "range" is commonly preceded by the adjective "open." Open range has long inspired the likes of poets and cowboys to search out their romantic dreams. In Minnesota, however, the Range is viewed as a natural asylum, a safe haven for a constituency of the state's social deviants more commonly known there as "hellraisers." A captive of this birthright, Bobby Zimmerman was compelled to get by on his imagination. As such, everything he encountered became a liberating symbol of life outside the Range. The radio, books, even the railroad tracks that bisected the north end of Hibbing, became links to the civilized world.

"When the train rolled through town you always looked at those faces that were peering out of the windows," Dylan reminisced in another interview. More times than he cared to admit, Bobby found himself killing time along the pebbled banks that skirted the endless stretch of train tracks, drawn there by some nascent impulse to free himself. It was as if he were just waiting for the right boxcar. . . and the right opportunity to ride it out of town.

Years later, Dylan would claim to have been a chronic runaway, hopping boxcars out west, as the stories go, only to be rounded up each time by a posse of burly truant officers who rode shotgun for his old man. In truth, Bobby might have once taken the family car, under the pretense of visiting a relative, and cruised the blues haunts in and around the Twin Cities. That *might* have happened once or twice after he was old enough to drive. But Bobby was too middle-class to run away from home. Like most kids, he was driven by the impulse to please his parents, which precluded him from acting out his rebellious fantasies. He was, by all accounts, a model child, and as drifters go, merely an itinerant dreamer whose worst offense was that he refused to deny the errant powers of his mind.

By the time he was thirteen, Bobby had begun to exhibit a strong creative streak. He was a whirlwind of artistic energy, spending bursts of time banging on the living-room piano, writing little poems, sketching pictures, and making up stories to entertain himself. Neighbors recall a kind of breathlessness in the way he attacked these interests, never sitting still long enough to develop any one talent. He was always off and running... doing... dreaming. It was all rushing at him at once, and he must have been overwhelmed by the new world that had suddenly availed itself to him.

At the same time, Bobby began to surmise that he was not like the people around him—that he had feelings and interests completely different from those of his closest friends or even his family. In Hibbing, this must have been like carrying around a dirty little secret. Especially at a time when most boys are fumbling around, trying to locate their identities. The message Bobby Zimmerman kept getting was that he somehow didn't fit in. So, in that respect, it's not difficult to look into the future and understand why, as Bob Dylan—folksinger, rock star, hillbilly, born-again Christian, Orthodox Jew—he'd be condemned to a never-ending search for his true identity.

It is not uncommon for gifted children, deprived of their ability to evolve in a natural manner, to retreat into a dark, private world from which they never quite reemerge. Bobby wasn't psychologically ready or even willing to wrestle with what Freud referred to as "those half-tamed demons" that torment the inner self. Nor was he about to reject his cushy, if unstimulating, home life. Instead, he escaped into the more accommodating world of make-believe which, for him, was epitomized by Hollywood-style entertainment.

Bobby loved going to the movies and went often since his grandfather and uncles owned Hibbing's largest theaters. In lieu of the twenty-five-cent admission, he was obligated to make small talk with his Uncle Mel, a sour-pussed martinet who patrolled the lobbies like a feudal baron, but it was a pittance in return for the education he received inside. Each week, Bobby spent hours slouched down in one of the threadbare velvet-covered seats in either the State or the Lybba (another *b* was added to the name on the marquee, perhaps to categorize the type of movies that played there), studying actors and the ways in which they carried themselves. A childhood friend remembers how Bobby seemed to transform himself after each matinee—not in body, but personality. Walking down Howard Street, he'd be coolly detached after watching Monty Clift in *The Young Lions,* cocky and shamelessly glib following a Bogart film, loaded with one-liners having watched Jerry Lewis diddle an unsuspecting Dean Martin, and flushed with John Wayne's bravado in the wake of yet another patriotic blitz. Bobby tried on each identity for size without much success. Lacking a strong role model in Abe, he was determined to appropriate any trait that seemed comfortable to him, no matter how theatrical or poorly contrived. Each actor made his unwitting contribution to the classic Dylan image, though it was an even more obvious screen idol who ultimately provided Bob with a clue to his now-legendary persona.

It was at the State Theatre, in the fall of 1955, that a movie and its enigmatic star gave Bobby the first peek at the combustible properties of attitude and self-expression. On a crisp autumn day, he sat mesmerized by the premier showing of *Rebel Without a Cause,* a stagy morality play about teenage restlessness in suburbia. Every minute of film pulled him deeper into the story and, most likely, prompted a keen identification with each of its central characters. Set in a neighborhood no different from Bobby's split-level ghetto, inhabited by pouty spoiled kids with parents much like Abe and Beatty, the film focuses on a teenager's first day at a new high school cast against a netherworld of romance, violence, and despair. The antihero portrayed by James Dean—decked out in an outrageously gaudy red zipper jacket and skin-tight jeans—projects an air of porcelain vulnerability as a smokescreen for the smoldering anger and confusion that torment his adolescence. By film's end, he is transformed into a Central Casting JD, misunderstood by parents and friends alike while courting their recognition, and retreats into a solitary fantasy world. The resemblance must have made Bobby sweat bullets.

If ever the term "born-again" applied to Bob Dylan it was then, following this celluloid revelation. He had gotten a glimpse of the future up on the screen in the form of James Dean, teenage rebel, and it appealed to his sensibility. He was inspired by the whole package—the defiant posturing, the attitude, the mumbling, and especially The Look. The look established a state of mind that allowed you to slip into the role with relative ease.

Up until then, Beatty had dragged Bobby into Kopple Hallock's shop twice a year for his ritual fitting of back-to-school clothes. Hallock, a jovial old haberdasher, would stand Bobby at attention in front of a three-way mirror while he ran his yellow tape measure up, down, and around the boy's body, clucking his tongue in wonderment at the degree of tailoring needed to reshape the various fabrics to Bob's husky frame. Then, under Beatty's watchful eye, he'd begin laying out an insipidly clean array of outfits befitting a Ken doll: khaki chinos, vests, polo shirts, argyle socks—the kind of stuff that makes you want to say to your mother, "If you like it so much, why don't *you* wear it?"

Rebel put an abrupt end to that farce.

Almost overnight Bobby metamorphosed from a wussy squirt into Hibbing's protopunk. He redid himself from head to toe, like a fashion model undergoing a beauty makeover. Along with another impressionable school chum, Bobby made a beeline for Feldman's basement, the uncharted blue-collar section of the store, where he picked out stiff Levi's, black biker's boots, and a leather motorcycle jacket similar to the one Brando wore in *The Wild One*. A real shit-kicker's getup. Then it was over to a hole-in-the-wall shoe repair on First Street to refine The Look. "Give us the biggest cleats you've got," they ordered the cobbler on duty there, who nailed disks the size of hockey pucks onto their heels. That would certainly do the trick. Mission accomplished, the boys shuffled across the street, heels grating in stereo against the pavement, to Stevens' Grocery, where they checked their appearance against the latest batch of James Dean fanzines stuffed into the racks. Jacket—check. Jeans—check. Boots—check. Thumbs hooked into pockets—check. Slouch—check. Lip-curling—that took a bit of practice. Still, something crucial was missing. After a bit of deliberation, they decided it was definitely the hair. Something had to be done about Bobby's ultra-wave locks. It was a dead giveaway and exposed him for what he really was: a Jew in goy's clothing. Nothing a little Vaseline wouldn't cure. Back home, Bobby applied a handful of gook to his unruly hair, and—presto!—in no time at all he had the makings of a gen-u-ine greaser.

This act of self-creation marked the genesis of Dylan's scruffy image and, for the time being, was probably as close as he'd come to blending in with the working-class Rangers. It would always take great effort for Bob to look the part of whatever group he was trying to belong to. Whether it was the New York folk scene or Carnaby Street, hanging out with Nashville cats or posing with Madonna for the cover of *Life,* he always required a bit of window dressing to pull off the masquerade. This probably explains why close friends throughout the years have claimed Dylan always looks so uncomfortable and out of place, no matter where he surfaces. The true social chameleon, cast in a different mold from his peers, spends his entire life trying to find ways in which to conform. He is ashamed of his natural identity, suffers from intense feelings of insecurity, and siphons off the traits of others in order to make himself more appealing. Bob Zimmerman's standing as the son of one of Hibbing's more prominent families put him outside the town's proletarian social circle. Luckily James Dean—and later on Woody Guthrie, Bobby Neuwirth, various Woodstock compatriots, even Jesus Christ—provided Dylan with the proper papers to make him feel like a member of the crowd.

In school, it was somewhat easier for Bobby to blend in with his surroundings. Hibbing High, which Bobby attended from seventh through twelfth grades, is a red-brick and concrete monstrosity that spans two city blocks on East Twenty-First Street, about a block and a half from the Zimmerman house. The school is one of Minnesota's architectural showplaces, built and endowed by the mining companies in 1921 as a form of penance for what they were doing to the environment. And, in fact, a visitor is immediately struck by the school's copious appointments: a Depression-era mural adorns an entire wall of the library, busts and friezes line the corridors in a setting not unlike a wing of the National Gallery, and mosaics and beveled glass enrich the building's elegant fixtures. There's even a concert-size auditorium fashioned after New York's old Capitol Theatre to showcase various student productions. Unfortunately, its curriculum has deteriorated into a residue of academic mediocrity, and the school is now noted more for ice hockey than for scholarship. (In the same vein, its local hero is Boston Celtics forward Kevin McHale and not Bob Dylan.) But when Bobby attended Hibbing High, it still adhered to the principles of learning and knowledge.

How much Bobby benefited from that program is purely a matter of speculation. He was your typical Robert-is-not-working-up-to-his-potential student, although even that is subject to debate; Bobby entered Hibbing High with the rather unexceptional IQ of 106 and had no trouble maintaining his place on the bell curve right on through to graduation. He earned mostly B's and C's in class, unable to carry an A past the ninth grade, although an F in physics lowered his grade-point average to a measly 2.73. Charles Miller, who taught twelfth-grade social studies, recalls Bob being more distinguished for his place in the classroom: "Last seat back there next to the window," he laughs. "Z. . . alphabetical order." Otherwise, Bobby did just enough work to glide through school in a respectable, if unremarkable, way.

Bobby's legacy at Hibbing High might have been trifling as well, were it not for the real source of his education: the radio. He was constantly perched in front of an ancient Zenith, cruising the dial for stations that played interesting music and brought the outside world right into his bedroom. What he heard was certainly more stimulating than any boring geography class he'd been forced to sit through—and obviously more vital to an imaginative boy of fourteen. Unfortunately, reception was horrible during the afternoon, due to interference from the mines. The only stations that came in clearly were those few from Hibbing and nearby Virginia, which limited their playlists to sappy balladeers and a surfeit of country & western fare. The patient listener waited until nightfall when Minneapolis and Duluth came in crystal-clear. Then, as the night wore on, one could pull in stations from as far off as Tallahassee and Denver, where radio personalities communicated in strange and curious tongues.

Sometime in 1955, Bobby's pal John Bucklen picked up a signal from a station in Little Rock, Arkansas, and immediately called his friend with the news. "You've got to hear what they're playing!" he remembers telling Bobby.

The next day, the two boys huddled to discuss their transcendental experience. Both had been dumbstruck by the music's driving beat, powered by electric guitars, stride pianos, and screeching saxes, not to mention the garrulous hipster whose rap between songs sounded like the auctioneer on the Lucky Strike commercials. At first it sounded a bit preposterous, as if it were a parody of the various Negro dialects you normally heard in the movies. But the more they listened, the more obvious it became that the patter of the music was somehow related to the intensity behind movies like *Rebel Without a Cause.* It percolated with that same energizing feeling that came from the wild-sounding music—something the announcer kept referring to as "rock 'n roll."

3

Jungle Music

Hibbing is, and always has been, a city of devoted churchgoers. Not the kind of people who drop their kids off at services Sunday morning on their way to the golf course. The Rangers were God-fearing folk. They lived by the Good Book and the Golden Rule and expected the same from their neighbors. They could, however, cope with a spot of whiskey every now and then. They could cope with a friendly wager at the track. Lord knows, they could cope with the blasphemous Republicans downstate (who everyone knew were really agents of Satan). They could even cope with s-e-x. What they couldn't cope with, it became clear, was the sinful music rattling around the walls of Bobby Zimmerman's bedroom each night at ten-thirty sharp.

To the pious Iron Ranger, rock 'n roll was an opiate of the devil. It was a manifestation of depravity. The essence of sin. Of course, this is exactly why it appealed to Hibbing's emotionally repressed teenagers. For them, the music provided a call to arms, a conspicuous ID badge, and, more importantly, a way to euphemistically say to parents something they'd been trying to articulate for years: Fuck you!

For Bobby, the discovery of rock 'n roll was a flat-out epiphany. It startled him out of his socks. That wild, wanton, rollicking music sent a charge through his guts that produced two seemingly disparate effects: it whipped him into a frenzy while, at the same time, soothed his doubts about what the future held for him.

Today's kids grow up with their music all around them. Back then, pop radio—as well as the recording industry—catered exclusively to an audience of anesthetized adults. It had probably never occurred to Bobby that anyone would make music specifically for listeners his age. The postwar generation had been weaned on a steady diet of Golden Records, which is okay as long as you're six years old. But all those moronic songs about chipmunks and honeybees engaged in moral dilemmas had absolutely no significance for a boy of fourteen. The same could be said for the drivel passing for pop music on the airwaves. At the time, radio was overrun by a sorority of lily-white, uptight vocalists whose colorless material served to mirror the more dismally colorless times. Ex-big-band singers like Giselle MacKenzie, Patti Page, and Rosemary Clooney inched into the spotlight with songs like "Papa Loves Mambo," "The Naughty Lady of Shady Lane," and "Hernando's Hideaway." Skidding along the dial you might expect to be entertained by a lyric as thought-provoking as "How much is that doggie in the window/ the one with the waggly tale?..." Which went to show there wasn't much difference between children's programming and the so-called Hit Parade.

Until then, Bobby had listened almost exclusively to country & western music, which was very popular in northern Minnesota. The twangy musings of hillbilly greats Hank Williams, Webb Pierce, Hank Snow, and Slim Whitman, among others, treated him to an uncomplicated view of the world told through a spare, plaintive style that would eventually show up in some of Dylan's earliest songs. But while the music held his attention, it didn't exactly light a fire beneath him.

Imagine how Bobby must have felt when, bored by musical pablum and numbed by his surroundings, he tuned into a staticky station located somewhere between 1050 and 1100 on the dial, and was blown out by the wildest sounding music he'd ever heard. An unmistakably colored voice grunted and growled through the interference. "Ain't that a shame, my teardrops fall like rain/ Ain't that a shame...." The voice, sounding like a car exhaust in extremis, kicked into a shotgun rhythm that caught the unsuspecting listener right between the eyes. "You said (bomp! bomp!) goodbye (bomp! bomp!), you know (bomp! bomp!) I cried/ Ain't that a shame...." Then, out of nowhere, a hardcore barroom-style piano snaked around the lyric like an irascible boa, squeezing out every last ounce of sass. "Ain't that a shame, You're not the one to blame. . . ."

Like most white teenagers first encountering rock 'n roll, Bobby probably didn't know what to make of the music, only that it was, in some extraordinary way, speaking to him. And he immediately fell under its spell.

Every night at ten o'clock, he'd steal off to his room and fiddle with the radio dial until he managed to tune into the station as clearly as that night's weather permitted. The show was broadcast over KTHS, a fifty-thousand-watt clear-channel station out of Little Rock, Arkansas, which at the time was considered the wellspring of southern communication to the outside world. Dozens of shows that originated on local country stations, jinxed by only enough wattage to power a flashlight, were co-opted by this megasaurus and beamed across the country, bringing a taste of good old-fashioned cornpone into the homes of fidgety northerners. For a measly fee of about five or ten dollars, KTHS licensed programs like *Lum 'n Abner* and *The Johnny Cash Show,* which made it possible for some radio freak, sitting in his kitchen in Chicago or Detroit, to hear an earnest-sounding cracker rattle on about rooooom-tism or hawg fodd'r or this here fahn-lookin' l'il Stooo-baker see-dan wi' nuttin' but wile stal'ins unner t' hood.

Around 1955, KTHS picked up a show out of Shreveport, Louisiana, called *No-Name Jive,* featuring a badass, burpgun-style disc jockey named Frank "Gatemouth" Page. In reality, Page was the same southern gentleman who co-hosted the widely revered *Louisiana Hayride* every Saturday night from eight to eleven o'clock, as well as a live show with Hank Williams every morning at a quarter after seven until the singer's death in 1953. But here he was incognito, disguised as your typical adenoidal speed freak, an unrelenting jive bomber, reeling off all the latest R&B hits.

Actually, the show had been on the air since 1949, the same year the term "race music" was abandoned in favor of the lustier and more inspired "rhythm & blues." *Groovy's Boogie*, as it was originally called, was an immediate hit on Shreveport's KWKH, thanks in part to the sultry music, but more probably to Ray "Groovy Boy" Bartlett, the show's host, who would grab a live mike, hang out the window of the Commercial Bank Building on the corner of Market and Texas Streets, where the show was broadcast, and scream: "Hell-*ooooo* bay-be—*blow yo' horn!*" Then, while traffic below wreaked havoc for the pissed-off merchants who'd come out to see what was going on, he'd segue into an appropriate hellraiser like Wynonie Harris's "All She Wants to Do Is Rock" or "Drinkin' Wine Spo-Dee-O-Dee" by Stick McGhee.

As a result, *Groovy's Boogie* became the number-one show in town. People of all ages tuned in every afternoon at four o'clock to get their dose of Groovy Boy as he spun platters by Stickhorse Hammond, Sister Rosetta Thorpe, Bobby "Blue" Bland, the Midnighters, and Howlin' Wolf. "Blow yo' horn!" replaced the rebel "Yee-hah!" as Shreveport's clarion call. And Ray Bartlett turned white kids on to the blues.

Frank Page, Groovy Boy's successor in 1950, slid behind the microphone with relative ease, and from the very first lead-in—"Here he is, folks, the Mouth of the South: Bru-thuh Gate!"—the show was resurrected. *No-Name Jive* (which the show would later be called) didn't attempt to duplicate the manic intensity of *Groovy's Boogie.* Whereas Bartlett had babbled at an incomprehensible clip, Frank Page hipped himself to the bebop language spoken by the city's musicians. His trademark became the way-out rap, an aphoristic ragout salted with street savvy, offbeat poetry, and the ultimate essence of "cool." While he wasn't a natural freak by any stretch of the imagination, Page managed to mimic the spade cats who populated Shreveport's underworld of blues haunts and chicken shacks that had been heretofore off-limits to respectable folk. He diluted their rap, conferring an insider's sensibility to the listener and making them members of this exclusive, oddball society. In time, this wordplay would develop into a universal language—a salvo of idiomatic jive talk laced with musical imagery.

But even as late as 1955, Brother Gatemouth was unique. It was a startling revelation to flick on the radio and hear a southern voice purr:

> Nothin's shakin' but the
> leaves on the trees,
> Wouldn't be shakin' were
> it not for the breeze.

Once he'd established the hypnotic mantra, verses rolled off his tongue at an amazing speed.

Nothin's boilin' but the
peas in the pot,
Wouldn't be boilin'
if the pot wasn't hot.

Then the deejay switched off his mike, and another voice that sounded like its owner was in the process of having his black ass dragged across hot coals interrupted the broadcast with a demonic shriek: "*A-whomp bop-a-loo-bomp, a-whomp bam boom!*" Little Richard's subhuman voice was fired up like an overheated Harley. He pounded the piano with both fists while screaming to be heard above Lee Allen's wild sax solo. "I've got a gal/ Named Sue/ She knows just what to do/ *Wooooo*. . . ."

Picture a fourteen-year-old boy in Hibbing, Minnesota, listening to this free-for-all. It would have struck him as the animalistic rumblings of Armageddon. Still, Bobby was an instant convert to Brother Gatemouth's jive-talking liturgy. He was stirred, as well, by the music's loudness, its barrelhouse rhythms, its outrageous lyrics, and its Lord-have-mercy style of singing. No doubt he felt the call that would eventually summon forth his burbling talents. For while Bob Dylan never materialized into a bona fide rock 'n roll star, he nevertheless used rock's R&B roots as a foundation for every form of music he ever made.

John Bucklen remembers that Bobby was absolutely floored by his initiation into rock 'n roll. "He couldn't believe it," Bucklen says. "The two of us were so hungry for anything, it didn't matter what it was, and then this sound comes along and sweeps us off our feet. We knew we were onto something that nobody else in Hibbing had any idea about—something very special—even though, at the time, we still weren't sure what it all meant."

Unfortunately, there was no place in Hibbing where the boys could buy these records. It took Stan Lewis, a swarthy, whippetlike Syrian who owned a cinderblock shoeshine parlor in Shreveport, to bring those records north. Lewis had struck up friendships with a contingent of fast-talking northern city dudes, a slippery crew of hipster entrepreneurs who, once or twice a year, rolled through town in rented cars, hustling their latest releases. Ahmet Ertegun, Lew Chudd, and Leonard Chess—the founders of Atlantic, Imperial, and Chess Records, respectively—all sold records to Stan Lewis out of the trunks of their cars.

They set him up in the kind of retail business that makes the IRS do cartwheels. Someone like Chudd, for instance, would lay a box of the new Fats Domino record on Stan, or a stack of Ernie Freeman singles. Stan would push a fistful of cash into Chudd's hand, and the books, as they say, were closed.

Stan's Shoeshine Parlor was transformed into Stan's Record Shop very nearly overnight. Coincidentally, Fred Watkins, the station manager at KWKH, had been looking desperately for someone to sponsor *Groovy's Boogie.* For the extravagant sum of one dollar a spot, Stan's earned the honor of becoming the show's exclusive sponsor. In between songs, the deejay would remind his listeners that, for the remarkably low price of three dollars and forty-nine cents, they could own a collection of the very same tunes he played on the air. Yes sir, for three dollars and forty-nine cents you'd receive "The Blues Special" or the "Muddy Waters Special" or "The Harmony Five Special" or any of them "Preacher" records ol' Groovy played on today's broadcast. Four to six records for three-and-a-half bucks was a steal to a boy who was deprived of a source close to home. As a result, many teenagers like Bobby culled their entire record collections from Stan Lewis's mail-order emporium.

In 1956, when the show expanded and changed its name to *No-Name Jive,* Stan Lewis became a household name. (It also helped Stan that he wrote the Dale Hawkins record "Suzy-Q," which became a number-one hit.) By this time the program reached anywhere from twenty-five thousand to sixty-five thousand listeners up and down the Mississippi River. Teenagers from Baton Rouge to Bismarck clung to the show for dear life. It became their single most important source of identity as the music confirmed their innermost fantasies. Blue-suede shoes, pink cadillacs, women with one-track minds and a whole lotta shakin'—no red-blooded American kid could have a more powerful incentive. But while the new culture was based on rock 'n roll music, its hard currency was records, and as such, Stan Lewis was in ecstasy.

Commercials for his records interrupted each broadcast with a frequency that would make Cal Worthington drool with envy. Unlike today's practice of bombarding a listener into submission, however, they never seemed obnoxious or intrusive. There was an absence of high-pressure salesmanship, none of the usual Madison Avenue razzmatazz we're accustomed to hearing on top forty radio. Stan Lewis managed to get his message across in such a straightforward, effective manner that he was regarded as an integral part of the show. Listeners identified him so strongly with the program that, in time, it became known unofficially as *Stan's Record Review.* Imagine that!—a sponsor becoming more imageworthy than a jive-talking disc jockey. It seems hard to believe in this day and age, though it was not so preposterous when you consider the dependency that was created between Stan Lewis and the show's listeners.

Look at it this way: What happens when a fourteen- or fifteen-year-old kid hears a song that knocks him out? The answer is easy—he decides he has to have it in his collection. Today that's as uncomplicated as buying a loaf of bread. You merely drive over to the closest mall, where several record shops compete for the trade, and pick it out of the appropriate stack. But in the mid-1950s that wasn't so routinely accomplished. The established labels like RCA and Capitol, which had begun to dabble in teenage music, had enough trouble convincing the owner of the sole record store in a particular town to carry their rock 'n roll issues. After all, adults constituted nearly one hundred percent of the record-buying public and it was a well-known fact they steered clear of rock music. So why should stores stock a lot of records no one was going to buy? Fortunately, the major labels were able to exercise some muscle and insist merchants carry rock 'n roll; otherwise they might find themselves slow in receiving shipments of the companies' top-selling artists like Perry Como or Tennessee Ernie Ford.

The independent labels were faced with much greater obstacles. Distribution for them was virtually nonexistent. If the owner of an independent label didn't drive cross-country dropping off records by hand, chances were his current releases would never see the inside of a store. Which meant that if a teenager in Fort Wayne or Peoria or ...*Hibbing!*...went into a record store looking for, say, "Little Girl of Mine" by the Cleftones, or for the Del Vikings' "Come Go with Me" on its original Fee Bee label, odds were he or she wouldn't find it.

This gave Stan's Record Shop a virtual lock on rock record retailing in the south and throughout most of the Midwest. The kids who regularly tuned into *No-Name Jive* knew Stan's carried these hard-to-find singles by virtue of his incessant ads, and so they didn't have to waste time searching for them all over town. What's more, it became clear that Stan could get you *any* title Brother Gatemouth played. His resources were that good. All you had to do was send in one dollar and eighty-nine cents per record, or save money by ordering one of his "special package" offers of three hits for "the itsy bitsy price o' $3.49," and in no time they'd arrive at your door.

Each morning, Stan trundled off to the post office, balancing a skyscraper of record cartons that represented the previous day's response to his ads. Waiting his turn in line, he liked to scan the mailing labels in order to gauge the demographics of his clientele. The bulk of the orders came in from the Mississippi Delta region and Texas—the areas immediately around the station's transmitters. Nevertheless, listeners from as far off as Mexico and Chicago became part of Stan's regular customers. They formed the basis of a devoted group of record collectors who he hoped would put this new music, as well as his mail-order business, on the map.

The demographics, for the most part, were predictable. He serviced medium-sized urban communities or southern boondock towns where the blues was an ingrained part of local tradition. One address that kept coming up, however, surprised him for its remoteness, a frontier town almost to the Canadian border. His shipments to Hibbing, Minnesota, were so steady, in fact, that it made him wonder about the kind of person who ordered all the obscure rhythm & blues titles—a teenager obviously, by the handwriting, who signed his notebook-paper letters "Bobby Zimmerman."

4

That Weird Kid

The records that found their way into Bobby Zimmerman's hands opened an inspirational floodgate and prompted him to seize upon the following conclusions: (1) despite his lack of training, he could play along with most rock 'n roll songs on the piano; (2) they gave him the drop on a new phenomenon that no one else in Hibbing was hip to; and (3) someday he was going to be a rock 'n roll star. To that end, nothing was going to stand in his way.

In the weeks following his discovery of rock 'n roll, Bobby confined himself to a corner of the living room, where he picked out a number of rudimentary three- and four-chord melodies on the family piano. From the start it dawned on him that, in this milieu, you didn't have to be Van Cliburn to find the right groove. He needn't endure tortuous hours of practicing scales or be forced to practice imbecilic warm-ups like "See the Pretty Bluebird" or "In My Sandbox" before getting to the real stuff. No, with rock 'n roll there was absolutely no discipline involved, a quality that must have struck Bob as enormously attractive. You were in there from the word "go," chording along with Jerry Lee Lewis, Little Richard, or one of the other exponents of the hard-driving rhythm style of piano playing. There was nothing to it; all you had to do was keep thrashing away at a particular chord on the upper register, while your left hand hammered the corresponding bass note. That alone provided him with a repertoire of more than a hundred tunes. With a song like "Lucille," he could drop the left hand altogether. So much for technique. The rest of it—the singing—well, you could do anything you wanted with that, a theory for which Bob was a shining example throughout most of his career.

Even as a child, Bobby never had a great set of pipes. He could carry a tune, but his singing voice was thin and wavery. It lacked the resonance of a confident vocalist who takes command of a melody, infusing it with his own phrasing and expression. Nor was it sweet and songlike; Bobby struggled awkwardly when it came to negotiating a lilting falsetto, which is the way students were taught to sing in grade school. Straddling the register between soprano and baritone, his voice never quite found a comfortable foothold. He was forced to slide into his notes rather than pouncing on them. His voice was tremulous and cracked in the throes of indecision, in much the same way a speeding car swerves out of control when you fail to apply the brakes with enough force.

That is no doubt why Bobby latched onto country & western music at such an early age. Relaxed and undemanding, it presented a viable alternative to a boy who loved to sing but was ill-equipped to deal with the dynamics of voice. There were no vocal tricks to interpreting the songs of someone like Hank Williams, none of the rising and falling glissandos that usually baffled Bobby. One only has to listen to a few bars of a Woody Guthrie recording to understand why Bob Dylan patterned himself after that wasp-voiced folksinger. But for the time being, rock 'n roll provided him with a whole new approach to singing, primarily because rock music came from the gut. It incorporated everyday expressions of emotion into the music—whoops, cries, and hollers. It was instinctive, improvisational. Bobby could shine merely by being himself.

Bobby sat at the piano every day after school, playing right up until it was time for dinner. He practiced whatever he'd heard on the radio the night before. Finding it was easy to remember the fairly homogeneous tunes, he played them with gusto, singing as much as he could remember of the lyric (often it was only the song's title shouted over and over again to fill up the melody line) or substituting his own words—"I got a yeah/ she can yeah yeah all the time"—without losing the overall feeling. Since most early rock songs expressed the same sentiments, lyrical content was not crucial to barreling through a song. Catchwords and key phrases were often enough to do the trick.

By the end of 1956, Bobby was confident enough with his ability to try it out in public. Until that time, he confined his piano playing and singing to the living room, and while Bobby never formally entertained anyone in his family, Abe, Beatty, David, and Florence nevertheless served as a kind of laissez faire audience. The only thing standing in his way was the lack of competent sidemen; Bobby needed a band.

Finding musicians who could play rock 'n roll in Hibbing at that time was nearly impossible. Not only weren't they playing it; they had very little knowledge of its tempos and cascading guitar solos. The closest thing to a talent pool Bobby could draw from was the high-school marching band. Having befriended Hibbing High's clarinet player, Chuck Nara, and a few other "straight" musicians, Bobby soon had the makings for what would become his first rock group.

"None of us had ever heard the music he wanted us to play," recalls Larry Fabbro, a ninth-grade trumpet player Bob recruited to handle the guitar chores. "Chuck and I were into jazz; Bill Marinac learned the string bass from a Yugoslavian folk-dance group in the area. But Bob came after us with all these records he'd gotten and introduced us to rock 'n roll." Soon afterward, Nara traded in his clarinet for a snare drum, Fabbro picked up a few basic guitar chords, Marinac learned how to "walk" a bass run, and together with Bobby's frantic piano playing, the boys brought Hibbing, Minnesota, into the Rock Age.

The group jammed in the Zimmermans' living room after school a few days each week. Bob would customarily play recordings of the songs he wanted to work on and then set about teaching his friends the riffs. "He was completely in charge," Fabbro remembers. "There was never any questions of our making a contribution (not that we could have, at the time). He knew exactly what he wanted us to play. If he didn't have the records he'd hum the parts until we got them down, then do whatever he wanted at the piano and expect us to follow him. We were strictly Bob's back-up band."

No sooner was the band ready than Bob came up with their first gig. He wheedled an invitation for them to audition for the College Capers, an annual talent show put on by students at Hibbing Community College, which held classes in a wing of the high school. Actually, this was nothing more than a parade of amateur talent thrown together by the student council. Such extravaganzas were very popular at the time in Hibbing, which had little else in the way of entertainment, and were usually well attended. This year, however, they were short on performers and opened up the contest to high school students.

The audition was held a few weeks later in the high school auditorium. Bob and the band arrived and took their place among the other hopefuls: tap dancers, acrobats, a girl who played "Carnival in Venice" on the accordion, a would-be opera singer whose piercing soprano must have sounded better at home in the shower. In all, they resembled a collection of *Gong Show* rejects. Watching them, as each took the stage, must have raised Bobby's hopes. The acts weren't even interesting, much less talented. He was going to shake up the proceedings with a couple of Little Richard songs he'd worked out with the guys.

When it was his turn, Bobby stepped up to the piano and launched into an uninhibited version of "Jenny Jenny" that rumbled through the cavernous hall. "Jenny, Jenny, Jenny, won't you come along with me/ Jenny, Jenny, *whoooooo,* Jenny, Jenny. . . ." Bobby sang with complete abandon as the band fought to hear him above the squall. "You know that I love you, we could live so happ-i-ly/ Jenny, Jenny, *whoooooo. . . .*" His performance must have sounded like a catfight to the jury of student council members sitting out front. They'd obviously never seen nor heard anything like it in their lives—a little tenth-grade boy, Abe Zimmerman's son, no less, shaking and screaming at the top of his lungs like. . .a berserk Negro! If that didn't beat all!

Luckily for Bob, the music was so loud it drowned out the laughter from the small audience who, nevertheless, applauded politely when he was finished. While a few student council members argued in favor of including the band on the bill as a shock-value act, the majority judged the act unsuitable for the College Capers.

Bobby took the rejection without the slightest evidence of misgiving or self-doubt. If anything, it seemed to have the reverse effect on him, as if the jury's failure to appreciate the music was actually an endorsement. The council members may have laughed at him, but it was out of ignorance. Hibbing was still oblivious to the music that was sweeping the nation, but Bobby knew that his performance was the coolest thing going, and the fact that it baffled these Rangers made it that much cooler. He was ultra-hip, avant-garde, the local emissary of rock 'n roll. If it was perceived as something outrageous, so much the better. "Trying to make life special in Hibbing was a challenge," John Bucklen says, "Rock 'n roll made Bob and me feel special because we knew about something nobody else in Hibbing knew about. That set us apart from the rest of the people there, who we called 'bongs.'"

If any concern was to remain constant in Bobby's life, it was this: knowing something—or pretending to know something—about which no one else was aware. Obviously, this was intended for both impressing and separating himself from the bongs, carving out his own identity. It conferred on him a kind of hip status that, in the 1960s, Dylan refined into an art form, albeit with malevolent consequences. He became a self-styled innovator by what French impressionist J. F. Millet called "a treating of the commonplace with the sublime." He pumped color into an otherwise gray environment. Occasionally, however, that meant stretching the truth in order to make his presence felt. A childhood friend from Minneapolis (where Bob often vacationed with relatives) remembers him as "a sullen, pouty kid" who continuously made up stories as a way of rising above the local playground continent. "The general impression we had of him was that he was a phony. He was always bragging about things he was supposed to have done that we knew he really hadn't."

Bobby's behavior was typical of a child who is not particularly outgoing or confident, but who wants desperately to be accepted and admired by his peers. He overcompensates by showing off. Like a magician, he needs his props to pull off a particular moment, be it the inside scoop on rock 'n roll or some other well-timed opportunity. He was, in effect, saying, "Look!—I can get your attention," making himself a threat as well as someone to be courted.

Through the music, Bobby had the new language, the divine words; his shocking performance at the College Capers audition was a way of coming down off the mountaintop and showing others the way. One might choose to dismiss the entire episode as a coincidence. After all, it was only a matter of time before rock 'n roll found its way to Hibbing, Minnesota. It could have been any one of the five-thousand-

or-so kids there who introduced the new music to his peers. On the other hand, Bobby demonstrated, as he did throughout his career, his knack for perfect timing. Whether it was serendipitous or he was in fact an idiot savant, Bob Dylan has always managed to strike chords in the deepest part of one's soul, and he has done it by always being a step or two ahead of everyone else. That is the mark of a true artist: to be able to intuit what was already in everybody's subconscious and to articulate it for them.

To think of a fourteen- or fifteen-year-old boy causing this kind of reaction with his very first public performance is to acknowledge that the young Dylan was an inspired and talented rebel. However, as Horace Walpole points out, even the wisest of prophets makes sure of the event first. Up to this point, Bobby had only *heard* rock's cultural mandate. It wasn't until sometime in 1956, when he sat through a movie at his uncle's State Theatre, that he got a chance to see it as well.

The Blackboard Jungle arrived in Hibbing months after it had already played most of America's first-run movie houses—perhaps simply as a consequence of scheduling, or perhaps a precaution against the frenzied effect town fathers feared it would have on their teenagers. (*The Blackboard Jungle* sparked a few minor skirmishes, which the press sensationalized as "teen riots," at early showings of the film.) Bobby saw the movie with his friend and classmate Leroy Hoikkala, another introverted, musically aware kid, and it made a profound impression on both of them.

The Blackboard Jungle is the story of a young teacher's first classroom experience at North Manual Trades High, a multiracial school made up primarily of working-class kids, set in one of New York's seamier neighborhoods. By today's standards the film would be considered predictable, derivative, melodramatic, and boring. But in 1956, it presented a disturbing and provocative look at the lost, angst-ridden teenagers who rebelled against the adult values and adult control of postwar America. What's more, *The Blackboard Jungle* introduced rock 'n roll to the movies (over the credits), linking the causes and making for one potent statement to its audience of impressionable young viewers.

"Bob couldn't believe it!" Leroy Hoikkala exclaimed when he recalled that afternoon. "We were walking home past the Alice School, and he kept saying, 'This is really great! This is exactly what we've been trying to tell people about ourselves'"—as if to say: Maybe now they'll believe us. "Looking back, that film really changed our lives," Hoikkala says, "because for the first time, we felt it was talking directly to us."

The Blackboard Jungle also defined two distinct crowds in American high schools—the do-gooders and the greasers, or JDs—and suddenly you had to decide which group you'd be affiliated with. For most kids, it was strictly a matter of economics and caste. Those who were financially comfortable strove for self-improvement and maintained a squeaky clean image. The poor, as Disraeli said, are ordered by different manners. If you were from the wrong side of the tracks, you were already cynical about your social position and were more apt to flaunt an attitude. Bobby's option wasn't so black and white. His middle-class Jewish upbringing and everything that went with it—a strong desire to please his parents, an impulse to do the right thing, irrepressible guilt—weighed heavily on his soul. The hoods, on the other hand, embodied his romantic fantasies with their motorcycles, tough chicks, and contempt for authority. Clearly, he was caught in a social vise.

Music provided Bobby with the wherewithal to straddle the fence as far as his image was concerned. There he was, a good kid, the perfect little gentleman, a budding musician who sat down at the piano *without even having to be asked!*—and what did he do? He played rock 'n roll! To make matters worse, it wasn't the kind of white bucks-and-crewneck stuff the teen idols were singing. It wasn't exactly "Love Letters in the Sand." No, it was chock-full of the meanest, most salacious lyrics ever to darken a public place. Imagine how confusing this must have been to the circle of decent, studious kids who deep-down felt something give way inside of them when Bobby began to play but were too uptight to let themselves go. What a threat he must have posed to them. His commitment to the music alone was enough to raise a few eyebrows. That boy was possessed! When he began talking in earnest about having a group and making records, even his band backed off. "None of us took it that seriously," Larry Fabbro says. "At some point, Chuck and Bill and I began talking about having real careers. Bob continued to hang out and dream about rock 'n roll, and we took the opportunity to go our separate ways."

No longer preoccupied with his band, Bobby struck up a friendship with John Bucklen, a big-boned ninth-grader who lived across town in one of Hibbing's less exceptional neighborhoods. John was the perfect foil for Bobby's aggressive fantasies. He was painfully shy, supportive of every wild scheme Bobby proposed, and a devoted friend. More pivotal, perhaps, was John's fanatical interest in rock 'n roll.

Together, the boys spent every spare minute pursuing their raison d'être. Each day after school they'd meet at Melrad's Cafe, a greasy spoon across the street from the Lybba Theatre, where, over cherry pie and coffee, music was discussed in the most reverential of terms. Bob and John preferred Melrad's over the more popular after-school hang-outs because none of their classmates—bongs to a man—came in there; it was theirs exclusively in which to dream aloud about the songs and the new crop of singers who were emerging as formidable heroes. One, in particular, they both admired was Gene Vincent, who, with his group, the Blue Caps, staged an all-out assault on America's teenagers by playing a brand of down-and-dirty *white* rhythm & blues that was rougher and more suggestive than that of their predecessors. (Until this time, only the Crew Cuts and groups like Bill Haley were considered white practitioners of the rock idiom, and by today's standards they'd be considered preppies. Even Elvis Presley was promoted as a good boy who was devoted to his parents. Vincent, by comparison, was a street tough, a hood.) Gene Vincent dazzled these country bumpkins with his urban-gutter posturing, DA haircut, mean guitar licks, and virtuoso singing.

How were two kids from Hibbing supposed to get a step closer to this fantasy? A cinch, Bobby suggested. All they had to do was find themselves a couple of blue caps and pretend they sang with Gene Vincent. All the stores were selling the kind of hat President Eisenhower made popular, even in a labor stronghold like Hibbing where Republicans were grouped in the same general phylum as reptiles. So it was over to Feldman's Department Store on Howard Street, where Bobby and John picked out a couple of smashing turquoise chapeaus, before embarking on an excursion into a relatively new phenomenon called lip-syncing.

"Be-bop-a-lula, she's my baby/ be-bop-a-lula, I don't mean maybe..." It was Bobby's turn to be Gene Vincent, going through a series of stagy gyrations in a corner of his bedroom that had been converted into a makeshift bandstand. John pantomimed a guitar two steps behind him, moving his lips whenever a background vocal was required. There, they covered all the hits of the day, from "Be Bop A-Lula" to "Roll Over Beethoven" to "Long Tall Sally," yanking the narrow brim of the caps over their eyes in the fashion of a small-time hood. "... be bop a-lula, she's mah babe, mah bay-hay-be now, mah bay-hay-be now, mah bay-hay-be now."

One afternoon, in the midst of a particularly rollicking "club date," Abe accidentally barged in on their act. He wore an expression of complete shock and disbelief. It was as if he had caught the boys jerking off. "Oh, my God!" he muttered. John Bucklen remembers Abe's reaction very clearly. "It wasn't simply surprise," Bucklen says now, "but more like disgust. He didn't try to hide the fact that he thought we were a couple of silly children. He couldn't deal with that and left the room shaking his head."

Bobby was thoroughly humiliated. The confrontation with Abe had clearly unsettled him, but he recovered in time to discourage any discussion of it with his friend. Instead, Bobby internalized it, as he did most personal matters. "He was very private, even as a kid," Bucklen recalls. Still, it was hard to mistake the colossal resentment and utter disappointment Bobby felt, camouflaged though it was in the petulant anger. "I think it was very painful for him to have to hate his father like that," Bucklen says. Undoubtedly, it is shattering for a boy of fifteen or sixteen to lose his father's respect, especially when his creativity is dismissed as complete foolishness. This put Abe squarely in the camp of people who didn't understand what Bobby was about, another face in the audience who laughed derisively when Bobby was struggling to express himself. Alas, he was just another ignorant Ranger.

Seemingly ostracized by his peers and his family, Bobby Zimmerman turned deeper into his music and the rebellious fantasies it inspired. He appeared oblivious to people's opinions of him. He became more independent—a loner, as some friends observed—in an effort to protect himself from the criticism and rejection of closed-minded individuals. To many, Bobby's behavior seemed eccentric, if not downright weird. There were certain social conventions Hibbing teenagers were expected to observe, and Bobby refused to conform. "He wasn't influenced by social pressures or peer pressure," says Monte Edwardson, a future sideman of Bobby's, who chose to view his friend's behavior as unique. "That wasn't easy, because Hibbing is a very cliquish community. Still, if he wanted to do something that wasn't socially acceptable in the area, he just went ahead and did it without concern for the consequences. At the time, it made Bob stand out as an oddball."

Now in tenth grade, Bobby was recognized by classmates as a renegade. Despite the gradual infiltration of rock music into the cultural mainstream, at school it continued to alienate him from the status quo. Bobby nevertheless went full throttle ahead along his alternative course of study. Each night he tuned in faithfully to *No-Name Jive* for its up-to-the-minute offering. He was a determined listener, developing an ear that was acutely sensitive to riffs and vocal inflections. This, in turn, rendered him an accomplished mimic. After hearing a new tune, Bobby could imitate it to perfection. The next day, he'd play the song almost note for note, word for word on the piano while John Bucklen captured the performance on his reel-to-reel tape recorder.

For the most part, Bobby memorized the songs he heard on the radio, lest he be forced to wait three months for them to arrive by mail. Crippa's, Hibbing's pitifully understocked record shop, hadn't yet begun to carry all the newest rock 'n roll records. Neither did WMFG, the local radio station, play them. And WEBC in Duluth played only the whitest of the top forty hits. The only breakthrough, as far as Bobby was concerned, occurred later that year when a Hibbing deejay named Ron Marinelli began hosting an hour-long teen program on a privately owned radio station. For the first half-hour, Marinelli ran down the national Top Ten before saying, "Now we go to Jim Dandy in Virginia." Then, by remote hook-up, another deejay took over, jazzing up the show's final segment with records by Lightnin' Hopkins, Howlin' Wolf, and a cross-section of other blues artists whose scatty vibratos must have been a revelation to the musically naive Rangers.

No sooner had Bobby heard them than Jim Dandy became the sole object of his interest. He wanted to know who this guy was and where he came from. Where had he latched onto R&B? How much did he know about music? And most important, was there anything Bobby could learn from him. There was another issue, too, that nibbled at Bobby's curiosity—Jim Dandy's slow, sulky twang. The dude sounded black. Could it be? Was it possible that a Negro could have slipped through the color lines and dared to settle where none had ever ventured before. The odds were unlikely, still. . . .

Bob and John Bucklen descended on Ron Marinelli's office, where their suspicions were confirmed. Sure enough, Marinelli told them—

ol' Jim's a colored guy. Hell of a nice one, too. Why, he wouldn't be surprised if Jim could teach the boys a lot about music, and he gave them his colleague's phone number in Virginia.

Virginia, Minnesota, is another of the bleak mining towns on the Mesabi Range—a once-thriving community picked over by the robber barons who exploited its natural resources before moving on—a half-hour's drive north of Hibbing. Bobby borrowed his father's car (he had turned sixteen that spring) and, with John Bucklen in tow, set out in search of their black messiah.

That a man like Jim Dandy landed in Virginia is one of those fortuitous strokes of luck that befall all great artists. A black man who played R&B for an audience of predominantly blue-collar workers whose tastes ran to country & western and polkas—you try to figure it out. Nevertheless, Jim Dandy had the kind of credentials that made him one of the genuine early influences in Bob Dylan's life. A slight, wiry man in his early thirties whose real name was James Reese, he was a disciplined student of urban blues and jazz, an eclectic audiophile whose record collection knocked Bobby for a loop.

Bobby gaped at the man's neatly lined shelves of records, not so much for their size, but for the extent of singers and stylists he'd never heard before. Big Bill Broonzy, Son House, Robert Johnson, Bukka White—the names swirled around him like a cyclone. Lester Young, Charlie Parker, Coleman Hawkins—where had these musicians been hiding? How could he get an immediate grasp on it? The analogy that can be made is to someone who has just learned to read and, stumbling upon a copy of *Crime and Punishment,* is told, "If you like this stuff, you ought to check out *Madame Bovary, Great Expectations,* and *The Sound and the Fury.*" Jim Reese introduced Bobby to an entirely new world of music, one that expanded the boy's already bountiful reach and helped him to define the roots of rock 'n roll.

Over the next year, Bobby made a number of pilgrimages to Jim Reese's home, the upper story of an old two-family dwelling, where he was always made to feel welcome by the deejay and his wife. They'd sit in the living room and talk for hours about every facet of popular music. Jim, the rabbi, and Bobby, his devoted student, the two engaged in rap sessions born out of a common love and necessity. Jim would play the records Bobby specifically wanted to hear, but it was no secret that the deejay held rock 'n roll in low esteem.

"I remember Jim telling Bob that rock music was nice superficially, but that jazz had a much deeper meaning to it," John Bucklen recalls. Standing at the shelves, Jim would pull out well-worn recordings of the great jazz artists and play the boys samples of his favorites. He impressed both boys with his knowledge of the musical idiom, elaborating on each song with a few words of theory and biographical information. From what we know, Bobby put these teachings to excellent use.

Bob Dylan, from his earliest years, was recognized as an accomplished interpreter of songs. His first album contains compositions written by people as stylistically diverse as Jesse Fuller, Roy Acuff, Blind Lemon Jefferson, and Woody Guthrie, yet in Dylan's hands each becomes unquestionably his own. Observers attribute this to Bob's natural instinct, but while there may be some truth to that, the simple fact is that Bob was and still is a superb listener and an eager student of all musical idioms.

By the time he was sixteen, Bobby had already opened up his ears to rhythm & blues, gospel, rockabilly, country & western, show tunes, and jazz (just as, later on, he would embrace spiritual and Middle Eastern music). He listened to everything he could get his hands on. Thus, he absorbed a wealth of sounds and styles on which he later drew, like a musical smorgasbord. This foundation no doubt enriched Bob Dylan's "natural instinct" and gave him a dimension other performers of his generation sorely lacked—the ability to be stylishly sophisticated. Jim Reese obviously recognized Bob's insatiable appetite and cultivated it.

Later on, Bobby took other friends along when he visited the disc jockey, but most found the experience too esoteric and interminable. Says a former girlfriend of Bobby's, "It was like sitting in a bar with an alcoholic who just wants one more drink. It was an addiction, and this was the only way Bobby had of satisfying it."

But talking about and listening to music quenched only a small part of Bobby's thirst. He wanted to play again, to perform with a band. Music, he realized, no longer had to be limited to his dreams. There was no law that said it had to remain a hobby. From now on, everything he'd do would fit into his plans for becoming a rock 'n roll star.

As it happened, Bobby knew just the guys who could help further his ambitions. Leroy Hoikkala and Monte Edwardson were classmates at Hibbing High, brawny country boys who worked after school at Feldman's, selling shoes and sweeping the floors. One afternoon, Bobby intercepted them as they were leaving the department store. "Hey, you guys like music," he said, as they ambled up Howard Street past the decrepit Androy Hotel. "We should do something. We should get a band together."

The idea sounded fine to the boys, both of whom had worked with other bands but had never played rock 'n roll. Hoikkala, a cynical, aloof kid, was a competent enough drummer. Monte Edwardson was the best guitar player in town, a flashy chorder who could bend over backward and continue to pick until his head hit the ground. (This stunt apparently complemented Bobby's penchant for dancing while he played the piano.) As the trio began to work together, they found an uncanny exhilaration in what they were doing. They became technically tight, and the intensity of the music fused with their dorky personalities and transformed them into punk studs. This regeneration, of course, was the narcissistic artifice of *attitude,* which was intrinsic to the rock 'n roller's persona. A mix of vanity, bluster, conceit, and smugness, it embodied the rebellious nature of the music and cut a defiant image that Bob would continue to project throughout his career. Here, however, it was contrived to give the boys a conspicuous identity. The Golden Chords, as they began calling themselves after Hoikkala's glittery-gold drum kit, gained notoriety as Hibbing's first rock combo. But as Hoikkala and Edwardson soon realized—like Larry Fabbro and Chuck Nara before them—it was Bob's band.

"He'd have listened to *No-Name Jive,*" Leroy Hoikkala remembers, "then would say to us, 'I heard some neat stuff, this is how it goes.' Since records hadn't gotten to Hibbing, he'd hum it for us—all the different parts—so we could get it down. 'This is what I want, try it this way,' he'd say. Then he'd dash over to the drums and show me what to do. He'd sing the guitar parts for Monte. Bob had complete arrangements worked out in his head and he used us so that he could hear them come to life."

The band's repertoire consisted primarily of R&B tunes culled from *No-Name Jive*'s homogeneous playlist. A special favorite was "Flirty Gerty" by the Jive Tones, which Bobby sang like a *houngan* voodoo demon. What's more, he had begun writing his own songs. With

Bobby calling the shots, the Golden Chords worked out a twelve-bar blues of his called "Big Black Train," which most likely stands as his earliest composition.

According to the Dylan legend, the Golden Chords performed for the first time at the high school Jacket Jamboree in the winter of 1957. This would have been an auspicious debut for the as-yet undistinguished band, since the Jamboree was regarded as the high point of the school's social calendar. Held annually, the Jacket Jamboree is a week-long festival honoring the winter sports teams that was patterned after the traditional college homecoming pageant. For five days, classes are interrupted for all kinds of competitive activities like tug-of-war and volleyball tournaments, culminating in a Friday afternoon ceremony at which a winter king and queen are crowned. A talent show, held the previous Monday, determines which lucky acts get to entertain the royal couple. Considering the circumstances of Bobby's previous audition, it should come as no surprise that the Golden Chords never quite made it to the coronation.

Their performance, in the words of an eyewitness, was "one of the most shocking bits of exhibitionism to hit Hibbing, then or since." This is an obvious overstatement, but nonetheless, the audience reaction to the band's audition foreshadows Bobby's reputation as the class weirdo throughout his remaining school years.

In fact, the performance was nothing more than a standard Bobby Zimmerman set, consisting of a couple of new rock 'n roll songs, followed by the requisite Little Richard impersonation.

That afternoon—one of the most blustery days on record—fifteen hundred students piled into Hibbing High's stately auditorium. A testament to the mine owners' Babylonian *anschauung,* the hall is a cathedral-like gilt-and-filigree amphitheater, suggesting a cross between a chapel and a dance hall. The sprawling interior boasts blue-velvet orchestra seating with a hand-scalloped overhanging balcony reserved for the ranks of disenfranchised underclassmen. Overhead, the vaulted ceilings are ornately carved and painted in the seraphical style of the Sistine Chapel, complete with a million-dollar pipe organ. As if all this isn't enough, the walls are trimmed with a webbing of rococo moldings; even the fire extinguishers are encased in stained-glass crypts. More impressive, perhaps, is the ebony eight-foot Steinway grand which sits center stage like a dignitary lying in state; with a boat like that,

Bobby could rock 'n roll with the major leaguers. In all, it was more spacious and elegant than the Carnegie Chapter Hall at which Dylan would eventually stage his New York concert debut.

The Golden Chords had agreed to appear near the end of the program to accommodate the equipment change. From backstage, the boys watched as the senior MC killed time between acts. The whole student body had turned out for the event, and anticipation ran high, despite the phalanx of teachers who sat custodially with their homeroom classes. For more than twenty years the Jacket Jamboree had served as a release from the rigors of classical education, and the talent show was the apogee for anyone with real or imagined talent. The program had a competitive *Amateur Hour* quality to it that tied in handily with school honor and tradition, and, as such, had presented acts from all walks of the performing arts. But until that afternoon, the audience had never seen the likes of what Bobby Zimmerman had in store for them.

William Law, who was to become the school's principal, got his first look at the city's future star that afternoon. He recalls being stunned by Bobby's performance. "I had always known him as your average, unassuming student," Law laughs in retrospect, "so that seeing him there was like a spirit had taken possession of his soul." Law remembers Bobby bounding on stage, singing rock 'n roll as loudly as he possibly could, to the total amazement of both teachers and students. Almost on cue, the audience began to laugh at the spectacle. Bobby Zimmerman was behaving like a lunatic again; he was out of control, only this time you couldn't even hear the singing above the roar.

John Bucklen, cowering in the balcony, was flushed with embarrassment for his friend. "Bobby was so wound up, going full steam," Bucklen says. "Today, his performance would be considered subdued, but those kids had never seen anyone play rock 'n roll before. To them, Bob looked like a comical cartoon character, a total nut. They just didn't understand what he was doing."

Halfway through the second number, an incident occurred that proved to be an even more memorable showstopper. "The pedal broke on the piano," William Law says. "Bob had been standing there, thumping on it so hard that it just snapped off with a clang." The audience titters now broke into uncontrollable laughter. Law recalls: "The teachers had a good laugh about it, too."

B. J. "Bonnie" Rolfzen, who taught eleventh-grade English, told journalist Toby Thompson years later that the earsplitting music was absolutely the loudest thing anybody had ever heard. His version of the episode has a supporting cast of moralistic teachers rushing backstage to shut off the power to the instruments. That, in fact, never happened. A more accurate picture is provided by Charles Miller, who retreated to the faculty lounge following the show. The teachers he found there were in a huff over Bobby's act. "One guy wanted to throw him out [of school]," Miller remembers, adding that other reactions were somewhat more tempered. "They made it clear that they weren't going to permit this type of music on the school stage anymore. It was too violent a departure from the norm for them."

Bobby was finally out of the closet, so to speak. No longer a bedroom rock freak, he had declared himself openly in front of the entire student body. His classmates were shocked. They couldn't identify with his wacky behavior. There was something irresponsible about it, something almost dangerous, although many were intrigued by the music.

As a result, the Golden Chords became a fixture of Hibbing's teenage undercrust. All that year the band played for kids who dared to declare themselves disciples of the emerging rock 'n roll culture. They played wherever they could—in garages and living rooms, in unheated basements, practicing new material in order to be the most current, the most outrageous, and just plain The Most.

Sunday afternoons, the band rehearsed at Collier's, a family-style barbecue joint, which was closed regularly in observance of the Sabbath. To a passerby the shuttered restaurant may have appeared God-fearing, but inside the place was jumping. The boys would enter the building circumspectly, hauling their equipment in through the basement where they stopped to watch the kitchen staff shoot hundreds of potatoes through an electric peeling machine. When the fascination wore off, they went upstairs to play.

Collier's wasn't what you'd call a happening place. It was nothing more than a long, narrow dining room set up to accommodate the folksy crowd. Owing to the volume of advance cooking in the kitchen, Sunday afternoon was hotter than an oven inside. Bob or Leroy would prop the front door open to cool off the room, and kids on their way home from church would stop by out of curiosity to hear what was going on. In no time, Collier's would be jammed with teenagers celebrating the Lord's day in their own deviant style.

Bobby finally got to perform his Little Richard numbers for an unhostile audience. He really let loose at Collier's, screaming and shaking to the music, his leg striking out at the piano keys every so often to whip up the crowd. Occasionally, they'd slow things down with a Buddy Holly or a Hank Williams number, but for the most part, rhythm & blues ruled the day, with the emphasis on rhythm.

Unfortunately, Bobby was unable to take full advantage of the liberating beat. He was shackled to the piano like a prisoner; he couldn't move with it and had to confine his energy on stage to a specific area. And perhaps more fundamentally, the band could play only in rooms that had pianos (which in Hibbing were few and far between).

For Bobby, this problem was easily surmountable. He simply asked Monte Edwardson to teach him a few chords on the guitar. "He picked it up in no time," Edwardson recalls. Thereafter, Bobby began switching off between piano and rhythm guitar to suit his mood.

Bobby used the guitar the way a ballerina uses a great dancing partner. It sharpened his talent as a performer, really brought him out on stage so that he was right in there with every note. Now he could play the music with his body, as well. He could wring every last ounce of energy out of a song. Act it out to the hilt. Getting off on the music. At last, he would be more visible, less a member of the band and more the focal point.

Bobby felt more comfortable with a guitar. Technically, it didn't demand as much of him as the piano. He didn't have to master it or reach beyond an elementary degree of proficiency in order to play at his peak. You could hammer out all the three-finger chords you liked on a piano, but at some point in every song even hellraisers like Jerry Lee and Little Richard broke into swirling arpeggios to wind out an instrumental break. Not so on the guitar. Bobby could play rhythm—a role that required little more than chording along with the melody—and still front the band. This method, in fact, was preferred by most legendary performers. Elvis Presley, John Lennon, Jim Morrison—none of them were extraordinary instrumentalists. They concentrated on songs and performances to put themselves across. They worked on the audience instead of an instrument, recruiting virtuoso accompanists who, for the most part, took a back seat to their exhibitionism.

In no time, Bobby had his own guitar, an assembly-line Silvertone he claims to have bought at Sears but, in fact, came from B&G Music on First Avenue for the extravagant price of twenty-two dollars. He also picked up a Nick Manoloff finger-exercise book to learn additional chords. Bob was too impatient, however, to stick with it, relying on Monte Edwardson to teach him the basics. Whatever Monte didn't know, Bobby glommed from others. "He'd run all over town with John [Bucklen] and pick up new chords for the guitar," says a high school friend of Bob's. "Anybody who played, he'd try to pick up something new. Then he'd share it with John, who was also learning to play."

Together, the boys set out to get the hang of their new instruments. Bobby was immediately the more disciplined of the two, almost to the point of obsession. He was always fiddling with the guitar, playing along with Hank Williams records even if he didn't quite have the chords down. He tried to pattern himself after Scotty Moore, whose trademark was a good, clean country lick. Other times he sat listening to the radio, cradling his guitar in his lap until a song came on that he could accompany. Then he'd strum along with it, mindful of each variant rhythm and the technique necessary to recreate it with his hand. Ten years later, young guitarists worldwide would go through the same ritual, painstakingly copying riffs off records by the Beatles, Rolling Stones, Yardbirds, and Animals. But Bobby's apprenticeship was a solitary one, without the luxury of thousands of peers or an environment to support and nurture his talent.

Bobby outgrew his Silvertone guitar practically overnight. If the truth be told, it was a junky little thing—the kind kids get when they sign up for group lessons at the local music emporium. A beginner's model. He could handle it well enough, but it'd never do for rock 'n roll. First of all, it was about as resonant as a tin can, producing more of a "sproong!" than a "twang!" The action, or fingerboard construction, was so preposterously high that you'd cut your fingers if you grabbed the strings the wrong way. Then, of course, came the aesthetics. Playing a Silvertone was like driving a Chrysler; there was nothing special or unique about it, nothing daring, or . . . raunchy! Someone like Gene Vincent wouldn't be caught dead with one in his hands. And more important, it wasn't electric.

Bobby and John cruised Hibbing's music shops in search of a more appropriate guitar. One of the places, a tumbledown joint in a reconverted bakery, had a selection of instruments unlike any other place on the Range. It was run by an old Finnish guy in his sixties named Mr. Hautela, who looked like a Bavarian brewmaster and had a personality to match. Stocky, with a 1930s German haircut, Coke-bottle glasses, and an accent equally thick, he entrusted the boys with a revolutionary new form of musical tablature he'd invented that utilized dots instead of notes. At a glance, the boys knew that it was absurd, although they forgave him his eccentricity. Hautela may have been a first-class nut case who waved his arms like a traffic cop when he talked, but he loved talking music with Bobby and John, and they appreciated his kindness. He also had a pair of Ozark Supros they coveted—black, solid-body electric guitars with a sunburst finish that fingered a lot like Fender Stratocasters but sold for a fraction of the price. "They cost us sixty dollars apiece," Bucklen recalls. "Hautela gave them to us at cost, because I remember Bob cackling, 'Wow!—did we ever get a deal!'"

Most kids would have waited to buy an electric guitar until they could afford an amplifier to power it. Most kids, but not Bobby Zimmerman. He was too impatient and improvised, instead, by holding the guitar against his bedroom window so that it would reverberate and simulate amplification.

This impatience was manifested most prominently in a physical characteristic that stuck with Bobby for the next twenty years. In the eleventh grade he developed a leg twitch that seemed to have a rhythm of its own and operated on a current of nervous energy. At any given moment, when Bobby grew bored, if he daydreamed or tuned out a companion, he'd hunch forward in his seat and jiggle his right leg at a spastic clip. He'd really let that leg fly: up and down, up and down, picking up steam in proportion to his restlessness. Sometimes, he'd be so preoccupied, so wrapped up in thought, that he was oblivious to the attention it would attract. Friends would sit at a table with him and make jokes about how he was liable to take off, just lift right out of his seat as a result of all the explosive energy building up in that leg. Twenty-megaton *spielkas.*

Later, when he achieved godlike status, friends would gauge

Dylan's moods by the velocity of his leg and adjust their interaction with him accordingly. For all his inexpressiveness and fancied profundity, he was that transparent.

Clinically, Bobby's twitch is similar to the habitual adolescent practice of masturbation to relieve tension. This reflex action may have arisen as a result of acute frustration due to any number of creative anxieties. From the start, Bobby had some other agenda that, however unformed, was always lurking in his unconscious, disturbing his inner *wa*; there was always something in his mind saying, "This is a colossal waste of time." Then, again, when you're in a situation that's boring and you want to entertain yourself, the most attractive and satisfying place to retreat is to your crotch. Sexual energy cannot be discounted, because at the same time Bobby began to fidget—right around his sixteenth birthday—he became preoccupied with the opposite sex.

5

Rebel Without a Pause

After rock 'n roll, Bobby's fondest passion was for women. Although no Lothario, Don Juan, or Casanova, he always had a girl around for companionship. Arousing in Bobby the deepest emotion he ever felt, they inspired in him the most brilliant imagery he ever created. And while they charged his mind with the energy to imagine his famous songs, they also wreaked havoc upon his ordered life and filled him with a compulsion to plumb the darkest reaches of his soul.

Bobby developed his first crush in the spring of 1957. Barb Hewitt was a dark-eyed comely bookworm, stacked to the rafters, with a thick Range accent who reduced her young swain to a babbling jellyfish. "Oooh, I love Barb so much," he'd pine to impervious friends. "Oooh, I'm so crazy about her." Unfortunately, Barb had ideas of her own and blew him off before a courtship ever got off the ground. It wasn't until October of that year that Bobby started going steady, and this time the object of his affections was as devoted to him as a cocker spaniel in heat.

Echo Star Helstrom was the quintessential girl from the wrong side of the tracks. A Dogpatch dazzler whose hillbilly father warded off many of her suitors with threats of physical violence, Echo devoted herself unconditionally to the fulfillment of Bobby Zimmerman's dreams. She became his spiritual Maecenas, his very personal cheerleader. She encouraged his creativity to such an extreme that most people considered their fancies a *folie à deux.* "You want to be a rock 'n roll star?" she sniffed. "—just do it. Why not?" Echo herself was determined to become a movie star in the tradition of her idol, Marilyn Monroe, so their respective dreams weren't that far off. And she believed they both had what it took to hit the top.

If ever anyone was made for Hollywood, it was Echo. She had an ingenue's name, the right attitude, and all the tinsel trimmings. High, wide Finnish cheekbones, Siamese eyes, pale, chalky skin, and a full steamy mouth that hung limply and begged for masculine sustenance of any kind—Oh Lord, she was a hot little number! Bobby was wild about her body too. Not that it was perfect, but Echo knew how to carry off what she had. And what she had was the promise of sex. Lolita incarnate. The Brigitte Bardot, Tuesday Weld, sex-kitten look, with a baby-doll voice, peroxide-blond hair, and a pork-chop figure she'd stuff into tight jeans or leopard-skin tights, or whatever outrageous get-up she'd find to make Bobby's mouth water. What a tease that girl was! She fancied herself "a real outlandish creature." The ultimate shiksa who haunted every Jewish boy's dreams.

Together, they cut a striking pair: Echo in vampirish makeup, a khaki jacket festooned with idiotic patches like "Kiss Me—I'm a Red-hot Mama," and scuffed biker's boots; Bobby as a *yiddishe* Hell's Angel. Weirdos, is the way John Bucklen claims they were regarded around town. "Everybody thought they were a joke," says another contemporary from the Mesabi Range. "They stuck out like a sore thumb, but then people were always threatened by anyone who dared to be different."

They'd meet after school and walk over to the L&B Luncheonette on Howard Street for a slice of Bobby's favorite: cherry pie à la mode. Echo chain-sipped Cokes and nibbled on greasy French fries. Smoking half a pack of cigarettes between them, they'd take turns punching nickels into the jukebox to hear their favorite songs, but when the check came, Echo always picked up the tab. "Bobby claimed he never had any money," Echo remembers, but even at the time she believed otherwise. "He'd be so convincing, saying things like 'How can you deny this little boy a hot dog?' or 'I'd kill for another slice of pie,' but he'd rather go without than pay for it himself." It was like a game to Bob. He wasn't so much a mooch as he was a schemer. He enjoyed finagling things out of people, no matter how well off he was at the time.

John Bucklen remembers a standard Dylan dodge when it came to smoking cigarettes. "Bob would customarily bum one off me. Then, minutes later, I'd see he had an unopened pack in his pocket," Bucklen recalls. "The funny thing was, when I called it to his attention he pretended not to hear me or made me feel as if I was a cheapskate." This perplexed Bucklen, who came from a family that Bobby knew was struggling. Echo, too, found him inconsiderate. Says she: "Here I was the poorest kid of the bunch, but I got a sense that he *liked* having someone in my financial condition pay his way."

Whether or not Bobby derived satisfaction from this practice, he gravitated to people who fell below his family's social station and even, as we shall see, went out of his way to be accepted as one of them. He took naturally to slumming, as one of his friends liked to say. Feeling more at home with Echo's family, Bobby hung out regularly at their place in Maple Hill, a stretch of tumbledown shacks and cabins a few miles outside of town. There amidst the clutter of cows, chickens, and rusted out junk that Echo's father, Matt, collected, Bobby would rummage through her mother's pile of 78s and play Matt's electric guitar. Martha Helstrom would make the kids root beer floats, while impressing Bobby with her expert knowledge of country & western music. Then, after exhausting the requisite pleasantries with Mr. and Mrs. Helstrom, Bobby and Echo would steal outside to gossip or neck.

The Helstroms must have held a perverse attraction for Bobby, their having few of the material indulgences his own family had. Forget about late-model cars and fancy furniture; as late as 1950, there was no hot water or bathroom in their makeshift house. They were dirt-poor, down-home country folk. Matt, as ornery and unpredictable as a rattler, made his living as a jack-of-all-trades when he wasn't poaching beaver out of season. He put in an honest day's work, digging wells, welding machine parts, or repairing objects that other people couldn't fix. In the tradition of the country's earliest settlers, Martha sewed her daughters' clothes. To Bobby, they were as simple and exotic as the Okies in the John Steinbeck books he loved to read. It was obvious to Echo that he felt more comfortable in their hayseed world.

Consider, in contrast, his own family synergy. Beatty was a socially conscious go-getter, risen from the ranks of Hibbing's common herd to one of the city's first daughters. She was loud and feisty, an organization woman who served as president of both the local chapter of Hadassah and the synagogue's Sisterhood organization. In other words, she had what was known as a "big image." She was a socialite, albeit on a small-town scale. What's more, Beatty engaged in a practice that was considered wildly profligate by Hibbing's standards: she sold her practically new clothes to rummage shops when she grew tired of them. This was unheard of in a town where hand-me-downs were a way of life.

Abe was another story altogether. By now, Bobby had nothing but contempt for his father and everything he touched. You'd think that Micka Electric's timely expansion into Zimmerman Electric and Furniture would have pleased Bobby, would have made him proud of his father's professional successes. Unfortunately, this wasn't the case at all. The business's growth—its branching out into furniture, necessitating a new, larger showroom—became, to Bobby, a symbol of greed and plunder.

The reason for his discontent was unmistakable. Since the end of World War II, the economy in Hibbing's mines had been in steady decline. Natural ore was running out, and the Pennsylvania industrialists who bought the raw material were forced to use more pig iron in their manufacturing processes. The shortage of crude created strikes and massive layoffs that sent shock waves to the warren of surrounding communities. Hibbing, whose economy rested solely on the productivity of the mines, was hit hardest of all. Subsequently, the town became engulfed in a debilitating recession that foreshadowed its demise. Young families, the town's greatest resource, simply moved as far away as they could. The blue-collar workers, however, who found themselves without steady income for the first time in their lives, had to rely on the good graces of the local merchants to see them through the crisis. Initially, this didn't pose much of a problem; there was a deep-rooted symbiosis between the miners and Hibbing's business community which fostered a mutual economic dependency. But as the recession wore on, as it became clear to everyone that the mines would never recover, the degree of goodwill slowly disintegrated.

Zimmerman Electric and Furniture had a long-standing relationship with Hibbing's bloc of mining families. The store's reputation attracted customers to its comprehensive range of affordable, quality merchandise which the Zimmerman brothers invariably stood behind. Maurie was a skilled, capable electrician who backed up manufacturers' warranties with his own technical expertise. Paul handled the floor sales. It fell to Abe, their no-nonsense bookkeeper, to set up credit and payment schedules for the bulk of their clientele, who bought on time. And consequently, it was Abe's duty to collect on delinquent accounts, or *ergo propter hoc,* to repossess their goods. In the wake of frequent mine foreclosures, the latter practice occupied much of Abe's time.

"The Zimmermans really leaned over backwards for a lot of people, they let it go right to the end," recalls Benny Orlando, who was the store's service manager for eighteen years. But the climax was inevitable. The list of deadbeats began to pile up. Abe would rack his conscience over an outstanding account until it was impossible for him to carry it any longer. Then, reluctantly, he'd send Benny Orlando or one of the other drivers to collect. "A lot of time Abe would have Bobby go with me when I went to repossess the stuff," Orlando says. "He'd sit in the truck and smoke until it was time to carry out whatever it was we were taking back. It really hurt him to have to do this, but Abe left us no other choice."

Usually these calls were routine, but once in a while Bobby got a taste of hardship that shook him to the quick. Orlando remembers: "We went to a few places where the women cried and begged us not to take something from their home. Others got real angry and threatened us." One man, in particular, blamed his misfortune on the money-hungry merchants who bled the troubled miners. Orlando remembers, "He made some pretty smart remarks about Bobby's father and his religion being the cause of things. Bobby was real quiet after that. He didn't talk to anyone for a long time."

It's not hard to imagine the effect this had on Bobby. Many of his friends and classmates were affected by the mining slump. Their families struggled to make ends meet. Adversity was all around him, contrasted with the image of Abe Zimmerman, *his own father,* lowering the boom. He saw Abe as a kind of new-world Shylock extracting a pound of flesh from the backsides of impoverished laborers, sapping their pride. No wonder Bobby became so estranged from his father. How could he love someone who didn't appear to extend love to his fellow man?

For the time being, father and son were content to coexist as adversaries. Abe misperceived his son as a shiftless bum who placed his music (if you could call it that) ahead of scholarship. No doubt it would have been difficult at that time for any man to understand a son like Bobby, considering his uncommon interests. On the other hand, according to friends and family, Bobby saw his father as a miserly tyrant. A greater lack of communication between two men would be hard to find.

In Echo Helstrom's opinion, Abe Zimmerman was nothing if not a nice guy. "He was your typical Jewish father who wanted his son to do something he could be proud of," she says. "Except that Bobby wanted to spend all his time playing music." From the start, Bobby laid down an unspoken rule that the subject of his father was strictly off-limits. "He refused ever to talk about him," Echo says. "But in spite of the fact that they didn't get along, his dad must have loved him like crazy. Abe always let Bobby borrow his car; that was never a problem. Then, with little to-do, he bought Bobby a car and a motorcycle! He wasn't a mean man; he just wanted what was best for his son."

Leroy Hoikkala vividly recalls both automotive episodes. He says, "Around 1956, Bob wanted a '50 Ford convertible something bad. There was a really prime one for sale in town, and he'd waltz around saying, 'I want that car. Gotta have that car.'" At first Abe was totally against it, Hoikkala remembers. "But a few weeks later I stopped by his house and the car was sitting out front." A customized job minus the nose piece, it had dual pipes, skirts on both sides, and fancy hubcaps, and was lowered dramatically in the back—the kind of wheels you'd see the greasers tooling around in, cruising the main drag of every town in America.

Later, after the fascination with his car wore off, Bobby demanded the ultimate badass machine: a Harley-Davidson motorcycle with all the trimmings. Once again Abe voiced his disapproval, but confided in Hoikkala, "You've got a bike, Leroy—make sure Bob gets a good one and, if you can, come with us when we pick it out." In no time at all, Bobby found a killer cycle lying around in someone's garage on the west side of town. Abe watched reluctantly as his son rode it home, and he followed, eating Bobby's dust.

The next day, Bobby and Hoik got themselves a couple of Harley hats, the same kind worn by Gestapo officers, and then strapped watch bands over the brim to complete the tough-guy image. It didn't work out quite the way they had planned. Young hellions on wheels, they were about as unruly as a couple of boy scouts. "Bob, John Bucklen, and I used to crash a lot of parties," Leroy grins in retrospect. "We'd always ride up and force our way in with a couple of guitars." Only instead of feeling like personae non gratae, they usually wound up being asked to entertain. Buddy Holly tunes seemed to go over best with the high school crowd, though Hoikkala remembers: "There were times the music was so loud that nobody could hear what we were singing. So Bob would make up the name of a song—sometimes it had words, sometimes no words—and instead of singing we'd moan and groan, as a joke."

Some of these early scenes correspond neatly with Dylan's lifelong practice of putting people on and giving all the squares what they deserved. Bobby had already broken free when he desecrated the Jacket Jamboree with an attention-getting dose of rock 'n roll. The other misfits in Hibbing who dug rock 'n roll never put together bands of their own because a smart Ranger knew "never to stick his neck above the crowd" if he expected to live there in peace.

Bobby always pushed things a shade too far, in John's opinion—"a guy who was so far out, who made it difficult to know when to take him seriously." Bobby put John through such embarrassing scenes. One time when they were hanging out in the Twin Cities, in a Jewish section called Highland Park, Bobby told friends they were in town to cut a record; John, caught totally off-guard, had to play along so as not to embarrass his friend. Another time Bobby dragged him into the all-black Selbydale section of St. Paul to swap tunes with a couple of blues brothers who dug his honky scene. And the various masquerades he perpetrated, the rock-star impersonations trumped up to impress his friends. Bobby Vee was one of Dylan's favorite impostures. A dainty-voiced crooner whose claim to fame was that he had stood in for Buddy Holly after the latter's death. Bobby shamelessly copped Vee's rising star.

"I formed a group and I'm calling myself Bobby Vee," he told Bucklen upon returning from a visit with his relatives in Fargo, North Dakota, where, coincidentally, Vee also happened to reside and once even let Bobby try out with his band. He flipped John a copy of the newly released "Devil or Angel" and waited for his opinion. Bucklen remembers that it sounded remotely like his friend. "I believed him," John says, "so he never denied it or admitted it was only a joke."

Bobby laid the same rap on Echo, who fell for it in an even bigger way. "One time he called me and said, 'I want to play you this song me and the guys made over the weekend,'" she recalls. "It was 'Do You Wanna Dance' [by Bobby Freeman]. I thought to myself, 'Wow, they've really gotten good!' I didn't realize until years later that it wasn't him."

Not even Crippa's, the leading record store, escaped Bobby's ball-busting. He and Echo spent many afternoons there, crammed into one of the three listening booths with friends and a stack of 45s to check out the newest hits. Bud Crippa liked having the kids around. They spent most of their allowance on records. They gobbled up the rock 'n roll singles, and occasionally he'd sell one of them a musical instrument or a hi-fi which he'd allow them to pay for in affordable installments. Still, Bobby had to have the upper hand with the store's salespeople. To achieve this, he constantly asked for records he knew were impossible for Crippa's to get. "Bobby'd say, 'Get a load of this,'" Echo remembers, as they stood outside the store on Howard Street. "Then he'd go inside and in a very sincere voice ask for records he knew goddamn well they didn't have. Afterward, he'd grab me by the hand and haul me out of there before he burst out laughing. That's the way Bob liked to have fun."

Bobby loved putting them on. Those two-bit Rangers would believe anything he told them! With such gullible friends, Bobby could say or do anything he wanted. He had free rein—in fantasy and reality. Why not play it for all it was worth. Because in no time at all, Bobby *Zimmerman* would no longer exist... just as Bob *Dylan* would have no past. Reality and fantasy would merge as one and the same thing.

Until then, Bobby contented himself with playing rock 'n roll and taking his motorcycle for long, carefree spins around the Hibbing streets. Leroy Hoikkala remembers an afternoon when he, John Bucklen, and Bobby hit the road for an outing and narrowly avoided a disaster. The boys were traveling along a stretch of train tracks in neighboring Brooklyn, cooling off after a morning under the sweltering sun. Bob was leading the pack on his Harley 45, with John Bucklen riding shotgun on the back of Leroy's bike, when they were halted by an automated railroad barricade at Fourth Avenue, signaling the approach of an oncoming train. Finally the train rushed past. It seemed endless, what with its string of freight cars bumping along like swollen sausages. Leroy shut off his bike lest it overheat. But Bobby grew restless. "He had trouble just sitting there, waiting for the train," Leroy recalls, "and he just kept revving his engine." At long last, the caboose rolled past. Bobby pulled up on Leroy's right and yelled, "Let's head out!" Without waiting for a reply, he lurched forward, unaware that there was an identical set of tracks behind the disappearing train and another freighter was barreling through from the opposite direction. Bobby couldn't stop in time to avoid it; however, his bike luckily skidded out of control and tipped over inches from the speeding locomotive's wheels, pitching him headlong into the gravel.

"Another six inches and he would have been underneath it," John Bucklen says in retrospect. "I remember the engineer hanging out of the train; he did a fast double-take and looked back to see if Bobby was okay, but it would have been impossible for him to stop."

When it came to music, however, Bobby was totally in control. He was the most knowledgeable cat in town, the mavin of rock 'n blues. It didn't matter that he was laughed at, chided, and spurned by his peers. Other guys might have waged a campaign to win them over to his side. They might have persisted, trying to hip those "bongs" to their electric legacy. Bobby didn't. He didn't try to lower himself to their conventional scene. Why should he cede his authority, feel less superior, or compromise his individuality? In Hibbing, being weird and aloof earned him a certain cachet, even if it meant being alone most of the time. The laughter was just a confirmation that Hibbing wasn't the proper place to exploit his talent. It was merely a testing ground, where he could be as low-keyed or as way-out as he wanted.

Bobby's last memorable appearance in his hometown came on February 14, 1958, at the Winter Frolic Talent Contest, and in the Golden Chords' opinion, it was a fitting tribute to the anniversary of the St. Valentine's Massacre. The contest, sponsored by the local Chamber of Commerce, was one of Hibbing's dozen-or-so yearly festivals designed to distract the arctic shut-ins from the town's three leading pastimes: drinking, incest, and family abuse. As we've already seen, the Rangers loved these old-fashioned amateur hours. It played right to their level of concentration. Bobby signed up the band as soon as the date was announced and began rehearsing what he considered to be an unbeatable set of tunes.

The Golden Chords were psyched to the teeth. They'd had a look at the competition and pronounced it, in a word, abysmal. In their eleven-and-older group, they were pitted against a thirteen-year-old acrobat from nearby Keewhaton named Rosemary Bellicotti; Raymond Reed, thirteen, Hibbing's answer to Marcel Marceau; and Stanley (who, like Dagmar, affected no last name), fourteen, determined to wow 'em with a stylish tap dance routine. To hear the band tell it, you had to be deaf, dumb, and blind not to be able to spot the winner a mile away.

Though Hibbing's Memorial Building hosted the local hockey games, band concerts, and trade fairs, its adjunct, the Little Theatre, was a hole in the wall. A forerunner of the epidemic quad- and octoplex cinemas occupying today's malls, the Little Theatre was a stark, box-like facility with sloe-colored walls suggesting the hold of a ship or, better yet, a mine shaft. All two hundred and fifty red velvet-and-black-naugahyde seats were filled the night of the Winter Frolic, causing the poorly ventilated space to be even hotter than it normally was. Backstage, however, Bobby was cool, collected, and extremely confident. Before the curtain was raised he told Leroy Hoikkala, "We're gonna whip this talent show! We're gonna take it!" Monte Edwardson, too, expected the Golden Chords to walk off with the top honors. "The audience was definitely ours," he says of the teenagers who made up seventy-five percent of the crowd.

What the boys forgot to take into account was their most formidable opponent: prejudice. The jury, which would award a trophy to the winner of each age group, consisted of a few of Hibbing's more eminent town fathers, who viewed rock 'n roll with about as much favor as they did the low-down venomous scum that sang it. Facing them, the band would be dealt the same kind of justice as accorded a black man accused of a crime in an all-white neighborhood.

The Golden Chords were scheduled last on the bill, behind the nimble-footed tap dancer. By the time they were introduced, the audience was nearly comatose, due as much to the oppressive heat as to the profusion of mediocrity that paraded before their eyes. From the band's opening chords, however, the place came alive. The two hundred-or-so teenagers began hollering and screaming and wiggling in their seats. Each number ended with a thunderous round of applause that segued into the next. In all, the reception was nothing short of rapturous approval.

When it came time to announce the winner, however, the band was awarded second place. "We got robbed!" Bobby protested, seething at the inequity of the judges' decision, but Leroy and Monte understood it. "They couldn't give us the trophy because we played rock 'n roll and that would have been like an endorsement of the music," Leroy concluded. "But it didn't matter because we *knew* we had really won." The Golden Chords had, at last, earned the acceptance of their peers.

Once Bobby had some respect, he grew even more sullen and removed. "Bob spent a lot of time at home by himself," Leroy Hoikkala says of his friend's last year in high school. "He was kind of trapped because he didn't hang out with a crowd, so he'd stay at home by himself and listen to music." Echo kept him company much of the time while he practiced the guitar. Other times they'd hop into the car, find a side road or head up to the gravel pits, and make out. "Bobby was so shy about it," Echo recalls fondly. "But he was always excitable and anxious, and he could usually talk me into doing anything he wanted."

During the summer months, they'd lie on the grass in front of Echo's house and fantasize about the future. All their dreams began with: "When I get out of here I'm going to . . ." Staying in Hibbing was never a possibility for either of them, and while Echo was undecided about her plans, Bobby talked only about how he was going to break into the music business. He was single-minded about it. The only two things standing between him and stardom were his hometown and his name: Bobby *Zimmerman* would never do for a rock 'n roll singer. *Little* Bobby didn't cut it; Bobby *Zee* was too close to Bobby Vee (who he was still claiming to be). "He was actively looking for a name to call himself," Echo remembers, and John Bucklen even recalls Bobby billing himself under a few long-forgotten stage names.

One afternoon in 1958, Bobby pulled up in front of Echo's house and hopped out of the car. He had a small book in his hand and waved it wildly at her as he walked up the front steps. "I've finally found a name. I'm gonna call myself Bob Dylan," he said, pronouncing it *Dial-in*. "Whaddya think?" Echo agreed it was a splendid name, although

Bobby never specifically acknowledged it corresponded to his discovery of Dylan Thomas.

The sudden identification with the brilliant Welsh poet, a man who ended his career in a succession of Greenwich Village saloons, is the first sign that Bobby had formulated the essence of his persona and was starting to envision a parallel image. Stir into this self-invention the distinctive features of Dylan Thomas's tragic legacy: he wrote poetry crammed with complex, surrealistic imagery based on sources as varied as social criticism, love, Christian symbolism, witchcraft, Freudian psychology, and personal myth; from his enormous commercial success at the age of twenty, Dylan Thomas lived both recklessly and notoriously and over the years passed from religious doubt to joyous faith in God. This romantic image must have captivated Bobby no end. At last he had discovered a role model worthy of his ambitions, someone to style himself after and apotheosize. Everything about the poet was attractive to Bobby. In the course of reinventing himself, he would even take his name.

Assuming this new name opened up a world of possibilities for Bobby. He could gradually put his past behind him. There was no longer any need for Bobby to assuage his conscience concerning the number of pathological lies he told. He no longer had to worry about being found out, for as we noted before, Bob Dylan had no past, just as Bobby Zimmerman had no future.

Before the metamorphosis could take shape, however, it was necessary for Bobby to unload some baggage. Echo Helstrom drew the first in a fistful of short straws. She was the perfect groupie chick but knew, in her own words, that "nice Jewish boys aren't supposed to marry girls like me." After taking her to the junior prom, Bobby began dating around (even with Echo's best friend, DeeDee) and this eventually ended their relationship. Bobby professed his love for Echo while openly betraying her in order that she would be the one to break off with him. Bobby Zimmerman, and Bob Dylan as we shall see, was very bad at ending things with the women in his life.

Bobby simply drifted apart from his longtime friend John Bucklen, and ultimately had no time for him. "The tragic thing about it," Echo says now, "is that Bob was such a hero to John. He considered anything Bob said or did to be the greatest thing that ever happened. Then, before we graduated, Bob wasn't there for him anymore and John didn't know what to do with himself."

Bobby began hanging out in Duluth, where he and a cousin formed a group called the Satin Tones. Despite an appearance on a local amateur-hour TV show, the band was short-lived. Duluth was no place for a comer like Bobby to dig himself in. He made no commitments to friendship, due, in part, to the confusion he caused by proffering numerous last names. Was he Zimmerman or Dylan? No one knew for sure.

The name Dylan signified a formal, if not final, rejection of Bobby's roots. The Iron Range had no trace of a Dylan lineage in any of its registries. Certainly no one would suspect him of being a Jew. Even more significantly, it signaled a sharp spiritual separation from his father. Denying the family name is perhaps the most powerful weapon a son has in his arsenal of rebellion. A fatal shot aimed at the heart. It would be hard to write off to coincidence Bobby's free-form confessional, "Oh, God said to Abraham, 'Kill me a son,'" despite the slight spelling modification of his father's name. Nor would it be possible to ignore any of the song's subsequent ironies, especially when the fictional Abe asks, "Where do you want this killin' done?" Implicitly, God replies it should occur on the same road that would soon lead Bobby Zimmerman far from Hibbing: "Out on Highway 61."

6

Joe College

In the opinion of those who knew him, Bob Dylan was pleasant enough but basically just another of the terminally wrinkled, no-talent folk-singers who passed through Minneapolis in the winter of 1959.

One of Bob's casual girlfriends from that period, Lorna Sullivan, says: "The Minneapolis intelligentsia thought he was just kind of a twit. They didn't appreciate what he did or find him very interesting. At this point, he wasn't a charismatic personality at all."

Bobby Zimmerman arrived in town in the fall of 1959. He was enrolled as a freshman at the University of Minnesota, where he burrowed into the anonymity of its assembly-line liberal arts program. And while he certainly wasn't a twit, appearances were deceiving, to be sure. He looked like he stepped right out of an Andy Hardy movie: a baby-blue button-down shirt peeking out from beneath his V-neck vest, khaki pants, Hush Puppies, curly fly-away hair. In the safehold of campus life, Bobby blended in nicely with the two-thousand-or-so Sanforized "frosh" who came there to receive instruction.

The truth is that Bobby may have looked like a college man, but he was anything but interested in a formal education. The University of Minnesota was a catchall for Hibbing High graduates who chose not to go into the mines or to the local community college—a springboard to the world at large. In Bobby's case, college was a ticket out of Hibbing. Not only did it get his parents off his back, but he actually pleased them by selecting a school which had recently graduated his cousins Charles and Howard, and where another relative, Mike Siler, was a big *macher* at the Sammy house.

As for Minneapolis, Bobby probably concluded that moving there wasn't the worst thing that could happen to him. A lot of his childhood friends lived there, as well as across the Mississippi River in St. Paul, where he'd spent summers visiting dozens of relatives. The city itself was harmless enough. Billed as "the cultural center of the Midwest," Minneapolis probably never achieved as much national prominence for anything else as it did for serving as the backdrop for Mary Tyler Moore's TV sitcom. Still, the arts flourished there in the form of regional theater, opera, and symphony. Rock 'n roll was featured on a few of the city's smaller AM radio stations. Bob Zimmerman knew his way around town and felt pretty much at home there. But the real attraction to Bobby was Dinkytown, where he could slip into blue jeans and just as easily slip into the character of Bob Dylan.

Dinkytown was the ideal matrix for someone about to become Bob Dylan. A funky-chic district near the university, Dinkytown boasted a full-scale hipster scene, like Greenwich Village or Cambridge, only pasteurized for the predominantly middle-class kids flirting with nonconformity. Dinkytown attracted a coterie of social deviants—beatniks, outcasts, revolutionaries, and freaks—who sought to entertain each other with their "radical" insights. A sordid little hangout of mostly coffeehouses and shops, it was a taste of the East Coast counterculture that seemed starkly out of place in the delta of Middle America. Bobby had certainly stumbled on the perfect environment for himself. In Dinkytown he could soak up the offbeat life-style and try on his new Dylan image.

Like an actor who goes to the theater each night and for two or three hours becomes another person, Bobby could actually lead two lives. By day he'd be Bob Zimmerman, tentative student who stalked the University of Minnesota campus in search of fellowship and knowledge; by night, Bob Dylan would surface, a collegian errant caught up in the riptide of urban bohemianism— Dr. Zimmerman and Mr. Dylan. This type of internal struggle is difficult to contain, but Bobby, for the time being, was compelled to develop both personalities concurrently until one declared itself predominant and pivotal to his future.

The conventional side of Bob's identity crisis was conducted on campus, where he was known only as Bobby Zimmerman. Before the school semester started, Bobby's name was given to the rush chairman of Sigma Alpha Mu, whose job it was to canvass the list of Jewish underclassmen for potential pledges. The Sammys—as fraternity brothers were known—had to work extra hard to attract incoming freshmen, since the two rival Jewish frats at U of M had houses that were virtual palaces in contrast to the Sammys' dump. That may explain why they rushed Bob Zimmerman, although as the cousin of two alumni brothers, he would have been given priority over men with no such pedigree.

The first Sammy to befriend the "wide-eyed kid from the Range" was Wayne Freeman. Wayne recalls Bobby coming around to his parents' house in Minneapolis a few weeks before school started to check out the college scene. As Sammy rush chairman, Wayne was in the process of writing a pledge skit entitled "Annie Get Your Buns" with three other brothers when Bobby arrived. "He immediately sat down at the piano and knocked out a few songs," explains Wayne, who was amazed at the boy's lack of modesty. He also made a number of preposterous claims—among them, that he was Bobby Vee and had played with Buddy Holly and Little Richard—embarrassing Wayne and the others, who knew at once that they were lies.

The Sammys rushed Bob in spite of his mendacity—probably, Wayne Freeman concludes, because they desperately needed out-of-towners to live at the fraternity in order to defray the house's operating expenses. Whatever the reason, Bob took up residence at the Sammy house in September 1959 and participated in the pledging ritual along with other candidates from his class.

The Sammys' motto may have been "Fast and Firm," but that certainly didn't describe their house at 925 University Avenue Southeast. From the outside, the place looked like a setting for a Stephen King novel: a green-and-white shingled monstrosity flanked by a ramshackle porch and great paint flecks that hung off its sides like Spanish moss. The interior was only marginally better off. The front door opened onto a foyer whose linoleum floor sported an inlaid replica of the crescent-shaped fraternity pin and was eternally sticky from the pitchers of beer poured over the heads of unsuspecting pledges. The living room stood off to the left, with an upright piano that instantly won Bob's affections. Downstairs was a knotty-pine dining area, next to which was a room called "The Hole," which doubled as a place to study and play cards and whose principal decoration was an applique of cigarette burns covering the rugs and furniture.

Bobby's room was the farthest from the stairs, on the righthand side of the second floor. He was the only house member who roomed alone—a condition owing to the fact that he was "an anomaly to the other fraternity brothers." Richard Rocklin, who had known Bobby since he was five years old, occupied the adjoining room and remembers his friend's awkward presence there. "He was a loner," Rocklin says. "The fraternity brothers thought he was strange because of the way he looked and acted. He always had the same silly smile on his face that invited the others to pick on him—which they did."

In self-defense, Bob kept to his room. He spent most of his time there locked away in the tiny sanctum which friends remember as being perpetually dark. He never turned on the overhead light. Instead, he preferred to sit at his desk, hunched over a perplexing anthropology book that he read by the solitary glare of his gooseneck lamp.

He wasn't the least bit interested in school. "It was as foreign to him as the moon," says Richard Rocklin, who occasionally helped Bobby cram for a test. Dylan later admitted that he didn't agree with school. In "My Life in a Stolen Moment," a blank-verse poem that originally appeared in a 1963 Town Hall concert program, Dylan romanticized his boredom by claiming he flunked out of school for refusing to participate in biology experiments and writing papers that were critical of his teachers. This, of course, was a fantasy; nevertheless it expressed his innermost feelings about school. Formal education wasn't for him. Not the regimented classes or useless information, not the textbook teachers or gym jocks or all that rah-rah shit they foisted on the kids. He had no intention of memorizing bluebooks jammed with trivial facts: the capital of Laos is Vientiane, the line on the weather map is called an isobar, mombin describes any tree of the tropical genus Spondias of the family Anacardiaceae.... Who needed all that crap! And what was he supposed to do with it anyway—work for IBM or Philco or one of the myriad accounting firms that swallowed up promising grads? Go into sofa beds with his old man? Treat gum disease? Some future that'd be!

To complicate matters, Bobby had absolutely no attention span. He couldn't sit still for two minutes, let alone through an hour-and-a-half lecture on Gilgamesh or the reproductive cycle of the antelope.

Five minutes into class his leg would start pumping, his eyes would glaze over. Doodles appeared in the margins of his notebooks. A profile of the cross-eyed chick who sat across the room. The beginning of a poem. Anything but what was going on in class.

Bobby felt even more alienated from his friends inasmuch as they were a studious bunch. The crowd he hung around with as a freshman was a residue of kids from the Hibbing–Duluth–Twin Cities Jewish community that he'd known since childhood. He'd gone to camp with Dickie Rocklin, Larry Keegan, Karen Katz, and Barry Goldman; now they were all U of M students, working diligently toward conventional professional goals. The same with Judy Rubin, whom he'd dated on and off since they were both twelve and who now lived across campus in the Sigma Delta Tau house.

Judy was an irresistible honey-blond with the-girl-next-door looks and a lithe cheerleader figure, spoiled only by a dopey midwestern twang. She'd first "paired-off" with Bobby at Camp Hertzl, a Zionist retreat in Webster, Wisconsin, where they'd both spent a number of summers away from home. "He was so cute and adorable, I couldn't resist him," Judy recalls, adding that it was difficult to draw him out even them. As a camper, he was acutely sensitive and private, preferring to express himself in the pages of a weekly newspaper the kids put out. Judy remembers Bobby always scribbling thoughts on scraps of paper, then tucking them into a back pocket. He rarely discussed them with her. Once, sitting around a campfire, Bob read a poem he'd written about a helpless dog, which was so touching, as Judy remembers it, that everyone broke into tears.

The Bobby Zimmerman who lived in the Sammy house seemed to have lost his frame of sensitivity. He was still introverted and restless, but the tenderness was gone. There were no soft edges to him. His customary good humor was oblique and biting. He enjoyed giving playful names to each of his friends that, beneath the surface, were often cruel and demeaning observations on their physiques. For instance, Karen Katz, who was mildly overweight, became "the squashed tomato that sat on top of the SDT piano." Others were even more demeaning, though always offered good-naturedly. "We pretended to be good sports," claims one member of the group, "but deep down it hurt."

Bob's blunt-edged hostility was an obvious reaction to his burgeoning alienation and his realization that college and a middle-class Jewish life-style held absolutely nothing for him. His role in fraternity affairs was virtually nonexistent. Brothers avoided congregating in his room. In school his attendance record dwindled steadily to only occasional classroom appearances. Bob and Judy were regular guests at the local Hillel House, where they mixed with other Jewish students and competed in friendly bridge tournaments, but emotionally Bob was miles away.

With nothing to feed his dreams of becoming a rock 'n roll star except an occasional gig at a Sammy party (where no one listened to him), Bob Zimmerman had nothing going for him.

Bob Dylan, on the other hand, was beginning to come to life. His internal identity—the fantasy person Bob Zimmerman wished he could be—had remained dormant for the first few months of school while he had a chance to study the scene. During that time he was drawn to the exotic pretensions of Dinkytown on the campus fringe where the hip crowd chewed over the sociopolitical fodder of the late-1950s. Hip in those days meant being perceptive, not the zonked-out hedonism that joggled the Sixties. Hip defined a kind of undeluded prehensile awareness, a cynical streetwise slant, that showed you were on to all the bullshit tied to middle-class norms. It gave you license to laugh condescendingly at all the squares who bought the company line and to pass judgment on contemporary affairs. For instance, a hip person knew beyond doubt that the government represented a corrupt, elitist club of aging bureaucrats, that Dwight D. Eisenhower was a gumptionless zero, and that Freud fathomed the essence of our privileged, neurotic existence.

Hipness appealed most to the college kids, who, disillusioned with their parents' uptight values, embraced it as a panacea for their boredom. And Dinkytown provided a funky, out-of-the-way roost for them to practice their idea of the "existential" life-style.

Until the mid-1950s, Dinkytown was an unprepossessing little neighborhood, run-down but recovering peacefully from its tenure as one of the earliest commercial centers in northern Minnesota. The railroad switching yards, docks, and loading platforms had all but disappeared after World War II when the action shifted to the other side of the Mississippi River, leaving Dinkytown a skeleton of mostly abandoned buildings.

The college kids discovered Dinkytown the way NYU students discovered SoHo and Berkeley grads resettled the Haight. They made favorable deals with owners of the tenements, renovated existing shops, and eventually opened small businesses of their own that reflected and catered to the new scene.

Toward the end of the 1950s, Dinkytown managed to inspire a certain cultural renaissance of its own. Adjuncts of university classes taught by John Berryman, Allen Tate, James Wright, Saul Bellow, and Robert Penn Warren spilled over into the cafe society that spawned within a three-block hive of provincialism built around the intersection at Fourth Street and Fourteenth Avenue. Their graduate students held court around tables at Bridgeman's ice-cream parlor, the East Hennepin Bar, or the Varsity Cafe, when the latter wasn't polluted by the bourgeois fraternity crowd. There they could sit over coffee and lionize their mentors, distracted only by the scene's hip signature—wine, jazz, and marijuana. One participant sums it up this way: "Dinkytown was filled with people who were around the edges of academia but were more devoted to drinking and fucking off."

Those aesthetics—intellectual thought and fucking off—were inextricably intertwined to foster the basis of a new sensibility among Dinkytown's ranking heads. Their "new vision," so to speak, personified what sociologist Morris Dickstein, in his magnificent book *Gates of Eden,* referred to as Romantic Socialism: "the Romantic vision of the redemption of the self, the libertarian socialist dream of a community of redeemed selves in the real world." In other words, they envisioned an alternative life-style that encompassed politics, morals, and even religion. C. Wright Mills called these harbingers of a new society "the young intelligentsia" and hailed them for their courage to rebel against the barren spirit of the Eisenhower era. This movement—a patchwork of middle-class college kids, Freudian radicals, and Marxist ideologues—discovered, according to Professor Dickstein, "not only new and transfiguring ideas but a new intellectual style—committed, inspiriting, prophetic—rich with the promise of salvation and the dream of a new world... [which] spoke to the ultimate issues of culture and personal destiny."

Those less inclined to take on society's problems subscribed to the Beat life-style of hanging loose which was endemic to Dinkytown. Al's Breakfast opened at five a.m. to attract the all-night crowd that the restaurant's namesake considered to be oddly fascinating. From there you could drift farther along Fourteenth Avenue to Yohanda Cleaners, where a card game was always in progress, or hit an art film at the Varsity Theatre. Daylight hours were reserved for playing chess or the guitar, or blowing pot to the turned-on plaint of a Charlie Parker album that invariably had to compete with the harsh din of traffic. Or you could just hang out on the street, where a whacked-out scene was always going down.

The most striking aspect of Dinkytown society was the interplay of cultural bohemianism and political militancy. They seemed to go hand in hand, inasmuch as one's status was measured in terms of social awareness. Most Dinkytowners waxed eloquent on the burning issues of the day: the Cuban revolution, the cold war, civil rights, the nefarious House Un-American Activities Committee, and the politics of sexual enlightenment. Young social critics launched an all-out assault on the prevailing social norms, but nowhere was their cynicism better expressed than in the breathless urgency of their music.

The music Bob Dylan heard in Dinkytown wasn't the rock 'n roll he'd come prepared to play. It wasn't jazz, or rhythm & blues, or one of the other urban motifs that influenced rock. It was folk music: the music of the 1930s labor movement and dust-bowl balladeers. Since the end of World War II, folk music had courted extinction as a medium of popular entertainment. People avoided its preachy ruralism in favor of the imaginative, kinetic sounds that accommodated advancement into the modern era. Jazz, with its impulsive energy and unstructured, elliptical arrangements, captured the haste and excitement of postwar America during those otherwise dull days, but the reigning bopsters soon confounded their audience with esoterically radical improvisations. And so people turned back to the comforting, melodious refrains of folk songs.

Until that time, folk music was something of a cultural pariah. The Weavers and Pete Seeger, its most eminent practitioners, had been hauled before the House Un-American Activities Committee in 1951 and blacklisted as communist sympathizers, casting a pall over the genre. In retrospect, it is ironic that the arbiters of morality chose to castigate performers who sang "This Land Is Your Land," "So, Long, It's Been Good to Know You," and a smorgasbord of similar compositions championing the people of America. Yet it is exactly that injustice which endeared them to the new generation of folk enthusiasts, returning them to the limelight.

The young crowd that gravitated into coffeehouses featuring folksingers felt alienated from traditional mores and shared a need to communicate their political and economic views. Folk music provided a perfect expression of the issues. It reflected the spirit of the times, linking all the populist elements of the 1930s with what would ultimately be embraced by the New Left. The college kids loved its missionary appeal. Singing and clapping about the open road, freedom, migrant workers, and southern chain gangs—lordy, lord!—they'd have to rush home and beg forgiveness of their parents' black maids now, wouldn't they?

But while the country bought into the folk craze, lines within its own ranks were already being drawn. Traditional folk jongleurs like Pete Seeger and Ewan McColl, who collected and interpreted the musical heritage of authentic rural prototypes, squared off against what they called the exploiters and folk expressionists. Theodore Bikel and Burl Ives booked their folk acts into Las Vegas-style cabarets. Harry Belafonte turned "The Banana-Boat Song" into a top forty shuck and jive by performing it on the Ed Sullivan and Perry Como variety shows. Even Josh White, heir to Leadbelly's ethnic acclaim, was accused of Uncle Tomming his repertoire of Negro spirituals to reach a broader audience. Every record label in the country groomed a glossy folk act to cross over into the musical mainstream. And in October 1958, the Kingston Trio's jouncy version of "Tom Dooley" became the number-one hit in the country.

Bob Dylan, with his electric guitar and amplifier, took one look at this scene and realized his dreams were history. There was no longer much interest in rock 'n roll. The doo-wop and rhythm & blues groups of the Fifties had given way to a group of white-bucked, white-skinned choirboys who projected decidedly wholesome, clean-cut images on the order of Frankie Avalon, Bobby Darin, Ricky Nelson, Dion, and Paul Anka. That certainly wasn't Bobby's style. Aside from Elvis, who moved on to Hollywood's bike-and-surf movies, the singers who'd inspired Bobby were disappearing from the spotlight; Buddy Holly was dead, Little Richard was becoming a preacher, and Gene Vincent had expatriated to Great Britain. It was clearly time for Bobby to reevaluate his direction.

If the truth be told, Bob Dylan got involved with folk music because it was the only game in town. To make it as a rock star in 1960 you had to have original material and a face. Not just a face, but a *FACE*—a sleek, square-jawed kisser, prettyboy looks, bedroom eyes, and a forehead destined for a spitcurl apropos of an Italian racecar driver. Not to mention one of those Troy-Rory-Dana-Jody names that roll off the tongue and sell records to preadolescent girls. Unless you were an empty-headed hunk like Fabian, the odds were stacked against anyone breaking in as a rock star.

Folksingers weren't boxed in by cosmetics or catchy tunes. On the contrary, they were blessed by volumes of traditional material which they performed over and over again. Audiences never seemed to tire of hearing version after version of "The Golden Vanity" or "Copper Kettle"; they'd cheer and clap along with "Sinner Man" even if the opening act performed it twelve different ways. Integrity carried more weight than polish. There was no need to perfect an act or worry about how you looked. You could have a face like Ernest Borgnine or sing like Alfalfa and still be considered a brilliant star. What mattered was the rapport a folksinger established with his or her audience, the ability to convey a real understanding of the material. There was no faking that. An audience knew instantly whether or not a performer was sincere.

The cherry on the icing was that a folksinger didn't need a band. That feature alone could have sold Bobby on this new solitary form of music. Since the beginning, he'd had trouble keeping a band. Either his sidemen weren't good enough, or they deserted him for a more popular group. Dylan told a *Rolling Stone* interviewer in 1984: "Lead singers would always come in and take my bands, because they would have connections, like maybe their fathers would know somebody, so they could get a job in the neighboring town at the pavilion for a Sunday picnic or something. And I'd lose my band." The Golden Chords disbanded because Bob's commitment to rhythm & blues prevented them from getting paying jobs. The Satin Tones fell apart when R&B died out. Nothing he did to keep a band together seemed to work. Folk music, however unexciting it seemed, would surely solve that problem.

It also made it easier for him to get a gig. New coffeehouses were opening up every day, especially around college campuses where the audiences were virtually guaranteed. Any storeroom or cellar would do. In fact, the grungier the space, the more status it held. Coffeehouses, lest you forget, were still primarily the haunt of beatniks, who felt right at home in such tenebrous surroundings. Black walls, filtered light, rickety seats, dirt floors—such was the elegance of the Ten O'Clock Scholar when it opened in Dinkytown in the fall of 1959. Dave Lee, a cocky hustler who fancied himself part of the Beat scene, bought the place to capitalize on the lucrative folk movement. Ideally located on Fourteenth Avenue between Fourth and Fifth Streets, it was nothing more than a storefront with a big plate-glass window, a long, narrow room with tables and chairs that were too high off the ground to be comfortable and an oversized benchlike section that stretched along the right side of the wall.

During the day, the Scholar attracted an in-group of Dinkytown's self-styled heads, presided over by Melvin McKosh, the Scholar's resident radical. A parlor anarchist who was a good ten years older than the rest of the crowd, McKosh ran an alternative bookstore a few doors away where fellow sympathizers gathered to play cards, philosophize, and rail against America's *Realpolitik* and the pretentious creeps who fed the system. McKosh dropped by each afternoon to host a daily browbeating of Scholar regulars, who feasted on his diatribes. Then there was the outcrowd: the dropouts, burn-outs, and hangers-out who whiled away their days in the Scholar, playing chess and scrounging change from anyone who bought their hardluck raps. And, of course, you'd always spot a few folksingers surrounded by cliques of adoring coeds.

Around nine each night, the lights would dim as performers took to the makeshift stage directly in front of the Scholar's window. The house act was an ersatz flamenco guitarist named Jerry Goodge, who called himself "Amigo" and ran perfunctorily through the half-dozen ham-and-eggs folk songs he knew. Between sets, a succession of polished-faced Joe Hills and Barbara Allens entertained while the young audience sipped coffee and chatted. In all, the Scholar was a fairly respectable hangout, a good deal tamer than what you'd find near most college campuses today. But it was loaded with "atmosphere" and, therefore, became the sort of joint your parents warned you never to set foot in lest you contact a communicable disease—like syphilis or imagination.

The Ten O'Clock Scholar was Bob Dylan's idea of Utopia. Finally, here was a place that catered to people who felt the same way he did about things. Guys sat around all day swapping guitar riffs and songs.

Families held no status, much less interfered with anyone's life inside the coffeehouse. No one gave a shit about school or making grades—everyone was welcome to hang out as long as they were cool about it. Like Dodge City, the Scholar's dictum was anything goes, even if it meant being there under an assumed name.

That suited Bobby just fine. Bob Zimmerman didn't exist for the Scholar crowd. He was Dylan there, a well-traveled drifter who'd played behind Little Richard and Buddy Holly and might even have been Bobby Vee. Most Dinkytowners knew he went to the university, but that was about all they knew. No one asked any questions. It didn't matter.

The only stumbling block proved to be the music. Rock 'n roll was passé. It lacked the substance necessary to please the savants. Folk music was their muse. It brought with it the prestige and the attention of even the most jaded head.

That was all Bobby had to hear. Almost immediately, he traded in his electric guitar for the folkie's standard ax—a brown Gibson flattop with steel strings. What a piece of machinery that baby was!—a considerably smaller guitar than Bobby was used to, handcrafted to produce a beautifully rounded, dulcet tone. Chording it was more cumbersome, but he adjusted quickly to it. The same with finger-picking, which was a technique everyone used underneath the plangent songs.

In all, Bobby gave himself a crash course in folk music. Starting each day at one of the folkies' apartments, moving on to the Scholar, and continuing at one of the all-night parties where guitars were passed from hand to hand like the Torah, he began to spend all his spare time with the Dinkytown crowd. School existed only as a formality; he occasionally went to class or attempted to study, but his mind was elsewhere.

That December of 1959, Bob finished his exams and went back to Hibbing for the semester break. There was so much excitement swirling around in his head, so many changes to contend with, that the vacation proved more stressful than he'd anticipated. Most pressing was the question of whether or not to return to school. College was a joke. Bobby wasn't learning anything there. One thing was for certain—he sure wasn't going back to the Sammy house. Those bozos were putting too much pressure on him to "go active" and pay back fraternity dues. If he went back at all, it would only be to please his parents and to have more time in Dinkytown while he decided what to do next.

Bobby spent that vacation looking up some of the old gang. Leroy was working for some electronics guy in the north end of town. Echo, to his amazement, had gotten married only a week before to some guy she hardly even knew. And to top it off, she was expecting a child. That left Judy Rubin as the only available woman in his life. To shore up his reserves, Bobby rushed her an expensive black velveteen outfit trimmed with brightly-colored appliques that Judy thought was the most gorgeous thing she'd ever seen. She was blown away by this incredibly decent Jewish gesture of affection! Only a few weeks before he'd insisted she wear a black leotard underneath a hip-high black skirt and black fishnet stockings to a beatnik party. To think of such a thing—Judy Rubin dressed like a tramp! Next thing she knows, this outfit arrives! Who could figure with a guy like Bobby. Who, indeed—her *parents,* that's who! They had his number. In their eyes, Bobby's influence on their daughter was despicable, and they insisted she send back the gift. A week later, Bobby was on the phone to Judy, pouring out his heart. He really laid it on thick about how much he loved her and how they were made for each other, he couldn't live without her, wanted to marry her as soon as it made sense, and that she should hop on the next bus to Hibbing—*anything!* Meanwhile, he'd be back in a few weeks and they could make plans for the future.

John Bucklen was still in town, playing rock guitar just like when Bobby'd left him—only Bobby hipped him to the news that rock 'n roll was no longer where it was at. "I'm a folksinger now," he informed John, who reacted to the news as if Bob had blurted out he was gay. "Electric guitars aren't in anymore." Then, as if to prove it, he showed off his new acoustic guitar and a contraption that, at first, confounded Bucklen: a neck attachment designed to accommodate a harmonica.

Bobby had changed all right. His hair was no longer stacked up in a pomp; the biker's getup was gone. But it wasn't the cosmetic about-face that intrigued John; it was the new music his friend played for him with such passion and commitment. Bobby had become an apostle of a woman named Odetta, a husky-voiced black folksinger whose blend of traditional ballads and urban blues cut a nice compromise between folk and the roots of rock 'n roll. For hours on end he rhapsodized about her earthy style, dropping her mysterious name as if she were an intimate acquaintance. Bucklen listened to Bobby strum through tunes like "Mule Skinner," "Jack O' Diamonds," "Water Boy," and "'Buked and Scorned," equally fascinated by their beautiful melodies and "the intellect of the songs." They dealt with the great questions of the time: love, freedom, and the size of tailfins cluttering up the new-model cars. Mostly, however, they conveyed an insider's take on life in general, kept in check by a good amount of cheek and wit.

These sermony serenades demonstrated to Bucklen that being a folksinger meant being smart, being perceptive, even being a bit profound. Far from being an instigator of rebellion (an image he would ironically come to epitomize), the folksinger seemed to fancy himself a social critic, historian, and offbeat raconteur. He was the hip philosopher, a street sage with an inside track on the vicissitudes of culture. A patron of the "livelier" arts that nipped around the edges of conformity without getting too square. The Scholar crowd quoted Allen Ginsberg and Lenny Bruce to each other, while Bobby boned up on the likes of Rimbaud, François Villon, and some of the more obscure French symbolists who were currently the rage. These were folkdom's role models, from whom Bobby would borrow liberally in his Greenwich Village years.

Bobby used those few weeks in Hibbing much as a Broadway producer gauges a new show—opening it quietly out of town and constantly revising and reshaping it until all the kinks are out. John Bucklen's enthusiasm oiled the rusty parts, and before long Bobby found himself with enough material to do a decent set of his own.

By the time he got back to Minneapolis in early January 1960, Bobby was ready to perform for a paying audience. There were a few coffeehouses where up-and-coming entertainers could play—the Coffee Break, Hillel House, a pizza joint called the Purple Onion. However, the Ten O'clock Scholar was generally regarded by folksingers as the best room in town. Naturally Bobby wanted to break in at the top. Dave Lee, who ran the place, is generally credited with giving Dylan his first gig as a folksinger, but if the truth be told, the Scholar's stage was anyone's for a song. Every night was amateur night. All you had to do was get up and play.

Bob Dylan's debut was anything but auspicious. He ran through a couple of folk standards—"Sinner Man" because it required exactly two chords and about as much technique to pull it off, "St. James Infirmary," and two or three others he'd picked up from Harry Belafonte, Jesse Fuller, and the Carter Family records. "He wasn't any good," Dave Lee recalls, "but he was just learning." That attitude—allowing would-be folksingers to learn their craft in front of unreproachful, appreciative audiences—encouraged amateurs like Dylan to keep plugging away at it night after night until they developed stage presence and some sort of a show. That was, in fact, the scenario Bobby followed for the next several months.

Every night he would leave the fraternity house, giving the brothers who ridiculed him a lame excuse concerning his absence, and head off to Dinkytown, a gaminlike noctambulist wrapped in an ankle-length black wool coat he'd picked up at the Salvation Army with a long scarf wound around his neck, lugging a plaid guitar case that looked like some young girl's luggage. Down University Avenue he'd walk to Fourteenth Avenue, then along Fourteenth to the Scholar. Once inside, he'd transform himself from a ninety-pound weakling into a poised, self-reliant young man, and the college kid from the Range would become Bob Dylan.

The Scholar was strictly a bicameral house, consisting of the university's "unitarians" as they called themselves—an older crowd of closet radicals who cast themselves as intellectual heavies—and a contingent of lightweight, but adoring, coeds. Dylan appealed to the college girls who didn't mind paying fifty cents for a peasant sandwich in order to sit through the show undisturbed. Occasionally, he'd camp out at one of the tables with Judy Rubin and a few of her apple-faced girlfriends and play from his seat. More often, though, Bobby would take his rightful turn on the stage. Walking up demurely, dressed in an old denim workshirt and pegged blue jeans, he'd half prop himself on a stool, the other foot toed on the rickety platform for support, and wait for the house to quiet down. He'd smile sheepishly into the lights. Sometimes he'd make a quip about the kitchen staff and would draw a few titters, or he'd affect some comical difficulty with the stool. Then he'd nervously tune the guitar until it suited his ears before beginning the set.

At the Scholar, Bobby had to limit his material to fairly straightforward, parochial folk songs, a considerable departure for a kid who, only six months ago, had done cartwheels off the high school piano.

"I was kinda combining elements of Southern mountain music with bluegrass stuff, English ballad stuff," was how Bob characterized his folk apprenticeship. None of that cutesy Kingston Trio–Limelighters–Brothers Four folk-pop crap that charmed the college crowd. Bob stuck close to the textbook, dosing his audience with sea shanties, Child ballads, field songs, and chants. Then there were the traditional broadsides like "The Golden Vanity," which he never failed to perform.

> There was a lofty ship, And she
>   put out to sea,
> And the name of the ship was
>   the Golden Vanity,
> And she sailed upon the low and
>   lonesome low,
> As she sailed upon the lonesome
>   sea.

All nine verses of it, sung in a rambling, unemotional drone. Still, Bobby put his own signature on the material in a way that gave his set an unusual lift. "He was dramatic when he sang," Lorna Sullivan recalls. "He would move his body in a way and strum his guitar in a way and he would sort of blurt things out in a way that was very different."

Dave Matheny, a third-rate folksinger who worked across town at the Purple Onion, grew jealous of Bob's ability to get so much mileage out of mere stage presence. "As a guitarist, I would look at Dylan's inability to play and sneer, but I just *had* to recognize that magnetism. It spilled all over the place when he performed." He also observed that, as Bob developed a small following, his ego swelled to disproportionate dimensions. "He became so goddamned self-centered," Matheny claims, "running over anybody who could help him get another step ahead in the game."

John Koerner, one of the all-time great urban blues guitarists who was also new to the Dinkytown scene at the time, remembers a night in 1960 that probably sealed Matheny's enmity. Koerner and a friend ran into Dylan on Fourteenth Avenue; he talked them into going to see Matheny perform at the Purple Onion. Bobby had his guitar case and harmonica apparatus in tow and kept them by his side even once they were seated inside the club. "You could tell Dylan couldn't wait until Matheny stopped playing," Koerner grins in retrospect.

Sure enough, the minute Dave took a break, Bobby hauled out his guitar, popped a harmonica in the metal holder around his neck, and launched into a folk song *from his seat in the audience!* The crowd immediately perked up. They started rearranging their chairs to get a better view of the unexpected sideshow, showering Bobby with applause as he finished the first number. Acknowledging their approval, Bobby sang another song, then another and another, until Matheny finally pleaded with him to stop so Matheny could go back on stage. Bobby ignored him, playing for another hour or so until Matheny used a microphone to prevail on him to stop. Koerner laughs, "Dylan wanted an audience and just took it away from Dave. That was his way in the early days; he took what he wanted."

Dylan's habit of laying claim to things was not limited to stage time. From way back he had a knack for conning people into giving him things and paying his way, much as he had aced Echo and John Bucklen out of cherry pie and cigarettes. Those were innocent enough peculations. You could even write them off as stinginess. Since hitting Minneapolis, however, Bobby's license for appropriating things seemed to exceed the bounds of rightfulness. "He was a ripoff artist," says a longtime Dinkytowner who belonged to the Scholar's inner circle. "He took things that belonged to his friends—most of it petty stuff. Still, it got so that none of us could afford to leave him alone in any of our apartments."

He took small things at first—guitar picks, pens, cigarettes—then books and articles of clothing. Says an old Dylan crony named Hugh Brown: "We were all getting by on money from back home. Bobby was, too, but he had this thing about scamming cigarettes and things that went beyond the objects themselves." It was almost as if the more applause he got, the more he felt he was entitled to—and took—in order to uphold his personification of the suffering artist.

Oddly enough, Bob's friends forgave him these transgressions. So he had sticky fingers! Okay, so there were worse things in life to worry about. After all, the kid had talent. He had charm. Forget about it. Let him work it out on stage, they seemed to say.

This was precisely the kind of treatment Bobby needed if he was to maintain his ascendancy. He had to stay in front of an audience, keep working on his show, expanding his repertoire—all of which he showed a real determination to do. A night rarely went by in which he failed to get up and perform or work out some aspect of a new routine. Even when he showed up and was preempted by someone from out of town who'd drifted in to play, he picked up new material or finger-picking variations.

His ambition naturally pissed off a number of the resident heads. Larry Sullivan, a blowhard who fancied himself Dinkytown's intellectual Grand Poobah, used to protest whenever Bobby took the stage. Intercepting Dave Lee during Dylan's set, he'd ask the club owner to can the music for a while so he and his pals could have a decent conversation. "We can't hear over the noise," he'd complain, nodding in Bobby's direction. Others echoed Sullivan's dislike of Dylan's voice—which was soft and sweet and not at all like the skreigh for which he became famous—but were still taken with his infectious stage manner. None of this appeared to affect Bobby one way or the other. Judging by his actions, he was oblivious to criticism or disdain—single-minded in his effort to become a professional folksinger.

Whatever animosity he may have felt, Judy Rubin was around to give him moral support. She really hung in there, long after the other Jewish kids deserted him for being too far-out. Faithfully at ringside for every show, she'd call out, "Bobby, sing this," and "Bobby, sing that." And he'd do it, too! He'd close his eyes, lower his head, and play all Judy's requests like... Wayne Newton at the Sands! He'd do anything to please her, she was so beautiful. And such a decent kid. The kind guys wanted to marry. Hell, *he'd* marry her in a minute. Only... Judy wasn't interested. Not that she didn't like him. "He was like a little lost puppy," she muses today, "very shy and romantic." But after all, she was a princess—a Jewish princess—and Bobby was hardly anyone's idea of a prince. Not even a knight—not by any stretch of the imagination. She wanted some kind of stability, and here this *meshugah* folksinger was talking about taking off for New York and making it as a singing star. Judy fed on that daydream for a good minute or two until she understood that Bobby was dead serious about it. But in the end, she was simply too uptight to follow a young punk's dream.

By mid-January, Judy had lost interest in the wild plan and got pinned to a degree-minded guy from St. Paul. Bobby was distraught. Here he'd fallen for a straight Jewish girl. He even humiliated himself by calling her five times a day, pledging his love, begging her to come back, promising to marry her, throwing out every line in the book, but... nothing doing. Judy knew it wouldn't work out, and the bottom line was that she plain didn't love him.

Without Judy, there was a gargantuan hole in Bobby's life. Friends recall him moping around Dinkytown like a lovesick puppy. He began smoking twice as many cigarettes, staying out every night. At parties he got drunk and obnoxious or quickly passed out. If anyone brought up Judy's name, Bobby pretended he didn't hear and immediately started tuning his guitar or just launched into a song. It was difficult to have a conversation with him. He turned further and further inward, committed solely to his music.

It was time for Bob to clean house—literally and figuratively. Judy was gone. He no longer had any connection to his studies. The next thing he had to do was split from the fraternity house. Within days, he gave the brothers notice and moved into a real shithole at 42 Seventh Street Southeast, along with John Koerner and an older guy named Harry Weber, who was a Ph.D. candidate at the university.

Dylan and Koerner were like Mutt and Jeff—Bobby being short and pudgy, John bashful and spindly, hence his nickname, "Spider." A more unlikely pair was hard to find, although the two struck a sympathetic chord when it came to their music. Koerner was a student of the blues. He'd listened to all the old Folkways albums and 78s that featured Negro spirituals, field hollers, spoken plaints, and delta blues. Leadbelly was his idol. Josh White, Robert Johnson, Memphis Minnie, Bukka White, Lonny Johnson, Sleepy John Estes—dozens of authentic bluesmen provided him with source material which he mastered to a nuance. But unlike the horde of imitators who impressed their audiences with "discoveries" of obscure blues songs, Koerner captured the feel of Negro music. There was nothing slick about the way he played. No apologies for the rough-hewn manner or orneriness of the idiom. No, "Spider" John played the blues as it was intended to be played, low-down and dirty. He duplicated guitar phrasing and vocal inflections until it was difficult to distinguish his midwestern growl from the real thing.

None of this was lost on Bob Dylan. It wasn't too long ago that he'd done the same thing with Little Richard and Fats Domino, so that his shift from rhythm & blues to pure blues was more a metamorphosis for him than a sudden, opportunistic shift of style. Koerner reignited Bobby's interest in the blues, embroidering it into the crazy-quilt fabric of folk music, and while Dylan did not choose to dedicate himself to it in quite the same way Spider did, he nonetheless could hold his own among the purists.

Bobby hooked right into the blues emotionally, too. All things considered, he was a depressed kid—misunderstood by parents and peers, recently dumped by a childhood sweetheart. The blues captured his pain in its lyrics, especially when John Koerner picked up a guitar and sang:

> Well when I see you baby,
> I just don't feel so well.
> I come down with a fever. You know I
> just can't help myself.
> I got the love bug, honey,
> I got the love bug, mama,
> I got the love bug, honey.
> Sho' gonna give it to you.

Critics rarely measure Dylan's oeuvre in terms of the blues, since his songs are not structurally analogous to a classical blues riff. The parallels lie in his lyrics, which incorporate elements of the blues in more subtle ways. Just listen to "Tomorrow Is a Long Time," "Don't Think Twice, It's All Right," "Maggie's Farm," "I Believe in You," "Can You Please Crawl out Your Window"—the examples are simply too numerous to list and would probably incorporate most, if not all, of Dylan's later work, with its emphasis on anguish and broken love affairs. Bobby's music expressed frustration, disappointment, foreboding, heartache, doom. He had the soul of a bluesman, and he bared it continuously for more than twenty-five years.

Koerner and Dylan rose quickly above the complacent Dinkytown folk scene. Each developed a unique style that eventually attracted the attention of audiences, and before long the two men were alternating weekend gigs at the Scholar. The pay was abysmal—a measly five dollars a night—but the experience was priceless. Bobby had finally become a *professional* folksinger, a promotion that entitled him to perks such as billing, attitude, and a healthy bit of posturing. He became a terror on stage, demanding quiet and respect from a crowd that came to bust loose after a rough week in school. They wanted to chat, play chess, table hop, eat, drink espresso, and take in the cheap entertainment; Bobby, however, insisted his set be construed almost as if it were a concert performance. He refused to play until the house quieted down. If they were slow to get the point, he'd tell them to shut up and occasionally even walk off stage. Some of the audience recognized his underlying talent and excused the annoyance, while others considered him a rude little asshole. The older segment of the crowd—the heads—weren't impressed. They felt he was a parasite of the worst possible order. He didn't read, he wasn't political, he had no charitable sense or universal ethic. What gave him the right to claim their respect?

Yet Bob Dylan oozed charisma. He was irresistible on stage. He knew how to look lost and cocky at the same time, affecting charm through ambiguity, the same way his hero, James Dean, managed to win young girls' hearts. He was a young punk with a streak of vulnerability. People who recall his Dinkytown performances easily remember Bob's urchinlike stage manner, an ingratiating impishness that begged for affection. "He always knew that you'd fall in love with that shyness," John Koerner says, "yet he knew how to rattle peoples' cages."

Dylan also developed a keen sense of comic timing that fit nicely into his stage image. He knew how and when to smile, when to punctuate a phrase, raise a curious eyebrow, or mumble something self-deprecating, all to get a laugh. The ninety-odd patrons who came regularly to the Scholar took the Dylan charm hook, line, and sinker. He wasn't singing anything that different from the rest of the folksingers; he merely *performed* it differently. The restless, antagonistic audiences began to listen. Before long, he attracted a cadre of faithful followers. Lauded more for his manner than for his singing, Bobby Dylan became the Dinkytowner people hated to love.

One of the first fans to actually befriend him was a local girl named Gretel Hoffman. A delicate, long-haired dancer from Minneapolis, Gretel had just dropped out of Bennington College and was trying to find herself in Dinkytown's mock-hip cafes. A rich girl doing the requisite rebellion trip—only Gretel wasn't your typical suburban princess. She wasn't timid or uptight or very concerned about what the relatives would think. And definitely not like most girls who did the weekend hipster scene—listening to jazz, reading eastern philosophies, wearing torn jeans and sandals, but clinging to clutch bags and department-store makeup. Gretel had graduated from an alternative high school and kissed off a college that, by reputation, babysat petulant *artistes.* She was into radical left-wing politics; her parents had been communist sympathizers, labor organizers, culture vultures, the whole post-war Jewish intellectual bit. You didn't run into girls like Gretel in Hibbing. It was easy to see why Bobby was quick to take up with her. They shared a lot of interests: books, poetry, folk music, a rejection (for the time being) of formal education. Bobby and Gretel had no expectations of each other aside from friendship (for the time being).

Throughout February, they hung out together almost every day. Gretel had a part-time job as a photographer's assistant, but come evening they'd meet at the Scholar or take in one of the many exhibits in and around the Twin Cities. Poetry readings, Israeli folk dancing, social mixers—Gretel was open to everything. During the day, Bobby wrote poetry and songs and worked on his music in a drab, one-room apartment over Gray's Drug Store in the heart of Dinkytown. His crash pad with John Koerner and Harry Weber hadn't lasted more than a few weeks. Weber had trouble dealing with Bobby, but in the end it came down to finances. None of the guys could come up with enough bread to pay the rent, so they pulled a disappearing act before the landlady caught up with them.

Nobody in Dinkytown ever had money to speak of—just pocket change, a couple of bucks at the most at any given time. Money wasn't of primary interest to the folkies. In fact, possessions was a word that was frequently bandied about in a derogatory manner, like "filthy rich" or "two-faced." These refugees of the bourgeoisie believed you should be able to stuff your possessions into a knapsack so you could hit the open road, be mobile, free to do your hard travelin'.

The folk movement and its disciples—most of whom were middle-class or upper-middle-class kids—sought to disassociate themselves from the assiduous 1950s work ethic that had consumed their parents. They glanced around and saw the incredible pressures mounting up to pay mortgages and educate the young. They witnessed the mad scramble up the professional ladder. They confronted repressed hatred in their parents' eyes and decided they wanted off the treadmill. Consequently, the folk districts that sprang up in urban centers became communal in spirit; someone passing through could always expect to find a meal and a place to crash for a couple days before moving on. Nothing fancy, mind you—maybe soup and a sandwich, followed by a couple of cushions on the floor. Nevertheless, you'd be well taken care of and, with a little luck, offered a gig so the local performers could hear what your stuff sounded like.

It was in this spirit that Bob and Gretel rollicked through the winter of 1960. They jabbered incessantly about books and poetry. They shared a lot of cheap meals—hamburgers, pizza, pancakes. But as Gretel recalls, "Music was the thing that really turned him on." Dylan lived and breathed music. He ate it, devoured it, studied it, and *played* it. God, how he played it—day and night, as though if he stopped for air he'd never get the chance to play it again. He worked by himself during the day, listening to records and trying out original lyrics which he copied in a childish circular scrawl into spiral notebooks left over from school. In the evenings he played the guitar with friends or informally in front of a Scholar crowd. But the litmus test was how well his music was received at one of the myriad parties that were the center of Dinkytown society.

Dylan worked the nightly parties without fail. He turned up, invited or not. Curling up in the corner of someone's living room or taking to the bedroom, Bobby would strum quietly, humming to himself until he'd attracted a following. "Not Dylan again!" someone inevitably groaned as the first thrum of "Johnny, I Hardly Knew Ye" came wafting over the conversation. Every once in a while he'd try out a song he'd written—which had a power those present still recall. But more often than not it was a reprise of the same lethargic stuff he'd sung the night before, and the night before that and *the night before that*—laments about bonnie lassies and faithful ponies.

One evening in mid-March, Gretel dragged Bobby to a party at the home of a girl she'd gone to high school with in St. Paul. The minute they got through the door it was apparent they'd walked into the dullest scene in town. Faculty types stood around in small circles, sipping cocktails over small talk about Khrushchev, the pill, and the military-industrial complex. Not a guitar or black leotard in sight. The usual bunch of squares. . . except for a wiry little guy named David Whitaker who darted around the room and came on like a pop-eyed hipster. Someone introduced him to Bob and Gretel, and it was love at first sight. Within minutes, the trio had split from that boring scene in favor of a smoky pad on Minneapolis's West Bank, where an all-night bash more suited to their energy level was already in progress.

David Whitaker was a truly special cat—wired, juiced, and ready to fly, not to mention an inspired storyteller who could go for hours spinning out tales about his adventures on the road. From the sound of it, he'd experienced things that people in Dinkytown only dreamed about. David was originally from one of the Twin Cities' Jewish ghettos, but that was the only ordinary entry on his résumé. The son of progressive ex-Socialist Party members, he had dropped out of school in 1957 and drifted to San Francisco in an attempt to join the Beats. Since then, he'd lived in Israel and Paris, where, after trying to enlist in the Merchant Marines, he'd carried on with the crowd around Giacometti and a contingent of American poets trying to recreate the West Coast scene *en français.*

Bobby, extremely susceptible to anyone who was daring, beguiling, and free-spirited, was immediately taken with David. Within days, he, Gretel, and David were inseparable. They spent every day hanging out together—David the teacher and philosopher, Bobby and Gretel his devoted students. A voracious reader, he insisted they read left-wing political writers, rhapsodized about Marx and Lennon, Dos Passos and Frank Harris, and introduced them to the experimental verse of Kenneth Patchen and Lawrence Ferlinghetti.

"David had the vision of a poet and insisted there was room for expressiveness, music, and creativity here and now in the real world," Gretel says. "He lived on the edge long before it became fashionable, and indoctrinated Bobby and me in the ways of the nonconformist." This required a purging of Bobby and Gretel's old ways, something to help liberate the uninhibited part of their souls. David's secret weapon was Heavenly Blue and Pearly Gate morning glory seeds, the immediate natural source of LSD, which in 1960 could still be purchased over the counter at local seed stores. All you had to do was to empty a fifteen-cent packet into a blender, add a cup of your favorite juice or a milkshake and in no time at all you had the fuel necessary to launch the first hipster into outer space. Man, how it cleared those sinuses right out!

David served as Bobby's first important guru. He opened the boy up to new thoughts and experiences, as well as to an existential, come-what-may life-style. "Dylan didn't know nothing!" Whitaker says today, recalling Bobby's unlicked psyche in Dinkytown. "He was like an empty vessel waiting to be filled." To that end, Whitaker reconfirmed Bob's suspicion that the education offered by the University of Minnesota was useless. All the knowledge that anyone could hope for was right out there on the street, any time of the day or night. The whole world walked by your front door, people brimful of practical experience—information, enlightenment, instruction. Experience life, man! Get out there and sample it! Communicate!

Whitaker pushed Bob to expand his horizons. He dragged Bobby to his first political demonstration—a rally against some local right-wingers who ran a forum called Operation Abolition. Together, they explored the music of Jimmy Rogers and other eclectics culled from Whitaker's enormous collection of blues records. Poetry occupied a good part of their conversations—Allen Ginsberg and Gregory Corso; hash and peyote deepened their appreciation. And books! Whitaker was famous for reading anything he could get his hands on, especially in the area of literature and politics. Word had it that you could go into the most obscure stacks at the U of M reading room and find Whitaker's name on a book card.

Accordingly, David was dismayed that Dylan didn't read. Bobby seemed put off by books. He was too impatient to struggle through all those pages when he could be . . . *doing!* Thoughts didn't entertain him so much as the experience. As a result, Bobby was often lost or excluded from the dialogues held regularly at McKosh's Bookstore. The heads would meet there each afternoon, passionately exchanging ideas, rapping about the philosophies they'd read, preaching anarchy, spouting opinions, comparing notes, searching for deeper explanations, burning, burning—and through it all, Bobby would remain mute. He was totally unfamiliar with the material that energized his friends. Dylan's obliviousness infuriated the armchair philosophers—except for David Whitaker, who sensed his young friend was taking in much more than he let on. He also knew that when Bobby finally came upon a book that intrigued him, he would fasten onto it with an unshakable hold.

That book surfaced shortly, when a whacked-out college professor handed Dylan an old edition of *Bound for Glory* by Woody Guthrie. It was as if Bobby had found God! There, between badly tattered covers, was the key to his very existence, a philosophy he could grab hold of and embrace. Guthrie, an itinerant folksinger and working stiff, had written a book in 1943 that championed the little man, full of folksy yarns and confessions. Comforting words for people unburdened by materialism or greed, which talked plainly to men of the soil—laborers, drifters, cowboys, *dreamers.* Free spirits! It zeroed in on the very essence of what "Bob Dylan" was all about, what he stood for. If Bobby had an idea of "Dylan" before, then *Bound for Glory* provided him with a blueprint from which he could build his new identity.

It is not difficult to understand Dylan's attraction to *Bound for Glory.* Guthrie's audience consisted mainly of society's outcasts, people who, for whatever reason, were ostracized from the cultural mainstream and took solace in living a carefree existence outside the bounds of social convention. Bobby saw himself in similar company, rejected first by his peers in Hibbing and again by the college crowd. He just didn't fit in and either was unwilling to compromise or didn't know how to. Guthrie's book told him that it was all right to be his own man, that nonconformity was a blessing. It gave him encouragement and provided alternatives. What's more, Guthrie tied it all together through his music. Folk songs conveyed an enviable sense of community, and Woody Guthrie, much like Bruce Springsteen in the 1970s and 1980s, chronicled the caste system in America with a repertoire of anthems that united the disenfranchised and downtrodden. It gave them something to feel good about and ultimately gave them hope. What better role model could Bob Dylan hope to find?

Bobby devoured *Bound for Glory* in one sitting. For days afterward, he was never seen without it. He thumbed through it on the streets, at McKosh's Bookstore, over at Whitaker's, and finally at the Scholar, where he was seen cutting pages from the book that eventually wound up in his back pocket. In no time, he could quote Guthrie verbatim, often reciting passages as if they were his own thoughts.

From Woody, Bob got a real feeling for the American heartland. Woody considered himself an Okie. He rode boxcars and sat around campfires with fellow drifters, swapping stories and committing their adventures to memory. He helped organize labor unions and was deeply involved with left-wing politics. A dust-bowl balladeer, he had the gift of plain speech—the spare, down-home patois of people who sweat for their suppers—and was able to communicate with them through the language of his music. In the 1960s, folksingers who wrote their own music were, for the most part, college students whose "folk songs" sounded as if they'd been written in collaboration with Bertrand Russell and Gene Autry. Woody's songs were straightforward and to the point, yet full of imagination. Listening to them, you were treated to richly drawn pictures of country life—the wide-open country, from California to the New York island, from the redwood forest to the Gulfstream waters.

Suddenly, Bobby's world opened onto yet another thought-inspiring vista. Woody Guthrie's music was a storehouse of experience and enlightenment and, as he quickly discovered, many Dinkytown friends owned fabulous Guthrie record collections which they made available to him. Gretel did her part by introducing Bob to a girlfriend whose radical father not only had the records, but had compiled manuscripts, sheet music, and folk magazines dating back to the early 1940s. Together Bob and Gretel rooted through the documents and listened to each song on the scratchy 78s, harmonizing along with the old masters. In no time at all, Bob had memorized dozens of Woody Guthrie songs, including "Pastures of Plenty" and "Go Down You Murderers," not to mention the endless epic, "Tom Joad," which he played every chance he got. Bob's repertoire grew to consist entirely of Woody Guthrie material. Later, his mannerisms and dialect began to reflect those of his new idol, too—the nasal twang and clipped Oklahoma phrasing. And Woody's single-note harmonica style. Just as he'd become Little Richard, Bob Dylan was transforming himself into a teenage version of Woody Guthrie.

Bobby was so engrossed with his study of Woody that he was oblivious to a new development going on under his very nose. David Whitaker and Gretel Hoffman had become involved in a hot, steamy affair. Before Bobby even realized what was happening, word got back to him that on May 20, 1960, his best friends had eloped. The news devastated Bobby. He had been secretly in love with Gretel and, despite their platonic relationship, he considered her his girl. And David his best friend. Now he felt betrayed, confused. How could they have done this to him?

Gretel insisted it wouldn't change anything; they would still be as close as ever. But Bobby wasn't buying it. Encountering Gretel on the street, he couldn't bring himself to look her in the face. "When you get a divorce, let me know," he shouted from a half block away, then spun on his heel and disappeared into a nearby store.

It took a few weeks before he had the courage to visit the Whitakers. The newlyweds had moved into a one-room apartment above McKosh's Bookstore, where Gretel, in her own offbeat fashion, attempted to set up house. David dreamed away the days, reading and theorizing with the irascible McKosh. When Bobby came by, the men huddled together in a corner of the room and talked among themselves. "I was isolated from their world," Gretel says. "It was a world without a time frame. It was whatever they wanted to make out of any particular day. Nothing was scheduled. David wasn't working, and Bob wasn't going to school." Poetry and music generally occupied their days, and every so often Whitaker managed to sneak in a political manifesto designed to keep Bob on his toes. Not long after, Gretel learned she was pregnant and very quickly got a job to support the household. The Whitakers moved to larger quarters in anticipation of their new family, and Bobby moved in right along with them, occupying a small alcove in the rear of their two-bedroom house.

He spent several weeks there, working on his music with an even greater determination than before. Through his study of Woody Guthrie, Bob got a glimpse of his own potential. His fantasies were enriched by the realization that someone older, wiser, and respected by the masses had done exactly what he wanted to do—run away from home, assume different identities, express himself in whatever way suited his mood. It confirmed all his dreams. Bob not only shared Woody's vision; he realized the possibilities that lay before him: the potential to combine words, music, persona, and emotion, and to bring them to life through the ministry of "Bob Dylan."

More important, it provided Bob with a new sense of purpose. Before, he was just another listless folksinger, lingering around Dinkytown's coffeehouse scene. Nothing was really happening; no one was going anywhere. Johnny Koerner—he was a great guitarist, a real talent, but destined to play out his career in the Twin Cities. The same with Dave Ray and Tony Glover, both of whom influenced Dylan's early artistry. David Whitaker had the goods to bust out and succeed in a big way—he was well-read, articulate, innovative, arrogant... everything except ambitious. Whitaker didn't have the one attribute necessary to put it all together: desire. Dylan, on the other hand, burned with it. He needed to see his dreams come true. Convinced he had the ability, Bobby began to talk about music and performing in terms of something more tangible—*a career.* He'd taken things as far as they could go in Dinkytown. It was time to see what was out there for him, time to hit the road.

7

Another Side of Bob's Dealin'

The Old West. A figment of every schoolboy's imagination, spurred on by visual images of cowboys in ten-gallon hats, sagebrush, guntoting desperadoes, the noon stagecoach, buckskin, and honky-tonks. Not the likeliest of places you'd expect someone like Bob Dylan to turn up. Matt Dillon, maybe. But Bobby?—ex-Ranger, ex-Sammy, exponent of the blues? It sounds pretty fantastic, but it's true.

Bob arrived out west in the summer of 1960, at a time when the fledgling folk music scene was expanding to the Rocky Mountain states. Coffeehouses, like color televisions and Metrecal, were becoming assimilated into the cultural mainstream. No longer were they frowned upon as sinister beatnik lairs. Nor were they situated only in urban centers where the "anything goes" mentality generally sanctioned an air of permissiveness. No, these once-dark rooms, where jazz and its vocally hybridized poetry had grooved to the patter of finger-snapping approval, evolved into the kind of well-run, popular nightspots frequented by college kids on a conventional weekend date. Three shows nightly, reservations taken by phone, proper attire required. Good, wholesome clubs providing good, wholesome entertainment. In most of these places no liquor was served, so you could even bring your younger brother or sister along for a hot cider or herbal tea and a fudge brownie. There was plenty of adult supervision. No need to worry about the show, either. Well-scrubbed performers traveled the coffeehouse circuit, and their music reflected the new, clean-cut atmosphere. For these reasons, among others, the coffeehouse phenomenon was as well received in Dubuque as it was in Da Bronx.

The experimental arts period which had rocked coffeehouses throughout the 1950s was over. Improvisational jazz, blank verse, abstract expressionist art, satirical stand-up comedy—the whole rush of innovative energies that had touched off a revolution in modern life-styles ground to a short-winded halt. Even rock 'n roll, chief opiate of the movement's insurrectionists, was temporarily neutralized; the 1959 payola scandal had provided the country's moral watchdogs with conclusive proof that rock 'n roll bred indecency and corruption, and for the time being, the kids bought their reasoning. It was as if the country had overdosed on creativity. So much artistic invention had been served up in such a short period of time that everyone's senses were overstimulated, and as a result, the whole manic phenomenon short-circuited.

What emerged in its place was what newspapers and magazines called "the folk craze." Aptly misnamed, it wasn't a craze in the fanatical sense. Rather, it was an entertaining distraction that caught America's fancy for a short period of time, a harmless infatuation with traditional music that was commercialized to such an extent that it appealed to everybody and offended absolutely no one. Of course, in any artistic idiom, when no one is offended, nothing exceptional is being produced. But that hardly mattered. The important thing was that folk music displaced the jazzy decadence of the coffeehouses, and for the first time in nearly a decade, teenagers who congregated there sang along with and harmonized to intelligent lyrics; they behaved in a civilized manner, and searched for an equitable link between music and the past. They behaved just the way their parents wanted them to! Folk music had *respectability* written all over it. It had. . . *significance.* Little did anyone realize that it was a dulcet preamble to the social upheaval of the 1960s—when songs would advocate uninhibited sex, good dope, independence, and revolution. At the time, "the folk craze" was just a welcome respite from the anomaly of Beat society and the chaos that was yet to come.

Folksingers, on the other hand, were still held in dubious esteem. Since the time when Woody Guthrie entertained the rank and file at impassioned union rallies, there had always been a scant though vigorous association between folksingers and the communist cause. Some were outright Party champions, like Sarah Ogan, who wrote and performed a song called "I Hate the Capitalist System." Others, like Pete Seeger, vocalized their ideological discontent through radical protest songs which, disguised as peace songs, ambiguously attacked America's imperialistic mien. Sometimes the folksingers were rediscovered Negro bluesmen from the Mississippi Delta, like John Hurt, Fred McDowell, and Son House, whose songs educated audiences about the southern black experience and intercut nicely with the resurgence of civil rights activism on campuses. Many folksingers, however, were politically naive but happened to belong to the post-Kerouac generation that was awakening to social issues. Somewhat bohemian in outlook and lifestyle, they turned to the coffeehouse scene as a very important stage in their development. Their uniform was less severe than their predecessors'—crewneck sweaters, chinos, and dirty bucks. Their commitment to political activism wasn't as strong. In fact, they were to folk music what Neil Diamond and Billy Joel would eventually be to rock 'n roll, but in the end, their clean-cut enthusiasm helped establish it as a popular contemporary entertainment.

Like the labor faction they immortalized, folksingers of every stripe and color agreed to join ranks and coexist in a peaceful manner. There was plenty of work for everyone. Coffeehouses were flourishing. In fact, a network of tiny clubs stretched from coast to coast, establishing a kind of alternative entertainment circuit. Folksingers with talent could develop quite a reputation as they worked their way across the country, playing popular clubs. Coincidentally, a handful of coffeehouses emerged as the "important rooms" one had to play on the way up. There was Folk City in New York, the Gate of Horn in Chicago, and in San Francisco, the hungry i and Ash Grove became essential links to the big time. Each major city had a coffeehouse or two where enthusiasts came to see folksingers on the brink of success.

In Denver, the place to play was a scruffy joint on Colfax Avenue called the Satire. Owned by an ex-football player named Sam Sugarman, it had begun as a blue-collar sports bar called Sugie's—a steady, well-run little place, no overhead, good for a couple grand a year. Except Sugie had a taste for nightclubs. He decided to upgrade the bar, maybe put in a few couches instead of tables and chairs. Charge a few bucks cover, hire a few girls to give it pizazz. And somewhere or other Sugie'd heard there was a buck to be made in folk music. He didn't know a thing about it, per se, but that didn't bother him a bit. If he had a folksinger or two, his instincts told him, the place would jump with crowds.

Rechristening his bar the Satire, Sugie put in a tiny stage and hired a guy called Lingo the Drifter to take over the club and play there. Lingo, an ex-businessman from Chicago who had dropped out, grown a beard, and lived out of the back of a pickup truck, did a folksy Burl Ives–Pete Seeger-type show that clicked with the local crowd. The Satire's business picked up almost overnight.

Right after the Satire "went folk," Sam Sugarman caught an act in nearby Aspen that turned his head—and, subsequently, his club—around. The performers were brothers whose only other professional gig had been at the Kerosene Club in San Jose, California. Tom Smothers played guitar, his brother Dickie slapped a stand-up bass that looked like it was always about to topple over on him, and their send-ups of traditional folk songs cracked up audiences that remained SRO throughout the entire two-week Aspen run.

Sam Sugarman loved the Smothers Brothers' show. It was tuneful, clever, and, at times, mordantly funny. Ironic, considering the brothers hated each other. In Aspen, they even got into fistfights over which songs to include in an evening's set. But they were sensational, nonetheless—a novelty act that lampooned the folk craze as much as it honored it—and Sam Sugarman smelled money.

Sugie's entree to the Smothers Brothers came through their warm-up act, a burly, albeit likable, black folksinger named Walt Conley, who hosted hoots across town at Sugie's competitor, the Exodus. He made them both an offer they couldn't refuse: an open-ended engagement at the Satire. He'd pay the Smothers Brothers the princely sum of two hundred dollars a week, and Conley would get one hundred twenty-five dollars to open for them and run the club. The trio didn't waste time thinking it over. They jumped at Sugie's generous offer, and in no time, the Smothers Brothers were the darlings of Denver nightlife, while a table at the Satire became the hottest ticket in town.

One night, not too long afterward, Bob Dylan wandered into the Satire, looking for Walt Conley. An ex-girlfriend of Walt's from Minneapolis had told Bob to look him up if he ever made it out west. Suddenly Bobby was in town, and he talked Conley into letting him play a couple of songs. This went against club policy, but Conley took one look at Bob and felt pity for him. "He looked very gruff, as rural as he could possibly look," Conley recalls. "And it was embarrassingly obvious that he was trying to look that way."

Bob had cloned himself off as a pint-size Woody Guthrie, complete with blue jeans, work shirt, and a brown corduroy railroad cap that fit snugly over his runaway curls. He'd also picked up an Okie accent somewhere between Dinkytown and Denver. Relying on his finely tuned ear, he now sounded more down-home and rustic than a steer-roping cowboy, combining an adulteration of Joad-family pidgin and something that Hibbingites called Rayncher. Much later Dylan would affect a literary style that apostrophized all present participles, so that *blowing* became *blowin'* and *thinking* became *thinkin',* and so on. But at the time, Bob actually spoke like that. "Been out ramblin' and talkin' to folks, learnin' some new songs. . . ." He wanted to do some playin', and it was apparent to Walt Conley that he hadn't done much eatin' or sleepin', neither.

Dylan appeared on the same bill with the Smothers Brothers, performing an eclectic mix of Woody Guthrie, Leadbelly, and Cisco Houston songs. Not the popular numbers either, like "This Land Is Your Land" or "Rock Island Line," but real "authentic" folk stuff he'd dug out of anthologies and obscure records. Songs that would impress the purists.

The Satire's audiences responded indifferently to Bob's set, however. They'd come to clap and sing along with all the folk "hits" Walt Conley played each night. Everyone knew the words to "500 Miles" and "Waltzing Matilda" and "The MTA." When Conley strummed the opening chords to "Jamaica Farewell"—as he did five times each night—you'd think it had replaced the national anthem prior to the opening game of the World Series. Suddenly, instead of their beloved song leader, their Negro Pete Seeger whose wit, charm, and personality catered to all their needs, there was this pudgy, introverted little "hobo" who wandered around morosely on stage picking out atonal, minor-key folk dirges they'd never heard before. In between songs, when Bobby rhapsodized about Everyman travelin' those hard roads, the audience revealed a lot about their devotion to folk roots. "Who gives a fuck! Play 'Michael Row the Boat Ashore'!" "Let's hear 'Tom Dooley'!" This was a crowd that idolized the Kingston Trio, adored the Limeliters, and canonized the Brothers Four. The thought of listening to the songs of Negro sharecroppers and Appalachian hillbillies appalled them. Riding the rail was about as romantic a prospect as commuting to work. They wanted entertainment, not social commentary.

Dylan's vocal style didn't improve his popularity any. No longer sweet and sepulchral as it had been in Dinkytown, Bob's voice was now gravelly and adenoidal, as if someone had taken sandpaper to his vocal chords to remove the resonant quality. It was wild, breathless, oddly syncopated, in the whoop-and-holler style of itinerant blues masters—rural and tribal, irreverent, and *irritating*. Tommy Smothers would stand at the back of the club and cringe with each rasp of Bob's astringent voice. "Aw, jeeze," he'd complain to Walt Conley, "this guy is awful. Can't you do something about him?" Patrons pleaded with Conley to cut Dylan's set short, and finally he concluded that Bob was "too rough around the edges and too ethnic" for the Satire.

Though Dylan's chance of a week-long gig was all but obliterated, Conley invited him to stay on at a house he shared with fellow folksingers in a commercial section of downtown Denver. The place was a legendary crash pad for folkies passing through the city. The bedrooms were already occupied by the Smothers Brothers and a banjo player named Dave Hamil. Nevertheless, Bob enjoyed the run of the house, whatever food was in the cupboards, and access to Conley's splendid record collection, which included not only folk music but a first-rate selection of Broadway soundtracks and spoken-record recordings.

Bob came and went from the house for a period of about three weeks. Conley is convinced Dylan was checking out the scene, to see if perhaps Denver was a worthwhile place for him to launch his career. Minneapolis was certainly out of the question. New York figured to be brutally competitive. Chicago, where Odetta reigned, hadn't reached its potential and was full of Zimmerman *mischpucha*. The San Francisco scene was finished. Los Angeles was an intellectual wasteland. Denver, on the other hand, was nice and inconspicuous. A perfect balance of country and city, still provincial enough to be taken by storm. Monte Edwardson, the Golden Chords' bass player, had moved there after school and had hipped Bob to the steadily developing folk scene. No "star" had emerged as yet from the Rocky Mountain region, although the Smothers Brothers had an outside shot, as did Judy Collins, a local teenager who performed regularly at the Exodus. But the territory was still wide open. Anybody with a modest amount of talent and plenty of ambition could lay claim to the city and move on from there.

It immediately became apparent, however, that if there was going to be a local folk hero, his name wouldn't be Bob Dylan. Denver was a bastion of slick, commercial folk-pop; behind those hearty outdoorsmen faces and dungaree-and-flannel facades lurked the soul and inspiration for groups like the New Christy Minstrels. Bob was a professed purist. "He was struggling to maintain authenticity," Conley says in retrospect. "He not only knew all the Guthrie songs, he knew what they were about, and that impressed me."

Dylan presumptuously lectured Conley about the importance of rediscovering the folk past and "not spoiling the music." "I felt guilty because I knew Dylan had all the commitment to the music that I lacked. Bob knew it, too. He was thoroughly disappointed in me," Conley says now. "Because I was black, he expected me to be a young Bill Broonzy or a young Leadbelly. Instead, he encountered a singing actor who knew his on-stage commercial worth. It was obvious to me that Bob thought I had sold out. To him, I was just another white nigger with a guitar."

As in Hibbing, and again in Minneapolis, Dylan was ostracized by the Denver folk circle. They ignored him, both professionally and socially. He was permitted to do an occasional guest spot at the Satire, but he was never paid for it. At parties, he was usually the last person invited to sing. The Smothers Brothers didn't like him. He wasn't going to get a break at any of the local clubs. The handwriting was on the wall: it was clearly time for Bob to move on.

Ironically, Dylan didn't have enough money to get out of town. "He was in desperate straits," Walt Conley remembers. "At the time, I think he didn't have ten cents to his name."

Both problems—money and travel—seemed to be solved by a phone call Conley received from a woman in Central City, Colorado. Sophia St. John ran a "honky-tonk" there called the Gilded Garter and wondered if Walt knew anyone who was available to sing folk songs for a two-week engagement. Conley hesitated for a moment before answering. Any number of his friends needed the work. Club dates were few and far between. But the Gilded Garter in Central City? That wouldn't be regarded so much as a referral as it would a sentence.

Conley knew the Gilded Garter only by reputation. Word had it, it was a horrible place to play, the worst possible booking. A real tourist trap, it was a cavernous room modeled after a Dodge City-type saloon in a restored frontier town. It featured a big bar and swinging doors that opened onto a crowded thoroughfare. College-student waitresses worked the floor in skimpy Gay-90s outfits and were instructed to serve by leaning into the customer's face, ignoring the inadvertent brush on the ass or stroke on the thigh. Because there was no cover, the place was always packed with the kind of people who wanted to get as much as they possibly could for the least amount of money. A lot of families with screaming kids. Loud-mouthed vacationers just off the tour bus. Coffeeshop food. And a sign that promised "Free Entertainment."

Working the Gilded Garter was enough to drive any performer out of his mind. Customers wanted to eat, use the rest rooms, and compare the junk they picked up at the souvenir shops out on Eureka Street. Nobody paid any attention to the music. The folksinger was practically drowned out by the constant clatter of silverware, the noisy cash register, and people hollering for more ketchup, another cup of coffee, and the check. On top of that, the stage was right next to the door, so it was hard not to feel like the Monkey Boy at a freak show, performing while the tourists stood at the door and gawked at you from the street.

Walt Conley couldn't possibly send a friend into that situation. Instead, he recommended Bob. "The kid was desperate for money," Conley insists, "but the truth of that matter is that I saw it as an opportunity to get rid of him."

The Gilded Garter is the famous "sleazy striptease joint" or "burlesque house" Dylan always refers to whenever he recounts his adventures in the Old West. The tourists are romanticized as ornery "drunks," the waitresses as "dance-hall girls" or "strippers." In all, Bob's "summer gig" lasted four or five days at the most. The official story is that he was fired, but in actuality he took off. At the end of the first week, Walt Conley got a call from Sophia St. John informing him that both Bob and twenty dollars that had been in her purse were missing. "I'm going to call the authorities," she told him.

Conley talked her out of pressing charges. He paid her back, figuring it was worth the twenty to be rid of Bob. Imagine how he felt, then, when Dylan returned to the house on East Seventeenth Avenue as if nothing had happened. "I told him he couldn't stay with us anymore," Conley remembers. "Enough stories had drifted back from Central City, and nobody wanted anything to do with him."

Somehow Bob got together enough money for a cheap room in a hotel next door to the Exodus, where Leon Bibb was playing a three-day gig. Not that he spent much time cooped up there. Bob would always be hanging out at the coffeehouses, scrounging a meal or the chance to do a couple of songs before the headliner took the stage. After the Satire closed each night, performers usually gathered at Walt Conley's house, where the music continued until three or four o'clock in the morning, and Bob would usually stop by to sing or strum along. His presence was tolerated by the others, but it was obvious that some discouragement was necessary to send Bob on his way.

It occurred a week later, when Walt Conley and Dave Hamil arrived home after a particularly stressful night at the Satire. Some holdovers from Sugie's sports bar had staged a drunken offensive against the folksingers, and Conley was forced to restore order with the blunt end of a bottle. That, and a number of taxing performances, had sapped him of any desire to socialize that night. Instead of partying until dawn, Walt and Dave decided to relax and listen to a few records. Flipping through the shelves, Hamil was the first to notice that some albums were missing from his collection. Conley's records had also been pruned, but strangely enough only the three-record boxed sets had been taken.

"Dylan!" Hamil declared, "—he took the records!" Conley disagreed. What would Bob want with albums like *Death of a Salesman, Othello,* and *Julius Caesar*? They were of no interest to him. Furthermore, Walt's Guthrie and Leadbelly records were untouched. The robbery just didn't have Bob's signature on it. Dave Hamil, however, remained unconvinced. He knew how desperate Bob was for money and considered that a strong enough motive.

"I'm going down to his hotel," he said. Conley glanced at the clock—it was a few minutes after three a.m. Figuring an investigation could wait until morning, he decided to go to bed.

He was awakened an hour later by the jangling of the telephone. Hamil was in Dylan's room and needed Walt's assistance. Conley arrived ten minutes later, surprised at just how sleazy a hotel Bob had been staying in—drunks and bums passed out in the lobby, hookers working the halls. A real two-dollar-a-night fleabag. Upstairs, Hamil was giving Dylan the third degree, convinced more than ever that he had taken the albums. Bob was curled up on the bed, pleading his innocence. He looked pathetic sitting there. Tears had streaked his cheeks. He wrung his hands, jiggled his leg out of control, begged the guys to believe him. Why would he steal their records? Bob asked. He'd never do anything to hurt his pals. Bob started crying, looking at Walt as if to say, "Save me!" Conley became disgusted with the whole scene and went home. As he walked in the door, however, the phone was ringing. "I've got the records," Hamil told him. "He had 'em all the time."

Hamil had momentarily left the hotel room and, upon returning, discovered Bob removing the records from beneath his mattress. Before Dave could reach him, Bob flung the records out the window. Ten stories down, the records lay strewn along a deserted alley. Many of them were broken, the covers destroyed. Hamil took one look at the damage and called the police.

It took Walt Conley until dawn to discourage Hamil from swearing out a warrant against Bob. The cops weren't eager to haul in some kid who'd pinched a few records, especially after most of them had been recovered. But Hamil was adamant. He wanted revenge, particularly because of Bob's ingratitude to people who had cared for and fed him—people who had trusted him with their belongings. It took a few hours to calm Hamil down.

Throughout, Bob sat on the edge of the bed, crying into his hands. No matter how many nights his idol, Woody Guthrie, had spent behind bars a-singin' and a-protestin', the prospect of going to jail terrified Bob. Sure, he'd set out to follow in Woody's footsteps, but missing one of two of them wouldn't hurt the image any. Not every card-carrying folksinger had to do time as a prerequisite for authenticity. Nor was it likely to reform him.

A year or so earlier, when Bob was scuffling around the Twin Cities, he was accused of a similar crime. John Pankake, the editor of a snooty Minneapolis folk rag called *The Little Sandy Review* and a friend of Bob's from Dinkytown, returned home from a weekend vacation and found about twenty of his records missing. After a brief investigation, Dylan confessed to the crime, but only after making up some cock-and-bull story about friends dropping them off with him for safe-keeping. The excuse he gave Walt Conley was every bit as lame. Bob claimed the records were meant to be a gift for Conley's ex-girlfriend in Minneapolis. "I was taking them back as a memento of you," he said. It was decided that the records would remain in Denver, but Dylan would have to leave.

He made good on that promise a few days later. Leon Bibb, whose stint at the Exodus had ended, had gotten an important last-minute gig back east, providing he could be there the following day. To make it in time, Bibb jumped on the next plane, but only after he arranged to have a waiter from the coffeehouse drive his car cross-country. Bob got wind of the plans and saw it as an excellent opportunity to hitch a ride out of town. The men could make the trip in three, four days at most, depending on the weather and stamina. Bob agreed to share the driving chores in exchange for free passage.

He'd had his fill of the Old West. The same with Denver and its "rising folk scene." It was nowhere. Just another paean to the marriage of folk music and free enterprise. And a bad marriage, at that. It was time for a change of scenery. Bob needed to go somewhere that he could fit into the community, where uniqueness was not only tolerated but encouraged. Where he'd have a shot at fulfilling his dreams.

That would require him to move into a completely different groove. Up to now, Bob's problem was simply the fact that he was turning people off. He hadn't even managed to polarize his audience. If he wanted to get anywhere, he had to find an audience that worshipped what he was doing as vehemently as the part of the audience that disapproved of it. He wasn't daring enough, or even outrageous. He hadn't gone far enough out on a limb. About all you could say for Bob was that he did a decent imitation of Woody Guthrie.

Maybe the change of scenery would do him some good. He could use the time on the road to play with a few ideas, come up with a new angle or even a couple of decent tunes. He needed some new tactic, that was for sure.

After all, they were on their way to New York.

Part 2

The Twerp

8

Stalkin' New York

There was no one waiting for Bob Dylan when he arrived in New York in January 1961. Like his previous pilgrimages to Minneapolis and Denver, he arrived in Manhattan alone, with his guitar, a sleeping bag, and two goals: to visit Woody Guthrie and to become a star.

The first objective posed no difficulty. Guthrie, who suffered from a rare, degenerative nerve disorder called Huntington's chorea, had been confined to Greystone Park State Hospital, a sprawling medieval institution in Morris Plains, New Jersey, since 1956. Bob had called him there from Minneapolis, only to be told that patients weren't permitted to come to the phone: there were regularly scheduled hours when they received guests, should he like to visit.

Bob, however, was determined to meet his idol. It was all he talked about—"Goin' t'see Woody." Most people thought the trip east was just another of his starry-eyed fantasies. Another self-delusion. The Dinkytown crowd had sniggered as he trundled off in pursuit of the great god Guthrie. The thought of Bob coming within a mile of the mythical folksinger inspired a volley of spiteful criticism. Imagine someone you know setting out to encounter Greta Garbo or J. D. Salinger, and you have a pretty good idea of how they felt. Dylan and Guthrie!—You couldn't say the names together without rolling your eyes. It was ludicrous!

Be that as it may, Bob immediately made the hour-and-a-half trip from New York to Greystone and was admitted to Woody's room without having to go through a lot of rigamarole. "There's a Mr. Dylan here to see you, Woody." "Hey, send him right in!" It was as easy as that. The next thing Bob knew, he was strolling into a visitor's ward lined with mechanical beds where the great balladeer lay waiting for him.

Bob was asked to play a medley of Woody's songs for the patient. It must have been a sobering experience for Bob. The Woody Guthrie he'd read and dreamed about was a scrappy little guy, full of defiance and exuberance. He was a guy who boasted of raising hell with the company man, of insatiable sexual appetites, capped off by years of hard drinking and cussing, carousing and practical joking. When Bob finally came face-to-face with his hero, it must have been nearly impossible for him to recognize Woody. Gray and gaunt from the debilitating disease, he was racked by uncontrollable spasms. His shoulders twitched, his arms flailed, his torso writhed in constant motion. His speech was slurred and often incoherent. Deprived of the very mannerisms that defined him—playing his guitar and writing—Woody Guthrie existed only in a physical sense; the indomitable creative forces had long since withered from his flesh.

So, too, had he been abandoned by most of his so-called traveling buddies. Aside from folksinger Jack Elliott, who emulated a healthy Guthrie, and Harold Leventhal, Woody's manager, nobody came to visit. At least, not on any kind of a regular basis. The closely knit folk circle—that earthy band of peaceniks, universalists, and goodwill ambassadors—wanted no reminder of their dying friend. "Better we should remember him *as he was,*" as the old saying goes.

Bob was nevertheless intoxicated by his encounter with Woody Guthrie. He was flushed with excitement. "It was all he wanted to talk about," recalls Mark Spoelstra, another aspiring young folksinger who met Bob during that first week in New York. "He'd just been to see him that first time and had a card Woody'd signed that said 'I ain't dead yet' on it."

Spoelstra, who had arrived in New York only six months before from Pasadena, wasn't as enamored of Guthrie. A student of the intricate twelve-string blues technique, he thought "Woody's guitar playing was rotten." Mark preferred the way Leadbelly tattooed a riff, working it up into apoplectic fits of minstrelsy. That suited Bob just fine. They also agreed on Josh White and Bill Broonzy, as well as the mainstay of inspiration for the blues idiom: women. If, as both men confessed upon meeting, their weakness was for the opposite sex, their undisputed passion was for music.

Though he was only twenty-one when Bob met him, Mark Spoelstra was a rather accomplished guitarist—not an innovator or a virtuoso, but a guy who could play along with anything after hearing it once. He'd been at it since he was a kid and had played professionally all over the country, including a few gigs that Bob heard recounted with great fascination. Mark had hung around with legendary bluesmen Sonny Terry and Brownie McGhee in Chicago and wound up jamming with them. He even took a job as their "white chauffeur," in order to stick by these cats. Lacking the kind of distinctive voice Bob was cultivating, Mark dedicated himself to playing traditional blues with the understanding that he was never going to be considered a world-class performer. First of all, he was white, and that just didn't sit well with the purists. His interpretation of blues standards wasn't exceptional enough to set him apart from the fifty-or-so other guitarists looking to make a name for themselves. Nor had he ever thought of himself as a professional entertainer.

No doubt Bob recognized a real opportunity for friendship. In Mark, he'd found someone his own age who was carried away with folk music and the blues, broke, allergic to work, droll, girl-crazy, playful, and *no competition*. He'd never challenge Bob for the spotlight. Mark was the perfect straight man, a foil for Bob's high-flying antics.

Soon after they met, they crashed the gate at the Café Bazaar, one of the high-spirited little coffeehouses on West Third Street which charged a cover at the door. Bob had this thing about the place—it was seedy, loud, a haven for hitter-chicks, the kind who'd take you home for the night without asking for your name and number, tolerant of rock 'n roll, offbeat, and off limits to the tourist trade. It was the natural joint for a night's play—except for the buck or two they hit you for at the door.

A block away Bob flashed on an idea to get them inside without paying. "I'm gonna be your manager, and you're gonna be 'the famous Mark Spoelstra,'" he explained, bristling with mischief. A here-we-go-again look crept over Mark's face, but before he could say anything, Bob snapped, "Just play along." Next thing Mark knew, Bob strolled up to the bouncer parked outside the door.

"Hey, man—how ya' doing? Hear you got a pretty nice scene going down inside." The ill-tempered greaseball, rocking back and forth to keep warm, glowered at the boys, but Bob was smiling and putting him on cheerfully, so they struck up a conversation. Pretty soon the guy was laying out his whole life story. "Hey, how about letting us go inside?" Bob asked in a low, palsy-walsy voice. The guy shrugged, explaining that he'd like to, but if he let them in he'd have to do it for everyone; the boss was strict; he kept an eye on the box office; he could lose his job—every excuse in the book. Astonished, Bob gasped, "You're asking *us* to pay to get in?"

"Well, yeah—everyone has to pay to get in."

"I know. But *us?*" Bob grabbed Mark by the shoulders and hustled him in front of the perplexed bouncer. "Don't you know who this is?" Bob became more and more excited. Words rattled out of his mouth like a rabid drill sergeant, snarling and accusatory, not even pausing for answers. "This here is Mark Spoelstra. Haven't you ever heard of Mark Spoelstra?"

"Not really. . . ."

"Oh, man—are *you* out of it! Everybody knows who Mark Spoelstra is. People come up to him on the street. They . . . aw—you're just putting us on!"

Right about then, the bouncer began feeling unsure of himself. Maybe he should have recognized this Spoelstra fella. Famous people were dropping by all the time. It gave the club kind of a mystique to have them spotted there. Once in a while it even wound up in one of the columns: "So-and-so seen stomping at the Café Bazaar." Now he'd gone and insulted some big star he'd never heard of before. The boss'd have his ass in a sling for this.

On top of that, the little fat-faced kid in the corduroy hat wasn't backing off any. Bob was really rolling, laying it on thick about how offended they were, how all they wanted was a place where they could sit quietly and not be harassed by fans and autograph seekers, away from the press, the crush of photographers always chasing after them. To make matters worse, the doorman couldn't tell a celebrity from a soda jerk! How ignorant could you get? "I don't even know why we stopped here in the first place."

The poor bouncer tried desperately to get a word in edgewise, but Bob showed no mercy. He lit into the guy for another several minutes before allowing the guy to finally sputter: "Okay, okay—you don't have to pay. You can go in."

Bob stopped short and stared at the beaten man. "No. We don't want to go in," he said, pulling Mark after him.

"Really—it's my mistake. I should have recognized you guys. Why don't you just go in and have a good time. I'll square it with the boss."

Bob and Mark couldn't even look back, they were so convulsed with laughter. They took off down the street, arms wrapped around each other's shoulders, giggling and wheezing like a couple of schoolboys who had just wired the recess bell to ring ten minutes early.

Nothing seemed to delight Bob more than undermining the power of an authority figure. *Intimidation!*—he had a real knack for it. Immediately upon meeting someone he knew what button to push or string to pull. Then he went to work on the person's insecurity the way a boxer worked over a wounded opponent—goading, needling, harassing, knocking him off balance. It was spooky, Mark thought, how once Bob got going, nothing else seemed to matter. He was fearless. His face and posture would undergo an alarming transformation—his puny body bent forward at the waist with his feet spread apart and his face set in a squinty, snarling leer. In no time, he'd be all revved up, moving in on his quarry while spewing indignation in a staccato barrage.

Bob wasn't a fighter in the physical sense; he possessed neither the strength nor the finesse for fisticuffs. But his words always packed a mean punch, and he had the inner resources of a bully. In time, he would sharpen these instincts further, but in 1960 Bob was already quite a master of rhetoric. "It amazed me how, after only a week or two in New York, he could carry it off," Spoelstra wonders in retrospect. "It eventually reached a point where I thought it was enough, but Bob was just getting started."

Mark Spoelstra was also amazed at how well Bob carried himself in the monstrous city. Although Mark had arrived there five months before Bob, he never had to take him under his wing. "It surprised me how he seemed to know his way around," Spoelstra recalls. "Bob wasn't intimidated by or curious about the city, he just kind of took it for granted. It could have been any city on earth, to him they were all the same. The way it seemed, the only place that intrigued him was Greenwich Village."

Greenwich Village was the folksinger's Mecca. A catacomb of mazy streets in downtown Manhattan, the Village, as it is called, attracted millions of adventure-starved visitors looking for the romance and mystery its name alone seemed to evoke. Originally depicted by Henry James as a curious microcosm of New York society, the Village came to symbolize the perpetual wellspring of bohemian culture, a dark world of smoke-filled salons, unconventional thought, and tragic genius. It was where Edgar Allan Poe wrote *The Fall of the House of Usher,* where Edward Albee saw the phrase "Who's Afraid of Virginia Woolf" scrawled across a bathroom mirror, where Marcel Duchamp astounded the art world by painting *Nude Descending a Staircase,* and where Kahlil Gibran wrote *The Prophet.* Here Brando studied "the method," and comics such as Bill Cosby, Woody Allen, and Richard Pryor staked their claims to stardom. Some of the greatest minds of the twentieth century flourished in Greenwich Village, including Theodore Dreiser, Willa Cather, Aaron Copland, Eugene O'Neill, F. Scott Fitzgerald, Edna St. Vincent Millay, Max Eastman, Leonard Bernstein, Jackson Pollack, Norman Mailer—the list seems endless.

It is safe to say, however, that none of the distinguished artists whose work prospered in the Village really affected Bob Dylan's decision to gravitate there. He was simply looking for a place to play folk music, and the Village offered more opportunity for that than anywhere else in the world.

Although the Village had a long tradition of folk music, it provided a curious showcase for Bob Dylan. Throughout the late-1940s and even into the late-1950s, the Village had nurtured a mainstream folk music that was for the most part international in flavor. Its prodigies came from a group of dark, serious-minded ethnomusicologists who collected songs from around the world and performed them in myriad styles and tongues: political songs of medieval minstrels, South African tribal chants, English broadsides and sea shanties sung in authentic brogues, Russian boat songs, German *Volkslieder,* Negro spirituals, flamenco flourishes, Appalachian hill music and blues, as well as nursery rhymes, lullabies, madrigals, serenades, and drinking songs. Occasionally a cabaret-style singer like Theodore Bikel, Cynthia Gooding, or Martha Schlame presented an evening of folk songs at one of the Village's intimate theaters. But aside from the feeble Folk Singers Guild, which held bimonthly Sunday-night concerts at the tiny Sullivan Street Playhouse to showcase new talent, Greenwich Village was a wilderness to a kid in blue jeans and long, curly hair with a fake Okie accent, whose ultimate ambition was to write and perform his own folk songs.

The few coffeehouses committed to hiring folk attractions booked one of the thirty-or-so performers with broad-based appeal—popular folk recording artists like Cisco Houston, Oscar Brand, Josh White, or Odetta, whose names brought in paying customers. Every so often one of the lesser-known traditionalists struggling to remain a part of the scene was charitably allotted a weekend gig. The competition was fierce. There was a crush of talented, dedicated folksingers in Greenwich Village scrambling to make ends meet. Ed McCurdy, a baritone with a straight-faced lumbering presence, sought to revive and popularize old English ballads; Jean Ritchie primly hammered out rural mountain songs on her handmade dulcimer; Roger Sprung doodled on an old-timey bluegrass banjo; John Winn serenaded audiences with endless songs from the Renaissance; Augustine Dembello thwacked away on a flamenco-style guitar; Gil Turner performed high-minded anthems with a group named the New World Singers; Casey Anderson sang medleys based on Haitian voodoo incantations; Logan English crooned to the operatic drone of primitive American broadsides. These are but a handful of the well-respected journeymen who perpetuated folk music in Greenwich Village as one of the most academic, humorless, leaden, *boring* forms of entertainment to straddle the Eisenhower era. This was hardly the type of extended family Bob Dylan wished to join. But by courting such highly regarded performers, Bob not only slipped into the front ranks of traditional folk music, he did so at precisely the moment this dreary medium was about to jettison to the forefront of contemporary pop culture.

The catalyst was a group called the Kingston Trio, a flagrantly collegiate-looking ensemble that had the foresight to combine folk music with a commercial pop sound. The trio—Bob Shane, Nick Reynolds, and Dave Guard—revolutionized folk music with a transfusion of lush harmonies, ridiculously lighthearted lyrics, and a Vegas-type act designed to get the audience humming and clapping along. "Oh,

I don't give a damn about a greenback dollar/ Spend it fast as I can. . . ." Their songs rocked back and forth with a jaunty white gospel flavor that snapped the corset off folk music's straitlaced girth. And the boys knew how to bring down the house. They could be sentimental one minute, wry and sardonic the next, or even shamelessly playful. Versatility broadened their appeal to embrace teenagers, college girls, and young married couples. And so the Kingston Trio touched off a phenomenon that made folk music—or, at least, the musical odds and ends *they* called folk music—the last word in American entertainment.

To the purists, who considered folk music a sacrosanct expression of suffering, anger, and social injustice, this was an act of heresy. This strident *popularization,* as critic Robert Shelton called it, created a market "glutted with folk music that was distorted, hoked-up, disguised, and distorted." The threat of assimilation—that their privileged enlightenment might be understood and appreciated by the masses—was too much for the folk purists to bear. They wanted people the world over to raise their voices in song—but it had to be folk music as *they* defined it.

Fortunately this supercilious attitude had little effect on the music's growing popularity. Greenwich Village was overrun by thousands upon thousands of tourists in search of Kingston Trio-type folk music. Friday and Saturday nights the police were forced to put up barricades, the streets got so crowded. Traffic was backed up for blocks. Yet nowhere could you find a couple of all-American boys belting out the current folk hits. They didn't exist. The Village coffeehouses still featured dour-looking folksingers in suits and ties, presenting their folk-songs-heard-'round-the-world sets. Requests for "Scotch and Soda," "A Worried Man," and "Sloop John B" were met with reproachful glares.

The conditions in Greenwich Village were remedied by a simple exercise of supply and demand. Village landlords took one look at the situation and concluded there was a fortune to made in the folk biz. As early as the spring of 1961, every available dilapidated nook and cranny zoned for commercial use in the Village was being converted into a coffeehouse: abandoned laundromats, pizza parlors, coffee shops, delis, and bars—even former "social cellars" that had been boarded up since Prohibition were excavated for the cause. The land rush was carried to tragic extremes when a local huckster named Von Emsen displaced a sixty-five-year-old shoemaker from his longtime storefront on Bleecker Street in order to open yet another hole-in-the-wall coffeehouse; two weeks later, the disgruntled old cobbler accosted Emsen outside the place and shot him squarely between the eyes.

Most folks, however, welcomed the surge of new coffeehouses. The steady influx of tourists to the Village provided businesses there with a rich new source of income. The folk enthusiasts had spending habits that weren't limited to briny cups of espresso and capuccino. They bought T-shirts and buttons and posters and records and just about every other piece of junk you could put in front of them. They were the most conspicuous of consumers in a neighborhood that was rapidly becoming service-oriented.

The rank-and-file folksinger, too, was especially encouraged by the Village's romance with coffeehouses. Suddenly there were two dozen new places to play. The Café Bazaar, an old coach house that had been part of Aaron Burr's country estate, was the first place to convert to folk music on a professional basis. Its success prompted the Village Gate, long a cabaret, to copy its format, followed in quick succession by Gerde's Fifth Peg, the Gaslight, and the Third Side, all of which hired folksingers to perform on the weekends. These were the legit rooms, where well-known attractions played regularly. These acts got paid on time, were given small dressing rooms, and enjoyed free meals and a tab (at the few clubs where liquor was served).

The rest of the rooms comprised a new wave of coffeehouses which disburdened their owners from having to shell out a nickel for entertainment. Called "baskethouses," after the practice of passing a wicker basket through the audience for pocket change to compensate the performer, these places became the foundation of the folk craze that was about to sweep America. They were the dead end of the show-biz scale, real no-frills joints. Notoriously small and poorly lit, they were crammed with tiny tables, were noisy, and served lousy overpriced food and gritty coffee. Yet these effects actually *attracted* people inside! No kidding. Tourists liked to *get down* with the beatniks. It was an adventure, something to talk about when they got back to their squeaky-clean tract houses in New Jersey and Long Island. "You'd never *believe* where we've been, Harry!" It was part of the mystique.

Working the baskethouses, on the other hand, was no picnic. Any folksinger with an ounce of self-esteem wouldn't be caught dead playing in one of them. Food was served throughout the show; there was no such thing as a PA system; and you had to split the basket with six or seven other acts who rotated on the night's bill so they could turn over the house every half hour. It was a pitiful gig. But it was a gig nonetheless, and it opened the door for hundreds with talent, giving them the opportunity to be heard—in Greenwich Village, no less—the folk music capital of the free world.

Some pretty big names started out playing the baskethouses. Tom Paxton worked a few on MacDougal Street while he was still in the military service. Dave Van Ronk played and emceed shows over at the Commons. You could catch Phil Ochs at the Third Side launching one of his topical assaults. Peter Yarrow, Maria Muldaur, Richie Havens, Tiny Tim, Eric Andersen—they were all trying to make a name for themselves years before anyone thought to connect folk music with a profit margin.

Mark Spoelstra had broken in performing at a Bleecker Street baskethouse called the Cock 'n Bull—later to be resurrected as the Bitter End—where he'd worked on an open stage (meaning anyone who wanted to could get up and perform) and did an occasional Sunday matinee in the weeks before Bob Dylan arrived in New York. Spoelstra was too easygoing a Californian to wrestle with other folksingers for a paying gig. He enjoyed singing and got a kick out of hanging out in the Village. It never dawned on Mark to promote himself the way other guys did. He lacked the bloodthirsty ambition that was necessary to separate himself from the burgeoning folk peer group. It was this ingenuous demeanor that naturally prompted Mark to invite Bob Dylan on stage with him one wintry afternoon at the Cafe Wha?.

The Wha? was an enormous, dark room at 115 MacDougal Street owned by a tough-talking guy named Manny Roth, uncle of the 1980s rocker David Lee Roth. At night, one of three well-paid "house acts" worked the Wha?—Noel Stookey, a stand-up comic from Michigan who, in 1962, was renamed Paul to create a more melodious logo with co-trio members Peter Yarrow and Mary Travers; Louis Gosset, Jr., whose decision to shuck folk music for acting eventually earned him a best-supporting-actor Oscar for *An Officer and a Gentleman*; and Fred Neil, a singer-songwriter who later composed "Everybody's Talkin'," the theme song for *Midnight Cowboy.* The three had a virtual lock on the Wha?'s stage and were considered "real entertainers" by the baskethouse stiffs. Business was so good, however, that Manny Roth saw fit to open the club during the afternoon as a possible hangout for NYU students. Not that he was about to do anything so foolish as *pay* for entertainment. As Dave Van Ronk said of Manny Roth: "By the time he got finished with a penny, you could no longer see Lincoln on it." No, folksingers worked the Wha?'s matinees for free; it was a place new acts could cut their teeth, and they got to play with no less a pro than Freddy Neil, who emceed the festivities and opened up with a few songs of his own.

Spoelstra and Dylan began playing afternoons at the Wha? in early February 1961. Mark interpreted urban blues numbers like "Sugar Babe," while Bob limited his set to a medley of Woody Guthrie standards and some traditional folk songs, such as "Barbara Allen." Later, they even served as back-up musicians for Freddy Neil, with Bob vamping on harmonica instead of guitar. Van Ronk, by this time well-known as one of the Village's rising young stars, remembers catching Bob's first New York performance there and being impressed with his musicianship. "His phrasing was so unique," Van Ronk recalls. "He staggered the words against the music in such an exhilarating way, and he had an absolutely wonderful command of it."

Van Ronk cites Dylan's rendition of "Hava Nagila" as a particularly glowing example of Bob's comic versatility. "He broke it up into nonsense syllables and you never knew when the next *ha* or *va* was coming in," Van Ronk says. "The harmonica chorus was even more eccentric. It was absolutely unpredictable and captivating. I knew at once that the kid had real talent, though I wasn't the only one who had that revelation."

Gil Turner, recounting Bob's Wha? show in a folk-music journal called *Sing Out!*, gushed over the newcomer's "magnetism." Said Turner, "There was apparent in his singing, playing, and lyric improvization [sic] an excessive freedom seldom encountered among white blues singers." In particular, *that voice!* Nobody had ever heard anything like it before. The New York Dylan bore no resemblance to his melodious Minneapolis counterpart. By the time he hit New York, Bob had perfected a tonsilly scranch, a dry, throaty tenor "with all the husk and bark left on the notes," which, if you weren't actually looking at him, sounded like a middle-age hillbilly with emphysema. Although it took some getting used to, Bob's voice was totally unique and it seemed to strangle the music like a pair of ten-dollar shoes. It was unsettling, which in itself lent a high drama to every stanza he sang. The songs themselves might be relaxed and folksy, but with a gut-nervous flurry of short breaths and releases, he created tension around the most tranquil of lines. Then he finished them off with that sandpaper rasp. The effect it had on people can best be defined by a single word—*jolting*.

It seems obvious that Dylan understood the power of his inclement voice from the way in which he thrust it out front. Most performers would have buried a harsh-sounding vocal beneath spectacular instrumental flourishes, working to draw attention *away* from this weakness by underscoring the stronger points in their act. Most performers, but not Bob. Repeatedly straining his voice into a high-pitched key, Bob held a note until it fluttered and faded; then, gulping in air at the last possible moment, he sprang off the fade into yet another pneumonic trill. It was a tour de force in the dynamics of breathing—perhaps the most inspired mark of his legendary style. And it was his unique voice that made him rise above the crush of young folksingers competing for recognition on the Village stages.

In the weeks that followed, Bob's unusual vocal style earned him a fair amount of attention. Word spread quickly along the Greenwich Village grapevine that a new kid *with talent* was working the Street, as the clubs on MacDougal were collectively known. Consequently, the baskethouses Bob played were often spotted with other folksingers who wanted to find out what all the fuss was about. Some, like Van Ronk and Tom Paxton, were genuinely impressed by what they heard, and they were secure enough to welcome another gifted young folksinger to their midst. Others, however, claimed they were left cold by Bob's quirky style, put off by his voice or, in many cases, weary of so tedious another Woody Guthrie imitator making a big splash. Eric Darling, a banjo player who later enjoyed some success as a member of the Rooftop Singers, refused to remain in any room Bob entered. "We already got one Woody Guthrie," he told a friend one night as he stormed out of the Gaslight. "The last thing in the world we need is another one."

Arthur Gorson, who was soon to become Phil Ochs's manager, claims the traditional folksingers were intimidated by Dylan's dogged individualism. Then a college student who hung out in Village coffeehouses after classes, Gorson now says, "Bob showed up in the Village with an attitude, a rebellious persona. At that time, no one [other than, perhaps, Jack Elliott] had a persona. Then, suddenly, this kid arrives talking and acting like Woody Guthrie—only tougher and more preconceived. He'd created a character, which was fine by most folks, but he always *stayed* in character. That's what shook people up, because no one knew how to deal with it."

Despite their closeness, even Mark Spoelstra was seldom able to read Bob's prevailing personality. "I never knew when he was playing a role or being himself," the ex-Californian says today, still perplexed by Dylan's inscrutable disposition. On stage, Bob functioned as a dead ringer for Woody. "He was so serious and intense about it that it often made him seem like kind of a hilarious figure," Spoelstra maintains.

One time, at the Wha?, Spoelstra broke out laughing during one of Bob's impromptu sets. He couldn't help it. Sitting at a table with some friends, Mark looked up and saw what he thought was certainly a parody: Bob had his head thrown back, flaunting that gravelly voice; he was decked out in gen-u-ine travelin' clothes with the exaggerated Okie twang—it was too much at one time.

It was easy to laugh at Bob. At nineteen, the image he cut was preposterous, to be sure. Beneath the veneer, however, was a gifted young man with enormous talent. No doubt many performers' laughter was released nervously to mask their own insecurity.

Everything that Bob Dylan failed to communicate in Minneapolis and Denver worked beautifully for him on the New York stage. The response to his initial performances confirmed everything he'd always believed about his ability to make it as a singer. The real payoff, however, was that it would get his name around to the major league coffeehouses—Folk City or the Gaslight—where a gig would guarantee him between a hundred and a hundred fifty dollars a week. Up to now, Bob and Mark were limited to playing baskethouses to make ends meet. They worked those joints every day through the summer of 1961, playing the first show in the early afternoon and often finishing at two or three in the morning. During the course of a weekday they were likely to pop up on the stage at three or four places on the Street. For this, they took home roughly fifteen dollars in change.

Weekends were another story altogether. On Friday and Saturday nights, the Street resembled downtown Las Vegas, with its crowds and carnival atmosphere. Barkers patrolled the club entrances, vying to steer people inside. "We've got what you've been reading about!" they shouted at passersby. "Authentic folksingers, right inside!" The coffeehouses opened early, but entertainment generally got under way around seven o'clock to accommodate the dinner crowd. By eight, the first rush was in full swing. Lines formed outside most of the tiny clubs, snaking fifty or sixty feet along the curb, where they remained steady until midnight, when most tourists called it a day. Bob could often play as many as four sets in that time. He'd begin at the Wha?, then scoot over to the Commons or Mills Tavern, maybe play a few songs at the Limelight, a couple at the Why Not?. Sometimes the managers at the Bazaar would let him do a set if the crowds were good.

Business slacked off for an hour or two around one in the morning. Usually the musicians stopped to grab a bite to eat or killed an hour playing chess. Bob quickly acquired a reputation for his unique style of play among the Street's late-night chess freaks. He'd mastered the moves but had little of the patience or concentration that the game required. After the third or fourth move, Bob would customarily begin to fidget. He'd scratch his head, drum his fingers on the board, get the ol' leg pumping—often all three at the same time! "It was like a bag of raw nerves sitting across the table from you," complains Dave Van Ronk, who often accepted Bob's challenge between shows. "He'd be playing up to his potential—which was above-average—and you'd be making mistakes you normally wouldn't make against any other opponent." A half hour into the game Bob would lean over the board and utter some sleepy-eyed conundrum like: "I'm not too sure how you play this game." Then he'd nonchalantly slide a piece into place and grin. "Oh, yeah—*checkmate!*"

Around three a.m. the folksingers returned to the stage to entertain the second rush of tourists, whose mood was far rowdier. Audiences at the late show consisted mainly of refugees from the nearby bars, which were required by law to shut down by two o'clock. Since most of the Greenwich Village coffeehouses chose not to serve liquor, they were exempt from the curfew. Therefore, as soon as the clock struck two, crowds of night owls thronged the Street in the hope of prolonging their predawn bacchanal. The music clubs served as the perfect place to coffee-up and catch a glimpse of the beatniks and folksingers they'd been reading about in the magazines and newspapers. "They didn't want to hear us, they wanted to *see* us," Van Ronk asserts. "For two hours, until the last drunken fireman was shoveled into the street, folksinging was one hellish ordeal."

For the effort, which meant finishing up no earlier than six in the morning, a performer could take home an extra fifty dollars a night. That was more than enough to see someone like Bob through the week. As a bonus, folksingers acquired the restraint necessary for playing to any kind of audience. Out of necessity, they developed a seasoned professionalism that took other performers years to perfect. Bob began applying all the things he'd learned in Dinkytown and Denver, refining his stage act with an offbeat flair for showmanship that lifted him to another plateau. Tapes that have surfaced from 1961 and 1962 reveal Dylan as a tenaciously evolving performer. He jazzed up his traditional repertoire with a potpourri of country blues and current popular styles, including a parody of adolescent rock 'n roll called "Acne." Another folksinger might have been accused of commercialism, but Bob's stage presence—intercut with measured sarcasm and sophistication—gave his shows an aura of hipness. He made audiences feel he was taking them somewhere special, letting them in on something only enlightened people could appreciate. He put them in a groove and nursed it along until even the stubbornest skeptics were in the palm of his hand. More extraordinary perhaps, was that he managed this feat months before writing the kind of original songs for which he is best known.

While Bob Dylan's creativity was beginning to bud in Greenwich Village, his showmanship was in full bloom. The spring of 1961 marked a tangible breakthrough in Bob's rush to stardom. Throughout these months, he worked often on any stage that would have him—baskethouses, open stages, hootenannys, revues, guest sets in which he played the harmonica or backup guitar on another performer's bill, folk-song society meetings, private gatherings. He passed up no chance to road-test a song or two in front of an audience. During the day, folksingers jammed in the back of the Folklore Center, a storefront on MacDougal Street. On Sunday afternoons, Bob played in Washington

Square Park where, every week, literally hundreds of folksingers tried out new material on the crowds of strollers and picnickers. Then, at night, he invariably turned up at one of the countless parties in the neighborhood.

The parties were, in effect, serious musical forums hosted by various patrons who fed and encouraged the community of young folksingers while they participated vicariously in some of the most creative "sings" in the history of Greenwich Village. Imagine sitting around someone's living room listening to Dave Van Ronk, Judy Collins, Peter Yarrow, Tom Paxton, Richie Havens, Buffy Sainte Marie, Phil Ochs, Mark Spoelstra, Jim Kweskin, *and Bob Dylan* play a round-robin of songs. If Bob Gibson or Odetta was in town, chances were he or she would stop by to say hello and contribute a few numbers, too. Sidemen like David Bromberg, Felix Pappilardi, Danny Kalb, and John Sebastian would often provide accompaniment. Mary Travers might supply a gentle harmony line or Maria Muldaur a violin glissando behind one of the soloists. What a dazzling array of talent under one roof! By today's standards it was certainly an all-star cast, a supersession of folk greats. Back then, however, they were merely a bunch of neighborhood kids, getting together out of camaraderie and a common passion for music.

According to longtime Village folklorists, Bob Dylan made his reputation not in the coffeehouses, as one might expect, but at these parties. The guests who attended regularly, most of whom considered themselves his peers, professed awe at Bob's ability to retell the fusty old ballads in a fresh way. Any number of folksingers on the Street performed "Makes a Long Time Man Feel Bad" or "The Great Divide," but in Bob's hands they became completely different songs. He sang them with a poignancy that suggested the pinings of an impressionable young buck who'd only recently encountered these feelings for the first time. His voice pitched and moaned; the guitar throbbed like an irregular heartbeat; the mood created was stirring and suspenseful.

Gradually, Bob became the center of attention at the nightly soirees. An air of expectancy greeted his arrival, much as when a celebrity enters a roomful of fans, and in no time the spotlight would shift to Bob from whomever was singing. Fortunately, a number of tapes exist of these parties, most of which were recorded at Cynthia Gooding's

Greenwich Village apartment in the spring and summer of 1961. What they tell us, more than anything else, was that Bob Dylan was becoming increasingly more confident with his material. Songs like "Ranger's Command," a Woody Guthrie variation on the traditional "Rye Whiskey" melody, became a playful parody in which Bob improvised new lyrics and transformed the chorus with an oscillating, scatlike coloratura. An old Delta-blues number, "When I Left Wichita," was camped up by a series of whoops and hollers that attempt to imitate and good-naturedly poke fun at the dialect of the old blues masters, while a vigorously syncopated guitar lick ran wildly up and down the frets. Close your eyes and you can almost see Bob's fingers hammering off the strings as if they were red hot power lines. When the instrumentation collapsed around a sloppy hit-or-miss cadenza, it actually augmented the satirical spirit of his performance. This burlesque showed Bob not only was more comfortable playing in this relaxed environment, but was taking once-hallowed songs less seriously.

One night in May, Bob and Mark left a party on Sheridan Square and began the long crosstown trek back to Mark's pad in the East Village. Usually the boys would stop at one of the coffeehouses on the way or grab a nightcap at the Kettle of Fish, but Bob made it clear that he wasn't in the mood to be around a lot of people. Nor did he feel like turning in for the night. It was obvious to Mark that something was on his friend's mind, but he knew better than to try to coax it out of him. Bob was an aggravatingly private person. If he wanted to share something with you, sooner or later he'd get around to it.

As it happened, they stopped at a place on Sullivan Street to play some chess. The room was fairly empty because of the late hour, and as the boys hunched over a table, Bob was uncharacteristically quiet. He couldn't keep his mind on the game, which was nothing new, of course, but this night his distraction wasn't betrayed by an outward show of impatience. He sat contemplatively in his seat, staring at the wall. He showed little or no interest in the game and was allowing himself to be outmaneuvered. After a while, Mark couldn't take it anymore. Pushing the board aside, he asked, "What's up, man? Is something bugging you?"

Bob looked up deliberately as if he were about to confess to a crime. "I want you to hear a few things I've been working on," he said with great significance. Mark almost laughed, thinking that Dylan was ridiculously one-dimensional. He held back, however, when Bob leaned across the table. For a moment, he thought Bob was about to grab him but noticed a beseeching look in his eye. "I've been writing," he added. "I've been writing my own songs."

9

Writer's Cramp

Bob's decision to write and perform his own songs was certainly creative in spirit, but in a larger respect it was also an attempt to wrest his career from folk music's languorous treadmill. For a singer-songwriter, the field was wide open at the time, almost unnaturally so. Few performers had the nerve, let alone the talent, to write their own material. Even folk music's most alluring young star, Joan Baez, performed the same worn-out traditional songs in a silver-tongued but straightforward manner. The road was clear for Bob Dylan to become the most original new voice on the folk scene, if not in all of popular music.

From the mid-1950s right up until Dylan's debut, there had been a decisive shift in the commercial hierarchy, in which young artists seized pop's lyrical mantle from the vise grip of Tin Pan Alley. Teen stars like Buddy Holly and Chuck Berry cranked out the idiom's earliest string of self-penned hits, tackling head-on such socially pertinent issues as high school, cars, and puppy love. These songs captured the hearts of American youth, and more importantly, they established a new lyrical sensibility that sought to depict the emotional ardors of adolescence.

Chuck Berry's lyrics, written in the same excessively wordy, run-on style as Bob's earliest electric songs, expressed frustration over some of the more mundane routines that bugged kids about their lives. Songs like "School Day" conveyed a creeping ennui among teenagers who had grown dissatisfied with their subordinate status in an adult world. For them, rock 'n roll became a form of self-expression; and as the years passed they longed for something more substantial, perhaps even more experimental, in the way of spiritual fulfillment and personal authenticity.

By 1961, however, the novelty of school days and heavy petting had begun to wear thin on the top forty. The new music had failed to continue feeding its audience in a way that was both animalistically gratifying and spiritually beneficial. Clever writers—like Gene Pitney or the teams of Carole King and Gerry Goffen, Barry Mann and Cynthia Weil, Jeff Barry and Ellie Greenwich, and Jerry Leiber and Mike Stoller—continued to deliver catchy toe-tapping rock hits, but the emerging prototypical teenager—the 1960s kid who had begun the struggle to express himself and to expect more direct expression from others—needed something to supplement his low-nourishment pop diet.

Folk music had already established itself as an alternative to the juvenile instincts of top forty rock 'n roll. But like its pop-inspired counterpart, folk had reached a pivotal juncture with its audience that threatened its prospects of broader popular acceptance and commercial success. The problem, as young folksingers saw it, was the absence of a middle ground between the Kingston Trio and the Smothers Brothers on the one side and traditional folk music on the other. You listened either to a superficial, kitschy brand of folk music or to the purists brooding mulch. Unfortunately, that left no room for the young audience which had outgrown—or merely had grown tired of—rock 'n roll.

In retrospect, it becomes clear that the folk scene as it existed in 1961 suffered most from a lack of new blood. That is not to say that there was a scarcity of new talent; certainly, an abundance of accomplished folksingers wandered the Village streets in search of coffeehouses to play. What folk music needed were performers who were willing to invest in it something unique and intensely personal.

Although Bob Dylan's music inspired the cultural insurgency of the early 1960s, it was not his intention to reinvent the folk scene. When he arrived in Greenwich Village, Bob was content to take his place among the troupe of gifted interpreters working the Street. He was keenly aware of the opportunity created by Woody Guthrie's failing health—Bob continued to visit his hero at Greystone Hospital each week—and structured his career in a way that made him one of the obvious heirs to Woody's legacy. One of the very first songs he wrote, in fact, was a sentimental paean entitled, straightforwardly enough, "Song to Woody," in which Bob pledges to his bedridden mentor that he'll carry on in the errant tradition not only of Woody, but of Cisco Houston and Sonny Terry and Leadbelly, as well.

"Song to Woody," written in 1961, stands as Bob's first fully developed song, reworking a traditional folk melody with a younger, more reflective eye. Bob had written songs in Minneapolis and Denver, but none that so thoroughly applied all the things he learned from the years spent meticulously listening to records. The chording is simple, the words are full of rural folk nuances, and the phrasing is as brusque and stubborn as the engine of an old jalopy refusing to kick over. The song, which could have been just another starry-eyed homage, bowled over the Village folkies, who were awed by Bob's instinctive artistry.

Bob introduced "Song to Woody" at the Gaslight in the spring of 1961. He'd gotten into the habit of stopping in at the club a couple of nights each week to do a guest set, which paid about twenty-five dollars and included a hot meal. Three songs were the maximum anyone was allowed to do, but the real perk was admission to the back room, where the performers hung out between sets playing penny-ante poker. The Room, as it was known, looked more like a broom closet crossed with a sty. Hugh Romney, a Beat comic who worked regularly at the coffeehouse, rented it as an apartment when he was in New York; otherwise, it was the folksingers' unofficial clubhouse. Noel Stookey presided over the on-stage festivities, while backstage Dylan, Van Ronk, Paxton, Spoelstra, Len Chandler, Johnny Herald, and anyone else who stopped by kept the poker game alive. A pair of speakers monitored the stage, and when it was your turn to play, you'd put your chips in your pocket, move to the sofa, and tune your guitar so the guy who'd just finished performing could take over your hand at the table.

That night, Bob played "Song to Woody" along with two Guthrie numbers, but quickly left the coffeehouse in order to perform at a chess club he frequented in Orange County, New Jersey. The next day he returned to the Gaslight and talked Noel Stookey into letting him do another set that, for Stookey, was a watershed.

Bob played his customary Guthrie songs, but instead of signing off with one of the ballads or blues tunes from his repertoire, he took a well-known, traditional folk song about trappers in the Canadian northwest and recast it with an unusual twist. In the original version, the trapper goes to get paid at the end of the season, only to be told the trading company he worked for has gone bankrupt; instead, he is paid in pelts, which he takes to the general store and trades for supplies to see him through the summer months. Bob prefaced the song with a bit about how he'd just played a chess club in New Jersey and wanted to share with his audience some of the pitfalls of singing. In this version, however, a poor, bedraggled folksinger attempts to collect his check following a week-long gig. The club owner, portrayed here as a "bossman," informs him: "We're too poor to pay you; we'll have to give you chess pieces." Out of desperation, the folksinger takes his chess pieces to the bar in return for food and gets two rooks and a pawn for change.

Stookey was blown away by Bob's inventiveness. "It floored me," Stookey remembers, "that someone could take an old folk format, update it with a personal experience, and turn it into something relevant. At the time, I thought it was an act of true genius. Nobody was doing anything like that, and it dawned on me that there was a lot going on underneath Dylan's little cap that wasn't immediately visible to the rest of us."

The key to Bob's "genius" lay in his ability to spin folk style songs from observation and personal experience. Bob seized little moments from his life, exaggerated them to fit a particular theme, and came up with a new, entertaining song. It was by no means an original concept. Writers, poets, and playwrights have made personal experience the very foundation of their art. But folksingers were bound by a tradition that presumed music was to be *handed down.* Like the Ten Commandments, folk songs were etched in stone and passed from generation to generation without any modification whatsoever. That occasionally a new folk song could be written was, at the time, a matter of hot debate in Greenwich Village. (Ironically, many of the academics who opposed the writing of original folk songs came from a radical background that saw new songs being tailored to chronicle current events all the time.) Woody Guthrie had gotten away with it, some say, because his songs grew out of oppression and political turmoil. So had Leadbelly and some of the civil rights activists. No one else had any business monkeying around with folk's holy scripture.

Bob Dylan escaped castigation thanks, in part, to the spirit of his performances. He sang these songs with such spontaneity and self-deprecation that the guardians of folk's dogma were momentarily disarmed. Whereas the Smothers Brothers used folk music as a springboard for their comedy, Bob commented humorously—with irony and imagination—through the folk idiom. He respected the music's traditional ethos, but infused it with a fresh new topicality.

A week after the chess-club debut, Bob did something else to rattle folk music's brittle bones. Noel Stookey had run across a newspaper article about several hundred people who bought counterfeit tickets to a family outing in upstate New York that ended in a fiasco. Stookey, who had an offbeat comic mentality, considered the incident deliciously macabre. Backstage at the Gaslight, he told Dylan about it and handed him the clipping. As Stookey remembers it, "The next day Bob showed up with a nine-verse satire called 'Talkin' Bear Mountain Picnic Massacre Blues.'"

Using one of Woody Guthrie's favorite musical structures, the song parodies both the event itself and the talking-blues form. Not to be confused with spoken-word recordings, the talking blues was an obscure Negro blues style revived to great response by Guthrie and other dust-bowl balladeers with halting voices. The trick to the talking blues was that you didn't have to sing at all—you just talked rhythmically over an unvaried three-chord progression whose tempo rose and fell like an old-timey hoedown. Woody had altered the syncopation to his liking, holding the final diminished-seventh arpeggio an extra beat or two in each verse so he would have enough time to cram in a punch line, often to great ironic effect.

The folkies pounced on the talking-blues form with great relish. Here, at last, was a musical structure that combined the cynical humor of the Fifties with the emerging folk culture. It was progressively political, full of high-minded opinions, and socially significant, and, for the purists, it had a bardlike quality inasmuch as each talking blues related a fully drawn anecdote told in a narrative. Now there was something a modern-day folksinger could really sink his teeth into!

Bob skillfully adapted the facts in Stookey's newspaper account into a grossly exaggerated yarn that had "dogs a-barkin', cats a-meowin'," and a supporting cast of picnickers who sounded more like extras for *Ben-Hur* than passengers on a Sunday cruise up the Hudson. Just as in Woody's talking blues, Bob polished off his fable with a wry observation in which the establishment gets a taste of its own medicine: What do you think we should do with the hustlers responsible for this catastrophe? he asks. Why, simple—put 'em on a boat and send 'em up to Bear Mountain. . . on a picnic!

When Bob delivers that final tag—"on a picnic!"—it was almost as an ironic afterthought. He spit it out in a huff—much the same way John Houseman explains how E. F. Hutton makes its money—and then vented more of his sarcasm with the help of a few bars of playful harmonica.

With "Talkin' Bear Mountain" Bob tapped the real power of folk music. He'd sung Woody Guthrie's songs over and over, conveying the lyrics' bittersweet messages, the not-so-hidden political manifestoes, the triumphs and defeats. But Woody's songs were mostly holdovers from the labor movement of the 1930s and 1940s. They were timepieces—historically relevant, but no longer vital to the younger generation. By writing new folk songs, Bob had a chance to say something compelling about the current scene and comment on his own life and times.

Meanwhile, friends were warning Bob to separate himself from the carbon-copy Guthrie image he was sharpening lest he always be known as an imitator—and not even the best imitator on the Street. Jack Elliott, an ersatz cowboy from Brooklyn who had knocked around with Woody, held that distinction. Still, Bob milked his urban-cowboy role for all it was worth. He clung to a pose that suited his romantic vision of what a folksinger should be, enhancing it with tales that strengthened his connection to Woody and a spurious but colorful past.

For a while, he even camped out at the home of a middle-aged couple named Bob and Sidsel Gleason in East Orange, New Jersey, where, each Sunday, folksingers gathered to pay their respects to the ailing Guthrie. For two years, the Gleasons had checked Woody out of nearby Greystone Hospital and brought him to their tiny, fourth-floor walk-up on North Arlington Street so he could spend a few hours visiting with family and old friends. The routine was invariable. Before noon, Sid Gleason would help clean Woody up, dress him, and answer fan mail. Then, family and invited guests arrived in droves—Woody's wife, Marjorie, with little Arlo in tow; Alan Lomax; Harold Leventhal; any number of Old Lefties who were lurking around, and, of course, a dozen-or-so prominent folksingers from the Greenwich Village scene.

The folksingers who showed up symbolized the generational shift that was reshaping folk music. There were the real legends like Pete Seeger and Cisco Houston who came whenever they were on the East Coast; they played songs, swapped stories, and generally held court in the cramped living room to Woody's spastic blandishments. The life of the party, however, was the group of devoted "kids" who vied for Woody's attention, up-and-coming folksingers such as Peter LaFarge, Logan English, Ernie Marrs, Jack Elliott, John Cohen, and Lionel Kilburg. They took turns entertaining their idol with faithful interpretations of his songs. Due to his celebrity status, Pete Seeger insisted on being the center of attention at the Gleasons' hootenannys, but eventually everyone got his or her rightful turn to solo before the group sat down to one of Sid's enormous feeds.

Bob Dylan turned up at the Gleasons' in the spring of 1962. He had hitchhiked out from New York and spent most of his first visit there in awed silence, curled up next to the couch where Woody was stretched out. Woody's health was deteriorating rapidly. Each week revealed a worsening of the old folksinger's condition. His speech was badly slurred, often unintelligible. He no longer had control over his motor reflexes, an impairment which triggered facial contortions and unpredictable bouts of paroxysm. He'd grown incredibly impatient, and there were times when he demanded out of the blue that someone stop singing and do another of his famous numbers instead. Remarkably, none of this cast a pall over the get-togethers; the guests always found something to celebrate, some way to shine a light on the shadow of Woody's sickness. Still, it was clear that the Sunday afternoons in East Orange were numbered.

For Bob Dylan, they were perhaps the most educational days of his life. If it could be said that he'd gotten his primary schooling from

Gatemouth Page's radio show, his bachelor's degree in Dinkytown and Denver, and his master's on the Street in Greenwich Village, then the Gleasons certainly provided him with the resources to fulfill his Ph.D. requirements. The well of creative talent there appeared to have no bottom. Each Sunday, the musicians played and discussed the character of folk music dating from the Middle Ages to the present. They traced countless versions of each song to its source, placed the songs in relation to the political and social climate in which they were written, and shared material they'd picked up all over the world. Here were individuals who actually lived through their music. They advanced a folk *sensibility,* a karma that combined humanitarianism with intellectual wisdom, critical protest, and utopian speculation in juxtaposition with music. Without that kind of commitment, Bob Dylan might not have been able to write his greatest songs.

The Gleasons recognized a kindred spirit in Bob Dylan, despite his young age, and in them Bob found not only a home away from home, but an extended family that finally understood his essential nature. What a sense of comfort that must have been for him—what a relief!

As the weeks passed, it also happened that Bob became Woody's favorite. "Is the boy gonna be there?" he'd ask first thing when the Gleasons picked him up at Greystone. Woody thought the boy sure knew how to sing those songs. He had the knack, if not quite the sophistication, to carry the torch. Sitting at his mentor's feet, Bob would rattle off any country & western song that Woody requested. There was never any question of his knowing the words. Woody would lie back on the couch with his eyes shut and his mouth wide open, or try to clap along. Occasionally, Bob slipped in a song of his own—a rough version of "Talkin' New York" or "Standing on the Highway"—and was saluted in turn by Woody's wholesale praise. "The boy's got it! He sure as hell's got it!" he'd cheer, grinning at the circle of open-mouthed guests. Talk about divine ordination!

With nothing to encourage *their* dreams other than an occasional nod or "howdy"!, the other young folksingers at the Gleasons grew resentful of Bob. He was stealing the show—*their* show. You could see it in their faces and in the way they reacted to him. "There was quite a bit of 'Why him and not me?' going on," Sid Gleason says, "—and not just in Bobby's age group, but among the older folksingers as well." A few guests complained privately to her, usually whining something on the order of: "Hell, he's just a kid. What's he got that I haven't?" Sid recalls that the two who griped the most were Logan English and Lionel Kilburg. She says, "Lionel had done just about everything in the world to make it and couldn't get anywhere. Logan managed to play some coffeehouses in Greenwich Village, but wound up serving as the MC at Folk City." They both became bitter and privately blamed Bob for their failure to attract any attention. "You see, once Bobby made it, the others realized that they would never make it," she observes. "They just didn't measure up. It was over for them."

Identical jealousies blossomed on the Street in direct proportion to Bob's growth as a songwriter. The Village was rife with musicians whose primary instrument was the pen as opposed to the guitar, but popular folk performers were required to do more than merely write and sing. During those summer months of 1962, show business reared its ugly head on MacDougal Street as folksingers of all ages and allegiances scrambled to satisfy the public demand. Their shows had to be fresh and entertaining. That meant appealing to a younger, hipper, more broad-based audience—developing an *act* as opposed to merely a repertoire of songs and working original material in with the proven favorites.

Bob Dylan, as we've seen, had it all. But for others, the "folk music revolution" caused a worsening turmoil on MacDougal Street. It resembled Hollywood in the late 1920s, when sound shattered the silent screen. Certain fixtures who'd been on the Street since the 1940s couldn't make the transition and subsequently found it impossible to get work. Some were put out to pasture; others decided to hang it up and get on with their lives in a more responsible, "adult" manner.

Dave Van Ronk, for one, faced the prospect of becoming a dinosaur in his mid-twenties. The frog-voiced singer had absolutely no gift for songwriting, and topical music was of no interest to him. His on-stage demeanor was likened to that of a wounded grizzly bear. To make matters worse, Van Ronk specialized in blues and "root" music—a respectable idiom, to be sure, but hardly the type of drawing card necessary to attract young crowds into a coffeehouse. The likelihood of his career growing in proportion to, say, that of his friend Bob Dylan's was beyond the bounds of reason.

"Around that time I got a call from Albert Grossman," Van Ronk recalls, referring to the man who was soon to become Bob Dylan's manager. "He was putting together a monster folk-pop trio and needed someone who could not only hold down a harmony but was reasonably strong on guitar." In an apartment overlooking Central Park, Grossman outlined the whole scam for Van Ronk. "He had [the producer] Milt Okun and Warner Bros. Records in on the deal before he actually got the trio together. The way he explained it to me, they were going to keep spending money on the project until everyone got rich."

Grossman already had two folksingers in mind for his group. Peter Yarrow was a student at Cornell University whom Van Ronk knew from a few solo gigs in the Village. Van Ronk says, "The set Peter was doing at the time consisted of a French tune called 'Les Pacifistes,' several syrupy ballads, and, of course, 'Puff,' which I hated. We all hated it. You *had* to hate that song even if you liked it!" The other candidate was a mercurial girl named Mary Travers, who lived upstairs over the Commons, a cafe on MacDougal Street. Mary, who had sung solo on the Street since she was fourteen, was blessed with having a boy's voice in a gorgeous girl's body. As Grossman saw it, the combination was unbeatable. Sex and sophistication—the two added an exotic spice to an otherwise bland repast. But his real trump card was *material*.

Like Bob Dylan, scores of young folksingers had turned to composing, and their material was a good indication of what lay ahead for the pop mainstream. Grossman was astute enough to realize that there was an abundance of fantastic new songs on the Street. A singing group with a major recording contract was bound to attract the choicest material, the result of which would be a hip successor to the Kingston Trio that reflected all the recent changes in the folk format. The winning formula, as Grossman and Warner Bros. saw it, called for a trio, and Van Ronk was offered the final spot.

Any mortal would have jumped at the chance to be part of this prefab folk music extravaganza. Albert Grossman fancied himself the Sol Hurok of folk music. Warner Bros. Records provided a glitzy legitimacy that was heretofore unknown to the genre. The timing couldn't have been more providential, especially for Van Ronk, who detected the odor of money and liked what he smelled.

His wife, Terri, however, had an altogether different opinion. "She couldn't stand Mary Travers," Van Ronk recalls, chalking it up to the jealousies induced by two tall, very good-looking women in the same milieu. Hooking up with Mary would have spelled certain catastrophe for the Van Ronks' marriage. "And anyway," Dave says, "I didn't want to spend the rest of my life with Peter and Mary."

Little did Van Ronk know that Grossman was offering the job around to any number of suitable prospects. Always one to hedge a bet, Grossman had approached Noel Stookey one night at the Gaslight with a similar proposition. Stookey had given one of the standout performances of his career that night. His comedy routine had been incredibly sharp, and he finished with a sound-effects version of "The Golden Vanity" in which he recreated the sinking of the Spanish Armada amidst a rush of off-color noises. The audience was still in stitches when Grossman beckoned the comedian over to his booth.

"I expected him to offer me a contract in Hollywood," Stookey remembers, "so you can imagine how deflated I felt when all Albert said was 'How'd you like to sing in a group?'" According to Stookey, they were going to be called the Willows. But when he joined the trio, they borrowed a phrase from one of the folk songs Peter Yarrow performed, called "The Oldest Man in the World." Stookey says, "It's got a line in it that goes: 'I saw Peter, Paul and Moses playing ring around the roses,' so the whole alliteration would work if I agreed to change my name to Paul."

Stookey gave in because of the rosy picture Grossman painted for him. Peter, Paul & Mary would enjoy an opportunity never before provided to any member of the Greenwich Village folk establishment—the opportunity to be a huge commercial success. The prospect of introducing the songs of young writers excited him almost as much. Grossman made it clear that he intended to cross-pollinate the artists he represented with each other's material. It was time to think of The Future. Clearly, folk music was moving out of the coffeehouses into concert halls and television studios. Stookey recognized, perhaps before many of his peers, that staying on the Street could wind up a dead end. The cultural revolution had officially begun, and God help the folksinger who couldn't conceptualize his own myth.

Bob Dylan had long since come to grips with that concern. Image was so inalienable an aspect of his persona, that it no longer seemed fabricated. Myth and reality had converged to form a seamless identity. Now songwriting would provide that image with another, more complex definition.

Bob began turning out material at a fantastic clip—a dozen, maybe two dozen, songs a week flowed from his pen. Tom Paxton remembers walking through Greenwich Village with him after the coffeehouses had closed, astounded by his friend's prolificacy. "Bobby was in another world," Paxton recalls, "hardly aware that I was even next to him, writing phrases and ideas on scraps of paper and stuffing them into his pockets. His mind was on fire. Between the club and wherever he was heading, he'd start as many as five songs... *and finish them!*"

Privately, Bob began telling friends that his goal was to record an album. The smaller, independently owned folk labels were turning their attention to the new crop of performers on MacDougal Street. Prestige Records had signed Dave Van Ronk; Elektra courted Judy Collins; Jack Elliott had struck a deal with Vanguard. The response to Bob's songs was so favorable that it was only a matter of time before he, too, was offered a recording contract. It was also acknowledged, however, that before Bob Dylan could make an album he'd have to move away from the Guthrie mold to which he continued to cling. He'd have to graduate to a more sophisticated level of composing and write about his own life and times. In the mid-1960s drugs would stimulate Bob Dylan's creative juices, but these simpler times required another kind of inspiration. And it was at Folk City, one night that summer, that he finally found her sitting at the bar.

10

Testing New Waters

Perhaps the biggest boost to Bob's career was a featured stint—his first—at one of the few coffeehouses in America that was successful in booking big-name folksingers: Gerdes Folk City. Dylan had appeared regularly at the club's free Monday night hoots, but it took considerable politicking on his and other friends' parts until Mike Porco, Gerdes' philistine owner, agreed to put him on the payroll as an opening act. Though relatively low-paying, the Gerdes booking represented a significant professional break for Bob: it not only provided him with measurable status on the Street, but also gave him instant credibility at the dozen-or-so "legitimate" coffeehouses across the country where college students thronged to hear folk music's most distinguished voices. With the right promotion, Bob could eventually tour the country as a "New York coffeehouse sensation" and trade on the Gerdes name.

Though Gerdes sounded prestigious to the out-of-town ear, at home it struck an ambiguous chord. "Playing Gerdes meant you were either on your way up," says Dave Van Ronk, "or on your way down." Come a certain juncture, a rising Gerdes star was expected to graduate to playing a modest-size concert hall in New York. Smartly managed performers like the Clancy Brothers, Theo Bikel, Jose Feliciano, and Judy Collins made that professional leap without much difficulty. But for most, Gerdes became the folksinger's graveyard. You were assured of a gig there every few months, although more than likely you'd be playing to a hundred and ninety people a night for the remainder of your career.

Be that as it may, a week at Gerdes remained the object of fierce competition. Yet which performers got booked into the coffeehouse was left solely to the discretion of Mike Porco, who knew as much about folk music as did, say, Admiral Nimitz. Porco, a thick-accented Calabrian immigrant who had originally operated Gerdes as a blue-collar bar, simply hired whichever act received the most applause during the Monday night hoots. The quality of music was of absolutely no consequence to him.

Porco cared only about one thing: each night's tally from the bar. In his thinking, a performer's popularity was measured by the size and thirst of the audience he or she attracted. If the crowd didn't drink, the folksinger was a bum. Plain and simple. And so it was that Porco had lost Peter, Paul & Mary's thunderous debut to the Bitter End: the trio was talented but lacked the required Alcohol Consumption Quotient.

For Porco, Bob Dylan was a particularly hard sell. How could a voice like that bring in customers? But Dylan had something important going for him: he came cheap. Porco offered Bob a scant ninety dollars a week, the rock-bottom fee he was permitted by law to pay a performer, and a date was set.

The real compensation was that Bob would be sharing the stage with John Lee Hooker, a legendary bluesman who'd been working almost exclusively in the Detroit area. Hooker wasn't some rubber-bellied folksinger with a slick act. He was respected, he was authentic, and what's more *he was black!* Talk about cachet! With John Lee Hooker, Bob had gotten the luck of the draw. For all he knew, he might have found himself stuck on the same stage with waspy Oscar Brand or Cynthia Gooding and her crinoline dress for two weeks—a fate similar to opening for Wayne Newton or Barry Manilow. But *John Lee Hooker!* Bob was in heaven.

Dylan opened at Folk City on April 11, 1961, the first of only two paid performances he ever gave in Greenwich Village. Earlier on that momentous day, Bob and Mark Spoelstra strolled around the streets, eventually cutting through Washington Square Park to a shabby

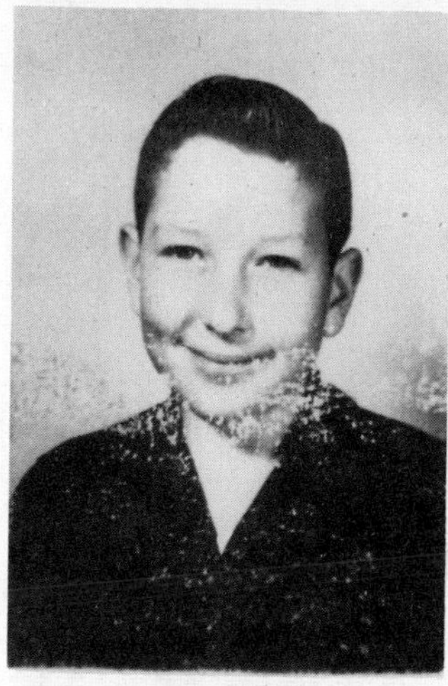

Sixth grade: class photo, 1952. (*Courtesy of Hibbing Senior High School*)

Twelfth grade: senior yearbook photo, 1957. (*Courtesy Hibbing Senior High School*)

At Camp Hertzl, 1954. (Judy Rubin is kneeling below Bob). (*From the collection of Judy Rubin Shaffer*)

Bob and Pete Seeger during those leaner times, 1961. (*Photograph by David Gahr*)

The debut at Folk City, 1961. (*Courtesy Irwin Gooen*)

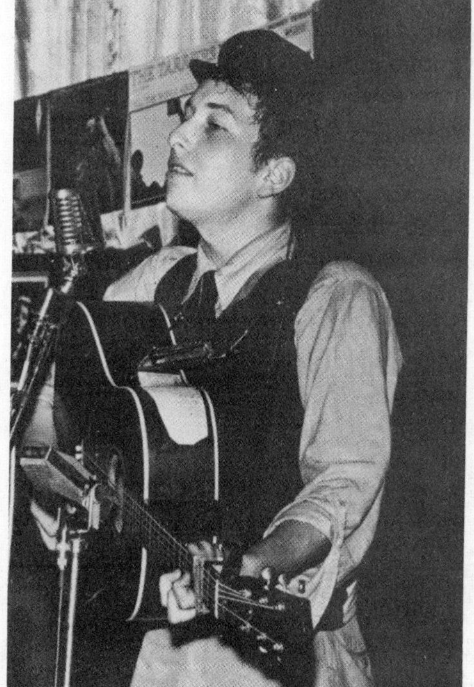

During a hoot, 1962. (*Courtesy Irwin Gooen*)

Richard Fariña and Caroline Hester, 1962. (*John Cooke*)

John Hammond, Sr., gives Bob a pointer during the recording of the first album, 1962. (*Courtesy John Hammond, Sr.*)

James Dean reincarnate—an early Columbia promo photo, circa 1962–1963. (*CBS Records Archives*)

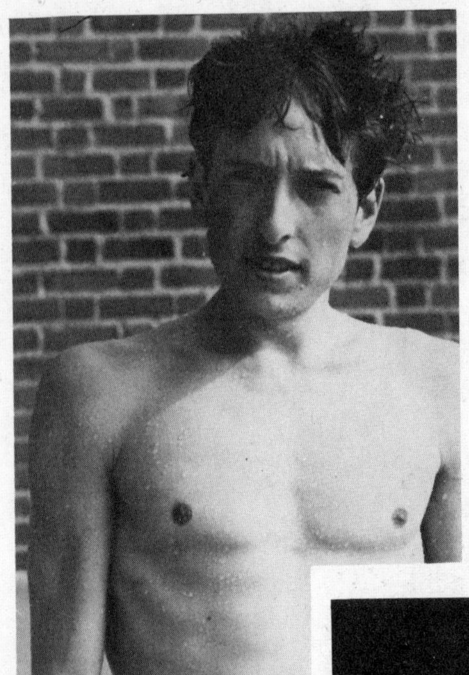

Olympic folkswimmer, Newport, 1963. (*Photograph by David Gahr*)

Bob's first Newport appearance, August 1963. (*Photograph by David Gahr*)

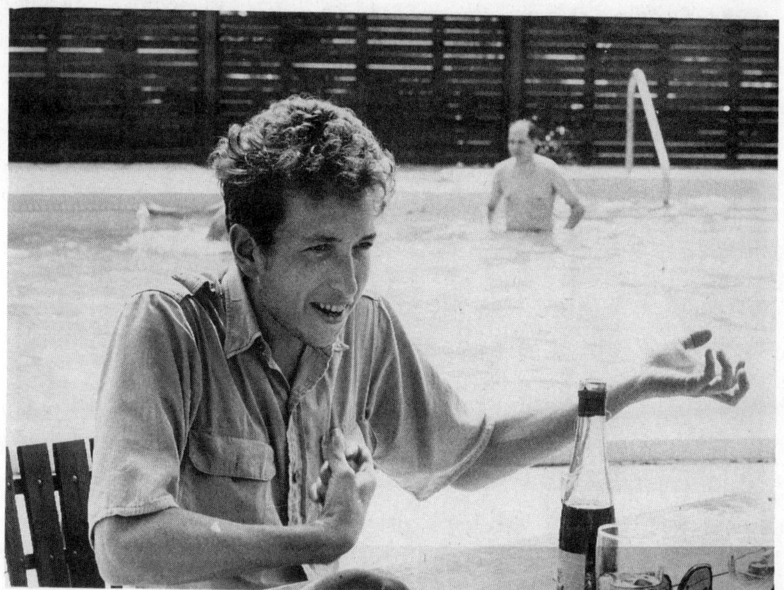

"It's this easy. . . ." Bob demonstrates his technique, Newport, 1963. (*Photograph by David Gahr*)

"Kitten with a whip," Newport, 1963. (*Photograph by David Gahr*)

The finale at Newport, 1963. Left to right: Pete Yarrow, Mary Travers, Noel Stookey, Joan Baez, Bob, the Freedom Singers, Pete Seeger, and Theo Bikel. (*John Cooke*)

Young Tom Paine accepts his award from Clark Foreman, November 1963. (*Arthur Swoger*)

little hotel where John Lee Hooker was registered. They'd stopped by to discuss an urgent matter with the seasoned pro. "Bob didn't have any clothes to wear," Spoelstra remembers, "and he was more nervous about it than that evening's show." Image, not artistry, was preying on Bob Dylan's mind. He wanted to look just-so for his New York debut and appealed to John Lee Hooker's sense of folk couture. One can only imagine what the relatively impoverished urban-blues guitarist must have thought of Bob's request. Nevertheless, he sympathized politely with Bob's dilemma and loaned the boy a pair of pants. Spoelstra donated a brown sportcoat several sizes too large for Bob, and the corduroy cap rounded out the eastern European rabbinical look he'd envisioned for the big event.

By all standards, Bob's Gerdes opening was a critical success. The tiny room was packed with friends and folksingers who turned out to give the kid a boost. Standing by the bar, Bob could see Dave Van Ronk and Oscar Brand kibitzing with John Sellers, Gerdes' MC. Tom Paxton shuffled in, along with Bob and Sid Gleason, Mel and Lillian Bailey (a Brooklyn couple on whose couch Dylan crashed a few nights each week), *New York Times* critic Robert Shelton, Mark Spoelstra, a couple of the Clancy Brothers, Logan English. What a hot crowd!

Ticket sales were stronger than usual. Word had spread that this new young folksinger was terrific. Certainly some of the excitement could be attributed to John Lee Hooker's appearance, but there was an air of expectancy created by the Village scene-makers who sensed Bob Dylan's time had come, and from the moment he walked on stage the crowd was his.

Dave Van Ronk had sat through dozens of Dylan's sets, but that night he was blown away by Bob's performance. "He was absolutely remarkable," Van Ronk recalls even now. "It was one of the most electrifying shows I have ever seen in my life. His delivery was letter perfect, he kibitzed with the audience. The songs sounded positively beautiful. Little bits he did with his guitar and stool were perfectly Chaplinesque. If ever a star was born, it was that night at Folk City."

Perhaps no one was more aware of the impression he made than Bob Dylan himself. Throughout the two weeks he was higher than a kite. His usually sickly-pale face was flushed with excitement, complimentary beer and wine was lavished on his friends (a gesture that pained Mike Porco inasmuch as the deal he cut with Bob included an unlimited bar tab). But once the thrill wore off, Bob plunged back to earth with a thud. Though his performance was judged a success, the reality was that not one record-company executive had caught his act, and neither had he managed to attract Robert Shelton's attention. Dylan had counted on a review in the *Times* to stir up record-company interest, but Shelton only had eyes for John Lee Hooker.

After his Folk City run, Dylan sulked around the Village. He'd become the new "in" folksinger, the Village crowd's favorite act to catch, but nothing else seemed to be happening to his career. Terri Thal, Van Ronk's wife, offered to shop a tape of Bob's Gerdes performance around to record companies, but at Prestige and Folkways, the predominantly folk labels, she couldn't get her foot in the door. They weren't the slightest bit interested. Columbia and Warner Bros. weren't interested, either. It was a total bust. Tom Paxton dragged Bob along to the Indian Neck Folk Festival, a performers-for-performers-only show in Branford, Connecticut, but that too seemed pointless. With little else to encourage him, Bob retreated to Dinkytown that spring, for a brief stay, where tales of his success earned him a much-needed moment of glory.

When he returned to New York, it was the same old story—making the obligatory rounds of hoots, hitting the parties, hanging out at the Folklore Center and in Washington Square Park—except that Bob flaunted a renewed self-assurance. According to Mark Spoelstra, "Suddenly he decided that he was Bob Dylan, the Great Writer. He, alone, had some mystical insight into folk music; the rest of us were pretenders." No longer simply confident, Dylan had become egotistical, arrogant. He openly disdained the Old Guard that presided over the Street. That was demonstrated one night while Bob and Mark were camped out at the bar at Folk City. Mississippi Fred McDowell was on stage, picking through a particularly smooth version of "Easy Rider Blues," when Dylan blurted out, "Aw shit, that ain't nothing. I can do that, and a helluva lot better'n that cat!" It was a ridiculous boast. But Bob was pumping himself up for the next round, even if he had to bully his way to the top.

As Bob realized from his long-standing fascination with James Dean and Woody Guthrie, when you stay in a role that demands more character of you than you're normally equipped to carry off, you actually assume the essence of that idealized persona. Certain mannerisms and attitudes are absorbed by constant imitation—a look, a stance, the way challenges are delivered. If you exaggerated it, the role model is reduced to a grotesque caricature and what is left becomes yours alone. That was the technique Bob used in order to attract attention and think of himself in terms of being Bob Dylan, the Great Writer. Boastfulness, impertinence, hubris, arrogance—these constituted a self-prescribed course in confidence building that succeeded in alienating even his closest friends while nonetheless arousing their curiosity. While Bob Dylan hadn't yet perfected this to the art it would eventually become, it was nevertheless becoming disturbingly effective.

Slowly but surely, Bob discovered that attitude was one powerful weapon. Attitude and mystery—the two went hand in hand. He'd already concealed his past in the labyrinthine guise of Dylan; now he set about embellishing the old alibis with outrageous flourishes. Bob hadn't just been on the road, he was *an orphan!* No longer content that Zimmerman had been erased, *he denied being Jewish!* Barry Kornfeld, a Greenwich Village mainstay, recalls a night he and Bob spent huddled over a chess board. Halfway through the match, Kornfeld's girlfriend brought out a tray of hors d'oeuvres and a famished Dylan went to town slathering chopped liver over the crackers. "Hey, man, that's great tuna fish!" Bob exclaimed, wolfing down his share.

The girl politely corrected him. "No, Bobby—that's chopped liver."

A few minutes later, Dylan looked up hungrily. "Hey, you got any more of that tuna fish?"

Mark Spoelstra quickly tired of Bob's latest pattern of behavior. The attention-grabbing stunts and lies were getting on his nerves. He couldn't figure out how anyone took such pleasure in jiving his friends all the time. It didn't make any sense. Bob was so bizarre, Mark thought, so completely into "being Dylan," and being Dylan fluctuated about as wildly as the specials at the Second Avenue Deli. Spoelstra might have dropped Bob entirely, were it not for Dylan's astonishing songwriting ability. Mark had tried his hand at writing, and while he wasn't a fraction as intuitive as his friend, he picked up a lot of technique simply by osmosis. He also profited greatly from Bob's finesse with women.

Mark loved catting around the Village with Bob. The streets were crawling with good-looking NYU coeds, and the boys—carefree and full of life—made such a great pickup team. Mark was trim, darkly handsome, and shy; Bob, with his squirrel-cheeked Jewish looks, came on like a hot matinee idol. Roberto Dylantino! Mark was constantly awed by Bob's nerve. When it came to women, Bob was incredibly aggressive and sure of himself. Spoelstra says, "He could get a girl's attention purely by his energy. Then he would come on to her with a kind of James Dean cockiness which gave her the impression that he knew all about her and could see right through her."

Intimidation! Bob was experimenting with an approach that would later become his signature. From the moment a girl showed interest he went to work on her self-esteem. As Mark remembers, sometimes it was playful puppylike teasing, but more often than not it was rank humiliation. "You think you can handle me, do you? *You* couldn't handle *meeeee.* You don't have what it takes. Never *gonna* have it." The poor girl would be so shaken that she'd trip over herself trying to get away from him. Any attempt to defend herself would be interrupted by: "Think so, huh? Yeah? *Yeah?*" He never let up, never apologized. The object was to push, push, push, challenging her to stand up to the inquisition. Once he got her on the hook the fun was over; the more she resisted, the crueler he got.

Every so often, Bob came up against a woman who was confident enough to give it back to him. Then the fireworks really started to fly. Nothing got Bob's attention more than a woman with balls. Spoelstra remembers, "There was this singer around the Village named Ann-Marie who we were both real curious about, a mysterious character who, like Bob, refused to talk about her past. One day, Bob and I were up at her apartment, and he launches into this intense rap about what she was trying to hide. He's really giving it to her, standing about two inches from her face, letting her have it. There's a lot of tension in that room. He's putting on a first-rate performance. Leg's pumping up and down like a jackhammer, when suddenly Ann-Marie says, 'You know, I hear that guys who move their legs like that are chronic masturbators.'" Bull's-eye! But Bob didn't even skip a beat. If anything, he turned it up a volt or two.

Bob was obviously shopping for a woman with spunk. Girls like Judy Rubin and even Echo, in her outlandish way, were too provincial for the New York folk scene; they had their hearts set on a traditional family life, with Bob as the housebroken hubby. "Hi dear, how was your day at the office?"—that'd never fit into his plans. No, he needed someone independent enough to let him be Dylan. Someone who was hip and cynical enough to play off of, being into him without looking for a long-term thing.

Bob never had a problem attracting girls—just staying interested in them. He spent his first few months in New York hanging out with a very attractive sidekick named Linda Fuch (Imagine what fun he had with that name!) who, according to sources, passed herself off as a professional thief. Now that was a racket that appealed to Bob's sense of mystery and adventure! Linda's successor, Averill, was cast more in the classic Dylan-girlfriend mold: dark, Reubenesque, opinionated, maternal—the kind of girl Abe and Beatty secretly wished he'd bring home, but never did. Averill was a prodigy of the Old Left, a farm-labor activist whose political convictions won her instant approval from the folk crowd. Bob moved into her East Fourth Street walk-up, where the couple entertained his friends from the Street, but in no time the arrangement proved too confining for him. "Averill was really in love with Dylan," Mark Spoelstra says, "but he was intimidated by her honesty and directness. That just wasn't his style."

Though Bob certainly exercised control over his women, he was never able to take the initiative when it came to breaking off a relationship. With Averill—and later on with Suze Rotolo, Joan Baez, and his wife, Sara—Bob let things degenerate to such a point that she finally had to walk away from him or suffer the open hostility and detachment of a disinterested lover. He perfected an ambivalence that protected him from intimacy.

Spoelstra recalls: "I walked in on them in a restaurant when Averill was breaking up with Bob. She resented being treated like that and really had him pinned to the wall. The gist of the conversation was that she wasn't pushing him into marriage, a casual affair suited her just fine. All she wanted was honesty. She was very intense about it. And Bob just kind of played the James Dean thing—very quiet, reserved, and cool, like he couldn't have cared less. The next day he left her a note and simply disappeared."

Bob resurfaced a few weeks later, holing up at Folk City or the Gaslight during the afternoons and most nights. For living quarters, he crashed at the Gleasons or the Baileys until too many demands were made of him. The Van Ronks provided him with a couch whenever things got rough, and for a few months he lived with a couple named Eve and Mac MacKenzie, whose leftist leanings clarified ideas that were beginning to formulate in Bob's mind.

One afternoon at Folk City, Bob bumped into a girl from Valley Stream, Long Island, whom he'd first met at the Folklore Center and then again at an NYU hootenanny at which he'd performed. Sue Zuckerman was one of Dylan's earliest fans. Still in her teens, she kept turning up at Greenwich Village coffeehouses to *watch*—as opposed to *hear*—him play the harmonica. She thrilled at the way he'd bend at the knees and lean back, the harp cupped gently in his hands as if it were a wounded sparrow. Then, eyes closed, he'd thrust the lower part of his body forward, undulating to the rhythm like a shameless bump-and-grind artist. What a turn-on! Sue was mesmerized and dragged her friend Suze along to witness the spectacle.

Suze (pronounced: Suzy) Rotolo was more into the way Bob made the harp speak than his scrawny physique. The way he played that thing really blew her away, but she couldn't bring herself to tell him that when Bob and Mark later joined the girls at one of the tables in the back. Probably because Suze was as interested in Mark, on whom she had developed a lingering crush.

It wasn't until August fifth, at a concert at New York's Riverside Church, that Suze's attention shifted to Bob. On a balmy Saturday afternoon, he performed at a twelve-hour benefit for the church's new radio station, WRVR-FM, along with Tom Paxton, Bob Yellin of the Greenbriar Boys, the Reverend Gary Davis, Molly Scott, Dave Van Ronk, Cynthia Gooding, blues singer Victoria Spivey, and Jack Elliott, who'd recently returned from a self-imposed European exile. After the show, Bob got a lift down to the Village with journalist Pete Karman. He squeezed into the back seat of the car alongside Karman's other passengers, Suze Rotolo and her older sister, Carla. Karman noticed a special chemistry brewing between Bob and Carla and assumed they'd eventually get it together. Therefore, he was stunned when, a few days later, he heard that Bob and Suze were officially "a couple."

Suze would have caught Bob's eye any day of the week. She was everything he'd been looking for in a woman—intellectual, passionate, cultural, and pretty in a way that required Levi's and cowboy boots—the perfect ol' lady for a folksinger who'd become excessively concerned with his image. Although Suze was only seventeen, she knew her way around the coffeehouse scene and was willing to make Bob's career the prime focus of their relationship. Like a lot of ol' ladies on the Street, she was as creative, well read, musically knowledgeable, and intuitive as her male counterpart. When it came to politics, however, Suze outshown Bob the way a beacon eclipses a flashlight. Although she wasn't as politically outspoken, Suze enjoyed the hip mystique of a radical, left-wing upbringing. By the time she was in high school, Suze worked to improve interracial relations at Bayard Rustin's Youth March for Integrated Schools Center in Harlem. During her senior year, she petitioned actively for A Sane Nuclear Policy and staged pickets outside Woolworth's to protest the chain's disgraceful treatment of blacks at their lunch counters in the South. Following graduation, she planned to study art in Italy before a near-fatal car crash delayed her trip abroad. It was while recuperating from a number of related injuries that she met Bob Dylan.

From the outset, Bob was completely captivated by Suze. For the first time in his life, he'd stumbled upon a woman with the potential to fulfill all the requirements of a satisfying and steady relationship. In the past, whenever Bob dated a girl, he eventually detected something lacking in her personality, a fatal flaw or imperfection, that prohibited him from focusing all his attention on her. Echo Helstrom was outrageous and encouraged his dreams, but without the attendant subtlety or class. Judy Rubin had the social graces but none of the free-spiritedness of a dreamer. And Averill, who was political, intelligent, and independent, wouldn't put up with Bob's bullshit.

Suze had the desirable attributes of Bob's former girlfriends, plus another important virtue: naïveté. She was an unformed and impressionable young woman, eager to be groomed. That meant Bob could have everything his way—a woman who inspired him yet was faithfully open to his suggestions. He could mold and create her the way he did a new song.

Suze seemed perfect in every way, but instead of showering her with interest, Bob was on his best typically detached behavior. "Why don't you come by Gerdes," he muttered by way of introduction. "Maybe I'll see you there." At Gerdes, Bob was on safer ground. What better way to impress a woman than have her see you on stage, under a spotlight, while the audience whistled and shouted at you in appreciation.

The following weekend, Suze turned up at the Greenwich Village coffeehouse to meet Bob Dylan. Because she was underage, Pete Karman acted as chaperon, but he left Suze to her own devices once they were inside. She remained on a stool at the bar for most of the night. The club was dark and noisy, but when Bob performed, the atmosphere grew deferential. Though he played only a short set, Suze was struck by his seemingly transformed personality. He wasn't abstruse or indifferent. Instead of playing it cool, like James Dean, Bob was warm and affectionate. Suze saw a completely different side of him, a side that was "funny and clownlike and whimsical and cute." She was completely charmed by this Bob Dylan, yet wary that he could play such entirely different roles.

Pete Karman shared Suze's suspicions, although in a much deeper, more mistrustful way. The journalist in him didn't buy any of Dylan's fantastic stories or the tangle of characters he portrayed in the course of an evening. Nor was he taken in by the little-boy-lost quality Bob put forth on stage. "There was a lot of bullshit flying around that night," Karman recalls. "And none of it made me feel very comfortable, especially because he was making such an impression on Suze." Not that Karman was alarmed. He didn't consider Bob to be dangerous. The worst you could say about Bob was that he was your typical Village folkie with a good line. Nothing unusual about that! Folksingers were notorious skirt-chasers. Nevertheless, Bob was coming on like gangbusters and Suze was easy prey. After all, she was only seventeen. In a roundabout way, her welfare had been entrusted to Karman, and he was determined to keep an eye on her in the company of a smooth customer like Mr. Bob Dylan.

In the days that followed, the invitations Bob extended to Suze became more frequent, less casual, and, in a mystifying way, increasingly emphatic. "Why not meet me at Gerdes" turned into "Come to Gerdes. I expect to see you there." "Be at the Folklore Center" at such and such a time. "Get over to the Figaro." "We're going out with the Van Ronks." He was all over her—in one sense sweet and demonstrative, in another full of demands and expectations. A more mature woman might have told him to fuck off, but Suze almost welcomed the regimentation. She longed for some kind of structure, some kind of discipline in her life, and understandably so.

Suze's father, a painter, had died when she was fourteen. Her bohemian mother, Mary, was the editor of an Italian left-wing newspaper and was wrapped up in her own affairs. Before the car accident, Suze's mother had relinquished the family apartment in anticipation of their trip abroad. Suddenly everything had changed; plans were delayed. Their life was a mess. In an effort to regroup, Mary Rotolo moved into a friend's apartment on Sheridan Square. Carla had her own West Village walk-up. And Suze, only months out of high school, was more or less on her own. Painfully shy, pitifully innocent, she was abandoned to the vicissitudes of city life until Bob Dylan appeared on the scene. Ironically, Bob provided a stabilizing influence for her. He was someone for Suze to learn from and to oblige.

At the same time, Suze served as the first real anchor in Bob's driftwood life. He, too, had been on his own since the age of seventeen, without any appreciable guidance. Without the benefit of a strong role model (aside from, perhaps, the surrogate teachings of Woody Guthrie), Bob stumbled through the years when young men most need good, sound advice. His father existed in name only. He had no true friends to speak of. Suze was someone Bob could talk to, someone who understood the pain and loneliness he felt.

"When I first met him," Suze says, "he told me incredible tales—about being an orphan and that he had run away from his foster parents in Fargo, North Dakota. My heart went out to him. I believed him, even though I knew deep inside that he romanticized everything."

Accordingly, Bob Dylan and Suze Rotolo found great comfort in each other's company. They shared many creative interests and, perhaps more out of self-protection than passion, became very exclusive very fast. As Suze remembers it, "We made a conscious effort of being by ourselves, shutting out the rest of the world." They retreated into an art-minded fantasy world, feeding each other the fruits of their individual sustenance. Bob introduced Suze to the nightworld of coffeehouses and jazz clubs. They sat through what seemed like a seamless cycle of shows at the Top of the Gate and the Village Vanguard, two of New York's most famous jazz haunts. During the day they went to the movies or holed up in various friends' apartments, sorting through the shelves of books and listening to records. As a result of her left-wing upbringing, Suze knew the entire Guthrie songbook. She'd listened to most of the legendary bluesmasters, as well as Odetta, Pete Seeger, Cisco Houston, Big Joe Williams—all Bob's idols. Her interest in poetry and theater uncovered a whole new fascination for Bob, and they pored through Suze's collections of Edna St. Vincent Millay, Dylan Thomas, Emily Dickinson, Rimbaud, Brecht, and Byron. In essence, Suze was a mirror image of Bob, dowered by all the knowledge and savvy he longed to absorb. And which, in time, he would.

How did Suze's mother greet the news that her seventeen-year-old daughter was spending every night in the company of a ragamuffin folksinger who had no home or substantial income? She wasn't thrilled, to put it mildly. On separate occasions Carla and Suze dragged her to Gerdes to see their troubadour prince in action, but Bob's performances left Mary cold. Afterward, when Suze introduced them, Bob floundered uncomfortably. It was remarkable that someone could express himself so eloquently on stage and yet come off practically incoherent in conversation. Mary was understandably concerned about her daughter's choice of young man. Nevertheless, she remained cordial toward him. "They were both kids, and it was something that I didn't feel would last," she says, remembering those bygone nights, "so I wasn't particularly worried."

A week later, however, when Suze brought Bob and a few friends up to her mother's apartment, Mary Rotolo pulled Pete Karman aside and asked him, "Who is this guy? He's scruffy, he's *disgusting.*" Karman gave her every assurance that Bob was a harmless character. What's more, he explained, Bob was well regarded around the Village and, in some circles, was considered to be one of folk music's rising young stars. Karman's testimonial temporarily alleviated her fears. It wasn't until later that same evening, when Mary questioned Bob about his roots, that she became disturbed anew.

"He said that he was left on the doorstep of a wealthy man in Chicago named Zimmerman who adopted him," Mary recalls. "When I asked him where he got the name Dylan, he said that it was his original parents' name." Borrowing a soupçon of fact, Bob also purported to have been sent by his adoptive father to the University of Minnesota, but he pushed things too far when he converted his nearsightedness into a degenerative eye disease that would inevitably render him blind. "Suze at seventeen might have believed in innocent good faith, but her old mother couldn't," Mary says. Once more, she cornered Pete Karman and implored him to look out for Suze's welfare. No matter what anyone said, the boy had presented himself to her as a chronic liar. Experience warned her not to trust Bob Dylan one bit.

* * *

Now that he had a steady girl, Bob set aside more time to concentrate on his career. That meant not only performing and writing songs, but listening to them as well—listening to ethnic folklorists in the hope of latching onto an obscure tune that he could "interpret."

Interpretation was the newest and toniest art form on the Street. In effect, it was a compromise that had been reached between the purists and those musicians dedicated to writing new folk songs. Interpretation, both schools argued, was a respectable method of updating our musical heritage. All you had to do was exhume an authentic folk song—one that hadn't been performed in, say, fifty or sixty years—change a few chords as a personal signature, and slip it casually into your repertoire. There was no status symbol greater than dropping a new song on the Street. Especially one with political overtones. Field hollers and chants accredited to slaves were all the rage; Spanish civil war songs *très chic.* When Dave Van Ronk introduced "House of the Rising Sun" as an honest-to-God relic from a Storeyville brothel, you'd have thought he'd uncovered Atlantis.

As an interpreter, Bob Dylan himself was no slouch. The songs he chose to rework reveal a liberal command of moods and styles that evoke America's musical ancestry. "KC Moan" and "Muleskinner Blues" were country standards he performed with all the fillips and creaky falsettos of a displaced southerner, although to his credit Bob never tried to imitate the drawly hokum of an Opry star. He substituted enthusiasm for mimicry, choosing instead to capture the flavor and tone of country music, so that his versions became playful rather than perfumy. The same can be said of his spiritual interpretations, most notably of "Poor Lazarus," "Gospel Plow," "Honey, Just Allow Me One More Chance," and "Deep Ellum Blues," which popped up repeatedly throughout his Gaslight and Folk City stints in the fall of 1961. Thankfully, in each of the aforementioned he refrained from exploiting the Amos 'n Andy dialect favored by other white folksingers. Instead, he gave the songs a free or loose translation, delivering them in the general vicinity of a particular idiom. And while they were imperfect as far as root songs go, they bore the unmistakable stamp of the singer.

As far as interpreting went, only Bob's accrediting of material was suspect. He claimed to have picked up songs from blues singer Mance Lipscomb, despite the fact that Lipscomb remained in Texas, a state that Bob had yet to visit, until mid-1962. Arvella Gray, a blind street singer and gandy dancer on the B&O railroad, was another of Bob's reported gurus. So was "a lady named Dink," who reputedly taught Bob "Dink's Song," even though musicologist Alan Lomax claimed to have learned it from an old black woman named Dink as early as 1904.

One of Bob's favorite sources was Big Joe Williams, a sixty-year-old delta blues singer and author of the classic plaint "Baby, Please Don't Go," whom Bob professed to have befriended when he was ten years old. As Dylan told it, he had run away from home and encountered Williams on a corner in Chicago. "I saw a Negro musician playing his guitar on the street, and I went up to him and began accompanying him on the spoons," Dylan avows. Indeed, if Bob Dylan had met Big Joe, it might very well have happened that way; as Bobby Zimmerman, however, there wasn't an ounce of truth to it. The story is pure "Dylan," and not a bad one as folk yarns go. Bob told it every chance he got, each time enhancing it with a spectacular new detail here and there to keep his pals entertained. By the time Dave Van Ronk heard it, Big Joe and Little Bob had jumped on a boxcar headed to Mexico, where the two amigos canvassed the territory playing their guitars. Van Ronk says, "We knew it was baloney, but it was the kind of baloney you swallow without studying the ingredients too carefully. And Bobby fed it up in such a good-natured way. Hell, we figured why spoil the kid's fun?"

Van Ronk and the boys anticipated fun of a different kind when word hit the Street that Big Joe had been booked into Folk City for a week-long engagement. As he remembers it, "A bunch of us who'd endured all versions of this saga grabbed Bobby and headed over there for a showdown of sorts. Surprisingly, Bobby was pretty cool about the whole thing. It didn't seem to faze him that he was going to be unmasked. All the way over there I remember thinking, 'When is he going to make his move? How's he going to get out of this?' But the kid never batted an eye." To make matters worse, Big Joe spotted

Bob first as he entered the club, rushed over, and roared, "Hey, Dylan! I haven't seen you since that boxcar in Mexico!" Van Ronk and the others watched open-mouthed while the two ex-hoboes reminisced. "To this day I'm dying to know how Bobby swung that one," Van Ronk laughs. "Until I find out, all of us are inclined to believe he got to Big Joe first and worked out the story."

Bob spent more time writing his own material, but the pressure was still on to come up with a new batch of little-known folk songs to work into his act. Besides Van Ronk, one of the most resourceful interpreters at the time was a Boston folksinger and commercial artist named Eric Von Schmidt, who ransacked the Library of Congress files in search of Negro blues standards to rewrite. Bob had already met him in May when Von Schmidt taught him one of his foremost finds, "He Was a Friend of Mine." (Bob later contended that he learned it from Arvella Gray.) The time had come to reacquaint himself with Von Schmidt in the hope of picking up another gem or two to balance out the gush of original songs.

Toward the end of the summer, Bob took off for Cambridge, where he found not only Eric Von Schmidt but a rival folk scene in full bloom. The coffeehouses there were studded with young talent from the surrounding universities. Performers like Tom Rush, Jim Kweskin, Debbie Green, Jackie Washington, Rolf Cahn, the Charles River Valley Boys, and Dick Waterman traded weekends playing at the city's two most important clubs, the Golden Vanity and Club 47. Boston's meal ticket, however, was a twenty-one-year-old siren named Joan Baez, who, in no subtle way, had commandeered the regional spotlight and was beginning to attract national attention. The local folkies talked about nothing else. It was "Joanie this" and "Joanie that"—you'd have thought she was part of the Kennedy clan.

Bob was naturally curious about the buzz. In Joan Baez, he'd encountered a folksinger who was making a big splash—his own star-spangled goal—*without any original material.* And in a tank town like Boston. There had to be something more to her than simply a pleasant voice.

Von Schmidt took Bob over to Club 47 on Mt. Auburn, where Joan usually sang, but she wasn't on that night's bill. Instead, Carolyn Hester, a Texas bombshell with a thrushlike voice, was the featured attraction. The place was packed, and Eric had to work his ass off for a couple of seats. Bob waited outside, peering in the big plate-glass window at the well-lit stage. Club 47 was a hot room. Unlike the liturgical Village clubs, it encouraged a partylike atmosphere. There was an obvious camaraderie among tables. Bob desperately wanted to perform there, but the 47's manager, Paula Kelley, had only that night turned him down for a booking. Like anyone else, however, he was welcome to play between Carolyn's sets. Bob seized the opportunity to show this gang what he could do. When the time came, he played "Talkin' Bear Mountain Picnic Massacre Blues" to the general delight of the crowd—the ulterior motive being that he might impress Paula Kelley enough to change her mind.

Afterward, he and Von Schmidt sat and drank coffee through the regular show. Carolyn Hester proved to be an engaging, if unremarkable, folksinger. Bob and Eric weren't particularly impressed with her set, although things picked up suddenly when she shared the stage with her husband, Richard Fariña, for an Irish ballad entitled "Johnny's Gone to Hilo." Fariña had an eerie stage presence, like a sulking cat. He sang with obvious feeling, but more interesting was the way he seemed to light a fire under his wife. He was intense, penetrating, and when they collaborated, Carolyn sang like a woman possessed. Bob and Eric were both fascinated by Fariña. Von Schmidt worked out introductions after the show and, without any difficulty, arranged for everyone to spend the next day together at nearby Revere Beach.

As it turned out, the day was as momentous as any one Bob Dylan could have possibly hoped for. Dick Fariña lived up to all of the previous night's expectations—he was an extraordinary character, taken by life almost as much as he was taken by himself. Though only twenty-three when Bob met him, Fariña had already lived on three continents and worked professionally as a journalist, songwriter, novelist, poet, performer, and political agitator. Dick was also an impulsive fantasizer who suffered from the inability to distinguish between romance and danger. He claimed to be friendly with Fidel Castro and Che Guevara, and supposedly trained with the guerrillas who sought to topple the Batista dictatorship. Later on, Dick became "involved"—as he mysteriously put it—with the outlawed Irish Republican Army in a little escapade that compelled him to pack a .38-caliber revolver wherever he went. Fariña spun such tales with all the blood and thunder of a professional raconteur, though Von Schmidt, for one, harbored serious doubts about their veracity. Some weeks earlier Von Schmidt had told Fariña about an episode he had in the army, which came back to him through friends as part of Dick's Cuban experience.

Dick Fariña lived for the scene and did anything it took to be part of it. "If tap-dancing was what you did this year, Richard would have tap-danced with grace and style," Carolyn Hester insists. When Irish ballads came into vogue, Dick studied them with breathless impatience. "One thing he had was plenty of balls. Richard was consumed with the Latin conceit of *machismo,* and he traded on it to transform himself into anything he wanted to be. Surprisingly, it never really put people off, most likely because he was glib and witty and provocative and entertaining as hell. He'd meet a complete stranger and, in no time, Richard could take over his soul."

Probably no one knew that as well as Carolyn Hester did. He'd done almost as much to her. Earlier that year in New York, Dick had cornered her at the White Horse cafe, wangled an introduction, and married her thirteen days later. The couple then proceeded to cut a striking figure on the East Coast coffeehouse circuit. Dick was dark, fiery, and intimidating; Carolyn, by contrast, possessed a sunny southern delicacy, along with dazzling beauty and frisky party-girl charm. And both were swimming in potential.

Dick saw himself as the existential hero of the times, determined to write about every abstract observation that haunted his own idealized destiny. He was incredibly prolific, dabbling in every literary form. He had studied with Vladimir Nabokov at Cornell and demonstrated an intuitive grasp of rhythmic and narrative structure. But unlike his teacher, Dick had the concentration of a firefly. Monday, he could begin work on a collection of free verse; Tuesday, his attention shifted to the plot for a morality play; by Wednesday, he was at work on an article intended to move Mencken to tears; there were *New Yorker*–type short stories to be written on Thursday; a folk song needed shaping for Friday night's gig; and the weekend was reserved for the cornerstone of his artistic empire—a novel in perpetual progress, which he had asked Eric Von Schmidt to illustrate. Since none of his undertakings had borne fruit as yet, Dick was left to managing his wife's career, which was further along the road to success.

Carolyn Hester, in fact, had enjoyed a profitable summer as a leading folk music attraction. Her gig at Club 47 was the last in a series of New England bookings begun back in early May, and she was taking a few weeks off before heading to New York for an October recording session at Columbia Studios. This was to be her third and most important album, inasmuch as it was the first for a major label. Her debut on Coral Records had been a homemade affair, produced under the aegis of fellow Texans Buddy Holly and Norm Petty and featuring Carolyn's father on harmonica. The next one was a solo shot for puny Tradition Records, produced by Tom Clancy. With any luck, this upcoming project would be her masterpiece, that is if she and Richard could pull together all the elements for it.

Spread out on a blanket at Revere Beach, Carolyn and Dick spilled all the details of the upcoming recording session. They were especially enthusiastic about its potential. First off, it was for Columbia Records—an industry giant which, until that time, had virtually ignored contemporary folk music, recording established stars like Pete Seeger and the Clancy Brothers while bypassing the younger coffeehouse set. Carolyn's deal there was considered a definite coup and an indication that Columbia might be willing to sign other new folksingers. More important, the recording session would be presided over by the legendary producer John Hammond Sr. Hammond undertaking your album was like Francis Ford Coppola directing your screenplay or Stephen Sondheim scoring your libretto. His involvement attracted almost as much attention as the music itself, and his reputation as a star-maker was undebatable.

Hammond discovered and recorded what has become the backbone of American popular music in the twentieth century, including the likes of Billie Holiday, Count Basie, Benny Goodman, Lionel Hampton, Teddy Wilson, and Aretha Franklin. He'd been shopping around for a folksinger for some time, having passed on Joan Baez whose demands proved too rich for Columbia's corporate blood. Carolyn seemed like a suitable understudy to Baez, even if she lacked Joan's fire. With the Hammond touch, Carolyn was guaranteed at least a fair shot at making a highly regarded, if not commercially successful, record.

By this time, Bob's tongue must have been lolling in the sand. Even money says he was thinking, "How can I get in on this action?" Here was Carolyn Hester, a perfectly inconsequential folksinger, talking about a recording session with John fucking Hammond! The situation reeked of opportunity. If ever there was a time for Bob Dylan to talk his way into a gig, the moment had finally arrived.

Bob was smart enough to know that it wasn't going to take much. Carolyn had developed a perverse attraction to Bob, so much so that, at the beach, she found it difficult to take her eyes off him. She'd never seen anyone who looked so unhealthy before. He seemed chronically wasted, stricken by a delicate madness, pale, dirty, weatherworn, and strangely effeminate. The guy was monstrously unusual. "The beach looked to me like the last place in the world he would be," Carolyn recalls. Yet she was struck by his acetylene voice, the way he committed himself to every song he played. And more important, she could tell Dick was taken by him. "I put a lot of faith in Richard's judgment," Carolyn says. "He was able to zero in on who was doing IT and who wasn't, and who was somebody we ought to be friends with. The fact that Richard was fascinated by Dylan was good enough for me. I knew the three of us were destined to become involved."

Fariña hammered on incessantly about Carolyn's forthcoming album. "Yeah, yeah—I'd like to do that," Bob said, picking up his guitar. "Here's a couple of songs I could teach you." Without hesitating, Bob launched into a medley of half-finished original tunes, one of which, "Come Back Baby," caught Carolyn's fancy.

"I'd been looking for a good blues to put on the record," she remembers of that afternoon, "something that required more than just a guitar and a good voice. Magazines like *The Little Sandy Review* were incredibly critical of what instrumentation you used on an album, and I felt that something with a bass and harmonica would fulfill my requirements and please the reviewers. I also thought that Dylan was going to have a great future and that somehow he would add to the album's mystique."

A few weeks later, Carolyn met Bob at Mary Rotolo's apartment on Sheridan Square, where he taught her the finished version of "Come Back Baby." They worked out a loose, bluesy arrangement which required a snaky harmonica fill that only Bob could play. Carolyn thought he'd give a lift to the album and invited him to a dress rehearsal before the recording session so that he could teach the song to her bass player, Bruce Langhorne.

Bob showed up for the rehearsal at a brownstone on West Tenth

Street early on the afternoon of September 14, 1961. Carolyn and Dick were already into the polishing process, working out a couple of charts with Langhorne, so Bob curled up on an antique wooden bench to await his turn. Fariña, naturally impatient, tried to rush his wife through the rehearsal, but Carolyn insisted on taking her time. She'd suspected for some time that Dick had grown jealous of her success and was determined not to let that interfere with this project. It was a touchy situation. Resentments started to rise and threatened to interrupt the music, when the doorbell rang.

Everyone was surprised to see John Hammond shuffle up the stairs. The producer hadn't been expected at the rehearsal; nevertheless Carolyn and Dick were pleased to see him, and Hammond's presence served to defuse the tensions that had been building. Probably no one was more delighted to see John Hammond than Bob Dylan. To him, Hammond was a connection between folk music and professional entertainment, the full spectrum of his desire. Bob moved over to the couch where Hammond was seated. He seemed very relaxed, almost calculating in his reticence. Carolyn remembers, "Every so often Bob would sneak a peak at Hammond. Then, when we began to play, Hammond would glance over at Bob. This went on throughout the afternoon—they were kind of casing each other out. Before he left, John made sure that Bob was going to be at the recording session."

The session was scheduled for September twenty-ninth, which Dylan repeated aloud as if to assure Hammond that he'd be there. But the assurance, in and of itself, was gratuitous. Bob had been granted an audience with John Hammond. Nothing short of nuclear war was going to stand in his way.

11

Hammond's Folly

Two weeks after meeting John Hammond, Bob opened at Gerdes Folk City for what would be the second and final club date he'd ever play officially in Greenwich Village. Mike Porco still wasn't convinced Bob could pull in the stalwart drinkers. Gerdes' bullheaded owner once again denied Bob the star billing he deserved, hiring him instead to open for the Greenbriar Boys, an ersatz bluegrass group whose yodels and yee-hahs really liquored-up the crowds.

Porco's lack of confidence in him to fill seats with guzzlers was no doubt a slap in the face. The nerve—having him warm up some dumb hillbilly act! After all the attention he'd been getting, you'd think Porco could've treated him with more respect. He knew that Bob was ready to headline. Everyone else knew he had the talent to carry two weeks at the club. But what was he going to do? Bob wasn't interested in bellyaching. And he certainly wasn't going to kiss Mike Porco's ass. Subconsciously, he must have sensed something else was going on, something that had nothing to do with whether he went on first or second at Gerdes. Secretly he must have known it didn't make a damn bit of difference. The fact of the matter was, Bob was on a roll; he had to devote all his energy to keeping up the momentum. If he paused to get pissed off at Mike Porco—what then? He'd fuck things up for sure. He'd lose the focus. Bob was too shrewd to make that kind of a mistake. Especially after all the time he'd invested in his career. There were more constructive things he could do to compensate for second billing. "Ac-cen-chew-ate the pos-i-tive/ e-lim-i-nate the neg-a-tive"—he'd sung the silly refrain over and over again as a kid, and there was no time like the present to practice what he'd sung.

It was time to take the bull by the horns. No more waiting with the rest of the MacDougal Street lightweights for someone to discover him. Working for a lousy eighty bucks a week. He could rot in a joint like Gerdes, die there like Cisco Houston, kicking off with a final chorus of "In the Sweet By-and-By." No, he had to get something moving. Summoning up every ounce of chutzpah in his bones, he picked up the phone and called Robert Shelton, the music critic for *The New York Times.*

Calling Shelton for coverage was about as cool a move as asking Earl Warren to fix a parking ticket. Musicians weren't supposed to court the press, especially for favorable reviews—particularly folksingers, who were by nature suspicious of the media. Occasionally critics and musicians developed a mutual admiration for one another, but from a distance so that it didn't constitute a conflict of interest. Otherwise, critics remained deliberately distant from their subjects. It was a way of saying, "I can't be bought." The latter, in fact, was *lex scripta* at the *Times,* which went as far as to forbid its writers from accepting lunch or dinner engagements with anyone even remotely interested in promoting something.

Bob Shelton was another story altogether. To the folkies, Shelton was family, part of the ever-expanding circle that hung out on the Street each night until dawn. He frequently dated Jean Redpath, a leading coffeehouse chanteuse. He was a *capo* in the Waverly Street "mafia" that included Dave Van Ronk, Tom Paxton, Noel Stookey, and Barry Kornfeld. (The folksingers lived in an apartment building at 190 Waverly Street, directly across from Shelton's pad.) If a card game was in progress at the Gaslight, Shelton could be counted on to sit in for a few hands before returning to his table downstairs. Or to buy a round or two of drinks at the White Horse, where he regularly entertained an entourage of friends—among them Carla Rotolo, Suze's older sister, who talked about nothing but Bob Dylan. No one ever came right out and said it, but Robert Shelton was *accessible.*

Shelton had caught Bob's act before—at Folk City, at the Gaslight with Dave Van Ronk, and again at the Riverside Church concert—but, admittedly, he never heard enough to warrant a full-scale review. There had been some kind of loose promise made, like "Call me when you get your next gig and I'll see what I can do," but to Shelton, Bob was simply another young folk music interpreter competing in an already overcrowded scene. Shelton promised to show up at his Folk City show, but, in fact, that gig clearly belonged to the Greenbriar Boys, who deserved some of his thoughtful attention.

When the momentous night, September 26th, arrived, Bob was running on pure adrenalin. He'd spent a good deal of the afternoon in front of Carla Rotolo's mirror, picking out the right getup—a blue shirt, black vest, khaki pants, and the ever-present corduroy cap—but by the time the show started, his clothes looked like he'd slept in them. He was a mess of nerves and, to more than one observer, a nervous mess. Not that his appearance was a clue to what was to come. Bob Dylan, as usual, was cool as a cucumber on stage. Once those lights hit him, the nervousness melted away, and he cruised through forty-five minutes of musical wit and ingenuity. He really brought down the house, and the remarkable thing was that he did it with a fairly straightforward set of blues and traditional songs. "I'm Gonna Get You, Sally Girl," "This Life Is Killing Me," "900 Miles," "See That My Grave Is Kept Clean," "Poor Girl," "House of the Rising Sun"—you could hear any one of those played up and down the Street, and by the original blues gurus like the Reverend Gary Davis or Josh White. But Bob's power lay in the *performance,* the trenchant way he communicated these songs to his audience. On stage, he took them further than any of his contemporaries had dared, singing with complete abandon, and gave the standards a distinctly personal and exhilarating reading.

To put it mildly, Robert Shelton was blown away. A few times during Bob's set, Carla Rotolo looked at the critic and found him transfixed, his eyes bugged open like an expectant puppy, hanging on Dylan's every gesture and nuance. "My God!—this is great!" he sputtered between two of the numbers.

Bob also slipped in a couple of new talking blues to liven things up and show off his talent for songwriting—a tactic which was daring and more than a bit arrogant, considering no other singers were performing their own *folk* songs as yet. But Shelton wasn't put off by this act of heresy. He bought the whole routine, shaking with laughter at Bob's well-timed wordplay.

Shelton remained at his table for the Greenbriar Boys' set. As soon as it was over, he made a beeline for the kitchen, where Bob was retuning his guitar between bites of a sandwich. There, in a grubby little galley strangled by the gamy aromas of coffee, French fries, and sauerkraut, Bob Dylan gave not only the most important interview of his entire career but one that would serve as an outline for every interview he granted over the next twenty-five years. There, he invented what would become known in journalistic circles as *The Bob Dylan Interview*—a put-on really, a pastiche of truths, half-truths, and boldfaced lies set forth in an elliptical dodge. There, he drew the shade on his personal life and celebrated the mythification of Bob Dylan.

Shelton played the indulgent straight man as Bob shoveled it on thick. He was born in Duluth—or maybe it was Superior, Wisconsin, he shrugged. At thirteen he ran away and joined the circus, cleaned up ponies, and ran steam shovels from Minnesota all the way to the southern border. Some character named Wigglefoot supposedly taught him to fret his guitar with a kitchen knife in Gallup, New Mexico. Of course, he'd recorded with Gene Vincent in Nashville, although, he was quick to mention, the tracks were never released. He dropped the name of his old pal Mance Lipscomb again. Bobby Vee, Woody Guthrie, Jesse Fuller. . . . On and on Bob went, hardly coming up for air, about his influences—every esoteric name in the book—and his travels to America's backwater paradises. To hear him tell it, Bob had seen, done, and committed everything analogous to a leathery old character out of Hemingway. *And to a reporter for The New York Times!* He kept right on fabricating his life, varnishing the myth with brand-new tales, until it was time for his next set.

Shelton's article wasn't scheduled to run for a few days, so Bob concentrated on the business at hand. From Monday through Thursday, he played three sold-out shows a night at Gerdes. Thursday evening, as he was finishing up at the club, Shelton appeared backstage. "Have you seen the *Times?*" he asked mysteriously. "Wait'll you see my review." He refused to say more, teasing Bob, then acting cool and imperious.

Bob grabbed Suze and ran over to the Sheridan Square kiosk to get an early edition of the *Times.* Across the top of page thirty-one, the headline for Shelton's review of the Greenbriar Boys read: "BOB DYLAN: A DISTINCTIVE FOLK-SONG STYLIST." In smaller type: "Greenbriar Boys Are Also on Bill with Bluegrass Music." Bob stared at it in disbelief. Shelton had gone berserk with praise—two and a half columns devoted to everything from his appearance to his voice to his delivery to his choice of material. "There is no doubt that he is bursting at the seams with talent," Shelton drooled at the top of the piece. "His music-making has the mark of originality and inspiration."

Dylan reread the words in a state of shock. The first article ever written about him—in *The New York Times* of all places—and *it was a goddamn rave!* Not only that, a photo of Bob holding his guitar drew even more attention to the review. The kind of space Shelton had given him was unprecedented for an opening act, let alone a newcomer to the scene. Bob and Suze bought a stack of papers and ran back to Mary Rotolo's apartment, where they committed Shelton's rave to memory.

Suddenly everything was changed. The next afternoon, September 29, 1961, Bob was due at Carolyn Hester's recording session, which now took on a new importance. John Hammond would be there, and when Bob walked in, it would be not only as an accompanist, but as one who had an endorsement from *The New York Times* in his back pocket. The call of opportunity thundered off the walls as he dressed for the occasion. He stood in front of the mirror for more than an hour, going through his entire wardrobe, fussing over each piece like Lauren Bacall on opening night. Denim shirt and khakis—hmmm, maybe. Or perhaps a pair of old jeans and a sweater was more appropriate. Or the wool shirt. He tried on each *schmatah* with his cap, studying his pose, shifting his weight from leg to leg to determine the effect. Juggling his shoulders, pouting, cocking his head to one side like Christie Brinkley. Suze watched the modeling session with a sense of presentiment. "He's so aware of the impression it'll make," she thought. "He knows what's at stake."

Bob was the last to arrive at the old Columbia Studios building on Seventh Avenue at 54th Street. Richard Fariña and Carolyn Hester were already laying down some tracks along with bass player Bruce Langhorne, and each had his own copy of the *Times* review. "Bob walked through the door with his guitar in one hand and the review waving in the other," Carolyn remembers. "He was flying high, really pleased by it. In fact, Bob showed more happiness about it than anything I'd seen him show before...or since." Even Dick Fariña, whose dander bristled at the slightest whiff of competition, was pulling for him. And Bob played it for all it was worth, blushing and squirming like he was sweet sixteen. Wasn't he the lucky one; maybe he didn't deserve it; he never saw it coming; isn't it a *bitch!* When he got those embarrassed eyes and noodling smile working, that shrinking bashfulness tugging at your heartstrings, that facade of clownish inarticulate self-consciousness, you could be sure he was up to something. Bob knew how to work any audience.

Bob handed John Hammond a copy of the review and then set about doing some harmonica warm-ups as if it were any other day of the week. "I could tell Hammond was hooked from the very start," Carolyn says. "The longer we worked, the more I could see Hammond's interest in Bob developing, until the two of them were thick as thieves."

Hammond's division of interest irritated Carolyn, although it has less to do with Bob Dylan than it did with the producer's personal style. Despite his sound creative judgment, John Hammond had a notoriously short attention span and an aversion to perfection. He was known as a musician's producer, someone who relied on spontaneous artistry to shine through a performance in lieu of his input and state-of-the-art technical assistance. If most producers were known to put their personal signatures on the recordings they made, Hammond remained conspicuously anonymous. He was the kind of guy who propped his feet up on the control panel, opened mail, read magazines, answered the phone, and let the "magic" happen on its own. There was no such thing as a John Hammond record, only a John Hammond artist. In fact, if you listen carefully to his masterpieces—most notably the recordings of Billie Holiday, Meade Lux Lewis, Albert Ammons, and later, especially, Bob Dylan—you'll be amazed by how many imperfections slide through. They're not the sound of performers in a recording studio. The musicians hit a lot of clams, vocals are occasionally muddy or off-key, a roving foot can be heard tapping out the rhythm or grazing the side of piano pedals—none of which detracts from the overall performances. If anything, it enhances them by emphasizing the honesty of the moment. All of which is well and good if you're a musician with a particularly strong sense of self-assurance.

Unfortunately for Carolyn Hester, this was not the case. The importance of making her third album a popular success was implicit and wrought with pressure. She wanted to reap the benefits of John Hammond's star-making powers. She wanted a strong creative producer. What she got instead was a mail-opening, phone-answering, magazine-reading nice guy *who was infatuated with Bob Dylan!* According to Carolyn, Hammond couldn't have shown less interest in her session. He rushed her through a string of first takes, including three songs on which Bob played harp—"Come Back Baby," "Swing and Turn Jubilee," and "I'll Fly Away." By the end of the week, three things must have become glaringly apparent to Hester: (1) she'd been shortchanged by John Hammond; (2) the resultant album wasn't going to do anything spectacular for her career; and (3) the real beneficiary of her Columbia session would be none other than Bob Dylan.

In fact, Hammond had pulled Bob aside and asked him to drop by his office at Columbia Records. "Listen," he said, "I think you have something for us here. Why don't you come by and tell me what you're interested in." Subsequently, the two men chatted informally about folk music—John devouring Bob's rebellious, underground pose—and, in effect, Bob was offered a recording contract solely on the basis of Hammond's intuition. Just like that! Hammond never asked to see him perform. There's even some doubt whether Hammond had heard Bob sing! He just liked what he saw—the whole Dylan package, the angry young folksinger. It hit the right chord.

No other producer would dare even try to sign an artist without an audition. John Hammond, however, wasn't just *any* producer. His track record had earned him extraordinary powers at Columbia Records, and he used them with great finesse. Hammond passed himself off as a befuddled eccentric, a mad genius indulged by his coworkers, but in reality he'd engineered many a company political coup and knew how to exploit the corporate machine. If he wanted Bob Dylan on the label, chances were good he'd let nothing stand in his way.

Why Hammond was determined to sign Bob is a consequence of practical, as well as artistic, reasoning. There is no question he saw in Bob exceptional character and talent. Like any record man, Hammond was a gambler—he traded in the futures market, recognizing artistic potential and capitalizing on it before a performer reached his or her maturity. Bob was a diamond in the rough.

But talent wasn't Hammond's sole criterion for pursuing Bob Dylan. Since rejoining the label in 1958,* he had become something of a company man, and he took an active interest in Columbia Records' welfare. That meant staying on top of the business and developing the label's roster of talent to ensure its presence in the recording industry.

In the early 1960s Columbia was a joke as far as the growing youth market was concerned. RCA had signed Elvis Presley and Neil Sedaka; Atlantic attracted the leading R&B groups; Warner Bros. grabbed the Everly Brothers and Peter, Paul & Mary; most of the popular teenage attractions were clustered on the small independent labels. Columbia had signed only one rock singer, Dion, whose biggest hits had already been released on Laurie Records. Mitch Miller, the label's Director of Artists & Repertoire looked upon rock 'n roll as one would a stray dog: ignore it and it would eventually go away. As a recording artist in his own right—and with his *Sing Along with Mitch* series—he, understandably, felt threatened. In 1960, at a Columbia Records convention in Kansas City, he issued a fiat that, in essence, said Columbia would never go into the rock 'n roll business. The people at Columbia, he made clear, were prepared to stick with their *respectable* roster of artists, which included Ray Coniff, Doris Day, Johnny Mathis, and a number of other mediocrities.

In time, this lack of foresight cost Mitch Miller his job. Rock was there to stay, and word eventually filtered back to Columbia's top brass that the record company couldn't deliver what people wanted to hear. As a result, Miller was replaced by David Kapralik, a refugee of Columbia's sales and promotion departments, who was instructed to beef up the label's "contemporary" roster. Kapralik's first coup was signing a young New Yorker named Tony Orlando. A couple of weeks later John Hammond burst through his door like a bookie with a hot tip.

"He was delirious about this kid I had to hear," Kapralik recalls of that afternoon. "The gist of it was that we had to sign Dylan immediately because he was going to be important—not just musically, but intellectually and politically, as well. Not a *recording* artist, but a recording *artist.* He seemed more excited about the kind of message Dylan conveyed and what he represented than about his music, which

---

*Hammond originally worked for Columbia Records in 1939. He left there in 1946 to work for Majestic, Mercury, and Vanguard Records before returning to the CBS fold.

was so unusual. There was no way he was going to let me get back to work until I said yes." Nevertheless, Kapralik maintains he wasn't muscled into signing Bob. He says, "When it came right down to it, I was an a priori believer in John's ears and knew better than to dismiss his enthusiasm as hype. If another A&R man had brought Bob Dylan to me I don't think I would have allowed him to be signed at that time. But with John I just said, 'Go ahead.'"

Little did Kapralik know that Hammond already had Bob cutting demos in the studio before a contract was tendered. "I wanted to get something down on tape and hear what Bobby was capable of," Hammond says in defense. The outcome must have produced considerable anxiety, especially after a few false starts. "In a word, he was *terrible,*" Hammond contends in response to a question about Bob's virgin studio experience. "Bobby popped every *p,* hissed every *s,* and habitually wandered off mike. Even more frustrating, he refused to learn from his mistakes. It occurred to me at the time that I'd never worked with anyone so undisciplined before."

That session was preserved on rare Columbia reference acetates that have surfaced in recent years. The records preview the kind of material Bob ultimately selected for his debut Columbia album, but at the same time they clearly depict Bob Dylan as a country blues singer. This was peculiar given the broad range of material he normally performed on stage. His sets were a miscellany of songs culled from the country, rock 'n roll, bluegrass, blues, and traditional and folk idioms, not to mention a growing inventory of original material. Yet his first solo session at Columbia consisted of unremarkable performances of the classic Kokomo Arnold song "Milkcow Boogie" and a ballad called "The Last Time I Saw Wichita," neither of which he explored with any new significance.

Even these one-dimensional songs were enough to convince John Hammond that Bob should do an album for Columbia. Bob naturally jumped at the opportunity. And as you might believe, Bob was willing to agree to anything that led to a record deal.

Eschewing the customary practice of having a lawyer or manager work out a contractual agreement with the record company, Hammond negotiated a deal with Bob on the spot. It was the standard contract Columbia offered all new artists: one year, with four one-year terms that the record company could exercise at its option. In return, Bob received about one thousand dollars as an advance against royalties and the exclusive services of John Hammond Sr. as his producer.

Since Bob was only twenty years old, still considered a minor in New York, Hammond insisted that Bob's parents cosign his contract. You can only imagine the chilling effect that news had on Bob. *His parents? Abe and Beatty?* He hadn't so much as communicated with them since dropping out of college. He didn't want any part of their life, and he certainly didn't want them interfering with his. The thought of Abe agreeing to endorse his son's career as a professional folksinger was absurd. One can only imagine hawk-eyed Abe squinting at the fine print of a Columbia Records contract while poor Bob waited anxiously for his father's decision.

"What's this clause here about promotional copies being given away to deejays?"

"That's just standard practice, Dad."

"Standard schmandered. If these deejays want one of your albums so badly, why can't they just walk into a record store like anyone else and *buy* one? Think about it, Robert. What would happen if I gave a toaster away to every customer of mine who wanted to test a loaf of pumpernickel? I'd go broke."

"But, Dad, this is a *record* contract."

"Records, toasters—they're one and the same thing when it comes to business. I don't know—I'm going to have to talk this over with your Uncle Maurie. . . ."

Bob wasn't about to let that happen. So he conned Hammond with the old orphan story, improving it by adding that his only living relative was an uncle named Dillon who dealt blackjack in Las Vegas. *Las Vegas!* Consider what effect those two words might have had on a man like John Hammond who, only a year before, watched as a Senate Judiciary Committee had a field day investigating payola in the record business. The names Gambino and Sicily would probably have been more well received. No, there wasn't any need to bring Uncle Dillon into the picture. So John Hammond, in a momentary lapse of common sense, decided to waive the legality and trust Bob to sign the contract on his own.

At last Bob had what he had worked so hard for: *a record contract.* And with Columbia Records, not one of the little *pishkie* folk labels hungered after by other singers on the Street. Columbia meant the big time—national distribution, major advertising, a multimedia organization behind him, perhaps a shot at TV.

To his credit, Bob soft-pedaled his triumph on the Street. He was aware of the jealousies already stirred by Shelton's review. And more than likely he was a bit embarrassed by it. Suddenly, he was thrust into the same league as Pete Seeger and the Clancy Brothers (both Columbia artists), when he knew there were other folksingers more deserving of the distinction. So while he mumbled down his contract with Columbia, he set about quietly laying the groundwork he hoped would ensure his album's artistic success.

By this time, Bob was spending almost every night on a couch in Carla Rotolo's apartment on Perry Street. Carla worked for noted musicologist Alan Lomax and consequently owned one of the best folk music reference libraries in the neighborhood. Every day after she went to work, Bob went through her record collection—which included most of the Folkways catalogue and Lomax's field recordings—searching for interesting material for his album. When he'd exhausted the records, books and anthologies provided a wellspring of new sources. He devoured Cecil Sharp's *Eastern Folk Songs from the Southern Appalachians; Songs and Ballads of the Maine Lumberjacks,* by Roland Palmer Gray; Lomax's *Folk Songs of North America; Coalfields,* compiled by A. L. Lloyd; the entire *Sing Out!* collection, and anything else Carla had lying around the house. Bob may have been a lousy college student, but he studied enough folk material to have earned a Ph.D. at any respectable university in the country. Even Dave Van Ronk was impressed by Bob's diligence. "I figured that by the time he was ready to cut the album, Bobby had more songs in his repertoire than the Library of Congress had in its catalogue," he says facetiously.

On that point alone, Bob Dylan's first album might be said to have been a tremendous disappointment. The songs he ultimately recorded were, for the most part, traditional and familiar. Everyone on the Street performed "Fixin' to Die" and "Gospel Plow." Jesse Fuller's "You're No Good," "Man of Constant Sorrow," and the Blind Lemon Jefferson dirge "See That My Grave Is Kept Clean" were songs Bob had done once or twice and then discarded, so in a sense he had no real connection to them. And "Pretty Peggy-O" he'd reduced to an outright parody; in the coffeehouses he often condensed the last line into about two beats while the audience rolled on the floor in stitches. No one took it very seriously, and even less so as an album track. All in all, then, *Bob Dylan* represented no great departure in the recording of traditional folk music.

Where it did connect was on the two original tunes that won spots on the record's final sequence. "Talking New York" and "Song to Woody" both stand as tributes to Bob's folk music mentor and characterize two very different faces of the genre. "Talking New York" is a witty, archly cynical *bouffe* that mimics Woody Guthrie's hallmark, the talking blues. Bob trips lightly across the syncopated stanzas, tipping his cap to a clutter of Woody's well-worn images—ramblin' and travelin', working for beggarly wages, joining the union, battling New York's callousness. He recalls an oft-quoted line from Woody's "Pretty Boy Floyd": "Now, a very great man once said/ that some people rob you with a fountain pen."* "Talking New York" expressed none of the new attitudes affiliated with the coffeehouse movement. If anything, it demonstrated Bob's willingness to continue writing in a traditional folk form out of respect for the old masters.

That wasn't the case at all with "Song to Woody." Generally acknowledged as the real masterpiece of the album, "Song to Woody" signaled a breakthrough, not only for Bob Dylan but for commercial folk music as well. The song is intensely personal and introspective. Simple images, stoic observations, strained ironies—they are embroidered with a persuasive, though naive, sincerity that gives the song its compelling force. Strangely enough, the words scan more like a eulogy than an elegy. In essence, Bob says, "Hey, Woody—you had the drop on hypocrisy. The world owes you a debt of gratitude, and we'll never forget you." No one who heard Bob perform this in the early 1960s was unmoved by the full emotional treatment he always gave it.

For the members of the folk community, "Song to Woody" was the first indication that they were in the presence of a major songwriter. Up to that point, songwriting was no more than a sideline with any of the professional folksingers. It would have been unthinkable for anyone to consider himself a songwriter, nor did it probably ever occur to Bob that he could get by solely on original material. "Song to Woody"

---

*"Now as through this world I ramble I see lots of funny men/ some will rob you with a six-gun/ and some with a fountain pen."

changed all that if for no other reason than the widespread support it received from his peers. The gang on the Street applauded the song for its eloquence as well as for what it represented: a clear and tantalizing transition away from the music of the folk song movement. "Song to Woody" used all the traditional vocal and instrumental techniques one normally applied to interpretation—there's a large element of folk *influence* in it—but it wasn't folk music. It was a new synthesis of music *in the folk tradition.* In time, this would lead to the establishment of a new school of performer known as the singer-songwriter, but for now Bob Dylan was content to dabble in it like anyone else.

Expectations soared as word of Bob's forthcoming album circulated on the Street. "We figured that if Bobby had a record deal, ours wouldn't be far behind," Tom Paxton recalls, echoing a sentiment voiced by several Village folkies. Dave Van Ronk was especially glad for his friend's good fortune. Not long after the Columbia sessions, he bumped into Bob at the Folklore Center and extended his congratulations over a glass of wine. While they were chatting, Bob asked if he could record Van Ronk's stylized version of "House of the Rising Sun."

Van Ronk, who was in the process of cutting an album for Prestige Records, remembers saying, "No, Bobby. I'd really rather that you didn't, because I'm going into the studio in a week to record it myself."

Bob looked uncomfortably at his hands. "Well, I've already cut it," he confessed.

"*You what?*" Van Ronk roared. Unable to contain his anger, he stormed out of the Folklore Center, swearing never to forgive Dylan for what he considered to be a gross breach of friendship.

Terri Thal recalls her ex-husband's reaction with amusement. "Dave decided not to speak to him anymore," she says, "except that Bobby called every night, crying and begging to talk to him. He wanted a chance to explain and probably apologize. And every fucking night I had to say, 'Dave won't speak to you.'" This went on for two months until Van Ronk eventually cooled off and forgave Bob. "But it is indicative of the way in which Bobby manipulated his friendships," Thal notes, "and from that point on we never quite trusted him again."

Terri already had every reason to doubt Bob's sincerity. For several months she'd served unofficially as his manager, throwing gigs his way whenever something opened up at an area coffeehouse. But by the end of 1961, word filtered back to her that Bob was being represented by Albert Grossman, a familiar figure on the Street who seemed to have his claws in all the young folksingers. "I was furious with Dylan," she says of the situation, "not because he'd jilted me, but that he hadn't the decency to tell me himself." Thal claims she would have gladly stepped out of the picture had Bob asked. She knew she was a lousy manager, hardly earning him enough money to starve on, and that it was only a matter of time before Bob required more professional attention. But Albert Grossman was a shark—a real ganef. She hated to see Bob take up with someone who was likely to bring out the worst in him.

Cryptic, arrogant, condescending, shrewd, underhanded, cutthroat, even diabolical to some people, Albert Grossman was known by the New York folk community not necessarily for what he was but for what he wanted them to think of him. And yet the images he presented in public were inconsistent. He was the loan shark with a list of personal charities, the hit man with a heart of gold. The contradiction is best expressed by Mary Travers, who was managed by Grossman for more than a decade: "Albert wasn't a very nice man, but I loved him dearly," she says without any irony whatsoever.

By the time Bob Dylan met him, Albert Grossman was one of only three managers in the music business who specialized in booking folksingers. The others—Harold Leventhal and Manny Greenhill—were gentlemanly impresarios whose dealings were governed in part by their political convictions and a strong commitment to the peoples' folk song movement of post-Depression America. Albert was neither a gentleman nor political. He was, by his own description, a "Jewish businessman," a cagey operator who lived by the Teutonic theory that those who strike first and fastest usually eat best. He preferred to remain vague and ambiguous to others so that they could interpret, or rather *mis*interpret, his actions in any manner that conveniently suited their purposes. Later, when it came time to commit to a formal agreement, Albert would shrug and say, "I never said that. That's what you *thought* I said."

As a manager, Albert was notoriously evasive. One of his favorite ploys was getting you to go on record in making a deal without ever going on record himself. When he owned a coffeehouse in Chicago, for example, he'd express interest in a manager's act and would maneuver the man into saying that his artist would appear there on a particular night for, say, six hundred dollars. He'd never say those terms were acceptable to him, only attractive or interesting or any other shadowy term that implied his general agreement. Nevertheless, he'd lead the man into believing a deal had been made and a signed contract would be forthcoming. Then, a few days before the date, the manager would discover that Albert hadn't sent him a contract. And when he finally got one—too late, of course, to change the performer's arrangements—the terms would be altered significantly in Albert's favor. At which point the manager had no choice other than to cancel his artist's appearance—for which he'd receive no money—or agree to Albert's revised terms.

Bob had heard all the stories going around about Albert. He knew people thought the man was sleazy. Manny Greenhill, Joan Baez's manager, had laid it out for him one night at Folk City after Bob told Manny about Albert's offer to manage him. Manny had, on several occasions, been burned by Albert Grossman and told Bob so, sparing none of the gory details. But he also considered Albert to be the most talented of all the managers in the folk field. "Whatever you do, be careful how long you commit yourself to Grossman," he advised Bob, sidestepping the issue of ethics.

Greenhill's warning was echoed by others in the folk community. Dave Van Ronk, for one, considered Grossman to be "an astute but very cruel man—extraordinarily cruel in a very cold and calculated way." He perceived Albert's interaction with the young Village folksingers as "a kind of Mephistophelian role," in which he guaranteed stardom in return for their integrity. "He corrupted Noel [Stookey] and was working on Bobby with a vengeance," Van Ronk notes. "Even though we all knew Albert was a man who could make things happen, his interest in Bobby made me uneasy and I was concerned for [Dylan's] welfare."

Van Ronk recounted his talk with Grossman about becoming part of Peter, Paul & Mary, as well as another illuminating encounter. As Van Ronk tells the story, "I ran into Albert at a party and before long we were off in a corner together, ruminating about the business. 'Dave,' he said, 'I know how I can make a fortune for you. If this doesn't work, I just don't know the business, and to show you how sure I am of it I will personally guarantee you a three hundred thousand dollars gross for your first year.' As Albert saw it, I didn't have to change my style of singing or my repertoire, I just had to change my name—to Olaf the Blues Singer—and I had to wear a helmet with horns growing out of it and pretend to be blind. I laughed, thinking the scheme was a marvelous joke, but he wasn't kidding. He wanted to turn me into a novelty act, not out of avarice or marketability, but because it would prove that I was corruptible. Integrity bothered Albert; he used to say that there was no such thing as an honest man, and it was merely a question of finding out what my price was, even if it cost him three hundred thousand dollars of his own money. That was the kind of guy Albert really was."

This splash of hubris was indicative of an attitude Albert Grossman had perfected since first appearing on the folk scene in Chicago. Around 1950, he and a classmate opened a nightclub there called the Gate of Horn, which attracted the cream of the city's bohemian artistes. Its success also drew a heady clientele that included Saul Bellow, Nelson Algren, Isaac Rosenfeld, Lionel Trilling, William Styron, and the Second City crowd, which had begun to make its mark nationally for producing inventive comic stylists. Night after night, Al Grossman played host to the Gate's mix of culture vultures and local celebrities. While a folksinger performed in the main room, Al chatted with the "dignitaries" out front at the long, crowded bar, working very hard to create an atmosphere of cultural sophistication. Taste, refinement, provocative conversation, political and intellectual savvy—these are the qualities Al Grossman sought to cultivate as part of the Gate's highbrow mystique and the same ones he eventually passed on to the performers he represented.

To those who knew him well, the mystery was not how, but *where,* Albert Grossman acquired his appetite for life's finer trappings. The son of a working-class tailor from the North Side of Chicago, Al was raised in a surprisingly common and unaffected manner. It wasn't until later on that he began developing a persona for himself. Much like his protégé Bob Dylan, Albert concocted an apocryphal autobiography, telling friends he graduated from the University of Chicago (he didn't) and walked away from a promising career in city government. In fact, it was nothing more than a briefly held tenure with the Chicago Housing Authority as a management aide for Deerborne Homes, an all-black public housing development on the city's impoverished South Side, from which he was summarily dismissed for "gross irregularities." Convinced that he was no longer employable, Albert persuaded college chum Les Brown (who later became *The New York Times* TV critic) to put up half the money to open the Gate, which, although only moderately successful in a financial sense, became *the* place in Chicago to make the scene.

Sometime during the fall of 1961, Grossman phoned his lawyer, Sam Freifeld, and announced that he was leaving Chicago and the nightclub business. "I'm going to New York to manage the greatest folksinger in the world," he told Freifeld, who was offered a chance to get in on the ground floor of this opportunity of a lifetime. "Be at The Bear [a small club owned by Second City cofounder Howard Alk] at eleven o'clock tomorrow morning. I want you to hear him."

The next day, Freifeld dutifully took a seat at one of The Bear's dark and deserted tables. As the lawyer remembers it, "Bobby Dylan was on stage with his guitar and harmonica performing for Albert and Howard. Nobody else was in the place. After two songs, I leaned over and asked Albert, 'Is that the greatest folksinger in the world?' He nodded and said, 'Yes.' To which I whispered in his ear, 'You're out of your fucking mind.' And I left."

Within weeks, Grossman sold his interest in the Gate of Horn and opened a New York management office whose official roster consisted of a number of distinguished folk acts, the least of which happened to be Peter, Paul & Mary and the still-unknown Bob Dylan. Grossman's objective, of course, was to fashion an entertainment empire from the nursery of talented folklings wandering the Street. Yet he also sought the kind of cultural mandate entitling him to turn out artists with an unmistakable Albert Grossman imprimatur. "Albert envisioned himself as a cultural messiah," says Chicago folksinger Bob Gibson, an early Grossman client. "For his artist, talent was always an incidental part of the package. The highest priority was given to *class.* You had to, in some way, embody Albert's elitist tendencies, which also meant taking regular instruction and criticism from him and assuming aspects of his personality."

No doubt, image was an important feature of Grossman's management technique. He enjoyed recreating the artists he represented to suit his messianic ambitions. With Bob Dylan, he was prepared to take his image-making one step further. Harnessing Bob's sense of inspiration, rebellion, exaggeration, peculiarity, posturing, and conceit, Grossman intended to create a *legend.* Bob's extraordinary talent already guaranteed him a retinue of fans. Albert's goal was to somehow elevate that enthusiasm to a level that separated his new client from every other performer, so that no comparisons could be drawn between Bob and . . . *anyone.* Dylan would be the king, like Elvis, but only in stature, because his appeal was intellectual as well as emotional, and that made him unique as far as Albert was concerned. In Albert's eyes, Bob was in a class all by himself, and he was going to make damned sure he remained there.

The easiest way to do that was to perpetuate Bob's image as an original and to see that it went unchallenged. Albert devoted most of his time to "the Dylan mystique," as he began referring to it. Like a motivational therapist, he conducted countless pep talks designed to reassure Bob how special he was, and how insignificant everyone else was by comparison. Albert had nothing but contempt for the other performers on the Street. They were *ordinary,* he said, pronouncing the epithet in the same tone of voice Ronald Reagan used to say *liberals.* Bob, on the other hand, was an artist, and it was about time he began carrying himself like one.

Grossman's formula for the Bob Dylan legend can be summed up in one word: mystery. People grow increasingly curious about an unknown quantity; give them no information about yourself and you wind up actually feeding their curiosity. All in all, it was a nifty piece of advice from a man who claimed to have studied philosophy with Bruno Bettelheim (but hadn't). As far as the press was concerned, Albert advised Bob to ignore all requests for interviews. He considered journalists nothing more than parasites, either bloodsuckers or sycophants who would take your words and use them to their own advantage. He concluded the press was useless to an artist like Bob, whose talent transcended conventional critical response. If he had to be interviewed, then by all means be vague, or better yet—*inscrutable.* God knows, Bob had a gift for that.

Another of Grossman's commandments was: Stay out of the public eye. Even at this early stage of the game he warned Bob about overexposure—in order not to dilute the mystery. And he advised him to separate himself from the riff-raff. Almost overnight Bob Dylan became a recluse. Suddenly he was unavailable to his friends, suspicious of their intentions—*paranoid.* The most widely asked question on the Street around Christmas 1961, was: "What's gotten into Bobby?" And who in the hell did he think he was? "I remember him when he was a nothing," someone at the Gaslight was overheard to say, to which Dave Van Ronk responded: "Funny—he's *still* a nothing."

Strangely enough, Van Ronk's assessment of Bob's status couldn't have been more accurate. Bob's October concert debut at the Carnegie Chapter Hall was a resounding failure. His disappointment and embarrassment over the handful of people in the audience caused him to perform with obvious indifference. Even more frustrating was his recording career. By the end of 1961, Columbia still hadn't released Bob's album, and people were beginning to wonder if the record would ever find its way into the stores. Bob couldn't get a straight answer out of anyone at the label. All he was told was that the powers-that-be didn't think it was the right time to introduce a new folksinger.

John Hammond Sr. was just as discouraged by Columbia's failure to release *Bob Dylan*. Word had gotten back to him that people within the company were put off by the record. Dylan's voice eluded them. He wasn't your obvious teenage heartthrob. They couldn't find a track with an ounce of pop-single potential, nor did it seem to have a prayer of getting any top forty airplay. They knew it was impossible to break out a new artist without a hit single. Why should they waste their time working on an artist who was never going to pay off?

Hammond was pissed off at the lukewarm reaction and put pressure on David Kapralik to give the album a decent push. Characteristically, Kapralik indulged Hammond—he gave him every assurance that his men were behind the album, that the sales force was enthusiastic, that the guys in the field were knocked out by it. All the usual bullshit. Then he put it out of his mind. Kapralik knew the score. Some of his staff were already referring to the project as "Hammond's Folly." The old guy might have picked winners in the 1930s, 1940s, and 1950s, but those golden ears of his were obviously out of tune with what was happening in the 1960s. There was no way Kapralik was going to put himself on the line for a stiff like Bob Dylan. The bottom line was that the album only cost about four hundred dollars to record—pocket money by current standards. It would probably be cheaper *not* to release it than to throw expensive promotional support behind the record.

Hammond was nobody's fool, however, and he could spot a brush-off a mile away. It wasn't the first time in his career that people who considered themselves in-the-know laughed at him. "It was the same way the first time I played Billie Holiday's record," Hammond recalled with glee. "So to me, this kind of negative reaction was almost a recommendation, and I was more determined than ever to get Bobby's album released."

Hammond knew Kapralik wasn't going to be of any help to him. He considered Kapralik nothing more than a shoe salesman, an industry term that meant a guy *sold* records but knew nothing about making music. So he went over Kapralik's head to his old friend and ally, Goddard Leiberson, who was not only president of the CBS record division, but, more important, a confidante of Babe Paley, the boss's wife. With Leiberson's help, Hammond gained the promise of a March 1962 release date for Bob's album and reestablished his political influence at the label.

Bob, of course, knew nothing of the controversy at Columbia Records. He was too busy preparing himself for stardom. He and Albert Grossman discussed plans for a concert tour and a music publishing company to exploit Bob's songs. Then, of course, there was the album cover to think about. Bob had his heart set on wearing a sheepskin jacket for the picture, because he liked the way Ian Tyson (of the Canadian folk-duo Ian and Sylvia) looked wearing one on his album. Bob and Suze combed the East Village head shops for sheepskin but found the real thing was out of his price range. Instead they settled on a jacket made out of phony suede with a pile lining, figuring nobody would be able to spot the difference on an album cover. In the meantime, Bob worked on liner notes for the record along with Robert Shelton, who agreed to write a glowing endorsement under the nom de plume Stacey Williams, since it would have been regarded as unethical for a *New York Times* critic to objectively review an album that carried his byline on its back cover.

Bob Dylan was finally released on March 19, 1962, with minimal fanfare. Aside from a few polite reviews, the album was overlooked by the media and record-buying public alike. Columbia, as expected and as it has demonstrated throughout the years, bailed out early, drawing the pursestrings on its promotional support. Only a few hundred copies were sold in the first six months. As several thousand had been pressed, the rest were quickly marked down and transferred to cutout bins in order to deplete the overstock.

John Hammond was enraged that *Bob Dylan,* "a masterpiece of intelligence and style," had been sabotaged by pencil-pushing Neanderthals. Shoe salesmen! He petitioned Columbia Records' legal department to pick up the option on Bob's contract so they could get to work on a second album. What was normally a routine procedure turned into weeks of bureaucratic delay until Hammond identified the obstruction: David Kapralik had begun filing the necessary paperwork to drop the folksinger's contract. Kapralik's disenchantment with "Hammond's Folly" was no secret around the Columbia offices. The record company had moved strongly into the pop music fold, and artists like Bob Dylan were standing in the way of his plans to revitalize the roster. Kapralik's position was bolstered by his young staff, which considered Bob too esoteric for their taste.

Once again, John Hammond staged a showdown with Kapralik. Cornering the A&R chief in the corridor, Hammond gave him hell for the way the record company had undermined Bob Dylan's record. To his credit, Kapralik stood his ground. He admitted his disinterest as well as his intention to drop Bob from the label as soon as the contract expired. "Over my dead body!" Hammond screamed, oblivious to the small crowd that had gathered near to where the two men stood. Kapralik, who was aware of the older man's heart condition, took Hammond at his word and backed down. The last thing he wanted was to be held responsible for killing one of the most beloved figures in the music business. If Bob Dylan meant that much to him, then so be it. Let the old guy fall on his own failures. In a few years, he reasoned, no one would remember the Bob Dylan name anyway.

12

The Look of Love

Suze Rotolo remained Bob's faithful cheerleader throughout the drought between record albums. From late 1961 until the following year she was the perfect "folksinger's chick": supportive, deferential, adoring, indulgent, nurturing, carnal, and *invisible.* She catered to Bob's most essential and neglected needs, inspiring in him the most beautiful songs he ever composed. But she also played into the hands of Albert Grossman and others who sought to isolate Bob from the old MacDougal Street mob and to groom the Dylan legend.

From the start, Albert urged Bob to think of himself solely as a *concert* artist. Coffeehouses were for schleppers. And Albert wasn't interested in handling anyone incapable of earning fifty thousand dollars a year. That must have sounded like an extraordinary sum to Bob, who was used to making seventy-five to a hundred dollars on a good week. Yet Albert assured him that financial success wasn't far off. He needed only to come up with the right strategy to attract national attention.

Consciously or not, Bob knew the answer lay in his ability to write songs. He would definitely have to sharpen his material if he was going to work in concert halls and produce hit records. The first album wasn't going to do the trick. Even before it was released, Bob regarded it with distaste. The songs were uneven; his performance was uninspired. Despite the warm reception it received from folk-pals like Dave Van Ronk and Tom Paxton, Bob knew the record wasn't anything special, and he began working on material for a sequel.

Determined not to sound like everybody else, Bob decided to rely entirely on his own experiences and what was going on in his head. Today, of course, that's a pretty routine practice. But in 1961 it represented an incredible departure. Back then, you'd have been hard-pressed to find a single songwriter saying anything personal or commenting on society in a way that provoked a listener's response. It took an incredible amount of guts for a twenty-one-year-old to put himself on the line like that. Or maybe just the opposite, maybe it took some impetuous young buck to jump off the deep end without giving too much thought to the process. Either way, as 1961 drew to a close, Bob Dylan began working on a portfolio of new songs that would eventually alter the direction of folk and popular music.

Suze remembers those days as some of the most productive in Bob Dylan's life. "He used to sit in a bar or at one of the outdoor cafes on Bleecker Street and write all day," she says of that time. "Then, at night, he'd get out a yellow pad or find a typewriter and go at it until he gave out. He was always working on something—*always*. Or listening."

Like most novelists, Bob had an ear that was finely tuned to conversation. He would eavesdrop on people and scribble down things they said. Or he'd lift ideas from rap sessions with his friends. "He absorbed things, like a *sponge,*" Suze recalls, using the most frequently employed word to describe Bob during that period. "Somebody would read or tell him something about a poet or an artist, and he'd use it to produce something uniquely his own. He'd take them over every trivial detail about it. Then, later, I'd hear what they said in a slightly different form in one of his songs. He was influenced by everything and everybody."

What Bob was doing was no more or no less than what most serious writers had done for centuries. "Use what you see around you" is the first lesson taught in any college writing seminar. Woody himself said: "The best stuff you can sing about is what you saw and if you look hard enough you can see plenty to sing about." So that calling the young Bob Dylan a sponge, an exploiter, and a professional vampire as it applied to his writing was a fair, if unreproachful evaluation of an exceptionally creative artist at work. Nevertheless, it augured a significant change in Bob—in the way he approached his work as well as the way in which he regarded himself—that drove a wedge between him and the gang with whom he lived on the Street.

Songwriting had become the new religion in Greenwich Village, and the popular belief was that Bob Dylan had somehow acquired The Word. His tunes were getting a lot of favorable recognition; he was attracting unparalleled professional attention. Suddenly, both his friends and the folksingers who usually avoided him began to take an interest in what he was doing. They wanted to talk about songwriting with him, perhaps collaborate on a few things. Maybe Bob could put in a good word for them with John Hammond or Albert Grossman or one of the other bigwigs responsible for his success.

"Bob grew basically paranoid and wary of people on the Street," Suze recalls. Very early on she was given instructions concerning friends who wanted to know what was up with Bob, such as "You don't talk about anything," and "You don't tell anybody anything." Says Suze: "He was suspicious of all the attention he was receiving. He thought it was basically false and didn't want anybody getting too close." Part of that was Albert's doing—keeping him separate from the other folksingers—and part of it developed as he recognized he was more talented than the rest of the crowd. That was something Bob wasn't naive about. From the beginning, he talked a lot about becoming very famous. But it was the professional jealousy that really contributed to his paranoia. "He talked a lot about friends being jealous of him—wanting something from him," Suze recalls. "And the more attention that was focused on Bob, the more he began to withdraw from the scene."

These changes in Bob's personality confused Suze, who had only just turned eighteen. As early as December 1961, she expressed difficulty dealing with the responsibilities that came with being "Dylan's girl." In a letter to her friend, Sue Zuckerman, she wrote: "Things are going fantastically unbelievably great for the Pig [her affectionate nickname for Bob]. Things are happening to him that only happen in the movies...take my word for it: they'll be selling Bob Dylan hats pretty soon....John Hammond, the guy who discovered the Pig and is doing all for him, completely flipped. I swear, if Dylan vomited into the microphone, Hammond would say, 'Great, Bob, but try it again with harmony.'

"I don't want to get sucked under by Bob Dylan and his fame. I really don't. It sort of scares me. I'm glad and all, but I just have a funny feeling about it.... It really changes a person completely when they become well-known by all and sundry. They develop this uncontrollable egomania. It's weird because it can happen to the humblest and inferior-complex person [sic] too. Something snaps somewhere, and suddenly the person can't see anything at all except himself and herself. And even if they see or are aware of other things it's only an awareness in relation to themselves and their enlarged ego.... I can see it happening to Bobby, and I've tried to tell him in so many ways but it's really useless, it really is. Each day it gets harder."

Sue Zuckerman was alarmed by the tone of Suze's letter. "She was obviously in trouble," Zuckerman recalls thinking at the time. "I was away at school and decided to go to New York and get in touch with Suze—maybe help her out with some of the problems she was having with Bob—but by the time I got there it seems they already had a place of their own."

Tired of crashing on people's couches, Bob decided it was time to take up permanent residence in the Village. One afternoon in January, he and Suze cruised the narrow streets west of Sixth Avenue and stumbled upon a tiny one-bedroom apartment in a walk-up on West Fourth Street. The neighborhood's trashy allure suited them perfectly—licks of honky-tonks, record stores, sandal shops, greasy spoons that were open until four in the morning. It was a five-minute walk to MacDougal Street, just around the corner from Suze's mother, and a couple of blocks from Carla's. A major thoroughfare for Bob's folk pals. And the apartment was cozy and pleasant, with enough Village charm to compensate for the lack of living space it offered. Without a moment's hesitation, Bob signed the lease, although, hesitant until she turned eighteen—no longer jailbait—he and Suze intended to live there together despite her mother's objections.

Mary Rotolo not only disapproved of their cohabitation, she loathed Bob and his dowry of lies. "I didn't trust him and I didn't like him and I certainly didn't want him living under the same roof with my daughter," she says in reference to Suze's decision. "I mean, there were so many things *not* to like about Bobby. He was terribly dirty-looking, he smelled bad, he was very unhygienic (we used to talk about his green teeth), he wasn't particularly generous, and his attitude left a lot to be desired. I had my daughter's welfare to think of. And I don't think it's out of line to say that Bobby Dylan was not the stuff of every mother's dreams."

But then Mary Rotolo wasn't anyone's idea of a typical mother. Relenting without giving them her blessing, she invited the kids to drop by whenever they pleased and doubled her efforts to have Carla keep an eye on Suze. Says Mary, "I figured there were enough people I knew watching out for her. After all, they were only kids and would eventually move on to other things. Certainly no harm could come of it."

For the first few months that Bob and Suze lived as a couple their life was happy and peaceful. Suze decorated the place with thrift-shop furnishings and chatchkas. Bob built in bookshelves and a TV cabinet. A tiny table he made stood in the kitchen portion of their living room—any minute you'd expect Ralph and Alice Kramden to waltz through the door. Everyone agreed the place had a homey feel to it. Suze's artwork perked up the faded walls. Naturally Bob kept his guitar and notebook lying around in order to seize the moment when inspiration struck. He taught Suze how to play the autoharp, and the lovebirds spent many nights harmonizing to their folk and rock favorites long after the coffeehouses had closed. There was a lot of happiness in that Fourth Street apartment during the early part of 1962. The folk scene was in full bloom, and everyone on the Street coveted an invitation to the Dylans' new pad.

"I remember Peter Yarrow hearing about the place and saying, 'Let's have dinner!'" Suze recalls. "I didn't even know how to cook a steak, but Bob wanted to impress him so I decided to give it my best shot."

That night, while Suze pfumfed around the kitchen, the phone rang. Bob picked it up and heard a familiar voice on the other end of the line. Mark Spoelstra, who'd been off doing a gig in Toronto, was at the airport and wanted to get together with his friends. Bob hemmed and hawed. "Yarrow was some sort of big deal to Bob," Spoelstra explains, sensing at the time that his call was an imposition. Bob's attitude wasn't difficult to assess: Yarrow was on his way up, while Spoelstra seemed happy to continue playing for nickels and dimes.

Bob was in the process of outgrowing his friendship with Mark, but he invited him to stop over anyway in time to witness Suze's culinary debut.

As Spoelstra remembers it, dinner turned out to be the least remarkable event of the evening. "I expected to find the same rascally Dylan that I'd hung around with in the Village," he says, "only when I got there, he and Yarrow acted like a couple of fat cats. I couldn't believe it. They were sitting around talking Big Bucks. Yarrow was going on about Peter, Paul & Mary's airplane, limos here and there, and how, in a few years, they could retire for life. There were Big Bucks to be made, everyone was going to be rich. Bob was really excited about that. He was drinking it all in."

Prosperity wasn't the only thing being swallowed at Dylan's table that night. Bob had a particular fondness for red wine and, to Dave Van Ronk's recollection, he enjoyed drinking *vino shitto* as well as any folksinger on a coffeehouse income. "But here was Peter Yarrow talking about *vintages!*" Spoelstra says. "They were smelling the corks of wines he'd brought to dinner, passing burgundies and bordeaux around like they were the crown jewels. You'd have thought I'd walked in on a dinner party of wealthy industrialists."

"I remember thinking, 'What the hell happened while I was in Toronto?'" Spoelstra says. "The object of our closely knit folk community had always been to sing and have fun. And suddenly it seemed as if everything had changed."

Spoelstra's observation carried the scope of "moment" with it—the moment when a historical transition could actually be seen by the human eye. Just as vacationers to Key West, Florida, report seeing a green flash at the precise moment the sun sets on the horizon, Spoelstra, too, was witness to an epiphany, only in this case it was the green flash of *money,* and it signified the point at which folk music merged with show business. Until that time, folk music, like the blues, was an art form symbolically identified with poverty. It was the music of the masses; it chronicled the struggle of the working class and was handed down orally from generation to generation. Woody Guthrie often referred to it as the "people's form of expression," and, in fact, it had been the populist elements of the Old Left that kept folk music alive throughout the last thirty years. Now, suddenly, folksingers sampled the nectar of prosperity and found that it tasted pretty damn good.

The notion that folksingers and money didn't mix was becoming obsolete. They were no longer playing the music of itinerant Okies. It wasn't even the music of America's poor and underprivileged classes. The folk being sung in coffeehouses was the music of middle-class intellectuals who'd been weaned on the principles of ambition, hard work, and prosperity.

As we know, Bob Dylan didn't set out from Hibbing to be a penniless troubadour; he was determined to be a *star*. Stars made big bucks, rode in fancy cars, and drank great wines. Anyway, Bob's earliest role models weren't folksingers but rock 'n roll stars who basked in their lucre. Elvis was always being photographed tooling around in one of his Cadillacs or showing off his mansion. Little Richard was a wardrobe junkie á la Liberace. And Jerry Lee Lewis displayed a genius for self-promotion. For now, Bob was satisfied just to be able to pay the rent on his tiny flat, but success was never going to pose much of a problem for him.

Neither were the folksingers on the Street who couldn't make the grade. In no time it became obvious to Bob that the lines were drawn between those who had what it took and those who didn't. Peter Yarrow had it; Albert Grossman certainly had it; Dave Van Ronk, Tom Paxton, and, later, Phil Ochs and Eric Andersen had it. Mark Spoelstra, on the other hand, was a perennial bystander or, as he says of himself, "the kind of guy who gets in the back of the line and waits." It was probably that very lack of drive which ultimately caused Bob to distance himself from Mark.

Spoelstra traces the root of their problem to a party one Sunday afternoon in the same Greenwich Village building where Suze's mother lived. Each weekend, the young MacDougal Street crowd gathered at the apartment of Mikki Isaacson, a woman who fancied herself a patron of the neo-Beatnik scene, where they passed the guitar and, in return, were guaranteed a great meal. Unbeknownst to anyone but Mikki, Spoelstra had begun writing his own songs, and when it was his turn up at bat she goaded him into playing one of them. Mark's selection was a typically forgettable ballad, a real hack job by his own admission. After that he ceded the floor to Bob, who strummed through an unfinished version of what was to become "Blowin' in the Wind." The group acted as if it had just experienced a divine revelation. Jaws hung open to the floor; a few of the listeners grew teary-eyed; there wasn't an impassive face in the bunch. When the praise died down, Spoelstra blurted out, "Hey—I'm not writing any songs that good!"

The look on Mikki Isaacson's face said, "No shit, Sherlock!" Maneuvering her two prodigies into a corner, she pleaded, "Bobby—help him. What's he doing wrong with his songs?" Bob gazed at their hungry, fawning faces and immediately checked into the twilight zone. "Uh, I dunno," he muttered, searching for a quick escape route. "How come your songs are touching and his aren't?" Mikki persisted. "Help him, Bobby—show him how it's done."

This was exactly the kind of situation Bob Dylan dreaded. It embarrassed him. He was in the midst of developing his own songwriting technique, working it out for himself, experimenting with a number of different voices. The last thing he needed was to coddle every folkie who wanted to try his hand at songwriting. Ever since the Columbia Records contract every nudnick with a guitar sucked up to Bob, hoping he would share his secret with them, his Betty Crocker Easy Songwriting Recipe. And when that didn't work out, they attempted to imitate him. Even today, Spoelstra admits he became a songwriter because Bob was having success with it. "I figured—Jesus, if he can do it, so can I," Spoelstra says, echoing a theory that, at the time, was common on the Street. From the beginning Bob identified this as a form of jealousy and went out of his way to avoid it. But people like Mikki Isaacson thought that Bob owed his friends a hand. "Give him a break, Bobby," she insisted. "Show Mark what he's doing wrong."

Bob shrugged and said, "Uh, I dunno. Maybe you're using too many long words. It's not necessary to get your point across. Try working simpler phrases to express the basic emotions." Mikki beamed at Mark as if he'd just been blessed by the Pope, then drifted back to her guests. When she was gone, Bob looked awkwardly at his friend. "Look, I don't know, maybe I'm wrong," he apologized. Then he quickly grabbed his guitar and left.

That kind of slobbering was the easiest way to alienate yourself from Bob. He detested being put on a pedestal; it turned him right off and served to do nothing more than arouse his suspicions. Friends interpreted this as a sign of paranoia. But more likely, Bob was protecting himself from the growing circle of no-talents and hangers-on who crowded into the scene. At some point, he must have looked around and realized that no one else could hold a candle to what he was doing. And no doubt it was a very lonely, albeit instructive, realization. Talent, as Bulwer-Lytton wrote, does what it can, while genius does what it must, and for Bob Dylan there was never any alternative but to isolate himself from the rabble and write.

Over the next few months, Bob produced a number of songs that established him as the premier folksinger on the Street. The first batch—"Ballad for a Friend," "Ballad of Donald White," "Let Me Die in My Footsteps," "Man on the Street," "The Death of Emmett Till," and "Mixed-Up Confusion"—were slapdash attempts at imitating his early folk heroes Woody Guthrie and Hank Williams. "Donald White," "Emmett Till," and "Man on the Street," all about men who were victimized by the system, illustrate the role of the modern folksinger in the act of exposing miscarriages of justice. The protest song had come of age. Still experimenting with his voice, Bob used lurid descriptions of wrongdoing to get his points across, but the songs were rife with simplistic images and a preponderance of moon-and-June rhymes.

It wasn't until April, when he completed "Blowin' in the Wind," that Bob incorporated the alchemy of poetry and metaphor to communicate more subtle messages in his songs. Familiarity has made "Blowin' in the Wind" a fixture of America's musical heritage and arguably the only song written in the 1960s that will endure a hundred years from now. Yet it remains as distinctive for its *lack* of substance as it does for how listeners interpret its meaning. A sequence of portentous social questions, it isn't so much a statement as an expression of abstract ideas. Bob doesn't presume to have the answers to these questions. They're all "blowin' in the wind"—a graceful, musical answer that suggests the zen notions of meditation and eternity. The song has a very soothing effect owing to its clever phrasing and cadence, as well as a beautiful melody. Critics, however, felt it was nothing more than a "grocery list" of histrionic social questions; shuffle them and the result is virtually the same—rhetorical rhyme without reason—regardless of the order in which they come up. Champions of the song argued that Bob merely verbalized questions that were on everyone's mind; the answers weren't as important as the song's power to get people to think about them. Therefore it is double ironic that the song—controversial for its *lack* of content—helped to establish Bob Dylan as the poet-philosopher of his generation.

Bob finished "Blowin' in the Wind" in one sitting at the Commons, a MacDougal Street cafe across from the Gaslight. Later that same evening, he took the song over to Folk City, where, between sets, he played it for Gil Turner, who emceed the club's Monday night hootenannies. Turner was knocked out by it and talked Bob into teaching it to him on the spot. They went over it a couple times in the basement. Then, when the show resumed, Turner taped a copy of the lyrics to the mike stand and announced, "Ladies and gentlemen, I'd like to sing a new song by one of our great songwriters. It's hot off the pencil, and here it goes."

According to custodians of the Dylan legend, the entire audience jumped to its feet and cheered as Turner stretched out the final palpitant "innnnn the wiiiind." Bob stood at the darkened bar like Rocky Balboa, grinning numbly as the spotlight fell on him. "Bob Dylan, ladies and gentlemen. How 'bout a hand for a great, new songwriter. Bob Dylan . . . " More applause thundered through the room, and in a manger on MacDougal Street a star was born.

That version has a pleasing historical elegance to it, although not everyone shared the same reaction. The following day Bob played "Blowin' in the Wind" for Dave Van Ronk over at the West Fourth Street apartment. Van Ronk listened politely and then bellowed, "Jesus, Bobby—what an incredibly dumb song! I mean, what the hell is 'blowing in the wind?'" Van Ronk dismissed the song as a throwaway. As he recalls, "I figured Bobby could grind out a tune like that on the worst day he ever had in his life." But maybe six weeks later, Van Ronk witnessed a scene that made him realize his mistake. "I was walking through Washington Square Park," he says, "and heard a kid singing: 'How much wood could a woodchuck chuck if a woodchuck could chuck wood/ The answer, my friend, is blowin' in the wind.' At that point, I knew Bobby had a smash on his hands!"

It would take practically a year for "Blowin' in the Wind" to evolve into the smash that Van Ronk predicted; nevertheless, the song earned Bob the respect of most of his peers and recognition as folk music's rising young phenom. By the beginning of summer, Bob was cranking out songs faster than a Detroit assembly line. He had written a few things with political overtones and was trying them out immediately in front of the socially conscious college crowd that packed into his gigs.

"Talkin' John Birch Paranoid Blues" was an early rap song that needled the rednecks with one-liners pigeonholing their superpatriotic exploits. Bob remained faithful to Woody Guthrie's talking-blues form but updated the lyrics with such familiar 1960s images as TV sets and the movie *Exodus,* which the Birchers had labeled Communist propaganda. And like Woody, Bob showed himself to be an effective social satirist. Presenting himself as an upstanding, flag-waving American citizen, he attempts to root out potential Reds, searching for them in the glove compartment of his car, up the chimney, even inside his toilet bowl—a hideout Bob proposes with deadpan earnestness. Driven to the brink by anticommunist hysteria, he "discovered they wus *red* stripes on the American flag!" Then, running out of Reds to point the finger at, he figures the only one left to investigate was himself. It was a delicious piece of commentary that delighted the audience every time he played it.

"Long Ago, Far Away," another topical song, was too primitive and sophomoric to be considered witty; yet it was equally popular for its message. In seven interconnected verses, Bob unreels the history of social injustice, from the crucifixion of Christ to slavery to world war to lynchings, with the sarcastic refrain that things like that don't happen anymore. The song's noisy conclusion didn't seem to matter. After all, the country's civil rights awareness was in full bloom. The papers were full of demonstrations and threats of sit-ins. JFK campaigned actively for racial equality. When Bob offered his two-cents worth in song, the audience ate it right up. Especially in New York City, where college kids were out front every night devouring what Bob said. Young, middle-class Jewish intellectuals, they hungered for someone to put ideas into their heads, someone who wasn't standing in front of a classroom, someone who shared their background and their illusions. When Bob sang, it seemed to cut through all the bullshit; what he said gave them something to chew on. They also dug the way he looked and acted. His was the voice of change. There were dozens of crusading folksingers on the Street, but most of them were self-righteous and had a hard time drawing a full house. Most of them patterned their shows after Bob's, mimicking his protest songs, his manner of dress, and his hipness. But these kids could see right through the cheap imitations. Why settle for rank substitutes when Bob Dylan was the real thing?

Now that the kids had discovered Bob, his peers started to come around more often. Van Ronk, Paxton, Buffy Sainte-Marie, Jose Feliciano, Judy Collins, Peter Yarrow, Richie Havens—they all loved Dylan's new stuff. Even the Old Guard, those ridiculously boring traditionalists whose days on the Street were numbered, no longer treated him like an insignificant twerp. Some even performed his songs in their own sterile way. It became chic to cop the newest Dylan tune, to be the first one on the Street to put one in your act. Whenever Bob played a set at Gerdes or the Gaslight, the club swarmed with folksingers who were appearing at nearby coffeehouses. Excuses were always made about how it was natural for them to catch each other's shows, but Bob had become the folksinger's folksinger and they were there to listen and learn.

Suze watched the metamorphosis with mounting apprehension. The attention being lavished on Bob seemed unnatural to her. The interest in his music was loaded with ambiguity. She didn't mind the boost to his career or the incentive it produced in him to write, but everyone seemed to have ulterior motives for their sudden attraction to Bob. It was almost as if the closer they got to him, the better their chances were that some of his talent and good fortune would rub off.

Suze also realized that being Bob's friend conferred affiliate membership in the MacDougal Street mafia—a clique whose privilege was not to be underestimated. Like the Beat writers and "sick" comics before them, the Village folksingers were a group whose time had come. Opportunity prevailed for anyone who looked the part and could write a few decent songs. Maynard Solomon, who owned Vanguard Records, revitalized his little jazz label with folksingers from the Village talent pool. Jac Holtzman, who ran a hole-in-the-wall record store on West Tenth Street, signed up plenty of Bob's pals to record for his folk label, Elektra Records. Club owners hired their acts from the close-knit circle of performers that had established itself as folk music's dominant voice. And Bob Dylan emerged as its spokesman. It paid to travel in his shadow.

In time, however, Suze felt that her identity was being eclipsed by Bob's lightning ascent. On the Village scene, she was Dylan's girl, plain and simple. When she went out, everyone's attention was focused on Bob. People pumped her for information about him—how he was feeling, what he was up to, where he was playing, who he was hanging out with, what he was writing, why he was ignoring them?

Their curiosity was unquenchable, but no one showed any real interest in her other than the latest dish about her relationship with Bob.

She confessed to her friend Sue Zuckerman that Greenwich Village had become a dreadful place to live, and that "one can get into a terrible, horrible rut [there]." It wasn't fun for her anymore. Suze had completely neglected her art. Bob didn't encourage her to paint or to write poetry; she sensed he regarded it as competition and so, for the time being, she suppressed her creative impulses. Occasionally he told her "not to look so good" when they went out, which she took to be a warning against upstaging him. Says Suze now, "I remember thinking, 'I am not giving myself over to him one hundred percent—I cannot become dependent on him. If I do, I'm no person at all—I'm a thing.' But there was a conflict because I wasn't strong or secure enough to assert myself. And I was scared." All the excitement and confusion began to pile up on her. Suze was clearly depressed, and she began to drink more than usual.

Privately, friends and family members suggested to Suze that she might be happier if she gradually broke away from Bob. The Village was full of armchair shrinks who dished out their opinions with impunity: "Dump the guy!" "You're too good for him!" "He's suffocating you!" "He's a *folksinger!*" Carla Rotolo, who'd begun as Bob's biggest fan, saw the destructive effect he had on her sister and urged Suze to take better care of herself. Her mother, Mary, was less tactful. She detested the relationship. She wanted it to end, even if it meant putting distance between Suze and Bob. Mary had standing plans to spend six months in Italy and decided to leave at once and to take Suze along with her.

Now Suze was more confused than ever. Emotionally drained, she had to get away for a while and find herself, but the bottom line was that she really loved this guy. Despite all the bullshit, they were soulmates. Still, maybe a couple of months abroad was what the relationship really needed. It would give her some time to think and to grow up, and Bob could further his career without worrying about her needs. Not that he did anyway, but at least it wouldn't be such a tug-of-war.

When Bob heard the news, however, he went through the roof. The way he saw it, Suze was abandoning him when he needed her most, just when things were taking off. He knew things had been tough, but they were going to change. She'd see. He'd be more considerate. He loved her! In fact, maybe they should get *married.* Married! Bob was really putting himself on the line for her. He'd asked her to marry him, and it went right to Suze's heart—even though she never for a moment believed he'd follow through on it.

Mary Rotolo simply wouldn't hear of it. "He could date her all he wanted, they could even live together, but under no circumstances would I have permitted Suze to marry Bobby Dylan," she says today. "I just mistrusted him too much, and I told him so. Besides, Suze was still in her teens. They were both too young, and neither of them knew what they were doing."

So much for Mom's blessing. Still, Bob refused to take no for an answer. He'd stop by the apartment unannounced, chat up Mary, then gradually pop the old question again. Says Mary, "Bobby was a real courter. He'd be very disarming and all smiles, very flattering. 'Gee, that's a neat dinner you made.' He could charm the pants off me when he wanted. Then he'd get around to marriage and I'd stand my ground."

"Well, why don't you want us to get married?" he asked one night after a dinner at Mary Rotolo's apartment.

"I have my reasons."

Bob's eyes narrowed, he refused to back off. "Yeah, but what are they?"

Mary said, "I've already given them to you. You're both too young, and I don't know anything about you."

"Yes, you do," Bob insisted.

"I only know what you tell me, and frankly I don't believe too much of it. You know, Bobby, I think Zimmerman must be your real father and not your adoptive father."

That was all he was going to take from Suze's mom. Bob leaped up and shouted, "The trouble with you is you're an anti-Semite."

If this were a movie, the script would dictate a smash-cut to Pier 44 in Hoboken, from which Suze and her mother set sail on the U.S.S. *Rotterdam* that June. After much anguish, Suze agreed to make the trip, and at the last minute the gang from the Street came aboard to wish her a bon voyage. Bob acted like a condemned man. He was a basket case. Lillian Bailey, who accompanied him to Hoboken, remembers Bob as being "shattered." His eyes were filled with tears. As they walked toward the ocean liner, she took him into a flower shop and instructed him to buy Suze a dozen yellow tea roses. Bob balked at the suggestion. "You *have* to," Lillian insisted. Reluctantly, he bought the bouquet, but he was so embarrassed at the gesture that when the time came, he thrust the flowers in Suze's face, muttered "here," and promptly jumped ship.

For the next six months, radical emotional extremes jostled Bob's young soul. His girl—his *inspiration*—had sailed off to escape him at the very moment his career appeared ready to burst wide open. Bob grew despondent, he couldn't concentrate. It was too hard for him to be around the Village; Suze was everywhere but nowhere, and he couldn't function properly while her specter loomed overhead. A short trip to Minneapolis provided Bob with a temporary diversion, but before long he was overcome anew with thoughts of the dear departed Suze Rotolo.

Dave Van Ronk recalls this period with tactful compassion. "I remember we got a phone call from him at four or five o'clock in the morning," Van Ronk says. "Terri picked it up. Bobby said he was standing in a phone booth some place in Minneapolis. It was nineteen degrees below zero and he was crying. 'I want Suze!'" Van Ronk assured him that Suze wasn't there, she was in Europe. "You'd better go to bed, Bobby," he told him, worried that his friend was ruining his health.

Others, too, were concerned. On Bob's return from Minnesota, it was apparent that he'd lost a considerable amount of weight. His baby fat was gone, and he looked gaunt and frazzled. He seemed withdrawn. Some friends speculated he'd turned to drugs, but more likely he was simply heartbroken. Not that drugs weren't part of the scene. Everyone and his brother smoked grass. Bob had even done some peyote with interesting results. He also talked a good high. But as for the harder stuff—probably not. Psychedelics hadn't hit the Street yet, nor was heroin in vogue. Bob hadn't developed his sweet tooth in time to assuage the pain. But he sure looked the part.

Carla Rotolo recalls bumping into Bob that summer in Washington Square Park, where he went to watch the old men play chess. "I barely recognized him," she says. "He cut such a sad figure, and he was melancholy and listless. I'd never seen Bobby so depressed. Like everyone else, I was concerned about him, but not worried." They traded what information each had about Suze. Carla was on her way to meet Suze in Europe, but to her amazement Bob seemed to have talked with her sister almost daily, often ringing up overseas calls at a hundred dollars a clip. "What else have you been up to?" Carla asked, before going on her way. Bob shrugged and mumbled, "Nothing." Then, almost as an afterthought, he added, "Writin' songs."

The songs Bob so spiritlessly shrugged off, those he subordinated to the burdens of his heart, proved to be some of his early masterpieces. He had obviously examined his anguish in verse, converting his feelings into the seminal food of all great poets, and finished them as songs. "Masters of War" stood as a biting, personal statement opposing the military-industrial complex, but the rest were indisputably about Suze Rotolo.

"Tomorrow Is a Long Time," "Boots of Spanish Leather," and the trenchant, unremorseful "Don't Think Twice" came tumbling out of Bob's tidal grief. Now *those* were impressive songs! They were eloquently wrought, vigorous and impressionistic, lyrically simple and romantic. No offspring of Woody's tunes, they were spun with the graceful, expressive imagery of modern poetry and signified a complete break with the folk tradition that had trundled over from the nineteenth century. Noel Stookey, who later sang the vocal on the hit version of "Don't Think Twice," saw a definite transition of form emerge from these songs. He says, "It was obvious to us that Dylan was stretching the folk idiom and traditionalists were no longer going to be upheld. A new spirit had come."

Of "Don't Think Twice," Stookey says, "I thought it was beautiful—a masterful statement." Albert Grossman had played him an early version of the song, and he knew immediately that it was destined to be a classic. The lyric, now as familiar as any pop standard, was touching and evocative. Young audiences identified with its realistic account of lost love, probably because for once the narrator refused to gloss over its disappointments. Bob was bitter, full of regret, and the least bit vindictive. Feeling rebuffed, he managed to take a few swipes at his absent girlfriend's character, insinuating that she was immature, greedy in love, and an artless mistress who wasted his precious time.

The straightforward, no-bullshit approach struck a sympathetic chord with teenagers inasmuch as it reflected both the youthful anomie and new sensibility that foreshadowed the Sixties. Bob had found a way to vent some of the hostility and aggression heretofore masked by rock 'n roll, while retaining a haunting romanticism. The messages of both "Tomorrow Is a Long Time" and "Don't Think Twice" are no different from Elvis's "I'm a-so lonely I could die." Bob merely layered them with a dramatic, narrative complexity summoned from personal experience and the ability to express himself poetically.

Bob performed these songs regularly through the summer of 1962, and while they broadened his popular appeal, their content raised more than a few eyebrows. The source of the controversy was twofold. First, friends familiar with his domestic situation felt embarrassed by such a public disclosure. "The minute I heard 'Boots of Spanish Leather' I knew what it was about," Dave Van Ronk says, "The same thing with 'Don't Think Twice.' Bobby was rolling it out like a soap opera for everyone to hear. It was pathetic. The songs were so damn self-pitying—self-pitying but brilliant." Another close friend to Bob and Suze found it difficult to sit through his performances "because the stuff he was doing was so transparent and Suze wasn't around to defend herself."

A more delicate wrinkle arose over the authorship of "Don't Think Twice." No one complained about the lyric; it was so damn original that folksingers admitted losing sleep over it. But the melody had a familiar ring to it. Word began to spread that Bob had lifted it almost note for note from Paul Clayton's ballad, "Who's Gonna Buy Your Ribbon Saw." That in itself wasn't a contemptible offense. By definition, folk music encouraged an element of borrowing from sources to preserve its traditional flavor. But Bob not only ignored his debt to Clayton's composition; he copyrighted the tune in his own name without acknowledging its origins or, as was custom, listing the melody as "traditional."

Several folksingers complained that Bob had done Paul an injustice. There wasn't any question of Clayton's contribution, nor was Bob able to wriggle out of it by feigning ignorance. Some time before the song appeared, he ran into Clayton, Van Ronk, and Barry Kornfeld, another Village folksinger, at which time he said, "Hey, man—I really dig 'Who's Gonna Buy Your Ribbon Saw.' I'm gonna use that." No one gave it a second thought. Clayton himself had copied it from an old music-hall number called "Who's Gonna Buy Your Chickens When I'm Gone." The guys figured, "Fair enough—Bob'll probably do a nifty variation on the theme." Unfortunately, "Don't Think Twice" is a dead ringer for "Ribbon Saw."

To his credit, Paul Clayton, who was popular among fellow folk-singers for his agreeable and gentlemanly nature, bore Bob no malice. Especially since he admittedly lifted traditional tunes for his "original songs" all the time. Barry Kornfeld recalls, "One of Paul's favorite lines was: 'If you can't write, *re-write;* and if you can't re-write, *copyright.*' "* That's the kind of guy Clayton was—wonderfully ingenuous. And prolific. He was a walking encyclopedia of folk songs. Chronically broke, he traded in folklore to pay the bills. You could pocket a deuce to cut an album, so Clayton invented the concept of theme albums. He spent every spare minute he had in the studio making records like *Ork Hunting Ballads of the Inner Hebrides as Sung by Paul Clayton.* "So poor Pablo would have to go into the studio and record fourteen dog songs," Van Ronk remembers. "He was as poor as a churchmouse. Still, all of us profited from his vast knowledge of music. Including Bobby. That's why the 'Don't Think Twice' business made us all think it wasn't fair that Pablo should be scuffling as hard as he was. You could see the soles of his feet through his shoes. The honorable thing would have been for Bobby to cut him in on the copyright. But that wasn't Bobby's way."

Bobby's way, at least for the time being, was self-serving—licking his wounds, unburdening his heart, relying on the sympathy of friends. At times he was positively miserable to be around, unintentionally inconsiderate. He roamed MacDougal Street like a stray dog. The gang wrote it off to a case of heartsickness—"the Suzes," as one Dylan insider called it—though there were side effects they couldn't overlook.

One involved Bob's relationship with Columbia Records. From the start, it had been an uneasy affair. No one at the company aside from John Hammond seemed to appreciate him. They had delayed the release of the album. Worse, no one bought it, airplay was sparse. The publicity department managed to dredge up a couple of interviews, but only at magazines for teenage girls, where he pontificated between the beauty tips and makeovers. Bob was understandably disenchanted with the whole mess.

Hammond, however, believed the next album would win over an audience and instructed Bob to collect material for another session.

---

*Ironically, Clayton's witticism echoes T. S. Eliot, who wrote: "Immature poets imitate; mature poets steal." (*Philip Massingel,* 1920)

But before they could get into the studio, a letter was delivered to Columbia's legal department attempting to annul Bob's contract. It began, "In view of the fact that I was a minor when I signed my contract with Columbia Records, I hereby demand the return of all metal parts, masters, tapes, etc., and declare this contract null and void." The letter bore Bob's signature, but to Hammond it gave off the unmistakable stench of Albert Grossman.

Hammond was furious. The words "trust me!" rang in his ears like sterile thunder. That ungrateful little twerp! Hammond bulldozed his way into the office of Clive Davis, who was then Columbia's general attorney. "Can he do this?" Hammond wondered, admitting that he knew Bob was underage at the time of their original negotiation. Davis nodded grimly. He also pointed out that Bob's twenty-first birthday was only a few days off; it was in Columbia's best interests to settle this matter before he legally became an adult. In his biography, *Clive—Inside the Record Business,* Davis writes: "I suggested that [Hammond] call Dylan—right away—and bring him into his office; then convince him that the company *would* get behind him in the future, find out if he was really *that* angry and, if he wasn't, get him to disavow the letter in writing."

Accounts of that conference vary, but Hammond claims that he and a publicist met with Bob in an office on the fourth floor of the CBS building, at which time he said, "Bobby, unless you repudiate this you're finished as far as I'm concerned." Another version takes place a few months after Bob's birthday and supports a standard legal interpretation—that as long as he had been in the studio since turning twenty-one, the original contract could be upheld. Either way, Bob signed a letter reaffirming his agreement with Columbia Records and promised to play Hammond a new batch of songs.

In the meantime, Albert Grossman unleashed another curveball, this time aimed at Bob's publisher, Dutchess Music. Prior to the release of the first album, Hammond had convinced Lou Levy, who owned Leeds Music and was an inveterate New York song-plugger, to advance Bob five hundred dollars against future royalties. Such deals were normally viewed as a crapshoot when they involved a writer with no track record. But Hammond relentlessly hyped Levy, assuring him that Columbia was determined to make Bob Dylan a star. For a paltry five hundred dollars which Bob desperately needed, Dutchess (one of

Leeds' subsidiaries) won the rights to publish Bob Dylan's songs for an unspecified number of years. In light of the fact that Bob's catalogue has since earned millions of dollars in royalties, this deal now seems about as equitable as the sale of Manhattan for a handful of glass beads. That, of course, was before Albert Grossman entered the picture.

Grossman was making a name for himself as one of the music industry's smoothest operators. Characteristically, he acquired a taste for the blood and power of competition. Friends say he loved nothing more than to outsmart his business adversaries, making them look like assholes. "But always in a cavalier way," says one of his longtime henchmen. "Albert passed himself off as the gentleman gambler, never without an ace hidden in his sleeve." A better comparison, however, might be the canny magician who misleads his audience with feats of illusion. "Watch carefully, ladies and gentlemen. The trick is that you're fooled not by what you see, but what you *think* you see!"

It was with this strategy that he set out to reclaim Bob's publishing rights from Dutchess Music. It's reasonable to assume that Grossman resented not being a part of the original deal. Managers traditionally treated themselves to a piece of their client's publishing, knowing it might eventually yield a considerable return. Albert suspected the royalties to Bob's songs would be immense. He also held a trump card out of sight of Lou Levy—"Blowin' in the Wind." Grossman sensed that that song alone was worth a fortune in royalties. It was being sung nightly in every coffeehouse in the Village. Bob intended to put it on his next album, as did several of Grossman's clients, including Odetta and Peter, Paul & Mary, whose version he believed had the potential to catapult "Blowin' in the Wind" onto the top forty.

Before any of this was revealed, however, Grossman went to see Artie Mogull at M. Witmark & Sons, another well-known publisher, and tipped him off. The aptly named Mogull was considered one of the shrewdest young music publishers in the business. He was cocky, ambitious, professionally high-powered. He'd also been instrumental in getting Peter, Paul & Mary a deal at Warner Bros. Records. So it had become a matter of one hand washing the other. Mogull heard "Blowin' in the Wind" and instantly recognized its potential. He wasted no time concocting a plan to wrest the Dylan catalogue from Dutchess Music.

As the story goes, Mogull presented Bob with a thousand dollars to publish his songs with Witmark—twice what he got from Dutchess. In a move reminiscent of *The Producers,* Bob had now promised his copyrights to two publishers. A nifty little business deal—if it weren't against the law. But Grossman and Mogull were one jump ahead. "Why not use half the Witmark advance to buy back your contract from Dutchess?" So Bob traipsed into Dutchess while Lou Levy was out of the office and presented the staff with a proposition. An administrative assistant checked the balance sheet, noticed the dismal figures for the Dylan account, and jumped at the chance to recoup their investment. It was as simple as that.

The era of gentlemanly enterprise that had artificially steered the music business for half a century was drawing to a close. The new gospel was intimidation. There was a perverse satisfaction to see how far you could push someone, to corner him into a deal. Not to mention the animal hunger to talk tough and bully weaker opponents. "There was always a lot of one-punch fight talk around Albert," says a longtime friend and coworker. "He used to tell all the younger guys, 'If you smell trouble coming, make sure you get the first punch off. Hit first and ask questions later.'"

Fortunately, Bob was isolated from the everyday hustle as a hedge against disrupting his productivity. New ideas were bursting from his hair-trigger pen, his latest invention an endless stretch of free verse that he reeled off one night on Hugh Romney's typewriter in the room above the Gaslight. Tom Paxton, who was waiting to go on stage that night, recalls, "Bob handed me the poem and asked me what I thought. It was a wacky, wild thing, the likes of which I'd never seen before. As a poem it totally eluded me, so I suggested he put a melody to it. A few days later I heard him perform it as 'A Hard Rain's A-Gonna Rain.'"

"Hard Rain" was immediately hailed as Bob's chef d'ouevre. Based on the epic minstrel "Lord Randal," it combined the disparate elements of French symbolist poetry and traditional music in an entirely revolutionary way. No popular songwriter had ever attempted such an ambitious exploration of popular songwriting other than perhaps Kurt Weill. Nor succeeded so persuasively. The song's kaleidoscopic imagery refracted into splinters of clear and powerful expression that caught unsuspecting listeners completely off-guard. Dave Van Ronk's recollection speaks for a majority of the MacDougal Street mob, which fondly referred to the song as "Dylan's *War and Peace.*" Says Van Ronk: "I heard it for the first time at the Gaslight. A very warm night in September. The joint was half-full. Bobby was doing a set—maybe two or three numbers—and there it was, just wedged between a few others as though it were nothing special. It absolutely stunned me. I couldn't believe he'd written it. It was a masterpiece from the word 'go.' All I know is that afterward I had to get out of the club. I couldn't speak—to Bobby or anybody else for that matter. I remember being confused and fascinated that night because, on one hand, the song itself excited me, and on the other, I was acutely aware that it represented the beginning of an artistic revolution."

Barry Kornfeld, who heard "Hard Rain" later that same week, attributes the folkies' strong reaction to the song's fluid dispatch of symbolism. "None of us were used to studying the lyrics of a song in order to understand it," he says. "So in that respect it opened up an entirely new world of songwriting to us—something, I think, a lot of us weren't prepared to deal with. Nevertheless, it gave Bob's career a whole other degree of respect."

Van Ronk agrees. "With that one song, Bobby was truly launched," he says. "Everybody was blown away by it. We all thought it was the greatest thing since sliced bread, and it made him want to go home and write more just like it."

The success of "Hard Rain," however, was only a contributing factor to Bob's latest surge of creativity. He was also writing to fill the void left by Suze Rotolo. Originally, she'd promised to return in October. But in August, Suze wrote to her mother (who had returned to New York), instructing Mary to get her winter clothes from the West Fourth Street apartment and send them overseas. Unbeknownst to Bob, Suze had met a man in Italy "who was crazy about" her, and she'd decided to stay through the fall. Delaying her return had undoubtedly provided her with a difficult choice. "I don't know what the fuck to do," she wrote her sister, Carla, in September. "I don't belong in that . . . community [Greenwich Village]. But then there's Bobby."

Lillian Bailey had dutifully kept Suze posted on Bob's condition, which, she described in a word, was *miserable.* Naturally, Suze was concerned about him. His letters sounded desperate. On the other hand, she now led a more gratifying existence. There were none of the Village crazies to contend with, climbing over each others' backs. No swollen egos to pamper. She was painting and drawing in Italy, something she'd done little of since hooking up with Bob. She was no longer depressed. Friends on both shores urged Suze to protect what she'd fought so hard to regain—namely, her self-esteem. "But," she wrote to Carla, "you can't leave something like this uncompleted. You have to resolve things—not just for me but for Dylan. So you see, my dear..."

The situation called for a showdown. On December 13, 1962, Suze set sail from Naples on the Italian liner *Leonardo Da Vinci.* That day, the deck of the great steamer was thronged with passengers waving madly to friends and family below who had come to see them off. The weather was especially mild for that time of the year, and it is likely that both the well-wishers and voyagers alike remained in place for some time as the ship glided effortlessly from the harbor. The crossing would take only five days. All things pointed to an uneventful journey back to the states. As Suze gazed out over the bow of the ship, out across the tranquil sea, how could she predict the chaos that awaited her back in New York?

13

Second Time Around

Suze Rotolo's long-awaited homecoming was forestalled by an ironic twist of fate. Bob, unaware of her return, had flown off to Europe with Albert Grossman and wouldn't be back in New York until the third week in January, when he was scheduled to be photographed for the cover of his next album.

Actually, Grossman was in London for the commencement of Odetta's multicountry tour. It was a significant breakthrough for his client—a black folksinger was still primarily a curiosity to European audiences—and he persuaded Bob to accompany him, sweetening the offer with a bit part for Bob in a forgettable BBC drama called *The Madhouse on Castle Street.* For Bob, the trip abroad was pure recreation. It was his first time overseas, his first sojourn in the company of his new manager-cum-role model, but even more important, the trip put him a mere day's-trip distance from his beloved Suze.

Within hours of setting foot on foreign soil, Bob called Suze in Perugia, where she was supposedly ensconced for the winter. As luck would have it, she had already made plans to sail for New York, thus abrogating Bob's excursion. Her romance with Enzo Bartoccioli had blossomed, and the unannounced visit would have no doubt proved embarrassing for everyone involved. Exasperated by yet another setback, Bob sought refuge in Rome. He spent a few days there, exploring the landmark sights and soaking in the ancient ruins rising beside modern apartments and offices, luxurious villas, and noisy boulevards that provided him with an animated distraction. The highlight, however, was the cafes where, restored with inspiration, he could sit and write for hours without being interrupted. Haunted once more by thoughts of Suze, Bob returned to his music and put the finishing touches on "Girl from the North Country" and a skeleton for what eventually became "It Ain't Me Babe."

Back in London, Bob encountered two of his favorite playmates—Richard Fariña and Ric Von Schmidt—who were fashionably passing themselves off as expatriate *artistes.* The ubiquitous Fariña, no longer with Carolyn Hester, had taken up residence at a wealthy painter's flat in South Kensington, where he was trying to finish the first draft of a novel. (The manuscript eventually became the underground classic *Been Down So Long Looks Like It's Up to Me,* published by Random House in 1964.) Von Schmidt, also newly separated from his wife, was preparing to record an album there for tiny Folklore Records. The new bachelors invited Bob to drop by and join their ongoing party.

Bob was thrilled to find his friends there. Bewildered by London's starchy traditions, its mannered exercise of courtliness and protocol, he elected to slip away from the pompous Mayfair Hotel every chance he could. But instead of throwing himself jubilantly on Fariña and Von Schmidt, he proceeded to cold-shoulder them. Arriving at their pad, he behaved contemptuously, practically ignoring his hosts, pretending instead to be distracted by the apartment's plush appointments.

Fariña and Von Schmidt were understandably perplexed. Was Bob pissed off at them? Was he under the weather? No, probably not. It was the same display of rude, insensitive behavior that Albert Grossman had perfected in his own dealings with people, the compulsion to throw someone off-balance in order to gain the upper hand. Grossman's tack was to convince a victim that he had some special knowledge obviously out of their lowly grasp. Bob's technique was more oblique. He pretended to be on his own mystical wavelength. Obviously he'd learned a great deal about projecting an attitude from his mentor.

Ric Von Schmidt recalls vividly that first time he came up against Bob's inscrutability. "After Dylan showed up, for some weird reason he pretended that he'd never met Fariña. Now, Dick was a competitive guy. He sensed Dylan was going places and wanted a little credit for helping him onto that first rung of the ladder. Dylan, unfortunately, was having none of it. Dylan wouldn't talk to him. For a while he wouldn't even acknowledge Dick's presence. Somehow, we ended up sitting in this odd position, with me on one side of the room and Bob and Dick on the other, facing me but separated by about ten feet. It was like I was doing the translating for them, and it went on that way for about twenty minutes before these two egos settled down."

Bob finally broke the ice by pulling out his guitar and playing "Don't Think Twice." Fariña, who hadn't heard the song before, pronounced it a brilliant piece of work. "Then," Von Schmidt recalls, "we ended up smoking a lot of dope and everyone got real friendly."

One might conclude from this scenario that Bob's strange behavior was a result of shyness or discomfort around these two inseparable buddies. Granted, he may have felt a tad self-conscious around Fariña and Von Schmidt, but his attitude, the mysteriousness and mind-fucking, was an acquired skill that would, in time, emerge as his lethal trademark. After years of being ridiculed by his peers, Bob Dylan was apparently no longer content to play the weirdo or feed off the private knowledge that he was more gifted than those who looked down their noses at him. He'd proved himself worthy of respect with the songs he'd written. What's more, Albert Grossman continuously stroked his ego, assuring Bob that he was in a category by himself. Everyone else was, to use one of Grossman's favorite put-downs, a *moron.* And it was perfectly all right for someone of superior ability to assert himself. He was entitled. He'd taken a lot of crap in the past. Now it was his turn to dish it out.

Fortunately, Bob decided not to put his pals through any more of his obnoxious antics. The remainder of his stint in London was spent in unusually high spirits. He, Fariña, and Von Schmidt dragged themselves from one end of the city to the other in the blustery, calf-deep snow. They were invited to parties—so boring that an original song was composed on the spot to describe the tedium: "They're doing the London waltz/ because they can't think of anything else," the trio chanted in a taxi after a stuffy reception in Bedfordshire. They invaded the network of dingy English coffeehouses—occasionally banishing local performers from the stage—and picked up a number of interesting new songs to play back home. Bob was particularly observant of the British balladeer Martin Carthy. On one occasion, they heard Carthy and an accompanist perform a folk song called "The

Franklin," about a ship that sailed around the North Pole. Von Schmidt watched Bob take down the chords, then grill Carthy about the arrangement, never for a moment expecting his friend to attempt more than the standard variation on the song. One can imagine Von Schmidt's surprise, then, when a few months later he listened to Bob's new album and discovered the melody for "Bob Dylan's Dream" was almost a note-for-note clone of "The Franklin."

With Bob there was always a hidden motive operating. For instance, while he was still in London, Von Schmidt asked Bob to play on the Folklore album they were recording in the basement of Dobell's Jazz Record Shop. It was an uncomplicated request—musicians played on their friends' albums all the time. But Bob claimed his contract with Columbia Records forbade him to appear on a rival label. He proposed a solution: Why not credit him not as Bob Dylan but as Blind Boy Grunt? The artifice was okay with Von Schmidt, who didn't give a damn what Bob called himself as long as he'd do it, and they cut five tracks there—"Cocaine," "Xmas Island," "You Can't Always Tell," "Overseas Stomp," and "Glory, Glory"—with Bob playing some manic harmonica and doubling on harmonies.

The session took only two days, but afterward Fariña admitted he had seen enough of Bob Dylan for an entire year. The bluff posturing had gotten to him. What's more, he'd been spooked by what he perceived as Bob's uncanny ability to alter his physique from day to day. Von Schmidt noticed it too. One day Bob resembled a scrawny kid, the next a hulking lumberjack. They never knew what to expect. Fariña began referring to him as Plastic Man, after the cartoon character who could transform himself into a pistol, then turn into jelly so that he could slide underneath the door jamb. Dylan was one eerie cat! That realization no doubt humbled Fariña, who had set himself up as the quintessential Man of Mystery. Even he was no match for Bob Dylan.

The physical transformation they imagined in Bob was certainly an optical illusion. Not to mention a consequence of the ridiculous quantities of dope they'd smoked. But there was also the recognition that Bob's inner nature was beyond their reach, no matter how long they hung out together.

Never mind, Bob had already designated Suze as "the true fortuneteller of my soul." No sooner did Bob get back to New York than he rushed off to see Suze. There was so much to tell her—he couldn't wait to see her. The European trip, all the songs he'd written while she was away, the new record...

Suze was less than eager to take up again where they'd left off. Italy had certainly changed her. She'd grown up, in both appearance and self-esteem. The gangly teenager who'd gone off to Europe had returned home a confident and poised young woman. To complicate matters, friends accused her of torturing poor Bob by her absence. Eve McKenzie, on whose couch Bob had spent many a miserable night, upbraided Suze for abandoning him. The folkies at Gerdes and the Gaslight cornered her with woeful tales.

Even before she set eyes on Bob, Suze was confused anew. Their relationship had become *public,* and viciously distorted. People followed their personal business like a storyline on *Edge of Night.* Everyone offered an opinion. "Take care of your man!" "Don't get involved with him again!" To protect herself, Suze moved in with her sister, Carla, and began working part-time with an off-off-Broadway theater troupe. For three weeks she immersed herself in this pleasurable project. It was exactly what she needed—to be artistic and independent and away from the voyeuristic folk scene. She even started pursuing new friendships. Life in Greenwich Village was becoming almost tolerable again—until Bob Dylan showed up.

Their reunion wasn't the steamy saturnalia one might have anticipated a few months back. Suze was nervous about seeing him and understandably reluctant to jump back into the fray. Bob, however, managed to be very persuasive. He turned on the old charm full force, declaring how much he needed her. He'd turn over a new leaf—she'd see. Everything would be different now that they were together again and his career was on track.

A lot of promises were made that cold January afternoon. This was the New Improved Dylan, with greater sensitivity and resilience. Listening to him, Suze felt all her defenses melt away. And that face! He looked better than she'd remembered. She'd forgotten how cute he was, how much she cared for him, her little RAZ, a pet name derived from Bob's natural-born initials. Maybe things would work out after all, she thought, while he paced restlessly back and forth, pleading his case. Suze had resolved not to move in with him again, but before anyone knew it she was back at the West Fourth Street apartment, once more the faithful chick.

Bob, meanwhile, was already hard at work on his new album. He'd been in the studio four times since April, laying down a variety of songs that he considered suitable for the final sequence. "Masters of War" was a possibility, as was "Tomorrow Is a Long Time," "Girl from the North Country," "Talkin' John Birch," "The Walls of Red Wing," and "The Death of Emmett Till." A number of traditional tunes had also been recorded—"Corinna, Corinna" (which Columbia had released as the flip side of a single with "Mixed up Confusion," to no great acclaim) and the country blues standard "Make Me a Pallet on Your Floor." Bob was still overflowing with ideas, and by the beginning of February only "Don't Think Twice" and "A Hard Rain's A-Gonna Fall" were certain to appear on the forthcoming album.

John Hammond insisted that "Blowin' in the Wind" also make the final cut. It wasn't clear at the time whether Bob would intentionally leave it off the album. If he did, it would have created a conspicuous absence since the song, much to Bob's chagrin, had developed into his "theme." It would have been a gutsy move not to have recorded it, but Hammond put his foot down.

Bob still valued Hammond's expertise as an A&R man, but as the sessions wore on he began to question John's ability to competently produce the album. It seemed like the old guy's heart wasn't in it. He was detached, preoccupied with mail and correspondence that littered the studio console. Worse, he never raised the slightest criticism of Bob's performance. Every take was fine with Hammond, despite the false starts and mispronunciations and vocal flaws that cropped up in the normal course of the recording process.

Bob, worried about the quality of his performance, complained to his manager. Grossman was equally concerned and showed up at the next session, along with his new partner, John Court, who recalls the unrestrained atmosphere in Studio A. "There was John, sitting in the control room, flipping through *The New Yorker* and recording the kid for posterity," Court says. "It looked to us as if he was handling [Bob] like an Alan Lomax Library of Congress recording. He didn't stop him for mistakes, feeling, mood, or anything. He just kept the tape rolling, and every once in a while looked up over the magazine to say, 'Okay, are you through, Bob? Is that it?'"

Grossman and Court both knew enough about music to detect the obvious errors. Rather than let Bob make a fool of himself, they repeatedly interrupted the session, pointing out mistakes and other problems the producer had overlooked. Hammond felt "as though [his] balls had been cut off," and he banished the managers from the studio.

As one might expect, Grossman took up the grievance with Columbia Records. He demanded that David Kapralik replace John Hammond as the producer of Bob's album. This was like asking to have Johnny Carson relieved as host of the *Tonight Show.* Hammond was the label's resident dignitary and top creative star. What's more, Hammond had clout and would use it to raise bloody hell inside the company. Kapralik attempted to defuse the potential blowout, but to no avail. Grossman wanted action. Bob didn't want to work with Hammond anymore, and since it was unlikely that Columbia could come up with another in-house producer who understood the artist, why not just let Bob out of his contract.

Why Columbia didn't take him up on the offer remains one of the music business's greatest mysteries. After all, Bob's first album was a resounding stiff, no one aside from John Hammond particularly cared for his music, and the kid had been nothing but a pain in the ass since signing his contract. Releasing him would have made everyone happy. As irony would have it, John Hammond stepped in and insisted that Columbia Records stand fast to their agreement with Bob Dylan. Hammond generally defended artists, but he was also a relentless company man, who had, if nothing else, a clear understanding of Bob's potential worth to the label. Dylan, he assured them, was a gamble that would ultimately pay off—all they had to do was find the kid another producer.

Kapralik went through Columbia's entire roster of producers without any success. Bob and Albert rejected every candidate as being either too pop-oriented or too classical-minded or just plain unhip. Bob didn't want some guy who produced Johnny Mathis or Doris Day calling the shots on, say, "Don't Think Twice." Next thing you know the company would want him to work with the Ray Coniff Singers or Percy Faith's orchestra. The whole thing didn't sit well with him. Kapralik flashed on a last, desperate suggestion. He'd just hired a jazz producer named Tom Wilson away from Audiophile Records and thought the chemistry might be right. Little did Bob and Albert know that the chemistry had nothing to do with Wilson's personality or his ear for music, but rather with the fact that he was black. Kapralik calculated that the Bob Dylan who'd written "Oxford Town" and

"Emmett Till" wouldn't dare reject a black man. It wouldn't look good. Fortunately his hunch proved correct. Kapralik kept Grossman busy in his office while Bob walked down the hall with Wilson, and by the time the two men came back they had agreed to give it a try.

With Tom Wilson at the controls, Bob's second album swung back into high gear, but the peace was only temporary. The difficulty arose over a guest shot on *The Ed Sullivan Show.* The idea of booking Bob had come not from Ed Sullivan but from his son-in-law, Bob Precht, a folk enthusiast who'd heard the first album and thought it was extraordinary. In those days, Sullivan's stage was the launching pad for hundreds of up-and-coming stars—comics, acrobats, opera singers, musicians. The ungraceful host prided himself on giving amateurs their first professional break, so Precht, who also produced the show, had no trouble convincing him to sponsor Bob Dylan's network TV debut. On the surface there was nothing controversial about the appearance. A kid with a guitar—it'd be a nice change of pace for Sullivan's Sunday-night audience.

A week before, when Precht and the show's staff interviewed Bob at their West 57th Street office, they found him to be "courteous and cooperative." He strummed through a few songs so they could determine if the material was appropriate for TV, got a unanimous vote of approval, and then left, promising to show up on time for the dress rehearsal.

The Ed Sullivan Show was an important guest shot for Bob. Few folksingers had been afforded such auspicious TV appearances. Network officials considered them too avant-garde, objectionably scruffy, and too closely associated with their beatnik forebears for the general public's consumption. The fact that many folksingers were known communist sympathizers was also taken into consideration. So it was doubly unusual that Bob Dylan—the self-professed protégé of political activists Woody Guthrie and Pete Seeger—was invited to appear on a show that was as important to American Sunday ritual as church services.

Bob surely recognized the show's value to him. With a new album on the way, this was a golden opportunity to goose Columbia Records' skeptical promotion team. He'd be seen by twenty million people! It would also place him another rung above his fellow folksingers on the Street. Not that the step-up was well received. A few days before the show, Bob stopped in at the Fat Black Pussycat, where Johnny Herald and his girlfriend were huddled over black coffee. He stopped at their table and, in a loud, whiny voice, announced that he was going to appear on *The Ed Sullivan Show.* Herald, a respected folk purist, threw his hands up in the air, and said, "*Ed Sullivan!*—you really went too far this time, man, you sold out! You really sold out!" Bob pointed an admonishing finger at his friend and sneered, "Yeah, but in a few years I'll be telling them what to do and say." Then, slowly nodding his head, he walked out of the cafe and, wisely, remained out of sight until the day of the show.

When the big day, May 12th—Mother's Day!—arrived, Bob was ready to knock 'em dead. He showed up early at Studio 50 on Broadway and 54th Street, tuned his guitar, and waited in the green room until it was his turn to walk through the show. The dress rehearsal was already under way, and he was far down on the bill—behind Al Hirt, Irving Berlin, Rip Taylor, Topo Gigio the Italian Mouse, Teresa Brewer, and comedian Myron Cohen.

Around three o'clock, Bob Precht was informed by Stowe Phillips, the CBS censor, that there were problems with Bob's act. "Blowin' in the Wind" was okay, but they couldn't permit him to do "Talkin' John Birch Paranoid Blues." It was too controversial, and there was an outside chance that it libeled members of the John Birch Society because they were compared with Hitler. Precht consulted the show's sponsor and got an identical reaction—"Let's not take any chances—get the kid to do another song."

In the Dylan legend, Bob, confronted with the censor's decision, throws a temper tantrum, refuses to change his set, and boldly storms out of the theater. According to Precht, however, who recalls the incident quite explicitly, that wasn't the case at all. There was no screaming or carrying on. "I explained the situation to Bob and asked him if he wanted to do something else," Precht says. "And Bob, quite appropriately, said, 'No, this is what I want to do. If I can't play my song, I'd rather not appear on the show.'"

Ed Sullivan blew the incident way out of proportion. The next Tuesday he gave an interview to the *New York Post,* in which he claimed to have fought for the song: "We told CBS, 'It's your network, but we want to state that the decision is wrong and the policy behind it is wrong.'" In fact, Precht says, Sullivan didn't utter so much as an objection, "probably because Bob wasn't that important to the show. He simply didn't mean anything to [Ed]."

The same could be said with regard to his record company, and Columbia soon followed suit. Bob received word that the label wouldn't permit him to put "Talkin' John Birch" on his forthcoming album. In a tersely worded decision, Columbia's lawyers concluded it would enable any member of the John Birch Society to indiscriminately sue the record company for libel. That's all CBS needed—five thousand bigots dragging the company into court, one by one. The song had to go.

This time, Bob's reaction was, indisputably, outrage. He demanded an audience with Clive Davis, then Columbia's legal affairs advisor, but from the outset of the meeting he was overcome with frustration. "What *is* this?" Bob demanded to know. "What do you *mean* I can't come out with this song? You can't edit or censor me!" Davis was clearly embarrassed. A liberal Democrat who had worked for Adlai Stevenson, he found himself in the unseemly position of protecting two strange bedfellows—a multinational corporation and the scurrilous John Birch Society—from the musings of a young social satirist. Bob perceived it as a conspiracy of establishment forces to silence him. It had nothing to do with politics or liberalism, Davis argued. It was simply a business decision. Bob got up from his chair and walked to the door. "It's all bullshit," he said with disgust and, with that, strode from the room.*

It was a particularly tricky situation from Columbia's point of view. Had the controversy arisen a few months earlier they might not even have tried to placate Bob. But since April, his stock had surged enormously in value. Bob was becoming a phenomenon in spite of his pitiful record sales.

The first indication of that came on April 12, 1963, when Harold Leventhal presented him in concert at Town Hall in New York. Financially, the concert was a risky venture; Bob's last solo outing had attracted an audience more suited to the size of his living room. This time out, he struggled to fill two-thirds of the largely papered hall,

---

*About three hundred copies of *The Freewheelin' Bob Dylan* were distributed with "Talkin' John Birch" on it before the album was recalled.

but the performance itself was a magnificent critical success. That night, the hippest of the hip turned out to watch Bob Dylan take possession of folk music's eminent sway. It was almost religious the way it was set up, with saintly Pete Seeger looking down from his seat in the balcony. The MacDougal Street disciples were scattered dutifully around the audience. And Leventhal, the producer—he'd been Woody Guthrie's manager! It was the stuff of show-biz legend.

The Village elders had handed Bob the necessary vestments. The rest, for a performer of his ability, was a matter of unerring determination. He had to earn the audience's respect anew. The show, over and above the music, had to signal a new milestone in his career. It needed to establish a new image, a new outlook. He couldn't wander on stage, the boyish comical Chaplin, and camp it up the way he had at Folk City.

In fact, the cuddly whimsical Bobby was nowhere to be seen that night. In his place stood a bold, solitary figure of such high intensity that he threatened to defy the principles of combustion. Bob Dylan came ready to perform. He didn't scratch or jiggle his leg. He didn't fiddle nervously with a stool. When he got into what he called one of his "finger-pointing songs" like "Masters of War," he straddled the mike and fired off each word from his gut so that it rang off the cinder-block walls. The audience was hypnotized by his aggressive command of the stage, fixed for the full two hours—even through the desultory, long-winded poem he read called, appropriately enough, "Last Thoughts on Woody Guthrie."

The Town Hall concert established Bob as *the* major new voice in folk music. A new star in the tradition of Joan Baez. Robert Shelton dashed off another worshipful review for *The New York Times,* this time comparing Bob to Rimbaud and Yevtushenko, proclaiming him "a young giant." He even extolled Bob's "excellent guitar" playing, though Bob's instrumental skills were a joke on the Street. The Village folk community buzzed with the tidings of Bob's success. He'd taken another giant stride toward becoming their spokesman.

Suddenly Columbia Records found itself with a hot artist on its hands. A number of formerly skeptical record-company execs began to beat the drums. Look what had fallen into their laps! The bandwagon picked up momentum a few weeks later, when Peter, Paul & Mary released a single of "Blowin' in the Wind" that catapulted to the top of the charts. Albert Grossman seized the opportunity to finagle Bob an appearance on Studs Terkel's popular radio show, "Wax Museum," on WFMY-AM in Chicago.

Terkel was the undisputed scion of talk radio, his show a "must" stop for any personality traveling through the Midwest. Those familiar with his broadcasts enjoyed the host's casual sophistication and avuncular wisdom, and bounty of Americana he shared every afternoon. His guests, by contrast, usually displayed the kind of radio flair necessary to maintain the show's smooth, chatty format and to plug their new products. But Bob Dylan wasn't your average radio personality—a fact which became clear in the show's opening minutes.

Following a jangly version of "Farewell," during which Studs introduced Bob as a young man who "looks like Huckleberry Finn but lives in the twentieth century," Bob fielded a barrage of questions that served to establish him as the spokesman for Disgruntled American Youth. They discussed everything from civil rights to the country's itinerant poor to the difference between good and evil, all in the vernacular of a twenty-two-year-old musician. Terkel was unmistakably impressed by Bob's social conscience and his precocious first-hand knowledge of grass roots America. Here before him was a contemporary of Frankie Avalon and Chubby Checker whose music symbolized not cars, surfboards, and girls, but a passionate sense of mission.

"Do many [of your friends] in their early twenties—nineteen, twenty, twenty-one.... How many of them feel as you do?" Terkel asked with brooding interest.

The question set up a truly introspective moment for Bob, in which he revealed a great deal about his separation from his friends and his past. Alluding to his pals from Hibbing and Minneapolis, he responded, "They still seem to be the same old way.... I can just tell by conversation that they still have a feeling that isn't really free.... They still have a feeling that's... tied up in the town, with their parents, in the newspapers that they read which go out to maybe five thousand people. They don't have to go out of town. Their world's really small."

This provided the perfect segue into an abridged version of "Bob Dylan's Dream," which gave a picture of Bob Dylan struggling with his own success. In a hokey dream sequence, Bob imagines himself in a room filled with his boyhood chums long before any of them faced the consequences of adulthood. Life was much simpler then, he muses. Everyone laughed and sang and talked and joked. It was easy to tell black from white and right from wrong. Now, corrupted by ambition and the outside world, he mourns the loss of childhood in all its innocence, offering the sum of ten thousand dollars to restore the virtues of yesteryear.

Knowing what we do of Bob's childhood, the song cannot be taken literally. Bob couldn't have romanticized the mean-spirited Rangers who ridiculed his music and ostracized him for following his dreams. But that dream—or, rather, nightmare—belonged to Bobby Zimmerman. Bob was interpreting Bob *Dylan's* dream in the song. Taken in that context, his message is perfectly clear. He'd gotten a glimpse of the future—and it looked bleak. The song expresses his disillusionment with success—the petty jealousies, the false sense of security, the inability to distinguish between friendships and envy—and its idealized alternatives.

A few weeks before his second album was due to be released, Bob pulled up stakes and headed to the West Coast for an appearance at the Monterey Folk Festival. Driving north from Los Angeles with Jac Holtzman and Jim Dixon (who later managed the Byrds), it must have struck Bob that he was venturing into uncharted territory. He was an unknown to the small circle of western folkniks (who were equally unfamiliar with New York's coffeehouse gang), and had been booked on the show only at the insistence of headliners Peter, Paul & Mary.

The trio introduced him to a relatively small audience that had assembled on the grass of the County Fairgrounds. That evening, Bob took to the stage with only his guitar and harmonica. Unlike the Greenbriar Boys, the Weavers, the Dillards, and Bill Monroe before him, Bob performed alone, and the diminished pitch worked to dampen the crowd's enthusiasm. That and his scratchy voice, the intellectual lyrics, the lack of clap-along choruses... they weren't buying any of it. The reaction was only lukewarm through his first few songs. "Hard Rain" nearly put the audience to sleep. Then Bob introduced "Blowin' in the Wind," and the place exploded. The song had become a coast-to-coast smash, and its impact on the audience was absolutely breathtaking. It dawned on them that this was the guy who'd written Peter, Paul & Mary's hit and—WHAMMO!—instant respect. Suddenly, he was someone worth listening to.

One person in the audience came to that conclusion long before Bob got to "Blowin' in the Wind." Joan Baez lived in nearby Carmel and showed up Saturday evening especially to hear his short set. There she was—the Queen of Folk Music, as *Time* had dubbed her, *in the flesh!* She and Bob had been introduced at Folk City a year earlier, but at the time neither had made much of an impression on the other. Bob hated the traditional crap she sang; and Joan was insulted because instead of kissing up to the queen, like a dutiful subject, he hit on her fourteen-year-old sister, Mimi. Joan forbade Mimi to go out with Bob. The next day she sailed for France, leaving any thoughts of Bob Dylan and his music on the banks of the Hudson River.

It was Manny Greenhill, Joan's manager, who redirected her attention back to Bob. Greenhill had been charged with the task of finding new material for her so that she could beef up her dainty repertoire. It was no secret that Joan's act had grown stale. She'd barely changed it in years—all those dreary Child ballads and post-Civil War songs. "Give me a copper kettle, give me a copper coil..." People were tired of hearing them. It had gotten so bad that folksingers even did a take-off on her, singing "Mary Hamilton" in a shrieky, wooden soprano like one of the zombies in *Village of the Damned.* Manny wanted to at least bring her into the twentieth century. Give her something that coincided with her interests, like war and peace and the bomb.

A few months before, Greenhill had been sent a series of acetates by Witmark Music that were intended to showcase Bob's songs. He was genuinely knocked out by what he heard. The kid had come a long way since he'd first seen him perform at Folk City. Bob's songs were fresh and clever and poignant. The political stuff was uncommonly perceptive. Greenhill urged Joan to listen to the demos, but to no avail. Finally, following a midnight concert she gave at Princeton University, he sat her down and played them for her. "Joanie was even more impressed than I was," Greenhill recalls. "She was completely overwhelmed. The next thing I knew, she'd gone to Monterey obviously for the purpose of talking to him."

Talking was most likely the last thing on Joan's mind. She practically mugged the poor kid as he came off the stage. "Your music... what a voice... manage to say the things I've always thought about... like nobody else... genius...." Who wouldn't be swept off his feet! It was infatuation at first sight. Well, second, if you were keeping strict score, but both were willing to let bygones be bygones.

Their attraction extended far beyond the professional level. In Bob, Joan recognized a kindred soul. It was almost as if God had chosen to create a male counterpart of Joan Baez, right down to the peculiarities. Joan knew, like Bob, that she had no competition. She was the best of the female folksingers, the most influential and respected, if not the most difficult. And, accordingly, she was proud, insolent, condescending, distant in the iciest of airs. Her humor could turn cruel and deadly as quickly as it was engaging. The whole package, of course, was intimidating as hell, and Joan was a "folk hero" whose attitude won her few close friends. Still, folksingers worked overtime to remain in her good graces.

The point here is that Bob Dylan was experiencing the same thing. Or if he wasn't, he soon would be. His songs were too good; his arrogance was in full bloom. He carried himself with the swagger of a Hollywood matinee idol; his ego was insatiable. Joan recognized intuitively a true genius when she saw one. And those songs of his drove her wild!

The next thing Bob knew he was on his way to Joan's place in Carmel for a couple of weeks. She had a place in the highlands, not too far from town, surrounded by mountain cyprus and pine trees. The house, a contemporary ranch trimmed with an expanse of windows and skylights, belonged to Brett Weston, the photographer, and gave her a panoramic view of the brown hills and, in the distance, the sea. Two Dobermans ensured her privacy. What better environment for writing folk songs?

Of course, there was Suze to think about. And her Italian temper—*mama mia!* He didn't want to deal with that. Bob knew how to handle it, though. He called Suze every day, sometimes twice, claiming he was off writing songs—which was true enough, right? She didn't need to know where. He was *in California. Out west! On the coast!* Suze knew better than to ask for specifics. In fact, Suze didn't want to know. She was enjoying the time away from Bob, getting back into circulation, out from under his eviscerating grip. They were both better off apart for a while.

In the meantime, Bob and Joan exulted in the creative nest they made for themselves. He wrote and played her songs while she rehearsed for an upcoming concert tour. They worked out a number of duets of his tunes. Adapted arrangements to suit her voice. Joan made no bones about it: she intended to introduce his songs to the world. Promoting Bob would be her personal crusade. Bob had very quickly defrosted her icy facade. He brought out all the female and maternal instincts in her. Joan felt compelled to take care of him, fatten him up, brush his hair, and clean his green teeth.

Before he left for New York, Bob wrote two songs that logged his Carmel sabbatical into the history books. "Love Is Just a Four-Letter Word," a title that conveyed a bluntly ironic admission, was quickly snatched by Joan to bolster her flimsy repertoire. The other song was a dirge inspired by a newspaper article he'd recently read about a remorseless Baltimore tobacco heir named William Zanzinger, who, in a fit of pique, killed his black housekeeper and was given a ludicrous six-month sentence. It was a clear-cut mockery of justice, and Bob was predictably outraged. To him the story typified everything that was wrong with American society—the corruption of money and power, wanton disregard for human life, a black person's helplessness at the hands of white justice. Bob's account was a chilling commentary entitled "The Lonesome Death of Hattie Carroll."

In this highly regarded song, Bob not only expanded the facts for dramatic purposes to movie-of-the-week proportions, but in his elaboration he also managed to indict the country's smug, liberal establishment whose lip service throttled the struggle for civil rights. "Hattie Carroll" stands as one of the most beautiful and evocative of Bob's early compositions. He rolls out the lyric with seething, judgmental clarity; the melody is as plain and haunting as a hymn. The strength of the narrative is further illustrated by the fact that not one line in any verse rhymes. Even after all these years—despite the song's droning familiarity—the stinging candor of the refrain still echoes with hard truth.

The Freewheelin' Bob Dylan was released on May 27, 1963, three days after Bob's twenty-second birthday. This time, the album had a life unto its own. It picked up excellent reviews, a decent amount of airplay, and an unexpected shot in the arm from Peter, Paul & Mary's pop version of "Blowin' in the Wind," which continued a steady climb up the singles chart.

Even the cover attracted attention. On it, Bob and Suze are posed arm in arm as they stroll idyllically along the slush-covered surface of Great Jones Street. Suze is flashing one of her grooviest smiles, her cheek glued devotedly to Bob's shoulder. The singer-songwriter appears deep in thought. They're both probably ignoring the fact that HIS FLY IS OPEN! The gang on MacDougal Street had themselves a good chuckle over that. After all, how cocky could he get, putting his girlfriend on the cover. Especially in light of his new bicoastal liaison with Joan Baez. If anyone questioned the album's hip, slangy title, they need look no further for an answer. That was *freewheelin'* man!

14

"A Folknik Hero"

The success of *Freewheelin'* established Bob as one of the country's most imaginative folksingers, but more important was the recognition it brought him as the leading exponent of protest songs.

In the early Sixties, protest songs were synonymous with freedom of expression. Those who felt strongly about an issue and could carry a tune or simply clap their hands had a stake in the protest movement. It was as populistic as fast food. And they protested *everything:* war, materialism, the bomb, discrimination, police brutality, political corruption. It was as if a crack opened up in our social system and all the complaints and hostility that had accumulated over the years came cascading out.

Protest songs vented the rage against the uptight social and moral repression of the Fifties. But it was unquestionably the younger generation, those next in line, whose voices cried out the loudest. Throughout the Eisenhower years, American youth had generally conformed to all the moralistic pieties of their parents. In his 1957 essay "The Young Generation," Norman Podhoretz detected "a certain justice in regarding the young generation as a non-generation, a collection of people who, for all their apparent command of themselves, for all the dispatch with which they have taken their places in society, for all their sophistication, for all their 'maturity,' know nothing, stand for nothing, believe in nothing."

What Podhoretz failed to envision, however, was the *emerging* generation of youth—the first generation of essentially nonimmigrant parents who were sent to college en masse for the purpose of sharpening their intellects and reshaping the American dream. This peer group, which came of age during the Kennedy era, took one look at their social inheritance and began raising hell. Just look at what their parents had in store for them: missile silos planted in the middle of Iowa cornfields, states where black people were considered legally inferior human beings, 16,800 Americans defending rice paddies in southeast Asia, a humor distinguished by the elephant joke—what a fucking mess! Parents! For Chrissake, someone had to protest!

Natural selection had chosen Bob Dylan to be the high priest of protest singers. He had an extraordinary ability to dramatize any injustice. He also had the built-in radar necessary to zero in on a golden opportunity, which this one definitely was.

Freewheelin' quickly earned Bob a set of very impressive credentials. *HiFi/Stereo Review,* one of his earliest champions, said, "It is beginning to appear that Dylan's music will become as much a rallying point for this era as [Woody] Guthrie's was for his." Its competitor, *High Fidelity,* concluded that the songs "so unerringly crystalize the fears and failures of a world, that, increasingly, is too much with all of us." And *Variety,* in its inimitable way, dubbed him "a folknik hero."

It wasn't long before Bob was branded "the spokesman of his generation" in almost every article written about him. What a drag that turned out to be! Every group promoting a worthy cause came knocking on his door.

In July, he endorsed a cause about which he felt passionate, and in a bizarre turn of events, he wound up regretting it. Theodore Bikel, a neighbor of Bob's in the Village, was involved with the Student Non-Violent Coordinating Committee (SNCC), whose drive to register potential black voters in the South was picking up steam. Bikel and Pete Seeger agreed to sing at a registration rally in rural Greenwood, Mississippi, and invited Bob to accompany them. Says Bikel, "I thought that since he was a spokesman of the next generation, if he wanted to paint pictures he should be closer to what was actually happening and experience it first hand."

Bob had no trouble putting his name to that. He thought discrimination was a disgrace. Through his music, he'd become more than a passive advocate of the civil rights movement. Suze would certainly be proud of his participation. And Joan, of course—this was her cup of tea. Even the implicit danger held a certain attraction for him. Bikel had warned him they'd be viewed down South as a bunch of no-good folk nigger-lovers. The atmosphere would be tense, someone might take a shot at them. "Count me in!" Bob told him, and they flew south.

The rally itself went off without a hitch. The folksingers entertained pockets of fieldhands who worked the cotton plantations along the murky Yazoo River. They sang all the standard freedom anthems, of which "Blowin' in the Wind" was now a star attraction, and they drew plenty of national media coverage. Bikel had been right—the realities of segregation had a startling effect on Bob, but his vision was blurred by the swarm of activists and organizers who subsequently lectured him on his responsibility to the movement. Jesus!—that bugged the hell out of him. "Everybody wanted to make a claim on him," Suze recalls, and that really turned Bob off. He had to protect his privacy, and from that day on he swore off political organizations.

Besides, Albert Grossman thought it was time Bob focused more attention on his career. "Blowin' in the Wind" was a smash. His album was walking out of the stores. His name was in the air. When Columbia Records invited him to entertain at their national sales conference in San Juan, Puerto Rico, Bob surprised them and accepted. Not that he'd forgiven those morons for dumping his first album. They'd missed the boat on that one due to their complete lack of faith in him. And now that he was hot, they had begun to come around. The company line was: "Oh yeah, Dylan, man, he's great—he's a monster, man—a fucking monster!" They were notorious front-runners, and for the time being Bob Dylan was their number-one man.

The San Juan trip started off as one big happy family vacation. Suze was invited to attend, and she and Bob asked Carla to join them for a few days of fun in the Caribbean. The gang checked into the glitzy new Americana Hotel—"Mr. and Mrs. Dylan" and their "sister-in-law"—then hit the beach, where they made small talk with the hookers who were on hand to provide a little entertainment of their own. The whole tone of the place was partytime. Columbia was enjoying a banner year, and all its new stars were flown in for the company bash—Tony Bennett, Andre Watts, Aretha Franklin, Bob. Someone paraded Cassius Clay through the festivities for pure spectacle. Bob was thrilled to be part of the scene. Beneath his scruffy folk exterior beat the heart of a Jewish businessman from Minnesota. He knew the value of self-promotion, and in an offbeat way he courted the establishment crowd when he thought that could help his career. All Bob really had to do was be seen and shake a few hands. And, of course, perform.

The "concert" itself was a farce. Bob Dylan—poet-philosopher, America's angry young protest singer, spokesman for the new generation—was part of the floor show at the Americana. If only the gang from SNCC could see him. The same Bob Dylan who, only a week before, sang freedom songs for Negroes on the cotton plantation, was now standing in front of a plush gold curtain on the stage where the hotel's girlie revue usually shook their cha-chas at the tourists. And if that didn't beat all, Bob chose "Oxford Town" and "With God on Our Side" for his set. Imagine how that went over with Columbia's southern sales force! You could practically smell their toupees smoldering as they sat there, having to applaud politely at the end of each number. And with Goddard Leiberson and John Hammond Sr., their esteemed leaders, beaming with pride. Twenty years of service to the company and what do they get for entertainment? Not Ray Coniff, not Patti Page, not even Mongo Santamaria, but some long-haired, college-educated, pimple-faced, nigger-loving pinko making fun of southern custom.

Criticism eventually filtered back to Bob, but it wasn't from the southerners; it wasn't from anyone at Columbia Records; it wasn't from Albert Grossman. It was from, of all people, Carla Rotolo. She really lit into him for pulling a stunt like that. The next day, too, when Bob refused to put on a necktie in order to have dinner with Goddard Leiberson, Carla complained about his behavior. She told him he'd acted childishly; he'd been rude. He ought to show people more respect. That did it! That was just about all he was going to take from Suze's big sister. Carla had a big fucking mouth, and he told her to keep it buttoned for the rest of their stay in San Juan. He meant it, too. Later that afternoon, he cornered Carla in his hotel room and hit her with all the stuff that had been building up over the months. He accused her of being a pushy little troublemaker, making life difficult for Suze, living vicariously through them. He was relentless, wagging his finger two inches from her nose, backing her up against the wall. She wasn't a human being, he screamed. Suze had all the talent, not Carla. Carla was nothing—a piece of shit.

Back in New York, relations between Bob and Carla went from bad to worse. He felt she was trying to alienate Suze from him and wanted nothing more to do with her. The trouble was, Carla was always around. She and Suze were extremely close, and the rift with Bob took its toll. Suze regarded her big sister as almost a surrogate mother. She depended upon Carla for advice, sought her approval, confided in her. Yet, Bob treated her sister with unmitigated scorn. Suze was caught in the middle.

It was during this time, as well, that Suze felt increasingly alienated from Bob as a result of his popularity. His album had created a sensation. He had become the darling of pop music critics, who analyzed his lyrics and discussed what social impact they might have. Profiled repeatedly as a rebel who "set about to dismember the Establishment, limb by limb," Bob was pressed to comment publicly on a wide range of issues. Regarding the United States, he observed, "Ain't nobody can say anything honest in the United States. Every place you look is cluttered with phonies and lies." On politics: "I'm not gonna vote, because there's nobody to vote for; nobody that looks like me, the way I feel." Summing up President John F. Kennedy, Bob concluded, "He's all right but he's a phony, pretending all the time." How utterly preposterous, Suze thought. The same guy her friends and family called "the Twerp" was carrying on as if he were Bertrand Russell.

Everywhere they went, people treated Bob like an enlightened prophet. Fans followed him down the street. They imitated the way he talked, the clothes he wore. They hung on his every word. "Hey, waiter—gimme a pastrami on rye." *What does he mean by that?* It had gotten to be that ridiculous!

Through it all, Suze became more confused and withdrawn. She felt herself slipping away again, being consumed by the ensuing squall. "My instinct told me there was no way he and I could co-exist as equal personalities," Suze remembers. "I had to be either 'Dylan's girl' or not his girl. I had to give my life over to him. There was clearly no room for compromise."

The Newport Folk Festival, held during the last week in July, proved to be Suze Rotolo's emotional undoing. Bob had been invited to close Friday night's concert, and they arrived at Freebody Park early enough in the day to wade through the crush of performers who congregated backstage. Most of them were friends or, at the very least, familiar faces—Bikel, Seeger, Jack Elliott, Joan, Tom Paxton, Peter, Paul & Mary, Van Ronk, Judy Collins, Paul Clayton. The Cambridge mob turned out in full force. Mississippi John Hurt and John Lee Hooker had been imported from the Deep South. The 1963 festival had attracted the cognoscenti of professional folk music, but Bob Dylan's name seemed to be on everyone's lips. A number of performers planned to sing his songs on stage; others, like Pete Seeger and Peter Yarrow, diligently sang his praises. It was one of the stellar weekends of his career, and the petulant attitude he adopted for it probably owed a lot to the fact that Bob Dylan came to Newport not as a festival rookie—which, in fact, he was—but in the role of a star.

No sooner had Bob arrived than he ran into a friend from Boston named Geno Foreman. Geno was a musician of sorts—not a performer or even a talent, but one of those people who hung around the folk scene and picked up an instrument any time someone jammed. The son of civil rights activist Clark Foreman, he'd had it up to here with politics and renounced anything remotely requiring social responsibility for the life of a gallivanter. Geno could be charming, warm, and generous, but the word that most accurately described him was *wired.* He acted out every sudden urge, no matter how incendiary or self-destructive, which is probably what attracted Bob to him in the first place. Geno Foreman was the flip side of Bob's dark persona, the dangerous, unrestrained facet of "Dylan" that simmered in embryo.

Geno took one look at Bob and grinned. "Got something for you, man," he said, and presented Bob with a huge, leather bullwhip. Bob slung it over his shoulder like a vaquero, then stole off to practice, vowing to work at it until he could flick a cigarette out of Suze's mouth at twenty paces.

Mark Spoelstra happened to be hanging out backstage when Bob moseyed over with his new toy. The old friends hadn't seen each other in a while and spent a few minutes catching up on the disparate progress of their careers: Bob, of course, was exploding, while Mark barely hung in there by his teeth. Elektra had signed him to a record deal, but it wasn't happening—at least not the way it had happened for Bob. "Listen, man," Mark said with some discomfort, "I could use your help getting tickets into the festival." Bob was more than happy to give him a hand, escorting him off in the direction of the office. They weren't ten yards from their destination however, when Mark spotted an old friend. "Hey, there's Joan Baez!" he said, unaware of Bob's fling with her. "C'mon, I'll introduce you two."

Mark gamboled toward her on some ulterior mission of his own. Years before, when they were teenagers, he had taken Joan dancing at the Pasadena Civic Center. They'd gone parking afterward, and Mark told Bob he still daydreamed of that magical night with her in the back seat of his car. Trouble was, he could never get Joan on the phone again. She'd brushed him off. Maybe this was the opportunity he'd been waiting for, the chance to pick up where they'd left off.

Bob strolled right past her on his way to the ticket booth. "Hey—give this guy some tickets," he barked at the attendant there. Mark had abandoned his pursuit of tickets in favor of Joan's memorable aroma. "Hi, Joan," he said with a glint in his eye, as Bob shuffled to his side. "Hi," she replied. "Say, who's this little tramp you've got with you?" Mark tendered an introduction while the two coyly continued to pretend they'd never met. "Are you part of Mark's singing group, or just his road manager?" she asked Bob. That was carrying the joke further than his ego could allow. Instantly, Bob was on top of her with insults. He really let her have it—not that Joan couldn't defend herself, but it was difficult taking that kind of crap from someone he was in love with.

Their little intrigue continued the next day at the Viking Motel, where the younger performers had gathered to chat and jam. Bob brought Suze with him, and Joan couldn't take her eyes off his immortalized girlfriend. "It was very intense," Suze remembers. Still, she had no reason to suspect there was anything going on between Joan and Bob. Their musical connection got to Suze every now and then; at times she felt left out because she didn't perform or write folk songs. But as far as romance was concerned, she assumed—as did the rest of the gang—that Joan was still caught up in a torrid relationship with one of the young girls who worked for her.

Suze had more important things on her mind—namely, her own screwed-up romance. It was obvious that things weren't working out with Bob. She wasn't happy anymore. Oddly enough, the festival brought that into sharp focus for her. Bob was Newport's out-and-out star. She watched as reporters and fans tagged after him like sheep. Folksingers fawned all over him, treating him like a spoiled prince. People who had been friends of theirs! It was disgusting. Suze no longer knew what or whom to believe—who was a friend, or who wanted to be close to her simply because she was Bob's girl. That very afternoon a woman wandered over to ask Suze if she was "Dylan's chick." As if she were an inanimate object. A *thing!* She had to somehow extricate herself from his clutches and decided that now was as good a time as any to start.

Sunday night's concert served to hasten that goal. The show belonged to Joan Baez, and the moment she stepped on stage the audience went wild. "Tonight is one of the most beautiful nights I've seen," she shouted over the clatter of worshipful applause. "I'm all up here with it. I feel sort of like exploding!" A new burst of applause thundered across the grounds as she launched into her set, and Joan had transformed what, so far, had been a lackluster show into euphoria. This was her crowd, too. They had embraced her at the age of nineteen, when she made her debut at the first Newport Folk Festival, and regarded her as the symbol of folk music's resurgence. Much later, Bob would say that "folk music is just a bunch of fat people," but for the moment Joan Baez, more than anyone, represented its youthful allure. She possessed a sultry beatnik beauty, a sharp mind, and a brassy stage presence that could come across ambiguously as regal and rebellious, political and passive. It was the perfect hybrid for a generation in search of an image.

Joan performed a number of Bob Dylan compositions, each time identifying the author with mounting admiration. Suze, sitting in the audience with friends, leaned over and asked Terri Van Ronk: "What kind of rumors do you hear about Bobby and Joanie?" "The same kind of rumors you hear," Terri replied. But Suze shook it off, convinced that Bob couldn't possibly coexist with someone whose popularity was greater than his. His ego wouldn't permit it. A moment later, however, Suze wasn't so sure. "Here's another Bobby song," Joan announced as she returned to the stage for an encore. "This is a song about a love affair that has lasted too long." Joan delivered a plaintive, ironic version of "Don't Think Twice." When she summoned Bob to the stage for a duet of "With God on Our Side," Suze was no longer in the audience.

Bob's two-timing was ultimately little more than his cultivation of a new sidekick to help promote his career. Joan Baez had a national audience and a concert tour that was scheduled to begin immediately following Newport. She had already suggested that he make a few guest appearances with her. Nothing elaborate—perhaps just wander onstage with her after the intermission and sing a few songs, promote his album, whatever he wanted.

What he wanted—and needed badly—was exposure. His name still didn't mean a thing outside of New York City and, now, Newport. True, he'd written "Blowin' in the Wind," but that was Peter, Paul & Mary's hit. He was still a relatively obscure protest singer with a couple of decent albums to his credit. Many of the critics didn't know what to make of him. Record-buyers were leery of that voice, and his attitude sure didn't help matters. The trouble was, he was still scoring off some underground word of mouth. He had to break out of the small-time coffeehouse scene, reach a larger audience, and concerts seemed the only way to go. If he went on the road by himself, he probably couldn't sell enough tickets to fill the Libba Theatre in Hibbing. Joan, on the other hand, packed concert halls wherever she went. Without hesitating, he accepted her offer and prepared to hit the road.

When Bob informed Suze about the tour, she was devastated. Soon after, Bob found her on the floor of the apartment, the oven's gas turned on full blast. He called Carla for help, but by the time she got there the emergency had passed. Suze had regained consciousness, and an anguished lover cradled her in his arms.

In Carla's estimation, Suze was still in desperate trouble. Life had somehow gotten away from this fragile nineteen-year-old. She had to get Suze away from Bob. This proved a lot less difficult than she assumed it would be. "Suze wanted to get away from an untenable situation," Carla recalls, "so she moved into my apartment on Perry Street."

It was just as well. Bob was preoccupied with making his third album, *The Times They Are A-Changin'*, and appearing intermittently with Joan Baez. As agreed, Bob was sandwiched between her two sets as an unannounced guest. Joan would introduce him, turn the stage over to Bob, and then join him again for several absorbing duets before an openmouthed crowd. Together, Bob Dylan and Joan Baez created folk music's moment of glory. They were young, exotic, provocative, and spellbinding. When they sang, you could almost see the sparks fly. To many folk enthusiasts, hearing Bob sing "Blowin' in the Wind," "Only a Pawn in Their Game," "With God on Their Side," and "The Times They Are A-Changin'" for the first time, was an epiphany.

To some, however, Bob's appearance with Joan was an intrusion. Following a concert at the Hollywood Bowl, a fan wrote, saying, "You can imagine my frustration and disappointment when it turned out that only half the program was Joan Baez and the rest of the evening was spent tolerating a very inferior and irritating singer." Another letter signed by eight young women complained: "After anticipating an evening devoted entirely to {Joan}, we were unhappy to have Bob Dylan, a singer with debatable talent, dominate the second half of a short program."

Joan, to her credit, wasn't deterred by the grumblers. She was resolved to introduce Bob Dylan to America, and by the end of her abbreviated tour he'd won over a good portion of her fans.

While Bob was away, Suze had regained her confidence and basked in the emotional tranquility provided by her independence. She'd resumed painting and tried her hand at writing poetry. She and Carla found an apartment they could share on Avenue B—a gaping tenement in what was then one of the seedier sections of New York City—and fixed it up. They took in a lot of off-Broadway theater. Says Carla, "Suze regained that wonderful spirit and youthful glow. We started having a lot of fun together. She got a job working as a waitress at a luncheonette on 12th Street. So it was finished with Dylan. Until she discovered she was pregnant."

Suddenly, Bob was thrust back in Suze's life again. She decided there was no choice but to tell him about the pregnancy, and Bob had Albert arrange for an illegal abortion in a doctor's office on the Upper East Side. "Suze was in terrible shape afterwards," Carla recalls. "She bled like crazy, but we couldn't go to a hospital, so it was really up to Bobby and I to attend to her." Carla nursed her sister with a variety of homemade treatments, but she says that Bob was paralyzed with fear: "He just sat there with his head in his hands," she says. "What he wanted was for Suze to support *him*. I wasn't really sure what to do. Albert was nowhere to be found. Suze was in a lot of pain. I wanted to *kill* him!"

Bob and Carla went at each other every chance they got, bickering, picking at each other. Carla made it clear she didn't want Bob around, but Suze refused to discourage his visits. He became a fixture at their Avenue B apartment, with Carla staying out until dawn each night to avoid the inevitable confrontations.

Unfortunately, Bob fared no better in the studio than with his domestic affairs. He had written a lot of powerful material for the new album, but he felt it wasn't being properly recorded. Tom Wilson, as it turned out, was no more inspired than John Hammond behind the controls. He was a total washout, another corporate flunky. And what Bob needed, most of all, was a strong creative producer.

To appreciate that need, it is important to understand how Bob Dylan worked. Songwriting, for Bob, was not what you'd call a disciplined process. There was no organization to it, per se—no method or formula that produced a finished piece. Unschooled in musical composition, he didn't follow a prescribed plan but rather wrote spontaneously, by stream of consciousness. He seized immediate images and rhythmic phrases that accommodated a particular chain of thought. He'd fit them into a song, then sit in a room for hours at a time, singing the words over and over until they rolled comfortably off his tongue.

Because Bob was guilty of jam-up—the practice of putting more words in a line than metrical feet would allow—he had to devise phrasing to compensate. The lines had to "lay" right. They had to flow. That is why his instrumentation was always simple; it was secondary to the performance. To Bob, what mattered was making the words sound unforced, natural. And often, after performing a song he'd recently written, a song he'd perfected maybe twice in his bedroom, problems would arise on the first take in the recording studio. That is why a good producer was essential.

Tom Wilson, a qualified jazz buff, knew nothing about the folk idiom. Worse, he had no feel for it and was ill-equipped to advise Bob. He settled for anything—first takes, inadequate performances—to keep the session rolling in as cost-effective a manner as possible.

The obvious solution was for Bob to have Wilson removed and

replaced with an experienced folk producer. There were a handful of such pros around who supervised sessions at Elektra and Vanguard Records, most of whom were on friendly terms with Bob and would have jumped at the chance to produce his next album. But in those days, if you were a Columbia act, corporate policy specified that you had to be recorded by a Columbia A&R man in a Columbia studio, using a Columbia engineer. There were no exceptions. Bob discussed the problem with his friend Paul Rothchild, who produced most of Elektra's folk albums, and invited him to attend the recording session. "Just sit on the couch in front of the console as if you were one of my friends," Bob told him. That way Bob would be able to see Rothchild through the glass partition which separated the control room from the studio. "Nobody'll have to know who you are."

Rothchild came in the next day and inconspicuously positioned himself between the producer and Bob. "I watched Tom produce, and I immediately understood Dylan's terror," Rothchild recalls of that session. "He read magazines, he constantly paged through *Billboard,* he was on the telephone to bimbos, he hung out with friends in the hall. And at the end of each take, he'd look up, realize the music was over, and say, 'That was great, Bob. Let's do a different one now.'"

As Bob finished each song, he instinctively gazed into the control room to await his producer's response. Now, however, his eyes dropped furtively to where Rothchild sat in order to pick up a prearranged signal. If the performance was first-rate, Paul flashed thumbs up; if it deserved a retake, thumbs down. And for the first time, Bob said, "Let's... let's do that one again. Okay?"

Wilson attempted to shrug off Bob's request. "There's no reason, Bob," he'd say. "It's great—*great!*"

Says Rothchild, "Wilson's philosophy was 'Get in and out—let's make the record.' He didn't give a shit because he was thinking small. He didn't regard Bob as anything other than just another kid making a record, and it made him angry that someone like Bob would challenge his authority."

The third album was paced by a series of similar confrontations. Rothchild would invariably get a call from Bob and rush over to the studio, where he'd find performer and producer locked in an ugly dispute over the quality of a particular take. As such, Rothchild became a fixture in Studio A for the remainder of the session.

Bob interrupted the final stretch of his recording session for a series of solo concerts at Carnegie Hall, Town Hall in Philadelphia, and Jordan Hall in Boston. The New York appearance, on October 12, 1963, was significant as much for its venue as for its merit. Carnegie Hall was world-renowned, a preeminent concert facility that signaled indisputable stardom. Tchaikovsky had performed there, Stravinsky, Gershwin, Chevalier, Robeson, Pete Seeger. Bob Dylan—only twenty-two years old—at Carnegie Hall was a spectacular accomplishment, indeed. It would catch the eye of the major news media, and Bob flew his parents in to witness the spectacle.

Abe and Beatty's presence in New York was an event in itself. It augured a change in Bob's attitude toward his family, a compromise that measured the extent his self-confidence had grown. Months earlier, he was outraged upon learning his parents had made inquiries into his whereabouts. Suze Rotolo recalls a telephone conversation Bob had with John Court, Grossman's partner, concerning a phone call from Bob's father. Apparently, Abe hadn't heard from Bob in months and called Court, wanting to know where his son was and if he was all right. "Bob was furious," Suze recalls. "He regarded it as an intrusion. He certainly didn't want his father in his life at all and called Hibbing to tell him exactly that." Suze remembers the emphatic rage he directed toward meek Abe Zimmerman. "You! Called! John! Court!" Bob screamed into the phone. "How dare you!" Suze says, "He didn't want anybody from anywhere else to touch him in New York—most of all anybody named Zimmerman."

When they arrived in New York, Bob stashed Abe and Beatty at a schlocky motel on Eighth Avenue while he gave interviews to a number of magazines. One, in particular, in *Newsweek,* was considered crucial to Bob's dramatic ascent. Often, a newsweekly's coverage, coming on the heels of a major New York concert, created enough hype to carry the message cross-country. Momentum now was everything, and soldiers in the Dylan camp, from Albert on down to the record-company drones, urged Bob to take full advantage of the spotlight.

The Carnegie Hall gig allayed their concern that Bob needed a boost from anything other than his guitar. On this night, Bob was totally in command. He strode on stage like Field Marshall Montgomery at Dunkirk, cooking with determination. You could tell he was pumped up. He was ready for them. A wave of applause carried him from the wings to center stage, where he seized the mike with the tenacity of a stand-up comic. Four tiers of fans—not Joan's or Peter, Paul & Mary's or Woody's or Pete's, but *his,* Bob Dylan fans—went wild. Carnegie Hall—WOW! Bob rose to the occasion and cut loose.

He tore through about twenty of his most recent songs—"Hattie Carroll," "Blowin' in the Wind," "Don't Think Twice," "Oxford Town"—and they echoed through the hall, rattling the ghost of Tchaikovsky. He sang with clarity, conviction, passion, introspection, remonstrance, exasperation, and honesty. Everything he did that night—from the polemics to the poetics—conveyed an urgency that inspired the young crowd. They hung on his every word, ready to laugh, applaud, cheer, coo, and sigh on cue. They even sat hushed and attentive through scattered harangues he soliloquized like a snarling, cynical rabbi. By the time the show was over, Bob was a confirmed star.

The audience left as if they'd witnessed Jesus withering the fig tree. The concert was *religious,* man! Outside, Beatty Zimmerman paced the corner of 57th Street and Seventh Avenue in a full-length mink coat. She was ecstatic, bursting with pride. It was every mother's dream come true. Her son, the musician—her Bobby—played *Carnegie Hall!* Like Andre Watts and Van Cliburn and . . . Pinchus Zuckerman, a *Jew!* What a mitzvah!

Beatty couldn't get enough of the euphoric rush. She wanted more. She wanted to hear from the mouths of strangers just how good her Bobby was. Tearing away from her family, Beatty accosted fan after fan, asking, "What happened here tonight? Who performed?" Following the anticipated answer, she beamed, "*Bob Dylan?* Was he any good?"

Finally, Abe and a few friends managed to pull her away from the crowd and hustled her around the corner to the stage entrance on 56th Street, where a throng of fans awaited a glimpse of their young sage. It was a beautiful night, and the Zimmerman entourage waited patiently by the curb, reminiscing about their own apocalyptic experience. "All that applause . . . what a voice . . . how good he looked . . . he wrote those songs *all by himself!*" The only disturbing note arose from the program they each clutched in their hands. "It says all these crazy things like he sang on street corners and hopped boxcars and ran away from home eleven times," a family friend mused. "Who do you suppose put those ideas in his head?"

Before anyone ventured a guess, the doors flew open and Bob rushed out onto the sidewalk. The crowd closed around him, but Beatty agilely elbowed her way inside to within a few feet of her son. "I enjoyed your performance tonight, Mr. *Dylan!*" she screamed above the squall. Bob took one look at her and quickly averted his eyes, refusing to acknowledge her presence. Within seconds, he disappeared into a waiting car and pulled off into the night.

A week after Bob's triumph, *Newsweek* hit the stands and neatly dismantled his halo. The story, entitled "I Am My Words," took Bob to task for attempting to manipulate the press. It refuted the interview Bob had given to the magazine in which "he denied that Bob Dylan was ever Bobby Zimmerman" and disavowed any knowledge of his parents. *Newsweek,* in fact, had interviewed the Zimmermans only days before Bob's Carnegie Hall concert and pondered, as a mystery, why he "should bother to deny his past."

When Bob saw the story, he flew into a rage. He had been unmasked as a fraud. His dirty little secret was finally out in the open. What a blow to his image! Feeling deflated and very pissed-off, Bob vowed to get even with those responsible for the story. Meanwhile, he banned friends, family, and business associates from consorting with the press.

This left Bob's buddy Robert Shelton in a precarious position. Up until now, Shelton enjoyed a double life as both a Dylan pal and a Dylan critic. He hung out, drinking and partying with Bob; he was a frequent guest of Albert Grossman's and a member of the MacDougal Street mob. He was also emerging as the leading authority on Bob Dylan and recognized an opportunity to chronicle music history from the inside. It would be suicide for him to jeopardize that position. So in an act of unabashed loyalty, Shelton publicly accused *Newsweek* of performing "a hatchet job" on Bob after he so nobly supplied the magazine with "two years' anecdotes about Mr. Dylan's rise to national popularity." Shelton defended Bob's right to obscure his past, suggesting that by uncovering his past the magazine demeaned Bob's distinction as a "non-conventional artist." In other words, they were guilty of printing the facts instead of the ritual Shelton "puff piece."

Shelton also deplored *Newsweek*'s disclosure of a rumor that Bob hadn't written, but *bought* "Blowin' in the Wind" from its de facto author, a fifteen-year-old high school student from Millburn, New Jersey. The story had been circulating around the Village for some time that Bob made a one-thousand-dollar contribution to CARE in exchange for the lyric, but few folksingers paid it any attention. The song was clearly Bob's creation, and eventually the claim was identified as a hoax. But Shelton, in his capacity as Bob Dylan's unofficial press agent and apologist, lashed out at *Newsweek* for reporting the allegation. What's more, he sent copies of his grievances "to fifteen writers, editors, and music-world leaders" in order to set the record straight.

Throughout the fall of 1963, Bob continued to perform, but he refused to cooperate with the press. He granted interviews, but nobody got straight answers from him. If he was asked to define the blues, Bob replied, "The blues is a pair of pants without any pockets in them," or "blues is a color." A request for his recollections of being a teenager prompted the response: "I don't remember being one."

Bob had become the master of the hip put-on. He delivered nonsensical answers with a deadpan face. Of course, the questions he was asked were equally inane. What do you expect when you ask a twenty-two-year-old entertainer questions like: "Bob, do you have any philosophy about life and death?" "Do you avoid close relationships with people?" "Don't you have any important philosophy for the world?"

It is an often overlooked fact that Bob Dylan was less effective as a speaker than as a songwriter. At no time was this more evident than on December 13, 1963, when Bob accepted the Emergency Civil Liberties Committee's Tom Paine Award at New York's Americana Hotel.

The idea for giving Bob the award came from Clark Foreman, Geno's father, who had been Undersecretary of the Interior during the Roosevelt administration and was a renowned civil rights activist and a ranking member of the New York intelligentsia. Foreman's choice of Bob for that year's award served two pressing purposes: foremost, it might encourage young people to become active in the struggle for civil rights; and, Foreman hoped, it would endear him to Geno, who distrusted and was estranged from his father.

This wasn't the first time Clark Foreman had appealed to folksingers in an effort to promote the movement. Nor was it Bob's introduction to the Emergency Civil Liberties Committee. On two occasions that summer, he and Joan Baez appeared at small, intimate fund-raisers for the organization at the homes of Bernard Brighton and Dr. Corliss Lamont. At that time, Bob became familiar with the committee's goals: voter registration in the South, the right to unrestricted travel to Cuba, and a campaign to end the draft, as well as one to declare the budding war in Vietnam unconstitutional. It was a charter that obviously appealed to him and was certainly compatible with Joan's pacifist nature.

The Tom Paine Award was given annually at the committee's major fund-raising event—a semiformal dinner that celebrated the Bill of Rights, followed by a presentation of eminent civil libertarians. It honored a Tom Paine-like nonconformist, a voice in the wilderness that cried out for justice in a dark hour. And the award was highlighted by an acceptance speech.

Bob Dylan was an unlikely choice for the award, in comparison to past recipients. A year earlier Lord Bertrand Russell had addressed the gathering, and before him the honor had gone to James Baldwin, I. F. Stone, and Alex Meiklejohn. Still, the ECLC's executive committee felt Bob's presence was crucial to help raise the consciousness of American youth, who, if politically active, were drifting toward the progressive labor movement and away from civil liberties. Their only reservation was the manner of Bob's address to the audience. Perhaps, they reasoned, because of his age and experience he should accept the award, say thank you, and sit down. Maybe the occasion called for him to perform, someone else suggested. Clark Foreman objected to exploiting Bob. "No, let's hear what he has to say," Foreman insisted. "Let's dignify him as a thinking person and not merely as a performer."

A mid-afternoon snowstorm foreshadowed the evening's frosty developments, but failed to deter the thousand-or-so rights advocates who tramped steadfastly into the Americana's Princess Ballroom precisely at six o'clock. Bob arrived at six-thirty, in time for cocktails, but it was clear he'd already participated in happy hour somewhere else. He was stoned and determined to get plastered, if the amount of wine he consumed was any indication. Edith Tiger, a member of the ECLC's executive committee, realized early that Bob was bolting down drinks at a suicidal pace. "He looked terribly frightened," Tiger remembers. "He was pale and nervous. Those of us who know him began to grow concerned. Then Geno Foreman showed up wearing an iridescent suit and we knew we were in for a long night."

Dinner was served promptly at eight o'clock. By nine, the festivities got under way with comments by Corliss Lamont; John Henry Faulk, the blacklisted radio personality; Mrs. Cyrus Eaton; and author James Baldwin. Bob was next in line to speak, but when Edith Tiger looked down the dais he was gone. A committee member reported seeing Bob duck into the men's room; however, it seemed unlikely he'd still be there after all that time. Edith Tiger wasn't so sure. She marched unswervingly into the men's room and let out a gasp. There was young Tom Paine—pale, drunk, and terrified—holding himself up over the sink. Taking him by the hand, she said, "Bobby, you're on," and led him zombielike back into the ballroom.

Clark Foreman presented Bob with a plaque for "his outstanding contribution to the struggle for civil rights and justice." It was now Bob's turn to address the crowd. He glanced at Edith Tiger and grinned. We're in trouble, she thought, he hasn't prepared a speech.

"I haven't got any guitar—I can talk though," Bob began shakily. "I want to thank you for the Tom Paine award on behalf of everybody that went down to Cuba. First of all, because they're young and it's took me a long time to get young. And now I consider myself young and I'm proud of it. I'm proud that I'm young. And I only wish that all you people who are sitting out here today or tonight weren't here and I could see all kinds of faces with hair on their head and everything like that—everything leading to youngness, celebrating the anniversary when we overthrew the House Un-American Activities just yesterday. Because you people should be at the beach. You should be...swimming and...just relaxing in the time you have to relax."

The audience laughed at this remark. Bob shook his head pensively and put both hands on the lecturn.

"It's not an old people's world," he continued. "It has nothing to do with old people. Old people, when their hair grows out, *they* should go out." The audience laughed again, but Bob squinted and grew serious. "And I look down to see the people that are governing me and making my rules—" He glanced at a bald man seated at one of the front tables who'd covered his head with his hands. "And they haven't got any hair on their head. I get very uptight about it."

Bob's voice assumed a sharp, holier-than-thou quality: "And they talk about Negroes, and they talk about black and white. And they talk about colors of red and blue and yellow. Man, then I just don't see any colors at all when I look out...." He shook his head again and sighed, "I've never seen one history book that tells how anybody feels."

At that point, Bob went into a song and dance about Negroes, the whole some-of-my-best-friends-are bit. Except Bob claimed *his* Negro friends wouldn't be caught dead in suits, like the Uncle Toms who organized the March on Washington. "My friends don't have to wear any kind of thing to prove that they're respectable Negroes," he said incomprehensibly. Looking oddly gaunt and awkward under the harsh lights, Bob then launched into a defense of the radicals who visited Cuba with a great deal of emotion, but not much coherence. Finally, he struck a penetrating pose, his eyes growing narrow and moody.

His head performed a slow, jittery sweep of the room. "I'll stand up and to get uncompromisable about it—which I have to be to be honest...I just got to be," Bob fumfered, "as I got to admit that the man who shot President Kennedy, Lee Oswald...I don't know exactly where...what he thought he was doing, but I got to admit that I, too—I saw some of myself in him." The room froze. The symphony of clattering silverware, clinking ice, and nervous chatter that underscored his speech stopped dead. The audience was numb. *Lee Oswald?* Was Dylan *insane?* Only three weeks had passed since Oswald had assassinated John F. Kennedy, and the name sent shivers up and down everyone's spine. Never mind the extenuating circumstances. Oswald reportedly visited Russia and championed Fair Play for Cuba; as many in the audience had flirted with communist or left-leaning causes, they feared a potential repercussion or, worse, a witch-hunt.

Bob, oblivious to the tension, was not about to stop now. He was on a roll. He'd finally found a hook for his after-dinner remarks and refused to prostrate himself to a bunch of useless old geezers. "But I got to stand up and say I saw things that he felt in me—not to go that far and shoot...." A volley of boos fluttered through the room. "You can boo," Bob snarled, "but booing's got nothing to do with it. It's a—I just, ah—I've got to tell you, man, it's Bill of Rights, it's free speech, and...."

"Time's about up," Foreman whispered, fidgeting in his seat.

Guests on the dais were gesturing frantically to one another. *Someone pull the goddamn plug!* In the audience, couples began edging toward the door. Veteran show-biz instincts warned Bob things were heading for disaster. It was time to wind up his set. Hastily, he said, "I just want to admit that I accept this Tom Paine award in behalf of James Foreman of the Students Non-Violent Coordinating Committee and the people on behalf of who went to Cuba."

An embarrassed hush settled over the room. Edith Tiger grabbed Bob as he prepared to walk off stage. Fearing that he might be harmed (by *pacifists,* no less!), she steered him to a corner of the room until Geno Foreman and her assistant, Phillip Loose, arrived. "Get him out of here," she instructed them, watching disconsolately as they guided Bob's rubbery body out of the hall.

Unfortunately for Tiger, the nightmare had not ended. The committee depended on contributions to see it through the year, and as was traditionally the case, the solicitation of pledges began *after* the presentations and speeches. As a result, she stood helplessly by as Clark Foreman attempted to remind those who remained what the object of the awards dinner was. Hardly any people went for their checkbook. How could they after the things Bob Dylan had said to them? After all, they were the standard-bearers of liberalism, the Old Left, the watchdogs of democracy. Many of them—Jews and former communists—had been blacklisted, they'd funded civil rights struggles, they'd fought bigotry and hatred. And now some smart aleck thought they should be exiled to Miami Beach. "Sorry," they seemed to be saying, "but we gave at the office."

Clark Foreman calculated Bob's behavior cost the organization roughly six thousand dollars in contributions, not to mention a hefty chunk of esteem. Another executive council member resigned in disgust. Edith Tiger, on the other hand, was strangely buoyed by the controversy. "I felt these people needed a good shaking up," she admits, years after the event. "We'd survived the Fifties and now most of the liberals had become silent. They never even told their kids they were liberals. Instead, they moved out to the suburbs where there was complete isolation from one another and soothed their consciences by making donations. So all of a sudden Bob Dylan confronted them and said, 'Look, either get up and do something or go play on the beach.' It wasn't very diplomatic, but it got the point across."

Bob, for his part, suffered a fair deal of remorse. He was disturbed by the audience's reaction, but was even more bewildered by his inability to communicate with people whose views were probably very similar to his own. And angry at himself for choosing to speak. Politicians spoke at fund-raisers; he was a singer, an entertainer. He should have known better.

Later that night, Bob sat at his typewriter and composed a mea culpa in the form of a poem which he sent to the Emergency Civil Liberties Committee. Entitled "A Message," he said:

> it is hard to hear someone you don't know, say 'this is what he *meant* t say about something you just said.'

Reevaluating his comments to went on:

> I should've remembered
> I am BOB DYLAN and I dont have t speak
> I don't have t say nothin if I dont wanna
> but
> I didn't remember...
> ...my mind blew
> up and needless t say I had t get it back in its
> rightful shape (whatever that might be...)
>
> oh God, I'd a given anything not t be there
> "shut the lights off at least"
> people were coughin an my head was poundin
> an the sounds of mumble jumble sank deep in
> my skull from all sides of the room
> until I tore everything loose from my mind
> an said, "just be honest, dylan, just be honest"
>
> an so I found myself in front of the plank
> like I found myself once in the path of a car
> an I jumped...
> jumped with all my bloody might
> just tryin t get out a the way

> but first screamin' one last song...

Bob claimed his reference to Lee Oswald was a metaphor for "the times" and not the deed. The times were sick, he said, and the business about everyone sharing the blame for social misfortunes, like church bombings and gun battles, was a bunch of crap. That was why he felt compelled to stand up and say "I—I saw some of myself in him."

> yes if there's violence in the times then
> there must be violence in me
> I am not a perfect mute
> I hear the thunder an I cant avoid hearin it
> once this is straight between us, it's then an
> only then that we can say "we" an really mean
> it...an go on from there t do something about
> it...

Bob made no pretense of apologizing for what happened. He did, however, offer to compensate the ECLC for any losses it incurred and requested the committee send him a bill, "for money means very little to me." The remainder of the poem was a lyrical expression of the limits of his talent and a declaration never again to speak in front of crowds.

That might have been the end of it had Bob in fact kept his mouth shut. But in an interview published in *The New Yorker,* he blasted the ECLC's members as people who "had minks and jewels, and it was like they were giving their money out of guilt." He said, "Those people at the dinner were the same as everybody else. They're doing their time....the only thing is, they're trying to put morals and great deeds on their chains, but basically they don't want to jeopardize their positions. They got their jobs to keep. There's nothing there for me, and there's nothing there for the kind of people I hang around with."

The tone of the interview prompted Clark Foreman to call in Bob's promise to reimburse the committee for its fund-raising losses. Albert Grossman responded, saying that Bob would be pleased to give a benefit concert for the ECLC. He even set a date, signed a contract, and went through the motions for the charitable event. A few weeks before it was to take place, however, Grossman's office canceled the show, and both Albert and Bob became unavailable when Foreman attempted to reschedule it.

For all his solemn declarations, Bob Dylan was either unwilling or unable to confront the people he had disappointed. Ironically, facing the music was one of the most difficult things for Bob Dylan to do. He found it was often easier to move on than to repair a damaged relationship. In fact, Bob had done a fair share of hard traveling, disconnecting himself from conflicts. Each journey offered the path of least resistance, a shortcut to peace of mind. In fact, there was only one road ahead, and that, too, led to a dead end.

15

Some Kind of Messiah

Suze Rotolo must have experienced a dark foreboding as the New Year—1964—entered. Christmas had been an utter disaster. She and Bob spent it across the Hudson River, in Hoboken, New Jersey, with her newly remarried mother and a few close family friends. But if the holiday fostered a spirit of peace and goodwill, that spirit certainly eluded their little celebration. Bob and Suze argued constantly throughout dinner, and when they called a truce, he went at it with her mother and, later, with Carla. It was a rehash of the same old dispute: the battle for control over Suze. She was being pulled from all sides, crippled by advice and insinuations. "He's no good." "She's a jealous monster." "She's the enemy." All things considered, Christmas might have been more joyful had they spent it in the DMZ.

Bob's new album provided a bright interlude. *The Times They Are A-Changin'*, his third record, was released on January 13th to rapturous acclaim. This was his first collection of completely original songs, and its strength surpassed any of his previous endeavors. The songs were vivid and straightforward, the language neatly embroidered with imagery, the delivery steely and uncompromising. Previously, Bob's vocals had been almost timid, held aloft by his tremulous, Guthriesque drawl, but on this album he practically thrust the words at his astounded listeners.

The title song established an edge and a tenacious gait that extended throughout the record. "The Times They Are A-Changin'" pulled no punches. It issued a direct attack against complacency and a clarion call for American youth to stand up for what they believed in. In effect, the lyric was a reconstruction of his Tom Paine speech, although here it was more adamant and unsympathetic. Parents were cautioned not to criticize what was beyond their command, including their kids, and were advised that a better solution might be for them to... go to the beach! Go *swimming!*

Whereas "Blowin' in the Wind" and "Don't Think Twice" are classics in an overall musical sense, "The Times They Are A-Changin'" assumes an extraordinary significance as a revolutionary political statement. Of course, political anthems weren't anything new. They'd been around since Adam defied God's command not to eat the apple. But "The Times They Are A-Changin'" invested an entire generation of largely disaffected teenagers, with the license to express themselves and *insist* that they be heard. Individuality and change were necessary for personal fulfillment, Dylan implied. Following in the footsteps of parents, philosophers, writers, politicians—anyone, for that matter—was an act of self-denial. The shackles of tradition had to be removed, and anyone who stood in the way of this cultural uprising would be unceremoniously shoved aside. "The Times They Are A-Changin'" was a powerful stimulant to the anomie of youth in 1964, much as *On the Road* had been to their predecessors. It stirred up intense yearning, provoked introspection, and capitalized on the tidal currents of social unrest.

The same could be said for "With God on Our Side," although its potency has diminished more with age. The song is a melodramatic antiwar ballad—probably influenced by Joan Baez, who performed it regularly with Bob—that parodies war and the people who glorify it. Derisively, the song presents a child's-eye history of American war as it's taught in school, which is to say rationalized by patriotism: "These are our enemies and we kill them in the name of God and country." The child, as Bob sang it, grows confused by the illogical argument and, in the end, arrives at his own conclusion that war is not only evil but contrary to any concept of God, as well.

"With God on Our Side" was a definitive protest song, in both content and melody. The lyric was about as unsubtle as TNT and cloyingly precious, while the tune shivered with emotion. It sounded suspiciously like the national anthem of Hungary. You could really get carried away singing it. "The Ballad of Hollis Brown" and "Only a Pawn in Their Game" suffered from the same obviousness.

At the time, the protest songs drew the most response because of their unorthodoxy, but aside from the title piece and "Hattie Carroll" the album's standouts were anything but topical songs. The two love songs that cushion the politics revealed a maturity in Bob's writing, and a masterful aptitude for imagery. "Blowin' in the Wind" had demonstrated his skill with metaphor, but in "Boots of Spanish Leather" and the gossamery "One Too Many Mornings" Bob embraced his lyrics with a rich, allusive romanticism.

Except for "Restless Farewell," which Bob wrote specially to fill up the album, the songs on *The Times They Are A-Changin'* attracted new listeners with their brilliance and diversity. It convinced them that Bob Dylan was indeed a talent of major importance—not only to music but to their own cultural and spiritual exploration. What Suze feared most was happening: Bob was becoming a pop idol—a "thing." In a poetic letter published in *Broadside,* Bob described how autograph hunters followed him down the street, while other fans pondered his writing as if it held some important secret to their universe. Clearly, he was grappling with the inconveniences of fame. "I am now famous by the rules of public famiousity," he jested in *Broadside;* "it snuck up on me/ an pulverized me.../ I never knew what was happenin." His contempt for the media, which circled him like a school of undernourished sharks, went undisguised:

yes above all the mumble jumble an rave
praises
an all the records I've sold...thru all the
packed houses I play...thru all the communication systems an rants an bellows an
yellin and clappin comes
a statement like "why do you do what you do"
what is this?
some kind of constipated idiot world?
some kind of horseshoe game we're all playin
respondin only when a ringer clangs

no no no
not my world...

It was obvious that, by virtue of his album's success, Bob had forfeited a considerable chunk of personal privacy. The press was hounding him. Acquaintances tried to cash in on their "close friendship" with him. Strangers treated him like royalty, seeking personal advice as if he were a modern-day King Solomon. "an what am I anyway? some kind of messiah walkin around...?" he wondered. "hell no I'm not." Bob insisted that he wanted to be left alone, but at the same time he craved the spotlight and the public forum which permitted him to pontificate endlessly on subjects such as social responsibility, wealth, greed, Pete Seeger, and his folkie pals. Admittedly, it presented a contradiction for him, to which Bob responded:

away away be gone all you demons
an just let me be me
human me
ruthless me
wild me
gentle me
all kinds of me.

One of the qualities he omitted happened to be "two-faced me." The oversight was corrected a week later when Bob was holding court at Suze and Carla's new pad over on Avenue B. A few friends had stopped by to watch TV, drink wine, and get high, all of which helped to cast a tranquil mood over the room—until Geno Foreman flew in from the cold. "Hey, Bobby!" he bellowed, oblivious to the other guests. "You fuckin' Baez, man? She any good?" Suze was walking in from the opposite end of the room and froze. Geno grinned like an orangutan as Bob attempted to cover up the gaffe, but the damage was done. Geno had only divulged what Suze already knew—that Bob and Joan were still an item—but the truth hurt like hell. Worse, Bob planned to leave on a cross-country tour that wound up in northern California and suddenly the destination made perfect sense to Suze. Baez country! The little bastard intended to hook up with Joan. If that didn't beat all!

Bob's aim was to drive to California by way of the Deep South, then through New Orleans in time for Mardi Gras, on to Texas, then to Denver (where he was scheduled to give a concert), and finally to Berkeley on February 22nd, in time for a show at which Joan would be *his* guest. The odyssey was destined to echo the cover copy on a paperback edition of *On the Road*: "A mind-expanding trip into emotion and sensation, drugs and liquor and sex, the philosophy of experience and the poetry of being... passionately searching for their country and themselves."

By January, the passenger list was nearly complete. Bob's only stipulation for a seat was "grooviness," although the complexion of the final gang was anything but hip. Closest to resembling that definition was Victor Maimudes, a dark, hulking young man whom Albert Grossman had hired to be Bob's road manager. Victor, in time, would double as Bob's valet, bodyguard, and all-around penitent slave, but for now his job was to handle most of the driving and to make sure the young star got to his gigs in one piece.

Another seat went to folksinger Paul Clayton, despite the protests of several of Paul's close friends. He expressed an eagerness to travel with Bob, and Bob was truly fond of Paul. He admired Paul's scholarship in folklore, but even more than that, he felt completely at ease around him. In contrast to the aggressive, cynical, hipper-than-thou folkies who populated Bob's entourage, Clayton was mellow, *spiritual*. Everything about him—his soulful eyes, soft expressive speech, delicate mannerisms, and contagious smile—bespoke a gentle nature. Unfortunately, they also camouflaged an inner torment that consumed him.

Paul Clayton was a mass of raging conflicts so mentally overwhelming, in fact, that friends worried constantly about his sanity. There were any number of reasons the journey with Bob might be detrimental to his welfare. Chief among them was his drug addiction. Clayton popped five-milligram dexies, one after the next, from the minute he got up until his body collapsed from fatigue, and the stress caused by traveling might prove too much for him. That alone wasn't enough to alarm friends, but Clayton experimented with other drugs, and their cumulative effect was slowly driving him insane. Says one close friend: "The drugs turned him into a ghost. Every time I hooked up with him it was like getting together with someone or some*thing* out of a Stephen King novel."

More distressing, perhaps, was Clayton's sexual conflict. He was engaged to Carla Rotolo, but everyone close to Paul—including Carla—knew he struggled with homosexuality, and the object of his affections was none other than Bob Dylan. "Paul was madly in love with Bobby," says a member of the MacDougal Street mafia in whom Clayton confided. "It was something he never came to terms with, yet he spent every moment he could in Bobby's company as if to torture himself. You can't imagine how much it tormented him."

Consider the effect it must have had on Carla Rotolo. Not only had Bob made off with her sister's affection, but now her fiancé was in love with him as well. No wonder she despised Bob. Carla tried to talk Paul out of the trip, but she knew it was no use. "He was determined to go," she recalls, "and in some way I hoped he might use the occasion to come to terms with everything."

That left one seat up for grabs. Suze suggested Pete Karman. To Bob, this was about as appealing as having your mother say, "Take your cousin Sheldon to the movies with you." Karman was about as uptight as they came and, what was worse, a close friend of Suze's. He'd probably report to her every move Bob made. How was he supposed to have any fun with a spy aboard? Yet to everyone's surprise Bob relented, and at last the crew was set.

Before they left, however, Bob detoured to Toronto for one of the strangest performances of his career: a guest spot on a local TV show called *Quest*. This was a glaring example of how ill-suited folk music was to a medium that sought to convert artistry into superficial entertainment. For that matter, the entire show was an anomaly. There were no introductions, no voice-overs, only the legend "The Times They Are A-Changin'" superimposed on the black-and-white screen. Then the lights came up to reveal a set right out of *Klondike Annie*. The stage crew had reconstructed the interior of a log cabin with all its woodsy accoutrements. Three rugged-looking lumberjacks hunched over a card game, while a fourth Neanderthal, worn out from a hard day's woodchopping, whittled a stick as his rocking chair teetered in front of an old-fashioned pipestove. In the midst of all this manly kitsch stood Bob Dylan with his guitar and harmonica. Dressed in blue jeans, boots, and the obligatory flannel shirt he looked like a dim-witted coolie who'd been ordered to entertain the men. What this scene had to do with protests songs like "Hattie Carroll" was anybody's guess, but for twenty minutes Bob strolled around the set singing selections from his three albums. Luckily, *Quest* would be seen by only Canadian viewers.

The next day, Bob took off on his sightseeing tour, which, to Peter Karman's amazement, had been set up as a business write-off. The object was for Bob to visit deejays and promoters along the way, dropping off his new album with them. Trouble was, Albert's office was out of albums and the caravan was stalled for a few hours until another game plan was devised.

They were also delayed by a shipment of clothes that Bob had agreed to deliver to striking miners in Hazard, Kentucky. A few weeks earlier, Bob and Suze had attended a rally hosted by activist-folksinger Hamish Sinclair to generate support and money for the miners' families. Bob wanted to do something for them, but he was uncomfortable putting his name to it—no doubt a side effect of the recent Tom Paine debacle. Suze suggested they round up clothing that Bob could deliver on his way to New Orleans. That way, he'd be involved in a benevolent way, but it took him off the hook as a spokesman. Bob heartily approved.

The itinerary for the first couple of days was ordinary enough. The guys cruised through Washington, D.C.; checked out the Lincoln Memorial; and then stopped for the night at Paul Clayton's country home in Charlottesville, Virginia, where they got stoned and played Monopoly until almost dawn. The next day, they picked up a couple dozen of Bob's albums; continued south through Roanoke, Radford, Abington, and finally pulled into Hazard, where the strike had apparently disrupted the community.

Hazard must have reminded Bob of Hibbing, with its ruptured topsoil and regiment of dog-tired, expressionless miners. The landscape had the same dreary look to it. It had been violated, its natural resources ravaged and withered, its spirit beleaguered by industry's reckless disregard. Earlier in the day, they had picked up a young hitchhiker who told Bob how dead the town was and how, for kicks, he and his friends cruised the main drag in a nearby hamlet, watching the Greyhound buses arrive. In a different time and a different place, that might have been Bobby Zimmerman had his dreams not prevailed.

Bob obviously made the same connection. He took the kid for a beer, then left him with a copy of his album and perhaps a spare dream or two for the future.

Bob's experience in Hazard was not so rewarding. When they arrived, Hamish Sinclair was embroiled in the strike action and had no time for his northern friends. Bob assumed they'd hang out, exchange ideas, maybe jam a bit, but no such luck. "Bob was very pissed-off," Pete Karman recalls, consulting extensive notes he took during the trip. "He was hurt and angry about being brushed off like that, so we decided to hit the road. As soon as Sinclair said he didn't have any time for us, we didn't have any time for the strike."

Victor Maimudes headed the procession toward the next destination: Asheville, North Carolina, where novelist Thomas Wolfe grew up and was inspired to write his brilliant autobiographical trilogy. Having unloaded the cargo of clothes, the station wagon's rear compartment provided ample office space for Bob, who set up a typewriter there and proceeded to bang out lyrics for several new songs. Clayton sat directly in front of him with a traveling salesman's sample case balanced on his knees—his stash—and every fifty miles or so he reached inside and grabbed a handful of pills which he consumed with ceremonious delight. "We had a traveling drugstore in the car," Karman recalls. "Everybody was stoned—too stoned to be scared of getting busted. But the possibility followed us wherever we went." Victor and Karman shared driving chores, and as the car rolled south into the heartland, a feeling of adventure and enchantment seized the young explorers.

Ahead of them lay the village of Hendersonville, North Carolina, a few miles drive off the main interstate. Bob had been looking forward to this visit with great expectation, for Hendersonville was the home of one of his idols—the renowned poet and folk musicologist Carl Sandburg. Bob, who so valued and protected his own privacy, thought nothing of arriving unannounced at the poet's doorstep. Getting there proved more than half the battle. Victor had trouble locating Sandburg's farm and wound up driving around in circles. Finally, they asked directions at a gas station, where the attendant said, "Nope, don't know if this Sandburg fellow's a poet, but I can tell you how to reach Sandburg the goat farmer." Sure enough, they were one and the same, and before long the guys had an audience with one of the world's most beloved lyrical voices.

Carl Sandburg was as unassuming in his appearance as his homespun but tasteful farm. He was dressed plainly, in an old plaid shirt, gray trousers, and work shoes. His hair was toussled, and he badly needed a shave. From the looks of things, he was more likely just milking his goats than reworking a quatrain. Still, he was impressive, even powerful-looking, and his presence had the mark of true authority.

Bob stepped forward as the group's unofficial spokesman. He introduced himself as a poet and said, "I've written many poems, and I have this album which I'd like to give you." With that, Bob presented a copy of *The Times They Are A-Changin'*, which Sandburg accepted graciously. Clayton offered one of his albums, too.

"Without looking at each other, I could tell we were equally amazed," Karman remembers of the meeting. "I distinctly felt like there was a passage of honor between the young prince and the old king. It was a sincere, no-bullshit, no show-biz moment, and we all noted it respectfully."

Sandburg gave the guys about a half-hour on his porch before he excused himself. That was Bob's cue to shift into action. What he really wanted, what intrigued him most of all, was a tour of the poet's study—to see where the great man unleashed his imagination, maybe compare work habits. It'd be a pity to have come all this way, to have actually confronted Carl Sandburg, and not see where he wrote! So Bob tried another angle: the colleague approach. Catching Sandburg's eye, he said, "I, too, am a poet," as if that'd capture his host's heart, but the old man would have none of it. He promised Bob and Paul that he'd listen to their albums, then promptly took his leave.

Several accounts of this meeting describe Bob's reaction as "sulky" or "annoyed," but Karman maintains that everyone left Hendersonville in a buoyant mood. "We had seen [Sandburg]," he says, "and there was a general excitement that carried us on our way."

They were also propelled by the effects of good dope, which was consumed from a seemingly endless supply. Pot, pills, and booze. The station wagon was a continuous party-on-wheels as it crawled through the South. Bob was stoned a good deal of the time, and the drugs had a galvanizing impact on his personality as well as his music. When he was high, he became more introverted, preoccupied. His disposition swung wildly to extremes. One minute he was fun-loving and exhilarated; the next he became the nasty, jive-talking denizen of the underground. It was difficult to predict exactly where he'd land. One thing was for certain, though—his frame of reference grew weirder.

"Time don't exist—it's an illusion, the other side of Dali's clocks," he told Pete Karman en route to Georgia. Later, he blathered, "The birds are chained to the sky. No one's free, even the birds are chained." Karman told Bob that his poetic double-talk was bullshit. "I don't get it," Karman said. "How do you write the stuff you do when you don't even understand what it means?" But Bob wasn't up to explaining himself. He merely buried his head in the typewriter and converted the imagery into lyrics.

The song in progress was "Chimes of Freedom," which he completed before the trip was over. It marks a turning point in Bob's development as a songwriter. Loaded with imagery and metaphor, it paints surrealistic montages, one after the next, using a concurrence of phrases and rhymes. The lyric percolated with jingling alliterations like "majestic bells of bolts," "mad mystic hammering," and "disrobed faceless forms." In one stanza, the "sky cracked its poems in naked wonder." More than ever, Bob was experimenting with the *sound* of words—combining, juxtaposing, and overlapping them, regardless of meaning, to create a mood. Not that "Chimes of Freedom" is meaningless. On the contrary, what evolved from it was a narrative full of substance and force. But the lyric, like the most splendid symbolist poetry, gleaned its significance from interpretation.

For nearly twenty-five years, students of "Dylanology" have feasted on Bob's cryptic lyrics. They've read into the metaphors great philosophical relevance rife with Freudian undertones. Robert Shelton theorized that in "Chimes of Freedom," Bob is "developing his favorite metaphor of tempest... he is extending love and identification." Another pundit called the song a modern excursion into "a Romantic, Blakean childhood... an emotional protest against emotional deprivation." But as Freud himself said, "Sometimes a cigar is just a cigar." Bob Dylan wrote songs whose lyrics were often amalgams of clever phrases that flowed poetically from beginning to end. When he told Carl Sandburg, "I'm a poet, too," he meant exactly that—he wrote stanzas chosen and arranged to create a specific emotional response through meaning, sound, and rhythm. However, in a song, the poetry is sometimes just part of the machinery used to keep the entire process in gear. And occasionally it derived entirely from good dope.

To keep the spirit alive, the guys replenished their stash in Atlanta by retrieving a package from the local post office. The next day, Bob played a concert at Emory University, which attracted not only a full house of fans but a contingent of the civil rights movement's dignitaries who came to pay their respects. The concert was a dressy affair, the audience was decked out in their Sunday best, and poor raggedy Bob, clad in his well-worn traveling clothes, floored them. Watching from a seat out front, Pete Karman shook his head in wonderment. Seems I appreciate him better on stage, he thought, bewildered by Bob's split personality. "It was an incredibly powerful concert," Karman remembers. "The civil-rights crowd took each song to heart, the college kids knew all the words, Bob was in complete control. It seemed bizarre that this was the same snot-nosed little kid who annoyed me so much in the car."

Bob spent that night with a student who caught his eye at a post-concert bash. Suze was in New York, the other guys were preoccupied with similar liaisons—no use passing up the opportunity. After a late start the next day, the guys drove down the Delta into bayou country—Hattiesburg, Mississippi; Pearl River, Louisiana—arriving in New Orleans in the midst of Mardi Gras pandemonium. Three drunken, dope-filled days later, Bob played a brief recital at Tougaloo Southern Christian College, attended by a contingent of freedom riders, then sped into Dallas for a look at the notorious grassy knoll before heading toward Colorado.

Driving west, Pete Karman grew uneasy about the relationship blossoming between Bob and Paul Clayton. "Paul was definitely attracted to Bob," Karman recalls. "He was very warm, solicitous and affectionate toward him in a way that was different from the kind of relationship you'd expect from two straight guys. Everyone knew Paul was in love with Bobby, but as the trip progressed I began to have an androgynous feeling about Bob, as well."

Although it's unsubstantiated that Bob ever experimented with homosexuality, the notion that Bob was reciprocally attracted to Paul is not as inconceivable as it sounds. Mark Spoelstra claimed that two years earlier, he declined an offer from Bob to share his bed, an offer which left Mark disillusioned and shaken. Certainly, Bob was aware of Clayton's feelings toward him. He even encouraged them. If Bob, in fact, remained platonic with Paul Clayton, it was a very cruel emotional game the two men played.

In Colorado, Bob did a show in Denver and then schlepped the guys up to Central City, the scene of his spurious honky-tonk experience. The town hadn't changed one bit since he'd last seen it—still a second-rate fake western tourist trap, overlooking the Rockies. Luckily for Bob, the Gilded Garter was closed for the winter, lest someone recognize him as the culprit who lifted money from the owner's wallet. As it was, he conducted his friends on a tour of the ghost town and maintained his exceedingly tall tale about playing there.

By the time they reached California, however, not everyone was buying into his story. Pete Karman had grown seriously disenchanted with Bob's behavior. All the wacky images that enriched Bob's songs gradually crept into his conversation, and you had to be stoned out of your gourd to appreciate it. Victor and Clayton were, and their dopey chuckles encouraged Bob. He went on and on about . . . *nothing.* And the mumbo-jumbo got weirder. It was as if he had become their guru. "More like their meal-ticket," Karman remembers thinking, as they headed toward Berkeley.

Most likely, Bob was sick of Karman as well. The guy was incredibly uptight. Always straight and so fucking responsible. Worried about the drugs and cops and covering his ass, being on time, acting maturely. A real killjoy. He might as well have brought Carla Rotolo along! What's more, Karman constantly challenged Bob—"What do you mean by this? What do you mean by that?"—trying to call his bluff. What a drag Suze's friend had become.

It seemed like Bob and Karman were always sparring, although Pete was no match for his agile opponent. "He had a style of attacking me that was indefensible," Karman recalls. "Rather than addressing anything specific, he'd tell me what was in my head. 'Where you're coming from . . .' Or, 'Where you're at . . .' The worst thing about it was he'd never try to engage me. I'm argumentative, I like to discuss things intellectually, and Bob knew that, so he continuously kept me off-balance with observations about my inadequacies. He'd bait me, then back me into a corner. I felt helpless against him. Trying to defend myself was like punching air. And before long I felt like I was going crazy."

The knockout blow came in Berkeley, when Karman tried to arrange tickets to Bob's concert for two friends. He asked Victor for passes and was promptly told to go fuck himself. Karman was stunned. "It was a college concert, there were plenty of seats, a lot of people usually watched from the backstage area," he says. "Two tickets were no big deal, so obviously I was meant to take it personally." When he confronted Bob, he was accused of being a parasite. "You're trying to use me, Peter," Bob stammered, bringing up a six-month-old grievance to support the accusation. Karman crumbled under Bob's harangue. He'd had enough of this bullshit and told Bob so. As a result he booked a seat on the next plane back to New York.

Following the concert, Bob spent a few days in Carmel with Joan, her sister Mimi, Dick Fariña (who married Mimi on the rebound from Carolyn Hester), what was left of Bob's car crew, and a wild, whacked-out Boston art student named Bobby Neuwirth who, in time, would become Bob's constant sidekick.

Mimi remembers that week for the strong gust of egos blowing through her parents' house. "It was laden with them," she says. "A gathering of over-developed personalities. Everyone was angling for the last, coolest, hippest word." But the group deferred to Bob's penetrating wit. Joan was in love with him, Mimi, only nineteen, was a pushover, Fariña stood in awe of Bob, Clayton was infatuated, Victor took orders from him, and Neuwirth craved acceptance. The only resistance came from Joan's father.

"My father's got an ego almost as big as Bob's and he wanted respect," Mimi says. Bob refused to cave in to authority figures. In fact, he delighted in needling them. That his rival happened to be Joan's father only served to double Bob's obstinacy. A showdown ensued at a coffeehouse in the Cannery, where everyone had gathered for a bite to eat. Bob ended up grabbing a guitar and, staring right into Alfred Baez's eyes, performed a scathing version of "The Times They Are A-Changin'." "Come mothers and fathers throughout the land, and don't criticize what you can't blah, blah, blah . . ."

That really fried the old man's ass. Alfred found the lyrics disrespectful, offensive. He pulled Joan aside and discussed the incident with her, but his disapproval fell on deaf ears. To her, Bob Dylan's message carried the most clout, and even her father was upstaged.

Though Bob was thoroughly enjoying himself, he left Carmel to appear on the *Steve Allen Show* in Los Angeles. The idea of inviting Bob came from a member of Steve's staff, since the host had certainly never heard of him. Her argument that Bob was a complete original and outspoken for his young age appealed to the gregarious Allen, who regularly presented people whose talent went against the cultural mainstream. But even Steve Allen wasn't prepared for the absurdity that characterized Bob Dylan's appearance.

On February 25, 1964, Allen's viewers watched one of the most bizarre guest spots in television history. Attempting to set the mood, Steve Allen led into Bob's spot with a wordy homage more suited, perhaps, to the introduction of a religious leader.

> He's one of those performers who seems to somehow be taken to the hearts of the young people who see him—the high-school age, college-age people who see him—they somehow seem to identify with him or with parts of him or part of what he does. . . .

The audience laughed, but Allen was dead serious as he sorted through Bob's albums, and promised to introduce "this very interesting young man" after the commercial break.

When they came back, Bob was standing next to Steve Allen, looking sheepish and out of place. Allen, ever the gracious host, admitted the show's varietylike format usually necessitated a hasty intro of guests. "We say a few words about their accomplishments, tell you where they're working currently, and say, 'Here he is!' We point to them and they go into their act. But I thought it would be instructive, in this instance, to tell you about this young man," Allen remarked.

Quoting from journalist Ralph Gleason's review of the Berkeley concert, Allen's eyebrows shot skyward to emphasize how impressed he was: "'Genius makes its own rules, and Dylan is a genius—a singing conscience and moral referee as well as a preacher.'" This stuff was being broadcast to ten million people—you couldn't buy this kind of publicity! Allen read another rave from *Billboard:* "Dylan's poetry is born of a painful awareness of the tragedy that underlies the contemporary human condition." Steve was really laying it on thick. Foolhardily, he'd decided to interview the genius himself. Turning to him then, he asked, "Bob, do you sing partly your own songs, partly other peoples', or where do you get your material?"

A barely audible sound rose from Bob's throat: "They're all mine now."

"You do all your own material," Steve translated, sensing trouble. "And how long have you been writing your own music?"

Bob considered this pensively. "Uh... for about—uh—two years."

"Just two years."

"And seven years before that," Bob added in a dopey Gomer Pyle accent.

Steve Allen's face registered exasperation. "This is going to be a long night," it said.

"But I quit writing and started copying about two or three years between."

Steve was completely confused. "What do you mean by the word 'copying?'"

"I quit writing and started singing what other people have written."

"Oh, I see," Steve said, but clearly he didn't, and the studio audience chuckled in sympathy. "Uh, I think it might be interesting for the audience if I quote a word or two from one of your poems." Steve picked up a copy of *The Times They Are A-Changin'*, the lights dimmed, and as he started reciting the second stanza from the liner notes, entitled "11 Outlined Epitaphs," his piano player tinkled atmospherically across the keys. What an abomination! Bob's beautiful, impressionistic prose, its stark vocabulary, syntax, themes, mood, and movement, sounded, in this context, like a lounge act at a Holiday Inn.

Bob was somewhere off-camera, but one needn't have seen him in order to visualize the agony on his face. Television—he should have known better.

After it was over, the interview really started going downhill. Bob announced he was going to sing "Hattie Carroll"—embarrassingly, only one person applauded in recognition—and Steve asked for the storyline. Bob answered him coyly: "The story I took out of the newspapers, and I only changed the words." Now, that line brought appreciative chuckles in concert, but on TV it sounded incredibly dumb—a fact which wasn't lost on Steve Allen. "You changed the words?" he asked. "I changed the words," Bob repeated.

"I don't understand. You took a story out of the newspaper...."

"It's a true story..."

"I see."

"...it happened in Maryland."

But Steve wasn't about to let him off the hook so quickly. "What words did you change?" he persisted. "I still don't know what you mean by that."

"I changed—uh—the reporter's view..."

"Um-hmmm."

"I *used* it—I used it for something I wanted to say, and—uh..." Bob started to squirm. "...I used his view—many of the reporter's views—to get what I wanted to say and turn it that way."

"Um-hmmm." Steve wasn't buying any of Bob's cosmic nonsense.

"I used it to get at a true story, that's all. I could have made up the story."

"Um-hmmm. Was the, uh, story—I mean, was the actual incident—did it concern someone named Hattie Carroll?"

Bob practically blurted out the word *yeah,* thankful he didn't have to expound on that, but he got convoluted again when Steve asked for a synopsis of the song. "Oh, I could tell you about it, I could sing about it, I could do anything. If I talked about it, I could talk about it for a very long time; if I sing about it, it would only take as long as the song lasts."

Relief crossed Steve Allen's face; finally there was a way out of this mess. Precipitately, he said, "Well, I imagine the song tells its own story. Here it is."

Bob was clearly unsettled by the disastrous interview, as his subsequent performance demonstrated. He sang a dreadful, screechy version of "Hattie Carroll," aggravated by poor amplification that made his harmonica sound like the brakes of a truck. When the show came back from a commercial, Bob was probably already miles from the studio.

The *Steve Allen Show* confirmed Bob's theory that folk music and television didn't mix. *Hootenanny,* a weekly series that originated live from college campuses, was successful as a result of the strictly commercial pop acts it showcased. But serious folk music wasn't pretty enough to please the average viewer. On the air, Bob came across like a gawky hillbilly. His serious approach appeared comical. And on top of that, television stripped a song like "Hattie Carroll" of all its intensity and meaningfulness. His experience on *Quest* illustrated just how inappropriately folk music could be presented on the tube; with Steve Allen, he'd learned that a folksinger's job was to perform, not converse. Wisely, he swore off TV and, except for an outrageous segment on the *Les Crane Show,* in February 1965, he didn't return to the medium until 1970, when he was influential enough to exercise control over the way he was presented.

Bob's natural habitat was the medium-sized concert hall, where he played to an audience of folk-heads willing to be stimulated and amused by his songs, open to the ironic, intellectual tenor of his lyrics, provoked by the issues he commented upon and the opinions he rendered. They most likely knew the words to his songs and appreciated his quirky instrumental style. And they tolerated his deadpan sense of humor. That was the effect Bob Dylan achieved in concert throughout his career, and it was the medium he instructed Albert to pursue for him when he got back to New York in March.

Albert, for his part, was already two steps ahead of his client. While Bob was away, he'd arranged for a concert tour of Great Britain to begin in mid-May. But first there was a domestic appearance that required Bob's immediate attention.

Suze Rotolo was no longer content to exist only as Bob's girlfriend. Bob had virtually ignored her while he was away, even dispensing with the ritual of nightly placating phone calls. As anyone who knew Bob could tell you, he was expert at juggling relationships, but when he grew tired of the deception, he simply cut himself off from the problem or pretended it never existed. With Suze, he employed both strategies, which bore him truly lousy results.

Suze had occupied her time away from Bob with various interests, but in the process she had become detached from her true emotions. "She seemed kind of wiped-out and generally distraught," says her friend Sue Zuckerman, in whom Suze confided during this time. "She told me about some knock-down drag-out fights they'd had and about her suicide attempts. I saw that she was on the verge of flipping out and needed to begin re-ordering her life."

The situation exploded the last week in March when Bob returned from his West Coast trip. On a chilly spring night he and Suze decided to call it quits—this time for good—but the separation was anything but peaceful. A discussion at the Avenue B apartment dissolved into an argument, and about one in the morning, when Carla got home, they were going at it like a couple of street cats. Carla took one look at the situation and disappeared into her room. "I'm not going to get involved," she remembers saying to herself. She picked up a book and tried to shut out their angry words, but the uproar eventually became too much for her to ignore. Besides, Carla was an inveterate busybody. When Bob ignored Suze's appeals for him to leave, Carla plodded back into the kitchen.

"Why don't you leave?" she asked Bob politely, trying not to divert his wrath. "Come back tomorrow and finish this. It's very late and I want to go to sleep."

An hour later, Carla reappeared at the battlefront. Suze was pleading with Bob to go away, and this time Carla insisted on his cooperation. "Can't you see what she's trying to do!" he screamed, pointing at Carla. "Don't you see?" Suze screamed back at him, then at Carla. She was losing control, and her outbursts soon turned to gibberish. Suddenly, she picked up a knife from the kitchen counter and threatened to kill herself. Before anyone could grab her, Suze let out a moan and collapsed on the floor.

Carla rushed to her sister and determined she was all right. The knife had missed cutting her. Suze, however, was in worse shape than she first appeared. She began to shake; she had no visible motor control. "At that point, Suze had basically checked out," Carla recalls. "I couldn't get through to her."

Bob continued to scream at Carla, hurling one accusation after the next at her. According to Bob, she was responsible for every iniquity under the sun. She was a venomous bitch, untalented, jealous, meddling...

"Bobby—help me get Suze up," Carla pleaded. "I want to get her on the bed."

...antagonistic, bitter, fucked-up...

"Okay, that's it. Get out or I'm calling the cops." Carla lunged at Bob and began pushing him toward the door. He pushed her back, no longer simply defending himself. Carla couldn't get her hands free to hit him. "We were really struggling," she recalls, the night indelibly etched on her memory. "The two of us were really going at each other as if our lives depended on it."

Finally Bob gave up and left. Carla looked at the mess and at her nearly comatose sister and knew she needed help. It was four o'clock in the morning. She started to call Dave Van Ronk but remembered that he turned off his phones at night. Barry Kornfeld was home, however, and promised to run right over. So did her mother and stepfather; it'd take them about a half-hour to get there from Hoboken. Once Barry arrived, Carla split. She couldn't stay there any longer and decided to spend the night on Barry's couch. Paul Clayton, who'd shown up with Barry, agreed to stay with Suze until her mother arrived. The next day Carla learned Clayton had immediately let Bob back into the apartment. When a frantic Mary Rotolo got there, she found Bob and Suze on the bed, crying in each other's arms. Prying them apart, she took Suze to a doctor in Hoboken, where she was to recuperate for an indefinite period of time, effectively ending her relationship with Bob Dylan for good.

Bob's version of the battle was preserved in "Ballad in Plain D," which appeared on his fourth album. Vengefully, he made little attempt to disguise the embattled cast. Suze appears as the "constant scapegoat," a "tragic figure" with "the innocence of a lamb" and the gentleness of a fawn, while Carla gained notoriety as the proud "parasite sister." The song, for the most part, was a mean-spirited reenactment of the night at Avenue B; however, in it, Bob admirably recanted the head trips and lies he wreaked upon the Rotolos so that Suze would remain faithful to him.

"Ballad in Plain D" was too personal to find an appreciative audience. The lyric is maudlin, the melody monotonous and dirgelike. In the end, the idyllic relationship with Suze Rotolo was squandered by petty name-calling and insults. Bob could easily list "Ballad in Plain D" as one of his most bitter "finger-pointing" songs, a sad, sordid footnote to his Village days, especially when contrasted with a dedication he inscribed inside the front cover of a book of poetry he'd given to Suze earlier that year:

> To you,
> from I, me, Bob
> on this holy day.
> I give you this here present
> that I purchased in the
> New York rain.
>
> —Lord Byron Dylan

Part 3

The Mad Years

16

In the Court of the King

The thin crowds were a disappointment for the historic Bob Dylan–Joan Baez concert that toured during the spring of 1965. The billing warranted the kind of sellouts expected of today's superstars—an arena filled to capacity, scalpers pocketing a hundred dollars for a seat behind the stage, gate crashers *shtupping* the doorman for a pass through the turnstiles. Though this was one of the great musical events of the decade, promoters had a hard time moving tickets, and, come showtime, most of the halls fell short of expectations.

Looking back, this becomes more incomprehensible in light of the relative brevity of the tour. Now, pop acts often remain on the road for an exhausting ten or twelve months at a clip. Any period less than three months of solid dates is unprofitable. Bob and Joan's run lasted a total of nine shows with no appearance scheduled back-to-back, at Joan's insistence. What's more, the halls were moderate in size—scaled anywhere from three thousand to six thousand seats. They should have sold out in a flash.

Why the lackluster turnout? It's difficult to pinpoint a reason, but from the outset, the entourage was pervaded by a creeping paranoia. For one thing, Joan's manager, Manny Greenhill, and Albert Grossman were about as compatible a team as Bishop Tutu and the Ayatollah. Neither trusted the other's judgment, much less his ethics. It would have been an easier job had both men been willing to jointly promote the shows, but Greenhill refused to consolidate their operations and consequently wound up having to handle the tour on his own.

A second dispute arose over billing. It was supposed to be fifty-fifty, with neither performer hogging the spotlight, but that created its own rash of niggling problems. Like whose name appeared where in the advertisements. Greenhill had commissioned Bob's friend Ric Von Schmidt to design a poster for the occasion—an impressionistic watercolor depicting the two performers singing a duet—but the result proved anything but harmonious. Grossman was disturbed by the size and location of names: Joan's came first and appeared a fraction bolder than Bob's. Still, his image loomed dramatically above hers, so it seemed a judicious balance had been struck. When Grossman showed the poster to Bob at a concert in Providence, however, it was rejected without explanation.

One theory was that Bob objected to the use of his famous poor-boy image: the Woody Guthrie get-up, complete with cap and harmonica holder. In fact, his image had changed. Since returning from California, he'd forsaken the Okie-hokey-folksy mien in favor of a more contemporary flair. He'd transformed himself into the hip philosopher—a fast-talking, hard-loving, rock 'n rolling, trendsetting visionary, able to deflate hypocrisy with his penetrating insight. He was the epitome of cool. James Dean with a guitar.

In March, Bob had completed his fifth album, *Bringing It All Back Home,* which was destined to change the course of his career. No longer confined by the bounds of folk music, side one of the record jumped to the tempo of an electric rhythm section, but it wasn't the instrumentation as much as the songs themselves that joggled listeners. They were infused with surrealistic imagery, but their energy was flat-out rock 'n roll. They were eloquent, witty, conceptual, reflective, and musically combustible—magnificent explosions of words and music. Folk and rock—the combination was so obvious, yet so staggeringly unique.

The remainder of the album was even more extraordinary. Just four songs composed one of the most remarkable sides of Bob Dylan's recording career, beginning with the transcendental "Mr. Tambourine Man," a masterpiece of style and vision. Musically it bred a kind of enchanted buoyancy that heightened the power of the lyric. The phrase "jingle-jangle" repeated in the chorus almost defined the song's spirit, accentuated by Bob's playful guitar accompaniment. The melody bounded forward, spinning compulsively along the wordy odyssey he'd constructed from rhythmic patterns and phrases. The lyric, line after line of it, was abstruse yet at the same time unforgettable—a burst of fragmented thought, popping so fast and furiously that whole images rush by in a blur. What ear can absorb all those wonderfully absurd, alliterative abstractions upon first hearing "Mr. Tambourine Man"? "Evening's empire," "ancient empty street's too dead for dreaming," "magic swirlin' ship," "skippin' reels of rhyme," "twisted reach of crazy sorrow," "circled by the circus sands".... The extravagance of such phrases made the song more of an experience than a statement.

In another sense, "Mr. Tambourine Man" augured the spirit of the times; it was breathtaking, indulgent, utopian, extemporaneous, hypnotic, cajoling, hallucinatory. Nothing could have symbolized the Sixties better than a Pied Piper, a guru, a—*Mr. Tambourine Man!*—whose disciple is willing to be directed, perhaps even reeducated, without any resistance whatsoever. If ever a song revealed the curious path of its author, "Mr. Tambourine Man" was it. For the first time since becoming a songwriter, Bob Dylan flirted openly with his muse, abandoning the usual themes of love and politics for honest introspection. As such, it was the only song Bob ever admitted attempting to duplicate—unsuccessfully to be sure. It was simply too personal and had evolved organically, instead of by contrivance—a quality that makes "Mr. Tambourine Man" a triumph of inspiration over the craft of songwriting.

The remaining three songs—"Gates of Eden," "It's Alright, Ma (I'm Only Bleeding)," and "It's All Over Now, Baby Blue"—were equally impressive, if not as pop-oriented as "Mr. Tambourine Man." Unlike his previous compositions, which were mostly topical, Bob concentrated on the poetry in each line, stretching his already superb command of imagist verse into the abstract and beyond. "Gates of Eden" and "It's Alright, Ma" extended his experimentation with strobelike flashes of imagery, however brooding and cynical, into epic-length extrapolations on the human condition. Part sermon, part free-form rap, all three songs were heavily moralistic. Their message was: the whole world's a mess. THEY fucked up, now WE have to live with it. All fifteen verses of "It's Alright, Ma" careen along the precipice of Armageddon, plucked from the brink of despair only by the witty refrain, "But it's alright, Ma. . . ."

Bob unloaded on whatever was bugging him at the time—organized religion, phony advertising, the rat race, our antiquated court system. His belligerence respected none of the establishment icons. He was pissed off at conventional society and its platitudes. In "It's All Over Now, Baby Blue," Bob took on relationships as well, but for all its pessimism the upshot was a recommendation to "strike another match, go start anew."

Collectively, the songs on *Bringing It All Back Home* reflected a radical departure from popular music. The album also changed the way Bob presented himself in public, which was evident from its stagy cover photo. Shot in Blithewood, an old Victorian mansion on the campus of Bard College, it was styled to give Bob a well-groomed, seductive look, right down to the same vaseline-on-the-lens effect used to beef up *Penthouse* centerfolds. The setting was elegant, chic. An ornately carved mantle glistened in the background. Antiques stood in conspicuous disarray. Except for a carefully placed album cover or two, there wasn't a vestige of folk music anywhere in sight. No guitar or peaked cap or denim work shirt or snowy Village street corner tamped down by the heavy footprints of bums who usually shuffled there for handouts.

And no Suze.

In her place, though, was a really frosty-looking babe—none other than Sally Grossman, Albert's new young wife—curled up on a daybed like a cat who'd just come in out of the cold. For all anyone knew, she could have been a department-store mannequin. Dolled-up in a slinky, red peignoir, Sally had struck just the right pose for the occasion: distant, untouchable, all business behind those Siamese eyes, holding a cigarette in the world-weary manner of a Faye Dunaway character. The waspish look on her face said, "Just try it, buster."

In the foreground, Bob sat hunched forward at her feet. He wore a sleek-fitting sportcoat and dress shirt with. . . *cuff links.* Bob Dylan was dressed to kill—what a sight for sore eyes. And he was groomed, to boot. His hair wasn't all over the place for a change. He looked alert and interested in the way he was being presented, not detached as he had been on his previous albums. This cover projected the image of choice—the sophisticated Bob Dylan—jet-setter, arbiter of taste,

The Angry Young Rebels, poolside at Newport, 1964: Tony Glover (dressed, with shades), Joan Baez, Bob, Tommy Makem, and Jack Elliot (with cigarette). (*John Cooke*)

The ultimate in coolness: Bob and Bobby Neuwirth take a hip dip at Albert's house, Bearsville, New York, 1964. *(Photograph by John Cooke)*

Another happy hootenanny—Albert Grossman, Bob (on Joan Baez's lap), and Mimi Fariña, Newport, 1964). (*Photograph by David Gahr*)

Bob (still on Joan's lap) and his Beaujolais, 1964. (*Photograph by David Gahr*)

Albert and Sally Grossman, entertaining Pop Staples, Newport, 1964. (*John Cooke*)

Paul Rothchild keeping "tabs" on Bob, Amherst, 1965—just look at that face! (*John Cooke*)

The First Annual Bob Dylan Look-Alike Contest? Left to right: Richard Fariña, Donovan, David Blue, 1965. (*John Cooke*)

That controversial band—Bob rehearses at Newport, 1965. Left to right: a stage aide, Mike Bloomfield, Jerome Arnold, Bob, and Al Kooper. (*Photograph by David Gahr*)

That Night at Newport, 1965. (*Photograph by David Gahr*)

Bob pointing out the winner of The Most Likely to Change Nose Contest? With co-contestants Sonny and Cher Bono, 1965. (*Don Paulsen*)

Mrs. Dylan-to-be: Sara Lownd's Playboy Bunny tailshot, circa 1961. (*Playboy*)

Phil Ochs speculates about the outcome of Bob's motorcycle accident, 1967. (*Ron Cobb*)

Bob reappears for Woody Guthrie Memorial Concert, January 1968. Left to right: Robert Ryan, Pete Seeger, Bob, Judy Collins, Arlo Guthrie, and several Guthrie relatives. (*Photograph by David Gahr*)

The return to New York City, 1969–1970. A. J. lurking in the garbage below? (*C. Andrews/Retna*)

Another Bob Dylan look, Isle of Wight Festival, August 1969. (*David Redfern/Retna*)

Recording with Leon Russell, 1971. (*Photograph by David Gahr*)

cultural aesthete. Not some hayseed folksinger, some schlump! Together, he and Sally resembled a couple of prehistoric Yuppies, surrounded by their possessions, looking oh-so-cultured and smug.

Once you got past the cover, however, it was impossible to argue with the goods. *Bringing It All Back Home* had a tremendous influence on the shaping of popular music. It inspired every rock 'n roller for the next twenty years, from the Beatles to Bruce Springsteen. Just listen to "She Belongs to Me" to discover where Lou Reed learned how to sing. Groups like the Sir Douglas Quintet and the Lovin' Spoonful co-opted the intentional garage-band sound. The Byrds dined out on Bob's songs and solidified their place in the pantheon of rock 'n roll. Everyone's lyrics suddenly improved, although no one managed to rival Bob's poetic skill.

Perhaps one of the reasons for that was a powerful new stimulus that drastically changed his head: LSD. Bob had begun writing under the influence of acid in the spring of 1964, when he was turned on by friends who were determined to launch their hero on an eye-opening tour of the cosmos. Paul Rothchild recalls in graphic detail the night that Bob crossed that imaginary border into a state of altered consciousness:

> It happened right after a New England tour. God, Dylan had been great. He was magical. He'd cast a spell over those audiences unlike anything I'd ever experienced before—or since.
>
> After the last show at the University of Massachusetts in Amherst, we drove straight back to Albert Grossman's new house in Woodstock, where Dylan had a room at the end of the hall. At this point, we were all smoking joints in the car. Everyone was relieved that the tour was over. We were mellowed out and happy to be going home.
>
> Then, when we got there, we discovered that Albert was out of town. Bob started smoking grass, everyone else was higher than a kite and *hungry*. We all had a serious case of the munchies. Sometime after midnight, Victor [Maimudes] was dispatched to the refrigerator where he found a couple tabs of acid wrapped in aluminum foil. He shuffled over to me with a twinkle in his eye, nodded in Bob's direction and said, "Let's do it! If there's two people in the world who can make him comfort-

> able, we're it. After all, someone's gonna do it to him." I looked at the sugar cubes and thought, "Why not?" So we dropped acid on Bob. Actually, it was an easy night for Dylan. Everybody had a lot of fun. And if you ask me, that was the beginning of the mystical Sixties right there.

There is no doubt that LSD was largely responsible for Bob's sudden lyrical shift. The hallucinatory property of acid opened up whole new areas of poetry to him. It introduced him to his own abstract, and as such, the quality of his lyrics changed. They became more personal, more perceptive. He'd begun the mind-boggling "exploration of self" that shakes up the senses and splinters into kaleidoscopic flashes of vivid imagination.

The influence of LSD is everywhere in *Bringing It All Back Home,* launched by the opening line—"Johnny's in the basement/ mixing up the medicine"—into brilliant imagery and ethereal allusions. "Ah, get born, keep warm/ Short pants, romance . . . " The guy was gonged out of his nut. "Better jump down a manhole/ light yourself a candle/ don't wear sandals. . . . "

The album's one false note was its title—*Bringing It All Back Home.* Naturally, Bob meant "back to rock 'n roll," his roots. But, literally speaking, as of the album's release date, Bob Dylan no longer had a home. He had moved out of his West Fourth Street pad—the place held too many memories for him—and reverted to crashing on friends' couches. For most of March he had been on the road, which precluded more formal sleeping arrangements, and afterward there was Albert's place up in Woodstock, a funky artists' hamlet on the fringe of the Catskill Mountains.

Bob headed for Woodstock right after the tour, inviting Joan and the rest of their entourage to meet him there for a brief furlough. It was April, and the dense mountain foliage already showed signs of summer splendor. The community was undiscovered by weekenders, its pace was slow, people there respected each other's privacy. There was no better place to recuperate from the road. "By that time, we had become a family," recalls Joan's sister, Mimi, who joined the fun at Albert's along with her husband, Richard Fariña. "We all felt very exclusive, as if the outside world didn't exist."

But as with any vacuum, their world began to collapse inward.

Rudeness and hostility had become the dominant currency at Albert's—making a fool out of someone from across the room in order to entertain the troops—and Bob, as usual, traded most actively in the medium of exchange. The more fragile someone was, the more insecure, the more fun he had with them, and to Bob's advantage he had a houseful of emotionally transparent guests.

Joan Baez was perhaps the most sensitive of the bunch. Bob had kept her off-balance during the tour—criticizing her and openly tormenting her in front of Bobby Neuwirth—and she sensed he was moving even further away from her. Not that she hadn't expected as much. For all her shortcomings, Joan Baez saw things astutely, and she knew the idealized relationship with Bob was fated to end—*badly*. It just wasn't in the cards.

Nevertheless, Joan had held out for some kind of reconciliation. The prospect of a future with Bob seemed so deliciously romantic. Wouldn't it be wonderful if they could tour together for the next twenty or thirty years—the King and Queen of folk music? They could have it all if they wanted. A couple of times a year they could take time off for Bob to write. Joan could pursue the nonviolence school she was financing, maybe have a few kids. It wasn't out of the question. They'd joked about marriage in the past. Who knows? Maybe time and maturity would work to calm the troubled waters.

Joan was encouraged in her fantasy when Bob invited her to accompany him on a tour of England slated to begin that last week in April. What a gallant gesture, she thought. She'd introduced him to American audiences; now he was reciprocating by including her in his show. As a matter of fact, Joan had scheduled a British tour for later in the summer; the appearance with Bob would help to plant some powerful seeds in the British press.

In the meantime, Joan had several concerts to perform on the West Coast. The night before she left Woodstock, the gang got together at a restaurant there to wish her a speedy return. Joan, Richard, Mimi, a companion of Joan's named Barb Warmer who was visiting from California, Fariña's Cuban pal Alfredo, and the ubiquitous Victor Maimudes—everyone was in high, *high* spirits. Only Bob had the power to undermine such festiveness. That night, his weapon happened to be cruelty. His target: Alfredo, who had a nervous twitch in his eye.

Throughout the meal, Bob mimicked the twitch, then exaggerated it whenever someone addressed him. The laughter it provoked, along with countless bottles of wine, encouraged his deviltry and sent poor Alfredo into spasmodic bedlam. Unsatisfied, Bob parodied Alfredo's eating habits, which had become more seriously afflicted by the woeful degree of heckling. Finally, Alfredo stood up and threw his napkin on the table. "I'm leaving," he shouted in a rage. "Nobody talks to me like this." Bob smiled with satisfaction as Fariña chased after his friend. The evening's entertainment wasn't finished, however. Not by a long shot. Next Bob lit into Joan, opening up old wounds, until she, too, beat a hasty retreat. Mimi slipped out behind her and walked down the road, where she found Bob's victims licking their wounds. Joan was in tears. Alfredo was still fuming, threatening to immediately drive off to California. Mimi looked to her husband for guidance. "What are we going to do?" Fariña shrugged. "The guy's being such a creep."

Mimi was furious. Her marriage to Dick was already on shaky ground, owing to her tender age and the narcissistic circle in which they traveled. They'd grown closer in recent days. Now that creep Dylan had to go and stir up trouble! Lately, he'd been unusually nasty to Joan, too, pecking away at her self-esteem as if he were testing her, trying to determine her breaking point.

Without telling anyone, Mimi doubled back to the restaurant and sat down next to Bob. Her hands shook with anger as he continued his bloodless character assassination by mimicking a retarded girl's eating habits. Finally, unable to control herself, she grabbed him by the hair and yanked his head back. "Don't you ever treat my sister that way again," she screamed. Bob started to laugh at her, so Mimi tightened her grip, throttling him. Tears welled up in Bob's eyes. "You understand me?" she yelled. Bob nodded with what little mobility he had left, struggling until Mimi let go. "Because I was a pacifist, the move was completely out of character," Mimi remembers. "Nevertheless it gave me great pleasure and to this day I hold it dear to my heart."

The next day, the incident appeared to be history. Bob, Richard, and Mimi drove Joan to the train station and saw her off, promising to reunite on the coast before heading to England. Back at Albert's house, Mimi went into a bedroom to change her clothes and heard Bob dialing the phone. Curious, she eavesdropped on his conversation. She began to shake with anger as she realized he was making a date with another woman. "Don't worry, she just left," he said into the receiver.

To this day, Mimi believes he was making a date with Sara Lownds, a friend of Sally Grossman's and the future Mrs. Dylan, but it could have been any of the women Bob was seeing on the side. There were a few Village chicks he hung out with in New York City. Occasionally, he raided the chicken coop at Bard. But when he was in Woodstock, Bob dated a seventeen-year-old at the Barlow School, a private institution for troubled girls from good families in nearby Amenia. She represented a particular "type" of woman Bob would seek out whenever a major affair was on the rocks: Jewish, intellectual, short, earthy but not beautiful, intense, neurotic. There were always plenty of exotic shiksas for him to choose from—Echo, Suze, Joan, backup singer Clydie King—but in troubled times Bob found solace with someone exactly like... *mom!*

Sara Lownds, on the other hand, was a rare bird. She wasn't funky or sharp-tongued or outrageous. Neither was she self-centered or glamorous in a way that would threaten Bob's public persona (although she'd been employed as a *Playboy* bunny). Sara was sexy to be sure, a twenty-four carat head-turner, but her beauty was natural and unaffected, with a warm elegance. Which is to say: Sara had *class.* Her features beheld an almost European countenance, dark and well-proportioned, like a young Sophia Loren, whom she vaguely resembled. Her eyes were almond-shaped and set wide apart, framed by a mane of billowy brown hair that looked almost black in certain lights. In fact, she was so striking in her appearance that to have brains on top of everything else seemed almost unfair.

Sara had come to New York in the late 1950s as an impressionable young model. Still in her teens, she married fashion-photographer Hans Lownds, who had sort of "discovered" her; she then enjoyed a brief, meteoric success as a triple-A-rated cover girl. Ironically, her career was shortened by two unforeseen forces: her divorce from Lownds and pregnancy. Sara moved out of Lownds' East Side townhouse, modeled until she began to show, and then took a job as a secretary at Drew Associates, a film production company which was part of the Time-Life Broadcast organization.

As for Bob, Sara met him in the early part of 1963, after she had moved to an apartment on MacDougal Street with a girlfriend. Later, she and Bob lived together at Albert's place on Gramercy Park, where she supported and looked after him during the time when he wrote "Mr. Tambourine Man." Their affair had blossomed right under Joan's unsuspecting nose. It happened naturally, without any public curiosity to interfere with it. Sensing the speculation it would arouse, Bob kept Sara out of the spotlight and away from the folk scene. Not even his friends were aware that Bob had a new lady love. Sara was special. Besides, he'd be in hot water if Joan ever got wind of her. They still had a number of concerts to do together, and he'd invited her to England, so the less anyone knew about Sara, the better.

Meanwhile, Sara divided her time between her daughter, Maria, and the ongoing circus at Time-Life Films. Drew Associates was in the midst of producing six documentary features, leaving the office administrative chores solely in her hands. It was there that she met Donn Pennebaker, an artsy experimental filmmaker who was in the midst of shooting a short subject about a drug-addict trumpet player at Synanon House. Pennebaker was a practitioner of the cinema-verité style of filmmaking; no script, hand-held cameras, grainy black-and-white film, quirky subjects. Previously, he'd shot critically well-received profiles of a young, ambitious senator named John F. Kennedy (*Primary,* 1959), followed by *Jane,* which chronicled La Fonda's disastrous Broadway debut in a play that opened and closed on the same night. Sara liked Pennebaker, she liked the way he communicated with his subjects, and mentioned to Albert that he might be a good candidate to shoot some film on Bob.

The idea must have touched off neon dollar signs in Albert's head. From the start, he'd groomed Bob for a career in the movies. The prospect of making films always came up when they discussed their long-range career plans. It was what separated superstars from mere folksingers. It was what created international legends. It was where the money was.

Albert also knew the average singing sensation lasted anywhere from two to five years. To cushion against the inevitable, he'd do well to get his boy into some compatible area of exploitation. Lord knows, the movies kept Elvis's career alive long after he'd stopped having hits. Rumor had it the Beatles were exploring film opportunities. The only obstacle to Bob's movie career was going to be finding the right vehicle for his *unique* talent. There'd be no *Beatnik Bongo Party* for Bob Dylan, you could bet on that. No *Hootenanny Hit Man.* No, Bob needed something completely different, something as exceptional and unorthodox as his songs. Something avant-garde! New York was aflutter over a rage called *underground* filmmaking. Perhaps that was the best way to show off Bob. The more Albert thought about it, Donn Pennebaker sounded like just the person to come up with the hook they needed.

Pennebaker describes his initial meeting with Albert Grossman as "exploratory." "The whole thing was so vague," he recalls. "Albert didn't have the slightest idea what he wanted to do. He never even mentioned the words 'movie' or 'feature.' He was simply inviting me to England to do some *filming.*" In talking with Albert, it became apparent to Pennebaker that he wanted footage of Bob for promotional use. Albert had studied the British scene and dug the way television presented film vignettes of popular rock groups. Everybody was doing it—the Beatles, Gerry and the Pacemakers, Herman's Hermits, the Animals. The bands camped it up, mugged through lots of silly gags, lip-synced to their latest releases, and, as a result, sold tons of records. The concept of promos was nonexistent in the States, but Albert was interested in breaking similar ground with his clients.

Bob Dylan, however, had more grandiose ideas. Having practically grown up in the Libba Theatre, he was enchanted by movies, and the prospect of starring in one excited him. The press had covered his infatuation with Woody Guthrie and Little Richard, but his heroes were James Dean and Marlon Brando as well. It wasn't that long ago that he and John Bucklen had pretended to be Monty Clift and Burt Lancaster in *From Here to Eternity.* His Chaplin antics had delighted the Village coffeehouse crowd. Friends were constantly touting his charisma. To hell with promo films—Bob smelled feature all the way.

Pennebaker arranged to meet Bob at the Cedar Tavern, a cafe near NYU that once played host to the New York art scene. Jackson Pollack, Mark Rothko, Larry Rivers, and the abstract expressionists had drunkenly cavorted there with fellow gallery owners, writers, jazz cats, and the beatnik crowd. By the Sixties it held nothing but memories of those mad days, but still Bob occasionally hung out there out of some sentimental attachment to its history.

From the start, the meeting was a typical Bob Dylan burlesque. Bobby Neuwirth served as straight man as the boys put Pennebaker through a couple of numbers to measure the director's coolness quotient. Because it was mid-afternoon, the bar was practically empty, but Bob had gotten it into his head that a woman drinking quietly there was Lotte Lenya. Pennebaker had seen Lenya in *The Threepenny Opera* and told Bob he was mistaken, but Bob couldn't take his eyes off her. "Hey, I'd know her anywhere, man. It's Lotte Lenya," he insisted. This went on for ten minutes or so until the woman herself assured Bob that not only wasn't she the chanteuse, she'd never even *heard* of Lotty "Lender."

Afterward, he and Neuwirth went through a few numbers for the director's benefit. "It was an attempt to put me down, see how I react, was I a fag—things like that," he recalls. In fact, their routines had a completely opposite effect on Donn Pennebaker. He says, "I recognized instantly, when I met Dylan and Neuwirth, that they had the same sense about what they were up to as we did about what we were up to, which was a kind of conspiracy. We felt as if we were out conning the world in some kind of guerrilla action and bringing back stuff that nobody recognized as valuable and making it valuable."

That was when Pennebaker came up with the film's central motif: hanging out. The music, he decided, was going to be almost inconsequential. Anyone could shoot miles of concert footage; there was no real art to that. What fascinated Pennebaker was Dylan's persona, his mystique. Trying to capture that on film presented a tantalizing challenge.

Years before, Pennebaker had been hired to film an adaptation of Jack Kerouac's *On the Road,* in which he faced almost identical obstacles. "I knew there had to be some way to translate Kerouac's particular angst, his fidgety enthusiasm and love of things around him, people around him, into film terms," he says. "From watching Dylan's absolute compulsion to somehow evolve from Kerouac I began to understand how to approach the film. Kerouac and Neal Cassidy lived at a hundred-mile-an-hour clip; Dylan and Neuwirth enjoyed their own fantastic life-style, and in a way, their essences were intertwined."

It'd be impossible to capture Bob Dylan with a script. He wouldn't respond to cues or preconceived lines of dialogue. "The only way to do it," Pennebaker concluded, "was by having no expectations whatsoever. I think Dylan really liked that because the thing that scared him about making the film was that somebody was going to try and lay a trip on him and say, 'Here's what you have to do, because we're making this movie and it's got to be this way and we can't take the time to figure out another way.' The idea that he could do anything he wanted, without any preconceived notions, was what really interested him."

Bob insisted, nevertheless, on having a certain amount of creative input as far as his film debut was concerned. Pennebaker flinched. He knew from experience that filmmaking was a collaborative art, but Dylan's wayward enthusiasm could get out of hand. There had to be some measure of restraint. Still, Pennebaker decided to indulge Bob, hoping to get a better sense of his character from things he said.

"The first idea he came up with knocked me for a loop," Pennebaker recalls. Bob wanted to open the film with a song, only he wouldn't be singing it. It would be a track from one of his albums, during which he'd flip over cue cards displaying snatches of lyrics. "It was fantastic, *exhilarating!*" Pennebaker says. "I remember thinking: What a strong, resonant character I have on my hands! Here was somebody who was willing to take chances and let me film things that other people might shy away from. He'd be acting out his own life. Changing and evolving. I'd be the not-entirely-dispassionate observer. There was drama coming on. I could smell it."

Pennebaker's sinuses proved to be acutely sensitive. *Don't Look Back* turned into a seriocomic soap opera of Bob Dylan's off- and on-stage antics, made at a time when private experiences were becoming part of the public myth. Full of pathological energy, it played like a contrived peepshow made by an exhibitionist who knew the audience was watching his every move. Yet for all its guile, the movie's subjects were not self-conscious or modest. They weren't camera-shy. Nor were they particularly careful about what was said and done. No one stopped to consider the repercussions of a scene before allowing the cameras to roll.

Bob's opening sequence turned out marvelously. The film faded in over a shrill, ear-splitting rendition of "Subterranean Homesick Blues," the same track that kicked off the album, only in a darkened movie theater the wailing guitar riffs had the same effect on your nerves as an ambulance shrieking through the night. Over the clatter of music, Bob appeared on screen, standing in an alley, small and waiflike as a gypsy boy whose goal is eventually to lift your wallet, peering into the camera with a devilish glint in his eye. Earlier that afternoon, he and Donovan had drawn up about fifty cards on which random phrases from the song were written—phrases that sounded comical taken out of context, like: BASEMENT, MEDICINE, HEAT PUT, WIND BLOWS, DIG YOURSELF, GET BORN—and as the soundtrack barreled ahead, Bob raced to match the cards to the lyric.

The rest of the movie faithfully chronicled the tour as it evolved over the thirty-eight days, from April 26, 1965, to June 2, 1965. Bob played a total of only eight concerts, the last two of which were his historic Albert Hall performances. In between, however, the days were crammed with mischief and mayhem. Bob set the tenor of the tour as the plane took off for England. He and Bobby Neuwirth, in high spirits, camped it up with their entourage and spent an hour or so trying to convince a woman seated across the aisle that they worked for the CIA. There were birthday cakes presented to friends who weren't celebrating birthdays, photographs taken of passengers with unloaded cameras. They were like a couple of high school kids on their class trip, out to see how much they could get away with.

About two hundred fans waited patiently in the rain for a glimpse of Bob as he deplaned at Heathrow. England was swept up in the frenzy of Beatlemania, but the press and public reaction to his arrival was not without its own hysteria. Newspapers and TV covered it as they would a foreign head of state's first visit to their country. Reporters swarmed all over Bob, smashing a glass partition and overturning baggage as police escorted him through the airport terminal into a cordoned-off waiting room. They were so preoccupied with him that Lena Horne, a huge star in Great Britain, accompanied the handful of arriving passengers on TWA flight 702 and slipped by completely unnoticed.

Bob suffered through the pandemonium with mild amusement. Dressed less than casually in a denim shirt, blue jeans, boots, black leather jacket, and sunglasses, he traded one-liners with the emissaries from Fleet Street's umpteen dailies. Asked if he intended to marry Joan Baez, Bob quipped, "I might marry her arm." They pressed on, however, determined to find out if she'd accompanied him abroad. "I think she came along," Bob said more earnestly, despite Joan's standing only a few feet away. To poke fun at the occasion, Bob carried a gigantic light bulb like it was a religious artifact, which soon drew the anticipated inquiry. "What's the light bulb for?" a reporter demanded. "No, I usually carry a light bulb," Bob replied with mock sincerity. Moments later, when another reporter wanted to know what his message was, Bob shot back: "My real message?—Keep a good head and always carry a light bulb."

The reporters eventually turned their questions to the subject of Donovan, a cliff-jawed folksinger from Scotland, whose ballad, "Catch the Wind," was currently racing up the British charts. The press was having a field day with what headlines referred to as "The Dylan-Donovan Conspiracy." *Melody Maker,* doffing its hat to the hyperbole of Walter Winchell, labeled it "one of the biggest controversies that has ever split the British music scene," and accused Donovan of "copying Dylan's every antic."

Undoubtedly, "Catch the Wind" was reminiscent of Bob's earlier folk style, right down to the gravelly phrasing and accompaniment, but the "controversy," so to speak, was an aimless war of words that typified the English media's passion for exaggeration and hyperbole. The worst that could be said of Donovan was that he sounded a little like Bob Dylan—the first in a long line of "new Dylans" who were introduced for two decades. His song was pleasant enough; it had a catchy pop hook—"ah, but I may as well try and catch the wind." A lingering melody. Bob couldn't have cared less about Donovan's so-called plan to capitalize on his success. But the press did.

"Have you ever heard of Donovan?" a reporter called out.

"Donovan what?" Bob asked coyly, but after persistent interest in their similarities, he joked: "Where is he, this Donovan? Let's get him out here—put him on the wall!" The chance to do that would eventually come, but at the moment the focus of attention was reserved solely for Bob Dylan.

A major press conference took place the next morning, April 28th, before a caravan of limousines took off for the first concert in northern Sheffield. For convenience, it was held in the Manhattan Room, an annex to Bob's suite at the posh Savoy Hotel. It was obvious almost from the start that the flock of unsuspecting reporters had been sent over to do the kind of gag journalism that was usually practiced on lightweight entertainers who mugged for their cameras. This was the same crew that could ask the Beatles a setup question and count on a whimsical, very quotable reply. Their manner paralleled the send-up of a press conference in *A Hard Day's Night* when a woman asks George Harrison what he calls his haircut and he replies, "Arthur." That was the way the press handled *singers,* as they called them. Either that, or they fed you questions and let you hang yourself. But, of course, they'd never dealt with Bob Dylan.

Bob sensed immediately that he was dealing with a bunch of nitwits. They expected him to behave and respond like one of their infantile pop stars. It was also apparent that few of them, if any, had the slightest idea what he or his music was about. To them, he was just another assignment, another celebrity interview whose silly quote would appear on page three alongside the daily cheesecake snapshot of a buxom secretary. His expression conveyed an immediate understanding of the game and his attendant annoyance at what was expected of him.

Bob was unpredictable when it came to the press, almost schizophrenic. He exhibited nothing but contempt for the ongoing media circus that swirled around him, yet throughout his career Bob regularly made himself available for press conferences. It was as if he liked to spar cruelly with reporters the way a cat paws a wounded mouse—or, perhaps more simply, he enjoyed giving a different kind of performance.

Whatever his motive, Bob was in top form that morning of April 28th when more than twenty reporters tromped into the conference room at the Savoy. Wearing an outlandishly loud pink-and-blue shirt, blue jeans, and his trusty black leather jacket, Bob faced the gallery of interviewers with weary-eyed impatience. He was tired, irritated by the previous night's monotony of insipid questioning. He was also angry with the hotel's management, which had warned him that if he wanted to be served in their restaurant he'd have to wear a tie. In defiance, perhaps, Bob began the press conference by lighting a cigarette and dropping the match on the Savoy's plush carpet. Then, for the next hour, he answered a barrage of foolish questions in his most elliptical and truculent fashion.

The old flaks, expecting a cooperative subject, were intimidated by Bob's antagonistic manner. They couldn't get a straight answer out of him, there was none of the usual give and take. For example, when asked about the inspiration for his songs, he answered, "I write about the things I want to write about." In regard to his political interests, he snapped, "I just be—I exist. What people think about me doesn't affect me." The reporters grew increasingly frustrated. Unsure how to handle the situation, they pfumfed over their questions. Many of them packed up and left early. Says Donn Pennebaker, "Dylan had succeeded in outflanking them. He conducted the session in such a way that the reporters could actually hear how stupid their questions sounded as they asked them and it stripped them of their composure. No one had ever done that to them before, and the atmosphere in that room was incredible. Everyone left feeling like they'd been knocked completely off-balance."

On paper, however, they regained their equilibrium and used the opportunity to put the little whippersnapper in his place. The *Guardian* criticized Bob for being "monosyllabic" and "impatient." "Happily," the reporter wrote, "he had the dark, beautiful, straight-haired singer Joan Baez with him to straighten the record for the more middle-aged and irritated reporters." The *Sun* voiced concern about his stage presence: "It is hard to believe, looking at this short, rough-haired, rough-voiced 23-year-old from Minnesota, that he can hold an audience for two hours or more."

That fear was allayed the instant Bob set foot on stage. His eight English concerts stood out as more workmanlike, thoughtful performances than those he had given back home. Unlike his shows in the States, there were fewer attempts at comedy, hardly any interjections of cynicism, and no political grandstanding to placate the folkie crowd. In Great Britain Bob had come simply to play.

For the fans, Bob presented a show of such Spartan proportions that many of those in the audience were caught off-guard. The stage was practically bare, lacking the mountain of amplifiers and drums they'd come to expect of the current wave of English pop performers. Props were limited to a stool, a guitar, and a glass of water. Similarly, Bob's appearance on stage was acknowledged by respectful applause. There were none of the untamed screams or fainting associated with the customary teenybopper fanatacism. A bobby or two stood by the exits; otherwise police presence was limited strictly to traffic direction. In all, Bob Dylan's performances had more in common with solemn classical music recitals than those of his English contemporaries.

There was little variation from show to show, including Bob's apparel, which was somewhat upscale for the occasion—his black leather jacket framed a gray crewneck sweater, navy-blue slacks, and brown suede shoes. Ambling on stage without ceremony, he led off with "The Times They Are A-Changin'," his current English hit, then segued into "To Ramona"; "Gates of Eden"; "If You Gotta Go, Go Now," a salty love song which, at the last minute, had been lopped off *Bringing It All Back Home;* "It's All Right, Ma (I'm Only Bleeding)"; "Love Minus Zero/ No Limit"; and finally "Mr. Tambourine Man."

During one intermission at Leicester's De Montfort Hall, the producer issued an announcement over the PA system for his upcoming show—"starring *Donovan!*"—and everyone booed. That provided Bob with a moment of inspired comic relief. When he returned to the stage, he launched into "Talkin' World War III Blues" and altered a line in the ninth stanza to: "I turned on my radio—it was *Donovan!*" The place shuddered with more boos. Bob smiled and mumbled, "Whoever Donovan is . . . ," which prompted another outburst and applause. Bob raced through the second set with "Don't Think Twice, It's All Right," "With God on Our Side," "She Belongs to Me," "It Ain't Me, Babe," and "The Lonesome Death of Hattie Carroll." Encores, when offered, were limited to "All I Really Want to Do" and "It's All Over Now, Baby Blue."

There was no doubt that Bob completely captivated his English audiences. Throughout the first seven shows in the provinces, they remained absolutely quiet while he was on stage, listening intently to the words of each song. There was a smattering of applause following each number, but it was cut off sharply the moment Bob introduced another song. It was spooky, the way you could hear a pin drop. The tomblike silence affected Bob, too. At Sheffield, after the first few numbers, his eyes swept the dark auditorium.

"It's mighty quiet. Where are you all?" he asked, leaning toward the crowd.

Later he admitted being somewhat distracted by the hush. "Silent audiences don't exactly worry me," he told a reporter from *Melody Maker,* "but I think a lot more about what I'm singing and saying when they're so quiet." He wasn't unnerved by it. "Thoughtful," was how Bob preferred to describe his reaction. "If I appeared nervous or tense, that was because I was kinda inhibited, y'know—standing there listening to everything I was doing."

That part of it—listening—was a new experience for these young audiences. "There was so much to think about," said a dazed fan, leaving the auditorium in Liverpool. "So many new ideas and new ways of saying things. I'm not so sure I understood everything Dylan said, or even everything he was talking about, but the music put a lot of things in my own mind together for me."

The shows made quite an impression on the press, as well. The *Guardian,* which only days before had run a negative piece called "Overcoming Dylan," now gushed with enthusiasm. It proclaimed the event the "second coming of Bob Dylan, the singing Messiah." The Messiah! The paper completely reversed its original opinion, writing, "With his voice, the lyrics are astonishing; without it, in print, they are poetry. . . ." *The Daily Telegraph* was even less restrained. "There are better singers, better guitarists, better harmonica players, and better poets," their columnist surmised. "But there is no other 23-year-old who does all these things with even a semblance of the power, the originality or the fire." Bypassing all the music that was sweeping its own country, the *Telegraph* called Bob's show "an astounding popular victory for the world."

No paper mentioned a word about the conspicuous absence of Joan Baez. Surprisingly, she never once joined Bob on stage. Or rather, she was never *invited.* She would stand forlornly in the wings through each show, as Bob ignored her. Somewhere along the way he'd decided that it wasn't necessary to share his spotlight with her, no matter that she'd done it for him. What she'd done for him was her business, he claimed. He didn't owe Joan Baez anything.

Clearly, their relationship was over. Bob and Joan no longer shared the same bed, and even their friendship was tenuous. Joan walked on eggshells when they were together. His temper was short with her, and friends could tell she annoyed him by her very presence. One time, en route to a show, the caravan of limousines stopped for gas. Joan gazed out the window and saw some gypsies lingering around the pumps. "C'mon, let's film this," she said to Donn Pennebaker, who shared her car. Before he could respond, Joan flew out of the car, determined to pat the mongrels on the head like a pack of stray pups.

Bob, who was riding in a car behind her, jumped between the camera and its subjects. Furiously, he turned on Joan. "Hey, I've lived with people like that," he snapped at her. "You can't play with them. Get back in the car. Get rid of that fucking camera!" He'd had it with her whimsy, and it was clear that he didn't like Pennebaker's complicity in the whole affair. Anyone else would have simply asked Joan to leave. But as was obvious from past relationships, Bob wasn't one to confront bothersome situations, especially those involving women. With Joan, as with Suze before her, he preferred to make life so miserable that she'd eventually get the message and leave of her own accord.

Bob still had two shows to do at London's Royal Albert Hall. Ensconced once more at the Savoy, he spent a day off greeting a number of local rock 'n roll dignitaries who came by to pay their respects. The Animals, who had recorded Bob's version of "House of the Rising Sun" and "Baby, Let Me Follow You Down," were early visitors, leaving keyboardist Alan Price behind to clown for Bob and the troops. Manfred Mann had a version of "With God on Our Side" on the British charts and dropped off a copy at the suite. Doe-eyed Marianne Faithful hung out there for a while. And the Beatles took time out from recording a new album to visit their new American friend.

Bob had met the Beatles the previous August in New York, after their gig at the Paramount Theater. At the time, he wasn't entirely known to the Fab Four. Paul McCartney had heard his albums in Paris and turned on the rest of the band, but of the four only John Lennon was intrigued enough to explore Bob's music. Lennon was fascinated by the Dylan sound—the gritty, gutsy, smart-alecky edge that gave fire to each song. He admired Bob's rebelliousness, too, the attitude in his music that seemed to say "fuck you!" It was something he'd probably have liked to say himself, but the Beatles' image wouldn't permit it. Ironically, this gave John an inferiority complex that delayed their meeting. John insisted that he be Bob's "ego equal" before a summit between them took place.

By August 1964, Lennon was apparently feeling more secure. The Beatles had five singles on the American charts; they were on the cover of *Life,* and following a number of local appearances they were the toast of New York. In the manner of a spoiled British monarch, John summoned *New York Post* columnist Al Aronowitz, a notorious pop-star lackey, to his suite in the Delmonico Hotel and, in effect, demanded: "BRING ME BOB DYLAN!"

Bob showed up the next day, driving in from Woodstock with Aronowitz and Victor Maimudes. After fighting their way through thousands of teenyboppers and police outside the hotel, the three men spent a pleasant evening with their hosts in a top-floor suite, at which time Bob made the astounding discovery that the Beatles had never smoked dope. Fathom that!—*virgins!* Not one to pass up such an opportunity, Bob rolled a couple of j's, used Ringo to demonstrate the proper way to inhale, and inducted the Beatles into the Stoned Age.

Now, almost nine months later, Bob returned the Beatles' hospitality in his suite at the Savoy. Bob had already spent an evening at John and Cynthia Lennon's pad in Weybridge. To close observers, it was clear that John was enamored of Bob. He saw Dylan the way Byron must have regarded Shelley—as a natural poetic genius, and therefore subject to all sorts of strange eccentricities. Lennon loved Bob's brilliance with words, the way they set a song into motion, and even admitted that he'd tried writing in a "Dylanish" manner. "I'm a Loser" was an attempt on John's part to cultivate and fatten the Beatles' sound. The same with "A Hard Day's Night," whose opening bars originally mimicked a well-known Dylan flourish. "But later," John told a reporter, "we Beatle-fied it before we recorded it."

George, Paul, and Ringo didn't quite know what to make of Bob. While John huddled with the Americans, the other three sat around the suite cracking jokes. They had no instinct for the vended cynicism of the others, innocents by comparison. "There was a lot of petty role-playing going on," Donn Pennebaker recalls of that meeting. "A lot of hip one-liners filled with innuendo were fired off every few seconds. If you opened your mouth to say anything, you'd get rolled right into the game." Allen Ginsberg, a sharpshooter in his own right, joined the festivities, gathering Lennon up into the fleshy folds of his lap on the floor, where he related in great detail the "adventure" of how he'd been thrown out of Hong Kong the year before. Bob Neuwirth kept the party rolling, entertaining George and Paul. Ringo dozed off for a while in a corner. By the time Joan Baez poked her head in the door, the playmates were scavenging the suite for food. "Would you look at this!" she snickered. "The room is full of millionaires who don't know how to order a roast-beef sandwich." The afternoon radiated with that kind of lighthearted harmony.

The four-star welcome was reserved for another guest whose presence had been felt since the tour began. Word filtered upstairs that Donovan had camped out in the hotel lobby in the hope of meeting his idol. In fact, the interest was decidedly mutual. Bob had been primed endlessly about Donovan, and his curiosity had finally gotten the better of him. Someone had delivered Donovan's album to the suite, and throughout the tour Bob spent considerable time listening to it. He especially liked "Catch the Wind," which he played whenever there was a minute of privacy to be had. For appearances, he poked fun at the obvious imitation, but he genuinely appreciated the young Scot's artistry.

Finally, Donovan found the courage to telephone the suite. "Can I come upstairs?" he asked somewhat timidly. Bob smiled mischievously into the receiver. "Sure, come on up, kid," he tittered.

"God, I'd better film this!" Pennebaker said, grabbing his camera. Before he could load the magazine, however, Bob put up a hand. "No, man, you can't film this," he said. Pennebaker looked at him and realized that for all Bob's kidding, for all his public wisecracks at Donovan's expense, he didn't want to make a fool of the kid.

"Here's what we're gonna do," Bob said, handing Pennebaker and Neuwirth a few Halloween masks. "Put these on, and when he comes in, pretend nothing's out of the ordinary." Moments later, there was a knock at the door. Donovan entered, saw three guys standing there in masks, and didn't say one word about it. Not a word! That was all it took to endear himself to Bob Dylan.

Before long, Bob, Donovan, and Bobby Neuwirth sat around the hotel room, playing songs. Donovan did a number he'd written called "My Darling Tangerine"—*exactly* to the tune of "Mr. Tambourine Man." Pennebaker and Neuwirth had trouble controlling their laughter, but Bob listened to the entire song without so much as cracking a smile. When it was finished, he said, "I kind of recognize the tune." Donovan beamed like a devoted puppy. "Yeah," he said, "I heard you sing it at a concert. I thought it was an old folk song." Bob grinned for the first time. "Actually, that's one I wrote myself," he said. There was a long pause, during which time Donovan looked back and forth between Dylan and Neuwirth several times. "Ohhhhhh!" he whistled, "I get it!"

Inexplicably, Donovan was spared Dylan's and Neuwirth's patented shock treatment. If anything, he was taken under their wing. He became their mascot, a harmless court jester. Bob even offered him a place to crash, and for the next few days Donovan slept on the floor in a cubicle adjoining Bob's bedroom. The gesture, as innocent as it was intended, wasn't misinterpreted by anyone who understood the way Bob Dylan operated. In an act of apparent generosity, Bob had reduced the ridiculous Dylan-Donovan controversy to a trivial joke. What better place for the impostor than *on the floor* outside Bob Dylan's bedroom.

You'd think Joan Baez, of all people, would have fared as well as Donovan. She'd been Bob's patron, his lover. No one admired his music as much as Joan, and she had used her position to spread the Dylan gospel. Why, in London she was regarded as a star in her own right. That should have counted for something—decent treatment, a little respect at the very least. By the second week of the tour, however, she was completely demoralized. Ignored by Bob, tormented by Bobby Neuwirth, Joan craved affection. She tried doing little bits to get Bob's attention, but they only increased his irritation, preoccupied as he was with Sara Lownds. Had he only explained that to Joan, it might have spared her further humiliation, but that wasn't Bob's style. What she got instead was more of the same—more neglect, more grief. She was treated no better than any other member of Bob's entourage. *Worse!* She'd been made to feel like another mouth to feed, without any function or purpose. Think of what it must have been like for a performer of Joan's magnitude to be denied access to the stage. To have to *watch,* of all things, while Bob played to packed houses of adoring fans. Fans she'd helped to cultivate for him.

There is a moment in *Don't Look Back* that serves to illustrate her predicament. In a dressing room following the Leicester gig, while the camera watches, Joan harmonizes gaily with Bob to a medley of country & western songs. In between numbers, Bob prods her: "'Long Black Veil.' Sing 'Long Black Veil.'" Clearly, he didn't mean it. "Long Black Veil," like "Copper Kettle" and "Mary Hamilton," were leftovers from Joan's traditional folk repertoire and part of the image she was trying hard to shake. On more than one occasion, Bob had publicly ridiculed her dependence on those songs, so that by requesting "Long Black Veil" he was obviously making fun of her. In fact, Bobby Neuwirth accurately sums up the situation when he adds, "Hey, *don't* sing it."

Joan, for her part, ignores them and continues singing a Hank Williams song, despite Bob's persistence: "Sing 'Long Black Veil,'" he demands. "'She walks these hills in a long black veil.'" Finally, he gives up and does a verse of "I'm So Lonesome I Could Cry," but moments later, noticing that it's two-thirty in the morning, Joan says, "Oh, God, I'm sleepy. I mean, I'm fagging out." That was all Neuwirth needed to shift back into action. Smirking at Bob, he replies, "Let me tell you, sister, you fagged out a long time ago." Joan attempts to clown away the remark, but Neuwirth, sensing a scalp for his collection, goes on. "Hey," he says to Bob, "she's got one of the see-through blouses that you don't even wanna!" Joan looks to Bob for defense, but he turns his back and begins writing. "God!" she says with disgust, before sulking off to the car.

The next scene, filmed in a limo en route to Birmingham, proves ominous as Joan sings a line about leaving from "It's All Over Now, Baby Blue." The message, while most likely unintentional, was painfully explicit. Joan was leaving the tour. She'd had enough. On film, she merely drops out of sight, but according to what she told her sister, Mimi, Bob finally found the courage to tell her, "I don't need you," and that gave her the necessary wings to split. Packing hastily, Joan flew to her parents' home in Paris, shattered and angry, before returning to the United States.

Says Mimi Fariña, "In retrospect, it's obvious that Joanie never had a chance in the company of such professional killers as Dylan and Neuwirth. They took pleasure in reducing her to nothing and had a wonderful knack for it. They had impeccable timing and knew exactly which buttons to press—a throwaway remark or a casual glance between them—that would devastate Joanie. But she was hopelessly in love with Bob, so, in a way, I'm surprised she was able to leave that scene at all."

With Joan out of the way, the spotlight belonged entirely to Bob. With perhaps his most important shows left to play—two sold-out concerts at Royal Albert Hall—Bob could concentrate on enriching his already magnificent reputation. Public expectation for the appearances was running wild. Tickets had disappeared in two hours, and word had it the auditorium would be packed with London's toniest celebrities. The Beatles had promised to attend. The Rolling Stones asked for tickets. John Mayall, Eric Clapton, the Animals—*Donovan!* What a star-studded extravaganza it promised to be.

The first show was Sunday evening, May 9, 1965. Earlier that afternoon, Bob was at Albert Hall, performing a sound check, when a security guard called from the stage door. "There's a friend of yours here, says his name's John Beeklin. Don't see him anywhere on the guest list." Bob had no idea who he was talking about. A friend named Beeklin? Could it possibly be . . . ? "Send him up," Bob instructed the guard. A few minutes later, Bob's boyhood pal, John Bucklen, strolled across the floor. "Heeyyyyyy!" Bob screamed, practically jumping into his friend's arms.

Bucklen, an officer in the United States Air Force, was stationed at a base outside of London. That morning he'd passed a poster advertising Bob's concert and decided immediately to head for Royal Albert Hall. Bob was thrilled by John's unexpected appearance. "You're staying for the show, aren't you?" he asked during a brief chat. Bucklen admitted he didn't have a ticket, but Bob arranged for his friend to sit in the second row. "I really want to spend some time with you afterwards," he told John. Then, before returning to the rehearsal, he clapped his friend on the shoulder. "I'm glad to see you. You look great."

Bucklen smiled, without returning the compliment. In fact, he was stunned by Bob's appearance. "He'd lost a lot of weight and looked haggard," John recalls of their reunion. "I remember thinking 'This guy really looks sick. What has he done to himself?'" He'd changed in other ways, too, John thought. Bob no longer resembled the rambunctious little elf he'd remembered from Hibbing. He wasn't very animated. "He seemed a lot more withdrawn," John says. "I remember walking up behind him and touching him lightly on the shoulder—he must have jumped about three feet into the air. He was very self-conscious, his nerves seemed shot."

Bob might have been high-strung, but he certainly hadn't lost his edge. That night, before the show, he'd consented to do an interview with Judson Manning, the London correspondent for *Time* magazine. Not your run-of-the-mill wordsmith, Manning was something of a celebrity in his own right, having covered Great Britain for the newsweekly during World War II. His byline was familiar to New York audiences, not only for his repertorial skills, but also because of his reputation as a fearless interviewer. Over the years, he'd conducted several brilliant interrogations of no less a subject than Adolf Hitler, as well as dozens of eminent statesmen, but none of that prepared him for a ballbuster like Bob Dylan.

Bobby Neuwirth escorted Manning into a deserted lunchroom above Albert Hall half an hour before the concert. Dylan was already there, and their meeting, full of rhetorical fireworks, progressed exactly as it's enacted in *Don't Look Back.* That segment of the film, known as "The Interview," became the movie's most famous, if not its most memorable, dramatic highlight, upstaging even the footage of Bob performing in concert. Manning had barely gotten seated before Bob lit into him like a ferocious spitfire.

"Are you going to see the concert tonight?" Bob asked his well-dressed guest. "Are you going to hear it?" Manning answered affirmatively, if the least bit hesitantly, to both questions. "Okay," Bob said, leaning bullyingly into the reporter's face, "you hear it and see it and it's going to happen fast. Now, you're not going to get it all, and you might hear the wrong words, and then afterwards, see, I can't... I won't be able to talk to you afterwards. I got nothing to say about these things I write. I mean, I just write them. I got nothing to say about them, I don't write 'em for any reason. There's no great message. I mean, if you know, if you wanna tell other people that, you know, go ahead and tell them but I'm not going to have to answer to it. And they're just going to think, you know, what's this *Time* magazine telling us? But then, you couldn't care less about that either. You don't know the people that read you."

Manning couldn't get a word in edgewise as Bob continued his assault. What followed was a rabid indictment of *Time* magazine and all the slick newsweeklies and papers that had freely used him as grist for their rumor mills. They'd interpreted his lyrics, labeled him, identified his "message," stereotyped his audience, analyzed his life-style, symbolized his importance, critiqued his performance, accused him of various self-advancements and betrayals. Now that Bob controlled the spotlight, he intended to have his revenge. Bob contended that Manning was going to write whatever he wanted about Bob Dylan, so why even bother with the interview. "Because," Bob argued, "the guy that's writing the article is sitting in a desk in New York. He's not ...he's not even going out of his office....He's going to put all his readers on." For that reason, Bob persisted, neither he nor any of his fans took a word *Time* said seriously.

On screen, Manning appeared impotent and awkward during the tongue-lashing. The camera was uncomplimentary and unforgiving. It's not difficult for a handsome young Turk, someone who is used to performing before an audience, to make an older man unaccustomed to being photographed appear foolish. Yet Pennebaker, who knew Manning and respected him, insists the reporter got off easy. "I thought Bob was very gentle with Manning," Donn says today of the rather one-sided interview. "*Time* was a heavy enemy, it was detestable to Dylan, and Bob's way of dealing with someone he had no regard for was to play with him like a little rabbit. But he put Manning's nose into the turd, then very gently took him off the hook and, by doing so, I thought it was one of the kindest things I'd ever seen Dylan do."

The publishers of the magazine disagreed. After the film premiered in California but before it opened in New York, *Time* sent a delegation of writers led by John Gregory Dunne to Pennebaker's office in the hope that they might convince him to edit the scene from the final print. "They were obviously embarrassed by their task," says Pennebaker, who naturally refused their request, "but it amazed me how far Time-Life would go in order to protect their reputation."

The show Manning eventually saw that night was a Bob Dylan extravaganza. Bob somehow harnessed all the energy, excitement, anger, and tension of the previous two weeks and hurled it back at the crowd. Without a doubt, it was his most electrifying performance of the tour. With song after song, he convinced the English fans and the press alike that Bob Dylan was one of the most important and influential young performers in the world.

No one in the audience was more impressed than John Bucklen. "Seeing Bob perform in concert was a shock for me," Bucklen remembers of that night. "The last time I had seen him we were sitting around his house in Hibbing, playing our guitars and bragging about how we were going to become famous entertainers. Now, here he was, standing on a stage, alone, at Royal Albert Hall, no less, while thousands of people cheered every verse of every song he sang. It was almost too much for me to comprehend."

At one point, Bucklen was distracted by a strange sound coming from somewhere around his seat. "I glanced at this big guy with a beard who was sitting next to me," John says, "and saw that he was weeping into his hands. Other people, too, had been overcome by Bob's performance and were crying. I remember muttering to myself, 'I don't believe this!' It was the exact fantasy he and I had always dreamed about as kids. Bob always said he'd become a big star. Now, at last, it had come true for him."

17

Getting Wired

Within two weeks of Bob's triumphant return from Great Britain he was back in the recording studio to begin what was to be arguably his most important, if not his most influential, album, *Highway 61 Revisited.* Unlike *Bringing It All Back Home,* which cut a halfhearted compromise, straddling the true course between folk music and rock 'n roll, *Highway 61 Revisited* was as unequivocally rock as any album ever made.

One thing was for certain: the record didn't come about by accident or through fanciful or tentative, experimentation. No, *Highway 61* was a distinct sound that had been in Bob's mind for a long time. Each of his last few albums had been working up to it, and the music that transpired thundered with impulse and conviction.

Highway 61 offered no compromise to Bob's diligent folk following. It is safe to assume that his fans were of no consequence to him and that he never set out to make a record that would appeal to different types, or, for that matter, *any* types, of audience. Instead of observing the traditional music-business wisdom, which says, "Don't fuck with the formula," Bob insisted on satisfying his own creative impulse. He had to keep moving forward. He needed to cut loose.

Saddled once more with Tom Wilson at the controls, Bob went to work on the song that would soon become his signature piece, usurping even the sovereignty of "Blowin' in the Wind." The structure for it, a basic three-chord progression, came to him one day in Woodstock while he was riffing at the piano. Finding a phrase that fit the groove, he began to sing, "How does it feel?" over the chords until a general feeling developed. Then he concentrated solely on the lyric.

The first draft of "Like a Rolling Stone" was six pages long. "It just came," Bob recalled years later, describing its origin. He just squeezed it out, imbuing it with all the energy, speed, anger, excitement, and sense of discovery that was churning inside of him. "How does it *feeee-eelll?*" The line burned with the whole hostile sensibility that emanated through the sixties. A kind of electrically charged nihilism that ironically ran against the generation's slogan of peace and love. Traditionally, the line presupposes a feeling of concern or consideration, as in "Does your stomach hurt?—how does it feel?" But Bob's use for it was anything but well-intentioned. Here, it conveyed more the perverse satisfaction one gets in seeing someone he despises suffer from pain or torment. It was a vengeful lament. "How does it *feeee-eelll?*" he snarled, wondering how the object of his animosity liked being alone, without inspiration or support or real incentive from an alien world.

Bob recorded "Like a Rolling Stone" on June 15, 1965, at Columbia Studios in New York, less than a month after his twenty-fourth birthday. He showed up there around two o'clock in the afternoon and, with little or no ceremony, plugged in a Fender Telecaster and played it once for his accompanists. That warm-up, if it could even be construed as that, fit the pattern for all future Dylan recording sessions that required backup musicians—no charts, no definite instructions, no formal rehearsal. Bob liked spontaneity. The songs evolved organically, with no polished edges, and God help the sideman who couldn't improvise or simply bluff his way through a riff.

Halfway through the first take, Bob stopped the session. Something wasn't working for him. After listening to the playback, he had it: the organ part wasn't effective enough. Disconcertedly, he asked Paul Griffin, his keyboard player, to try it on the piano instead. That left a vacancy at the organ. Al Kooper, a young song hustler who had been invited to the session by Tom Wilson, wandered out of the control room and sat down at the unattended instrument. Had Wilson not been preoccupied with another matter, he might have warned Bob that Kooper had never laid a hand on an organ, but the situation allowed an instant audition for him and in true rock fashion launched a luminous career. With Kooper at the organ, Bob recorded "Like a Rolling Stone" in one afternoon—a six-minute single that many people predicted no radio station would play in rotation—and sowed the seeds for an instant and immense success.

That night, Bobby Neuwirth called Paul Rothchild at the producer's office at Elektra Records. "Get over here right away," he told Rothchild, directing him to Albert Grossman's apartment on Gramercy Park. "Bob wants to see you."

When Rothchild arrived, he found a truly wasted Dylan and Neuwirth, grinning like a couple of cats who'd swallowed canaries. They were sitting in front of a tape recorder, having just finished listening to a rough mix of "Like a Rolling Stone." Rothchild recalls, "They told me they'd already played it twenty-five times before I got there. Dylan just sat in a chair with a smile plastered on his face and his leg going a mile a minute. He was grooving on the knowledge that he'd made a great record. Then they played it through for me, and I was practically blown out of my seat. I couldn't absorb it all, and made them play the fucking thing five times straight before I could say anything.

"What I realized while I was sitting there was that one of US—one of the so-called Village folksingers—was making music that would compete with all of THEM—the Beatles and the Stones and the Dave Clark Five—without sacrificing any of the integrity of folk music or the power of rock 'n roll. As a producer, this was an awesome revelation for me. I knew the song was a smash, and yet I was consumed with envy because it was the best thing I'd heard any of our crowd do and knew it was going to turn the tables on our nice, comfortable lives."

"Like a Rolling Stone" was the perfect number to kick off the session, because it gave the other musicians on the date an attitude that they were in on something very special and important. The feeling was unanimous. None of them thought the song was anything less than amazing, so that the next day, when the session resumed, the ensemble zipped through takes of "Queen Jane Approximately" and "Tombstone Blues" like they'd been up all night studying for them. They were wired!

Bob's impromptu recording process allowed musicians to dig in and contribute to the arrangements, playing what they felt and heard rather than what they were told. It created excitement in the music and utilized the combined innovative talents of his sidemen rather than condemn them to the same tired patterns they played on other dates. It may have been unorthodox, but it worked. They'd already rolled through three difficult songs in two days. Everything pointed to a speedy, trouble-free gig. You can imagine everyone's disappointment, then, when Bob announced that because of a previous obligation there would be a fifteen-day recess before they reconvened.

So much has been written about the highlight of that interim period—the 1965 Newport Folk Festival—that the facts have been obscured beneath layers of romantic fantasy, myopic eyewitness accounts, and pure fiction. Two versions are generally regarded as being integral to the Dylan legend. In the first, Bob Dylan, bored by the hypocrisies of the protest movement and its oppressive responsibilities, turned on by the more hedonistic pleasures of life, namely the Beatles and drugs, a prisoner from his rock 'n roll past, broke the long-standing festival taboo prohibiting amplified music on the concert stage, and, armed with nothing more than an electric guitar and a pickup band, converted a field of folkies into liberated rock-heads.

The second version preserves the traditional folk ethos in a retelling of the event not unlike the Crucifixion. In it, Bob was booed soundly for having sold out to the golden calf of fame and therefore abandoned his electric set, returning to the stage with only his trusty guitar and harmonica. Both versions contain a smidgen of truth, but to put it into any kind of perspective we must examine that historic weekend in July not only from a front-row seat in the audience, but from behind the scenes as well.

To do that, it's important to have some understanding of Newport's busy three-day agenda. The star-studded concerts took place on successive evenings, but equally important were the workshops that were conducted through each of the weekend's mornings and afternoons.

The workshops were one of the festival's primary attractions. At scaled-down stages set up around the vast grounds, anyone with a ticket could walk right up and watch his or her favorite performers conduct a seminar on any of a variety of subjects. There was an international music workshop with Pete Seeger and Theodore Bikel, one devoted to topical songs with Phil Ochs and Tom Paxton, an Appalachian music workshop with Jean Ritchie, a bluegrass workshop, a stringed-instrument workshop. One of the best-attended of these was the blues workshop that took place on Sunday afternoon in a corner of Freebody Park called Bluesville. In the past, fans had gathered there to watch such eminent blues stalwarts as Lightnin' Hopkins, Sonny Terry and Brownie McGee, Jesse Fuller, Dave Van Ronk, Josh White, and Koerner, Ray & Glover try out new material. The blues workshops were also filled with expectation for their customary introduction of "new" legendary artists, like Mississippi John Hurt and Skip James, both of whom had been rediscovered after decades of obscurity in the rural South.

This year's blues workshop debut was prompted by another kind of stimulus: record-company hype. Each year around the time of the festival, Elektra Records issued what it called a "folk sampler"—an album featuring ten or twelve of its up-and-coming stars—for the unbeatable price of ninety-nine cents. The record was incredibly popular among the Newport crowd, which considered itself radically au courant and worked ferociously to stay up on the scene. Usually the record sold anywhere from twenty thousand to sixty thousand copies. But the 1965 edition rang up well over two hundred fifty thousand in sales due to a track on it called "Born in Chicago" by the Butterfield Blues Band. Folk, blues, and rock fans were knocked out by it. The song, produced by Paul Rothchild, was Elektra's initial entry into electric music and showed the company that a major shift in its folk-oriented audience was about to take place.

After a bit of lobbying, Elektra managed to get the Butterfield Blues Band booked onto the blues workshop, and suddenly, instead of the usual two hundred fifty purists who showed up each year, the stage was besieged by five thousand curious onlookers.

The 1965 workshop featured the usual eclectic mix of urban and delta blues interpreters. After each had taken his or her turn in the spotlight, the amps were set up and Alan Lomax, the celebrated folk musicologist and one of the festival's most popular directors, stepped up to the microphone. Visibly angered, his face an unhealthy shade of purple, Lomax went into his jive white-liberal-establishment bit. "There was a time when a poor black farmhand would take a cigar box, string some wires across it, sit under a tree and play beautiful music," he said, throttling the mike stand. He jerked his head in the direction of the band. "Well, here we've got a bunch of guys from Chicago with these big amplifiers [they were little boxes by today's standards] and plenty of power. Let's see if they have what it takes to play the blues!" Out of loyalty to Lomax, the audience booed.

Lomax walked off the platform and stood nearby, waiting to hear Butterfield's performance. As the band began to play, Albert Grossman walked over to him. "What kind of a fucking introduction was that?" Grossman demanded, displaying his usual finesse. Lomax, a big grizzly of a man, scowled at him "For fucking assholes!" he replied. Albert shook a finger in Lomax's distorted face. "Never," he yelled above the music, "*never* do that to a performer. I don't care if it's my act or not. Never treat an artist that way." Lomax puffed out his chest and moved nose to nose with Grossman. "Oh, yeah?" he asked. "Who's gonna make me do that?"

Albert, the first-punch advocate, was finished talking. Without warning, he swung at Lomax's face. Lomax ducked but lunged at Grossman, and before anyone knew what was happening, the two folk potentates were rolling around in the dirt like a couple of nine-year-olds. Neither man managed to land a punch, but the crowd they attracted cheered the performance as if they were watching Hulk Hogan and Andre the Giant settle a grudge match. Interestingly enough, the onlookers were thick with performers and managers who refused to break up the scuffle. Peter Yarrow stood off to the side, giggling with amusement. Ric Von Schmidt rooted for a quick pin. Recalls one bystander: "There were a lot of folk notables there watching the melee with great, *great* joy."

Others considered it the "perfect confrontation"—a metaphor for the weekend, if not for the entire era. Lomax, a member of the Old Guard, was being terrorized by the notion that the New Guard was going to render him obsolete. And Lomax knew that included his friends Pete Seeger and Theodore Bikel, who also served on the festival's board. All of a sudden, forces beyond their control designated them as the folk movement's stodgy right wing, and it was unconscionable, never mind cruelly ironic, that those old activists had to represent themselves here as the establishment.

Albert Grossman, who was one of the festival's seven directors, had remained scrupulously nonpartisan until that afternoon. For one thing, Albert was a manager whose job was to represent the artist, not the music. As such, he could cater to the needs of Odetta and Josh White as easily as he could to Peter, Paul & Mary and Bob Dylan. But as a businessman, Albert read the trends as skillfully as he read the daily stock market report, and wisdom told him not to neglect the potential of electrified music. He loved what Bob was doing with it; Ian and Sylvia, another of Grossman's 'folk' clientele, were also putting a band together. He'd be a fool to bite the hand that fed him. Besides, Albert regarded any new medium as a promising area of exploitation. He'd moved Bob into film at a timely moment. There was a book publishing deal in the talking stages. Perhaps now was the time for him to expand his interests into rock 'n roll.

Almost in response to that notion, Albert made up his mind to sign the Butterfield Blues Band to a management contract. "I'm going to take over as manager right now," he told them that afternoon, following his title bout with Alan Lomax. In all likelihood, Grossman made that promise only partly out of provision for the band. It was more probably his suspicion that their continued presence at the festival would force another confrontation, and his new role as their protector certainly appealed to him.

No doubt Butterfield's encore performance was the cause for Albert's concern. The band had been scheduled to open Sunday evening's gala concert, a slot noted for its inconspicuousness. They went on about six-thirty, as the audience began filing onto the field. How were they supposed to know that an hour earlier Pete Seeger had sauntered onstage to dedicate the entire show as "a message from today's folk musicians to a newborn baby about the world we live in." Picture Seeger's face as he watched five electrified speedballs raise hell about life on the streets of Chicago on *his stage.* Somehow that wasn't exactly the message ol' Pete had in mind.

Infuriated by this blasphemy, Seeger raced backstage. There he encountered the other festival directors and ordered them to put an end to the band's noisy set. *Immediately,* he demanded! Anyone else would have been kicked out of there, but Pete Seeger was folk music's undisputed holy man. The powers-that-be—George Wein, Alan Lomax, Peter Yarrow, Theodore Bikel, and Albert Grossman—debated the various aspects of his request while Seeger's blood continued to rise.

In the background, the raunchy music built to a nerve-wracking crescendo. Overwrought, Seeger couldn't wait any longer. Before anyone could react, Pete Seeger—Mr. Pacifist—grabbed a fire ax from off the wall and screamed, "Get them off the stage or I'm going to chop the power!" The cables buzzed with thousands of volts of juice. Peter Yarrow started to intervene, but Seeger was standing too close to the main power line for him to risk a stupid mistake. "Take it easy!" Yarrow shouted, looking behind him for help.

No one moved. George Wein, the festival's promoter, suggested that someone cut the power on stage until they reached a decision. "You do that and I'll sue you," Grossman barked using his favorite line. Lomax begged Seeger to give him the ax—*so that he could have the pleasure of severing the power himself!* The place was in a wild uproar. The men were screaming at one another, hurling insults back and forth. Sides had been clearly chosen: Wein and Lomax stood on one side of the fracas, Grossman and Yarrow on the other. That cast Theodore Bikel in the unlikely role of swingman.

Hardly a part of the contemporary scene, Bikel seemed to personify folk music's anachronistic conventions. He was the Old Guard—*the past.* What did he know about Chicago blues? Or, for that matter, rock 'n roll. The Bob Dylan he knew in the Village didn't exist anymore. And here was Pete Seeger, looking to his old friend to defend folk music's tradition. His eyes beseeching: *Theo, for Chrissake—tell them. Set them straight!*

"Peter," Bikel said, stepping forward, "put the ax down. This band, these rebels—they are us. They are what we were twenty years ago. Remember?" Seeger stared at him like a trauma victim. "Why don't we give them a chance and let the audience be the judge?"

An hour later, the backstage crew witnessed a virtual reenactment of the bickering. Cousin Emmy, a hillbilly singer, had just brought the house down with a hokey version of "Turkey in the Straw," and the crowd stomped and whistled for more. Instead of an encore, however, the lights dimmed and a crew of stagehands scurried around like moles, setting up another round of the cursed amplifiers. As far as anyone knew, the only electrified act—Paul Butterfield—had already performed. A quick check of the festival program confirmed that fact. Alan Lomax, who had been watching from the performer's circle, darted backstage and hovered over Paul Rothchild, who had taken over the soundboard. "What's going on here?" he demanded. "Who's on next?"

The answer, of course, was Bob Dylan, but no one had any idea what the star had planned. It was a doozie, to be sure. Unbeknownst to anyone but a handful of friends, Bob intended to play a set of his new rock songs from *Bringing It All Back Home* and the upcoming *Highway 61 Revisited.* That shouldn't have been a shock to anyone who'd listened to a radio in the last couple of months, but Bob anticipated some resistance from his die-hard folk following and preferred to surprise them instead. Even Al Kooper was let in on it only at the last minute, after Bob encountered him on the festival grounds late Friday afternoon. Since then, Bob had been holed up in a Newport mansion with the Butterfield Blues Band, Kooper, and session keyboardist Barry Goldberg, rehearsing a short medley. Rothchild, too, had been recruited just that afternoon when it was discovered he was the only one there capable of doing what recording engineers had only recently started calling a rock 'n roll mix. But due to the secrecy of the performance, Bob was forced to go on without even the benefit of a sound check.

As the rock equipment was turned on, sections of the audience began to boo. The MC, Peter Yarrow, strode quickly to the microphone. "It gives me great pleasure to introduce—" he said, pausing to give the crowd a chance to settle down, "Mr. Bob Dylan!"

The spotlights exploded, and there was Bob on stage in a psychedelic getup *with a rock band!* The crowd was momentarily stunned into silence. They were baffled. The hero of the last two festivals, the voice of their entire generation, the man responsible for revitalizing, if not rewriting, the course of modern folk music, was riding the body of one nasty-looking Telecaster. This must have been someone's idea of a joke.

If it was, Bob Dylan wasn't laughing. His face was set in iron, his eyes fixed relentlessly on the band. Turning his back on the audience, Bob nodded to guitarist Mike Bloomfield, then barreled into the opening chords of "Maggie's Farm." Backstage, Rothchild boosted the sound to maximum level, and it went cranking out across the floodlit field like rolling thunder.

Once more, Lomax charged the soundboard, this time with Pete Seeger nipping at his heels. Both were determined to stop the desecration once and for all. Pete tried several times to yank Rothchild's hands off the board, while the engineer struggled to maintain the levels. Stagehands had come to Rothchild's aid. Albert came screaming from around the stage—"Blah, blah, blah, I'll sue you!" Peter Yarrow, who had been watching the show from the wings, glanced at the fracas and bounded over to the board as Seeger once more lunged for the controls.

"Pete," Yarrow declared, pointing decisively at Seeger, "if you touch him again I'll press charges against you for battery." That declaration produced an instantaneous cease-fire. No one could believe his ears. Scrawny Peter Yarrow, a mere guitarist in a pop trio, taking that tack with... with *the son of God!* He must have lost his senses. "I looked up at him then," Rothchild recalls, "and remember thinking, 'He really means it. The fucker really means it. He's going to stand his ground with these heavies.'"

It took Yarrow at least another five minutes until Seeger and Lomax finally backed off. By that time, he and Albert had rounded up a number of Bob's cronies who were willing to form a cordon around the board until Bob got off stage.

Out front, however, things weren't in much better shape. The sound was awful. It wasn't balanced at all. One minute the guitars drowned out the other instruments, the next verse was overpowered by bass runs. Because there were no monitors, the drummer, Sam Lay, lost the beat for a few bars. Instruments were out of sync, as well as out of tune. The whole mess smacked of the Jacket Jamboree at Hibbing High.

The people in front of the stage began shouting, "We can't hear you! Turn the sound down—we can't hear the words!" That touched off a ripple of complaints, and by the time it reached the back of the field the grumbling had turned to boos. "Play folk music!" someone shouted, as Bob tuned up between songs. "Get rid of the band!"

Maria Muldaur, who had performed earlier that night with the Jim Kweskin Jug Band, recalls being furious at the so-called purists who called out for the "old Dylan." Muldaur was sitting close to the stage, with the other performers, and says, "They were a bunch of goddamn hypocrites. I knew most of them from Cambridge and New York and, like me, they all loved Muddy Waters. We listened to early R&B, not to mention Elvis and Chuck Berry. The music Bob played that night wasn't any different except that it was folk-type lyrics put to an incredible beat. They just needed something to be pissed-off about, and Bob provided them with an earful."

The boos rose a couple of decibels through the next number, "Like a Rolling Stone." The band really cooked, but it was obvious they were losing the battle to an unruly audience. After struggling through "It Takes a Lot to Laugh/ It Takes a Train to Cry," Bob and the band beat a hasty retreat.

Talk about hostility! You'd think someone had called in the riot squad. Half the audience booed loudly, the rest were on their feet shouting for more. Then, the factions squared off and began shouting at each other. Eric Von Schmidt remembers thinking the scene was "perfectly Dylanesque."

The shouting continued for about fifteen minutes while the stage remained dark. Backstage, Peter Yarrow pleaded with Bob to continue the performance. Too many people had bought tickets specifically to hear him play. Impossible, Bob told him—that's all he and the band worked out together. There was no more. After some more tactful cajoling, Bob finally agreed to return by himself with an acoustic guitar. Says Von Schmidt, "The only trouble with that was a lot of people in the audience interpreted it to mean they had won—they'd succeeded in driving the band from the stage. Bob had somehow come to his senses and abandoned the crazy rock sound."

The audience greeted Bob's reappearance with a thunderous ovation. This was the Bob Dylan they knew and loved. Taking a few minutes to tune, he ignored the sporadic heckles that drifted through the humid Newport air. His face remained turned away, ear to the frets, as he struggled to adjust the pitch. As he stepped to the mike, a lone voice cried out: "Mr. Tambourine Man." "Okay," Bob mumbled, "I'll do that one for you." "Mr. Tambourine Man" was a likely compromise—a quintessential folk song filled with rock and drug imagery. Afterward, he rushed through "It's All Over Now, Baby Blue," then quickly left just as the applause began to swell.

As Bob came charging off the stage after his now-legendary ordeal, he appeared shaken and confused. He hadn't anticipated such a hostile reaction to the band. It hadn't been his intention to shock the audience, to ram rock 'n roll down his listeners' throats. But his listeners had misunderstood; they'd closed their mind to new sounds.

They wanted him to stay the same, to stop growing or exploring music with its infinite variables. They wanted to hear *protest songs.* "Blowin' in the Wind" over and over and over again. Be Woody Guthrie or, at the very least, Pete Seeger. Except that he wanted to be Bob Dylan, and Bob Dylan was evolving as a person and as a musician.

That night, the party that traditionally celebrated the end of the festival was unusually loose and informal. There was a feeling among the performers there that something consequential had transpired. It was as if someone had given them a tremendous shove, turned their heads in another direction. A new world awaited them. As such, the party was marked by the kind of wanton promiscuity that one experiences after a revolution, a sense of "anything goes." The younger performers were in incredibly high spirits. An abundance of good dope changed hands. They'd demanded—and *gotten*—booze for the first time instead of the customary beer. Even the entertainment suggested a decisive break with the past. Rather than records or an ensemble hootenanny, the Chambers Brothers played rock 'n roll to the delight of several hundred dancers.

By one in the morning, most of the stragglers were pleasantly plastered. Richard Fariña, sweaty and stoned, leaned over a table and began beating out Latin rhythms in time to the peppery music, and it had a wild effect on the group's already steamy passions. Pretty soon, ten or fifteen pals joined him in the drumbeat. *Bomp a-bomp a-bomp-a-bomp-bomp! Bomp a-bomp a-bomp-a-bomp-bomp!* The whole place was drunk on cheap booze and excitement.

Maria Muldaur remembers dancing like it was the first time she'd been set free. "We were having the time of our lives," she says of the festivities. "The band was hot, the place was jumping, and there was an odd feeling that if we stopped and went home, everything would come to an end." At one point, Fariña grabbed her and danced off to one side of the room. Turning her around, he gestured to a corner of the room where Bob sat glumly nursing a drink. He was hunched over in the chair, one leg crossed over the other, staring at the floor. "Check out Dylan," Fariña said to her. "The guy looks positively miserable. Why don't you cheer him up and ask him to dance." Maria, who had known Bob ever since he arrived in New York, had never seen him dance so much as a step, yet the poor guy looked like he needed a lift. A dance seemed as good an idea as any.

Approaching him vivaciously, Maria grabbed his hand. "C'mon, Bob—let's dance," she said, trying to drag him onto the floor. His body remained planted like a lead weight. He looked up at her, and it was then that she noticed a well of tears in his eyes. The guy was really hurting. "I'd dance with you, Maria," he said, almost whispering, "but my hands . . . my hands are on fire."

My hands are on fire!

What a convoluted response, Maria thought. It was full of all that cosmic crap that had taken over everyone's lives. She gazed wistfully at Bob and flashed on an earlier, less complicated moment, when they were both just starting out in Greenwich Village. She'd been Maria D'Amato then, a foxy little teenager who sang a Carter Family–type duet with a woman named Annie Bird at a coffeehouse called the Third Side. One afternoon, while they were rehearsing a new number, Bob rushed in as if there were an emergency of national importance.

"He was all upset that he'd cut his finger," Maria recalled. "So we washed it off with great ceremony and put a Band-Aid on it, then sat with him over coffee until he'd recovered." After he realized that surgery wouldn't be necessary, Bob asked, "Want to hear a song I just wrote?" He picked up a guitar, and without any further ado played "Only a Pawn in Their Game" for them. "He sat there and sang it in that dark little coffeehouse and it just cracked my wig right open," Maria remembered. "That song made me aware of things I never thought about before. But when it was finished, he just laughed. He *laughed.* And we all joked around before heading off to our respective gigs."

What a wonderful experience that had been, she thought. The Village had been a wonderful place to come of age in the early 1960s, full of music and foolishness and camaraderie. The days were so carefree, the nights stretched on like one continuous party. Everybody shared what little worldly wisdom he or she possessed. They rooted for each other. There was a lot of love on the Street.

Looking around the room that night, looking at Bob, Maria got a sense that it was all drawing to a close. The Village had been a precious nest, but the boundaries and everything within them had changed. They weren't kids anymore. There was a lot at stake in the day-to-day club scene. Performers coveted a hit record, competed for managers, covered each others' songs. There were no rules anymore, except maybe: Everyone for himself. Even the music had changed . . . was still changing.

"That night everything seemed up for grabs," Maria thought. "Life, as we had known it, was out of control." And more tragically, perhaps, something forewarned her that they were about to get exactly what they'd bargained for all along.

18

The Hippest of the Hip

The controversy touched off by Bob's performance at Newport was nothing compared to the uproar that followed it. The folk press, minuscule as it was, came practically to blows over the dramatic show. Irwin Silber, *Sing Out!*'s bombastic editor, called the festival "a tasteless exhibition of frenzied incest," likening it to a "carnival gone mad." A completely different view was expressed by his *younger* colleague Paul Nelson, who argued that Bob's set provided one of those pivotal moments "that freezes the blood and sparks the brain into the kind of excitement that stays forever in one's memory." Public opinion couldn't have been more divided.

"Make no mistake," Nelson warned his readers, "the audience had to make a clear-cut choice and they made it: Pete Seeger. . . . They were choosing suffocation over invention and adventure, backwards over forwards, a dead hand instead of a live one. . . . It was a sad parting of the ways for many, myself included. I choose Dylan. I choose art."

But critics and friends alike were outraged by Bob's new sound. "Next year he'll be writing rhythm & blues songs when they get high on the charts," Izzy Young commented in *Sing Out!* "The following year, the Polish polka will make it, and then he'll write them, too. By then, he'll be so mired in the popularity charts that he'll be safe enough for the State Department to send him to entertain the troops at whatever battlefront we're on at the time." Don West, a relatively obscure and fusty poet, used the same publication to denounce Bob as "a phony." West claimed he wasn't opposed to the right of a laborer to his wage. "But making a lot of money from folk music just isn't genuine," he complained, neglecting to mention at the time that he ran a business called the Highlander Folk School in Georgia.

The so-called purists bemoaned any exploitation of "the people's music" as a breach of public trust. They were "troubled" and "saddened" and "embarrassed" by Bob Dylan and his imitators, but more than likely they were jealous and frightened—jealous because they'd never earned so much as fifty cents from their music, and frightened by the auspices of change.

The most ill-conceived pounding came from Ewan McColl, a Scottish singer and postwar folk revivalist, whose contribution to the folksong movement never amounted to anything more than an asterisk in the annals of popular music. McColl was now teetering on the precipice of extinction. To McColl, folk music had no future. The American songwriting spree threatened to destroy a heritage steeped in "the disciplines of traditional music." He considered it a movement full of flabby sentimentality and self-pity, and its ringleader, Bob Dylan, "a youth of mediocre talent."

"Only a completely noncritical audience, nourished on the watery pap of pop music, could have fallen for such tenth-rate drivel," McColl said of Bob's songs. In response to the critical popularity of Bob's image-filled lyrics, McColl asked rhetorically, "What poetry? The cultivated illiteracy of his topical songs or the embarrassing fourth-rate schoolboy attempts at free verse? The latter reminds me of elderly female schoolteachers clad in Greek tunics rolling hoops across lawns at weekend theater schools."

McColl's philippic caused a minor schism in the chummy folk community. *Melody Maker* devoted a series of weekly editorials to Dylan's defense. "It's sad to see Ewan McColl making a damn fool of himself," it responded in a subsequent issue. "He must be terribly upset that songs are being actually sung by people instead of being neatly parcelled on the shelves of his beloved folk museums. . . . He's got a bad dose of our society's most widespread ill—sneering sickness. Shame on him." A follow-up article, entitled "Just Who Does Ewan McColl Think He Is?" rounded up a number of pop celebrities, such as

Marianne Faithful, Manfred Mann, and New Faces' Charlie MacKay, to uphold Bob's position. Only Paul Simon, whose grudge against Bob dated back to a Folk City tiff when Bob talked through his show, put in a good word for McColl.

By mid-1965, however, college audiences were no longer interested in anything the old folklorists had to say. In their eyes, unamplified folk music was SQUARE. The new badge was MOD and HIP. For example, the Kingston Trio was SQUARE; Wayne Fontana and the Mindbenders were HIP. Hootenannies?—the square root of SQUARE; discotheques were HIP. Curiously HIP, according to a *Time* magazine survey, was pint-sized Brenda Lee, a sugary sweet pop-and-country singer, perhaps best remembered for her seasonal standard "Rockin' around the Christmas Tree," who the newsweekly said "outranks Folksinger Joan Baez [SQUARE]...on the college popularity polls."

Bob Dylan, on the other hand, was the hippest of the hip, and his influence was everywhere. If he wore a leather jacket, the Village head shops had a run on leather jackets. High-heeled shoes appeared on the feet of every folksinger. Words like "groovy" and "uptight" that swept through his interviews became part of the cultural patois. And by the end of 1965, all his folk cronies had electric backup in their acts.

In fact, nowhere was Bob's influence more deeply felt than in the world of popular music, where everyone rushed to imitate his new sound. Amplified bands purged the Village coffeehouses of its angry young troubadors, and by September, folk-rock dominated the scene. Since then, of course, volumes of scholarly analysis fraught with sociological overtones have been devoted to folk-rock, but what *Newsweek* hailed as the "NEW SOUND" was simply the natural evolution of folk-style songs fused with the beat of rock 'n roll.

The relationship between the two genres was inevitable—folk being a respectful retelling of the past, rock the energy behind a contemporary pop culture. Once folk music entered the commercial mainstream, its fate was sealed. Protest songs had caught the public's ear, and now there was a call for more aggressive action. Enough with singing sweetly or passively about discrimination or lynchings, the draft or the bomb. It was time to make yourself heard, insist upon results. Rock 'n roll was meant to shake foundations; it was musical terrorism, a revolutionary, attention-grabbing sound that played to people's emotions. And folk music was its perfect foil.

The MacDougal Street mob were eager converts to the electric muse. Eric Andersen, a handsome Dylanesque balladeer, immediately put a band together, grew long hair, and reissued an entire folk album of his, *'Bout Changes and Things,* as a rock record called *'Bout Changes and Things, Take 2.* Judy Collins added a full ensemble of session musicians to her act. Tom Rush cut a Bo Diddley single. John Sebastian, a member of the Even Dozen Jug Band who played harmonica on dozens of traditional folk albums, formed The Lovin' Spoonful. Another Village stalwart, Felix Pappilardi, who played second guitar for everyone from Peter, Paul & Mary to the Chad Mitchell Trio, performed with Mountain. Stephen Stills and Richie Furay appeared as the Go-Go Singers before forming Buffalo Springfield. The Mugwumps were made up of the Lovin' Spoonful's Zal Yanovsky and folksingers Cass Elliott and Denny Doherty, who together eventually founded the Mamas and the Papas.

For other performers, the sudden shift from folk to rock wasn't so smooth. Paul Rothchild recalls how frustrated his friend Jim McGuinn became as the Village coffeehouse scene began to collapse. "McGuinn was a banjo player I'd used on a lot of recording sessions," Rothchild says, "and a well-known performer who worked coffeehouses on MacDougal Street." One night he cornered Rothchild and asked the producer for some advice on keeping his career afloat. Says Rothchild, "I told him what I'd do if I were him, and the next day he showed up at one of the clubs and sang one or two of the Beatles' songs that were on the charts. Well, the audience booed his ass, and when he came off stage he looked at me and asked, 'Now what?' I said, 'If I were you, I'd sell the banjo, buy an electric guitar, and get out of town.'"

A year later, McGuinn's version of "Mr. Tambourine Man," with his group, the Byrds, legitimized folk-rock as a full-fledged commercial phenomenon and gave Bob his first number-one charted rock 'n roll hit. In retrospect, the Byrds' record is a mousy whitewash—slashing three of the four verses from the original lyric, slowing the tempo in order to sell the refrain. Unlike Bob's compelling vocal, McGuinn's solo is whiney and unemotional. It lacks passion. On the other hand, he opened up the arrangement with an unforgettable twelve-string guitar riff reminiscent of the Rolling Stones' "The Last Time" or the Beatles' "She's a Woman," which lingered long after the record had ended and delivered "Mr. Tambourine Man" to a much broader audience.

As a result, the Bob Dylan catalogue blossomed into one of Tin Pan Alley's hottest commodities. Warner Bros. Music mined his copyrights as source material for any rock prospector in search of a folk-rock hit. In July 1965, Cher recorded "All I Really Want to Do," a month before the Byrds released their version of it. Dino, Desi, and Billy cut an awful recording of "Chimes of Freedom," the Turtles had a hit with "It Ain't Me, Babe," and Stevie Wonder was at work on an R&B version of "Blowin' in the Wind." Even the Four Seasons got into the act, recording a castrato version of "Don't Think Twice" under the *nom de phew,* The Wonder Who.

Imitators were also grinding out what the recording industry called "Dylanesque" singles to capitalize on Bob's success. Lou Adler, a resourceful West Coast producer, gave a sixteen-year-old songwriter named Phil Sloan a copy of *Highway 61 Revisited* and told the kid to see what he could come up with. A week later, Sloan reappeared in his office with ten songs, one of which was an infantile antiwar ballad called "Eve of Destruction." Barry McGuire's angry recording of this "first rock 'n roll protest song," sold six million copies and sent the record industry scrambling for more of the same. Tom Wilson, Bob's producer at Columbia Records, was given the master tapes of a folkie act and was instructed to make them sound more commercial. The first song on the tape was a thoughtful ballad called "Sounds of Silence," beautifully accompanied by Paul Simon's acoustic guitar. To counteract the song's heavy-handed imagery, Wilson overdubbed it, adding an electric guitar, bass, and drums before releasing it as a single, then he sat back and watched as it shot up the charts.

Both "Eve of Destruction" and "Sounds of Silence" were packaged as "message" songs, though their insights into human nature spoke primarily to fourteen-year-old kids. Bob, meanwhile, had had it up to his ears with all this heavy philosophical crap. "Messages are a drag," he declared in a March 1966 *Playboy* interview. "Myself, what I'm going to do is rent Town Hall and put about thirty Western Union boys on the bill. I mean, then there'll *really* be some messages."

As far as Bob was concerned, finger-pointing and politics had become boring. The protest songs—much of his early repertoire—reflected somebody else's world, not his. And folk music took itself too seriously. It had become too predictable for him. On stage, he found himself just going through the motions, his mind drifting. Rock 'n roll was a challenge. The sound was bigger and more complicated. It allowed him to interact with other musicians and add variable textures to the sound as well as to the lyrics. And it kept the audience on its toes.

Newport, as it turned out, provided only a mild sneak preview of Bob's new act. It was an experiment—a couple of songs thrown together at the last minute, no real equipment to speak of, nothing to suggest commitment or continuity. Even the band—an ad hoc ensemble of musicians on loan from other groups—functioned as a working hypothesis. Now, with Newport behind him and *Highway 61 Revisited* on the charts, it was time for Bob to make clear where he was headed.

A month after the festival, he kicked off a tour at the Forest Hills Tennis Stadium, a fifteen-thousand-seat amphitheater in Queens, New York, that had previously presented sophisticated entertainers such as Frank Sinatra and Barbra Streisand. Forest Hills was a giant step up from the roach-ridden coffeehouses and compact concert halls played by more folksingers. It offered a performer the opportunity to make vast amounts of money. And it offered prestige. Any folksinger could now play concert halls. Joan Baez, Pete Seeger, and Peter, Paul & Mary traveled a circuit of classy stages that were once restricted to classical artists. Even Phil Ochs sold out Carnegie Hall—it was no big deal. But an *arena* was serious business. It broke new ground for folksingers who were willing to reach out to a broader pop music audience. Which is exactly what Bob had in mind.

For Bob, Forest Hills promised to be different from Newport, inasmuch as he would have more time to work the crowd and they had some advance warning of what to expect from him. Rumors had been circulating that he had his own band. Privately, Bob was telling friends to expect "some electricity" at his upcoming shows. For loyal fans, however, the prospect of Bob Dylan playing anything but folk music was unthinkable. They believed that rock 'n roll was superficial and anti-intellectual; it was apolitical; it appealed to the animalistic streak in every juvenile delinquent. Furthermore, it was inconceivable to them that Bob Dylan would sell out to commercialism, trading artistry and integrity for the Almighty Dollar.

A full moon hovered prophetically over the stadium that night. Then, half an hour before the show, a chill August wind blew in off Long Island Sound, sending the temperature plummeting to the low fifties. Ticketholders hugged themselves, huddling together like penguins on the dark rows of cement seats, as they waited for Bob to appear. There was something in the air, all right, and it was a lot spookier than the usual bubble of anticipation.

As if that weren't enough, some idiot let Murray the K, a slick top forty disc jockey, introduce Bob. "It's not rock! It's not folk! It's a new thing called *Dyl-lllllan!*" he shrieked into the microphone, while fifteen thousand fans gasped in horror. "Dylan is *definitely* what's happening!" he reassured them, thankfully omitting the customary "ba-by!"

Murray the K was wrong. The first half of the show was undeniably folk, with Bob performing seven of his most recent songs on acoustic guitar. The audience cooed in ecstasy. The lone performer on stage was definitely the Bobby they knew and loved. He was *exactly* as they remembered him—exactly as they wanted him to remain. Exactly! All that talk about electric guitars and amplifiers must have been the work of some jealous kook. Maybe Ewan MacColl started it. Or Phil Ochs!

Had the audience suspected what awaited them it was doubtful they would have shown Bob as much appreciation as they did. Apparently, Bob knew it too. Earlier that afternoon, while he went over songs with his band at Carroll's Rehearsal Hall and again at the stadium, he had warned the musicians about a possible backlash. "I don't know what to expect out there tonight," he told his bass player. "These are my hardcore fans. They're not used to the electric part of it. Anything could happen."

No matter, by the end of rehearsal everyone had been completely psyched. The band really cooked together. They were turned on, not only by the music, but by the chemistry of the group, which was unusually tight for the short time they had been together. Bob had put together a first-rate band for himself. Al Kooper had developed into an imaginative keyboard player since winging it on the *Highway 61* session. Kooper never sat down and worked out an arrangement; his input came right out of the music. It was totally kinetic. He colored riffs and organ flourishes, using tremolo and the Leslie baffles on his B-3, to augment Bob's haunting melodies. Unfortunately, Bob felt that Russ Savakus, who had played bass on the album, couldn't cut it, so he was replaced with a childhood friend of Kooper's named Harvey Goldstein, whose only experience had been playing society gigs and backup for a Trini Lopez soundalike. Mike Bloomfield, the album's brilliant lead guitar player, had left to play the blues with his former sidekick, Paul Butterfield, and drummer Bobby Gregg split soon after to fulfill an overload of studio commitments. In their places were a couple of guys from a Toronto band, the Hawks—Robbie Robertson and Levon Helm.

Between them, Robbie and Levon had enough experience to carry the rest of the group. Robbie had been on the road with Ronnie Hawkins since he was fifteen, first as a roadie, then, in quick succession, on bass, rhythm guitar, and finally lead guitar, which he picked at with a subtle, funky twang. Levon, at the age of twelve, played drums for a high school band before he, too, joined Hawkins' Dionysiac road show. Hooking up with Hawkins aged those young bucks overnight. Ronnie fronted what was known, even then, as the quintessential bar band, the rowdiest bunch of cats alive. The Hawks played one-nighters in every shitty beer joint from Anchorage to Alabama—boogying all night, getting plastered, then prowling the streets for townies willing to party until dawn in the back of the group's equipment van. They were one of the earliest bands to perfect the ethic of sex, drugs, and rock 'n roll as an alternative life-style, some of the heaviest players of the period, jamming and drinking and boosting each other like one of the house bands on a Fifties' doo-wop show. Bob had heard about them from someone on Albert's office staff, then got a glowing reference from Johnny Hammond, Jr., who had used them on his 1965 album *So Many Roads*. Bob's idea had been to snatch the whole group away from Hawkins, but he settled for Robbie and Levon until the others could find a reason to leave their steady gig.

The difference between Robbie Robertson and Mike Bloomfield was night and day. Mike was one of the greatest natural lead guitarists working in music, a free-spirited cat who played every note from his soul. When Mike bent the last, breathless notes of a blues riff the guitar howled in pain. Robbie was more restrained. He played "locked-in" riffs, a series of fills built tightly around the melody of a song so as not to detract from the rest of the arrangement. And he composed his parts in advance. Levon played in direct contrast to Robbie's meticulousness and opened up the beat. Whereas Bobby Gregg was a disciplined drummer who performed much like a metronome, Levon improvised at will and kicked up a rhythm like an unmuzzled machine gun. "Levon breathes in his playing," says Harvey Goldstein. "He kept the songs nice and relaxed."

Bob was convinced this band would eventually win over his fans, but the Forest Hills audience remained dubious and unmoved. "Sitting backstage through Bob's acoustic set, we could feel that crowd—there was a frightening coldness coming from them," Goldstein recalls. "When the instruments were set up during intermission, the fans began to buzz. The message we got was: 'Dylan, you're deserting us!' We nearly shit our pants."

The second half of the show—the electric half—was more like a confrontation than a concert. From the opening chords of "Tombstone Blues," the crowd was *involved,* responding to each verse with a volley of insults and boos. "Get off the fucking stage!" "We want the old Dylan!" "Traitor!" "Sell-out!" Impervious to the criticism, Bob pushed tenaciously through the song, refusing to back down. "The more they screamed, the more determined he became," says Goldstein, who was growing more unnerved by the crowd. "It was as if he drew strength from the uproar. And from the band. Bob played as if he had a fucking army behind him. That night, he was in command. He was in complete control."

Maybe so, but the audience was a mess. Some die-hard folkies stormed out early in indignation, while others hurled fruit at the stage, along with imaginative insults. They felt truly let down, angry, and utterly bewildered. How, they wondered, could they be expected to absorb the poetic eloquence of "Gates of Eden," then rock out with a song as absurd and flimsy as "Tombstone Blues." He was making fun of them. Worse, packs of young kids were on their feet *dancing to Bob Dylan!* Had they no respect?

The rock 'n rollers couldn't have cared less about how the old fans felt. This was the night they really discovered Bob Dylan, and everything they'd heard about his offbeat brilliance was true. What a head he had for abstractions! He'd taken all the stuff they loved about the English groups and refined it about six hundred percent, matching their intellectual restlessness to the driving beat. It was like being on an acid trip without the risky side effects. Fuck the folkies! Let 'em listen to Joan Baez, Phil Ochs, and Pete Seeger. From now on, Bob Dylan belonged to rock 'n roll!

Not everyone was willing to concede that point so quickly. A number of folk music loudmouths persisted in heckling Bob throughout the night on the off chance that he'd get the message and abandon the silliness. After all, they thought, that's what happened at Newport.

As Bob hit the intro for "Ballad of a Thin Man," a chorus of catcalls and hisses rang out across the amphitheater. Bob turned to the band and yelled, "Keep playing the intro over and over until they shut up!" The same ten notes stretched into what seemed like an eternity on stage. In his autobiography, *Backstage Passes,* Al Kooper claims, "We played it for a good five minutes." In fact, it ran just under a minute and a half, but the point was that Bob wasn't backing down no matter how long the audience screamed and hollered. Newport was old news. Besides, he loved playing with the band and was confident that his new material was as good as, or better than anything else he'd written. From now on, he'd play what he wanted to play—the audience could take it or leave it. After they'd quieted down, he leaned across the piano into the microphone and spelled it out for them: "Something is happening here, but you don't know what it is, *doooo yewwwww?*"

As the night wore on and Bob got deeper into the groove, the kids who dug his new sound grew progressively more restless. They weren't used to sitting still through a show like it was a formal state dinner. Folkies might go to concerts and applaud like schoolteachers at the end of each song, but at rock concerts the fans went wild. They shrieked and pulled their hair and beat their chests like Iranian fanatics during Ramadan. They fainted from pleasure and lit candles, and when they really got worked up, they *charged the stage!*

That night, the last thing any of the musicians expected was to confront the unruly crowd. From the stage it was impossible for them to see the audience, not only because of the spotlights trained in their eyes, but because the seats and the stage were separated by the stadium's two famous tennis courts. The police had set up barricades around the courts so that all the musicians could see was a rectangular green area directly below their scaffolding. It was like playing to an empty arena, with cheering and booing piped in to create the feeling of a crowd.

Halfway through the second set, however, the band members noticed people running around on the tennis courts, trying to get over the barricades to the stage. Says Harvey Goldstein, "I shot a glance at Kooper that, in effect, said, 'What the fuck is going on out there?' Suddenly, there were kids everywhere around us, running and dancing, jumping up and down. Who knew what to expect from the crowd."

It dawned on Goldstein that the promoter had put too much distance between the audience and the stage. The kids wanted to see Bob up close, so they'd come down out of the stands, onto the turf, and right up to the stage. When Goldstein turned back to see how Kooper was dealing with it, the keyboardist was gone—he'd vanished!

Actually, what happened was an overzealous fan had dashed onto the stage and accidentally pulled Kooper's chair out from under him. Kooper was on the floor, trying to avoid being stampeded by cops who were running around attempting to tackle kids. Bob kept playing through the melee as Al struggled to his feet and slipped back into the chorus of "Like a Rolling Stone." Surprisingly, no one on stage blew his cool. "Kooper and I just sort of looked at each other and laughed," Goldstein remembers. "We were having the time of our lives. It was fun, gleeful, from the heart, exciting—an experience we'd never had before."

The entire concert was an extraordinary phenomenon. The booing, the insults, the wild applause, fans charging the stage under the full moon, *Bob Dylan playing rock 'n roll*—it was like a scene out of *Marat/Sade.* Afterward, Bob was pulled into a waiting limousine to escape the frenzied crowd, but Kooper and Goldstein, who had parked in the stadium's public lot along with everyone else, shared the audience's enthusiasm as they walked to their car. *"Oh, my God!* What happened there tonight?" they kept asking each other as they weaved through the dwindling crowd. "How could music have that kind of effect on people? What does it all mean?"

One thing they knew was that Bob Dylan had somehow upset the balance of popular music. He'd successfully crossed over all musical lines and, without actually announcing it, declared his independence from the folk community.

The MacDougal Street mob—or what was left of it—was relieved to see Bob move on. Ever since he'd returned from England, he'd become a real pain in the ass, instigating the kind of troublesome routines that Albert Grossman enjoyed running on people to make them look foolish. Weird and flaky, but not exactly funny. For a while, Bob and Bobby Neuwirth acquired the habit of walking around Greenwich Village with unloaded cameras, taking pictures of their friends in unflattering positions. Thinking it was very "cutting-edge" stuff. Chuckling up his rock pals. The attitude he projected was that of a guy who was so hip, so cool, that anything he did was what was *happening*.

Guys with lesser talent did their best to imitate Bob's wise-guy attitude. Bobby Neuwirth, David Cohen (an ex-dishwasher at the Gaslight who studied Bob's persona before transforming himself into David Blue), Al Kooper, Victor Maimudes, a prodigy of Albert's named Nick Casey, the future Max's Kansas City crowd—they carried themselves like smug deputies and hired guns, but the number-one gunslinger was unquestionably Marshall Dylan.

Bob was constantly looking to add scalps to his belt, and the best place to do that was the Kettle of Fish, a grimy little joint on MacDougal Street populated by musicians and neighborhood stiffs who preferred to watch TV at the bar instead of at home where their old ladies invariably had the last word. The mob practically lived at the Kettle, as they called it. All the serious young stylists dropped in between their gigs. It was nice and funky—sawdust on the floor, ketchup stains on the menus. A grade Z show-biz scene, right down to the eight-by-ten headshots of local entertainers tacked up around the bar. The folksinger's version of Toot Shor's.

Bob Dylan held court at the Kettle. Night after night, the mob would gather around one of the back tables and wait for Bob to make his move. Eventually he'd choose a victim from among the assembled cast and then unmercifully pick him apart, zoning in on the guy's insecurities like a kamikaze analyst. He ridiculed his prey's music. If someone had wife or girlfriend problems, the victim was treated to Bob's sitcom parody of them. Maybe the way a guy walked or talked or ate was exaggerated in broad slapstick, or his stage act was lampooned. Another tactic he enjoyed was setting folksingers straight about their public image. "You think what you do is so important? You think anybody cares? Nah—you're a joke, man." That was one of Bob's favorite openings. "You don't have it, man. Never did." One of the gang nicknamed it "entertainment by torture." The deeper his knife probed, the more Bob amused his entourage.

"There were guys he could do that to and they would just collapse," recalls Dave Van Ronk, who spent many a bloody night mopping up at the Kettle. Van Ronk names Eric Andersen and Phil Ochs as two of Bob's favorite playthings. "Phil idolized Dylan," Van Ronk says. "He thought that Bobby was the greatest thing since sliced bread—which made him a marked man." Bob routinely ripped Phil's music to shreds, making fun of lyrics and the nasal way in which he sang. "You're not a folksinger, Ochs, you're a *journalist,*" Bob chided him, making it sound cheap and shameful.

"It was a real combat zone," recalls Artie Gorson, Phil Ochs's friend and manager. "If you couldn't deal with it, you weren't a man, or so the nightly rules went. And the sincere guys, the real sweethearts, bore the brunt of it." Like Eric Andersen, for instance. Says Gorson, "Eric was a naive romantic, a beautiful songwriter with a sweet voice who was tortured by the comparisons people made between him and Dylan. But it was nothing compared to the way Dylan and Neuwirth tortured him."

The shock treatment would usually begin with Bob saying, "Hey Eric, you can't use that line in your song. I use that line. You can't use that word, man. I already used that word yesterday." Then Neuwirth would say, "How's Debby, man? [Andersen's girlfriend, Debby Green, a member of the Cambridge gang, was Neuwirth's ex-lover.] She's great in bed, isn't she?" The one-two combination was brutal.

Not even Van Ronk was spared Bob's playful malice. Says Van Ronk, "I was at the Kettle one night when Bobby came in with some of his spear-carriers—Neuwirth, Victor, they were interchangeable parts. Anyway, Bobby had been listening to me do some Old English and Irish ballads and he started in on me about how I should stop singing the blues and become a ballad singer."

"It'll make you rich," Bob teased his friend. "You can make a fortune. Stop this blues business. It's ridiculous."

"In other words," says Van Ronk, "*I* was ridiculous, because everyone there knew how much I loved singing blues and was committed to it. He kept needling me for about ten or fifteen minutes, announcing to his cronies that if I gave up the blues he'd produce an album for me. He'd make me *respectable!* And Victor and Neuwirth were laughing. Finally I looked at him—I wouldn't let him look away or obliterate me—and I said, 'Dylan, if you're so rich, why ain't you smart?' And I left. But he'd gotten to me. I admit that, at the time, coming from Bobby it really hurt."

The folksingers were easy prey. Casualties of the British musical revolution, their glory was rapidly fading. They were big, clunky dinosaurs clinging to an unfashionable tradition, and the Street was suddenly crowded with the walking wounded—folksingers with acoustic guitars strapped to their backs, looking futilely for work. Bob Dylan was their last connection to fame and fortune. Being his friend, or at least claiming to rub shoulders with him every now and then, was an occupational necessity, and no one was willing to relinquish that resource—no matter how much shit they had to take from him.

19

Collision Course

After Forest Hills, Bob was ready for the road again. He'd rehearsed his recent songs with all of the Hawks, and he was dying to try them out on the new fans who flourished in almost every major city in the country.

By this time, the drug culture was in full bloom. Kids everywhere were stoned out of their skulls on grass and experimenting with hash and acid. When Bob hit them with his psychedelic-induced lyrics, he knew he'd cause another sensation similar to the one he triggered with the protest material. Even in places like Cleveland and Lincoln, Nebraska, he'd become the rogue guru of the in-crowd. Kids in rural towns who sensed something extraordinary happening, who recognized the seeds of a counterculture being sown in major cities across America, felt a connection with Bob Dylan. His music validated their longings in the same way that, a decade earlier, rock 'n roll had transformed his dreary youth in Hibbing. Its vitality liberated them from their dull, humdrum existences.

As Bob crisscrossed the country—playing thirty-six concerts in the final months of 1965—he was enjoying unparalleled personal success. His shows had never been so exciting, nor his stage presence more commanding. He won over audiences wherever he played, even in a town like Dallas, which wasn't exactly the seat of cultural enlightenment. "Desolation Row" and "Positively 4th Street" were among the greatest songs he'd ever written. Nothing wordier, wittier, or more scathing had ever been performed in front of an audience weaned on the vagaries of rock 'n roll. All the attention Bob attracted made him a tremendous media phenomenon, but if the press expected him to play by the rules, they were in for a rude shock.

Bob's attitude toward the press was worse than ever. Lately, he'd taken his licks in more than one of the tour's daily rags—"It stank," the *Toronto Daily Star* said of his show at Massey Hall, while the *Cleveland Plain Dealer* complained that "he often sounded exactly like a southern hound dog baying for a raccoon"—but the put-downs bounced off him like rubber bullets. They were ridiculous critiques dashed off by people who didn't have any idea what they were talking about. Rock critics hadn't yet been invented, so the assignments fell to staff reporters who were merely filling space. That was okay with Bob, but it didn't mean he had to cooperate with them. And when he did, more often than not he was misquoted, or, worse, the statements attributed to him were completely bogus.

The real challenge, though, as Bob saw it, was not how he could make the journalists understand him, but how he could make their lives as miserable as they made his. After reading several infuriating interviews, he decided the best defense was to become more inscrutable than ever. A few days later, a reporter in Austin, Texas, was given the full treatment, during a typical question-and-answer session.

REPORTER: Are you trying to accomplish anything?

BOB DYLAN: Am I trying to accomplish anything?

REPORTER: Are you trying to change the world or anything?

BOB DYLAN: Am I trying to change the world? Is that it?

REPORTER: Well, do you have any idealism or anything?

BOB DYLAN: Am I trying to change the idealism of the world? Is that it?

REPORTER: Well, are you trying to push over idealism to the people?

Bob Dylan: Well, what do you think my ideas are?
Reporter: Well, I don't exactly know.

Bob was an expert at dodging idiotic questions, but if the situation called for it, he had the unreluctant talent to lie with a straight face. The day of his sold-out concert at Chicago's Arie Crown Theatre, Bob was interviewed by Joseph Haas, a reasonably articulate writer whose features ran in *Panorama,* the Sunday supplement to the *Chicago Daily News.* Their conversation was unusually straightforward, with Bob explaining quite agreeably why he abandoned folk music and felt separated from the bulk of mainstream America. Except for one item about his personal life, the interview might have gone down as as honest and forthcoming an exchange as one could hope for from Bob Dylan. But that one item was a whopper.

Asked whether he ever hoped to settle down, get married, or have kids, Bob replied, "I don't hope to be like anybody. Getting married, having a bunch of kids, I have no hopes for it." The joke was obviously intended to amuse the handful of friends who, only two days before, had witnessed his marriage to Sara Lownds at an impromptu, private ceremony in a judge's chambers in Mineola, Long Island. Incredibly, not a word was leaked to the press, and even most of Bob's closest friends were kept in the dark. Dave Van Ronk recalls bumping into Dylan a week afterward at the Kettle. "There was this lovely woman with him," Van Ronk says of their encounter. "Bobby introduced me to her and we talked for about a half-hour before they left. The next day I discovered he had married her, and he never said a word about it."

Such was the extent of Bob's hard-fought struggle for privacy. Since *Highway 61* his life had become an open book. Albert's office was besieged with requests for interviews, and in every city along the tour newspapers and local magazines expected wide-open access to Bob to coincide with stories about his show. Like vultures they pecked for tidbits about his parents ("I don't have any family, I'm all alone."), his personal wealth ("When I want money, I ask for it. When I spend it, I ask for more."), and his philosophy of life ("Philosophy can't give me anything I don't already have."). Someone had the nerve to ask Bob if he considered himself a good Christian. Did he see the world as chaos? What happens when he becomes a has-been? Does he avoid close personal relationships? Each question seemed more nosy than the last.

Why Bob made himself available to those pests is anyone's guess. It would have been classy for him to refuse each and every request and remain above the verbal jousting that cluttered most media sessions. He should have remained as enigmatic as his songs. That's what he should have done—but he didn't. Instead, he played coy with the press, and thus perpetuated a swirl of speculation throughout his career.

And yet it was inevitable that Bob should play footsie with journalists. That they should interpret his lyrics and he should make them feel inarticulate. That they should pursue his essence and he should feed them lies. That, in effect, he should recreate the pattern he'd established a long time ago in Hibbing, where he'd alternated as dreamer, exaggerator, and provocateur. Bob acted as if he longed to be misunderstood. As if he thrived on it. But, eventually, he was left to the only devices capable of clarifying the whole mess: music and drugs.

"I wouldn't advise anybody to use drugs," Bob told Nat Hentoff in his hilarious *Playboy* interview conducted during the fall of 1963. "Certainly not the hard drugs; drugs are medicine. But opium and hash and pot—now, those things aren't drugs; they just bend your mind a little. I think *everybody's* mind should be bent once in awhile." Bob got his hipster public-service message out of the way, then jumped immediately to the self-revealing message simmering beneath the verbal smokescreen—namely, that LSD, that chemical road map to what's inside your head, had produced some nasty side effects on him. LSD wasn't for groovy cats, Bob concluded, in his offhanded way. *"It's for mad, hateful people who want revenge."*

In what appeared, at first, to be simply another throwaway observation, Bob uttered probably the greatest public confession of his entire freewheelin' existence. That various trips he'd taken had produced a collection of the maddest, most hateful, vengeful music in the entire American songbook. The lyrics to "Like a Rolling Stone," "Ballad of a Thin Man," "Desolation Row," "Positively 4th Street" and others all seemed to flow from the same poison pen. Acid had twisted his entire perspective. It pulled him so far inside his own head—into the darkest, moodiest, most gut-wrenching corridors of his psyche—that he'd eventually found the voice to unload his personal anger.

Yet if music served as a release for much of Bob's hostility, his life-style sizzled like a firecracker. More like a *thousand* firecrackers, when you took into account his round-the-clock schedule: the endless one-nighters, interviews, staying up all night writing songs, plugging the most recent album, traveling, rehearsing, getting himself together for gigs. It took a lot of motivation just to go out on that stage every night. He had to pump himself up, get the adrenalin going, maintain an energy level. Sometimes he could hook right into the music and ride the highs and lows like an agile surfer. Other nights were held aloft by umpteen mils of speed and caffeine—whatever it took to keep him in top form.

Lately, it seemed as if form and style had begun to carry more weight than content did. In fact, as the Sixties passed the halfway point, all of American culture shifted away from cognitive substance into the froth of pop commercialism. The avant-garde, which sparked the early Sixties with its great gales of wit and wisdom, had pooped out. Jazz and folk music were finished. The art world was in fractional disarray. Next to the high-gloss party fever rampaging through swinging London, American culture seemed drab and lifeless. The action had shifted overseas to where fashion, attitude, and appearance now dictated one's social standing. The discotheque craze was in full bloom. Carnaby Street's trashy allure replaced the somber dress codes of its sexless, post-beatnik predecessors. What the British had—and the Americans sorely lacked—was *style.*

Style was the word on everyone's lips at the beginning of 1966. It was the ultimate test of hipness. It was what everybody lived for. "Oh, she's got such style!" was the highest compliment you could pay someone. By rightful succession, the cultural icons were no longer writers, political satirists, and philosophers but the exemplars of style: fashion models, cafe owners, and photographers. How else could someone like Vidal Sassoon—a middle-aged hairdresser—become a pop idol? Or, for that matter, a shoe designer like Andy Warhol?

Ironically, rock 'n roll, which for years was construed as empty and vulgar, became the new superconductor of style. It was "The Sound of the Sixties," as *Time* announced on its normally sedate cover, "the international anthem of a new and restless generation, the pulse beat for new modes of dress, dance, language, art and morality." It also served as a link between the music and the art world, especially in New York where the city's action painters had traditionally been tuned into jazz. The times called for a new deal between music and art—one that reflected their symbiotic life-styles—and the pop establishment moved in to claim its piece of the rock.

It was not, therefore, a completely alien turf onto which Bob Dylan was moving with his new blend of arty lyrics and rock 'n roll. His music augured the galloping rise of self-conscious experimentalism—the move away from heavy social content into the suggestive go-go milieu of pop commercialism. It was aggressive, cynical, hard-edged, highly mannered, and surrealistic—the actual content of his songs being inconsequential.

Like the pop crowd itself, with all its self-awareness and sophistication, Bob's songs were full of that "up-your-ass" attitude indicative of the mid-Sixties rock scene. They were outrageous and cocky, spectacular and bitchy, and they demanded attention. It's not surprising, then, that Bob was considered one of the shining stars in the pop-art firmament. True, Bob Dylan didn't have the class or style of, say, Truman Capote or even Baby Jane Holtzer, two of its moving forces, but he was trashy in a uniquely stylish way. He represented their dark sides, that perverse fascination society has for rogues and misfits. And in the eyes of the pop-art world he was the complete exhibitionist, which was the ne plus ultra of the pop-art life-style.

Before long, Bob was traveling with a new, energetic crowd of New York personalities. Gone were the schlumpy, severe-looking folksingers, his former pals from the Street. For that matter, the Village itself had become frighteningly déclassé. To be in vogue meant you had to go either uptown or downtown of Greenwich Village. SoHo lofts were the ultimate in-joints because to be admitted to a party there, one had to be invited. Otherwise, the hottest little nightspot was a dive in the commercial section of lower Park Avenue called Max's Kansas City. A narrow, unfinished-looking restaurant, with nothing going for it other than an old bar, twenty-odd booths with linoleum tables, and a great jukebox, Max's was one of the favorite late-night hangouts of the "beautiful people," as they began calling themselves. The Warhol gang moved in there, with its bizarre mix of artists, underground stars, and assorted media freaks. Celebrities like Faye Dunaway and Jerry Schatzberg held court each night with a select cadre of restless, disaffected young actors who lived on the fringe of the New York entertainment community. Rock 'n rollers congregated in the back section, near the kitchen, along with a trickle-down of bikers, drug dealers, groupies, and assorted low-life. And the remaining bunch was made up of intense young artists.

Oddly enough, it was the artists with whom Bob Dylan seemed most at ease. Not the media whores like Peter Max or Roy Lichtenstein, who occasionally breezed through Max's on their way to somewhere more dignified, but the *serious* painters—the mad, passionate abstract expressionists and minimalists, along with the sculptors, neon and fluorescent artists, collagists, and experimental filmmakers. The artists who explored and expanded their media in the same way Bob opened up his music, who weren't afraid to drop a little acid or take mushrooms in order to delve more deeply into their work. Bob's connection to these weird cats was none other than his friend and road manager, Bobby Neuwirth.

Another, less self-centered star would have backed away from someone like Bobby Neuwirth, but to Bob he was an extraordinary individual. "Neuwirth was the eye of any storm," says Ric Von Schmidt, who knew Bobby from the early days in Cambridge, "the center, the catalyst, the instigator. Wherever something important was happening, he was there, or he was on his way to it, or rumored to have been nearby enough to have had an effect on whatever it was that was in the works."

An art student from Ohio, Bobby studied at the University of Ohio, then at the Boston Museum School, where he became involved with people like Jim Dine and Robert Motherwell. Neuwirth's rep there was that he had enormous talent, extraordinary vision, and absolutely no focus to develop into a dedicated painter. He wanted to be everywhere at once—immediately! Exhibiting in galleries, playing the guitar in coffeehouses, working on documentary films—he showed promise in every medium but due to a lack of concentration was unable to distinguish himself in any one of them.

Ah, but he was definitely the life of the party. "He'd always be up for some adventure," recalls Maria Muldaur, another early pal who credits Neuwirth with being the first person to encourage her to perform. "It was impossible to sit around with a bunch of complacent ideas when Neuwirth was in the room. He wouldn't permit it. He'd pull off a hilarious stunt or have everyone involved in some crazy scene—you never knew what he was going to do next, but you could be sure it would be something deliciously wild."

In the Sixties, Neuwirth fit right into New York's riotous party atmosphere. He made himself the star of every wild scene. Referring to Bobby as "the most extremely charming and manipulative" person she'd ever met, Mimi Fariña says, "His favorite put-on was to find two people he could toy with and bring them to a point where they were on the verge of throwing punches before saying or doing the perfect thing that would defuse the tension. The next moment, everyone would be laughing as though nothing had happened. He'd run that one again and again for his friends' amusement. I think he got enormous pleasure from seeing how far he could push someone to the edge, before rescuing them from disaster. He loved the attention it brought him, and with Dylan he had what was undoubtedly his most appreciative audience."

Together they were an explosive team—Bob with his taste for psycho-style drama, Bobby able to whip something up from the most trivial interchange. They'd sweep into Max's, usually drunk or stoned—or both—slit-eyed and ready to roll. Squeezing into an empty booth, Bob always sat with his back to the room. Every head in the joint would turn and stare, while Neuwirth ran down the scene for him. It wouldn't take long until sparks started to fly. Someone would get up the nerve to sit down with them, or Neuwirth would pin somebody from the crowd and wave him over, and then—BAM—the boys had their victim. They'd get the poor sap to reveal something personal, click their tongues in sympathy—sure, sure, they understood. A real pity. Then, before the guy knew what hit him, the table would be full of friends and Bob and Neuwirth were using the stuff the poor schmuck had told them in confidence to entertain the troops. Needling the guy until he either left in a huff or got abusive, in which case Neuwirth bought a conciliatory round of drinks or steered him safely out of Bob's path.

No one was safe from their torment. The more famous someone was, the deadlier they could become. Like the night at Ondine's, when Bob lit into Andy Warhol like a snarling pit bull. He ripped the frail artist to shreds, savaging his paintings and life-style. To his credit,

Warhol shrugged off the attack. But others, like the Rolling Stones' Brian Jones, weren't so fortunate.

Jones was the perfect patsy for the two Bobs. He was frightfully insecure, an emotional naif with a string of mental problems hampered by drug and woman habits that heightened his paranoia. And, worse, he openly admired Bob Dylan. One night at Max's, Jones made the mistake of falling into Bobby Neuwirth's exotic web a moment before Bob pounced on him. Bob detonated every one of Brian's emotional buttons—the Stones were a joke, Jones had no talent, he was a mediocre musician with a lousy voice, no wonder they never let him sing, the band would be better off replacing him, what a little weakling, he had the wrong image for the group. It went on and on until Brian cracked. He broke down crying, which gave Bob another vulnerability to jump on. What a pathetic scene.

Often they preferred to have fun in private—over at Albert Grossman's place, or at the fashionably seedy Chelsea Hotel, where Bob and Sara maintained an apartment. They could lure some chick up to the place and run a number on her for laughs. And women were so much easier to humiliate. The two Bob's had a contempt for women that protected them from any residual guilt which might arise later, after one of their scenes got out of hand.

One time at Albert's, their party guest grew progressively more disturbed about the orgy the boys were planning for her. All the talk about swinging and about fucking her simultaneously was more than she'd bargained for. Freaking out, she ran into the bathroom and locked the door. She was in there an unusually long time when it dawned on the guys that it was too quiet. She wouldn't respond to their exhortations. "Hey, y'know—we were only kidding. The whole thing was just a joke. Now come on out and we'll take you home." Finally, Neuwirth broke into the bathroom and found she'd escaped out the window. The guys loved to tell stories like that one to bolster their legendary status and set the tone for much of the nastiness that underscored the late Sixties.

With Bobby Neuwirth, Bob continued to operate at a ridiculously fast pace. The first half of 1966 was jam-packed with one-nighters that took him on a dizzying pilgrimage across three continents. He was definitely at the peak of his performing career, and though he wasn't caught up in an insidious romantic imbroglio—the inspiration for so many of his brilliant songs—it proved to be one of his creative zeniths as well. So commanding was the momentum he had built up over the past year that even during this period of extreme cockiness and mean-spiritedness and uninterrupted dope-partying, he could still pull himself together enough to produce another masterpiece.

As people close to Bob in those days recall, he had been working on songs for *Blonde on Blonde* since the Newport debacle. Driven by his transcendent success and a convulsive burst of drug-skewered fantasies, he dove into his writing almost obsessively, jotting down bits and pieces of songs whenever a spare moment arose. To accommodate this surge of creativity while there was virtually no spare time for writing, he burned the candle at both ends. On tour, he didn't sleep. After grueling performances, in which he turned himself inside out on stage, Bob grabbed a notepad and went to work. He wrote while members of the band slept, during long stretches of travel, instead of eating or relaxing. Adrenaline alone wasn't enough to keep up this pace. It required substantial subsidies of artificial stimulants—such as speed, bennies, dexies, B-12, caffeine—any form of "powerful medicine," as Bob referred publicly to drugs—to keep him "up" and self-absorbed.

What makes *Blonde on Blonde* so great is simply the fact that it was Bob Dylan confronting his tumultuous rapport with sex, drugs, and rock 'n roll. The only subject matter in which Bob was ever well versed encompassed the affairs of his microcosmic offstage world: the musicians and the managers and the performers and the club owners. And, of course, the affairs of heart. Every song that he wrote reflected his ability to convey the Zeitgeist of that private, idiosyncratic world to his inquisitive public. But now it was rife with drugs, paranoia, a smirking attitude, backbiting, recklessness, and endless bullshit—not to mention marriage and passion—and it took amazing dexterity to sift all that madness and introspection into such an accessible and self-revealing album.

Actually, the recording itself began on a disastrous note. Bob went into the studio on January 25, 1966, intending to lay down a few tracks, but the session was a bust. Something crucial was missing—crucial, yet undefinable—and that worried Bob. John Hammond suggested that he move the session to Nashville, where Columbia maintained an enormous recording studio and the relaxed atmosphere might be more conducive to his concentration. After some lobbying by his new producer, Bob Johnston, Bob was persuaded to give it a try.

If Nashville seems an odd place to record Bob Dylan, the choice of Bob Johnston as his producer was even more off-the-wall. Johnston was a veteran songwriter for Hill and Range, a man whose claim to fame was the music he'd penned for some of those Elvis Presley girls-girls-girls! movies. Hoping eventually to produce records, Columbia dumped Patti Page in Johnston's lap, instructing him to come up with a hit for her. Actually, the record company didn't expect much. The days of female pop singers were just about over, and Columbia was preparing to drop Page's contract. Then Johnston got her the title track to a movie called *Hush, Hush Sweet Charlotte,* and suddenly Patti Page was back on the charts. As a reward, the record company paired Johnston with Bob Dylan and the two men agreed to see how things worked out.

At the beginning, Johnston hadn't the vaguest idea who Bob Dylan was. "I simply woke up one night and found myself in a studio with Dylan staring at me," he says today. "Tom Wilson had already produced 'Rolling Stone,' there was a conflict between him and Bob, so I took over what remained of *Highway 61*. I knew there'd also been trouble with Bob and John Hammond, but my attitude was if Dylan wanted to record under a palm tree in Hawaii with a ukulele, I'd be there with the tape machine. I'm an artist's producer. I give my artists lots of freedom, and if they fuck up—it's their life."

So began one of the more successful artist-producer marriages in modern history. They made seven albums together, the first two of which are generally considered to be Bob's best: *Highway 61 Revisited* and *Blonde on Blonde*. Johnston claims it was he who first suggested that Bob record in Nashville. "I knew the turf," he says, "and told Dylan that I thought the musicians there cared more than anywhere else. What's more, I told him they were looking for a break and that he could be the person to crack the town wide open. In effect, he was the first young outsider to record in Nashville, and it was Bob Dylan who eventually opened the door for everyone since."

The *Blonde on Blonde* sessions were scheduled to begin on February 14, 1966. Bob arrived in Nashville directly from Norfolk, Virginia, where he'd completed a series of one-night stands. That afternoon, the backup musicians who'd been hired for the session—some of Nashville's most celebrated session men—met in the parking lot outside Columbia's new studio complex. "Who are we recording with today?" asked Wayne Moss as he unloaded equipment from the trunk of his car. Charlie McCoy replied, "Bob Dylan." "Who?" asked Kenny Buttrey, the drummer. "Bob Dylan," McCoy repeated, "—some guy from New York."

Actually, McCoy knew a little bit about Bob's style. He had played guitar on "Desolation Row," but he wasn't overly familiar with the rest of Bob's material. Says McCoy, "Dylan was practically an unknown in Nashville. He had no real following, no respect—at least not from us as yet—and we probably regarded him the way we felt about anyone from outside our small circle: as an interloper."

Yet as McCoy spent more time with Bob and observed the songwriter's eccentric routine in the studio, he began revising his own procedures for making a record. What most impressed him was Bob's method of letting a song take its shape as the session progressed. Nashville's musicians weren't used to that kind of creative extravagance. Consummate professionals, they usually came prepared to cut four songs in an hour. They played from prearranged charts, kept their mouths shut, pocketed their paychecks, and went home. When the musicians saw the schedule for Bob Dylan's session, McCoy and the others thought it was someone's idea of a joke. The call wasn't by the hour, as was customary, but for the entire week! Each day they were booked from two in the afternoon until one the following morning.

Once they realized the schedule was for real, everyone showed up feeling extra sharp and ready to play. Everyone, that is, except Bob. He came in two hours late, cornered McCoy, and said, "I haven't finished writing the songs yet. You guys just hang loose, and when I'm finished writing it, we'll record it." As Charlie McCoy remembers it, "We went downstairs wondering what in the hell this guy was trying to pull. We played Ping-Pong, we played cards, we drank tons of coffee." Around eight o'clock the musicians started getting restless. "The conversation was: 'Where is this guy? What's going on?' I got to thinking, 'God, this must be some song he's writing!'"

At four o'clock in the morning the band was finally summoned from the lounge. Their nerves were shot, they were wired from gallons of caffeine. Then blinding fatigue began to set in. Bob, looking energetic and unperturbed, paced back and forth in front of a music stand strewn with pages of illegible lyrics. "Okay," he said, "this is going to be like a couple of verses and a chorus and an instrumental. Then I'll come back in and we'll do another couple verses, another instrumental, and then we'll just see how it goes. Okay, guys, here we go."

"Hey—wait a minute," Kenny Buttrey, the drummer, interrupted. "You mind telling us the name of the song?"

Bob looked up over the lyrics and muttered, "'Sad-Eyed Lady of the Lowlands.' Now, just follow me."

As if the long wait weren't bad enough, the musicians were now confused by his Spartan instructions. The least Bob could have done, they thought, was to play through a couple of verses until they'd gotten the hang of it, maybe establish a few cues to guide the band along. But without further ado, the tape began to roll. Lucky for everyone the band was tight. They'd played together for years, and they knew each other's style and could instinctively predict each other's moves. Buttrey looked at his watch and thought, "All right, Kenny boy, settle down, stay alert. In three minutes the whole thing'll be over and you'll be able to get some sleep."

Two minutes into the song, however, Buttrey began wondering how Bob would reconcile an ending in the thirty seconds or so he had left. So far, they'd recorded only one verse of the song and he had gotten the impression there were several more on those pages. Three minutes later he wondered if this guy Dylan had any concept of a song's normal length. Record companies observed strict guidelines for that—three, maybe three-and-a-half minutes at the most—so a song fit into commercial radio's playlistings. Buttrey remembers the other musicians sensing disaster as the song dragged on and on. "Man, people were looking at their watches and squinting at each other as if to say, 'What *is* this—what the hell's going on here?' We'd never heard of a song taking more than two or three minutes, much less *fourteen*. I have to admit, I thought the guy had blown a gasket and we were basically humoring him."

Says Charlie McCoy, "We were all fighting hard to concentrate and stay awake. I couldn't see straight. I desperately tried not to make any mistakes. Hell, the only thought running through my mind was that I didn't want to fuck up and have to do it all over again."

Amazingly enough, "Sad-Eyed Lady of the Lowlands" was recorded live and in one take. The Nashville musicians heaved a collective sigh of relief as the song faded, though they were still spooked by the night's bizarre twists as well as its seemingly remarkable outcome. The song had incredible power. The performance, the tune—*those lyrics!* What a conglomeration of mad, magnificent passion.

The sun rose over the surrounding office buildings as they stumbled out to their cars. Nobody said a word as each contemplated the task that lay ahead. The session was going to be a motherfucker. It'd either be the most expensive catastrophe the music business had ever known or a monumental breakthrough. "See you guys later this afternoon," Bob said, as the musicians prepared to drive off toward their respective homes for some sleep.

The local musicians were wary when they arrived for the second day of recording but this time there was an altogether different mood in the studio. Bob was on time and, by all appearances, raring to play. He seemed more easygoing and personable, though still a far cry from any creature they'd ever encountered before. Other musicians were also on hand to liven up the atmosphere. Bob's pals Al Kooper and Robbie Robertson had arrived, and to everyone's surprise they weren't the kind of pushy, stuck-up creeps who were usually flown in from New York to "dignify" the country-style session. They were a right neighborly bunch of guys as far as the locals could tell—loose and goosey, which was the feel that gave Nashville its inimitable sound.

As the day wore on, the musicians fell into a real groove. The Nashville cats meshed nicely with the city slickers, and because Bob didn't rehearse or follow charts, the work took on the free-and-easy aspect of a jam session. Everyone contributed to the various arrangements; Bob handled suggestions from his sidemen as if they came from Toscanini himself. "It was a collaborative effort," recalls Charlie McCoy, who was enthralled by the ease with which Bob assimilated their ideas into the songs. "He was open to anything," says the producer, Bob Johnston. "By the early evening, when Bob started playing something, everybody would click in, even if they'd never heard the tunes or been given the chords. A camaraderie started to develop—the musicians began to trust Bob, at least as far as his being a fellow musician—and the barriers between them started to come down."

Johnston removed some physical barriers as well. He'd grown frustrated with the studio, a cavernous, sterile room sectioned off by towering dividers between the musicians to prevent the sound from bleeding into the sensitive microphones. The setup might have facilitated technically proficient recording, but it did nothing to encourage the ensemble sound he was looking for. Johnston wanted the men to *play together,* as opposed to playing individual parts, so he ordered most of the barriers ripped out. Kenny Buttrey attributes the album's distinctive sound to that change. "It made all the difference in our playing together, as if we were on a tight stage, as opposed to playing in a big hall where you're ninety miles apart. From that night on, our entire outlook was changed. We started having a good time. We started eating together, we took breaks together—that never happened on any album I'd worked on in the past. Dylan made us feel as if we had a personal stake in the album, and we began to play our asses off for him."

About ten o'clock that night, Bob decided to record a new song and talked about putting an unusual edge on it. "Maybe we ought to get a Salvation Army band for the tune and record it out in the parking lot," he suggested. Ken Buttrey laughed and shook his head. "You don't know Nashville, man. The Salvation Army band we got here sounds every bit as good as the Marine Corps band," he said. "It seems to me that you're talking about some playing that sounds nonprofessional or pretty dumb." "Right," Bob agreed. Buttrey grinned and waved his arm across the studio. "Then give us a chance. We can play pretty dumb if we put our minds to it.'"

Bob Johnston said, "What we need is a trombone and a trumpet for this song." Charlie McCoy knew a trombone player named Wayne Butler who could be roused out of the sack at midnight. Since the sound was expected to be rough, McCoy, a guitarist and mouth harp virtuoso, volunteered to play the trumpet himself. "One method of doing this that might be fun is if everybody changed instruments," Buttrey suggested. With that, Al Kooper switched from keyboards to tambourine. The bass player lay on the floor and pumped the organ pedals with his hands. Someone pulled the slide out of Wayne Butler's trombone, so the instrument would sound awkwardly out of tune. And Buttrey took apart his drum kit, laying the bass across two chairs, tying the cymbals onto a music stand, and rat-tat-tatting the head of his snare so it would sound dead and hollow, like the drums in a high-school marching band.

"This is called 'Rainy Day Women,'" Bob announced. "Let's run it down once or twice and see what kind of sound we get."

What they got was one of the sorriest sounding combos imaginable—the kind of off-key, zonked-out thumpers you hear outside Woolworth's every Christmas season. The horns bleated like hungry sheep, the piano jangled, the drums clattered with the resonance of rusty hubcaps, and when Bob came in with the lyric, the band broke into howls of laughter.

> Well, they'll stone ya when you're trying to
> be so good,
> They'll stone ya...

It was one of the funniest sounding songs they'd ever heard. Everyone in the room was whooping it up, hollering, shouting things back and forth. After a minute or two, Bob Johnston interrupted with an announcement over the intercom. "Hey, let's stop and go back to the beginning before we lose that feel," he said. "And keep that excitement going." Johnston was knocked out by the impulsive sound they were getting and didn't want to chance dampening it with self-consciousness and reexamination. The musicians were having the time of their lives. No one worried about timing. There were no attempts to cover up mistakes or clams. As far as the Nashville contingent was concerned, the song was a big goof. Besides, no one dreamed it would ever surface on a record. "'Everybody must get stoned?'—not a chance," Ken Buttrey recalls thinking at the time.

As they had done with "Sad-Eyed Lady of the Lowlands," the final version of "Rainy Day Women #12 & 35" was completed on the first take. They learned *and* cut the song in seventeen minutes flat.

Everyone's mood following the recording of "Rainy Day Women #12 & 35" was exceedingly high, but the exhilaration was short-lived. As before, Bob hadn't completed the remaining songs, though there were bits and pieces of things he liked—a verse here, a chorus there. Until he was finished, the band members were banished to the lounge where they once again took up a vigil likened to the selection of a new Pope.

Says one disgruntled musician, "Bob would tell us to take a break, which for us usually meant five or ten minutes but for him turned into five or six hours. We'd go out to dinner, come back, and he'd still not be ready for us. Guys were passed out on the floor, taking naps. Then word'd come down that he had something and we'd jump up to record."

Bob Johnston, somewhat naively to be sure, was compelled to defend his artist's strange recording habits. "After a while," he says, "everybody was certain Dylan was a junkie. He locked himself in the studio for twelve hours at a time, writing. He never got up to go to the bathroom. Food for him was a solid stream of malteds and candy bars. I've got to admit, the set-up had a lot of us second-guessing him."

Says another musician: "At the time, the whole session seemed like a childish joke, but somehow it turned into a piece of musical history that all of us are proud to have been a part of."

In all, *Blonde on Blonde* took about forty studio hours to complete, which for Nashville, in those days, seemed like a recording marathon. Listening to it today—at a time when solo artists spend months on end laying down as few as six or eight tracks of overprocessed pap—one is struck by how dynamic and instantly engaging the album sounds. And how honestly delivered it is, from the first jarring blast of "Rainy Day Women #12 & 35" on through to the final sigh of "Sad-Eyed Lady of the Lowlands." In between, the songs are as good as Bob Dylan got in his first twenty-five years of recording. They're full of wit, passion, rich poetic language, vitriol, double entendre, bravado, high and low camp, *chutzpah,* and charm.

For the longest time, it has been fashionable for critics to knock *Blonde on Blonde* for possessing too many good songs for one record, while not quite enough to sustain two, but a closer examination proves them hasty to beat the gong. Too many stand today as classic Bob Dylan, if not classic popular, songs: "Just Like a Woman," "Most Likely You Go Your Way and I'll Go Mine," "I Want You," "Stuck Inside of Mobile with the Memphis Blues Again," "One of Us Must Know (Sooner or Later)," "Visions of Johanna," "Sad-Eyed Lady of the Lowlands." Each is distinctive, unpredictable, always fascinating to the ear. Even a seemingly superficial number like "Leopard-Skin Pillbox Hat" spotlights the songwriter's arch humor much as "Talkin'

World War III Blues" and "Bob Dylan's Blues" enlivened earlier albums; he merely updated the form, giving it a decidedly mid-Sixties bite.

More than anything else, however, *Blonde on Blonde* dramatized a near-perfect collaboration of music, lyrics, and performance. The accompaniment, while spare and slightly off the hinges, is superb. Never had such a mongrel band played so harmoniously and with such critical deliberation. Bob called it "that thin, that wild mercury sound," but that was so much theatrical blather. The sound was pure, unadulterated rock 'n roll. The bluesy guitar fills, the rippling keyboards, the staccato, metallic-sounding drums—all fit Bob's songs like a warm lingering embrace. And yet the music-making was so obviously playful and festive. The band rocked out, especially on "One of Us Must Know (Sooner or Later)," "Stuck Inside of Mobile with the Memphis Blues Again," and "Most Likely You Go Your Way."

The singing was notable for its resonant simplicity. Once again, Bob Dylan's phrasing and saw-toothed delivery gave each song poignant accuracy. He was in extremely fine voice, maybe as fine as he ever displayed on record—rich and full and reverberating with personality. Mockery and wickedness drifted disturbingly through his vocals. The belligerence of songs such as "Just Like a Woman" and "Leopard-Skin Pillbox Hat" was underscored by his insinuating, strung-out slurs of words and notes. But these were upstaged by the passionately sung "I Want You" and "Sad-Eyed Lady of the Lowlands."

Ambiguous and complex, *Blonde on Blonde* was a magnet for every pseudo-intellectual and neurotic analyzer of lyrics. For them, *Blonde on Blonde* was a lyrical Rorschach test. Critics waxed clinical with profiles of Bob Dylan's psychology. Michael Gray, in his fuzzy, abstracted *Song and Dance Man: The Art of Bob Dylan,* proposes: ". . . the album is a whole and the individual songs are only parts; and it doesn't matter that sometimes the chaos seems to be America and sometimes to be the city life of particular sorts of people. It doesn't even contradict the spirit of the whole that a couple of the songs evoke a chaos that is inside the emotions of the narrator." Singling out "Pledging My Time," Robert Shelton, the songwriter's personal Freud, postulates: "Through the shadow and smoke we feel his doomsday imprisonment, as he pledges his will to go on living, loving, and singing."

Suddenly Bob Dylan's lyrics unlocked the mysteries of western civilization. An army of armchair philosophers turned his images inside out in an attempt to fit them to their nutty theses. Take a song like "Rainy Day Women #12 & 35." Could it possibly be simply a comical send-up of a generation getting stoned? Not according to Wilfred Mellers, a British music professor and noted Dylan authority, who contends: "The words pun playfully on two meanings of 'stoned': the honest man or woman, an outsider because of his or her freedom from conventional values, will have stones hurled at him or her by the conformists, even when 'tryin' to be so good'; he or she will also get stoned on whatever it might be, partly as a consequence of this outlawism, partly in an attempt to discover truer values through the Blakean Doors of Perception." *Whew!*

Bill King, another self-styled "academic," interprets "Just Like a Woman" as a treatise on "the failure of human relationships because of illusion created by social myth." And Ellen Willis, writing in *Cheetah,* deduces: "The fashionable sybaritic denizens of *Blonde on Blonde* are the sort of people despised by radicals and apologists for the system. Yet in accepting the surface that system has produced, they subvert its assumptions. Conservative and utopian idealogues agree that man must understand and control his environment. . . ."

Like Chance, the gardener, in Jerzy Kozinski's *Being There,* Bob Dylan was hoisted up as the reluctant arbiter of wisdom and insight. He became not only the generation's chief spokesperson, but its redemptive sage—misquoted and misinterpreted as a matter of convenience. Not that the reverence was without outside influence. Indeed, most teenagers who flipped a Bob Dylan album onto their turntable preceded it with a few hits of grass, maybe a tab of acid, some mushrooms, or even a jug of cheap wine, so that before a song was through the lyrics were teeming with dizzy, disoriented symbolism. They were fucking religious, man!

Consequently, thousands of fans flocked to Greenwich Village looking for their eloquent rabbi. They camped outside the Chelsea Hotel, on the curb in front of Folk City, inside the Kiev delicatessen or the Feenjon, where the Great One actually ate. Dylan fans peered inside the Kettle for a glimpse of him at rest or stared across the room at Max's. Die-hard freaks even made a pilgrimage to Hibbing in the hope of seeing family or friends. It got so that Bob couldn't go anywhere without confronting someone who was completely obsessed with his songs. People took them so seriously. They knew all the words by heart. Figured out what each song *really* meant. Perfect strangers talked intimately about Bob's friends and acquaintances as though they were characters on an afternoon soap. "Y'know, like in 'Ballad of a Thin Man' when you say 'you walk into the room like a camel. . . .' Well, that's gotta be about Victor—right?—because I saw a picture of him in a magazine and he was smoking Camels, even though Ric Von Schmidt used to smoke 'em, but he switched to Lucky Strike round about '64, so it couldn't be Ric. . . ." It was bizarre how much they knew about him and his circle of friends.

The more famous Bob became, the more his paranoia increased. He became increasingly uptight around the gang, always on edge. To people who approached him in public, Bob could be downright rude. He accused close friends of secretly wanting something from him, attaching themselves to his star. He suspected promoters of cheating him. The record company, he was convinced, fudged his sales figures. His "agents" had their hands in every pocket. Long-lost relatives called to put the touch on him. "I'm sick of giving creeps money off my soul," he complained bitterly to an interviewer early in the year. Even the press was out to "expose" him.

By the spring of 1966, Bob was clearly spinning out of control. He was on a collision course, working around the clock—on new songs, on his book, on a TV special, on a new tour and perhaps another movie—and the pressures of stardom were closing in on him like a vise. To those around him, he looked shockingly sick. San Francisco critic Ralph J. Gleason, an early Dylan partisan, warned friends that he thought Bob was on the verge of a breakdown. Drugs had become an indispensable part of his life. Amphetamines kept him going; downers and alcohol put him to sleep. In between, there were psychedelics to inspire his creativity. Although he has never admitted publicly to using heroin, he bragged to some friends about it. "Bobby tended to fall asleep a lot at the wrong times and I knew he was playing with heroin," affirms Dave Van Ronk. "He wasn't an addict. I knew addicts and he wasn't one, but he was flirting with it and wanted us to know—as if it would shock us." Or to send a message for help.

Around the same time, Suze Rotolo ran into Bob at the Kettle of Fish and was appalled by his woeful appearance. No longer the sweet, bashful Bobby who'd courted her, this Bob was an urban lizard. He was painfully thin and jittery, his pale, haggard face ravaged by abuse. His eyes were sunken and leaden, his skin waxy and gray. Suze was hip to Bob's erratic moods, but that day he was fatiguingly fast and loose. He was going a mile a minute. A speeding bullet aimed at some far-off target only Bob could bring into focus. Finally, when Victor and Bobby Neuwirth walked to the other end of the room, Bob admitted to Suze that his drug habit was careening out of control. "I've got to get cleaned up," he told her, wringing his hands. "Somehow I've got to get cleaned up."

No doubt his concern was prompted by several tragedies that had struck too close to home. Many of Bob's friends had died recently, all victims of reckless disregard. In April, Richard Fariña was decapitated in a motorcycle accident while on the way home from a publication party for his book, *Been Down So Long, Looks Like It's Up to Me.* Folksinger Peter LaFarge, a longtime pal who'd first befriended Bob at the Gleason's Sunday hootenannies for Woody Guthrie and was a fixture of the Village coffeehouse scene, overdosed. Paul Clayton went slowly insane from drugs. Broke and at the end of his rope, poor Pablo jumped into the bathtub holding an electric radio. Geno Foreman was wasted beyond all hope. Paul Rothchild had been busted and was doing time. David Blue, the funniest, coolest, craziest, and quickest-on-the-draw of the bunch, was also its most ardent junkie. Bobby Neuwirth was a mean-spirited alcoholic. Bodies were piling up faster than Bob cared to admit, the statistics spelling certain doom. Despite his steady momentum and luck, he knew he couldn't keep up the current pace and live to tell about it. What's more, he now had a wife to consider. And Sara's daughter, Maria, too—Bob had grown incredibly attached to her. He wanted kids of his own someday. Somehow, Bob had to find a way to cool his jets before they burned up and disintegrated.

Unfortunately, he was already committed to a tour of the West Coast and Canada, followed by a couple of shows in Hawaii, two weeks in Australia, and a month schlepping around Europe and the British Isles with the Hawks. He knew it was going to take a heap of medicine to keep him pumped up to face those fucking crowds night after night. Man, he couldn't be expected to do two months on the road *straight*. Not if he wanted to be in top form on stage. SydneyBrisbaneMelbourne-

AdelaidePerthStockholmCopenhagenDublinBelfastBristol—how the hell was he supposed to make a trip like that without a little extra assistance?

No, too many people were waiting to see Bob on this tour. He was finally an international star. This time he wasn't going overseas begging full houses. This wasn't going to be some bus-and-truck tour where the act had to change in the men's room. There were no crummy halls in the boonies to play. No bowling alleys or beer joints, no converted movie houses. Albert had booked all heavy "class" dates that would be sold out weeks in advance. Everyone was waiting to hear what the new electric Bob Dylan sounded like—and the new Bob Dylan songs. Fans in Australia and Europe were teeming with expectation. No longer a cult act, Bob Dylan was an international media event. He'd be expected to say and do the outrageous. To lay the newest, hippest sensibility on his audience. To deliver something that'd blow people's minds, shuffle their psyches. Alter their perceptions of reality.

At the awkward age of twenty-five, Bob Dylan had an awful lot to live up to—and a lot more to live down.

20

Dylan's Last Ride

The last week in March 1966, Bob and his gang left on what proved to be his final concert tour until 1974. After a week of previews in the Pacific Northwest, crossing briefly into Vancouver, British Columbia, this tour was scheduled to stretch more than halfway around the globe, barnstorming through Australia and Sweden before retracing much of the 1965 trek through England and the British Isles. Unlike the last go-round, however, Bob was emphatically a star in each of the countries he prepared to visit. He was idolized by audiences worldwide for the artistic and social importance of his songs (whose every word they had, by now, committed to memory), as well as for his ideas, which had provoked an upheaval in their traditional values. All of which goes to explain the scorching response when Bob ultimately failed to live up to their expectations.

Once again, the harsh reaction was prompted by Bob's errant musical path. A majority of his fans were still unwilling to accept Bob Dylan material other than his folk or protest songs. Ironically, *change*—the principal theme of those cherished early songs—was okay for anyone but Bob Dylan. From him they expected the old familiar civil-rights anthems mixed in with an assortment of love ballads and Woody Guthrie tunes. No surprises. Since his purpose wasn't to disappoint fans—only to stir them up a bit—Bob opened each show with the obligatory forty-five-minute acoustic set. Then, following intermission, the band joined him on stage, and Bob Dylan proceeded to rock the house.

The first few nights should have provided a clue to the stormy months ahead. In both Portland and Seattle, the cheers pulsing throughout his acoustic set turned quickly to catcalls and boos when the band plugged in. Each night, more than two hundred folk music stalwarts stormed out in disgust before the concert ended. The dissenters who remained were clearly at odds with the shaggier, more spirited fans who danced by their seats. No doubt the conflict was disorienting to the disparate fans, for in the past different types of popular music appealed to distinctly different generations. In the Forties, the bobby-soxers squealed at Frank Sinatra while their parents brayed in dispute. In the Fifties, the generations were divided over Elvis Presley. Here, however, were two contingents of Bob Dylan fans of *the same age* who seemed incompatible. They dressed differently, they acted differently, they wanted different experiences from a musical concert. William Littler, a music critic for the *Vancouver Sun,* neatly summed up that phenomenon in his review of the show, entitled "Eccentric Dylan Turns to Banality." "Bob Dylan has me buffaloed," he admitted in his opening comment. Praising the acoustic set for its "conscience and feeling," Littler wrote: "They were the kind of songs I could identify with . . . but then something happened. Intermission. And after that, nothing seemed quite the same. Gone was the guitar and in its place Dylan held an electric guitar. . . . I didn't like it. . . . It all spelled something I did not want to read or admit—that America's foremost folk voice may have sold out to the jukebox."

The show drew an identical response in Hawaii—more boos and more conflicting reviews—so that by the time the tour landed in Australia, Bob was pissed off and ready to bite back.

Bob's notion of Australia—most likely gleaned from B-movies and H. Ryder Haggard stories—was provincial, by most standards. As one interviewer reported, Bob saw Australia as a country "just like Texas"—an annexed territory, in this case a former Crown penal colony, inhabited by sheepherders and ranchers who shared the vast plains with wild packs of kangaroos. The people had no sense of hipness and were descended from disenfranchised convicts, degenerates, and other undesirables.

From the moment Bob set foot in Sydney, his attitude toward the country was revealed. "Australia is not a very nice place for a lot of people—like Orientals or Negroes," he chided Australian newsmen at an airport press conference. "I mean, you don't even have any baseball here." He had already goofed on the fans who herded out to greet him by signing autographs as "The Phantom." Members of his band and road crew, dressed condescendingly in sombreros and sunglasses, encouraged his antics with closed-mouthed grins.

The press considered him a disrespectful wiseguy. Sprawled across a couch in the airport lounge, dressed in skin-tight pants, a polka-dot shirt, and high-heeled boots, with a three-day patchy growth on his chin, Bob responded to their questions with a flurry of "huhs?" as the repartee grew increasingly ridiculous.

"Isn't this protest music a fake?"

"Huh?"

"It's a phony, isn't it?"

"Huh?"

And, later: "Are you a professional beatnik?"

"Huh?"

"Why don't you see more of your parents?"

"Huh?"

The simplemindedness of Bob's responses was exceeded only by the ineptitude of the reporters' questions. The press were united in their total lack of regard for their subject. But, as usual, Bob couldn't resist baiting them with infantile comebacks. To make matters worse, Albert Grossman suggested that Bob interview himself, and laughed loudly and condescendingly as his client ridiculed the reporters. Small wonder, then, that Bob was flayed by Australia's most prominent newspaper and television barons. They attacked him in the kind of blaring headlines usually reserved for national soccer matches and royal visits. His drug-riddled, indifferent performances didn't help, either. Bob stumbled blindly through his nine Australian concerts as though they were jam sessions. He was out of it, as only a mid-Sixties rock star could be in front of fifty thousand people.

From Australia, the tour flew to London where it was joined by Donn Pennebaker and a film crew, then connected to a flight bound for Stockholm for the kickoff of the European segment. Pennebaker was initially reluctant to come along but had been talked into it by

Bob before the group left New York. Since the *Don't Look Back* outing, everyone's concept of a tour film had changed, and its evolution didn't appeal to him. It had become slick and very preconceived. Pennebaker wanted to make a film similar to *Don't Look Back,* almost as an epilogue to that tour, where all the action came from within the film. But Bob wanted to use actors, dream up outrageous situations for them, and perhaps use a script to control some of the action. Bob was even determined to direct part of it himself. Finally, he and Pennebaker reached a compromise: the scenes would make themselves, and everybody would direct himself, so that there would be some acting and direction but enough spontaneity to give the film authenticity. Unfortunately, Albert Grossman had also made a deal with ABC-TV for a Bob Dylan concert special, and suddenly there was talk of bringing Pennebaker in on that too. Maybe combine the film and TV special and get those dumb schmucks from Sixth Avenue to cough up a fortune for the cheap black-and-white footage he'd already provided for. Or maybe even splurge for color. Rock 'n roll outsmarting the business sector at its own game—that was the kind of scam Albert loved to run, and while Pennebaker agreed to participate, he knew that the arrangement was liable to blow up in his face.

He also realized—pretty much from the start—that what the film was really going to be about was drugs. Says Pennebaker, "When I met up with them, there was an enormous amount of grass being smoked—it seemed like pounds of it. Also, Bob was taking a lot of amphetamines and who-knows-what-else, and he was scratching all the time. He was very edgy, very uptight, and he stayed up for days on end, without sleep." As a result, Pennebaker says, Bob was in an incredibly strange mood. "He could turn on you in an instant, without any warning, which made it hard communicating with him," the director recalls. "I was good at a fair degree of spontaneity and was fascinated by a subject's mood swings, but I had no idea how to steer something as flaky as that—something so tenuous and uncontrollable—and as a professional filmmaker that worried me."

They had no sooner landed in Stockholm when Pennebaker got a firsthand look at the type of situation he dreaded most. Bob was behaving in an outrageously wild way. He was going at a hundred miles an hour, flashing on ideas in fugues, with such tremendous impatience that no one understood what he was talking about. Amphetamines had kept Bob awake all day and night, into the early hours of the morning. He was going through them faster than a box of Good 'n Plenty, and to some members of the entourage it seemed like he was never going to sleep. Of course, if Bob didn't sleep neither did they, and as the sun began to peek through the Scandinavian nightscape, his playmates struggled desperately to hang on.

Mad passion and amphetamines were the magnetic poles pulling Bob along like a firecracker on its way through a beautifully landscaped park. Ideas were smoking out of his mouth like staccato guitar riffs; he wasn't even listening to hear how they sounded. He'd lost contact with Robbie Robertson, Bobby Neuwirth, Pennebaker, and the others and was steamrolling forward on some psychedelic trajectory of his own. Suddenly, out of nowhere, he and the others came to the docks. An American destroyer was anchored to a jetty there, rocking in its wake. Bob started framing the whole scene with his clumsy fingers—was he Vincent Minelli directing *The Caine Mutiny*?—and instructed Pennebaker to set up the camera.

Paranoia swept through the entourage like a brushfire. There were about ten tour members accompanying Bob, and it dawned on them all at once that their noisy celebration might attract the wrong kind of attention from the ship. It was well known that most sailors hated music freaks, especially those who wore flashy faggot clothes, and they would probably love nothing more than to bust some hippie heads. And who knew what any of the guys might be carrying on them at that moment; pot, hash, bennies, acid. Any trace amount, any false move, could land them *collectively* in the brig for a two-to-ten stretch.

Just as they'd headed Bob off in the opposite direction, reveille sounded on board the ship and hundreds of skinhead sailors poured onto the main deck. Shit!—morning assembly, what a lousy break for the guys. There was still plenty of time for them to slink off unnoticed, but before anyone could put a gag on Bob, he'd attracted a crowd. Scores of midshipmen began hanging over the railing, gaping at the musicians. Someone grabbed Bob and tried to drag him across the street, but he was having none of that. "Oh, man, this place is outta sight!" he babbled incoherently. "What a scene this'll make! Let's get it on film!"

Pennebaker looked up from the camera just as the gangplank was lowered and the captain strode formally down the ramp. "Now we're in trouble," he said in a hushed aside to Neuwirth. "Let's get Bob out of here before it's too late." The director was certain they'd be busted on the spot and stopped filming so as not to provoke the captain. Bob got furious when he heard the camera's motor wind down. "Hey! What are you doin', man? Keep shooting! Turn the fuckin' camera back on!"

Before Pennebaker could respond, the stern-faced captain demanded, "Are you Bob Dylan?"

Belligerently, Bob spun around on his heel and came face to face with the ship's first officer. The guy was the archetypal Navy slob—pug-faced, severe, patriotic, proud, a real Otto Schmidlap face, decked out in miles of gold braid and medals. Bob, zonked out of his gourd, must have flashed on every childhood role model: Douglas MacArthur, Farragut, John Paul Jones, Horatio Hornblower, Charlie Alnutt, Captain Bligh, Queeg, Ahab, Crunch. In one bystander's words: "He looked like the Arresting Officer of the Sky." Undaunted, Bob stuck out his chin and said, "Yeah, I'm Bob Dylan. What's it to you?"

The captain glanced over his shoulder, then broke into a mischievous grin. "I just wanted to tell you that I wrote a novel called *One Too Many Mornings.* Your song was the most incredible thing I ever heard. It changed my life, and I wanted to thank you myself." Then, flustered by his goofy admission, the captain stuck out a big paw, pumped Bob's hand a few times, and walked swiftly back to the destroyer.

The rest of the guys turned around and stared in astonishment across the dock at the imposing vessel. Bob grinned at them like a Halloween pumpkin. He was really wasted. Pennebaker doubted he had any idea what had just happened or how close they'd all come to disaster. "This time we were lucky," he thought. Still, they couldn't take that kind of chance again. Someone would have to sit on Bob, keep him out of trouble. Neuwirth was already running what they jokingly referred to as "damage control," but in Bob's condition it wasn't going to be enough. Not if they wanted to get him back to the States in one piece.

Bob was going to get them all killed, Pennebaker thought. That disturbing possibility and the fact that the film was slipping away from him set the stage for yet another dreary confrontation. Bob had invited his friends Howard and Jones Alk on the tour and gradually turned over to them many of the filmmaking responsibilities usually handled by Pennebaker. Howard had made a film in Chicago with the Black Panthers which Pennebaker liked, but it was clear that Howard's friendship with Bob blurred his objectivity and interfered with the strategy Donn and Bob had agreed upon in New York. And Pennebaker was unwilling to fight for control of the camera with Howard. So after another day or two of game playing, in which Bob deliberately toyed with each of the filmmakers, Pennebaker left the tour and went to Cannes with a work print of *Don't Look Back.*

Life on the road may have been an ongoing horror show, but on stage Bob Dylan was as magical as ever. In fact, more so. The European shows—beginning in Stockholm on April 29, 1966, and ending nearly a month later in London—were so moody and spontaneous, so immediately honest, that to this day his longtime fans consider many of them the finest all-around performances of his career. A self-styled "Dylan collector," whose tape collection comprises nearly every one of Bob's professional shows, claims that listening to the 1966 tour is still a "frightening experience" for him. "The guy was *possessed!*" he says of Bob. "All this new music, these new sounds, were inside of Bob—like it was poison and he had to spit the stuff out before it afflicted him."

Hyperbole aside, the group sounded like no other band before them, with a newness and urgency about their music that happens so seldom in art. The lyrics, music, and instrumentation were only partially responsible for the shows' fiery dynamics. Somehow, through the haze of drugs, Bob managed to harness other components that sharpened not only his performance at any given time but also the pure ideal of the rock 'n roll rebel in those wild, seminal years before the business grew up and became a cliché.

First of all, there was a gusty blast of hostility howling through those European concert halls in 1966. The so-called "Dylan controversy" raged on, and for many in those audiences Bob had about as much right to hold an electric guitar in his hands as he did a submachine gun. In England, an electric Dylan was as scandalous as the months-old Profumo affair. *Melody Maker,* which only a year before proclaimed Bob the demigod of popular music, labeled the new show "a disaster." Wrote the venerable music weekly: "It was unbelievable to see a hip, swinging Dylan trying to look and sound like Mick Jagger and to realise after the first few minutes that it wasn't a takeoff...for most, it was the night of the big let-down."

Bob became the object of scorn from practically every audience along the tour. From Dublin, right through to Paris and back to London, fans refused to accept the second half of each night's performance, when Bob appeared with the band. It was too unsettling, too experimental. In frustration, they wound up either whistling or booing or screaming out an obscenity to cover their bewilderment, and if that didn't suffice, they eventually up and left.

Make no mistake, Bob was equally frustrated. He was bored stiff performing without a band. The acoustic set, which began every show, was a concession of sorts to his earliest fans who had followed his career since the first album. Warming up with those songs was a way of easing them into the new stuff. But it was, in effect, the same set he'd done the year before—the same familiar folk style, standing alone with his guitar and harmonica—and you could see by his face what a drag it was.

During the acoustic set, the influence of drugs on Bob was also embarrassingly evident. He spoke abnormally slow. Introducing each song, he could barely get the words out, and when he finally did, they tumbled over his tongue like a schoolboy practicing a Demosthenic exercise. "Thisssong—useda be called—'Vizzins of Jo-haaaannnnn-aahhhh,'" he announced in Bristol. "Now—[long pause] it's called—'Muther Revisited.'" *What the fuck is he talking about?* people seemed to be asking each other. Even the die-hard fans were spooked by his manner.

In Dublin, where traditional ballad singing was going through a renaissance, an unruly audience clapped slowly and steadily between songs. "Oh, man—*what a drag,*" Bob complained during a moment of candid introspection. Shouts of "traitor!" echoed back at him. Bob shook his head and waved them off in obvious disgust. "It was the climax of mutual contempt," *Melody Maker* reported in its review of the show, "—Dylan for the audience and the audience for Dylan's new sound."

It wasn't until Bob reappeared with the band that his attitude improved. In fact, he seemed positively transformed—hopping onto the stage when the lights came up, grinning from ear to ear. He pranced lightly like a leprechaun on white-hot coals. The sound was hot and high, and with Robbie Robertson's goading guitar, the two men pushed the music to thrillingly frenzied heights.

At last, Bob seemed like he was having some fun. Performing with the band excited him; it allowed him to play from his cock instead of from his head. The words were great—sure!—but who needed to be weighted down by all those lyrics when the electricity simply picked you up and carried you into outer space for an hour or two. And Bob, already chemically high, soared like the proverbial kite. He needed a big blast—although not one quite as thunderous as a disgruntled fan in Sheffield promised when he telephoned a bomb threat to the box office. The reaction to his band, however, was just that violent.

Donn Pennebaker rejoined the tour in Glasgow, where he found Bob at the top of his form. "He was singing great songs, really enjoying himself," Pennebaker recalls. "I've never heard better concerts." That evening, after the show, the director joined Bob and Robbie Robertson in a room at the hotel where he witnessed "one of the most amazing feats of creativity ever to pass before my eyes." The scene defies thirdhand description, so it's best simply to let Donn Pennebaker's eyewitness account serve as the record:

> We'd been up all day and night, but that didn't seem to bother Bob or Robbie. They had no interest in sleeping at all. They were taking whatever you take to stay awake, and I was thinking, 'Okay, fellas, let's see what you can do with this custom-made energy.' The effect it had was that Bob worked at ten times the normal speed, but the stuff he got was ten times as fantastic. He and Robbie must have written thirty-five songs right in a row—one, two, three, four. Making up the words as he went along, like *The Basement Tapes.* The trouble was, they were so far into what they were doing that they had no time to write any of it down. Occasionally, Bob would stop and make a note, but he just played it and I assumed at the time that he'd remember it later. Unfortunately, I saw him at the piano the next day trying to remember stuff, but without much luck. It was really pitiful to think the songs had disappeared overnight like that. There were a couple songs he'd begin that'd break my heart, but he'd stop and shrug, realizing

that he couldn't remember any more and I never hear them again.

In Paris, on May 24, 1966, Bob Dylan turned twenty-five, and some friends speculated privately the birthday could be his last. He had grown accustomed to taking generous doses of "medicine" to maintain his blistering pace. Powerful stimulants kept him going through the day. Then there were those that got him up for the show and, afterward, special drugs to see him through the night. He was "up" literally twenty-four hours a day. He just kept going and going until he crashed from fatigue, living as if at any moment an alarm would go off and his time would be up. And yet there were stark paradoxes in Bob's behavior that contradicted the profile of chemical dependency. Most drug addicts are driven by erratic bursts of energy, interspersed with long stretches of depression as they drift back into the bleak horror of reality. Usually, they perform sluggishly and unenthusiastically, like they're under water, digging their own, secret little world. Highs and lows, highs and lows—drugs turned most performers into human roller coasters of emotions. That wasn't the case with Bob. He was dynamite on stage. Though he was synthetically pumped up each night, he was relentlessly on target and always looking for ways to tighten up his act. After most shows he tackled people with questions about the sound clarity. He shuffled song sequences and inserted new material to keep the energy flowing at peak level. Drugs certainly motivated him to perform night after night in front of hostile fans, that was for sure. But Bob got his main boost from a stimulant even more powerful than amphetamines, and that was *music.*

The historic Paris concert was unusually intense—Bob wired taut as the electric instruments, the audience on the edge of its seat—but it was panned in unison by the French press. Most dailies attacked his new material with the same old arguments, but the appreciable criticism took him to task for unnecessary rudeness. Bob was in a disagreeable funk and wasted no time conveying that to the audience. At several intervals, he antagonized the crowd with harsh and thoughtless remarks, suggesting they go home if they didn't like what they heard, or, better yet, open a newspaper and read. Another time, he snapped: "Don't worry, I'm just as eager to finish and leave as you are." The reaction to his unprofessionalism was summed up by a headline in *Paris Jour,* which read simply: "BOB DYLAN, GO HOME."

Before he could comply, however, Bob was due to play two concerts at London's Royal Albert Hall, which were eagerly anticipated by his devoted British admirers. The British seemed to have reinvented rock 'n roll, and by 1966 its clubs and music halls were literally bursting with talent. There were the Beatles and the Rolling Stones, of course. But the supporting cast consisted of illustrious bands like the Who, the Animals, Gerry and the Pacemakers, the Kinks, the Yardbirds, Herman's Hermits, and the Dave Clark Five—all the more reason why an electric Dylan should have captured their hearts. Logic notwithstanding, the result was cataclysmic.

Londoners should have gotten a clue to what was in store for them from Bob's press conference, held at the Mayfair Hotel two weeks earlier, as the tour left for Scandinavia. Unlike the previous year's media blitz featuring campy put-ons and humor, this one was marked by ambiguity and petulance. Even such a friendly newspaper as *New Musical Express* labeled it "Dylan's Press Deception" and described Bob as bored, his answers as "monotone inanities." His contrariness might very well have been a side effect of withdrawal, because, for all appearances, Bob faced the press drug-free. His eyes were tired rather than slits, as they'd been in Australia, and he seemed alert and responsive, so to speak. But his disposition suffered from being straight.

Robert Shelton, in his one-sided book, apologized once again for what he referred to as Bob's "quizzical style," blaming it on the inferior questions hurled at the star. The only source he cites as having attended the press conference was an inconsequential music weekly called *Disc and Music Echo,* which described Bob as "a very sympathetic man with a vast sense of humor." But here is a sampling of the repartee at the Mayfair:

REPORTER: We know that you'll be playing with a band. Could you tell us how many musicians are in your group?

BOB: Oh, fourteen, fifteen...

REPORTER: Could you tell us who they are?

BOB: You want names?

REPORTER: Yes.

BOB: Oh, George, Harry, Fred, Jason...

REPORTER: Could you tell us whom you consider to be one of the best folksingers today?

BOB: Peter Lorre.

REPORTER: Why do you write songs with titles that bear no relation to the lyrics? Like 'Rainy Day Women Nos. 12 and 35.'

BOB:: Oh it's related to the song all right. But it's hard to explain unless you've been in North Mexico for six straight months.

REPORTER: Are you married?

BOB: I don't want to lie to you. It would be misleading if I told you 'yes.'

REPORTER: Do you have a marriage certificate?

BOB: Why are you so interested in what I've got?

REPORTER: Is it Joan Baez?

BOB: Joan Baez was an accident.

He claimed his toenails didn't fit him, that he'd completed a book in one week's time about *spiders,* that he didn't see well on Tuesdays—the tap dance went on for about twenty minutes until most of the reporters got fed up and left. *Melody Maker*'s correspondent, an early Dylan advocate, tried to rationalize Bob's rudeness by ridiculing the personal questions that were asked, but concluded: "It's harder to see the equivocation on the subject of what instruments he'll be playing on the tour....he makes it clear he's not out to win friends and influence newsmen." The question most often asked outside Bob's hotel suite was: Why give a press conference at all if you don't want to talk? They needed to dig deeper to see that it reflected the spirit of the Dylan camp, instilled originally by that great humanitarian Albert Grossman—namely, that all journalists were peckerheads, and rather than ignore them, it was more fun to gather them together and goof on them. A little diversion to keep Bob amused for an hour or so.

It would take a good deal more than press conferences to keep Bob out of trouble, however. Once back in London, the drugs became routine again, and Bob treated himself to a generous sampling of what was available on the street. He was sick, caught in the vise grip of dependency. As the situation grew progressively worse, it terrified his friends, not the least of whom was John Lennon, who became a constant sidekick during Bob's brief visit. Lennon, certainly no stranger to the vagaries of drugs, was at the time still a virgin when it came to the hard stuff. Like anyone else, he smoked a lot of dope, but his visibility, mixed with a healthy dose of paranoia, kept him from jumping into psychedelics and narcotics for at least another year. John was dumbfounded by Bob's wanton consumption. He knew Bob was out of control, but he appeared helpless or unwilling to do anything about it.

A scene from *Eat the Document* (the film chronicling the 1966 tour), which for reasons that will become apparent wound up on the cutting room floor, starkly portrayed Bob's and John's disparate relationship to drugs. In the footage, the two men are crouched in the back of a limousine, both "disguised" in dark shades, on their way back to the Mayfair Hotel. Bob is wasted beyond belief. His head lolls ponderously on his neck like a broken marionette, a glazed-over look weights down those lazy, feline eyes. A close-up reveals that Bob is zooming well beyond the range of Thai-stick euphoria. He's drug sick and growing increasingly worse off as the camera continues to turn for posterity.

Distractedly, Bob glances out the car's large tinted window. "There's the mighty Thames," he announces, stifling a transparent slur. "Isn't that what held Hitler back?"

"Right," John says humorlessly.

"John, I think I'm gonna turn you into Tyrone Power." He laughs at his own mumbling absurdity. "I'm gonna turn you into Ronald Coleman." Furtively, Lennon inches away from Bob the way a passenger creeps off when a pervert squeezes next to him on the subway. John, trying to be cool in this situation, has decided not to yuk it up or encourage Bob. With any luck, they'll zip back to the hotel in time for Bob to sleep off whatever has gotten into his system and let nothing more be said of it.

Only Bob's not going to let John off the hook so easily. He's adrift in the ozone and craves a playmate for his narcotized fantasies. Indifferently, he grabs at a subject that guarantees Lennon's participation—rock 'n roll stars. It's time to trash their idols—beginning with Johnny Cash, especially the way Johnny moves, ungracefully and awkwardly like Frankenstein's monster. Stuporously, it dawns on Bob that Cash is a close friend of his and he says to Donn Pennebaker, who is recording the action from the front seat, "Hey! We'll have to cut this out of the film." In time, he'd recognize the whole scene would have to go, but for the moment there were plenty of laughs left to record.

Bob can't seem to get his words together. He paws at his face, almost spastically, as if the nudging will somehow dislodge the cloud cover and organize his jumbled thoughts. "John, I sure wish I could talk English."

"Me too, Bob," Lennon replies with cool impatience. Ironically, that exchange parodies a long-running joke between the two men, which always begins by Bob's teasing John that he should have been an American. The idea usually made Lennon laugh, and he'd break into his comical American accent—a dozy Texas drawl that delighted anyone who heard it. Now, however, the contrast makes John extremely uncomfortable as he realizes the degree of Bob's sickness.

Bob's speech begins to make even less sense; he is clearly starting to fade. "I come from the land of paradise, man," he says to no one in particular. His words are badly slurred. His mockeries of George Harrison, Paul McCartney, and the Mamas and the Papas makes no sense whatsoever. "I'm getting very sick, man. I'm glad [the ride is] almost over 'cause I'm getting very sick."

From the look of things, Bob has crossed the line into some dismal, dizzying galaxy. He cradles his head in his hands and complains about being cold. He's freezing in that toasty back seat and turning a shade of gray that matches the car's plush interior. "How far are we from the hotel, Tom?" Bob asks the uniformed chauffeur.

"Permission to land, Tom," Lennon utters dryly, in a kind of *Hard Day's Night*–like aside.

Bob, for his part, is oblivious to the humor. "I've done everything else into that camera," he moans. "I may as well vomit into it." But it is clear he'd rather avoid that last bit of cinema verité.

"*Awgrh!*" he grunts, rubbing his eyes. "*Hurry!*" The directive, however, sounds in vain. Unable to control himself any longer, Bob bends over and throws up into the back seat, while his pal Bobby

Neuwirth, in a Howard Cosell-like color commentary, describes all the frothy action.

John Lennon is visibly disgusted. He moves out of the way and grimaces, offering neither condolences nor encouragement as Bob knuckles his eyes, but for John you can see Bob's patina slowly discolor. Lennon made no secret that he revered Bob's enormous talent, but his admiration was seriously shaken by that incident. Bob's vulnerability was too plainly visible; the fatal flaw struck some identifiable failure deep inside of John that more than foreshadowed the days to come.

"He was really confused by Bob's condition," Donn Pennebaker recalls of that day in London. "Dylan was too sick for Lennon to make sense of it. It was too sordid a scene for him." The two men carried Bob upstairs to his room, stopping twice on the way while Bob continued to throw up; then they went for a short walk around the block. "I think the whole thing hit John squarely between the eyes, because as we walked he kept asking me if Bob was going to be okay, if he was going to make it, and I could tell he equated the drug business with life-threatening circumstances. He didn't know how to deal with it."

The Beatles, as a group, were perplexed by Bob's audacious lifestyle. Later that week, Pennebaker treated them to a private screening of *Don't Look Back* in a basement room provided by the Mayfair Hotel management. The ninety-minute film left them speechless. Other than John, only George Harrison showed any interest in it, and that was slight at best. Paul and Ringo seemed baffled by it. "I don't think it was what any of them expected in the way of a movie," Pennebaker surmised. "They were thinking of something along the lines of *A Hard Day's Night,* with lots of gags in it. *Don't Look Back* was too serioso."

John, as well, pronounced the film too personal for his tastes. Some time later, he told Pennebaker, "It was amazing that Dylan let you get into those things—he didn't care what you filmed." To Lennon, a film was something for the public that never trespassed into one's most private affairs. In fact, during the filming of *Don't Look Back,* Pennebaker began shooting footage of the Beatles' visit with Bob, and Cynthia Lennon got incredibly uptight about it—so much so that John ordered him to turn off the cameras.

Still, the Beatles kept their eyes on Bob Dylan's star. A few days later the Fab Four crept into a darkened box at Royal Albert Hall to catch the second of Bob's fiery performances there. From the start, Bob was embattled by hecklers who were intimidated by the much-publicized rock set. Requests were shouted out between each song, the audience squared off into opposing camps—the concert was about as orderly as a Lite Beer commercial: "More Folk!" "Less Rock 'n Roll!" "MORE FOLK!" "LESS ROCK 'N ROLL!" By the time the band wandered on, nearly a quarter of the audience had left the building.

Citing the Royal Albert Hall bootleg that has circulated since 1967, Robert Shelton says it was "technically brilliant" and in his book quotes rock critic Dave Marsh, who considered it "the most supremely elegant piece of rock 'n roll music I've ever heard... royal music." In fact, it has come to light that the Royal Albert Hall bootleg was recorded not in London, as originally thought, but in Manchester some weeks before the last show took place.

Actually, Bob's Royal Albert Hall concert was a second-rate performance in which he sounded distracted by the crowd. A lousy P.A. system contributed to the problems; often he was drowned out by the band and unable to pick up the monitors. He was also worn-out from the arduous tour—not to mention from abusing his body—and in an uncharacteristic soliloquy delivered center-stage, he let the audience have a piece of his mind. "I'm not going to play any more concerts in England," he announced, just prior to beginning "Mr. Tambourine Man." "So I'd just like to say this next song is what your English musical papers call a drug song. I never have and never will write a drug song. I don't know how to. It's not a drug song—it's just *vulgar.*"

After the band joined him on stage, he continued to browbeat the audience in a voice reminiscent of a fundamentalist preacher. "The music you are going to hear—if anyone has any suggestions on how it could be played better, or how the words could be improved...?—we've been playing this music since we were ten years old. Folk music was just an interruption and was very useful. If you don't like it, that's fine!

"This is not English music you are listening to. You haven't really heard American music before. [He must have been hallucinating!] I want now to say what you're hearing is just songs. You're not hearing anything else but words and sounds. You can take it or leave it. If there is something you disagree with, that's great. I'm sick of people asking: 'What does it mean?' *It means nothing!*"

Bob was full of fire and brimstone standing beneath the hall's hot lights. To much of the audience, he was also full of shit, and they let him know that by shouting insults at him, to the dismay of his many supporters. Once more a melee broke out that was carried on throughout the remainder of the show and picked up in the press. The reviews of Bob's Royal Albert Hall appearances were scathing, and the London entertainment columnists joined forces with music critics to roast the impertinent Mr. Dylan. This was one Yank from whom Great Britain had declared its independence.

As if that weren't enough, Bob began distancing himself from loyal and trusted friends when they didn't behave as he wished them to. A case in point: Geno Foreman was waiting for him after one gig, and from the look of things, he was in worse shape than Bob. The once-vibrant hipster whose friends had at one time considered "the incarnation of potential energy" couldn't hide the fact that drugs had done a number on him. The poor guy looked ghastly. His face was hollowed by dissipation, his lips twisted and quivering, and those once-famous eyes that could take over a room with their intensity now appeared dead to the world. His hair and his beard, long remembered as his pride and joy, were long and stringy. If ever a cat looked totally wasted, Geno Foreman was it.

Bob and Geno went back a long way, but now Bob pretended he didn't recognize him. He walked past his stick figure of a friend, slipping into the back of an idling limousine as if its dark interior provided sanctuary from the past. "What the fuck's going on?" Geno wanted to know. "What's gotten into you, man?" He started tapping against the smoked-glass window, trying desperately to get Bob's attention. "I need a little bread, man. I'm really in bad shape. Can't you help an old pal?" It was pathetic. Even Bobby Neuwirth, who had known Geno from as far back as Cambridge, was too embarrassed by Geno's condition to intervene. Nobody would take it upon himself to get rid of Geno, and it was clear Bob didn't want to have to deal with him. Geno was a guy they had truly liked as a friend. A real firecracker, he'd at one time ignited everybody's mind with his crazy schemes. He'd been a lot of laughs, but now he was no longer a laughing matter.

Finally, Bob dealt with Geno the only way he knew how—he turned on him. So viciously, in fact, that Donn Pennebaker had to turn his head away in shame. "It was one of the worst scenes I've ever witnessed," he admits today. "Bob just told him to go away in a very abusive way. We were all kind of amazed—it seemed so heartless, and yet afterwards it seemed like the only way he could have handled it."

Says Pennebaker, "The next I heard of Geno, friends of mine had made a little feature about him called *Head,* and right after that he was dead of an overdose."

When Bob got back to New York, his main objective was to get some rest and time off with his new wife. *Blonde on Blonde* had just been released to ecstatic reviews, and the publicity it generated gave him a few weeks leeway to settle down either in Woodstock or at the Chelsea Hotel before hitting the road again to promote the album.

Bob needed rest more than anything else. In Australia and Europe, he had pushed himself to a near-breaking point, and he wore the self-abuse about as inconspicuously as a sequined suit. His sallow face was disfigured by dark circles that rimmed his bone-weary eyes like grease-paint. He was unusually antsy, even for Bob, and his concentration dwindled to the length of an eye-blink. To make matters worse, he smoked like a fiend, he polished off as many as two or three bottles of beaujolais a night, and his drug use went unabated. Two weeks at Albert's place would have been a godsend. But within a week of his return, Bob was confronted by a mountain of new obligations.

Unbeknownst to Bob, Albert Grossman had booked an additional sixty concerts to carry him through the fall, including a colossal extravaganza at Shea Stadium toward the end of the summer. *Sixty concerts!* It must have sounded like a punishment to Bob, who had barely made it through the last stretch. What was Albert trying to do—kill him? Playing rock 'n roll was the culmination of Bob's life's ambition, but he needed a break—if not simply to recuperate, then at least to put all the craziness into perspective.

The concerts alone would have been a daunting encumbrance, but Bob's agenda rivaled that of an air-traffic controller at rush hour. He was contractually obliged to promote *Blonde on Blonde*; every major magazine and newspaper clamored for an interview. Columbia Records was badgering him to undertake a media blitz in conjunction with its publicity machine. Two separate film projects commanded his attention—he wasn't about to let those slip away from him.

Donn Pennebaker had showed Bob a rough cut of *Don't Look Back,* and because of it, Bob was determined to edit the 1966 tour film himself. "In his eyes, *Don't Look Back* was my film, and he had his own ideas about what the next one should be about," Pennebaker says. Originally, Bob had asked Pennebaker and Bobby Neuwirth to cut the next film, which they were tentatively calling *You Know Something's Happening Here.* Says Pennebaker, "The way Neuwirth and I saw it was that we'd take a twenty-four-hour period where no one had any sleep and start from there, but before long there were outside pressures Bob had to deal with."

For one thing, executives at ABC-TV had gotten an early look at the footage and rejected it as any fulfillment of their agreement for a TV special with Bob. It was too rough, too bleak, too lurid for their simple prime-time audience. The language alone was enough to curl the toenails of the network's censor. So Bob had to come up with another show they deemed suitable in order to avoid a serious lawsuit.

Then there was the little matter of his book, *Tarantula,* which was long overdue at his publisher. What started out as a serious literary project had become a millstone around his neck—an obligation, *another goddamn obligation.* Macmillan and Company's poetry editor evaluated Bob's first submission, originally entitled *Side One,* and declared it too "inaccessible." The symbolism was too convoluted, the material too thin. Bob might have been better off shelving his project until he cleared his head, but Macmillan demanded revisions, probably to capitalize on the tremendous swirl of publicity the new album generated, and the publisher began hounding him for the manuscript.

Albert asked Bob what he wanted to do about the book. Did he want to do something else for ABC? How did he intend to cut *Eat the Document?* Did he want Pennebaker or Howard Alk to edit the film? Would he agree to reporters' requests for interviews? Would he be available to promote *Blonde on Blonde?* Could he lay down a few tracks for new songs he'd been working on? Would he do a benefit for this or that civil rights group? Would he prefer to fly or drive on the upcoming tour? Spend the weekend in New York or Woodstock?...

TILT! TILT! TILT!

All this—this commercial gluttony—it was too much for Bob. The poor guy was coming apart at the seams. He looked like shit; he acted like an asshole to his friends who were more cautious than ever about what they said or did around him. They never knew what was going to touch him off. And yet he was constantly surrounded by a bunch of characters who groveled at his feet and hung on every word and took all his abuse with a smile, because even in New York, where every street corner beheld a three-ring carnival with a cast of fabulous freaks, the Bob Dylan Show, that real-life soap opera, was still the freakiest, zaniest, wildest, fieriest, most orgiastic psychodrama in town. So what if the leading man bordered on physical and emotional collapse? It wouldn't be the first time a star freaked out to the cheerleading cry of "The show must go on!"

Brice Marden, the painter, who at the time was married to Joan Baez's sister Pauline, ran into Bob sometime during the last week in July. "It was during that night-after-night scene-making spree, when all you had to do was take one look at Bob's face to realize how out-of-control he was," Marden remembers. That particular night, Marden was hanging out with Edie Sedgwick, Bobby Neuwirth's not-too-steady girlfriend, and they were set to rendezvous at Bob's pad in the Chelsea Hotel before another night on the town. The Chelsea is undoubtedly one of Manhattan's most startling residences. A ten-story Victorian building on West Twenty-Third Street, it has the rather dubious distinction of being both a tenement and a landmark, thanks to its rococo facade. Under that one roof, at that particular time, lived the most incredible mix of oddballs and prodigies that science has yet to observe: a who's who of rock stars, call girls, failed writers, drug dealers, ex-matinee idols, and assorted wackos who give the Chelsea what its tenants euphemistically refer to as *color.* No wonder Bob felt right at home there. "His place looked like it was in a state of perpetual disarray," Brice Marden says, "to the point that Robbie Robertson seemed to be road-managing the rooms."

When Brice and Edie arrived, most of the guys from the band were camped out in the living room, having a high ol' time. A lot of drinking, a lot of drugs, everyone was comfortably involved in his own excess. A pretty decent blues riff emanated from the stereo speakers, despite the fact the guys were watching Paul Robeson and Ethel Walters harmonize on the tube. In the middle of this scene lay a comatose Bob Dylan dressed in black-and-white striped pajama bottoms and a red, brown, and gold polka-dot top. "I took one look at this," Marden recalls, "and flashed on ancient Rome around the time of Caligula." Bob was dead to the world—the degree of deadness demonstrated a few minutes hence, when Brian Jones wandered in along with a willowy nymphette attired in an outrageously revealing bodystocking. Marden says, "Dylan's sleeping, and this party girl crawls all over him, sticking her tongue in his ear and who-knows-where-else, and Bob doesn't move a muscle. He's out cold—oblivious."

Later, after the girl got bored and passed out on the floor herself, there was a knock at the door, and in strolled Mick Jagger with a bunch of his boys. They were dressed to the teeth, Mick decked out in an oversized black-and-white checked suit, white socks tucked under spats—he's *very serious* about the way he looks. Everyone else, though, was trying hard not to laugh at him. Mick and Bob had never met, and this had been set up as some grand artistic summit meeting to introduce the two music masters. Of course, that was difficult at first because Bob was lying in state in the middle of the room, which meant that someone had to shake him awake and, in contrast to the exquisitely appointed Mick, he looked like a court jester.

Watching the ceremony, Brice Marden remembers thinking that Bob lived what must be a life of complete absurdity. Cosmic highs, subterranean lows—soaring and sinking to all levels in short-lived gusts, like a kite constructed of spit and tissue paper. One moment Bob was wiping the sleep out of his eyes, yawning like a hound, the next he was jumping around the room like a high-strung chicken. Up, down. Up, down. It was turning into an around-the-clock performance. No time for sleep, other than a few stolen minutes between parties. Can't break the rhythm. Working harder and harder to take himself higher and higher. Except that when he'd start to come down again, he'd realize the parties no longer mattered, the highs were no longer satisfying, the lights no longer shone—he was emotionally exhausted.

All performers experience burnout at some time in their careers. The music stops, the lights go out, and no matter how much applause there is it doesn't mean a thing. For many stars, it's the end of the road—a way off the roller coaster. Some, like Brian Jones, take a big blast of heroin or pitch themselves off the balcony of a luxury hotel.

Others swallow pills or the butt-end of a shotgun, or wind up married to a bottle of Jack Daniels. And still others, like Cat Stevens, become Buddhist monks and hole up in the Andes Mountains. Bob Dylan had been moving so fast for so long that some kind of tragic finale seemed overdue. It was *fated,* some people said. They *expected* him to explode. To self-destruct like a supernova.

Who knows what state of mind Bob was in a few days after meeting Mick Jagger, when he tooled around the back roads of Woodstock on his Triumph 500 motorcycle. Or if he was even on a motorcycle at all that Friday afternoon. The official story went that Bob was on his way to have his bike repaired when the back wheel locked and he went flying over the handlebars. Another version had him doing wheelies in his grassy backyard. In an account attributed to a close friend, Bob was showing off a few blocks from the house when he miscued, and Sara, who was nearby in her car, scraped him off the street and took him home. Any of the stories sounds plausible; most likely none of them is true. The only thing we know for sure is that Bob Dylan used whatever excuse was necessary to remove himself from the public eye for a little over four years. Either subconsciously or intentionally, the choice was clear: he could go on living, or he could die living the way he had been—as a twenty-five-year-old legend with no better hope than to get the better of himself.

Part 4

A Brief Intermission

21

Business as Usual

The pale winter sun had already dipped below the Catskills when the stretch limo carrying Mort Nasatir edged onto the New York State Thruway for the trip back to the city. The temperature had dropped to a teeth-chattering fifteen degrees, but Nasatir felt warmer than he had been in months. Positively glowing, in fact. And gloating, too, like a gluttonous little boy. Once more, he ran his fingers over the sheaf of papers clutched in his hand. Over the signature with its childish scrawl and curlicues. With a forefinger, he traced the round, slanting strokes that swung above and below the mimeographed line. D-Y-L. . . He could hardly believe his good luck. . . . A-N. No doubt about the name there. Bob Dylan—signed, sealed, and delivered.

Nasatir heaved a sigh of relief. So it hadn't been a hoax, after all. The offer, incredible as it sounded, had been on the level. Bob Dylan *was* leaving Columbia Records, and he was signing with MGM. *He'd already signed!* There hadn't been a blockbuster like this since the Yanks snatched Babe Ruth from the Boston Red Sox! Since the Nets got Dr. J. from the Kentucky Colonels! And the record company wasn't getting damaged goods, either. That had been the purpose of Nasatir's trip to Woodstock—to make sure Bob hadn't suffered any brain damage in that motorcycle business. To see if he could still play the guitar and write those fucking hit songs of his. After all, why else would

Columbia pass up a chance to resign its number-one recording star—the most important American artist on any label. Unless, of course, he was a . . . a vegetable.

Two weeks earlier, that had seemed like the only logical answer. That accident everyone was talking about must have snuffed out the left side of Bob Dylan's brain. Or left him confined to a wheelchair like Lieutenant Ironsides, so that he could never perform again. Those were the rumors. Whispers abounded that Bob wasn't half the Dylan he used to be.

Nasatir's suspicions had gone wild when Al Grossman called him and suggested that Bob *might* be willing to record for MGM Records. "Let's just say he's available," Grossman intimated, in the same way George Steinbrenner shopped a utility infielder he was dying to trade. "There's a possibility Bob would move under certain conditions." *Yeah, like a fifty percent controlling interest in* The Wizard of Oz *and your tacit agreement to replace Leo the Lion with a likeness of Andy Warhol. And you can throw in a date with Connie Francis for good measure!* Nasatir knew Bob Dylan wasn't going to come cheap. Grossman would squeeze him for every cent he could get—and then *more.* Still, it'd be a deal at any price. Bob Dylan! It was like a chance to acquire the *Mona Lisa.*

Though he probably didn't come out and say it, Nasatir had to admit to himself that MGM needed this deal in the worst possible way. To add a superstar like Bob Dylan to the roster would change the company's image overnight. It would have credibility. Prestige. *Instant respect!* Not that MGM was a shithouse. It had always managed a respectable showing as far as top forty was concerned. Connie Francis had been its number-one breadwinner for over a decade, and the Righteous Brothers and Herman's Hermits each had a decent string of hits. Then, of course, the Lovin' Spoonful, on MGM's subsidiary label, Kama Sutra, was nothing to sneeze at. But when it came to image, MGM came up short.

One reason was that it was the only Hollywood label in an industry of city street toughs. Its artists reeked of show-biz glitz tending to represent Hollywood's *idea* of what a garage band or acid rock group should look like, rather than the real McCoy. There was something superficial and *suburban* about their sound. Something that was hard to put your finger on, but nevertheless precluded groups like the Doors and the Rascals and Big Brother and the Beach Boys from signing with it. Unlike the major players—Columbia, Warner Bros., Atlantic, Elektra, and Motown—whose company presidents maintained a savvy rapport with rock musicians, MGM Records answered to a board of directors. Bankers and real estate moguls and . . . *Republicans!* . . . called the shots. So the company wound up signing the Cowsills and the Osmonds rather than, say, Cream or the Bee Gees or the Turtles. MGM's "heavy" act was a group from Maryland called Orpheus, whose "smash" hit, "Can't Find the Time to Tell You," never even grazed the national charts. All of which fired up those rumors that Bob Dylan was suffering from brain damage. Why else would anyone in his right mind leave Columbia Records for the dregs of the record business?

Mort Nasatir thought the likely answer was money. Dylan's interest in MGM was strictly bottom-line: points. At MGM, Dylan would earn a decent royalty for the first time in his career. He'd be in the position to make some real money—not that pocket change Columbia paid him. At Columbia recording artists received a paltry five percent of their album sales, and half that on records sold overseas. Now that Bob's contract had expired, Albert wanted more—something in the ballpark of, say, ten percent for domestic sales and five for foreign. Columbia was notoriously cheap, owing, in no small part, to a favored-nations clause in its contracts that stated no artist would receive a higher royalty than any other, so that if Bob got ten percent, then every other two-bit Columbia artist would automatically be raised to ten, too. So in a decision similar to the one the network would use ten years later to precipitate the retirement of Walter Cronkite, Columbia decided it could continue to be a dominant force in the music business without Bob Dylan.

MGM spent more freely when it came to signing acts. It'd given the Righteous Brothers an $800,000 advance, even though they'd already peaked with "You've Lost That Lovin' Feeling," and paid the Lovin' Spoonful a ridiculously high royalty of ten-and-a-half percent across the board. For Bob Dylan, Albert wanted $1½ million on signing and twelve percent, and in a moment of what must have been temporary insanity Mort Nasatir said yes. He knew such a deal would preclude MGM Records' ever making any money on Bob's albums. But it'd be a wonderful "loss leader" for MGM; what it would lose on Bob's records, it would make up for on the other artists Bob would help attract to the label.

For Bob Dylan, the news of switching record companies must have come as a terrible shock. MGM Records was the Miami Beach of the record business—it was where fading rock stars went to die. It was the bottom of the rock pile. Bob was only twenty-six-years old, in reasonably good health. Why would Albert Grossman condemn Bob to virtual obscurity for a few lousy points and front money? To understand Albert's motivation, you'd have to look beyond the deal itself in an effort to see what else was at stake here. For instance, you'd want to examine the artist roster of Verve/Forecast, a subsidiary label set up under the MGM banner only a few months earlier. Two of its first signings were Richie Havens and Gordon Lightfoot—both represented by the Grossman office. Ian and Sylvia, another Grossman act, who had been released from their contract with Vanguard Records due to sluggish sales, had just made a lucrative deal at MGM. And the label was also negotiating for the rights to another of Albert's artists—a female singer named Janis Joplin. So, in effect, the success or failure of MGM Records was largely connected to Albert Grossman's fortunes, and the power he wielded there was considerable. Bob Dylan would be the insurance policy he'd use to protect his other investments.

The only stumbling block might be Bob himself. Albert warned Mort Nasatir that Bob must be made to feel comfortable with MGM prior to signing any formal agreement. He suggested Nasatir visit Bob at his home in Woodstock to sound out the deal.

Nasatir feared the worst; even to him Dylan and MGM seemed wildly incompatible. Then he hit on a brilliant idea: *Hank Williams!* Through an associate, Nasatir learned that Bob was a Hank Williams freak, and he remembered a conversation he'd had with the late troubadour's publisher, Wesley Rose, about a trunkful of lyrics Hank had written but never set to music. The prospect of a Bob Dylan–Hank Williams collaboration could be his ace in the hole. Maybe they could even borrow one of MGM's old horror-flick promos: *From Beyond the Grave!*

Their meeting, from Nasatir's point of view, had been utterly delightful. Bob was ambulatory, he noticed from the start, and that was an encouraging enough sign. In fact, Bob was moving around pretty smoothly for a guy who'd recently taken a death-defying spill. He was working on a new draft of *Tarantula.* And intermittently he sat hunched over a moviola, attempting to edit scenes for his ABC-TV special. There was even a new batch of songs on the griddle. "The guy was operating in three different media at one time," Nasatir remembers. "It was a feat of energy that'd daunt even a healthy man. He couldn't have been in that much pain and still have maintained that level of activity." Not to mention steer a car, which Bob operated with apparent ease as he drove Nasatir back and forth between his house and Albert's place a few miles down the road.

All the while, the two men discussed the future. By now, Bob didn't seem at all bothered by a prospective move to MGM Records. One label was as venal as the next, and he felt no real allegiance to Columbia. There was nothing to keep him there, and there were good reasons why he should leave. The royalty rate, for one. But even more attractive were those Hank Williams lyrics Nasatir had mentioned. The thought of putting them to music really turned Bob on. He kept steering the conversation back to the lyrics—always to *the lyrics*—begging for more details. To him, it was like discovering a number of unpublished Shakespeare sonnets. Just to get his hands on them. . . . The music would be a piece of cake. God knows, the last couple years had left him feeling pretty tapped out. Taking time out to work on an album of country & western songs would provide both a creative and an emotional relief.

Nasatir promised other incentives as well. For one thing, there was complete freedom in the studio. Bob could record in Nashville or even Woodstock if he liked. And he shouldn't overlook MGM's stock-in-trade—*movies!* Bob could land a juicy part in any of the studio's upcoming projects or write music for them. Hey, and guess what? We just hired your old buddy Tom Wilson, so he can produce your albums for us, just like old times. *Tom Wilson!* When Nasatir mentioned his name, Bob must have shit a brick! It had taken him long enough to dump that loser. Still, he could always have Albert wriggle out of that one for him. Tom Wilson wasn't going to be a deal-breaker in this negotiation.

In the end, Nasatir left with Bob's signature on an MGM contract. No fuss, no delay. "On the one hand, I felt it was a new era for the company," Nasatir says of that fateful day, "but in my heart I knew his signature wasn't worth the paper it was written on." He felt almost certain the contract wouldn't be honored—and not by Bob

Dylan or his representatives but by the bureaucrats who ran MGM Records.

Ironically, the MGM brass bluffed their way through the deal using the same gambit that Albert Grossman often employed in his dealings with other managers and concert promoters. Says Mort Nasatir, "MGM held the position that anyone should be thrilled to be associated with such a prestigious company, and that gave them a tremendous bargaining position. It went back to the early days of moviemaking when contracts were meaningless. The producer would sign a contract and MGM would simply ignore it. Yet the producer could still get his picture made on the basis of a handshake. That was when the studio wielded fantastic power and, as late as 1967, they attempted to operate their record division on the same principle. So when I presented Bob Dylan's contract to the board, they said, 'All right, you've signed him and we'll honor it, but we're not going to countersign a contract right now. We're going to sit on it.'"

Albert should have known the origin of that swindle was none other than the birthplace of the fast deal—Hollywood! Still, as far as anyone knew, the deal was chiseled in stone. Bob Dylan was added to the MGM Records roster, and Mort Nasatir announced his acquisition at the company's annual sales conference in Mexico, gaining him headlines in all the trades.

Unfortunately, as the company was celebrating its good fortune, a melodrama—Hollywood style—was unfolding behind the scenes which threatened to undermine its power base. MGM, once the cornerstone of Hollywood royalty, found itself in the midst of a proxy fight involving its takeover by a real estate magnate. Suddenly two factions emerged inside the company—those loyal to management, and a nucleus of opportunists whose positions would be greatly enhanced by the takeover—and everyone was buying up its stock. Enter Allen B. Klein, a notorious entertainment gunslinger, whose personal clients had included the Rolling Stones, the Beatles (except for Paul McCartney), Sam Cooke, Bobby Darin, and Donovan. Klein was a VIP at MGM, having at one time or another managed most of its top acts—Herman's Hermits, the Animals, Bobby Vinton, a percentage of Connie Francis—and, thus, he was considered an important ally to management. He also owned a sizable chunk of MGM stock. What Klein said was taken very seriously there, and what he was saying now was that the deal MGM had made with Bob Dylan *stank.*

The Records Division was bewildered by his position. MGM's A&R staff appreciated Klein's enviable experience and wisdom, yet they knew he fully understood the value of Bob's contract to the label. Why would he try to throw back a prize catch like that?

Mort Nasatir, predictably outraged, cornered Klein in an office there and demanded an explanation. Had we a photograph of that confrontation, it would probably tell us all we needed to know about Klein's business comportment. He was a stumpy little bully whose knack for throwing his weight around was equal to that of a Sumo wrestler. Nasatir, by comparison, was a minnow. Klein devoured guys like Mort Nasatir in his sleep, and his rebuttal was fairly belligerent. He claimed a source close to Columbia Records told him that, in retaliation for the deal, CBS was prepared to flood the market with Bob Dylan albums made up of outtakes and live concerts it owned dating back to 1961. "CBS is sitting with enough tape on Dylan, so that every time you release a new album they will kill you," Klein told him. "They'll put two of their own out, they'll undersell you, they'll outmarket you and confuse the public so that anything bearing the Dylan name will be worth shit."

Now Nasatir was thoroughly confused. He'd raised that very possibility during negotiations with Albert Grossman, but the subject had been carefully shunted aside. Had he been suckered by Bob Dylan's manager? Grossman swore not. "They've got nothing in the vault but one acoustic album—and a *poor* one—that was recorded in the U.K. That is all they have. There isn't anything else. You have my word on it," he told Nasatir in response to Klein's insinuations.

His *word!*

As usual, Albert's word represented only part of the larger sentence. CBS *was* holding onto an unexceptional tape of an English concert it had considered releasing as a live album, but its audio cupboard was anything but bare. There were masters on file of several dozen songs Bob had cut but never released, and they could hardly be construed as swill. "Positively 4th Street" had been released as a single but never included on an album. The same with "If You Gotta Go, Go Now" and "Can You Please Crawl Out Your Window," both from a session in late 1965, plus two versions of "She's Your Lover Now" and a slew of stuff left over from *Blonde on Blonde.* And it was hardly a secret that a live compilation from various 1963 shows had been mastered as a *Bob Dylan in Concert* album, complete with artwork for the cover. In practice, a record company wouldn't dare alienate an artist like Bob Dylan by releasing material from its vaults without his consent, but legally it was theirs to exploit. And the little shit was walking away from Columbia, the company that had built his career from *nothing!* Who knew what Columbia's position would be if, months from now, he helped to turn MGM Records into a strong competitor.

More than ever, Allen Klein campaigned furiously at MGM to dump the contract, claiming Columbia had as many as twenty albums in the till ready for release. The number was most certainly an exaggeration and Klein knew it, but his uneasiness was fueled by a conversation he'd had a few days earlier with Columbia Records president, Clive Davis. Davis had intimated that Bob's album sales weren't on par with his reputation, and what MGM *really* bought for $1½ million and twelve points was the Dylan legend. Columbia, the industry leader as far as earnings went, could afford such luxuries. But could MGM? Despite its logo, it wasn't exactly the lion that roared.

Davis had obviously attended the same business school as Albert Grossman. The University of Hocus Pocus. For he gave Klein only a *partial* account of the facts. Bob's sales figures *were* lower than other artists in his league, but he spent practically nothing in the studio compared with Columbia's other premier artists. And that made Bob's albums wildly profitable.

Not only that, Bob's albums were fixtures of the Columbia Records catalogue; they continued to sell *years* after their release, whereas most albums had a shelf life of maybe eight to sixteen *weeks.* So the return on the Dylan catalogue was rock-steady and perpetual. Allen Klein should have known that—he *should have*—but his emotions got in the way. Clive Davis attributes Klein's miscalculation to the time-consuming MGM proxy fight, but Mort Nasatir blames it on ego. "If Bob Dylan recorded for MGM, Klein's prestige and clout would suffer," he speculates. "He'd no longer be The Most Important Person at the record company, and I doubt Klein's ego could have tolerated that."

The momentum had suddenly shifted at MGM Records. There was an outbreak of cold feet in the executive suite at 1350 Avenue of the

Americas. Now, instead of crowing about their new acquisition, instead of looking for data to support the Dylan deal, some staffers were aggressively searching for a way to back out of it. They'd be happier if Bob Dylan *didn't* record for their company. Imagine that, if you can. Of course, MGM could simply have refused to countersign the contract, but that would have invited litigation. After all, it had negotiated in good faith and tendered a verbal agreement. Besides, it would totally lose what standing it had in the industry if it reneged on the offer. Managers who avoided MGM in the best of circumstances would never bring an artist there! There had to be some other way to dump Dylan and still save face.

Talk at MGM turned to incrimination. If it could somehow make Bob look worse than the company, the deal might fall apart on its own. In fact, there was a rumor that one day a week Bob paid a very suspicious visit to a home in upstate New York, and everyone knew what that meant: DRUGS! The guy obviously had a habit. Or maybe he was already in detox. "The implication was that he was mentally unstable," Nasatir remembers being told. So what did the MGM Records president do? He hired a private detective and had Bob Dylan followed. He put *a tail* on Bob and turned up this startling piece of information: On the same day each week, at exactly the same time, Bob Dylan visited the apartment of a sick buddy and spent the afternoon chatting. So much for incrimination. There had to be a better way to dispatch the deal.

Maybe the most practical tactic was to let nature take its course. After all, the contract was studded with more loopholes than a crocheted potholder. Maybe Bob would overlook one that MGM could use to back out of the deal. It would simply hold up its end of the bargain until Bob balked. Knowing the habits of most young stars, chances were MGM wouldn't have long to wait.

The most obvious hurdle for Bob would be the time clause. "He had to deliver an album within six months of signing, and another one nine months after that," Nasatir recalls. "Otherwise we could walk." In addition, MGM wasn't required to advance a cent of money to Bob until the company had a finished tape. Says Nasatir, "When Bob delivered product, that's when the cash register rang." And, knowing Bob's frame of mind and his reluctance to be coerced into the studio, Nasatir feared he wouldn't record for a long, long time.

But within two months, word drifted down to the city that the prophet was moved to create. At Bob's request, MGM sent a recording crew up to Woodstock so he "could give them a feel for what he was doing." Surprisingly, the results helped the opposition at MGM. The tapes it got sounded like they were made in Dylan's *basement*, of all things. They were frivolous and trifling. And get this: not every number on them was sung by Bob Dylan! He'd let some of the guys in his band take turns singing lead. And on some songs the vocal sounded suspiciously like... *Tiny Tim!* In fact, after a few listens the MGM crew were certain it was Tiny Tim warbling a cover version of "I Got You, Babe" (he sung Cher's part, need you ask) in a duet with Robbie Robertson.

Nasatir wanted a real record and fast, to silence the naysayers at MGM. If they were going to salvage the deal, Bob needed to deliver product in time to bolster the MGM fall schedule. Nasatir explained his predicament to Albert Grossman, who replied: "Bobby isn't ready to record yet." As the six months' deadline approached, Nasatir received the same news. Bob wasn't about to go into the studio until he was ready, and no amount of outside pressure would change his mind.

Nobody, other than perhaps Albert Grossman, knows the sequence of events that ultimately rewrote Bob's record contract, but the right ingredients fell into place for all of the involved parties. Grossman knew Columbia's interest was strong to reacquire Bob, so if MGM belabored the point on album delivery he could tell the company to go fuck itself with some assurance. At the same time, Nasatir was making subtle overtures that would enable Bob to get out of his new contract without any legal difficulties.

Clive Davis, in his biography, claims that Grossman and David Braun, Bob's attorney, approached him with an offer to sign Bob to a five-year deal for absolutely no advance money in return for no guarantee of an album ever being recorded. Bob was supposedly having "second thoughts" about his contract with MGM, which the record company *still* hadn't signed. So if Columbia made a terrific offer, there was an outside chance Grossman might be able to pry Bob loose.

That was the *half* of the story Clive Davis got. What Grossman failed to tell him was that Nasatir had already been given the opportunity to rescind MGM's deal with Bob, and he'd advised Albert to shop around. The proxy fight had split the company in two, and Nasatir was already at work on an early draft of his own resignation. In any case, he told Albert, "You're free."

Or maybe that was Nasatir's *half* of the story. Albert Grossman, a master in the art of corporate intrigue, schemed to play both sides against each other to obtain a more lucrative contract for his client. MGM, for its part, was happy just to unload Bob's million-dollar guarantees. It didn't want anything to remind it of the embarrassing entanglement. Albert was welcome to any souvenir from it that he wanted—including that atrocious demo it had paid for that sounded like it was recorded in Bob Dylan's basement.

22

Catskill Skyline

The summer of 1967 diverted public attention away from Bob Dylan and toward another cultural phenomenon—the hippies. America's flower children had captured the spotlight and challenged their social legacy through sexual and artistic expression, spiritual exploration, a demand for relevance and political conscience, incipient experimentalism, and a myopically romantic vision of the future. And the language that united their odyssey was rock 'n roll.

Unquestionably, the music made during that Summer of Love, as it was billed, stands collectively as rock 'n roll's finest hour. The songs remain as fresh and exciting today as when they were first released: Aretha Franklin's "Respect"; "Light My Fire"; *Sgt. Pepper's Lonely Heart's Club Band;* "For What It's Worth" by the Buffalo Springfield; Marvin and Tammi's "Ain't No Mountain High Enough"; "Groovin'" by the Rascals; "The Letter" by the Box Tops; Stevie Wonder's "I Was Made to Love Her"; "Somebody to Love" by the Jefferson Airplane; new singles by Simon and Garfunkel, the Beach Boys, the Who, the Rolling Stones, the Mamas and the Papas, as well as debuts by Jimi Hendrix, the Steve Miller Band, Janis Joplin, and *Rolling Stone* magazine. It was an outpouring of visceral, nonstop musical energy the likes of which haven't been experienced since. Music loaded with originality. Music made to last. Yet from the counterculture's undisputed oracle, Bob

Dylan, holed up at his Woodstock retreat, the rock explosion got nary a spark.

Despite this conspicuous silence, Dylan's preeminence as a writer, performer, and provocateur went unchallenged. It may even have increased. He remained, in absentia, rock's reigning bard and brainteaser, and his daring lyrics continued to be studied and disputed like perplexing Talmudic riddles. The songs themselves—those prescient, profound elegies—seemed almost to improve with age. And the assistance of some lethal weed could take them to an even higher plain. No one else came close to composing such multitextured passages, nor consistently displayed such heavy musical artillery. As a result, Bob remained the heaviest cat on the scene even though he wasn't anywhere on the scene at all.

Naturally, Bob's music was the primary source of his acclaim. Despite the new releases of 1967, Bob's catalogue continued to receive tremendous airplay and sold at a corresponding clip. You could set your watch to the recurrence of "Rolling Stone," which blared almost hourly from thousands of underground FM stations. *Blonde on Blonde* was still doing a number on everyone's psyche. College kids sat around dorm rooms each night, mesmerized by his voice, spacing on the wordplay.

But there were additional factors that preserved Bob's reputation during the hiatus. First and foremost was *Don't Look Back,* which finally premiered in the summer of 1967. The film had languished in a can in Donn Pennebaker's office for nearly a year before Bob grudgingly approved its release. Word had it that he wasn't thrilled with the result, but in the end he agreed to let audiences decide for themselves.

Bob wasn't the only one displeased with the film portrait. Sometime that summer, Donn Pennebaker was informed that Abe Zimmerman awaited him in the reception area of his editing room. A polite, soft-spoken man bearing an unmistakable resemblance to his famous son, Abe introduced himself as "Mr. Dylan's father." Pennebaker was immediately touched by the man's deference and invited him inside. Asked to explain his unannounced visit, Abe said, "Mrs. Dylan and I came to New York for a brief stay and everyone's been so nice to us." *Mrs. Dylan!* "And I wouldn't want anything to alter their opinion of us." Says Pennebaker, "The whole gist of it was that he hadn't seen the film, but a number of his friends had seen it and they all commented that his son—Mr. Dylan—used a lot of four-letter words and would I mind taking them out. The guy was so polite and understanding that it was difficult for me to say no to him, but I tried to explain as best I could that people who the film is for would be disappointed if they heard Bob talking in a way they knew he shouldn't."

As it turned out, language was the least of the reviewers' complaints. Most critics found the film too unrevealing in its depiction of Bob Dylan, too guarded when it came to dealing with his personal feelings. Even Richard Goldstein, a staunch defender of Bob's, complained, "*Don't Look Back* is a finely wrought antique which offers no insight into Bob Dylan in 1967." Writing in *The New York Times*, Goldstein argued that the Dylan who cradled an acoustic guitar and declared "the times they are a-changin'" bore no resemblance to an electric Dylan who subsequently hissed "something is happening and you don't know what it is, do you, Mr. Jones?"

The film's audience, however, was made up, not of critics or unappreciative adults, but of *fans*, and to them the Bob Dylan who tore across the screen, singing and stinging victims, was exactly *on target*. Finally Dylan fans could *see* as well as hear Bob. The film added a visual dimension to his music—not that his songs lacked that quirky personality before, but now they took on a more lifelike resonance. The teenage films made by Hollywood were filled with paste-up characters and predictable situations. The Sam Cohn films were worthless. The Beatles acted like a bunch of silly adolescents. Even renegades like James Dean parroted the sentiments of fifty-year-old screenwriters. But *Don't Look Back* looked and sounded just right to its youthful viewers. It captured their scene without any phony, high-gloss, moralistic shellac, and it gave them something to emulate.

Bob also became daily fodder for the emerging rock press. For the first time, Bob's peers wrote about him in articles that conveyed a real understanding and a passion for his music. These weren't the entertainment hacks who covered all forms of music for, say, *Variety*, *Stereo Review*, or the *New York Post*. They weren't disgruntled folkies left over from *Broadside* or *Sing Out!* These were card-carrying rock freaks—writers close to Bob's own age—whose stock as legitimate journalists was rising fast. Since the counterculture was fashionable, people wanted to read about it, and even the establishment press hired rock-genre writers to compete with the sudden surge of underground papers. Overnight, glossies like *Life, Esquire, Playboy,* and *The Saturday Evening Post* boasted coverage of the hippie scene. *Rolling Stone* became the voice of young, hip America. And Bob Dylan emerged as its subject of preference.

Some writers enterprisingly turned their stories about Bob into a cottage industry. Nat Hentoff, for one, had been regularly churning out pieces on him since 1964, when his profile of Bob Dylan-the-Angry-Young-Folksinger turned up in *The New Yorker.* Hentoff followed that one with articles in *Stereo Review* and the *Evergreen Review,* to mention but a few, and even put his byline to a *Playboy* interview in which he somehow got away with allowing Bob to ask and answer his own questions. Of course, Robert Shelton continued to publish a volume of articles about Bob, banking on his reputation as a member of the fabled inner circle. And now Ralph Gleason added his name to the list of admirers who gushed shamelessly over Bob's every cough and sneeze.

Gleason was a curious newcomer to Bob's bandwagon. For years one of the country's leading jazz critics, Gleason was smitten by the blank-faced flower children who roamed his native San Francisco, and he began babbling endlessly about making love not war, rock 'n roll, the New Youth (as only he capitalized it), and Bob Dylan. Bob was his Ezekiel, his Zoroaster, his *Lenny Bruce.* Just as Lenny had converted Gleason to hip orthodoxy, Bob divined his regenerate spirit. Ralph Gleason, ensconced in his mid-fifties, was born again as a groovy, hip-shooting, Dylan freak, and articles galore appeared in praise of his favorite subject. Gleason's sermons had all the subtlety of a hand grenade. To him, Bob was never just a great songwriter: "He is the first poet of that all-American artifact, the jukebox, the first American poet to touch everyone, to hit all walks of life in this great, sprawling society. The first poet of mass media, if you will." In one fatuous slurp, Gleason managed to compare Bob to Rimbaud, Ferlinghetti, Ginsberg, Eliot, Pound, Cole Porter, George Gershwin, and Oscar Hammerstein. He even managed to toss in Shakespeare!

Thus began an era of curious relationships between rock critics and their intimate subjects. Writers like Shelton and Al Aronowitz were frequent weekend guests at Albert Grossman's Bearsville estate, where Bob was officially housemember-in-spirit. Daniel Kramer, who published a book of photographs and critical (but uncritical) text on Bob, as well as numerous spin-offs, profited greatly from their friendship, to the extent that his wife was on Albert's payroll. In 1965, when Bob faced an auditorium filled with San Francisco's press elite, who was his escort? None other than Ralph J. Gleason, who stood off to the side of the room, beaming like a spinster aunt, while his drug-eyed protégé handled himself like the town fool. Ah, yes—in an era that fostered the sexual revolution, the press was jumping into bed with Bob faster than a stage-door groupie.

How all this camaraderie affected Bob is a subject of great disagreement. Bob wasn't the type to chuckle up to some half-grinning writer in order to gain a favorable review. As we've already seen, Bob regarded the media as an evil necessity. So what was this cabal doing hanging around Bob Dylan in Woodstock? Well, they weren't, for one thing. They were *Albert's* pets. Albert, who loathed the press even more than Bob. He was their patron saint, their meal ticket. Albert spread his tailfeathers as this educated audience billed and cooed. They gaped and giggled as he ran his hand over a houseful of highly polished antiques and recounted their impressive provenances. Or unveiled his collection of Alaskan pewter, or his larder of splendid food.

While Albert held forth in the manner of a grand duke, inveigling the peanut gallery with his patrician tastes, Bob retired into his own private world inside Byrdcliffe, an artists' colony on the fringe of Woodstock. Little did he care about lacquered sideboards, Ming vases, or Queen Anne secretaries. He'd developed no taste for Vidalia onions, smoked Coho salmon, Belgian endive (*ahn-deeve!*), 1961 estate-bottled Bordeaux, or any of the other delicacies with which Albert gorged himself and his guests. He'd set aside this time for introspection and healing, not self-indulgence. To protect himself, he proffered creative excuses. Like the surgical neck brace, for instance. Bob wore one of those pink spongy neckpieces that lawyers handling accident cases instruct their clients to don for effect. An inconvenience, but necessary, since his brother, David, told inquirers that Bob had broken his neck. And it served its purpose well—the purpose being to delay Bob's tour and TV obligations.

The same was expected for *Tarantula*. Macmillan issued an announcement that the book was postponed again due to the motorcycle accident. "He couldn't use his eyes for a period of time and it made it difficult for him to work," said his editor, Robert Markel. An unlikely story. Nonetheless, Bob was off the hook with these people for the time being.

That left him free to reorganize his priorities, like his health, his family, his friends, and his music. The days of the high life were over. He was no longer the notorious party animal that stalked the in-spots while zooming on medicine. In fact, Bob's sole outing seemed to be the frequent drive he made to a large Victorian home on Doctor's Row in nearby Middletown, where he went to consult Dr. Ed Thaler.

Ed Thaler was the perfect person to treat Bob's disabilities. A longtime friend of Odetta's (who had referred Bob to him), Thaler was an early example of the type of spiritual, intellectually well versed doctor who befriended artists and treated their peculiar afflictions. And he came with all the necessary credentials: Thaler was an iconoclastic, outspoken civil rights activist, an extreme leftist who had studied medicine in Oklahoma, who not only played the guitar but knew the Guthrie and Almanac Singers songbooks backward and forward. At a time when doctors had come under scrutiny for their closed-door practices, Ed Thaler refused to be board-certified, calling it "the usual bureaucracy." No doubt Bob was grateful for another of the doctor's well-known practices—discretion. When conversation turned to the subject of his patients, Ed Thaler would become brusque or even mute. In fact, his closest neighbors, an investigative journalist and the editor of the Middletown newspaper, knew nothing of Bob's visits—including a time when Bob was a permanent houseguest there and the neighbors spent social evenings with the Thalers in a dining room situated directly beneath his room.

Ed Thaler was only the first of many steps Bob took toward recuperation, but an important one, to be sure. Without his strong and uncompromising commitment to treating Bob's unspecified illnesses, Bob might never have recovered enough to resume his career. But another priority critical to a more firmly grounded life-style was Bob's renewed dedication to his family.

During the first year after the accident, Bob became a confirmed homebody. He stayed close to the nest, reading and drawing, while Sara handled most of the chores. They also conceived two children—Jesse, a boy, and Anna, both born in 1967. (Sara and Bob had two more children. Seth was born in June 1968, and Samuel in 1969.)

Friends say that fatherhood touched off a period of intense focus and peace of mind for Bob. "He shut out the world of show business and all the Manhattan craziness and turned into such an ordinary guy that he was actually a little boring to be around," says friend and neighbor Happy Traum, who often dropped by Byrdcliffe to chat and play music.

Bob also struck up a brief friendship with flower-freak Tiny Tim, whom Bob met at the Little Theatre, a California cabaret run by Hugh Romney and his wife Bonnie Beecher, Bob's old college flame for whom reportedly he wrote "Girl from the North Country." He came in to catch Tiny's bizarre act, which at the time consisted mostly of Irving Kaufman and Arthur Fields songs—"When Will the Sun Shine for Me," "We Are Just the Type for a Bungalow," "Yes, We Have No Bananas," and "God Gave the Wise Men Their Wisdom"—sung in a screechy falsetto. Learning Bob was in the audience, Tim improvised a Jolson-like rendition of "Positively 4th Street," in which, at the end, he got down on one knee and boomed: "It's not 8th Street, 7th Street, 6th Street, or 5th Street, but Pos-i-tive-leeeee *Fourrrr-tthhh* streeeeet!"

That performance won Tiny Tim an invitation to Chez Dylan in Woodstock during the spring of 1967. Originally, Bob wanted him to play the part of Phillip Granger, a down-and-out drifter, in *Eat the Document,* but when Tim arrived there in March, the production was temporarily on hold. Instead, the two men spent several evenings at Byrdcliffe discussing American popular songwriting, including the masterwork of Tiny Tim's idol, crooner Rudy Vallee. Tim thought Bob was the modern incarnation of what Vallee was to the 1929 pop scene. "Mr. Tim," Bob said, switching on a tape recorder, "Tell me about Mr. Vallee." That was all Tiny Tim needed to hear, since beneath his ghoulish persona Tiny Tim was a walking encyclopedia of American popular song—beginning with turn-of-the-century ballads and stretching into doo-wop, which he had performed in the 1950s under the stage name Larry Love. Bob listened raptly as Tim performed an extended medley of Vallee's hits from 1929 to 1931 on his trademark Favilla ukulele. As an encore, Tiny did his impression of Vallee singing "Like a Rolling Stone," then followed it with a deadly imitation of Bob performing Vallee's hit, "There's No Time Like Your Time." That was the kind of lighthearted entertainment that kept Bob Dylan amused through the remainder of 1967.

It wasn't long, however, before the novelty of retirement began to wear thin. Earlier that year, Bob had recorded what would eventually be released as *The Basement Tapes* with the Hawks (who now called themselves simply The Band) and Tiny Tim, but there was some movement toward a more formal work-in-progress that was launched officially when Bob Johnston, his producer, was summoned to Woodstock in the spring of 1968.

Johnston remembers the get-together as a strangely speechless experience. As he tells it, "When we got to his place, he hugged me and my old lady, Joey, then nodded and went over and sat down on a couch. Joey and Sara talked for a couple of hours, while Bob and I sat there and watched the fire. He never said a word, and neither did I. Every so often he just looked at me and smiled, but otherwise that was it. Finally, I said, 'Well, I've got to go now,' and Bob said, 'Oh, no, man, don't go, this is great. I'm having such a good time.' But conversation between us was, for the most part, unnecessary, and a few weeks later when it came time to go into the studio, there was an unspoken understanding between us that made our work there almost effortless."

The album was *John Wesley Harding,* and Kenny Buttrey, who played drums and percussion on it, attests to the session's relative ease. "I ran into George Harrison some time after the record was out, and he told me the album was one of his all-time favorites, but he imagined it must have been a bitch to record," says Buttrey. "He wanted to know how long it took to do the damn thing. So I looked at my watch and said, 'About six hours.' Then he said, 'Well, how long did it take to mix?' and I said, 'That *was* mixed!' We just put it down and Columbia threw it out. Nobody ever went into the studio to mix a note."

Buttrey was relieved by the smooth-running session. When he got the call for the date, he flashed on the *Blonde on Blonde* marathon and steeled himself for a similar no-doze adventure. "I did nothing but rest before this one," he still recalls today. "Slept fifteen hours a day. Then, I located every truck driver I knew to see if they had any amphetamines so I wouldn't be falling asleep at two or three in the morning. I was ready for Dylan to go all night again, figuring that's the way he operated every time he did an album—and wouldn't you know it, the guy speeds through the damn thing in *six hours flat!*"

For all its simplicity, *John Wesley Harding* took Bob's fans completely by surprise. The music on it was by no means an extension of *Highway 61 Revisited* or *Blonde on Blonde*, nor did it evolve from his latest rash of songs—unless you were hip to the unreleased basement tapes. Instead, *John Wesley Harding* was as concise and low-keyed as the sessions which produced it. The songs were closer in spirit to his earlier work than to rock 'n roll, closer in style to the dust-bowl ballads of Woody Guthrie, who had died a few months earlier at Greystone Hospital, where Bob had first gone to visit him. They were *folk* songs, of all things, and there was no rock band on the album. Folk songs in an era of acid rock and soul music. Who else but Bob Dylan would dare to travel his own contrary path, to disregard popular trends, and not worry about losing popularity.

One explanation is that Bob was actually admired for his nonconformity. His fans were finally willing to accept something offbeat and fascinating as a main component of his music. They expected something unique, regardless of what was happening in the world of pop music. And as a result, they even tolerated his intellectual revisionism. Let us not forget, too, that the album was released in January 1968, more than a year after he'd dropped out of sight, so its very appearance was cause for celebration. And then, of course, there were the songs themselves. Of the twelve standard-length tracks, at least three—"All Along the Watchtower," "I Pity the Poor Immigrant," and "I'll Be Your Baby Tonight"—were for the ages. The love song "I'll Be Your Baby Tonight" was tender and playful in a way Bob had never really been before. Bob set aside the snide, sexist insinuations that usually littered his lyrics and instead channeled his strengths into more romantic expressions, using a distinctly Hank Williams influence for the melody.

Gone, too, was the profusion of surrealism and drug imagery, displaced here by religious allegory and philosophical musings. No longer cryptic and bitter, *John Wesley Harding* reflected the positive energies of Bob's year in seclusion. Obviously he'd been reading the Bible. As the reviewer for *Time* observed, "Several of [the songs] are suffused with religious feeling—a sorrowing series of meditations on the Christian ethic, outlined in a language that is close to simplistic." In recent interviews Bob had demonstrated a new pragmatism, a more introspective, more empathetic and self-assured attitude, and this carried through to his lyrics. Unlike the abusive declarations found in previous songs, the wisdom he imparted on *John Wesley Harding* was profoundly moralistic. The title character, Bob sang, "was never known to make a foolish move." In "Dear Landlord," he stressed a fundamental creed: "If you don't underestimate me, I won't underestimate you." And elsewhere he advised listeners: "Don't go mistaking paradise for the home across the road." Despite its humble appearance, there was a lot to absorb in the album's thirty-eight minutes of music.

Most encouraging was this solid evidence that Bob was working again. The album proved he hadn't lost any of his creative momentum, and a low-key appearance at a Carnegie Hall tribute to Woody Guthrie that January dispelled rumors of physical impairment and stage fright. In fact, Bob looked great. He had put on a few pounds, shed those flashy Carnaby Street clothes for a sportcoat and *slacks*. His trademark curls were trimmed to a modest length, in harmony with a clean-cut beard. Bob even wore a pair of rimless glasses, relinquishing his vanity so he could *see* for a change. And he sounded in fine voice—maybe even a little too fine for some tastes.

Listeners agreed that Bob sounded *different*. Not feeble or flabby, not vigorous, but—*different*. Bloodless, maybe. Perhaps more sensitive. Not refined, but reformed. Less throaty, more resonant and still rugged without the steely underside that provided him with an instrument of subtle revenge. He sounded *different,* and it suited his new songs, showing off their musical scope rather than emphasizing any single element such as irony or social significance or even electric accompaniment. His wonderful phrasing was downplayed—he was more in control of it—and the instrumentation was relaxed, but as effective as ever.

Curiously absent, however, was an aspect of Bob's voice that once characterized his self-styled persona: social conscience, anger—*protest*. Long ago Bob had scorned the label "protest singer," insisting it was just a phase he went through, something to help him "make it" in the music business. Yet there was never a more timely moment to protest social injustice than during the months immediately following the release of *John Wesley Harding*. In the briefest of intervals, both Martin Luther King and Robert Kennedy were assassinated, the U.S. death toll in Vietnam ballooned to 19,700 men with another half-million troops stationed in southeast Asia, Richard Daley ordered the Chicago police to "shoot to kill" anyone caught demonstrating in his city, and the students at Columbia University took over their campus, inaugurating a chain reaction of student unrest. Where was Bob Dylan in the midst of all this chaos? He was in the studio back in Nashville, appropriately enough, but the songs he recorded there gave off no residual heat of the times.

Bob Johnston recalls the 1968–1969 sessions as being premeditated and workmanlike. Unlike Bob's previous Nashville sojourns, he had already composed enough material for the album before he even stepped off the plane. "I went over to the Ramada Inn, where Dylan was staying," Johnston remembers, "and he played me all the songs—just like that. We discussed a list of prospective musicians, and the only thing left was to record the damn thing." The usual suspects were rounded up for the date—Charlie McCoy, Kenny Buttrey, Pete Drake—as well as Charlie Daniels, a friend of Bob Johnston's who was in town trying to make it as a session player, and Norman Blake.

The recording process may have been steady and systematic, but from the start the musicians were mesmerized by one glaring modification: Bob's voice. *Different* wasn't the word to describe its timbre this time out. He sounded like a nervous pigeon, all throat and no diaphragm, like a country crooner! Kenny Buttrey spent a few jittery days trying to work up the nerve to say something about it. Finally, he confronted Bob and asked, "Your voice, man—what happened to it? Are you changing it for any particular reason?"

"No," Bob replied calmly. "It's just that all these years I've been real nervous and scared in the studio. I'm getting so accustomed to you guys and so relaxed that it's time I sing relaxed, too."

Buttrey asked, "You mean to tell me this is the way you sing *all* the time?"

"Yeah," Bob said, smiling, "this is my normal voice."

His response was a classic Dylan dodge—half truth, half fiction. There wasn't an ounce of evidence that he had ever been scared in the studio. But this was probably as close to his normal singing voice as we'll ever get to hear. Tapes that have been unearthed, dating back to Hibbing and Minneapolis, disclose yet *another* Dylan voice: low-pitched, sweet, and resonant. The songs on them—traditional folk standards, like "Johnny, We Hardly Knew Ye"—sound like early demos made by Billy Joel. They reverberate with clarity and a rich, if somewhat monotonous, droning. "With drums and guns, and guns and drums/ harooo, harooo. . . ." You'd think it was sung by someone overly concerned with the graceful presentation of his voice. Which isn't exactly what we've come to associate with Bob Dylan. Yet here he was in Nashville, the Country Music Capital of the World, flaunting those golden pipes as if he were Merle Haggard or Charlie Rich. No wonder Kenny Buttrey was baffled.

For Buttrey, it got even weirder when Bob started playing down the chord progression for "Lay Lady Lay." Buttrey was searching for a drum part, but the tricky rhythm made it too elusive. There was no obvious beat. Stumped, he asked, "Bob, you hear anything on there for drums?" Bob, who was hunched over his guitar, looked up and said, "Cowbells."

Riiiiiigghhtt! "I probably didn't hear you correctly," Buttrey chuckled. "I thought you said—*cowbells.*"

"Yeah, I did."

Buttrey thought to himself, "Well, I'll just blow that one off." He let a few minutes pass before wandering into the control room, where Bob Johnston was going over some last-minute mike setups. "Hey, Bob," he asked the producer, "what do you hear for drums? Got any ideas what you think I should do on this?" Johnston glanced up and gave Buttrey one of those vague, don't-bother-me-now looks. "Bongos," he said dismissively.

Bongos, cowbells—*goddamn!* Two helpful hints, the drummer thought. Muttering under his breath, he traipsed back into the studio, where a janitor was straightening up around the equipment.

"Hey, Kris—wanna do me a favor?" he asked the wiry custodian.

Kris Kristofferson smiled and said, "Sure."

"See that funky little set of bongos lying in the corner?" Buttrey pointed to a pair of souvenir bongos someone had brought back from Mexico, the kind with little tacks stuck in the naugahyde to keep the heads on. "How 'bout holding them for me, along with the cowbell. I want to show some guys what a rotten idea of theirs sounds like."

A few minutes later, Bob counted off the intro to "Lay Lady Lay," while Buttrey, smiling grotesquely, switched back and forth between the bongos and the cowbell. "I'll give you wiseguys exactly what you asked for," he said to himself. All of a sudden, his smile faded. "This can't be!" Buttrey thought, as the opening eight bars slid into the verse. "You can't play bongos and cowbells and expect to get something this *good!* I'll be damned!" It was as if the part had been carefully arranged for the song. Cowbells! Bongos! "I'll be damned," Buttrey said again, out loud this time. "This is the tastiest drum part I ever played!"

The rest of the album flowed every bit as smoothly, with a seamless crossbeat between folk, rock, and country music worked into the melodies. The sidemen on the date enjoyed themselves immensely, including Johnny Cash, who turned up the final night of the session to sit in on a few tunes with his old pal.

Unlike the legendary Sun sessions that supposedly united Cash, Elvis Presley, and Jerry Lee Lewis, the Dylan-Cash collaboration is best forgotten by discriminating listeners. At best, it is a keepsake of a unique and long-standing musical friendship, a buoyant jam session conducted by two bold stylists whose voices find no easy harmonies. Still, many of the duets are enjoyable for their impetuous spirit, especially "Ring of Fire" and the old Arthur Crudup standard, "That's Alright, Mama," which sparkles with Pete Drake's magnificent pedal-steel fills. And a reprise of "Girl from the North Country," which Bob saw fit not only to include on the album, but to open it as well.

The album was destined to be a crossover phenomenon, with heavy sales expected in the South, but Yankee response was far from rapturous. Upon hearing the title—*Nashville Skyline*—Columbia Records grew skeptical. It was one thing for Dylan to record there; most people didn't pay any attention to that kind of detail. But putting the word "Nashville" on the cover—on a Bob Dylan album—was too much.

Says Bob Johnston, "Before we did *John Wesley Harding,* CBS expected something really heavy, and when they got an album with steel guitar, bass, and drums on it, they freaked out. So this time they weren't taking any chances." Midway through the *Nashville Skyline* sessions, Clive Davis called Johnston and insisted on hearing the tape before it was mixed. "I sent it up to him," Johnston claims, "and before long I got another call telling me to do all this shit to it—you know, add this, get rid of that—but it wouldn't have been the album Bob intended to make. So instead of fucking with it, I locked the master in a vault and stood my ground. Needless to say, a lot of crap hit the fan over it, but in the end they couldn't and *didn't* do anything we hadn't planned on at the time."

Davis, for his part, claimed only a disaffection with the album's regional salute. "It was a *limiting* title," he says in his 1974 biography. "The 'Nashville' idea might be a turnoff to great numbers of city people." He attempted to persuade Bob to change the title, which, to hear Davis tell it, he *did*, but alas it was too late to hold up the record's shipment.

The album's initial reviews were curiously mixed. *Billboard,* the record industry's usually docile watchdog, hated *Nashville Skyline,* saying, "Dylan, the satisfied man, speaks in clichés and blushes as if every day were Valentine's Day. . . . So goodbye Bob Dylan, I'm glad you're happy though you meant more to me when you were . . . confused like everybody else." *Rolling Stone* was also lukewarm, but the newsweeklies gushed their approval. They raved about his voice. They loved the material, calling it "mature" and—"*charming.*" The establishment media welcomed an album that was unencumbered by earsplitting lead guitars and Wagnerian drums. It appealed to their button-down sensibilities, and coming from a source as unlikely as Bob Dylan, they hailed it as one would a signal from God.

Perhaps *Nashville Skyline* augured the impending musical renaissance which eventually brought to prominence a slew of gentle songwriters like James Taylor, Cat Stevens, and Jackson Browne. Not more than four months after the album's release, a mass hippie migration to a farm thirty miles from Woodstock for a festival called, of all things, *Woodstock* (out of promoter Michael Lang's deep admiration for Bob Dylan), brought to a propitious end the Sturm and Drang of the psychedelic rock era, sending pop music scuttling back to its folk and country roots. Country music was thrust into vogue, and the fallout from the attention it received shot Bob's new album's sales well over the million-unit mark.

The musical shift, combined with a number of climactic occurrences, put Bob at something of a personal crossroads. The previous May, his father died suddenly, cutting Bob off from a link to his identity that was patently unresolved. No matter how divided they had been during Bob's formative years, time had brought them to a point of profound mutual respect. Abe took great pride in Bob's success, and he graciously referred to himself as "Mr. Dylan" on the occasions when it would benefit his son's career. Consequently, Abe's death hit Bob like a ton of bricks. At the funeral in Hibbing, he remained sequestered in his limousine, stoned on grass and grief, shunning most of his relatives other than to promise his Uncle Max that, as the eldest son, he'd say Kaddish for his father.

Without his father, Bob was haunted by his lack of roots. He claimed little connection to an ancestral bloodline—not even a family name. Woodstock, his current homestead, was an alien outpost; he was bored by its rustic cachet and disgusted by its gentrification. There was bad blood between him and his surrogate father, Albert Grossman, brought on by a dispute over Bob's publishing rights and the inevitable renegotiation of their management contract. Their proximity in Woodstock made life difficult. Bob couldn't go anywhere without bumping into one of Albert's many admirers. As a result, he toyed with the idea of moving to Nashville. During rehearsals for a Johnny Cash TV show on which he appeared, he spent a day with Bob Johnston looking at real estate there, but nothing ever came of that. Still, it was evident that an upheaval of some kind was in the works.

The time had come for Bob not only to reassess his career, but also to make some important decisions concerning his personal life. He was mentally and physically healthy. Staying off the road and out of the fast lane had done him a world of good. He'd settled down, and in doing so had grown up, begun a family, and turned his career around so that it pointed in new and vital directions that were exempt from the drug culture. He was making music again—actually, he'd never stopped; it merely wasn't open to public inspection—and felt the old inextinguishable urge to play it in front of an audience. In late August, he'd performed before a crowd of nearly two hundred thousand Europeans at a music festival on the Isle of Wight. Viewed as something of a comeback, Bob enjoyed performing with the Band again and alluded publicly to the possibility of a tour. A tour—after so many years of seclusion, it was a scintillating prospect for his legion of steadfast fans.

Still, the initiative had to come from somewhere other than his base in Woodstock. That's where he had gone to get away from it all. It was his snug harbor in a maelstrom of wild abandon. But Woodstock had outlived its usefulness to Bob. It no longer provided him with the necessary elements of inspiration. So that by the end of summer it had become clear which road Bob had to take. He was going back to where it all began for him, back to New York City, to a home in the heart of Greenwich Village.

23

You Don't Need a Weberman to Know Which Way the Wind Blows

"BOB DYLAN TURNS THIRTY!" There it was in black and white, splashed across all the major papers—*The Times, The Voice, The Jerusalem Post*—who treated the story as if it were some kind of cultural milestone. An entry suited for Ripley's *Believe It or Not! Bob Dylan. . . . thirty. . . .* Could two phrases sound so fundamentally inharmonious, so patently heretical, so undeniably apocalyptic? Oh, the symbolism of it! Bob Dylan—the spokesman for the generation which advocates "Never trust anyone over thirty"—was now a victim of his own doctrine. The occasion, while certainly cause for celebration, was full of delicious contradiction.

Though hardly a traumatic experience, turning thirty must have given Bob a momentary rush of apprehension. Careerwise, his twenty-ninth year had been an unmitigated disaster. Two albums were slapped together and released to varying notices. The first, *Self-Portrait,* issued in June, was an anomaly to most Dylan fans—a double album consisting mostly of cast-offs from the Isle of Wight festival and unrelated sessions in New York and Nashville. The New York dates were piloted by Bob Johnston. Down south, Charlie McCoy and Kenny Buttrey were once again recruited to provide instrumentation, but to their surprise the tracks were to be done *without* Bob Dylan.

"It was a real strange session," Charlie McCoy says of that experience. "Dylan sent the tapes down [to Nashville] with instructions that we were to just play over what he'd already recorded on it. I listened to it and thought—uh-oh, trouble. The tape was mostly other people's songs and it sounded like he was experimenting with them. The tempos didn't hold together real well and he wasn't real steady with his guitar, either. In any case, I assumed they didn't mean much to him and it was just stuff he'd thrown together for the heck of it."

To make matters worse, McCoy and Buttrey couldn't coordinate their schedules to be in the studio at the same time. Recalls Kenny Buttrey, "If I had another ten o'clock session but Charlie was available, he'd go into the studio and overdub his part and leave his charts on the music stand for me, with little arrows pointing up or down where Dylan might have speeded up or slowed down a bit. As a drummer, that made it all the more difficult to come up with a good part because I was the only person in the studio and had no one to play off of. Worse, I didn't even know if the vocalist liked what I was doing because *he wasn't even in town!*"

Not in town—and out to lunch was the verdict handed down by the die-hards who actually slogged through the record's four dismal sides. Fifteen of the album's twenty-five songs were covers of golden oldies, among them Gordon Lightfoot's "Early Morning Rain"; two Everly Brothers hits, "Take a Message to Mary" and "Let It Be Me"; a tongue-in-cheek version of Paul Simon's "The Boxer" (with Bob overdubbing himself à la Art Garfunkel); "Blue Moon" sung in a syrupy malaise as only Bing Crosby might have done it; Paul Clayton's exuberant "Gotta Travel On"; and the traditional folk ballad "Copper Kettle," which Bob had once criticized Joan Baez for hanging onto for too long. Mixed in with the standards were reprises of "She Belongs to Me" and "Like a Rolling Stone," as well as a few originals that were instantly forgettable.

Self-Portrait was greeted with not only dislike but *resentment.* Dylan fans felt they'd been ripped off, and the rock press—by this time a fraternity of professional skeptics—did nothing to discourage that reaction. *Rolling Stone*'s initial evaluation—which it so eloquently began: "What is this shit?"—concluded that the album was vapid and marketed on the strength of the dwindling Dylan myth. "For all the emotion usually found in his singing, there is virtually none here," one of its anonymous pundits decried. (The *Rolling Stone* review of *Self-*

Portrait was written collaboratively by eleven reviewers; however, none of the opinions in the piece were attributed.) *Crawdaddy* and *Creem,* muffled their dissatisfaction, but the *East Village Other,* a New York underground weekly, summed up the public response with its brief but poignant opinion: "This album sucks!"

Crucified by fans and critics alike, a penitent Bob had rushed out an album of eleven original songs, *New Morning,* which was released in October 1970. Coming on the heels of *Self-Portrait,* the album was received as a masterpiece; perspective, however, reveals *New Morning* to be as thin and unnourishing as canned soup. The songs measure up to the level of an album like *Nashville Skyline,* but individually and collectively they pale in comparison with his earlier, vital compositions. The imagery lacks teeth. The rhymes fall off witlessly into limping meter, free of any remarkable emphasis. The instruments are often out of tune. A Bob Dylan album cannot always be brilliant, nevertheless it typically demonstrates inventiveness and some special insight, and *New Morning* offered little, if any, of either quality.

Still, the appearance of a new Bob Dylan album was occasion enough for the critics to convene a tribunal. All the wizards of rock 'n roll listened and listened, then probed and projected and analyzed and meditated . . . and meditated some more . . . before they articulated their insightful conclusion: Bob Dylan was *back.* He had lived up to their expectations, therefore he was *back.* Back from what? From the grave, from seclusion? Back from mediocrity? Back from Brazil? They didn't say. But he was *back*—the same way he'd be *back* following the release of *Blood on the Tracks* and *Infidels* and *Biograph.* The same way he'll be *back* after any exceptional album in the future. Of course, what it really meant was that they'd prematurely written him off, and now had to retract their obituaries like hastily made New Year's resolutions.

"Well, friends, Bob Dylan is back with us again," began Ed Ward's review in the October 26th issue of *Rolling Stone.* In case anyone missed the point, the same magazine ran another article beneath the headline: "WE'VE GOT DYLAN BACK AGAIN!" in which the irrepressible Ralph J. Gleason blubbered over Bob like a twelve-year-old schoolgirl with her first crush.

Back in New York is what Bob was—back in Greenwich Village of all places, on the second floor of a renovated brownstone on MacDougal Street just two blocks from the love nest he once shared with

Suze Rotolo. Declaring Woodstock "a daily excursion to nothingness," he and Sara and the kids moved away from the country—and away from Albert, with whom he'd broken in a disagreement over financial affairs—in search of some place to call home. Bob and Sara sought a more complete environment for their family, a place with the promise of good schools, intellectual stimulation, proximity to work, invigorating nightlife—the whole American Dream. But as everybody who lives there knows, New York is no place to raise a family. The air is filthy, animals roam the streets in yellow cabs, and if you're Bob Dylan, chances are the fans will demand a significant slice of your privacy. In fact, no sooner had Bob returned to the city, than he got a typical New York welcome in the person of one of its screwiest denizens, Alan J. Weberman.

A. J. Weberman must have seemed the incarnation of Bob Dylan's worst nightmare. A schlumpy, munchkin-faced Jewish pseudo-intellectual, an only child from Brooklyn, he was a throwback to the type of spiral-eyed misfit that roamed the Village in the late Fifties: an angry and seriously misguided communist sympathizer fraught with all the rhetoric of the movement, such as "Workers of the world unite." Friends argued that A. J. was a harmless guy trying to find himself, but he had a history of drug-related arrests and nothing to fill his vacuous life aside from an obsession with Bob Dylan.

Weberman was a Bob Dylan junkie who tried to hook other fans. He was certainly no simpleton—on the contrary, A. J. was the kind of highly educated and thoughtful freak you'd find in the executive ranks of religious cults—but his actions misfired with paranoid distortion, and that's where all the trouble began.

A. J. claimed his goal in life was to explain Bob Dylan, but in practice he strove to *expose* him. This tactic wasn't particularly a novel one to Bob. Only months before, a groupie named Toby Thompson, who had masqueraded through Hibbing as a hip journalist and reportedly interviewed Bob's family and friends, published an infantile but highly publicized account of his exploits. Bob considered Thompson's underhanded reporting an invasion of his privacy, but it was nothing compared to what A. J. had in store for him.

Most parasites feed on a host, and A. J.'s, startlingly enough, was an unwitting *Broadside* magazine. The same *Broadside* which first published Bob Dylan back in 1962. Gordon Freisen, the magazine's eld-

The opening night of Tour '74 in Chicago, with Robbie Robertson. (*Photograph by David Gahr*)

Phil Ochs, Bob, Dave Van Ronk, and Dennis Hopper reflecting . . . soberly at the Chile concert, 1975. (© *1975 Bob Gruen/Star File*)

Serenading Mike Porco with Rob Stoner, Joan Baez, and Eric Andersen, Folk City, 1975. (*Mary Alfieri*)

Phil Ochs and Bob in a typical encounter, 1975. (*Mary Alfieri*)

The king and queen at the end of their later reign, San Francisco, 1977. (*Robert Matheu/Retna*)

During Rolling Thunder II, Houston, May 1976. (*Photograph by David Gahr*)

Bob and *Infidels* producer Mark Knopfler. (*Greg Noakes/Retna*)

Bob and longtime friend Eric Clapton jamming at Wembley Stadium, 1984. (*Michael Rutland/Retna*)

The face that launched a thousand tours? (*David Redfern/Retna*)

David Zimmerman, Sara, and Bob enjoy a warm family moment, Minneapolis, 1984. (*Greg Hegelson*)

Bob with Dinah Shore at the Songwriters' Hall of Fame dinner, 1982. (*Walter McBride/ Retna*)

On tour with Tom Petty, 1986. (*Robert Matheu/Retna*)

. . . and alone, with an intimate crowd, 1986. (*Michael Rutland/Retna*)

Mugging to "Hollis Brown" at "Live Aid" with Ron Wood and Keith Richards, 1985. (*Scott Weiner/Retna*)

Feeling right at home. . . . "The Gershwin Gala," Brooklyn Academy of Music, 1987. Left to right: Tommy Tune, Larry Kert, Christopher Walken, Chita Rivera, Gregg Burge, Madeline Kahn, Harold Nicholas, Bobby Short, Michael Tilson-Thomas, Mikhail Baryshnikov, Drew Barrymore, and Bob. (*Larry Busacca/Retna*)

The one and only. . . . (*Howard Rosenberg*)

erly founder, who obviously longed for the days when folksingers were celebrities and celebrities were activists, had dedicated several issues as early as 1968 to A. J.'s misguided interpretations. Weberman became *Broadside*'s resident Dylanologist, a term A. J. coined and exploited. A. J. convinced Freisen that Dylan was still the militant radical *Broadside* had nurtured back in 1962, only now Bob disguised his message in metaphor, and only he, Weberman, could decipher the "mysteries of Dylan."

Freisen was no innocent bystander, as he later tried to claim. He was *into* A. J.'s kooky rap. Dissecting Bob's motives behind naming an album *John Wesley Harding,* he himself deduced: "John Wesley Hardin was one of the sorriest outlaws we ever had, a bumbler who spent half his 42 years behind bars. And Harding was about the most incompetent president this country ever had. . . . Could there be any significance in the fact that the man who killed John Wesley by shooting him in the back of the head was successfully defended at the trial by A. B. Fall, who as Harding's Secretary of the Interior went to jail for taking bribes?" Nothing less than the theme song to *Twilight Zone* should accompany such a *folie à deux.*

The piece grows even more bizarre, as Weberman imbues every "if," "and," and "the" with mad, twisted meaning. He saw government conspiracy and collusion behind every line of poetry. According to A. J., the word "lady" in Bob's songs really meant "oligarchy," just as "Maggie's Farm" was used to describe "capitalism" and "rain" symbolized violence. In his analysis of "The Ballad of Frankie Lee and Judas Priest," A. J. free-associated to arrive at the following insight: "FRANKIE LEE, Frankie Lane, Frankie Lyman—it's Dylan the rock 'n roll singer." One might think that, even in America, the chances of a nutcase like Alan Weberman becoming a media star are slim—but that is precisely what happened.

By 1971, Weberman was teaching college courses in "Dylanology." He was featured regularly on several New York talk-radio shows. *Broadside* published his wacky annotations of Bob's songs. The *East Village Other* gave him a weekly column. He was interviewed by national magazines. Even *The Tonight Show* tried to book him! Once a likely straitjacket candidate, A. J. Weberman had become the country's leading authority on Bob Dylan.

The truth of the matter is that every celebrity encounters his share of overzealous fans, sickos, starfuckers, who live vicariously through their heroes, and most celebrities learn to accommodate this. Perhaps Bob Dylan should have simply ignored A. J.'s hijinx until the guy got tired and disappeared. With A. J., however, that was easier said than done. By late 1970, he had turned his Dylan fixation into a profitable gig. Somehow he had got hold of the five-year-old galleys to *Tarantula* and mimeographed thousands of copies which he sold at two bucks a pop. A small price for fans who'd been waiting for the book since 1965. Immediately, *Tarantula* became an underground best-seller, providing A. J. with a tidy annuity he used to expand his new venture, The Dylan Liberation Front.

The book that Bob had no intention of ever publishing was being read, yet he wasn't seeing so much as a cent from it. Worse, the profits were being used to finance Weberman's sick trip. To put A. J. out of business, Bob allowed Macmillan to rush *Tarantula* into print, which stopped the bootlegging quickly enough, but even that failed to muzzle his antagonist.

A. J. merely stepped up his activities, establishing the Dylan Archives (a collection of bootleg tapes and records) in his roach-infested Bowery loft and circulated two five-hundred-page manuscripts in which he analyzed every word in every Bob Dylan song known to exist (and some that didn't). His obsession began to get very weird—and *nasty.* Eager to get Bob's attention, he launched a campaign to prove Bob was a heroin addict. The songs, he theorized, no longer contained symbols of revolution, but rather of smack. Words like "morning," "nighttime," "wind"—they really meant "dope." "Saddle me up a big white goose"—"dope." "Sand"—"dope." "Sea"—"dope." Weberman enlisted members of his Dylan Liberation Front to help promote the folly, their motto: "Free Bob Dylan from Himself." Their goal: steering their hero back to politics and the poor man's struggle against capitalist slavery. To accomplish that, A. J. needed some kind of tangible proof that Bob was a drug addict so A. J. could confront the problem head-on. He ran a classified ad in the *East Village Other* that read: "If anyone has a sample of Bob Dylan's urine, please send it to me c/o. . . ."

Pretty funny stuff, right? A send-up, a prank? Maybe so, but then A. J. stumbled on a treasure trove of evidence, and that was none other than Bob Dylan's—*garbage!*

Bob's garbage turned A. J. into an overnight media star. He became a household name—or, at least, household initials. Straight cats on Wall Street and the Upper East Side knew that A. J.—*A. J.*—was THE MAN WHO ANALYZED ROCK-STAR DYLAN'S GARBAGE. He captured New Yorkers' wicked sense of humor and their cynicism. In a city whose residents were jaded by publicity stunts, garbage seemed the perfect antidote. They could identify with it. It made the rich and famous living among them seem like anybody else forced to cart a two-ply polyurethane forest-green bag down to the curb each night. Cut it open—you could learn a lot about your neighbor, especially if he happened to be Bob Dylan.

What A. J. found, however, wasn't particularly revealing, nor was it unearthed in the spirit in which people initially interpreted it. *Dogshit!* Yeeeeeeeeeeeeeeeeecch!!!" he squealed to a reporter from *Rolling Stone* who recorded the excavation for posterity. Another vulgarity vilified Bob's mutt, Sasha, who was apparently not housebroken. "Fuckin' bitch . . ." A. J. spat.

Weberman wasn't trying to be cute. He wasn't innocently vying for ratings. He was looking for *syringes*. Drug paraphernalia. Prescriptions. Night after night, A. J. crept along the curb in front of 94 MacDougal Street in search of something with which he could nail Bob in the underground press. The closest he came to it was a prescription for a commonly prescribed muscle relaxant.

Had A. J. at all valued his booty, the Dylan garbage could have provided a fascinating biographical sketch of the artist. There in the ruins lay some notes on the outtakes of *Self-Portrait,* a drawing of Jimi Hendrix that Bob made on the day of the rock legend's death, an unfinished letter to Johnny Cash and his wife, snapshots of Bob with some friends, others with him and the kids, an original poem. Had A. J. written at length about any of these findings, the expedition might have been valuable, or, at the very least, amusing. Instead, he used the garbage and the publicity it brought him as yet another means of harassing Bob.

The assaults on 94 MacDougal Street stretched into the spring of 1971, and as they did, Weberman's tactics grew more hostile and further from his original mission. He conducted crowded tours to the front of the house. Demonstrations became daily occurrences that often required police intervention. Bullhorns were used to antagonize anyone inside the brownstone. Sara and the kids were intimidated by members of the Dylan Liberation Front who camped on the doorstep. Anything to disrupt Bob's privacy was encouraged in the guise of a revolutionary expedient. They published his address—and his phone number! Music was no longer A. J.'s inducement, if it had ever been that at all. His psycho-babble about lyrics and poetry had given way to screwy soliloquies concerning establishment propaganda and profits and the underclass—the usual buzzwords that spring from all the revolutionary crap guys like Alan Weberman gorge themselves on, the standard, banal mumbo-jumbo that usually begins "It is the goal of the common man to rise up and overthrow the rich and corrupt oppressors who constitute the Ruling Class. . . ." No, Weberman wasn't interested in art. His obsession with Bob's songs had been supplanted by a preoccupation with Bob's *money*.

"Hey, hey, hey, Bob Dylan—time to give away your millions!" A. J. boomed from behind a police barricade as the DLF marched down Sixth Avenue.

"FREE BOB DYLAN, END ROCK RIP-OFF, FREE BOB DYLAN!"

"Bob . . . the kids on the street think you've turned into a fucking sellout. . . . people are saying you've turned into a capitalist pig, that your wealth has corrupted you. . . . You ripped off their music! *You owe them quite a bit!*"

There it was again—that word: *owe*. Bob had heard it repeatedly for the last ten years. He *owed* his fans certain debts. Hadn't he a *responsibility* to them? That attitude drove him right up the wall. He'd answered those questions hundreds of times over the years and always with the same response: "No, man, I don't *owe* them anything."

The fans were of absolutely no concern to Bob Dylan—not in any kind of personal way. He never wrote music with them in mind. He wasn't sending the fans any hidden messages, nor did he mean them to take personally anything he said in the songs. He couldn't worry about a stranger's deluded belief. God knows, there were two or three million fans out there who played Bob's records. If he had to stop and think about even one of them every time he wrote, he'd never complete a new song.

The only person Bob could worry about was himself. He had to get his career back on track and that meant concentrating on his music. There was to be a lot of it over the next six months, not the most even or representative work of his career; nevertheless it was interesting for its rummaging of various styles and sounds.

By March 1971, Bob was back in the studio, this time with a group of top-flight L.A. session men led by Leon Russell. The material from those dates wasn't meant for an album, and Bob had to cut through considerable red tape to hold it outside the purview of Columbia Records. For privacy, Bob selected a fledgling outfit named Blue Rock Studios, which operated out of a tumbledown SoHo loft. "He simply knocked on the door one day and said, 'I was in the neighborhood—mind if I look at your place?'" recalls Joe Schick, who managed the studio's affairs. "I didn't recognize him at first because he was wrapped in a parka and was wearing a Chinese-Communist border guard hat with flaps covering every side of his face. But it was Dylan, all right, and after walking through the place it was obvious he was raring to get started."

The sessions comprised only two days, during which time he recorded eight songs. Two of them—"Watching the River Flow" and "When I Paint My Masterpiece"—appeared on *Bob Dylan's Greatest Hits, Volume II,* which Columbia released in late November 1971. The songs were upbeat and vigorously sung in the style of his *Blonde on Blonde* period, finished off with a sassy edge reminiscent of "Leopard-Skin Pillbox Hat." Bob rides the jouncy beat with daring vocal glissandos that worked dynamically against Leon Russell's trademark piano strides. "*What's* the *mat*ter with *meeeeee?*" he brays, and the old excitement is at work. The performance on "Watching the River Flow" is so full of drive and good humor that it conveys to the listener a camaraderie between Bob and that band that actually was quite transitory. Joe Schick recalls that Bob and Leon Russell got along respectably enough, but there was no real chemistry there, no magic, and as a result any talk of an album was scrapped.

Unfortunately, some stupendous performances from the Blue Rock sessions wound up on the cutting-room floor. Most notable was a cover of "Spanish Harlem," which had been a hit for Ben E. King in 1961 after he left the Drifters. Bob's version is much sparer than King's, without the advantage of lush strings and a female backup. Yet Bob's rich, hoarse delivery established a real feeling for the song and its bleak urban scenario. "I love that one," he sighed to a musician after a false start, and his subsequent performance left little doubt of his sincerity.

Bob also tried a rendition of the Ray Charles ballad "That Lucky Old Sun," with somewhat less success, but two blues standards—"Alabama Bound" and "Blood Red River"—captured the spirit of Bob's partnership with this band, however fleeting, in all its rollicking energy.

That summer, he also showed up for a concert to benefit the war-relief effort in Bangladesh, which George Harrison organized at New York's Madison Square Garden. Bob was only a rumored participant prior to the concert, and until his appearance the main attraction was to be John Lennon, who hadn't performed on the same stage with George Harrison since the Beatles' demise. Lennon was set to perform three solo numbers, when suddenly Ringo Starr's name was added to the bill. The New York tabloids ran wild with the story. "If George, John, and Ringo showed up, could Paul McCartney be far behind?" they speculated. "Would the fabled Beatles finally reunite?" Not if John Lennon had any say in the matter, they wouldn't. According to his biographer Albert Goldman, "At the last minute John flipped out over the possibility he'd find himself in the middle of a Beatles reunion. He totaled his hotel room, beat up Yoko, and begged her to put him on a plane—*anywhere.* So just hours before the concert began, she sent John to Paris."

As it turned out, John might have thrown a killer tantrum had he been forced to follow Bob Dylan that August afternoon. The Concert for Bangladesh was one of Bob's finest hours, not only because it was his first time on an American stage in five years, but also because his performance was so aggressive and exciting.* He sang his heart out, playing "Hard Rain" and "Blowin' in the Wind" by himself before returning with a band made up of George Harrison, Ringo Starr, and Leon Russell. (For the evening show, he also strummed through "Mr. Tambourine Man.") He blew the crowd away, ducking a ten-minute standing ovation that was a measure of the demand for his return to the concert stage.

Bob was just getting used to the sound of applause again when a rampage of events caused him to push the panic button and retreat once more. The first, a hearsay piece in *Time* purported, according to

---

*Actually, Bob appeared on stage with the Band at a May 1969 concert they were headlining in Evanston, Illinois, during which Bob reprised his Hibbing High performance by singing "Long Tall Sally" and "Rip It Up."

"his friend and annotator, A. J. Weberman," that Bob had donated a sizable chunk of his income to the fanatical Jewish Defense League. No sooner had the magazine hit the stands than the theorists started weaving together a tapestry of circumstantial evidence to support their conclusion that Bob Dylan was a rabid Zionist. They found evidence of it buried in the lyrics to all his most recent songs. A vacation to Israel with Sara and the kids snowballed into rumors of gunrunning and emigration. Friends hinted that Bob had undergone a spiritual transformation during his seclusion in Woodstock. Because Bob suggested to a journalist he was returning to his roots, *Time* concluded he'd soon be changing his name back to Robert Allen Zimmerman and mentioned Bob's "great admiration" for JDL renegade Meir Kahane without explaining that Kahane had been Arlo Guthrie's neighborhood rabbi years earlier in Far Rockaway and the two men had been introduced purely on an informal basis.

Combine that with the consensus that even his music wasn't safe from outside tampering and you begin to understand Bob's compulsive need for privacy and isolation. Actually, Bob exercised complete artistic control over his recording sessions and seemed impervious to criticism of them. Moreover, his latest studio effort had been generally well-received. *Greatest Hits, Volume II* was a critical success if for no other reason than Bob's audacious inclusion of six previously unrecorded songs—one of which, the lushly melodic and haunting "I Shall Be Released," became an instant classic. A single, "George Jackson," issued in the fall of 1971, reawakened interest in Bob's political ministrations. He produced an album for Texas cowboy Doug Sahm that appealed to a small, but influential, audience. Even his frivolous soundtrack for the Sam Peckinpah movie, *Pat Garrett and Billy the Kid,* in which he played a relatively insignificant character was salvaged by the unforgettable hit song "Knockin' on Heaven's Door," and sold well despite horrible reviews and threats from Columbia Records to withhold the album. Consequently, by November 1973, Bob was encouraged to begin work on a new album of original songs, the first with his old pals The Band.

The sessions were to be held at Village Recorders in Los Angeles, where Bob had relocated with his family. The entire recording industry had begun to move west (except for stubborn, urban Atlantic Records), and Bob followed swiftly in its wake. Though he had always gone his own musical road, Bob Dylan was completely devoted to the scene. Being where it was, taking advantage of it. Jac Holtzman, the first record mogul to abandon his New York operation, always told Bob that the future of the music business awaited him on "the Coast." "Someday," he predicted like a Jewish uncle, "*someday* you'll all move out here." Now—reluctantly—the Dylan brood settled temporarily into a ranch-style house just outside the Malibu gates while their garish two-million-dollar domed mansion was under construction further down the beach.

No sooner had Bob relaxed in the studio than word came to him that CBS had announced the immediate release of a new Bob Dylan album, whose title was simply *Dylan.* "That's news to me," an engineer at Village Recorders recalls Bob saying, convinced it was merely another in a series of rumors issued by the record company to whet the fans' appetites. By day's end, however, the album had been shipped.

Columbia had buggered him, but good, finally getting back at Bob for his refusal to renew his recording contract. His deal with the CBS-owned label had expired in 1972, and once again Bob threatened to change record companies to get more favorable financial terms. For six months, David Braun, Bob's lawyer, and CBS Records' president Clive Davis had haggled over a new contract. Back and forth they went, dickering like a couple of garment manufacturers over the price of chintz. Royalty increases, incentive clauses, signing bonuses, limits on cross-collateralization, extended payouts—you'd think they were concluding a foreign-aid package. Finally the two men came to terms on a five-year agreement. They had the proper papers drawn, initialed all the riders and addendums and subclauses and appendixes and codicils. And after all the *i*'s had been dotted and the *t*'s were crossed and the corporate seals were affixed, when the only thing lacking was Bob Dylan's signature for it to be duly constituted under law—word came back that he'd decided not to sign. The thought of tying himself into a five-year relationship was too much for Bob.

Corporate hairs were pulled from corporate pates as Columbia Records executives racked their corporate brains for a quick solution. The CBS Records division *needed* Bob Dylan. First off, their big breadwinners were an endangered species. Janis Joplin was dead, Blood, Sweat & Tears was splitting up. So was Simon & Garfunkel. Sly Stone had drug problems. Laura Nyro had retired. The networks had canceled the respective TV shows of Andy Williams, Johnny Cash, and

Jim Nabors, which left little doubt about the future of their album sales. Who was left? Poco? Dr. Hook? The Mahavishnu Orchestra? Chicago's albums still sold remarkably well, but the band members were behaving like prima donnas. Columbia had to find some way to get Bob Dylan signed. And fast.

Davis and Braun went back to the bargaining table and looked for a way to resolve the mess. For another six months these men held power lunches and met over drinks, they huddled and conferred, and each time they met they bemoaned the fact that Bob Dylan and Columbia Records were like an institution. The two belonged together like... like bagels and lox. It was a *classic* combination. It was—*forever!*

To his credit, Clive Davis proposed a loxy deal in which he'd cede the rights to Bob's earliest albums in return for a two-record contract without any time restrictions. Bob could then either lease his early albums to Columbia, sell to another label, or take them out of circulation altogether, if that's what he desired. Bob jumped at the offer, as both men obviously knew he would. But before he could sign the proper papers, CBS Records fired Clive Davis and reneged on the Dylan deal almost at the same time, claiming it was too rich for its blood.

CBS's intention, after restoring order in its ranks, was to offer Bob a more reasonable deal. In the meantime, however, he was approached by David Geffen with a deal that ultimately made him feel more appreciated. Columbia's mistake didn't all boil down to dollars and cents. No, greater damage was done because it had failed to pay Bob the *respect* owed to someone who not only had sold millions of albums and remained hot after more than a decade in the business, but had changed the sound of popular music. Columbia failed to consider a very important factor: the artist's ego. And artists' egos happened to be David Geffen's stock in trade.

Geffen had a résumé that seemed custom-made for the rock music business. Rising out of the William Morris Agency mailroom like a crew-cut Godzilla, he'd courted performers and songwriters, attending to their business interests and insecurities, often becoming involved personally with them, until he'd organized the most impressive and influential management firm of its kind. In a few short years, Geffen managed to sign Laura Nyro; Crosby, Stills, Nash & Young; Joni Mitchell; Jackson Browne; the Eagles; and at least a dozen other top stars. And when he became bored with that aspect of the business, he formed Asylum Records, with an equally impressive roster of artists. Then, in 1973, he had a shot at Bob Dylan, who lived nearby him in Malibu, and Geffen made his most convincing pitch yet—which was no pitch at all. A master of artistic foreplay, he understood Bob's reticence about complex agreements and took an extremely low-key approach with him, offering Bob a completely unstructured, open-ended deal; they'd work together on an album-to-album basis, with absolutely no pressure on Bob to deliver product and likewise no pressure on Geffen to come up with a big advance.

Once Columbia got wind of Geffen's offer, the giant music conglomerate stepped up its efforts to resign Bob. At almost the same time, "Knockin' on Heaven's Door" broke out of the *Pat Garrett & Billy the Kid* soundtrack—an album Columbia initially marked for the cutout bins—and suddenly Bob Dylan had a hit single on the charts. The people at CBS knew they had to move fast in order to salvage the deal. It would be embarrassing for them to lose Bob at a time like this. Unfortunately, their new president, Irwin Siegelstein, was a former television executive who failed to jump to the tempo of the rock music business, and before he could say "Who's David Geffen?" Bob had cut a deal with Asylum Records. Columbia had lost one of its most important and most durable stars due to stubbornness and bureaucracy. When, adding insult to injury, Columbia released the *Dylan* album without his authorization, the company eliminated any chance at a reconciliation.

The only thing to be said about *Dylan* is that it was an unfortunate record album. A hodgepodge of outtakes from *Self-Portrait* and *New Morning,* it reflects a period of indecision and experimentation in Bob's career. None of the songs are his own—at least, he wasn't credited for any of them. One song, "Sara Jane," was most likely written by Bob although it remained unsigned and was excluded from his two books of lyrics. The others—an unfathomable medley of standards such as Joni Mitchell's "Big Yellow Taxi," "Mr. Bojangles," and two Elvis Presley hits ("Can't Help Falling in Love" and "A Fool Such as I")—reveal neither plan nor purpose, and, in fact, they were no more the intention of Bob Dylan than they were of the producer or engineer who sequenced them together from old tapes. The performances aren't embarrassing as much as they are pointless, nothing more than expensive demos not meant for public ears.

Officially, *Planet Waves* would be Dylan's first studio album in almost three years. Bob was in a rush to get it done, and he was obviously concerned about how the finished album would be received. Throughout the sessions he vacillated between relentless determination and an almost schizy indecisiveness, recording some songs as many as three or five different ways before shelving them. He was also unusually attentive to criticism, allowing even a stranger's thoughtless remark to influence him.

During the playback of "Forever Young," Bob's old camp buddy Lou Kemp dropped by the studio with his girlfriend, and they were invited to sit in with the band and crew. The song had been a particularly difficult one for Bob to nail down. Earlier that afternoon, he'd told Rob Fraboni, the engineer: "You know, I've been carrying this song around in my head for five years, but I've never written it down," he admitted. "And now that I'm going to do it, I don't know *how* to do it." So he recorded five versions of "Forever Young," each one completely different from the one before.

On the first take, Bob played it like a man possessed. He was wired right into the lyric and let the melody carry him away. Says Rob Fraboni, "The musicians came in [to the control room] to hear it back, and nobody said a word to each other—honest to God!—nobody spoke. It was so moving that it kind of paralyzed everyone a little bit. Then everyone left. They just wandered out without saying anything—nobody even said goodbye to anyone else."

Bob left the studio without requesting the usual feedback from his sidemen. Instead, he walked across the street and slipped into an artsy movie theater that was showing a François Truffaut film. Fraboni locked up and walked around the block with Ken Lauber, who had played congas on the date, then returned by himself to the studio. "The song was driving me nuts," Fraboni says. "I *had* to hear it again. I *wanted* that song the way a guy wants a woman, and I wanted to listen to it in private, without having to worry about anyone else's reaction." He monitored the playback tipped back in a chair, with his eyes closed. When he opened them again, Bob was standing there, smiling at him. "Ummmmm—yeah," he purred. "Sounds like the real thing, huh Ron?" Then, without waiting for an answer, he wandered back into the studio and cut it again. And again. And again. And again.

Afterward, Bob decided—or *in*decided, as the case may be—that two versions of "Forever Young" were unique and strong enough to deserve being on the album together. That intense first take on side one, and a fluffy, countrified version of it to lead off side two. It was a novel idea, but the band members encouraged him and it seemed like a fait accompli—until Lou Kemp and his girlfriend walked in.

Bob played them the two "Forever Youngs" he'd selected for the album. After the slow version finished, Kemp's girlfriend said, "You're getting mushy in your old age, Bobby."

Bob's eyes narrowed, his shoulders slumped. He got up listlessly and wandered out of the room. An hour later, he instructed Rob Fraboni to drop the second take from the final sequence.

"*What?*—you're out of your mind!" the engineer stammered. "Listen, man, you've got to leave them both on the master." But Bob was adamant. "I don't know, man," he mumbled, before dashing out of the studio. "Maybe it's not meant to be."

Fraboni eventually talked Bob into restoring both versions to the master, and the remaining work progressed with little or no interruption. Like its predecessors, the music on *Planet Waves* occurred spontaneously, sometimes materializing out of a few remote chord changes. The Band had rehearsed only four of the eighteen songs they eventually cut for the album. For the rest, Bob would start playing a riff, they'd watch his hands to pick up the chords, and the rest was history—no retakes or overdubs; the impromptu jam evolved into a song that often became the first and final take for the album.

They breezed through the final record in only four days' time. "Dylan kept things moving during the recording," Fraboni recalls with great admiration. "We'd come in to do a song and Bob would say, 'Okay, c'mon, let's go. *Let's go!*' The guys in the Band wanted to sit around, smoke a joint. They did things in a relaxed manner, had a lot of fun there. But Bob was wired and kept them in motion."

Most recording artists ease themselves gradually into a session. The first fifteen hours or so are often a write-off. Sometimes the first few days. The guys sit around unwinding, drinking coffee and talking about what they've been doing since their last gig together in the studio.

New instruments are shown off and passed around for approval, along with pictures of the wives and kids. Microphone setups are worked out. Riffs-in-progress are previewed. It is a process that is often compared with moving into a new house. You have to adjust to new surroundings, reacquaint yourself with old furniture. Get into a groove. All of that takes time, and at two hundred or even four hundred dollars an hour, it can run up the cost of an album by as much as ten percent.

No one could accuse Bob Dylan of wasting precious studio time. The very first day yielded seven finished songs. Levon Helm hadn't arrived on time from a vacation in Arkansas, but never mind—Bob moved Richard Manuel from the piano to drums, and the gang sailed through an electrified warm-up of "House of the Rising Sun" before moving onto the new material.

The second day was equally productive, which took some of the pressure off Bob. He began to relax, his playing loosened up, and his attitude with the guys took on a less businesslike manner. That night, in the new spirit of *glasnost,* everyone ate dinner together in the studio. During dessert, Garth Hudson mentioned that a Barbra Streisand special was on the tube and Bob's eyebrows shot up to the ceiling. He immediately sent one of the engineers out for a television set. Sure enough, there was Barbra mugging through some corny old Fanny Brice *schtik.* Bob pointed at Fraboni, who was in the control room, and shouted: "Roll tape!" Says Fraboni, "For the next hour he had me rolling twenty-four-track tape with an open mike while he and the Band sang duets and camped it up with Barbra Streisand." ". . . are the *luhhk*-iest *peeee*-pul in the *wuhllld. . . .*" Then it was back to business, although on a decidedly lighter note, and the effects can be heard in their subsequent breezy rendition of "On a Night Like This."

By Friday night, November 8th, Bob had finished the seventeen songs he'd set out to record with the Band. Saturday afternoon had been reserved for listening and sequencing, and when Rob Fraboni and Robbie Robertson arrived at the studio, they found Bob already there, lying on the floor in a corner of the control room. He was holding a tablet over his head, scribbling furiously on it with a felt-tipped pen. "Later on I might want to record something," he noted to Fraboni, before plunging back to work. Fifteen minutes passed. Then another fifteen. Suddenly Bob sprang to his feet, ripped off a sheet of paper, and said, "Okay, I'm ready." As Fraboni remembers it, he barely had enough time to get fresh tape on the board. Forget about mike levels, Bob was already in motion, running through the intro, and without any rehearsal or even time to see if his new words fit the music in his head, he closed his eyes and sang the beautifully evocative "Wedding Song." The album was complete.

The songs for *Planet Waves* had been cut in record time, but the album was still a long way from being delivered to an antsy, but enthusiastic, David Geffen. The tapes had to be mixed and mastered, and as luck would have it, Bob came down with a serious relapse of indecision. He sequenced the finished master seven or eight times. Even as the record was being pressed, he stopped it twice to change the order of the songs. Then he grew unsettled over the packaging. Originally, the album was going to be called *Wedding Song.* They'd shot a cover photograph of Bob on a chair in the back of a pickup truck, looking into the camera, but something didn't sit well with him. He agonized over the cover for days, playing with various themes from the songs, until, down to the wire, he ended up doing a charcoal sketch for it himself.

After three years and what seemed like a lifetime of obstacles, Bob Dylan finally had a new studio album set to go. What a wonderful feeling it must have been for him—almost a new beginning now that he was liberated from Woodstock, Albert Grossman, A. J. Weberman, and Columbia Records. He was genuinely pleased with the results. He liked all the songs, and his work with the Band had been pleasurable and productive. He was really proud of this album. It rang true. Yet there was something that continued to gnaw at him, a bit of unfinished business he had to take care of in order to feel completely at ease with it. He wanted to show off the new album. He wanted people not only to hear it but to experience it. Which meant that after eight years, it was time to hit the road again.

Part 5

The Second Coming

24

From Nowhere to Nowhere

Bob Dylan's return to the road in 1974 marked what was perhaps the most critical juncture of his career. His other milestones—Newport '65, Forest Hills, *Blonde on Blonde*, and, to some extent, even the Rolling Thunder Revue in 1976—occurred when he was riding a crest of popularity. Each found Bob performing vigorously, with an almost relentless determination, combining a tight schedule of concerts and interviews to promote new albums and introduce the bold songs he'd written to an impressionable audience.

Remarkably, as 1973 drew to a close, Dylan's appeal seemed stronger than ever—remarkable because it had nothing to do with what he was writing or singing at the time. How could it? After all, he hadn't appeared in concert in nearly eight years. The last five albums he'd released failed to stimulate any great interest or expand his craftsmanship, and, in fact, two of them—*Self-Portrait* and *Dylan* had antagonized all but a faithful few of his fans with what was perceived to be his cavalier attitude toward making records. Dylan was still presented as a folk hero in the rock press, nevertheless people were bewildered by his apparent inability to say anything new or powerful with his music. They blamed his creative mortality on the chaotic Sixties, which had laid waste to a pantheon of young heroes. Whereas Jimi Hendrix and Janis Joplin succumbed to the road's lethal adversities, Bob Dylan had apparently burned out. He had peaked early, then nose-dived into mediocrity, so that his fans—and they remained legion—were forced to idealize the past. They carried the torch for a phantom Bob Dylan, a Bob Dylan who, as a twenty-five-year-old renegade, had become the reluctant spokesman for his generation, but who, at thirty-two, seemed complacent and out of step with the times.

Like Elvis Presley, Bob had walked off the stage in his mid-twenties, at the height of his popularity, and in his absence was elevated to legendary status, with all its artistic constraints. Bob was remembered exactly the way he looked and wrote during the six months preceding his 1966 "accident." The college students who continued to wear out the grooves on his albums played *Highway 61 Revisited* and *Blonde on Blonde*, not *New Morning*. "Like a Rolling Stone" remained a staple of every FM playlist. It was as though he were preserved in a time capsule, a captive of his own mythic legacy. Certainly Elvis experienced a similar phenomenon on his return to the stage. The King had mounted a successful comeback in 1970, filling arenas and stadiums from coast to coast. But it was a financial, rather than a critical, success, for the Elvis audiences encountered bore no resemblance to the swivel-hipped rock 'n roller of "Hound Dog" fame, but instead was a pathetically awkward Vegas act that appealed mostly to suburban housewives.

That image of Elvis as a has-been had to have been fresh in everybody's minds as the dates for Bob Dylan and the Band's *Tour '74* were released to the press. Encompassing twenty-one cities and forty shows, the tour's announcement brought out all the cynics, who questioned its relevance at a time when rock was once again metamorphosing its sound.

"Who the hell wants to see Bob Dylan in concert in 1974?" asked Gary Stromberg, a prominent Hollywood music publicist. "He's history."

And to some extent so was the essence of what constituted rock 'n roll. By 1974, rock music was a fractionalized art form that had evolved in sound and in scope. No longer defined as strictly *teenage* music, it embraced three generations of fans whose tastes were as varied as their ages and experiences. Each wanted its own distinct flavor of rock 'n roll, and so the music became more heterogenous and more sophisticated. Financed by what was now a thriving commercial empire, experimenting artists created a vast palette of styles—actually idioms within the idiom—to spread the music's message to an unprecedented number of people.

The swiftness and extent of the change were breathtaking. By the end of 1973, rock 'n roll had splintered into at least five offbeat categories to keep the customers satisfied. There was *progressive rock* (Yes, the Moody Blues, Jethro Tull, Pink Floyd, and Emerson, Lake & Palmer); *hard rock* (Lynyrd Skynyrd, Grand Funk, Humble Pie, the James Gang, Deep Purple, and Led Zeppelin); *art rock* (David Bowie, T. Rex, Roxy Music, and Mott the Hoople); *singer-songwriters* (James Taylor, Cat Stevens, Elton John, Bruce Springsteen, and Billy Joel); and, of course, *R&B* (Barry White, the O'Jays, Isaac Hayes, and the Jackson Five). Reggae was introduced that year when Bob Marley and the Wailers made their first U.S. appearance as an opening act for Bruce Springsteen at Max's Kansas City. The first few months of 1974 also brought the release of two records which were to divide the rock audience even further along social and economic lines: "Rock the Boat," by the Hues Corporation, and George McCrae's "Rock Your Baby." These singles touched off the *disco* craze that swept pop music circles in the 1970s and reestablished the art of ballroom dancing as a cultural badge. Considering the revolutionary change taking place it's no wonder Bob Dylan wanted to go back on the road to keep from missing out.

Even so, he couldn't just pick up where he had left off in 1966. Concerts were no longer the respectful recitals that characterized Bob's previous tours. They were mass media events that required stadiums and arenas to meet the demand. And that, in turn, required a performer to present a more spectacular kind of show. Playing great music had become only a part of the overall presentation. Fans expected flash and special effects—something to transform those lifeless cinderblock arenas into a visual feast. *They wanted their money's worth.* And that took considerably more effort than throwing a band on stage for a rehash of the hits.

Practically all the people who bought tickets to the Bob Dylan/Band *Tour '74* claimed that what they wanted to see was the old Bob, the pesky troubadour who strode onto stage to assault the establishment with his verbal artillery. A witty, intellectual show. But, in fact, had Bob given the fans exactly what they'd asked for, the show would have proved uncomfortably dated and dull. It would have been received as a throwback to the Sixties. The places he was playing in the Seventies prohibited that kind of intimacy. They barred an entertainer from establishing a chummy rapport with his audience. Why, they weren't even called concert halls anymore, but *facilities*. What was Bob supposed to do—go on stage at a place like the Spectrum or Madison Square Garden and start singing "Hattie Carroll"? No, he knew that would only echo the thud produced by his *Dylan* album. It would also serve as a bleak admission that he was tapped out and had to rely on his decade-old hits, reducing Bob to another act on the rock 'n roll revival circuit. "This show is definitely not nostalgia," he told an interviewer from *Time*. "To my mind, I deal with certain problems. It's an up-to-date show."

Bob wanted to do the old songs, but he had to integrate them into a presentation that would be considered relevant to the times. Not that he had to resort to using lasers the way ELO did or imitate the Tubes and ride a motorcycle on stage. Bob needed a more practical device to get his songs across: *communication*. He had to make songs like "Blowin' in the Wind" and "Forever Young" ring true in a place that was built to feature ice hockey. And he had to overcome the curse which haunted him of being misunderstood in large arenas.

Huge houses had been scenes of nightmarish frustration for him. At Newport in 1965 the fans booed when they were unable to hear him, and at Forest Hills they had rushed the stage more out of a desire to see him than to actually touch any of the performers. Both catastrophes were the result of poor staging rather than his performance. They were tactical mistakes. Of course, a repeat of those incidents could be avoided if Bob stuck to small halls. Plenty of folk and rock acts opted for intimacy as opposed to extravaganza. And *money*. In 1974, a solo artist could make a hundred grand for one night at the Garden, instead of the pocket change you got at a place like Symphony Hall in Boston or Philadelphia's Academy of Music. Bob would have had to play ten one-night stands to equal that, requiring a long, arduous road trip. And you could forget that.

Bob also had an image to uphold, an image that required a bit of pomp and grandeur. Bob always thought of himself as the crowning point of a triumvirate: "It's the Beatles, the Stones, and *me*," he'd brag to friends. "Everyone else is in a different category." Could a star of that magnitude cower at the thought of playing arenas?

As it turned out, *Tour '74* was an inevitable chapter in the Bob Dylan story. He wanted to prove that he wasn't washed-up, and he wanted to perform. Performing was an addiction that Bob Dylan could never lick. It burned in him now the same way it had propelled a raw-boned Bobby Zimmerman onto the stage at Hibbing High School. Performing drove him to reckless extremes, but it also transformed his personality. Like so many brilliant songwriters, Bob always encountered difficulty as a conversationalist. He could rattle off a lethal put-down or expertly outjoust an interviewer, but when it came to everyday speech Bob's tongue corkscrewed the words into a blur of broken sentences. You'd never know it was the same guy who wrote all those poetic songs. In front of an audience, however, Bob was eloquent. "I'm only involved in communication when it's live," he told a journalist in a 1975 interview. The stage was the one place where he was able to unwind and feel completely at home.

Touring would be good therapy for him. Besides, he'd have plenty of friends to provide moral support. Members of the Band had been with him in some capacity or another since the middle of 1965, and by now they anticipated his every move. Bob was known to quixotically change the key of a song, or even an entire melody, at the last minute, and as if by magic, they'd be there alongside him, without missing a beat, playing as if they'd rehearsed it that way a hundred times. On stage he could even call for a song they'd never *heard* before and expect precision accompaniment. Precision, that is, wrapped in a roughhewn gunnysack of a sound that was as quirky and unpredictable as it was original, versatile, and bright-spirited. One critic complained that the Band's approach to music was marred by a "blasé professionalism," but that looseness, that seemingly disjointed, devil-may-care tempo they batted out, was exactly their hidden strength.

Three months before the tour, Bob and the Band held an impromptu rehearsal at a studio in California. Actually, "rehearsal" is a euphemism for what transpired that November afternoon. They *jammed* is what they did, and even that was too formal a description of the event, since neither Bob nor the musicians were disciplined enough to work out specific arrangements. What they did was to play bits and pieces of about eighty songs, one right after the next, often ending a number after the opening twelve or sixteen bars with the remark: "Yeah, that's it." Or: "We know that one—*next.*" No endings were worked out to anything; they'd take care of that on stage, in front of the audience. As for jotting down each song's key—forget it. The key was meaningless since Bob would change it nightly, depending upon his mood. He'd simply turn to Robbie Robertson, call out "'It Takes a Lot to Laugh'—B flat," and the song was under way. As usual, spontaneity would be standard operating procedure. And after a single, four-hour run-through, Bob said, "That's it," and not another note was "rehearsed" until the boys hit the open road.

Planning the tour, however, wasn't so easy. The last time Bob played concerts it was the Dark Ages of the rock music business. Back then, you simply announced your desire to perform, called up the usual promoters, and took off, lugging your instruments under your arm. By 1974, however, every group worth a gig had its own *organization* behind it. People to attend to the niggling details that were part of modern-day tours.

To play rock 'n roll, you needed lighting directors, staging designers, and sound engineers, and they, in turn, needed their *staffs,* so that by the time you got on the road, the entourage approached the population of Tongonoxie, Kansas. For instance, the sound technician begat the mix-down engineer who begat the wiring contractors who begat the equipment handlers, and so on down the line until, if you were Bob Dylan, you found yourself with eighteen sound and equipment men alone. Next you hired a tour director who hired a tour coordinator who hired a tour manager, and they, in turn, chose lieutenants like the press director who was responsible for flying in, housing, and providing tickets for the army of journalists whose requests for interviews with Bob were eventually processed by the press *associate.*

The trouble was, Bob Dylan didn't even have a manager to handle the most basic business arrangements for him. Since dumping Albert Grossman, he'd relied on the husband-wife team of Ben and Naomi Saltzman to oversee things like copyrighting his songs and depositing royalty checks in the proper bank account. Naomi had been one of Albert's assistants, but at that point she knew nothing about negotiating contracts. She wasn't hip to the hustles and dodges that were Albert's forte. And where was Bobby Neuwirth when he was needed? Bob hadn't seen hide nor hair of his old sidekick since the last tour, back in 1966. Word had it that Neuwirth was in Los Angeles working on his art and recovering from Edie Sedgwick's drug-overdose death, but, in fact, he and Bob had had a falling-out and were consciously staying out of each other's way. So that when Bob decided he'd tour again, there was no one to make the proper arrangements.

Robbie Robertson came up with a suggestion that ultimately saved the day. He'd mentioned Bob's dilemma to David Geffen, and Geffen directed them to an organization in the person of one Bill Graham. Graham was rock's ultimate entrepreneur—a hip-talking pitchman with a garment-center mentality. Once the kingpin of San Francisco's underground rock scene, Graham had put together a national network of post-hippie production, management, and record-company affiliates whose landmark Fillmore East and West were the psychedelic poles for his vast entertainment empire. Graham seemed like the perfect salve for Bob's problematic tour, and without any coaxing he agreed to put it on the road.

It was Graham who was responsible for turning the tour into a TOUR. He was in business to make money; and not one to mince words, he demanded they play only the biggest arenas and charge accordingly. Bob Dylan warranted top dollar. Until that time, seats at most rock shows went for a high of seven dollars, with rafter tickets scaled to three dollars and fifty cents. Graham argued that Bob Dylan could fetch at least nine dollars and fifty cents, maybe even ten dollars, the same price Elvis commanded for his comeback tour. Why, with a little promotion Graham bragged he could ask twenty dollars and still sell out each house. As it was, the tour was scaled to gross about five million dollars, which was quite a sum for its day.

The press concluded that ticket prices were outrageously high. Fans might boycott the tour in protest—that is, if they were even interested in seeing Bob Dylan in the first place. His box-office appeal was still a matter of speculation. Considering the shift in music, there was a chance only old hippies and peaceniks would give a damn. To almost everyone else, Bob Dylan was a relic of the Sixties. His name didn't mean a thing to young rock fans, many of whom were in diapers the last time he performed. They wanted to see musicians who smashed their equipment to smithereens as an encore or bit the heads off live chickens. They wanted the promise of—*sex!*

If there was any doubt about people wanting to see Bob Dylan in 1974, it was eliminated the moment tickets went on sale. The response was astounding—unprecedented. In New York alone, Graham received one-and-a-half million requests for the fifty thousand tickets available at the Garden. Chicago brokers sold thirty-seven thousand seats in two days. In Miami, fans caused a nine-mile traffic jam outside the Hollywood Sportatorium. San Francisco provided special mail centers to handle the demand. And in Philadelphia, where the Flyers still had trouble filling the stands, Bob sold out three consecutive shows at the Spectrum. In all, the tour received ticket requests amounting to over ninety-two million dollars, prompting one of the trade papers to calculate that roughly seven-and-a-half percent of the American population sought tickets to see Bob Dylan and the Band.

Only one question still hung over the tour: Could Bob Dylan live up to the fans' expectations? Could he still cut the ice? The lingering doubt annoyed everyone connected with the tour, but there was a degree of validity to it. First off, Bob was out of practice. He was a rusty hinge. Eight years between gigs took its toll on even the most natural of performers, especially one who had last trod the boards at twenty-four and was now pushing thirty-three. It took a lot more than confidence to entertain an audience in the Seventies. You couldn't just show up and sing; you had to convince them you were *hot*—the new American measure of quality. And there was a lot of competition out there. In the months immediately preceding and following Bob's show, the country's arenas were booked with acts like Rod Stewert, Jethro Tull, Elton John, the Rolling Stones, the Moody Blues, the Eagles, the Who, and the Edgar Winter Group, all of whom could work crowds into a frenzy. How were these same audiences going to react to a guy who came out and sang a six-minute monologue like "It's Alright Ma"? They weren't interested in political messages or thought-provoking songs. The last thing they wanted to be reminded of was the Sixties. Would Bob be able to engage the old fans anew? Not to mention that portion of the audience which was young enough to be his kids—the teenyboppers who bought tickets primarily because it was a media event and fuck the music, a Bob Dylan concert was the current place to be seen.

And how did Bob intend to work such immense houses? The stage would be two or three times larger than any he'd performed on before. His puny body would be a liability. Someone like David Bowie, who was also unnaturally short, distracted the crowds by wearing miniskirts and prancing across the stage amongst a chorus line of papier-mâché spiders. Elfish Elton John danced on top of the piano. And Iggy Pop stuck pins in his body and flung himself into the crowd. Alas, Bob Dylan had no gimmicks. He didn't have a choreographer or throw scarves, he didn't enter by wading through waves of dry ice or have a huge black saxophone player to play off of, and he wasn't a stud by any stretch of the imagination.

What it all came down to was his music. People had forgotten how much his songs expanded to fill a monstrous space. The songs had their own built-in dynamics, not the least of which was Bob's assertive voice. He'd learned how to use it as one would a fine instrument. Slipping into L.A.'s Forum to do a sound check/dress rehearsal, he learned how to project inside a nonacoustical arena. He kept apace with the megawatt amplification that drove the Band's equipment to near-ultrasonic pitch, so that come concert time the lyrics would carry to the uppermost seat. Then, of course, there were the songs themselves creating their own electric energy. When the organ broke into the opening vamp of "Rolling Stone," sparks flew in all directions. It produced the same jolting reflex that reached inside your craw as when Eric Clapton played the intro to "Layla," or Keith Richards picked out the eight-note feed into "Satisfaction." Bob could also do that with "Ballad of a Thin Man," "All Along the Watchtower," "Rainy Day Women," and a dozen other favorites. They were magical in any environment. And with the Band pumping out the music, all Bob had to do was to show up and be himself.

Opening night, January 3, 1974, a brittle nor'wester blew across the Great Lakes and sent the temperature in Chicago plummeting to single digits. Typically, Bill Graham grew panicky that the weather would fuck up his arrangements, but it didn't stop the masses from streaking to Chicago Stadium an hour before the show. Even outside the hockey arena, *Tour '74* was a typical Bill Graham production. Parking-lot attendants, clutching bouquets of dollar bills, directed cars to available spaces as an army of blue-jeaned vendors converged on their eager prey. Before a concertgoer even got to the gate, he or she was bombarded with concessions. Bob Dylan T-shirts in all colors and sizes went for three bucks, while hundreds of different buttons were hawked for a dollar apiece, about the same price as the bumper stickers and other festive Dylanware. Inside, concessions were replaced by security. After all, Graham was the guy who employed the Hell's Angels to police his

San Francisco promotions. There was no telling what kind of terrorist device a fan might sneak into a Bob Dylan concert, so anyone looking the least bit suspicious was pulled aside and patted down by one of the hulking, squinty-eyed goons that were stationed by the portals.

The inside shell of Chicago Stadium buzzed with anticipation. Fans who had waited years for this night were racked by two conflicting emotions: the expectant thrill of seeing Bob Dylan on stage and pure anxiety over the task facing their hero. Everyone there knew it'd be either a night of resounding triumph or a complete bust. All week, the Chicago papers debated Bob's ability to pull off such a comeback, and indeed many of the fans expressed identical concerns as they waited for the show to begin. "I'm real nervous. I'm dead scared he's gonna blow it," one of the ticketholders told a British music journalist. "He goes into obscurity, almost, then comes back to do this monstrous-sized tour. Just hope he doesn't shatter all our memories."

The fans, however, checked their fears when the lights dimmed. A deafening roar shook the arena as eighteen thousand people jumped to their feet. When the spots lit up the stage they revealed the Band standing poised behind their instruments. Then, without a word or announcement, a small figure swathed in a woolen muffler climbed the stairs behind the stage and walked to the microphone. The crowd let out another shriek of recognition as Bob Dylan strummed a few chords on his electric guitar and adjusted his harmonica brace. The continuous racket was louder than for any goal ever scored there by the Chicago Black Hawks, that was for sure. Bob looked petrified. Fixing his gaze on a point in the rear of the arena, he leered into the audience until the applause died down.

Speculation abounded over what song he'd open with. Some fans were convinced he'd blow them away with "Rolling Stone" or "Watchtower," while others knew he'd save them for the end. There were any number of classics that would electrify the audience and set the pace for his show. Bob began strumming in earnest as the audience struggled to identify the song. Was it "It Ain't Me, Babe" or "Mr. Tambourine Man"? For a moment it sounded like "Memphis Blues Again." Then the Band kicked in with a cool blast of rhythm, and it wasn't until Bob was halfway through the first verse that the real Dylan freaks in the crowd realized he was singing... "Hero Blues." An outtake from *Another Side of Bob Dylan!* A folk song! Was he out of his fucking mind? People clapped and bounced their heads up and down in time with the tempo, but the uniform expression on their faces was bewilderment. Eight years off, and the guy plays "Hero Blues." If that was an omen of things to come, it promised to be a helluva lot colder in Chicago than the thermometer indicated.

Once the initial shock had passed, Bob served up a menu of assorted Dylanesque treats that would remain his pattern for the next fifteen years: a full spectrum of the hits intermixed with R&B standards and the occasional outtake only a few die-hards would recognize. Almost defiantly, Bob revised the arrangements for most of his familiar songs, changing not only their tempos but often the tunes so that they were unidentifiable to the untrained ear until a well-known phrase shone through. From above, the audience resembled a massive chain reaction. You could actually read the confusion on peoples' faces.

"What's he doing now?"

"I'm not sure yet."

"Is it...'I Don't Believe You'?"

"I don't know. I think I heard him say something about roads."

"Roads...yeah, I think you're right. It's...it's...*'Blowin' in the Wind!'*"

Occasionally Bob slurred the words so badly that even the lyrics failed to identify the song. And his phrasing had been turned inside out. His voice ended "up" at the conclusion of each line so that the words hung in midair like so many unanswered questions. At first, people were annoyed by the realigned tunes. They took it personally, as if Bob were trying to confuse or make fun of them by disguising their favorite songs. In retrospect, however, it was a brilliant move on his part. If he'd sung the hits identically as he performed them eight years earlier, it would have reduced the concert to a golden oldies festival, or, more appropriately: Two Hundred Ways of Singing "Blowin' in the Wind." By changing the arrangements, he kept the audience off-balance and gave the songs a new dramatic sense by bringing them into the Seventies.

Still, neither Bob nor the Band was satisfied with their performance in Chicago. The pacing was all wrong. The momentum died after a few numbers, and the band began to work against itself trying to recover the excitement, which, most performers know, is suicide.

After the concert everyone gathered in a room at the Park Towers and tried to figure out what went wrong. A tape of the concert was played, and, as the musicians listened intently, Bill Graham and David Geffen exchanged nervous glances. Both men were thinking the same thing. Had they overestimated Bob's ability to entertain the jaded crowds? Was there a chance he couldn't carry it off and the tour would bomb? The Chicago papers had liked what they'd heard, and *Rolling Stone* delivered a rave. (Predictably, their critique of the show began: "Bob Dylan, praise him, is back."). But the reviews could be deceiving. An old hoofer like Graham knew the fans in 1974 were immune to hype. If the next few concerts were dull, they'd put the word out on the grapevine, and by the time the tour reached San Francisco, the Bob Dylan Show would be about as relevant as last week's stock quotations.

Were that to happen, David Geffen emerged as the person most likely to take a bath. He was sitting on seven-hundred fifty thousand copies of *Planet Waves* that were waiting to be shipped to record stores. Those albums had suddenly turned into a keg of dynamite. The original release date had been set for January 3rd to coincide with the tour, but due to a last-minute cover change it had been pushed back to January 17th. Usually, an exciting tour spun exultant audiences from their seats into the nearest record store, increasing an LP's sales by as many as a million or more units. That was why record-company logic determined that albums had to be in the stores a week before opening night. That way, if the tour stiffed, they'd still have a week or two headway to sell albums on hype alone before word leaked out to the fans. Not so, however, if your album wasn't coming out until the third week of the tour. If Bob couldn't pull the show together in time, it was conceivable that Geffen would eat six-hundred fifty thousand copies of *Planet Waves*. Couple that with the prospect of displeasing, and ultimately losing, Bob Dylan as an Asylum Records artist, and he had a potential disaster on his hands.

Bob and the Band, along with Rob Fraboni, Graham, and Geffen, dissected the taped performance until four that morning, when it became clear to everyone where the problem was. With great relief they concluded that it wasn't Bob's performance that weighted down the show. Nor was the Band deadwood; their music was hot and explosive when it came to reinforcing Bob's voice, and they proved a credible attraction in their own right. No, it was something more conspicuous and evidently simpler to correct: the show's *pacing* stunk. It was wildly uneven and, as such, proved too distracting for the audience.

The way the show had been laid out, Bob would play a few songs, then remain on stage while the Band featured a medley of numbers from their recent album, after which Bob drifted back into the spotlight until it was time for intermission. Then, he'd stroll out with an acoustic guitar and play a short solo set before being rejoined by the Band. As it turned out, the sequencing never allowed any one performer to establish his ground for a comfortable length of time and left the audience feeling as if it were on a roller coaster. Eventually, Bob would work around to "Like a Rolling Stone," but by that time he'd already lost the audience's attention.

The next night they broke it up differently, so that Bob and the Band each had a chance to establish their own ground. Bob appeared on stage, and—BOOM!—the songs hit you like a Mack truck: "Lay Lady Lay," "Just Like Tom Thumb's Blues," "It Ain't Me, Babe," "Tough Mama," "Ballad of a Thin Man," "All Along the Watchtower," one right after the next, each one harder-hitting and leaner. By intermission, the audience was dazed and somewhat out of breath. When Bob came back for an encore with "Like a Rolling Stone" and then "Maggie's Farm" the response was deafening. The fans danced on their seats and lunged at the stage in a display of hysteria right out of the early days of rock 'n roll.

As the tour zigzagged across North America, the pandemonium rose in pitch, and almost proportionately, Bob Dylan grew more relaxed. He regained his old confidence on stage, often straddling the mike, legs thrown astride, in the manner of Elvis or Gene Vincent. Occasionally, he appeared in whiteface or pancaked his cheeks with glitter, and on those brazen nights when the stage seemed like the last safe place on earth, he permitted his eyes to be limned with blue eyeshadow and mascara. And as Bob loosened up, the Band plugged into the excitement and turned up the musical heat a couple hundred degrees. On stage they rocked with an intensity rarely demonstrated by a backup group. And offstage they provided just the right touch of relief.

The guys in the Band were frisky little devils. At some point one of them decided to restructure the post-concert groupie situation. Too often they were besieged by homely women anxious to win an invitation back to one of their hotel rooms. It was awkward saying "no" to someone who had you cornered over a roast beef sandwich, so invariably the guys'd get stuck spending the night with someone they weren't interested in, when the backstage area was a feast of eligible young dazzlers. How do you avoid facing a roomful of unsorted candidates? Easy. One of the Band members bought a Polaroid camera and instructed an assistant of Bill Graham's to photograph all the women who wanted to come backstage. In no time, the guys had a female smorgasbord spread out on a table in their dressing room. "Okay, this one can come back, get rid of that one, give this chick to one of the equipment men..." The Band kept the tour moving with carefree good humor.

There was only a moment of distress brought on, in part, by an old friend, and that occurred as the entourage reached Oakland, California. For weeks, the press had stirred up interest in Bob's alleged ties to Israel. Most reports cited his "pledge" to send fifty percent of the tour's net to aid Israel in the Mideast war. *Newsweek* quoted no less a reliable source than A. J. Weberman, who said, "He is an ultra-Zionist. He is doing the tour to raise money for Israel. He has given large sums of money to Israel in the name of Abraham [sic] Zimmerman." Mostly, this was Weberman's specialty—garbage. But it stuck a thorn in the side of one spiritual foe.

Mimi Fariña was still smarting over old wounds from the Sixties when she reread Weberman's accusations. Mimi, who worked alongside her sister Joan at their Institute for the Study of Nonviolence, in Berkeley, was incensed that Bob Dylan, of all people, would commingle the virtues of music with a cause as hideous as war. Especially after everything Joanie had taught him about peace and resistance and the struggle to improve human rights. What a shitty thing to do, she thought. Money from the pockets of people who paid to hear him sing was being used to perpetrate war and killing. She fumed, "Well, that little prick—I'll get him. I may not have his power, but I've got some friends in the press who'll help me make a point." Picking up the phone, she called a reporter at the *San Francisco Chronicle* and told him that she was going to write an open letter to Bob Dylan.

It must have smelled like good copy because two days before Bob's Oakland concerts, Mimi's letter ran in a box on the *Chronicle*'s Op-Ed page. In it, she questioned his right to contribute tour profits to a foreign war and argued that Bob owed his fans an explanation. "The money you earn is the money we are willing to give you," she wrote. ". . . if it is going to support the taking of more lives, we should know that before we buy our tickets. Perhaps the question could be clarified by a statement to the press."

Fat chance of that ever happening. Bill Graham ordered the crew to keep the paper out of Bob's hands, and he barred the press from conducting interviews with Bob before the first Oakland show. "Knowing that it gave a guy like Bill Graham a little bit of a twinge was satisfaction enough for me," Mimi says today. "Also people credit Dylan with having more strength than he actually has and the fact that they had to keep the article from him reveals just how weak and powerless people really think he is."

A portion of Mimi's letter was eventually read to Bob, but it had absolutely no effect on the way he performed. In Oakland, just as in every city along *Tour '74*'s itinerary, he was a feast for sore ears and a revelation to the fans. Clad in a sportcoat and skin-tight jeans, Bob Dylan proved he was still the heavyweight champion of rock 'n roll. In an era devoid of personal commitment and political causes, fans still searched his lyrics for hidden meaning. Flashing an OK sign over his head, the spokesman for many generations strummed through a final chorus of—what else?—"Blowin' in the Wind," then sauntered peacefully off the stage. His message for the Seventies was clear: "There's a lot more left to come."

25

Chile and Hot Times

Bob was on the road when the news broke that the government of Chile had been overthrown by its military. Though the story probably eluded him, it had a devastating effect on other members of the New York folk community.

Pete Seeger, for one, had informal ties to members of the now-deposed Allende government and performed several Chilean folk songs in his repertoire. For Phil Ochs, the revolution meant a more personal and tragic loss. Ochs had maintained a close, albeit long-distance, friendship with folksinger Victor Jara, who was often described as "the Bob Dylan of Chile." As a result of the coup, Jara had been classified an enemy of the state, then dragged into Santiago's National Stadium where he was tortured and finally executed by members of General Pinochet's ruling junta.

Ochs was severely shaken by the news of Jara's death. Immediately, he set out to organize a concert to benefit the Chilean refugees and, in no small part, to embarrass CIA officials, whom he blamed for the coup. "I'm gonna pull this thing off if it's the last thing I do," he told a friend one night over drinks at Max's Kansas City. "I've already lined up the Felt Forum. And we're gonna have John Denver and Joan Baez and Bob Dylan and Frank Sinatra and Shirley MacLaine." Ochs then proceeded to get completely wasted and passed out, a condition that augured the concert plans themselves.

Ochs was in no shape to promote a folk concert, much less sing at one. His career had been in a kamikaze nosedive, brought on by fits of self-destructive fantasy. He struggled with alcoholism, manic depression, paranoia bordering on madness, and, worse perhaps, he had lost his voice as a result of having been mugged in Africa. Unable to sing, Ochs masqueraded as a political radical until the Chilean benefit materialized, and his Janus-like personality found a new focus.

The trouble was, nobody gave a damn about Phil Ochs or his concert. As an activist, he was a Model A in an era of hatchback sedans. He was an old hippie, struggling to keep the movement alive at a time when it was already considered long dead and buried. Politics was anathema to a generation of budding art-rockers who were content to entrust it to the politicians. To them, Sixties phenomena like drugs, Woodstock, peace, were relics of primitive man. The last thing they wanted to hear about was a Marxist politician from South America and the problems of Spanish-speaking refugees. And so, two weeks before the gig, only four hundred of the six thousand seats at the Felt Forum had been sold. The way it was shaping up, Phil Ochs had a major disaster on his hands. Not only wasn't he going to raise any money for the Chilean refugees, but his friends who'd put up a fifteen-thousand-dollar guaranty for the show were going to take a whopping bath.

His biggest problem was the entertainment. So far, only Pete Seeger, Dave Van Ronk, Melanie, and Arlo Guthrie had committed themselves to perform, and in 1975 they were comparable to the floor show at a Jewish hotel in the Catskills. John Denver was unavailable, Frank Sinatra was uninterested, and Joan Baez—to hear Phil tell it—was just plain uncharitable. Joan declined on the grounds that she had other things to do that night, which really infuriated Phil, considering she'd had her only hit single with his song "There But For Fortune."

"She's a no-class *bitch!*" he told Faris Bouhafa, the assistant manager at Max's, who was helping him with booking the talent. That night, at the club, the two men commiserated over an endless succession of drinks. The concert was in trouble, they both knew it, and it seemed they'd either have to come up with a last-minute miracle or pull the plug. Ochs, blinded by booze, began paging through a tattered copy of the *Village Voice* that someone had left on the table. In the music section, he squinted at an ad for Buffy Sainte-Marie, who was playing across town at a new club called the Bottom Line. "Hey, man, what have we got to lose? Let's go over there and see if Buffy wants to do our show," he suggested. "Maybe she can help us sell tickets."

Obviously, it was the act of a desperate man. Buffy Sainte-Marie might bring in five or ten old folkies, but a serious block of fans? Not a chance. The time was long past when a folksinger could draw a crowd in New York. Still, Ochs and Bouhafa stumbled over to the Bottom Line in the hope that they could pad the passenger list of their sinking ship.

When they arrived, Buffy was finishing the last few songs of the late show. The room was fairly light, there was a straggler or two at the bar, and Ochs walked over there to order a drink before last call. He was already drunk and reeling, barely able to stay on his feet. Then, as he inhaled the tumbler of vodka in his hands, Phil started to stare at a guy standing a few feet away from him at the bar. The last thing Faris wanted was for Phil to start up with someone, but before he could intercede, Phil was pointing with excitement. "I know that guy!" he insisted.

Bouhafa put a restraining hand on his shoulder. "C'mon, man—let's watch the show."

Too late. Phil walked over to the stranger and jabbed him in the ribs. "Hey! You're that kid from Minnesota who wrote a song about South American miners, right?"

Bob Dylan grinned at his old friend and said, "Yup."

"Well, I'm giving a benefit for those miners in two weeks and you're gonna be there!" Bob seemed startled and didn't answer. "When this show is over I want you to come over to my house and hear something."

There is no doubt that Phil's request was facilitated by the ridiculous amount of alcohol in his system. Bob and he hadn't spoken in almost ten years, and their last encounter had ended disastrously. It had been in 1966, after one of Bob's appearances at Carnegie Hall. Backstage, he played Phil the final mix of his new single, "Can You Please Crawl out Your Window," and was told it wasn't up to snuff. Enraged, Bob invited Phil to a post-concert party and offered him a ride so that he could order his limo driver to pull over and throw Phil out of the car.

Phil had always idolized Bob and gauged his own limitations as a performer against Bob's mega-success. After that rift their friendship was based on two incompatible emotions: love and hate. Around Bob, Phil always managed to say and do the wrong thing. He gushed over Bob's songs *in the press*—where everyone could see it. Phil was an aggressively passionate man whose obviousness left him wide open to the emotional punches, and during the mad years nobody had a more effective one-two combination than Bob Dylan.

Now, ten years later, the two men were able to face each other as friends. All that had gone before them suddenly melted away as Bob accompanied Phil to his tiny apartment on Prince Street. Little, however, did Bob realize what lay in store for him. He admitted he knew nothing of the events in Chile or their repercussions. That was an invitation for Phil to roll out a five-hour chronicle of South American history in song and sketches. He literally put on a one-man show for Bob, describing the Marxist regime of Salvador Allende in all its splendor, how it transformed Chile into an allegory for humanitarianism despite CIA interference, and gave the country its first real glimmer of hope. Then, for an encore, he reenacted a perfect recitation of Allende's ill-fated inaugural address. Bob was overwhelmed by Phil's performance and pumped him for more information about Chile, until the sun came up, the wine ran out, and the two men went their separate ways.

Faris Bouhafa waited until a decent hour, then telephoned Phil at his home. "What happened?" he asked excitedly. "Is he going to do the concert or isn't he?"

Phil said, "He told me there was a ninety-nine percent chance that he was coming."

"Phil, we need a more definite commitment than that. We're two weeks away from the concert. We've got over four thousand seats to sell. From where I sit, ninety-nine percent assurance isn't good enough."

"Oh, yes it is," Phil replied, and Bouhafa could almost see him grinning over the phone. After hanging up, Phil called the *Village Voice* and offered them a scoop in return for a short feature on the concert. The next week the paper ran an item which ended with a quote from Phil saying, "Dylan told me that there was a ninety-nine percent chance he was coming." That was good enough for the New York public, and within twenty-four hours the Felt Forum was a complete sellout.

Recalls Faris Bouhafa, "Now we've really got a problem. We don't know what condition Phil was in that night or what Dylan told him. What we *did* know was what condition Phil had been in for the last two weeks—crazy, maniacal, out of control, constantly drunk—so it was possible he had imagined it or was making it up or had done it as some kind of suicidal joke. And we did know one other thing: that we were going to have close to five thousand people who bought tickets to see Bob Dylan, and if he didn't show up our ass was in the ringer."

Bouhafa figured his safest bet was to confirm the date with Bob. After several phone calls, he dialed the concert office. "*He's split for California!*" he near-shrieked to a tranquil Phil Ochs. They continued trying to reach Bob, but to no avail. He covered his tracks better than an international terrorist, and no one connected with his office was willing to act as an intermediary. "Relax," Ochs sighed confidently. "There's nothing we can do about it now anyway, so just keep your fingers crossed and be cool."

Cool, he said. *Cool!* The concert was sold out. The media were covering it as a major social and political event. The State Department had pledged its assistance should any of Pinochet's thugs try to interrupt the show. A dais of luminaries had promised to speak to the audience. And all because Phil Ochs, town drunk, claimed Bob Dylan said there was a ninety-nine percent chance of his making an appearance. Sure, Bouhafa thought, he'd be cool—when his body turned up in the morgue after the audience got through with him!

The morning of the concert there was still no word from Bob Dylan. The equipment vans pulled up in front of the Felt Forum about ten o'clock. At noon, musicians started to arrive for a sound check. Not a word from Bob. By two, even Ochs's confidence started to unravel. He'd gone through a hip flask of liquor and sent Bouhafa out to see if he could rustle up a few fifths. As Faris turned the corner of Seventh Avenue, a short man with a guitar case walked up to him.

"Hi. You got any idea where the stage is?" he asked.

Bouhafa pointed to a small door on Thirty-Third Street. "Right there," he said. "But you've got to show some ID or find someone who knows you if you expect to get past the guard."

The man wrinkled up his face and shrugged. "Nobody told me nothing about that. My name is Bob. I'm supposed to be here for a show tonight."

Bouhafa did a double-take and nearly passed out. Bob! It was Bob all right. Bob Dylan actually showed up! They were saved. "Something tells me you won't have any trouble getting inside," Bouhafa said, barely able to contain his excitement.

The air inside the Felt Forum's torpid stage area became instantly cool and refreshing as Bob Dylan strolled through the door. Everyone's pulse rate returned to normal, aside from that of Phil Ochs, who was operating at a manic pace. Teetering on the brink of insanity as the clock ticked toward concert time, he had worked himself into a state of nervous exhaustion over Bob's uncertain appearance. He nearly collapsed when the big moment finally arrived.

"Deep down, I think Phil was sure that Bobby would show up," says Dave Van Ronk of that frantic afternoon. "But, then, Phil was an optimist; that was his curse. I'm naturally a pessimist, and knowing what I do of Dylan's politics I really didn't think he would show." Nevertheless, Van Ronk smiled proudly when Bob walked in—proud, not so much that he decided to do the right thing by the Chilean refugees, but that he bailed out his friend Phil Ochs.

Van Ronk dragged Bob off to the balcony, where they reminisced and traded slugs from a bottle of wine. By late afternoon, both men were asleep on the other's shoulder. Then, around six o'clock, they crept off to the Iron Horse, a commuters tavern in Penn Station, where they hooked up with actor Dennis Hopper and proceeded to get shit-faced drunk. When the concert finally started and Ochs introduced his pals from the stage, it resembled a benefit to combat chronic alcoholism. Bob and Van Ronk looked like a couple of derelicts who had wandered in off Seventh Avenue. They were off their nut. By the time they got to the finale, a jug of wine had been uncorked on stage, and as the ensemble broke into "Blowin' in the Wind," Van Ronk had to keep whispering the lyrics into Bob's ear.

The Chilean benefit signaled a momentous shift in Bob's career. What a relief it had been not to be a spokesman or a prophet, but just

Bob again. Just one of the guys who had gotten good and drunk and jammed with some friends. He was back on a New York stage without the Band and it felt great. A throwback to those wonderful, innocent days on the Street.

If Bob was indeed trying to recapture something from his past, the ball was set in progress a few days later when destiny took another twist. Ron Delsener, New York's foremost concert promoter, took a call from Phil Ochs that shimmered with promise. "Let's meet in the Carnegie Hall Tavern," Phil said. "I want to talk to you, Bob wants to talk to you." Fashionably two hours late for the meeting, Bob and Phil sat down with a hot proposition: they wanted to tour together.

Delsener's first reaction was that they were pulling his leg. Bob Dylan and Phil Ochs—in concert? What a preposterous double bill. Why, Ochs wasn't well enough to get on an uptown bus by himself much less undertake a major tour. And as if that weren't absurd enough, they proposed to do only small halls and coffeehouses and to donate the proceeds to charity.

This was one of the seeds for what eventually became the Rolling Thunder Revue. And even though Ochs's dream tour was postponed, in the summer of 1974 it was enough for Bob to flirt openly with recapturing the past.

For the time being, he had more substantial matters on his mind. Namely, his recording contract with Asylum Records, which was drifting dangerously toward the rocks. Bob made no secret of the fact that he was unhappy with the way *Planet Waves* had been handled. Geffen had shipped 771,000 copies, and the album had enjoyed a swift, if fleeting, success; however, Bob expected sales to exceed several million units considering the number of requests they'd had for concert tickets. Alas, he failed even to outsell other Asylum albums released at the same time by Carly Simon and Joni Mitchell. In the end, *Planet Waves* sold a meager 600,000 copies, which Geffen considered "fantastic for Bob."

It was that kind of condescending remark which ultimately sent Bob packing. He'd had enough of Geffen—his hogging the spotlight, his shooting off his mouth at the most inopportune times. In fact, Geffen's main concern seemed to be hanging out with Hollywood celebrities—especially Cher, whom it was rumored he would marry—

and that wasn't Bob's way. Unfortunately, Bob had a live album from the tour ready to be released, and it was essential he get it out before the excitement cooled down. Should he be forced to negotiate with another record company it was likely to take too much time. And even if he signed with someone else, the new company'd never have enough time to gear up a proper promotional campaign. Geffen was willing to put the album out immediately on Asylum Records. He had all the machinery in place, and it provided a consistent identification factor, what with Bob and Asylum's well-publicized recent partnership. Still, it rankled Bob to put another album into David Geffen's hands.

Returning to California following the Chile benefit, Bob searched for an alternative to releasing the album through Asylum. Before long, he and Robbie Robertson came up with a novel approach that suited their cynical impression of the record industry: they'd sell the album through late-night television, as though it were a Veg-O-Matic. Close your eyes and you can almost visualize the ad campaign...

It's after midnight, Johnny Carson finishes kibbitzing with Zsa Zsa Gabor about alimony payments, and he breaks for station identification. An ad comes on for Toro lawn mowers, and then... Bob Dylan, *the snarling darling of late-night TV, walking along the beach at Malibu. At once, he stops and smiles*—smiles!—*directly into the camera. "Friends," he says in that familiar Mesabi Range drawl, "were you one of the countless millions who sent in for tickets to my last tour, only to be told it was...* sold out? *Are you tired of missing out on those once-in-a-decade extravaganzas? Well, now, for a limited time, you, too, can experience the breathtaking excitement of hearing Bob Dylan in concert, with my new album*—Before the Flood." *At which point the song titles begin a rapid crawl over the screen. The scene dissolves to a closeup of a young couple, arms entwined in the orchestra section of an arena, as they squeal in obvious delight to an off-screen encounter with Bob singing "Positively 4th Street." Cut to stock footage of Bob and the Band riding the Log Flume at Disney World, their arms flailing in the air as the car plunges headfirst into the water. As ten seconds from "All Along the Watchtower" plays, we see Bob atop a horse, cantering along the crest of the Hollywood Hills, which segues into a shot of Bob and Sara at sunset, overlooking the surf, to a snatch of "Knockin' on Heaven's Door." "And that's only a fraction of what you'll get," he says, over live concert footage of the tour. "There's*

'It Ain't Me, Babe,' 'Just Like a Woman,' and that grand, old favorite . . . 'Blowin' in the Wind.'" At which point he intercuts a clip from the March on Washington, with thousands of people singing "how many roads must a. . . ."

That'd get 'em, all right. He could sell millions of copies on nostalgia alone. It provided him with a built-in market, unlimited potential, and absolutely no record-company participation. The increase in profits, alone, would be enough to warrant the extra effort. Let David Geffen play mogul with Carly Simon's records.

Incredibly, Bob might have gone ahead with this outrageous scheme had Clive Davis not talked him out of it. Davis, who had been living in virtual seclusion since his ouster from Columbia Records, proposed yet another method by which Bob could retain control of *Before the Flood*—by bypassing the record companies and selling it directly to rack-jobbers and distributors. Usually, that was the last resort of an artist whose tape had been rejected by the major labels, although in Bob's case it was unlikely to be misinterpreted as an act of desperation. Davis convinced him it was classier than huckstering the album on TV and more profitable, and Bob would have gone ahead with it had Geffen not kicked up a fuss.

Geffen objected that since he had helped put the tour together, Bob owed him the album. It was a moral obligation that he expected to be honored. And how would it look, after all that work and publicity, if Bob walked out? Even Clive Davis admitted Geffen would lose face if he didn't get the next Dylan album. Bob clearly didn't know how to resolve the problem, and his dilemma intensified when Columbia Records reentered the picture.

Columbia regretted having let Bob slip through its fingers and designed a nifty deal to win him back. It offered him a higher royalty, amounting to about sixty cents more per album, plus incentives, and dangled the old sweetener in which ownership of his masters reverted to him at the end of five years. It was hard to pass up an offer like that. Geffen couldn't possibly match it, but he wasn't about to make it easy for Bob. He agreed to match Columbia's royalty figure, and leaned even harder on the so-called "moral obligation." It was a ludicrous ploy, but in the end Bob prevailed by making a deal with . . . *both* labels.

Geffen got *Before the Flood*; Columbia would put out Bob's future albums, though his outrageously high royalty rate precluded either label making much of a profit. What each won, however, was the "honor" of including Bob Dylan on its artist roster. Three years later, Geffen put that word in what he thought was its proper perspective: "I trusted him, and he fucked me."

All the wheeling and dealing must have made Bob homesick for the studio because he seemed in a hurry to get back to work. That September, he notified John Hammond Sr. that he'd like to book time at Columbia Studios—a four-day sweep beginning on September 12th. Hammond pointed out that the 12th happened to be the first day of Rosh Hashanah. Bob shrugged with exaggerated indifference. "Why not? It's the New Year, isn't it?" he responded, and the dates were set.

That morning, Eric Weissberg, a guitar player who'd made a name for himself by playing on the hit single "Dueling Banjos," bumped into his friend, producer Phil Ramone, on the street outside of Columbia Studios. Ramone complained that he was supposed to do a Bob Dylan session that night, but, incredibly, the songwriter had yet to book a band. "Are you and the guys available, just in case?" he asked Weissberg. "Sure," Eric replied, although with some hesitation. He and his band, Deliverance, were one of the highest-priced session groups in New York, and as such, they had been in and out of studios, working steadily for nearly a week. They needed some time off. But the chance to work with Bob Dylan was too great a temptation to pass up. "We can make it," he shrugged, confirming the date, and the stage was set for a long, circuitous session that would eventually produce the great album, *Blood on the Tracks*.

The session started off as a typical Bob Dylan production: no charts, no rehearsal, no preparation. Just the usual, "Okay, let's get started. Here's how the first song goes. . . ." The musicians had no trouble following him, but as the night wore on, they couldn't click into the proper groove. As Weissberg remembers it, "I got the distinct feeling Bob wasn't concentrating, that he wasn't interested in perfect takes. He'd been drinking a lot of wine, he was a little sloppy, but he insisted on moving forward, getting on to the next song without correcting obvious mistakes."

At no time was that clearer to Weissberg than after they'd laid down the tracks to the first song, "Simple Twist of Fate." "We were listening to the playback—not in the control room but in the studio,"

Weissberg recalls, " and in the middle of it, Bob starts running down the second song for us. He couldn't have cared less about the sound of what we had just done. And we were totally confused, because he was trying to teach us a new song with another one playing in the background. I was thinking to myself, 'Just remember, Eric, this guy's a genius. Maybe this is the way geniuses operate.'"

Despite the distractions, they managed to lay down four songs in roughly three hours. Says Weissberg, "The stuff sounded great, and we were satisfied. We were also told to show up the next day to continue work on the session, but that morning someone called telling us not to bother." Instead, Bob began working with a new cast of session men, including Paul Griffen and Buddy Cage, who completed work on the album.

At least, that was what everyone thought.

Columbia was set to release *Blood on the Tracks* on December 25, 1974. Test pressings had been sent out to radio stations, a cover was printed which included liner notes written by New York journalist Pete Hamill, and an ad campaign to support the record had been approved. As this was Bob's first album since returning to Columbia Records, everyone at the label was psyched. Columbia had great expectations for it. The only trouble was, Bob Dylan wasn't satisfied.

Bob had spent the holiday season visiting his family back in Minneapolis. It was while he was there that he and his brother, David, listened to the tapes and grew completely disenchanted with what they heard. Both men agreed that something was missing. The songs were terrific as songs went, but they had no life to them, no drive. They sounded similar to the sessions Bob had done for *Nashville Skyline* or *The Times They Are A-Changin'*, and the last thing he wanted to make was another folk album. He couldn't let the new album go out sounding that way, so the night before it was to be released he called Columbia and had it hold up pressing the record.

The album needed a drastic overhaul, but time, as Bob had been forewarned, was of the essence. The press and radio stations were expecting a new Dylan record, and any delay would be attributed to artistic difficulties. Still, he was determined to take as much time as was necessary to perform the songs to his satisfaction. That could be a week, a month, six months, or maybe he'd wind up scrapping the album and start anew.

It was David Zimmerman, of all people, who came up with a reasonable solution. For years, David had been struggling to build his own identity among the Minneapolis music community, first as a composer, then as a manager and record producer. He'd enjoyed some minor success with a Canadian folksinger named Michael Lessac and another country-rock performer, but for the most part his success was overshadowed by the fact that his older brother happened to be the poet laureate for an entire generation. That haunted him, so that in 1974 David had all but abandoned the local music business in favor of a career that demanded less of BOB DYLAN'S BROTHER, but he still had tremendous resources in Minneapolis. He was convinced Bob could find what he was looking for without traveling back to New York.

With Bob's blessing, David assembled an exceptional group of local musicians, two of whom—Bill Berg and Bill Peterson—were considered great jazz artists in their own right. Kevin Odegard, another of David's recruits, had cut several records as a pop act but was working as a brakeman on the Chicago Northwestern Railroad when he was called for the gig. And Greg Imhoffer, a piano player, and guitarist Chris Weber worked sporadically in the burgeoning Minneapolis pop scene that would soon sprout the likes of Prince and the Replacements. David's greatest inspiration, however, was the studio—Sound 80—a state-of-the-art facility situated across the river from Dinkytown in the Seward section of the city. Minneapolis's great experiment in professional recording, Sound 80 was big, lush, and beautifully laid out, and as technically advanced as any New York studio Bob had ever worked in. Plus it was *private*; there were no groupies or press lackeys hanging around, no record company representatives dropping in to make sure things were on schedule. Only his brother, David, whom Bob had grown to rely on and trust.

Bob showed up at Sound 80 on Friday, December 27, 1974. As usual, the charts for the songs were all in his head, but he'd actually prepared the lyrics to "Idiot Wind" on a series of pink "While You Were Out" message slips, which he spread out across a music stand like cue cards. The band ran through it once. Then Bob walked off to the vending machines and came back with a new verse he'd written while having a soda. They did a second take incorporating the new lyrics and immediately hit the groove. It was like a jolt of pure energy. Bob had finally managed to unlock the song and was turned on by the musicians' fresh, if somewhat raw, imput. David suggested a retake, but Bob wanted to move on. "Tangled Up in Blue" had given him nothing but headaches, and he wanted to give it a try while the band was hot.

Again, almost miraculously, a song was rescued from inertia by enthusiastic advice from his young group. Kevin Odegard listened to a run-through, then suggested that Bob transpose it up a full key, from G to A, which would give his performance more energy and allow him to jump on the lyrics and spit them out with more authority. David, meanwhile, rewrote the drum figures, adding an exaggerated high-hat and snare to push the rhythm section behind his brother's voice. "We were going for a real hybrid sound," recalls Kevin Odegard, whose job it was to teach the song to the rest of the band. "Bob had chosen to use a stand-up bass, brushes on the drums, and a Hammond B-3 organ, which he overdubbed later that night, so that in the end, it was a real mix of old and new sounds, though it was specifically made clear to us that Bob wanted to duplicate the sound he'd gotten on *Highway 61*."

By the end of the day, Bob Dylan was on fire. The songs which had eluded him in New York were finally coming to life, they were beginning to sound the way he'd originally envisioned them. The emotion and the irony shone through the busy arrangements; Bob's voice was sharp. The band was good enough to get by with, and with his brother riding shotgun for him in the studio, it wouldn't be long before he could wrap up the project.

In the end, all it took was another day of recording to achieve that formidable goal. He'd given the band the weekend off, and when they regrouped on Monday the momentum proved every bit as supercharged and productive. The band breezed through a single take of "You're a Big Girl Now." That was all it needed as far as Bob was concerned; the imperfections that remained attested to the record's spontaneous atmosphere—perhaps capturing that "thin, wild mercury sound" he pursued ten years earlier. The next song, "If You See Her, Say Hello," proved more troublesome, if only for an awkward instrumental line that rode above the melody. Bob had always wanted a mandolin to play in counterpoint to his guitar and instructed his brother to book another musician. David responded by hiring a local virtuoso named

Peter Ostroushko who played with many of Minneapolis's top performers. Halfway through the first take, Bob stopped to call attention to a problem: the mandolin wasn't playing in a high enough register to complement the melody. He asked Ostroushko to play further up the neck of the instrument, but the musician refused, complaining that it would hurt his fingers. Besides, he argued, it was a physical impossibility to hit notes clearly that high on the neck.

Bob shook his head in disgust. Walking across the studio floor, he took the mandolin out of Ostroushko's hands and signaled the engineer. "Let's take it from the top," he said, pressing the chunky instrument to his chest. Then, leaning into the horizontal microphone he picked out the mandolin part himself, with all the flutters and flourishes, and finished the song in a single take. They added two versions of the epic "Lily, Rosemary, and the Jack of Hearts" and called it a day.

Blood on the Tracks wrapped in only two days of additional studio time—in Minneapolis, of all places!—relieving major anxiety at CBS. "Four of the songs, with the exception of 'Idiot Wind' were all session mixes," recalls Paul Martinson, who engineered the Minnesota dates. "Which means they were made the night we cut the tunes. They were only slightly better than rough mixes. I made a tape copy of the day's work for Bob and David to take home and study, and those were the mixes that ended up on the record."

Columbia rushed out *Blood on the Tracks* in early January 1975, to only a tremble of popular excitement. As it was the third Bob Dylan album to appear in under a year, the anticipation was comparatively muted—perhaps even suspicious, considering the haste with which it was made. Thinking Bob might be trading on his myth and not his music, the fans approached the album with misgiving, and as a result, they were staggered by what they heard.

Blood on the Tracks wasn't simply another of Bob's cut-and-paste jobs with a few decent songs surrounded by filler. It was a gem. Ten songs, each rich in language and musically inventive, constituted not just a magnificent album but a phenomenon. It was revolutionary in a distinctly 1970s sense of the word. Its imagery wasn't freaked-out, defiant, outrageous, rebellious, or another of the other mid-Sixties adjectives that defined vintage Dylan, but rather intense and moving, playing on a wealth of personal emotions. The poetry of the songs was remarkably confessional, and Bob sang them with a frightening openness.

It was easily his most stylized and powerful album since *Blonde on Blonde,* and as such, it touched off a dramatic public response. Disc jockies programmed the album as if it were an occasion of historical significance, often playing complete sides without interruption. Media barons, in their insightful eloquence, proclaimed that Bob Dylan was...*back!* Not only did the album receive the usual attention from the press, but it became the subject of serious scrutiny in *Rolling Stone,* beginning with a five-page critical analysis which ran in the March 13, 1975, issue. *Stone* pulled out all the stops for this piece, printing not one, but *two* lengthy reviews of the album, as well as the requisite idolatrous rave by Ralph J. Gleason, and abbreviated opinions by no fewer than thirteen of the country's most "influential" rock critics.

The reviews were more revealing for their comment on the wildly self-indulgent state of rock criticism than for light shed on the album itself. They served as a showcase of sorts for the elitest pack of supercilious "underground" pundits whose favorite music was no doubt the sound of their own voices. To most of them, rock 'n roll was the whipping boy for their literary frustrations—a subject rife for sadistic character assassination, rank erudition, and the venting of personal hostilities.

Rolling Stone entrusted the review of *Blood on the Tracks* to two of their deepest and most recondite arbiters—Jonathan Cott and Jon Landau. Cott's critique, divided into Roman-numeral subsections, read like a dissertation for a course on the Enlightenment.

Fans who wanted to read about the new album might have paged through this wordy morass wondering *"What in God's name is this guy talking about?"* Finally Cott worked around to it on the last page and pronounced it...okay. But that opinion had to be extracted from beneath so many layers of gratuitous bullshit that by the time you pushed past his monologues on Verlaine and Marcuse and Proust and Theodore Reik and Guido Cavalcanti and...*Dante,* by the time you finally reached the end, you'd forgotten what the piece was about.

At least Jon Landau had an ax to grind. He didn't like *Blood on the Tracks,* and not because the songs weren't great, but rather because Landau thought Bob had a lot to learn about making records. Says the reviewer, "He has made no single cut to equal..." and names ten of twelve pop songs that Bruce Springsteen might cover, including Joey Dee and the Starliters' "Peppermint Twist." It's not that Landau failed to consider such an obvious classic as "Like a Rolling Stone" in the same category as, say, "Breathless" (and not even the far superlative "Whole Lotta Shakin'"), but to dismiss it as not being a great single is pure nonsense. To make matters worse, of the thirty long-winded paragraphs that constituted his review, Landau devoted a total of *two*—the last two, if one read that far—to the actual subject of *Blood on the Tracks*.

Bob's appeal to a record-buying audience in the mid-1970s was a question that prompted *Los Angeles Times* critic Robert Hilburn to ponder aloud, "Entertainment, diversion and discos now reign. And there's not much you can dance to on *Blood on the Tracks*. Dylan's artistry remains, but I wonder how many people will be listening." Hilburn's fears were allayed before the issue of *Rolling Stone* which carried his quote even hit the stands. By the beginning of March, *Blood on the Tracks* had already shipped more than a million copies, with reorders sending Columbia scurrying back to press. The album reestablished Bob commercially, if not critically, as an artist of authenticity, vitality, and deliberate growth. Before the year was out, he'd strike out on another road that would set the remaining skeptics on their ears.

26

Man About Town

Love and work, that diabolical duo of human nature, played havoc with Bob Dylan as 1975 continued to unfold. Indeed, by midsummer, he must have wondered if it would ever be possible for him to combine the two. The last time he tried, in 1966, his career skidded to a halt. To be the kind of model husband and father his family needed, Bob had confined himself to Woodstock for five years, during which time he spun out mediocre albums. Now, in the midst of a professional renaissance, his marriage was on a precipitous slide toward the divorce mill. The masterminds of psychiatry could say all they wanted about love and work, but for Bob Dylan the two were about as compatible as the Everly Brothers.

What a hell of a time for his marriage to collapse! Musically he was at the top of his form. *Blood on the Tracks* had become one of the year's most important albums, and for weeks on end it juggled for top position on the charts with newer, cheekier rivals like *Born to Run, Caribou,* and *One of These Nights.* It attracted a new and alien segment of the public which, until now, had all but considered the name Bob Dylan ancient history. It must have satisfied him to no end knowing new audiences were buying his records. Considering that the Beatles had been supplanted by Paul McCartney & Wings and the Rolling Stones were reduced to making innocuous disco records, it looked as though Bob was going to be the only member of his "musical triumvirate" to find relevance in the Seventies.

As they say in the music business, Bob was "happening" again; he was *hot*. But if you examine the balance sheet carefully, you'll see the extent of this recent success was mostly on paper—or, more specifically, on vinyl. He was doing brisk business, only he himself was confined to the sidelines, watching as the rave reviews piled up and his album dominated the charts. Meanwhile everyone of importance, the singers who really established new directions and started new trends, were out there shaping the scene.

The scene was what Bob Dylan really missed. He craved the hands-on excitement of the old days—listening to live music, hanging out with fellow musicians, jamming until dawn, cruising the clubs where performers tried out their new material and fed off each other's enthusiasm. That was where he felt most comfortable—not in an unfinished two-million-dollar mosque in Malibu, bumping around the cavernous rooms like a bored houseguest. It drove him crazy to spend more than a week or two around the house with Sara and the kids. He couldn't sit still. He was like a junkie in need of a fix—a fix of the scene. Without it, he behaved like an animal, stalking his cage.

In her way, Sara tried to help Bob through these fallow periods. She'd dealt with this type of discontent before and each time managed to keep him preoccupied with bits of mundane household business. In Woodstock, they'd gone about their lives as any ordinary young couple on a multimillion-dollar income. For eight years, Bob and Sara carried on peacefully. They raised their five kids and enjoyed a life of virtual anonymity on the backroads of upstate New York. But the family idyll couldn't last. Bob demanded more of the scene, and Sara just couldn't sit around and talk rock 'n roll all day long. It wasn't her second language. Nor was the scene her natural habitat; she came off as aloof and uncomfortable around the manic shudder of perpetually turned-on musicians. She wasn't a role player like Yoko or Linda McCartney. She harbored no secret ambition to perform. No, Sara was cursed with being a dedicated wife and mother whose neediest dependent happened to be a superstar husband in constant motion. And she'd finally run out of patience.

When it came right down to it, Bob's rock 'n roll life-style was the only role he ever sought for himself. Sara, on the other hand, needed domesticity and stability. Two separate life-styles demanded to be pursued. For a while, they decided, it might be best if they led separate lives. Sara chose to stay in Malibu with a couple of the kids while Bob whisked back to New York. (Three of their children were sent to Minnesota to spend the summer with Bob's brother, David, and his wife.) Before they split, however, they discussed the seriousness of their decision. Neither of them wanted to rush into a divorce. Both admitted they still had a lot of feeling for each other and weren't prepared to sacrifice everything over a rash miscalculation. Careers like Bob's tended to wear hard on a marriage and often demanded a heavy sacrifice. So they decided to live apart for a while, to stay in touch and work hard at resolving their logistical differences, and see what happened.

As it turned out, Bob's departure was the beginning of the end of their nine-year marriage. The scene is what ended it. Sara just couldn't compete with the sideshow allure of New York. Greenwich Village was Bob's inspiration, the place toward which his fantasies raced ever since that bitter December night, thirteen years before, when he first hit the grime-caked pavement. The city was somehow the key to his whole personality: his subterranean songwriting and his mysteriousness and his own bizarre and stinging persona, being alone, on the road, and traveling incognito with his pickups and music pals, like a band of Hungarian gypsies.

Now he was back in New York, searching for the future in his past, at a time when the city itself was experiencing a mid-life crisis. Especially in Greenwich Village, where Bob had once again landed somewhat aimlessly and displaced. The Village—*his* Village—had drifted seriously out of vogue, a victim of the still-smoldering Sixties and its vagabond casualties who panhandled cigarettes and change from the daily procession of Japanese tour buses. The smart action had moved uptown to the discos and cabarets where flash and trash promoted voyeurism as a cultural prescriptive. The intersection at Bleecker and MacDougal was like the dead zone. It was a disgrace. The coffeehouses and clubs had been shuttered, and in their place stood a chain of grimy falafel joints and schlocky Indian clothing stores that doubled as head shops. Here and there a piano bar lingered on, but for the most part the Village's courtly tradition as a music and poetry oasis had vanished.

Bob moved back into the MacDougal Street pad, then bounced around the Village for several weeks, looking for some kind of a foothold. The old gang was still around, but they were involved with their own complicated lives now and he wasn't about to ring any doorbells. There were still plenty of places he could hang out until word got around that he was back in town. The Kettle attracted its usual residue of characters eager to chat, and the Bitter End had been reborn as a club and adjoining restaurant, now called the Other End, where musicians could relax without having to buck the steady traffic of fans. But Bob's thoughts were occupied by Sara and the kids. He missed them dearly, especially in that empty apartment, and was determined to distract himself from the domestic anguish the only way he knew how—by writing songs.

During the day, Bob holed up at MacDougal Street working on new material. It was the most creative stretch he'd experienced in New York since 1965, when he traveled the same Village street, lugging around his guitar and notebooks. Throughout the month of June, he poured out ten or twelve songs that were to carry him through the next year and a half. One of them, "Isis," he previewed for Jacques Levy, a raffish off-off-Broadway director who'd directed *Oh! Calcutta!* and had written a couple songs with former-Byrd Roger McGuinn. Levy had the nerve to critique Bob's song, and before anyone knew what was happening, the two men grabbed paper and pens and went to work rewriting the stanzas. They worked all night polishing a new version of "Isis," slept through the next afternoon, then resumed the collaboration, moving on to other songs.

Writing with a partner was a completely new experience for Bob. No one had ever said to him, "That's not good enough," or "Get rid of that adjective," or "Reverse those lines and it reads better." He'd never had to compromise his craft before. But they were getting great results, and Bob was actually enjoying himself. He and Levy cruised the club scene at night, then spent the afternoons writing songs with a vengeance. They grew so dedicated to the partnership that they actually moved out to Levy's house in East Hampton to avoid the myriad distractions. There, in the short span of two weeks, Jacques and Bob wrote most of the material for what would eventually become the album *Desire*.

Back in the city, life in the Village settled into what, for Bob, would become a familiar pattern. He'd hit the clubs at night. Go to bed around dawn. Sleep until two or three. Then someone would stop by the apartment—usually Jacques or one of his new playpals like Sheena, an amateur songwriter who was tight with the pack of younger musicians trying to make their name on the Street—and they'd go over to the Other End and try out the new songs. Grouped around one of the rickety tables, Bob would whip out his guitar and play a rough draft of something he'd recently written, just like the old days at the Kettle. Musicians would drift by, sit down for a few minutes, maybe even pick up the guitar if they were brave—or drunk—enough. Kick around a few ideas. Solicit *Bob Dylan's advice!*

Throughout the summer of 1975 an incredible scene developed at the Other End. Only months before, the place sheltered out-of-work musicians who loitered drowsily, with anemic faces, over bottles of lukewarm beer while they pined for one of the scarce twenty-five-dollar-a-night gigs left on the Street. Suddenly the place was electrified by the presence of Bob Dylan and his entourage. Dave Van Ronk might stop by to pay his respects. Or Loudon Wainwright III, who headlined at the Bottom Line, would rush in between sets to grab dinner and shoot the breeze. Invariably, Phil Ochs stumbled over to Bob's table, worked up over some secret government conspiracy or another. You could always count on Jack Elliott to put in an appearance when he was in town. Even a spacy dude like Ian Hunter, late of Mott the Hoople, cabbed downtown to join the fun. It was obvious they were determined to reinvent the Village scene, to bring it into the Seventies, and with Bob's presence, to raise the speculation that the community was on the verge of a major creative resurgence.

It also raised the standard of talent that played the few "live music" rooms operating along Bleecker Street. Through the early Seventies, as the vintage Village scene was going under, club owners had been less than discriminating about the acts they hired to entertain there. It was more a matter of having someone occupy the stage than what they did on it. The signs on the street announcing "Big-Name Folk and Rock Acts" were a ruse to attract only the dumbest tourists hoping for a peek at the past. No one had any experience, much less talent, and anyone with a voice was warned against wasting it singing in a dark cellar for no money and no audience. Now, however, due largely to Bob's reappearance on the scene, a lineup of fresh, young faces started popping up in the Village clubs. Folksingers like Steve Forbert, Willy Nile, and Cindy Bullens put together acts that attracted their own faithful followings. These kids had real talent, and in no time at all the record-company A&R men dropped in on their shows, offering words of encouragement, and, in some cases, private auditions.

One of the hottest new acts was an extremely skinny, boyish-looking poet named Patti Smith, whose hip verse blew madly like the cool breeze of instrumental jazz. Patti was appearing at the Other End with a backup band when Faris Bouhafa, who now worked for Columbia Records, dragged Bob inside to catch her show. "He had never heard of her," Bouhafa recalls, "but I felt Patti was sort of his alter ego. She reminded me of what he must have been like when he was that age, running around the Village, and I was determined to introduce them to each other."

Bob and Faris waited until the audience was seated, then slipped into one of the booths along the back wall of the Other End as the house lights dimmed. The instant Bob laid eyes on Patti, he was fascinated by her. She was so far out, and yet—what a stylist! She had her own individual sound—a blend of aggressive rock energy and free-form rap—and it cut right to Bob's deepest fascination with music. "His eyes were glued to that stage. He didn't say a word through her entire forty-minute show," Bouhafa remembers. "Afterwards, I went backstage and introduced them and they appeared to hit it off pretty well, but the real payoff was that Patti inspired Bob to comb the clubs in search of the new music spirit that was shining through the tired scene."

Bob began to conduct nightly processions of the Village music haunts. With a gang that now included Patti Smith and violinist Scarlet Rivera (a Chicagoan born Donna Shea whom Bob picked up one night walking along First Avenue), he turned up regularly at places like Folk City, Reno Sweeny's, and the Other End, listening and hanging out with a succession of new friends. At the Bottom Line he even jumped on stage to play with legendary bluesman Muddy Waters and a clarinetist named Perry Robinson, before crashing an all-night party at singer Victoria Spivey's house out in Queens.

It was there Bob met a pretty, young writer named Madeline Beckman who immediately captivated him. Madeline wasn't like the usual streamlined airheads with their trashy mouths and low-life, all-action attitudes. This chick had real class, *presence.* She wasn't gorgeous or hot, but rather lovely—a lot like his old college flame Judy Rubin—

and on top of everything else she was cultured. She'd read all the right books and been to all the right places. At one time, Madeline had even performed with a modern dance company, and before the night was out he talked her into dancing while he and Scarlet Rivera provided the musical accompaniment.

A week later, Bob and Madeline made a date to get together. What did she suggest they do? Did she want to be wined and dined or taken to a Broadway show? Was she out to be seen on his arm in some trendy public place, or invade his inner music circle? Not Madeline. She wanted to get to know Bob, so she invited him to dinner at her place. That really threw Bob for a loop! It had been a long time since he'd enjoyed a home-cooked meal or spent a quiet, easygoing evening in the comfort of a pretty woman. Not that he hadn't had a date since leaving Sara. There were always plenty of women around to provide a reasonable distraction. For a while, he'd commiserated with John Sebastian's ex-wife, Lorey, who was newly separated and on her own in New York. And groupies were always making plays for him. But dinner at a young woman's home! A really nice woman with no ulterior motives and a big brain! Now that was a date he intended to keep.

Even the location of Madeline's apartment held exotic promise. She didn't live in a sixth-floor walk-up like most aspiring rock singers who hung out in the Village. Nor was she the kind of Jewish princess who demanded a doorman building on the Upper East Side. No, Madeline lived in a loft in TriBeCa before it was anything other than a district for spice and fabric warehouses. Back then, nobody actually lived in TriBeCa—the streets were deserted at night—and as Bob entered the "working space," as they called it, he was blown away by the extraordinary layout. The place—one gigantic room—was the size of a basketball court, but furnished like an apartment out of *House Beautiful.* The furniture was tasteful but funky, the walls were lined with books and records, and what seemed like acres of polished wooden floors gleamed under the fluorescent lights. Soft music was on the stereo—something in the right groove, like John Renbourn or Emmylou Harris. An amazing smell drifted out of the battery of pots and pans percolating on the stove. And the one thing Bob couldn't take his eyes off of shimmered under the lights. Not Madeline, who was standing in the doorway looking perfectly radiant, but a *trapeze,* a real circus trapeze that hung invitingly from the old wooden rafters.

"That thing really work?" Bob asked, thrusting a magnum of cheap red wine into her arms. Madeline laughed and said yes. As he walked into the room, staring up at the trapeze, she noticed he'd been in the same clothes all week—brown corduroy pants, a blue-striped T-shirt, and a black leather jacket. He'd probably even slept in them the way they looked, like a kid who's been away at camp for the first time in his life. The guy really seems lost, she thought. His eyes darted nervously at everything in the room—at the records and plants and posters placed just so—and it made Madeline uncomfortable. What was he up to? But then she knew he was hurting and alone, and she resolved to make the night an easy one for him.

Madeline could tell Bob wanted to talk. "This was a time of real reflection for him," she recalls, as she reads through a journal entry from that night—July 9, 1975. "He was in New York to write and record, but also to put things in perspective." As they ate dinner, Bob began to loosen up and talk about his life. About Sara and the marriage, which he thought was screwed up beyond repair. Madeline says: "I could tell from the way Bob talked that he was still hooked on Sara. He said he wished he could 'find' his wife, but that it was a lost cause. I couldn't help feeling uptight about that. It was obvious he really missed her. He was there with me, but I realized that I was only filling in spaces in his life. Temporarily soothing the pain. That summer, the album and the eventual tour, even the women he attracted—they were all a way for him to exorcise the past."

And to come to terms with his kids. "He missed the kids so much," Madeline remembers. "It seemed like all he talked about and it was killing him. He was so connected to them, and to think he'd be without them was almost too much for Bob to bear. The way he talked, they were his only anchor—the kids and his music. But it was clear that, despite two of them remaining with Sara [the other children were still visiting David and his family], he had no intention of ever going back there."

Bob was already looking beyond the marriage, and as he talked that night, it became apparent his priorities lay in some kind of revision of his personal life. "It was as though he were trying to determine what was essential and important to him," Madeline surmises from her handwritten notes. "He was really examining his past for simple truths that might help him to sort out where he was headed." Like Minnesota, for one. Bob told Madeline about how he felt a tremendous spiritual pull back to the north country, where he'd recently purchased a farm. He and his brother wanted a place they could use as a retreat, where their respective families could vacation and find relief from the remorseless Dylan publicity machine.

David, too, had been on Bob's mind a lot. He was feeling particularly close to his brother, perhaps unnaturally so, and over dinner Bob romanticized his brother's modest life-style in contrast to his own public spectacle. "David's got it all," Bob told Madeline, "a good marriage and a family and... *anonymity.* Wish I had some of what he had—especially privacy. That'd be real nice right now. Publicity always fucks up everything. In the music business, everybody wants a piece of you until there's nothing left to give."

The guy was really laying it on thick. He went on and on about how lonely he was. How his dreams haunted him and what a drag the city was, except down on Orchard Street where he loved to shop for bargains and wander through the stores talking to the Chasidim. Poor Bob, Madeline thought—he has a serious case of the blues. Finally, she got him onto a more gratifying subject—his drawing. It seemed Bob was even more wild about drawing than he was about playing rock 'n roll. He'd been taking sketch classes with a famous New York artist and learning the difference between what you see and what you draw. Very interpretive stuff, but he loved it. He loved sketching peoples' *souls.* Heavy! Interpreting what lay beneath a model's skin. In fact, he wanted to try his hand drawing Madeline. Now, if she'd just slip out of her clothes.... But she wasn't buying that line.

Oh, he was a cutie pie when it suited him to be that way. The father of psycho-imagery, the author of word puzzlers like "Positively 4th Street" and "Just Like Tom Thumb's Blues," Bob begged, in Madeline Beckman's words, to be "puppy-doggish" and "cuddly." She says, "he wanted to play like a little boy. There was almost a desperation for him to be able to behave like a normal person—not to have everything he did interpreted and regurgitated in the press." With Madeline, Bob felt comfortable enough to swing on a trapeze or season a casserole or play Spanish music on the guitar while she danced, without worrying about an audience. They watered the plants and read aloud from a collection of Dylan Thomas stories. Later, after smoking a little dope, they circled the loft on a bicycle—Bob peddling and steering around the furniture while Madeline balanced on the handlebars, like Butch Cassidy and Etta Place. "He was having a ball!" Madeline says fondly. "I saw an enormous weight gradually lift off his shoulders, the weariness disappeared."

They played and talked until 4 a.m., when it became clear that what Bob Dylan needed most was to be held. He looked at Madeline with intense longing, that kind of hot, suggestive look you give a woman only after sharing such a wonderful evening with her that anything other than bed would be an insult.

Once she extended the offer for him to stay, Bob grew awkward and shy. He fumbled with the zipper on his leather jacket. "I don't even know you," he mumbled, avoiding her eyes.

Madeline smiled and took his hand. "Do you think that you don't know me—or it is that you think you shouldn't know me?" Then he fretted over what would be proper bed-wear. Madeline looked down at his feet and smiled again. "If you just take off your boots, that'd be fine," she said, turning off the lights. Slipping under the covers, they negotiated a mutually agreeable sleeping arrangement: Madeline's head on the pillows, Bob's at the foot of the bed. Like brother and sister. At least, for now.

Somewhere outside they could hear the first wave of trucks rumbling up to the cast-iron loading platforms, their centipede tires raking over the centuries-old cobblestone streets like an enemy tank battalion on the Champs Élysées. The pioneers of TriBeCa awakened uneasily to the predawn industrial growl, but for once, Bob Dylan slept like a baby.

Not all of Bob's summer nights ended so blissfully. He was living fast and furiously again, and most of June and July were paced by long, boozy parties where time wasn't measured by conventional days and nights. On one occasion, an eating and drinking spree at the Other End stretched on well past the official 4 a.m. closing time, when a squad car of cops finally helped to empty the joint. Bob, Ian Hunter, violinist David Mansfield, Faris Bouhafa, and another half-dozen hellraisers loitered outside on the sidewalk, refusing to call it a day. Finally, someone steered them over to Rocky's Venus Club, an after-hours mob hangout on Thompson Street, where they were free to indulge themselves as long as they liked.

Around 6 a.m., Faris Bouhafa remembers feeling someone grab him roughly by the arm. He turned around, ready to swing a fist, and encountered an impish-looking Bob Dylan motioning him toward a corner of the room. "Hey, I got a great idea," he said in a familiar aura of *eau d'alcohol.* Lowering his voice to a near-whisper, he said, "Here's what I want you to do. See all these people, the musicians? I want to take all of them in a bus and go all over the northeast part of the country and we're gonna go to colleges and we're not gonna tell anybody we're coming. Get it?"

Bouhafa got it, all right. Somewhere during the last couple shots of tequila, Bob Dylan had gone off the deep end. He was talking a mile a minute, slurring his words and sounding like a little kid planning incredible mischief. "We're gonna sell all the tickets ourselves—we'll print our own tickets—and we're gonna arrive in town and call up the college radio stations and tell 'em, 'We're gonna play tonight, announce it on your station,' and that's all the publicity we'll do. We'll do the show, then pack up and hit some other town. All unannounced. . . ." Bob stopped just long enough to gulp down a breath before mapping out the rest of his strategy. "I don't want no agents involved," he said. "Nobody's gonna make money off this thing or have any control over us. I want you and [Columbia Records staff producer Don] DeVito to handle everything."

Humor him, Bouhafa thought. Ask him specifics—for instance: who's going to pick up the tab, and how can you keep the lid on something that sensational? But Bob immediately disappeared into the crowd. The next morning, when Bouhafa ran down Bob's proposal again, he concluded, "That was a drunk talking to me last night." DeVito hadn't heard anything about it, nor had Bob notified anyone at Columbia Records that he was considering another tour. "Listen, I've got a session scheduled with Bob tonight," DeVito told Bouhafa. "Stop by the studio and we'll ask him about it."

That night, when Faris Bouhafa arrived at Columbia Studios, Bob was busy tuning his guitar and Faris could tell he was stone sober. "Hey, Faris," he shouted across the room, "have you started working on the tour?" Hastily, Bouhafa replied, "Well, I'm thinking about it, but, you know, man—like it was a long night last night." Bob put down his guitar and walked into the control room, his eyes narrowed with concern. "Listen, man, I'm serious about this thing. I want to do it right after we finish the album."

"Yeah, well there's going to be a lot of competition out there," Bouhafa warned him. "Paul Simon's promoting his *Fifty Ways to Leave Your Lover Tour,* and we're also getting tours ready for Loggins & Messina and. . . ."

Bob cut him off with a wave of the hand. "I don't care about Paul Simon. I don't care about any of those other people. We're gonna do real well," he argued. "And, anyway, we're gonna have so many great performers on this tour that no one else is gonna compete with it."

Bouhafa figured he better start making serious notes; otherwise Bob would give the responsibility to someone else. "Okay," he said, "who do you want to take on this tour?"

"Well, you know, I want Joan and Jack Elliott and Scarlett and Patti and McGuinn and. . . ." Bob stopped and rubbed his chin in contemplation. "Sounds like it's gonna be a lot of people on one stage, so if it comes down to it I'd rather have Patti than McGuinn. But, you know, like the cast can change. We don't always have to have the same people. It can be like—I'll start it off with some of my friends. Go for three weeks or so. Then maybe I'll take a rest and go back to California cause it'll be time for my kids to go to school. I know I can get someone like Eric Clapton to fill in while I'm gone. He'd love to get involved. Then, when everything's straight, I'll fly back to wherever in the country the tour happens to be and join up with it again."

Bob explained he wanted to sponsor a show that would never stop touring. That way, he could perform as often or as little as he pleased without committing himself to an exhausting grind. The personnel would constantly change to suit individual needs and to keep the show fresh. And all the top rock performers would know they'd always have a gig if they felt like working for a few days. "What I want," he said, "is to have a sort of traveling carnival that would eventually have its own tents and railroad cars. Something like Ringling Bros. does, only with musicians and their families."

This wasn't the first time Bob had fantasized his own three-ring extravaganza. Maria Muldaur recalls an evening she and her ex-husband

Geoff spent with Bob in Woodstock, in 1972, when he first proposed plans for a musical roadshow. "We were up at Bob's house," Maria recalls vividly, "and he had just spent time talking about his songs when suddenly he said, 'Wouldn't it be great if we got a train and put a revue together that would travel across the country? The two of you guys could come along, and we'd get Johnny Herald and me and the Band and Eric {Andersen}.' He wanted to pattern it after a circus—just arrive in a town and set up and do the show."

In fact, Levon Helm and Rick Danko remembered Bob's talking about a revue of one sort or another since they first hooked up with him in 1965. He was always intrigued by the concept, presumably as a result of the early rock 'n roll tours that passed through Hibbing when he was a kid. Back then, no fewer than five or eight acts were packaged to headline a month-long gig. Everyone traveled together; all the acts used the same band and switched off performing with each other to keep the show exciting over a period of time. Those kids always looked as if they were having a blast. All that camaraderie and jamming—that was what had first attracted Bob to the music scene and was, ultimately, what he longed to recreate. Rumor had it that Paul McCartney tried to do the same thing as the Beatles were breaking up. Not having performed in front of an audience for years, McCartney schemed to put up signs at high school gymnasiums advertising sock hops featuring Johnny & The Jokers or some ridiculous pseudonym. Then, when the kids showed up, they'd find the Beatles there. Wouldn't that blow their minds! But John Lennon dismissed the idea as sheer lunacy and refused to participate.

Bob, like McCartney, loved playing music above everything else. He was what professionals called a "pure performer," a guy who dug working for the pleasure of it, no matter whom he shared the stage with. He was a natural. At this point in his career Bob Dylan certainly didn't need to pad the bill in order to help him pack a house, but he enjoyed playing with people who turned him on, and his ego was such that he could do it without experiencing any insecurity.

While plans for the Montezuma Revue, as it was being called, pushed ahead, Bob was recording *Desire,* his twentieth album in fourteen years. The first session was held on Monday evening, July 28, 1975, at the old Columbia Studios on Seventh Avenue. Bob had recorded there on numerous occasions, but they never resembled the scene that transpired that night. By seven o'clock, Studio B was crawling with the most bizarre collection of musicians ever assembled under one roof: Eric Clapton, Dave Mason and his entire band, Yvonne Elliman, an eight-piece English R&B group named Kokomo whose first album on CBS was going nowhere, Village folkie guitarist Eric Frandsen, Scarlett Rivera, Emmylou Harris and her husband-producer Brian Aherne, musician Sugar Blue who played the mouth harp for spare change on the street, Bob's pal Sheena who danced around playing finger cymbals and Hare Krishna-type percussion, New York session men Hugh McCracken and Vinnie Bell, Rob Stoner (whose rockabilly band, Rockin' Rob & The Rebels, had caught Bob's eye at the Other End), and a dozen other musicians, freaks, transvestite lovers, and record-company drones who managed to crash the chaotic session.

In the midst of this musical Babel sat Bob Dylan, trying to record behind a barricade of soundproof baffles. He was laying down a track to "Hurricane," the Levy-Dylan tribute to boxer Rubin Carter, only it sounded more like a primal therapy session. Bob was competing to be heard over Kokomo's four-piece rhythm section, their four horns and three background singers—a *big* R&B band—whose style and his obviously didn't jive. Kokomo was a very slick, very structured band accustomed to split-second arrangements. Bob, as we know only too well, utilized the Polaroid method of recording—just snap the shutter and the picture appears. After an hour or so, their respective frustration grew, until it affected everyone's performance. Bob was losing his concentration—you could hear it in his voice. Despite the fact that he was reading the lyrics to "Hurricane" off a crib sheet, he was having problems with the words. Something would distract him and he'd lose his place. The band began to get pissed off and started whispering about his "lack of professionalism." It was a mess.

Even the constantly cool Jacques Levy started to sweat. Levy was scurrying back and forth across the studio, supplying the musicians with printed copies of lyrics in order to pick up the pace. This album was going to be his meal ticket, and no doubt he was aware that if the project deteriorated much further there was a good chance Bob would say "Fuck it!" and do an album of rhythm & blues favorites instead of the songs they cowrote. So Levy, doubling as the session's overheated cheerleader, struggled to boost morale.

The vultures were prepared to dine out on the Dylan name—literally! Adjacent to Studio B was an old radio room from which *The Arthur Godfrey Show* had been broadcast and where, now, thirty-odd musicians, their girlfriends, and an assortment of freeloaders attacked a buffet table that had been set up to feed the band. Eric Frandsen, whose career as a speedy flat-picker limited him to playing spot gigs behind washed-up folkies, balanced a mountainous three-decker sandwich on his plate as he crossed the crowded room to sit down. Pulling up a chair next to Rob Stoner, Frandsen leaned over and said, "Gee, Rockin' Rob, it looks like our price in the Village'll go up about thirty bucks a night. Don't you think?"

At that point, Stoner recalls, he considered packing up and leaving. A Dylan gig was admittedly a once-in-a-lifetime shot, but the spirit of it had sunk to new depths. "I remember thinking, 'This is out of control, man. What's going on here is not professional,'" Stoner says. "I was sitting there listening to Bob struggle through the third version of 'Hurricane' and figured I was better off not being a part of it, when the scene took a drastic change."

Don DeVito cleared out the buffet room, then sent Kokomo home. The others were eventually asked to leave, and by eleven o'clock the cast had been reduced to a manageable size. Eric Clapton sat down; Stoner picked up a bass; Frandsen was asked to handle the acoustic guitars. The only other people who stayed on were Emmylou Harris, a bebop trumpet player named Mike, Scarlett Rivera, and Steve Faroun of the Average White Band, who sat in on drums.

Bob Dylan was immediately relaxed. He and Clapton kicked into a bluesy groove, and it was obvious to everyone there that these two mega-powers could relate to each other in a productive way. Bob was finally in a familiar surrounding. He had an intimate group of musicians at his side—real pros—who weren't afraid to do something *once* and move on without a lot of fancy overdubs and retakes. Just like the old days. They warmed up with some straight-ahead blues—a few riffs that Bob and Jacques had been fooling around with—that were recorded as "Wiretappin'," "Money Blues," and "Catfish." Surprisingly, Eric Clapton remained subdued and held off playing his signature leads, but Frandsen contributed some tasty fills and the rest was sewn together by Scarlett's violin and Bob's wailing harmonica. They worked through a couple of instrumental numbers, then a take of "Romance in Durango" that was ultimately used on the album, before Bob sent this contingent packing as well.

Afterward, Bob grabbed Rob Stoner and hustled him into the control room where they listened to a playback of the night's work. Something was still seriously wrong with the tracks—all of them. They sounded flat and lifeless, empty. "How come it isn't happening?" he asked Stoner.

To Rob, the answer was obvious. Bob had let the music get away from him by going after too big a sound. He'd gone out of his element, and it had overwhelmed him. He'd lost his objectivity. Stoner had seen it happen dozens of times during his short career as a session man, and he explained that to Bob as tactfully as he possibly could. "The answer, man, is to go into the studio fresh tomorrow night with a small, tight little group and start from the beginning," Stoner told him. Rob recommended they try recording with an unrehearsed ensemble—say, just him and Bob and maybe Scarlett Rivera, whom Bob doted on despite her mediocre hand with the violin. Bob insisted upon using a drummer he knew—L.A. session-musician Jim Gordon or his old Nashville sidekick, Kenny Buttrey—however, both were unavailable and Stoner was able to talk him into using his friend Howie Wyeth.

Wyeth was a tall, clunky drummer who fascinated Stoner partly because of his heritage—he was Andrew Wyeth's nephew; Stoner's father, Arnold Rothstein, was the celebrated still-life photographer whose portraits and landscapes enriched the pages of America's most prestigious magazines, so there was a common ancestry between the two musicians. "Hey, man—we're gonna play with Bob Dylan tomorrow," he told Wyeth on the phone later that night.

"Yeah, sure—he'll probably cancel," Wyeth sighed. "Ten-to-one he called every drummer in the phone book."

"No, man, just be there. There's this situation you won't believe!" Stoner recalls telling his friend.

The next night Rob arrived early to act as MC of sorts as well as a peacemaker in case Bob changed his mind. To his relief, Bob was already there, and as soon as Stoner walked in, Bob sat down at the piano and pounded out some throbbing boogie-woogie patterns. Wyeth showed up a few minutes later, as Bob shifted into a familiar Little Richard medley.

"Tutti frutti, *aw-roooотti!* Tutti frutti, *aw roooотti!*"

"I knew right away the guy was in an amazing mood," Stoner says now. "He was wailing away. I joined him on bass, and before I realized what was happening, he'd broken into a take of 'Isis,' which, of course, no one knew since we'd never heard it before. But it was the same three chords over and over again, so I fell right in with him. Scarlett fell in with the fiddle. And Bob hit the lyric."

Just as soon as they clicked, however, Bob lost interest and segued into "Mozambique." Stoner says, "Meanwhile, I don't know this song from Adam, but Bob was attacking it with real emotion. He'd tunneled right into it... only Howie hadn't finished setting up the drums yet. You think that mattered to Bob? Unh-uh. He was actually recording it for posterity, and if you listen to the record you'll hear the drums don't come in for a while because Howie hadn't set them up."

After the first take, Bob bounded over to Stoner and stuck out his hand. "That was great, man! It's exactly the sound I wanted," he said. "Let's keep going." That was around nine o'clock. "By two in the morning," Stoner says, "we knew we had the entire album down." Bob breezed through eight Dylan-Levy songs—"Isis," "Mozambique," "Hurricane," "One More Cup of Coffee," "Joey," "Oh, Sister," "Black Diamond Bay," and "Rita Mae" (which was left off the album but was eventually issued as the B-side of "Stuck Inside of Mobile" from the Rolling Thunder Revue).

The only problem they encountered that night was with Emmylou Harris, who was brought in to sing backup vocals. Emmylou was a perfectionist, accustomed to working out a part and sweetening it until it shone—the prescribed formula in any recording studio other than one occupied by Bob Dylan. The trouble was, Bob never sang a song the same way twice. Now if you're Joan Baez and you've worked with him over a period of fifteen years you develop a system which enables you to at least follow him. Joan learned how to stem the vocal moguls positioned along the treacherous Dylan melody lines, laying back when he hit a field of trills, flutters, trembles, and clinkers, covering for him when he forgot the words. Emmylou hadn't the luxury of fifteen years' experience. Nor did she have the opportunity to rehearse with Bob, and she was so intimidated by working with him that she never even asked him to sing the melodies for her. Jacques Levy merely shoved a lyric sheet in her hands and wished her good luck.

She needed every bit of it. No sooner had they started than Emmylou stumbled over the words. She found it impossible to squeeze them into the astonishingly brief meter. Bob shot her one of his famous dirty looks. Explains Rob Stoner: "The mind-set of a Dylan session is excruciating. People become so terrified by the *potential* that they freak out. You tell yourself, 'I might be preserving the classic Bob Dylan song for all time at this particular second in the universe and I'm not going to be responsible for blowing it.' The next thing you know, you're fucking up a lyric and he has to start over again. Hence the dirty look. That's what Emmylou was going through all that week. Every time she blew a word she came down so hard on herself that it created unbelievable pressure for her. That woman was under a lot of stress that night, and the way Bob chose to record her did nothing to help matters."

Usually, a backup singer is brought into the studio after the lead vocals have already been recorded, and he or she sings over a track. That way, the singer can redo a performance as many times as necessary until everyone is satisfied. The featured artist doesn't even have to hang around while the overdubs are made. In the case of a live recording—when the lead and backup parts are sung simultaneously with the band—the vocalists are separated by a wall of soundproof baffles to prevent them from "leaking" into each other's mikes. That technique allows the engineer to record each voice on a separate track which he can later mix to achieve a complementary balance. If the vocalist hits a bad note it can be shaded down, or, through the wonders of technology, erased completely from the master track. But Bob was a sucker for atmosphere in the studio. He insisted that the lights be dimmed and Emmylou Harris sit next to him on a barstool, facing him as they harmonized to each song on *Desire.* A bottle of tequila was passed back and forth as they sang. The mood was soft and sexy. It may have looked good at the time, but the result was disastrous for Emmylou. Occasionally she'd hit a bad note, but because their mikes were "open"—meaning they picked up both singers' voices—it was impossible to cover her mistakes. Emmylou knew they'd stick out on the album, and it distressed her. After each take she'd sulk off to a corner of the studio where her husband, Brian Aherne, did his best to console Emmylou, but the damage was already done. With her luck, she'd be the only artist whose reputation would suffer as a result of having worked with Bob Dylan.

The studio was booked for another two evenings, but as far as Bob cared, the album was in the can. "But come in anyway and we'll listen to it," he instructed the band before sending them home to sleep.

That night, the atmosphere in Studio B was light and festive. "Bob was exhilarated," Stoner recalls. "He was relieved to be finished with the album and grateful that we'd cut it in a single night." He must have been elated because, to everyone's surprise, Sara was with him and they seemed to be enjoying each other's company. The band and a few invited guests smiled broadly as each song was played. It sounded much better on a night's sleep. And by nine o'clock, the party started to break up. Bob dragged the band into the studio to attempt a new song called "Love Copy," but it fizzled.

"Let's get out of here!" Don DeVito boomed from the control room.

"Hold on a second. I got another song I want to do," Bob replied.

DeVito shrugged and loaded fresh tape onto the spindles. "Okay, what's the name of this one?"

"'Sara,'" Bob growled into the mike, "'Part One.'"

A nervous hush fell over the room. Everyone there knew Bob and Sara were having marital problems—he'd made no secret about how they were living apart. Says one observer, "Bob obviously wanted to surprise her with it. He hadn't told anyone he intended to record it, not even the band who were expected to follow him. Those of us sitting in the control room stopped talking and froze. Nobody moved, not a word was said. Bob had the lights dimmed more than usual, but as the music started, he turned and sang the song directly at Sara, who sat through it all with an impervious look on her face. It was as if she had put on an expressionless mask. The rest of us were blown away by it, maybe even embarrassed to be listening in front of them. He was really pouring out his heart to her. It seemed as if he was trying to reach her, but it was obvious she was unmoved."

There was dead silence after the song ended. Nobody knew what to say, and everyone was afraid to look at each other lest it provoke a humiliating response. The only movement came from a young woman who'd been high all night and kept propping herself up on an elbow. Faris Bouhafa, who'd never seen her before, assumed she was one of the musicians' girlfriends or an acquaintance of Bob's. "When you're working with Dylan, you never know if it's a relative of his or someone he picked up on Ninth Avenue just before the session," he says. "So out of courtesy to Bob no one bothered to ask her who she was. Little did we know she was a groupie who'd managed to crash the session, and as the song finished she turned to Sara and said, 'I don't know who this Sara chick is, but she better hurry up before she's six feet under.'"

Listening sessions were proving more hazardous than life on the Gaza Strip. A few nights later, Jacques Levy invited some "members" of the Gallo family to stop by the studio while they were mixing Bob's paean to "Joey." Don DeVito, by coincidence, invited his brother to the same session—a perfectly innocent gesture, aside from the fact that his brother headed the Anti-Crime Squad of the Brooklyn Police Department. Imagine the scene outside Columbia Studios that night as a yacht-size Cadillac discharged four of the most notorious thugs in New York *at exactly the same moment* DeVito's brother pulled up with some of his buddies—*all of whom were cops!* Needless to say, Levy had to do some fancy footwork in order to convince each faction that the other was a friend of Bob Dylan's.

Some people prove more adept than others when it comes to exercising the powers of persuasion. For his part, Faris Bouhafa was having a hell of a time convincing the brass at Columbia Records that Bob was serious about this . . . *revue.* No one at CBS paid him much attention when he raised the prospect of a Dylan tour. Undaunted, Bouhafa began compiling detailed information to support Bob's maverick scheme. He called promoters, hall managers, ticket companies, sound technicians, bus lines, motel chains—all the components necessary to put such a show on the road. Then he prepared a two-page memorandum, laying out the tour, describing how it would coincide with the release of Bob's forthcoming album, along with all the financial details, and submitted it to his boss, Sam Hood. The memo was promptly returned to Faris with the notation "Bullshit—this will never happen!" scrawled in the upper left-hand corner.

Bouhafa was understandably dismayed by the record company's reaction. It was absurd. They were complete assholes, he concluded. Bob Dylan was offering to play every jerkwater town in America—during the bicentennial year, no less!—and they weren't interested.

Who could figure it? Worse: how was he going to explain it to Bob? That very evening he was due back at the studio to deliver a progress report. Bob was expecting good news; his mood depended on it. Faris was terrified that what he had to tell Bob would cast a pall over the mixing session. Bob would sulk instead of concentrating on his music. DeVito would blame Faris for interfering with their work.

That afternoon, Bouhafa was walking down Bleecker Street, bemoaning his fate, when he ran into someone he hadn't seen in the Village since the late 1960s. Bobby Neuwirth was back in town, and as fate would have it, he had pulled down a gig playing at the Other End as a way of easing himself back into the music biz. Leave it to Neuwirth to sniff out a new scene, Faris thought. That guy had fucking antennae when it came to anticipating where and when the next hotspot would spring up. It was spooky. You could throw a bash in the Gobi Desert and before long Neuwirth would ride by on a camel. "I was in the neighborhood and heard you guys were blah, blah, blah. . . ."

Faris remembered Neuwirth from Max's Kansas City and invited Bobby to join him for dinner at Pete's Tavern, just off Gramercy Park. As the two men talked, Neuwirth tiptoed around questions about his long absence. The best Bouhafa could make out, Neuwirth and Dylan had a falling out in Europe sometime after the *Eat the Document* tour, and they hadn't spoken to each other since. Even Neuwirth wasn't absolutely sure what had prompted it. It could have been anything—a sarcastic look, a misplaced opinion, a disagreement over an artistic matter. Maybe Sara was jealous of his relationship with Bob. That certainly was possible, considering he and Bob were inseparable during that time. Sara might have decided Neuwirth was a lousy influence on her husband and laid a trap for him. It wouldn't be the first time a jealous wife drove a wedge between two close friends. As Bobby saw it, it was anyone's guess.

Bouhafa was fascinated with Neuwirth's conversation but was forced to excuse himself. "I've got this appointment uptown around eight o'clock and have to hit the road," he said.

Neuwirth looked curious. "Yeah—what's going on? Maybe we can continue this later."

"Well, I think I'm going to be busy all night," Bouhafa hedged. He felt bad about not being more up-front with him. It was clear Neuwirth didn't even know Bob was in town. "Look," Faris said, compelled to clear his conscience, "I'm going to level with you. To be honest, I'm going to a Dylan session. I feel awkward about it because it's a closed session and you guys haven't been in touch all these years, but let me make a call and see what I can do."

Slipping off to a phone booth, he roused Don DeVito at the studio and explained the situation. "Well, Bob's not here yet," DeVito told him, "but bring him up and we'll see what happens."

As Faris Bouhafa recalls the events of that night: "It began with one of the most incredible cab rides I've ever taken. Neuwirth got uncharacteristically serious. I don't think I'd ever seen him that way before, but he was going through some major anxiety as we rode uptown, and as we wound through traffic, bits and pieces of the real story started coming to the surface."

As it turned out, there was more to the Dylan-Neuwirth rift than Bobby had led Faris to believe. Neuwirth had his shopping list of reasons, but a lot of it had to do with what he perceived as a lack of credit for his contribution to the Dylan legend. "He told me that, thinking back, Dylan owed him quite a bit," Bouhafa says. "Apparently, they'd written a lot of songs together and Bob had taken all the credit for himself. For example, in 'Just Like Tom Thumb's Blues,' Neuwirth claims he came up with the line 'When you're lost in the rain in Juarez, And it's Eastertime too.' Dylan wrote the rest of it, but Neuwirth felt he'd given him the song's strongest line. He said the rest of the song was nothing without it. And there were other songs, too, that he felt he had more to do with than Dylan did, but he'd always kept his mouth shut and taken a back seat to Bob."

Bobby Neuwirth was always too smart and too self-assured to claim any part of Bob Dylan's success. He knew there was a tremendous gulf between coming up with a line and being a composer, having the creative vision necessary to put the line to good use. Many of the world's leading artists depend on friends and real-life experiences to provide them with inspiration. Writers are forever jotting down personal conversations for their imaginary characters, just as some of Bob Dylan's lyrical brainstorms were seeded by dialogues he overheard in coffeehouses or between his buddies on the Street. A composer seizes a phrase—or even an entire line, as the case may be—that unlocks the mysteries to a brilliant song. He co-opts them, as Dave Van Ronk likes to describe the process. Plays with them, turning them this way and that, until the finished expression bears no resemblance to the context in which it was originally used and becomes rightfully his.

Bobby Neuwirth was more familiar with the creative process than most people. He'd been around artists and songwriters nearly all his life and recognized the license which allowed them to cannibalize conversations and experiences with impunity. Still, Bob's lack of gratitude rankled him. They'd collaborated on a number of classic Dylan songs without so much as a thank you. Not to mention the mystique attributed all these years to Bob—the bits of attitude and posture that distinguished Bob Dylan from the common herd. The whole hipster shuck and jive—that was pure Neuwirth. So were the deadly putdowns, the wipe-out grins and innuendos. Neuwirth had mastered those little twists long before Bob Dylan made them famous and conveyed them to his best friend with altruistic grace. That's just the way it happened at the time. Neuwirth could have easily saved everything for himself. There are scores of people in Cambridge and New York who say to this day that he had all the credentials to become a star in his own right. Bobby Neuwirth was the Bob Most Likely to Succeed, a wellspring of enormous potential. He possessed all the elements, except for one—nerve. That was what always held him back from climbing onto stage. He couldn't take the chance of being rejected, which was one of Bob Dylan's major strengths. It never once concerned Bob whether audiences laughed at him or not. If they didn't "get" his performance they eventually would, or they could drop dead. Bobby Neuwirth, on the other hand, cared about how he "went over." He savored *reactions*—especially those prompted by one of his bits, and in show business that was tantamount to professional suicide. So at some point in The Early Development of Bob Dylan story, Neuwirth chose to be a foot soldier instead of a star. He'd confined his artistry to the shadows, where Bob Dylan could watch and mimic him without worrying about betraying the source of his influences. "And I guess that's what's been bugging me all these years," he admitted to Faris, as their cab pulled to the curb in front of Columbia Studios. "Bob's never once acknowledged that debt."

Neuwirth had lived with that grudge for ten years. During that period, not a week went by when he didn't contemplate reestablishing contact with Bob, but he could never quite figure out how to do it. Suddenly the button was being pressed for him, and as he and Faris waited for the elevator that would carry them upstairs to Bob, Neuwirth regarded the metal doors the way a convict eyed the corridor connecting his cell to the gas chamber. Maybe Bobby's taxicab confession would help prepare him for the momentary meeting, Faris thought as he stood next to Neuwirth like a prison guard. Or maybe I'm cutting my own throat by inviting him here.

No sooner had he flashed on that possibility than the doors opened and the two men strode hesitantly into Studio B. Bob was already there, along with Sara, and he looked up as they walked inside. There was a flicker of tension in Bob's face as he recognized his guest before he offered him his hand. Neuwirth grabbed it too quickly and shook it once. "Hey, how've you been, man?" he asked casually. "Pretty good, pretty good," Bob replied.

Says Bouhafa, "Ten minutes later, Neuwirth was running the session. It was amazing—he just walked in and took over. Opinions started flying, suggestions—he had a hundred of them, and Bob really listened to what he had to say. After playing back each song, he'd turn to Neuwirth and ask, 'What do you think?' And Neuwirth shot back, 'Maybe *we* should do this. . . .' *We,* he was saying! 'That doesn't work at all, try it this way. . . .' It became clear to me that Dylan had enormous respect for this guy, so much so that within an hour he had displaced Sara from her seat alongside the producer, and he was more or less sending DeVito out for coffee!"

Neuwirth evidently saw the *Desire* session as his opening. In no time, he took over as master of ceremonies of the resurgent Village scene. From the stage of the Other End each night, he introduced an endless procession of folksingers and rock stars who bounded up during his set to help out with a couple of numbers. Jack Elliott, Roger McGuinn, Patti Smith, Mick Ronson, Ian Hunter, Phil Ochs, Bette Midler—everyone in New York was dying to get up on that stage. Superstars who sold out the Garden and had never set foot in the Village before made the trip downtown, looking for the Other End. It was *the* place to be, the center of New York's musical nightlife, no doubt because once each evening Neuwirth would coax his "good buddy" Bob Dylan on stage to perform and that was as good as a blessing from the Pope. Better, in fact. Oh, Neuwirth really had that joint hopping. He was in the driver's seat again, and it wasn't long before he set his sights on the jewel of the moment—the Rolling Thunder Revue.

After *Desire,* Neuwirth was in on every meeting for the tour. He provided nonstop input, always full of crazy ideas, and left those involved with the feeling he was now running the show. Bob had taken off with Sara to visit family in the Minneapolis area, but when he returned to New York he was alone, and from then on Neuwirth was invariably by his side. They were inseparable again, hanging out at all their old Village haunts and scoring chicks. And planning, always planning another phase of that magical fantasy tour.

There were so many details to be worked out, but once the men grew tired of the spadework, their talk always turned to the one pleasurable chore: selecting the talent. Who were they going to take along with them?

Jack Elliott was a lock, that was for sure. There was never any debate about including Ramblin' Jack, whose cowboy-errant life-style, conducted out of a jerry-built trailer home, paralleled the Revue's vagabond ideology. Besides, the New York folk community privately noted—and Jack Elliott himself frequently griped about—how much Bob owed him for some of the broader aspects of his career. As a prominent member of the MacDougal Street mafia sees it, "Very early on, Bobby appropriated Jack's vocal style, his stage persona, his repertory, and his closest friends without giving any credit where it was due, so the Rolling Thunder Revue was viewed by many of us as a way of his paying Jack back for the tremendous debt he owed him." Whether or not that was actually the case, Jack Elliott became one of the first members to join the traveling cast.

Patti Smith was eliminated by her own choice when it was decided that all performers would share the use of a "house" band. Accommodations were limited on the road and thus prohibited every headliner from taking along his or her own musicians. At a meeting in Howie Wyeth's loft, Neuwirth selected a versatile-enough ensemble that included Bob's *Desire* backup—Rob Stoner, Howie Wyeth, and Scarlett Rivera—as well as L.A. songwriter Steven Soles, ex-Quacky Duck member David Mansfield, David Bowie's sidekick Mick Ronson, and jazz percussionist Luther Rix. This band, which could adapt itself to any style or sound, would eliminate unnecessary expenses and hassles when it came to moving eight or ten acts on- and offstage each night. But Patti Smith and her band maintained an unusually tight partnership. She felt her band was intrinsic to her success and had stuck by her when she was playing freebies to make a name for herself. So out of loyalty to her band she turned down an invitation to join the Rolling Thunder Revue, opening a spot for Roger McGuinn by default.

Neuwirth had no trouble getting some of his other friends in on the action. Convincing Bob to take Soles and Ronson was easy enough, and before long Neuwirth tacked on rock 'n roller Cindy Bullens and a guitar player from Fort Worth, Texas, named T-Bone Burnette, whom he knew from the Coast. Others happened to be in the right place at the right time. Says Rob Stoner, "One night I'm playing at the Other End when Ronee Blakeley wanders in. She was hot at the time as a result of her performance in *Nashville,* so a lot of heads were turning and people were pointing at her. Next thing you know, she's up on stage and singing 'Your Cheatin' Heart' with my band—which, believe it or not, she bankrolled into a spot on the tour." David Blue wanted to go along, and of course Phil Ochs was under serious consideration, but they wanted another headliner, someone who could take the pressure, as well as the spotlight, off Bob.

What possessed them to approach Joan Baez was anyone's guess. Certainly the two Bobs recalled the events of their last tango with her, when, driven to tears, Joan bolted the *Don't Look Back* tour under a cloud of humiliation. Sure, it had been ten years ago, but they'd done a masterful number on her, they made her eat a lot of crap, and it left enough scars to last any sensitive person a lifetime. They must have been insane to think she'd even listen to them.

"Actually," says Mimi Fariña, "for a very long time Joan entertained a secret fantasy of going on the road with Bob again. She'd hung in there all those years out of some kind of really wild feeling for him, and had even made a series of phone calls pursuing him, which, in his normal fashion, he sometimes answered, sometimes didn't. It drove her crazy, but it also kept her interested, as that kind of behavior does with Joan."

When Bob finally contacted Joan in 1975, it was to pitch her the Rolling Thunder Revue. Mimi picks up the story as it unfolded, one afternoon in late summer:

Dylan arranged to meet her in New York City, where, after many days of waiting for him in a hotel, he finally came and brought Neuwirth with him. I happened to be in New York at the time, singing with Tom Jans, so it turned out to be a summit meeting between the four of us—Joanie, Bob, Neuwirth, and me. And suddenly the tour is a reality. All they have to do is decide what to sing.

Guitars appear out of nowhere, then just as quickly Dylan loses interest. Joanie's going through the agony of him pretending to listen and then not listening, and Neuwirth's encouraging him from the sidelines, with 'Hey, that's a good song, man, do that! That would be great!' Jollying things up with us, which is his role in this thing. Then, as it's Joanie's turn to sing, Dylan peels a banana and begins to walk around the room eating it in a very crude way. Neuwirth's shooting him snide little glances, he's digging the scene as it's going down. And things are only beginning to get worse!

Dylan sits down so Joanie can begin a song, then interrupts her as she starts it, then gets up and walks around the room again, and as the afternoon wore on I watched my sister sink physically lower and lower into the couch until she almost disappeared beneath a cushion. She's just falling apart. Dylan can't decide what he's going to sing, or if he'll even sing with her, as he'd promised. He's really toying with her. I'm boiling and about to take a stand, when finally—*mercifully*—Dylan decides to leave. He goes without giving Joanie any kind of commitment about the tour. Just—"See y'later."

Now it's just Neuwirth and me sitting there. Joanie's in the next room, probably crying, and I'm feeling a terrific responsibility toward her. It's been a tormenting afternoon—three or four hours of nonstop harassment and teasing, teasing, teasing, with Joanie buying into every bit of it. And all I want to do is go talk to her, console her, when Neuwirth grabs me. He gives me one of those sexy looks of his and says, 'Hey! Where you staying tonight? What are you doing tonight?' And all I want to do is to hit him, but I say nothing.

Meanwhile, he's engaged in trying to kiss me. I'm burning with anger and most of me wants to get to Joanie and see

> if she's all right, but I'm also being flirted with and I'm kind of digging that. I'm really torn. Neuwirth picks right up on that—he *knows!*—and so there's more flirtatious talk. He gets closer and closer to me and finally kisses me. But in the middle of the kiss I sense he's not there, so I open my eyes and see he's looking up over me at the front door, kind of smiling . . . because *Dylan's been standing there the whole time,* watching this go down. And they're both loving every minute of it.

Despite the sick psychological games, Joan Baez consented to add her name to the Rolling Thunder Revue. No doubt Joan thought she could detach herself from all the bullshit because she was older and had spent enough time in therapy working out her problems with Bob. But she wasn't being honest with herself. All those years and she was still hung up on Bob Dylan. She was so overwhelmed by his talent that she could never stand up to him or simply walk away when he acted like an asshole. He had incredible power over her, and like an abused wife she put herself into situations which allowed him to use it with impunity. Joan Baez was his trusty punching bag, his door mat. That was the ironic price she paid for introducing him to the public in 1964.

With the talent virtually intact, Bob concentrated on hiring a staff to get the Rolling Thunder Revue on the road. His first selection was Lou Kemp, an introverted, standoffish guy who had gone to Camp Hertzl with Bob in the early 1950s and, since then, had made millions overseeing a number of fish-processing plants he owned in the Duluth, Minnesota, area. Lou was on hand for no other reason than to provide Bob with a psychological anchor. Bob could relate to Lou; he found him a calming presence. Born and raised in Minnesota, Lou shared Bob's uneasiness about being thrust into the midst of a mostly gentile, mostly barbaric troupe of musicians, and he shielded his friend from the hustlers who constantly nipped at his heels. The two men spent a lot of time together, but they rarely talked. They just sat silently, soaking in the vibes.

It was Lou Kemp who hired Barry Imhoff to actually run the show. The two men had met during Bob's 1974 tour with the Band, when Imhoff served as one of Bill Graham's lieutenants. In the interim, Imhoff had struck out on his own, but his only real experience as a tour manager was on the 1975 George Harrison tour, which, unbeknownst to Kemp, was an unmitigated disaster. Be that as it may, Imhoff got the job of coordinating the itinerary as well as the logistics of over fifty technicians who were needed to mount the colossal undertaking.

Bob judiciously distanced himself from the preliminary operations to fulfill an outstanding obligation. He'd been invited to perform on *The World of John Hammond,* a segment of Public Broadcasting's *Soundstage* series, as a tribute to his old Columbia Records mentor. An all-star cast of Hammond's discoveries had been assembled to perform that night—Benny Goodman, Teddy Wilson, George Benson, and Helen Hume, among others—but, typically, Bob had put off responding until three days before the show. At the last minute, he grabbed Rob Stoner, Howie Wyeth, and Scarlett Rivera and flew to Chicago, where the show was being taped. "We're doing a gig there," he told them, neglecting to mention what it was or even to rehearse any material with the band. In fact, Bob never decided which songs he'd perform until air time, when it was already too late to ask the musicians if they even knew them.

Hammond was stunned that Bob showed up in Chicago. "I really didn't expect them," he told me during an interview in 1985. Before the show, John rushed backstage to thank his young prodigy for coming and to make sure everybody was comfortable. That was thoughtful of him, considering the cool reception they'd received from the other performers awaiting their turn to play. "I got the distinct impression these jazz cats were resentful of the rich pop songwriter," Rob Stoner says. "No one said hello to us; they treated us with disdain. Some of my biggest heroes in the world! I remember riding there in a car with Teddy Wilson, and the minute he heard me and Howie were with Bob he tuned us right out." Later, Joe Jones threw a tantrum when Howie Wyeth rehearsed with his drum kit. Says Stoner, "As a group, they weren't the kind of guys who'd appreciate the communal spirit of the Rolling Thunder Revue."

Due to taping difficulties, Bob's set was delayed until almost two o'clock in the morning. Hammond and the other geriatrics were beat, but Bob rocked the near-empty house with explosive versions of "Hurricane," "Simple Twist of Fate," and "Oh, Sister." The band really cooked for such a skimpy group, probably because they were petrified. "We didn't know what Bob was going to do until we were on,"

Stoner says of the experience. "He didn't even ask us if we knew the songs. Fortunately, 'Simple Twist of Fate' had been on the radio a lot, otherwise I'd have been sunk. And right before 'Hurricane' he leaned back and whispered to me, 'Sing Emmylou's part.' Well, hell, man—I didn't know the words, but I sang them off-mike to bluff my way through. It was a totally 'anything goes' type of performance, but a pretty fair preview of what lay ahead for me."

The band was scheduled to fly back to New York on an early-morning flight. Stoner knew he'd never make the plane if he went to sleep, so he decided to pull an all-nighter at the hotel bar. Coincidentally, Bob had the same idea. "You want to walk, man?" he asked Rob. Then, without waiting for an answer, he said, "I got to get some fresh air, see how the city looks."

At three o'clock in the morning, in a city once referred to as "the most dangerous place on earth," Bob Dylan and Rob Stoner went on a walking tour that lasted until the sun came up. "We just wandered around until dawn," Stoner recalls. "Bob staring off into space with his hands in his pockets, walking with a bounce to his step. Taking it all in. Later I learned that this was something he did in every major city in the country. No one recognizes him and it allows him to feel completely free and relaxed."

As usual, Bob was preoccupied with plans for the tour, but mostly they talked about obscure rock 'n roll songs. Stoner was a connoisseur of old rockabilly standards. He owned a priceless collection of R&B 78s, including the entire Sun Records catalogue and hundreds of southern "race" records, and as the two men walked they tried to stump each other with a list of their favorite titles and corresponding singers. Bob was no slouch when it came to rockabilly. "He knew almost everything I threw at him," Stoner remembers. "Not just the titles but the entire lyric, too. He'd go into a verse like he was singing it only a couple hours before. The extent of his knowledge was mind-boggling."

Very cautiously, Stoner broached a subject that had been nagging him for some time. "Ever hear a tune called 'Bertha Lou'?" he asked Bob.

Bob nodded confidently. "Sure. Johnny Burnette and his trio. 19 . . . 57."

"Fifty-six," Stoner corrected him, "but that's pretty good, man."

They walked another hundred feet or so in silence. "The reason I asked is because it's really similar to one of your songs." In fact, it was almost a note-for-note duplication of "Rita Mae," from the *Desire* sessions. The melodies were exactly the same, and Bob's scansion followed Burnette's pattern to a rhyme.

"Oh, yeah?" Bob remarked, but it was a closing statement if Stoner had ever heard one.

"He never even asked which song of his I was referring to," Stoner says nonplussed. "He didn't care, and at that moment I realized that the line between plagiarism and adaption was so blurred that it wasn't even an issue for him."

The real issue that bright, balmy night was *longing,* a bottomless need Bob had to belong somewhere and to someone who cared. Stoner realized that as they gravitated toward Lake Shore Drive, a wealthy residential area on the waterfront, consisting of beautifully appointed homes. Bob lectured Rob knowledgeably about the architectural characteristics of each house in relation to its aquatic environment, but it was clear he yearned for what lay inside. Says Stoner, "Families were asleep inside those houses, and Bob walked right up to some of them, staring in the picture windows for long periods of time. At first, I thought he was some kind of peeping freak, but I think he was trying to imagine families sitting around those darkened living rooms—*his* family, perhaps—because afterwards he got this really sad, wistful look in his eye and we walked the rest of the way without saying a word to each other."

Back at the hotel, Bob thanked Stoner for keeping him company. "It was great, man," he said as they ventured through the tranquil lobby. "We're gonna do something to try and get it like this from now on. Get things freer than the way I been doing it up till now." Bob continued fantasizing about this elusive concept of freedom he'd been pursuing, but Stoner knew it was a smokescreen for the most important thing on Bob's mind—the Rolling Thunder Revue.

27

Thunder on the Highway

One of the most flagrant misconceptions about the Rolling Thunder Revue was its purpose. If you followed the story in *Rolling Stone* or *People* or one of the myriad "insider's" books that were published afterward, the tour was launched to embody the lost idealism of the Sixties. Bob Dylan was depicted initially as an enigmatic and reclusive pop star, the most profound songwriter of modern times, whose lyrics had influenced everyone between the ages of four and forty. Then, in the type of whimsical plot shift you'd expect from an old James Stewart movie, he was transformed from a cranky eccentric into a moderately congenial Everyman whose chance brush with the masses in Greenwich Village staggered him to his senses. According to this popular account, Rolling Thunder represented either Bob's sudden passion to be out among the people; a publicity stunt to promote *Desire*; an excuse to make another underground movie; a goodwill reunion to repay his patron, Joan Baez; or his obsession to vindicate Rubin "Hurricane" Carter. All these rationales contributed to the soundness of the Bob Dylan legend, but, as usual, the media had missed the point.

Bob's aim was hardly to get down with the common folk. At least, not in any personal way. Throughout that year on the road, he made no effort to befriend anyone he met out there, least of all any member of the audience. Security was such an overriding priority that any fan who imprudently approached Bob would have been hustled off without so much as an apology.

Nor was *Desire*'s success dependent on the paste-up illusion of hype. Thanks to *Blood on the Tracks,* advance orders for the new album ran well ahead of Bob's usual pace, and from all indications it promised to be his biggest seller yet. That is not to suggest he wasn't concerned with his status as a recording artist. One of Bob's constant beefs was his inability to pull down hit singles. On many occasions, he'd corner a buddy and press him to explain why a group like the Rolling Stones, who came up at approximately the same time as he did, kept breaking into the Top Ten with the same boring shit. "Why can't I get hit records?" he'd blubber. "How do these guys manage to be such commercial successes? What do I have to do?" Invariably, the advice he received was the same: Make a careful, modern-sounding record instead of simply going for the moment. To which Bob would scowl and say, "Yeah, yeah—I know all about that stuff, but I can't do that. I do what I do." So in the end, he wasn't a perennial on the singles chart, but he'd stumbled over a fair share of hits. Even "Hurricane" was a certified smash as the tour began—and that baby was cranked out in one night!

"Hurricane" was Bob's first protest song since his "George Jackson" single stiffed in 1971. He'd read *The Sixteenth Round,* a book about Rubin "Hurricane" Carter, the outspoken middleweight contender who was doing time in Rahway State Prison for the alleged 1966 shooting of three white men in a tavern in Paterson, New Jersey, and decided that Carter was framed. It was shades of Mississippi all over again. A black man had gone up against white justice and got screwed by the system. What a perfect subject for a song! Rubin was right up there with Emmett Till, Donald White, Davie Moore, Hattie Carroll, Hollis Brown, and George Jackson. More fodder for the protest mill. The next thing anyone knew, he'd cut an eight-and-a-half minute version of "Hurricane" and people were *dancing* to it. Imagine entering a disco and hearing "Get Down Tonight," "I Want to Do Something Freaky to You," and... *"Hurricane"!* Girls in Spandex tops and hot pants were doing the hustle to it, bumping and grinding to Bob Dylan's epic protest song, which goes to show just where the nation's social conscience was in the mid-1970s. Bob pulled out all the stops for that record. Still, while it had heaped attention on Hurricane's legal plight, it was by no means the focus of the Rolling Thunder Revue. As a matter of fact, Bob rarely discussed Hurricane Carter while he was on the road.

The conversation aboard the tour bus was devoted to the pursuit of fun, fun, fun. Which steers us to the real purpose of the Rolling Thunder Revue: companionship. For the musicians and performers, the temptation of traveling across the country with people they could relate to was irresistible. The communal spirit that filled the Sixties was over, and for a lot of people that meant the collapse of their safe, carefree world. They were suddenly alone—and lost. Especially in the otherwise clannish rock world, where the nationwide club circuit had once perpetuated a life-style of liberties and esprit de corps. That, too, had fallen apart. No longer could they book into a place like the Fillmore or the Electric Factory and play on a bill each weekend with four of the country's hottest acts. The club scene had evolved into a complex of mastodonic arenas and two-hundred-thousand-dollar-a-night gigs, where to visit with your opening act it was necessary to board a jitney and travel through two miles of concrete tunnels connecting the dressing rooms. What kind of life was that!

For many of those who survived the Sixties, it was a confusing and impersonal time. Reputations had faded, finances dwindled, and it became impossible for once-famous rock stars to nail down a paying gig. Bob Dylan wasn't affected professionally by the cruel generational shift, but he certainly ached for the good ol' days. And the camaraderie. His own family was falling apart. He was lonelier than hell. And so, as a result, he manufactured this big musical family to help fill the void.

Suddenly Bob Dylan was surrounded by old and new friends. They turned up from his childhood, from the Folk City years, from the psychedelic Sixties, from Woodstock, and from the night before. It was a great "spiritual reunion," as *Rolling Stone* portentously dubbed it. One big "family scene" that was likely to show up at any time and play "in your living room." And while the symbolic nature of the tour was to recreate a tightly knit family, the spirit of it was patterned after summer camp.

It was that rollicking atmosphere that prevailed as the tour's three chartered buses left New York on October 27, 1975. The Rolling Thunder Revue chugged along I-95 toward New England, boosting the camplike spirit with an infusion of fun and laughter. In unfamiliar form, Bob chose to sit amongst the other performers, swapping songs and singing with Joan Baez. The two stars continued to work over a lot of new material, like "Honey Love," one of those early Drifters hits filled with sexual innuendo, and some traditional folk songs—"Handsome Molly," "Ramblin' and A-Gamblin'," and the old Irish ballad "Purple Heather." As everyone noticed, their vocal chemistry was perfectly balanced—a quality of two old lovers who, after years of being apart, still intuited each other's moves. Their interaction was professional and bonded by what appeared to be mutual respect.

The rest of the troupe entertained themselves with ritual standard to the first day of camp. They exchanged their favorite songs, named the main tour bus—"Phydeaux"—and established a seductive team spirit. "All for one and one for all!" Bobby Neuwirth shouted from his window seat. What an infectious mood that aroused in everyone's soul. Not to mention their libidos. It wasn't long before the performers and musicians realized that one aspect crucial to summer camp had yet to be addressed—bunkmates! *Yaaaaayyyyyyy!* They hadn't hit Connecticut before the aging campers began to pair off. A mass mating game was set in progress that continued through the next few days. "Everyone wanted to make sure they had a bunk and someone warm to share it with," observes one of the Rolling Thunder musicians.

The tour newsletter specified that each person was entitled to bring his or her spouse or lover along, but only half took advantage of the invitation. Roger McGuinn summed up the general attitude cavalierly when he explained to a writer: "My old lady's upset about me being on the road and balling other women, and all that. I told her to go out and get laid, it wouldn't bother me. I could've brought her on the road, but I didn't want to." He knew that would have ruined everything. The unwritten rule in every male musician's life was that touring gave him license to go wild. It was the place where, for one or two months out of the year, he was free to get all those freaky fantasies out of his system before settling back into fidelity with the little woman and the kids. What you did on the road was your business. It was like being a member of the musical masons. "Sorry, baby, I can't divulge what goes on there—it's a *secret*."

Not only was the tour loaded with eligible prospects, but the itinerary held much promise for crazy scenes. All those small towns whose womenfolk were struggling against the yoke of repression were sexual time bombs waiting to go off. The Rolling Thunder Revue rolled into town and—WHAMMO!—teenagers and young moms suddenly found themselves doing things they'd only read about in *Penthouse*. Leave it to rock musicians!

The action on the road was so wild it could never be reduced to a couple of descriptive paragraphs. Still, many of the troupe members were content to bunk with their counterparts on the tour. Bob immediately picked out his roommate—a pretty young thing who ostensibly handled the publicity. Steve Soles moved in on Joni Mitchell, and Ronee Blakely made a play for Mick Ronson—a choice all the more unusual considering his wife, Susie, also traveled with the Revue.

In retrospect, Ronson was a peculiar addition to the Rolling Thunder Revue. A man of fitful ingenuity, Ronson had the unfortunate good luck of creating much of the character for Ziggy Stardust, while David Bowie rode it to stardom. Ronson languished in Bowie's band for several years, a capable if unremarkable guitarist, waiting for his chance to grab the spotlight. That moment came in the summer of 1973, when Bowie announced the first of his annual "retirements" from performing, and Ronson, the logical heir, was given a greater shot than even he had anticipated. That was during the heyday of hype, and within six months he'd landed a lucrative recording contract with RCA, his own billboard on Times Square, a world tour, full-page ads in all the trades—the full superstar treatment. Only Mick didn't have the chops for it. He was a sideman, not a star. Glitter and glamour, his only bankable assets, weren't enough to sustain an act, and his tour disintegrated into a major show-business embarrassment. Subsequently, Mick lost his nerve and adopted a lowly profile until he was prevailed upon to join the Rolling Thunder Revue.

Unlikely as it seems, it was Ronson who emerged as the mainspring which updated the band's secondhand sound. Once a flashy stylist, he developed into a straightforward, blue-collar guitar player whose glittery antecedents modernized the band's otherwise dated country-rock effect. It remained a delicate process integrating his sinewy leads into the type of compatible accompaniment that would accommodate not only Bob's songs, but those of Joan Baez, Joni Mitchell, Roger McGuinn, and the rest of the Revue's ragtag headliners. They'd rehearsed for several weeks in New York, but with only three days left before opening night the band had yet to find a distinctive groove.

Part of the problem lay in the staging of such an elaborate show. With over a dozen performers sharing the spotlight, it was like a minefield just getting bodies on and off the stage. Once the entourage got situated at the Seacrest Motel in North Falmouth, Massachusetts, the main consideration was to synchronize the show. The motel's tennis courts were converted into an outdoor soundstage, and Jacques Levy directed a dress rehearsal as if he were fine-tuning one of his off-Broadway extravaganzas.

Using a stopwatch and a clipboard, he conducted a sketchy run-through of the Rolling Thunder Revue, sequencing the acts and their songs in order to give the stage and lighting crews their cues. A natural flow emerged from this technique, which allowed Levy to calculate the length of each set, individual logistics, and a rough blueprint for shuffling equipment around the stage. Within hours, things had fallen together with remarkable ease. "Let's take it through the show from top to bottom," he urged the weary performers, rounding up an audience from among the motel's bewildered guests and employees. For the first time, the Rolling Thunder Revue performed as a complete and seamless ensemble, and the result was a musical tour de force. Bob, Joan, Roger, Ramblin' Jack—they worked beautifully alone and together on that clay-and-concrete stage. There was a definite magic in the flow. The only problem was that Levy had seriously underestimated how long the show would run, and after they all had taken their turn at the mike, the Rolling Thunder Revue was clocked at a length of over *eight hours of music!*

Paring down the show developed into a major headache. Everybody's set had to be trimmed without ruining the varietylike appeal, and some acts were sacrificed completely until they could be worked back into a sleeker version of the Rolling Thunder Revue. Allen Ginsberg, who had been performing "Howl," was cut. Cindy Bullens got dropped out of the regular lineup. Neuwirth's set was reduced to a single song. They all were willing to do what was necessary to get the first few shows under their belt. Only Ronee Blakely posed a problem after the initial cut had been made. Her set had been reduced to two numbers in the first half of the show, and it was clear she was dissatisfied. Every time the piano bench was empty, Ronee would sit down as if she were a member of the band, or appear mysteriously to sing harmonies behind Bob as he worked through his set. Eventually, she had to be restrained from hogging the stage. Otherwise, though, everyone pitched in to get the show down to its final four-hour length.

The Rolling Thunder Revue was slated to make its debut on Halloween night, in Plymouth, Massachusetts. Barry Imhoff had secretly booked it into Plymouth Memorial Auditorium, an eighteen-hundred-seat town hall, for a measly two-hundred-fifty-dollar rental fee. He instructed the town fathers that it was to be a Joan Baez concert, although before long handbills started circulating which featured pictures of Bob Dylan, Joan, Bobby Neuwirth, and Jack Elliott, under the banner for the Rolling Thunder Revue. As word leaked out, Dylanophiles scrambled to make the still publicly undisclosed scene. Carloads of fans canvassed the area for spare tickets, while the media descended on tiny Plymouth like plundering pilgrims.

Back in New York, Faris Bouhafa decided it was time to alert the Columbia Records regional staff in the New England area. His relay man there was Sal Angatti, the tireless Northeast branch manager, who worked out of the record company's Boston office. Angatti was a fixture of the CBS Records field force, a silver-haired paisano who spoke like a Brahmin and wore double-breasted blazers with the company logo stitched over the breast pocket. He'd peddled the label's acts since the invention of stereophonic sound, hyping even the worst shit as if it were a national treasure. Bouhafa was relieved the Revue was opening in Angatti's territory. Because of the show's eclectic format, he depended on an old workhorse like Sal to give it the company's red-carpet treatment.

Bouhafa delivered the good news like a giggly teenager. The silence on the other end of the phone line was curiously labored. What was holding up Sal's customary enthusiasm? he wondered. Finally, in a strong, angry voice, Angatti barked, "*Goddamnit!* That little punk has to start his tour in my market!" Faris, shocked by the outburst, listed a half-dozen reasons why he considered the Rolling Thunder Revue to be such a prestigious concert event, but Angatti wasn't buying it. "I got a million things on my mind and a million things I've got to do," he bristled. "I don't need that—that *punk*—interfering with everything else."

Bouhafa calmed Angatti down and then slowly, obsequiously stroked him until it became clear why the branch manager harbored such tremendous hostility toward Bob. The problem dated back to an incident that occurred exactly eleven years ago to the day, when on October 29, 1965, Bob played a concert at Boston's Back Bay Theatre. Angatti, ever the dutiful company drone, showed up to provide what is euphemistically referred to as "label support"—a perfunctory handshake, some idle expression of encouragement. "Keep up the good work, son, and blah, blah, blah." "And that little *punk* didn't move a goddamn limb," Angatti complained more than a decade later. "He just looked at me and grunted. He refused to even talk to me!"

It was obvious to Bouhafa that Angatti intended to repay Bob's inhospitality by snubbing the Rolling Thunder Revue. Well, fuck him! Bouhafa thought. Fuck all those assholes who predicted with defiance that Dylan would never pull it off. Bob didn't need those corporate lemmings. Through a battery of well-placed spies, word had reached Faris that the show was a killer. It had exceeded even Bob's fanciful expectations. And Bouhafa knew it was only a matter of time before his fellow workers were climbing over each other to take credit for its success.

When the big night finally arrived, Bouhafa was standing in the wings as the ancient wood-paneled Plymouth Memorial Auditorium filled to capacity with wide-eyed Yankees. "Bob's gonna blow these fuckers away," he tittered to no one in particular, trying to steer clear of the frantic backstage hustle. Canvassing the room, he noticed it wasn't the usual star-studded audience that turned out waving "comps" for opening nights in New York. The place was packed with bona fide fans. People who had shelled out seven dollars and fifty cents to see Bob Dylan and his friends play in a town that probably never hosted a big-name rock show before, a town that once denounced the music as blasphemy. And here it was being played in the venerable town hall, of all places. How times had changed! Even the press had been denied access to the first show—officially, that is. Bouhafa had slipped *New York Times* critic John Rockwell inside under an assumed name. And the *Rolling Stone* reporter assigned to the tour prostrated himself for a couple of passes. Otherwise the concert was free of the jaded every-nighters and freeloaders.

Consequently, the performers were every bit as excited as their audience. And unquestionably apprehensive. It was more than simply a case of opening-night jitters, because the show hadn't yet been entirely worked out to everyone's satisfaction. It was still dreadfully long and disorganized. The sound check had been marred by confusion. And the musicians were visibly exhausted. Since arriving in Massachusetts, they had put in a succession of twelve-hour rehearsal days in which they were barely given time to take a leak between performances. One headliner would finish rehearsing and the next would jump right in without giving the band time to take a break. So it remained to be seen how sharp they'd be through yet another four-hour stretch. All these factors played havoc with the outcome of Rolling Thunder; nevertheless, as showtime rapidly approached, the only option was for everyone to wing it and hope it all turned out for the best.

Susie Ronson, who had been hired to do the cast's hair, took some of the edge off by encouraging the band members to try their hand at makeup. Not theatrical pancake, but a garish facial treatment right out of *Phantom of the Opera*. It was Halloween night, she argued—that gave them license to go whole hog without being accused of any glitter-band hysteria. Halloween! In the confusion, it had slipped everyone's mind. No more had to be said. The entire ensemble queued up outside the dressing room as Susie applied whiteface and glitter to their weary jowls. It livened up everyone's disposition. A lot of pointing and laughing broke the tension. Even Bob wore a mask on stage, and from that night on, the performers and musicians appeared in an array of elaborate disguises for the remainder of the tour.

When the Rolling Thunder Revue finally appeared on stage, the audience and performers alike were astonished at how smoothly the show ran. It seemed to pilot itself, steering neatly around the obstacles that confounded them in rehearsal. As Bouhafa predicted, the tiny SRO crowd rejoiced in the unpretentious nonstop riot of music that was paraded before their eyes.

Bobby Neuwirth opened the evening with a Valium-fueled country number that established the dozy pace. Then each band member got to do a solo turn that showed off his individual style—Soles the sensitive singer-songwriter, Stoner the rockabilly cat, T-Bone the honking delta bluesman, and Ronson the decadent blade who threw the night's first curveball by playing "Is There Life on Mars?" In any other setting, these opening acts would have been soundly encouraged to cede the spotlight, but the Plymouth crowd was unnaturally worshipful, despite the fact they were unfamiliar with the band members' names. Ronee Blakely could have recited the federal tax tables and received a thunderous hand. As it was, she gave two strong performances, one a solo and one in tandem with Bobby Neuwirth, and then introduced Jack Elliott, who breezed through a witty, four-song set that brought the crowd to its feet.

Bob obviously owed it to his image to follow Jack on stage and remove himself, once and for all, from the auspices of his folkie roots. Jack Elliott was unswervingly a funky cowboy whose songs romanticized the disappearing prairie and plains. In another time, Bob might have wandered out bemusedly, scratching his head and grinning; he might have told a couple stories in the sing-song fireside style Jack had patented, and from which he, himself, had benefited during those formative years in the Village. But Bob was more temperamentally suited to scowl and spit out his flint-edged lyrics with intimidating force; he was more in tune with the times than a storybook dreamer like Jack was. So when Bob emerged from the shadows, strumming his guitar and adjusting his harmonica holder, there was no mistaking his inimitable presence. That posture was as much a part of the cultural landscape as a chiaroscuro of Judy Garland at Carnegie Hall. "Here's another old friend," Neuwirth announced almost incidentally, and before the last word was out of his mouth, the house had erupted in cheers.

Bob rarely took advantage of such a riotous, fervent ovation. He always detached himself from it or blew it off by staging an awkward delay: retuning his guitar or whispering a last-minute instruction to someone in the band or adjusting the mike. Only when he was nervous, when he performed in an undeceptive setting and the adrenalin burned through his veins, did he lock into the energy level set by the audience. And when that happened, he gave the most unforgettable performances seen in modern times.

By the time Bob got deep into "It Ain't Me, Babe," the congregation of oddly assorted New Englanders hollered out the "no, no, no" coda as if it were a Gregorian chant. Ten years after the mast, he still commanded a liturgical response. The songs remained fresh in everyone's minds, not out of constant repetition, but because they carried the ring of truth. Their poetry was as timeless as that famous rock which sat a few miles up the road.

"Bob Dylan!" Bobby Neuwirth strained to be heard above the applause. "*Bob Dylan!*" The two friends grinned at each other as the band ricocheted into a throbbing version of "Hard Rain," and Bob was instantly reactivated by the music.

"Hard Rain" was one of those epic configurations of words that Bob often forgot in mid-course. He frequently blew a line or two, rearranged the words, or just plain made up new ones as he cruised through the difficult verses. In the 1980s, these verbal lapses would become so prevalent that, like a magician, he developed an illusion with which to distract the audience: slurring his words. Listen to tapes of his recent performances, and you'll hear a man who sounds as if he's suffered a stroke. Even a litany such as "Like a Rolling Stone" oozes like literary porridge. "You ussa be sammuzed/ Ana polyin rah rah rah ana lanny he used . . ." The technique has become so ordinary today that it has actually altered his vocal delivery—he *plays* to the slur. But that night each word popped with crystal clarity. He spit them out with a fierceness that suggested he had just written the song. Not that it would have made a goddamn bit of difference—because *the audience was singing along with him!* To "Hard Rain," of all things—not exactly an effortless little sing-a-long.

Bob capitalized on the standing ovation he received to slip in a couple of new songs—"Romance in Durango" and "Isis," from the *Desire* album. He had sung the old favorites with unexpected enthusiasm, but he'd never performed the new material before a live audience. Both were difficult songs to carry off, too. Not your everyday toe-tappers, they demanded that listeners pay close attention, and that was almost too much to ask from an overexcited crowd. Nevertheless, he sold them with a sidewalk pitchman's gift of persuasion, then fled to the wings, ending an impressive first half of the Rolling Thunder Revue.

Throughout intermission, the audience buzzed with ecstasy. The show had exceeded everyone's wildest expectations, and an almost palpable how-can-he-top-this curiosity wafted through the hall. Any doubts were disposed of as the curtain went up on the second act, revealing the legendary silhouettes of Bob Dylan and Joan Baez.

Their appearance together was the first indication that times indeed had changed. The Joanie who had appeared on the cover of *Time* in 1961 and at subsequent Newport festivals was a hippie sylph. She displayed an innocent, wide-eyed countenance as she stood barefoot, skinny as a stick, before her fans, the famous black Mexican hair flowing in waves to the small of her delicate back. Even her rumored toughness, bluntly disclosed in that icy soprano, was instrumental to the gypsy spirit she evinced.

In Plymouth, however, Joan appeared vulnerable and reserved, as if she'd been the victim of a feminist joke that had backfired. Her manner of dress was retro-fashionable—almost butch—in a French T-shirt and designer jeans. Even in the background she seemed wary of upstaging her scruffy singing partner. Bob carried the charge, leading her through a moving, if understated, version of "The Times They Are A-Changin'" that was unblemished by their former onstage battle of egos. As usual, though, Joan managed to prick his mirthless dharma when she lifted a water glass in a toast to him between songs. That was a tactical mistake, and he let Joan know it at once by leering at her until she ditched that ridiculous glass and returned to the mike. Strumming the guitar through her little business, Bob's impatience could be monitored by the acceleration of his wrist. The anxiety-producing strokes seemed to be imploring her: "Are you finally ready to sing?" Within seconds she was, and it turned out to be another Dylan-Baez time capsule—"Hattie Carroll"—which seemed to have become more poignant with age.

It was one of those magical moments, but they always had their dark side. Despite their apparent chemistry, Joan served as Bob's foil for one of his favorite onstage games of one-upmanship. This occurred regularly during their duets, many of which required holding a long, obligato note at the end of a verse. To cement his reputation as Old Leatherlungs, Bob would challenge her to see who could hold the note the longest. It was a very subtle head trip to remind her who was boss, and Joan, to her credit, never complained about it, but you could tell it unnerved the hell out of her. It destroyed her rhythm. Instead of concentrating all her energy on the performance, Joan was forced to anticipate when he'd drop a particular note and dive into the next line so she could stay with him and not look like she'd muffed a cue.

The harmonies were equally obstructed by Dylan roadblocks. No one who sang with Bob was ever certain how he'd execute a vocal part until they were smack in the middle of it. You never knew if he'd choose to sing the root, the fifth, or the middle figure of a chord.

Invariably, he sang whatever popped into his mind at the moment. And the poor harmony singer had to seize whatever note Bob *wasn't* singing—which presented problems for even the most versatile accompanist. Says one veteran of Bob's vocal duels, "It's an incredibly tough maneuver. You try to hear which note's coming and then nail whatever ones are left. That means you keep your eyes glued to his mouth and his throat in an effort to gauge his wind so he doesn't leave you hanging there. And, of course, you don't want to leave him hanging, nor do you want to sound like an asshole hanging on after he's stopped singing. So it becomes a constant game of cat-and-mouse that ultimately detracts from the show."

Eventually Joan could predict his every move, but that night Bob constantly eluded her at the mike. His vocal pyrotechnics exploded everywhere around her—grace notes, tremolos, raspy coloraturas, vibrato, inverted turns and flutters. He hit her with all the artillery at once. For Joan, it was like being on a runaway horse—you just hold on for dear life and pray you're still on him when the beast pulled to a halt. Bob was apparently pleased with the results. They had thrusted and parried their way through "I Shall Be Released," and as the song segued into applause, he grinned broadly and patted the side of her head before darting toward the wings.

Far from signaling an end to the gala, Bob's exit provided a release from the various tensions stirred up in his appearance with Joan. Now everyone could relax and enjoy the rest of the show. Still to come, in fact, was an embarrassingly old-fashioned solo set delivered by Joan Baez. Roger McGuinn strummed through a few old Byrds hits that were built around his showpiece, "Chestnut Mare." Bob and the band reappeared to introduce four new songs from *Desire,* and, finally, at ten minutes before midnight the entire cast, including Allen Ginsberg and David Blue, joined him on stage for two encores—"Just Like a Woman" and appropriately enough Woody Guthrie's "This Land Is Your Land"—before the curtain rang down.

The way the Rolling Thunder Revue really ended, though, was not with a finale but with a prophecy. Having dodged the stilted concert establishment—having spurned its box office and mercenary greed, its obsession with formalities and its utter disregard for the public it depended upon—Bob Dylan vowed, with the revolutionary tactic he dreamed up, to disassociate himself from mainstream show business.

The fat cats could walk through their shows in front of twenty thousand fans at a clip, they could perpetuate the company line that their music was a binding force, that it cauterized the national wounds when, in fact, it had disintegrated into nothing more than empty-headed, self-serving noise. They could kiss the asses of the mindless promotion men who came backstage in order to sell "the product" and tighten the screws that operated the record business. But the Rolling Thunder Revue sent a courageous message that Bob was having none of it. That was the prophecy implied in the show's rousing encore—that it was still possible to produce something sincere and honest in our junk-food society—and it was with that that he sent the audience whistling into the night.

After that first night in Plymouth, every small town in America lusted after a date with the Rolling Thunder Revue. The press wasn't sure what to make of it. There was the usual hodgepodge of raves and sour grapes—"delicious," "a rip-off," "totally unpredictable." *Rolling Stone,* the barometer of pop taste, found itself in a ticklish position when word reached its New York office that Larry Sloman, who was sent to cover the tour, had given Bob editorial control over his quotes. The stories he filed were "pure fluff," according to managing editor Chet Flippo. Sloman was promptly removed; however, in *Rolling Stone*'s rush to strike an editorial balance the magazine swiveled a hundred and eighty degrees by conducting an investigation into what it believed was the tour's main consideration: money.

Stone was righteously miffed over the sudden enlargement of the houses the Revue had chosen to play (such as the 10,500-seat Veterans Memorial Coliseum in New Haven, Connecticut) and subsequently reported that many in the audience "felt cheated." The magazine estimated the Revue grossed a bountiful $641,085 in its first thirteen shows, but came up with nothing more incriminating than Jack Elliott's whimsical confession: "All right, I want some fuckin' money. I want a boat. . . . I've wanted a boat since I was fourteen years old." Failing to turn up anything more concrete, even the supercynical *Rolling Stone* had to conclude that the Revue was "one of the more satisfying musical presentations to come down the pike in some time."

Between November and January, the Rolling Thunder Revue

played a total of thirty-one shows in some of the most incongruous joints ever to make up the offbeat rock circuit. One such "joint" was exactly that—the Correctional Institution for Women in Clinton, New Jersey, whose most celebrated inmate was none other than "The Hurricane" himself—Rubin Carter.

By the time Bob and the Revue trooped into the prison, "Hurricane" had already peaked at #33 on *Billboard*'s "Hot 100" chart. Still, the tour had helped to keep the song's message out among the people, and a steering committee worked diligently behind the scenes in an effort to get Carter a new trial. In its own right, the record had managed to stir up a good deal of judicial attention for Hurricane. The New Jersey Supreme Court was rumored to be reviewing the facts of the case and, if all went well, might rehear it before the end of its current session. A few months earlier, Bob's lawyers conducted their own examination of the evidence and concluded that as far as the facts were concerned, their client had better get *his* straight.

In his haste to get the record out, Bob had taken certain liberties with the musical retelling of the incident—placing the wrong witness at the scene of the crime—a minor oversight which not only threatened to bury him in litigation but could conceivably force a mistrial were the case to be retried. On the advice of counsel, Bob re-recorded the song with a corrected lyric, however, in 1979 he was sued in a U.S. District Court in Florida by Patricia Ann Valentine, who appears in a recurring role throughout the song.

The case holds little significance as far as the Bob Dylan story is concerned; his deposition, however, allows us a rare look at the writing habits of a man who otherwise *never* explains his songs. Most of the testimony contained in the sixty-four-page document is a miscellany of Bob's usual dodges. For instance, for the record he cannot recall whether or not he has legally changed his name, and when counsel for the plaintiff asks him if he is known by any other name besides Bob Dylan or Robert Zimmerman, Bob responds, "Not here. Not on this earth." Later, when he was ordered to recount the way in which Patty Valentine enters the song, Bob coyly testifies, "She enters into the song—she discovers the bodies." "Okay," the lawyer prods him. "And she's got a beautiful name."

These exchanges were the same that made Bob out to be one of the world's most difficult interviews. When he put up that protective shield, you could go on for days without getting a straight answer. At the same time, Bob was making this statement for his own protection, so that when the plaintiff's counsel raised the meaning behind certain lyrics, Bob felt compelled to explain them.

ATTORNEY: I must ask you first. In stanza 9, line 2, "The trial was a pig circus." Are you referring to policemen there?

DYLAN: No. First of all, I don't write many songs with a collaborator, so I don't remember who wrote what on this. ["Hurricane" was cowritten with Jacques Levy.] "The trial was a pig circus" would mean, most likely, that it was a spectacle, you know, for show, some type of abomination in a courtroom. I really couldn't tell you exactly what it means literally.

ATTORNEY: What do you mean by the first line, "All of Rubin's cards were marked in advance"?

DYLAN: Well, there again, you'd have to read up to Verse 8 to see that that would make sense—or be the truth.

ATTORNEY: What do you refer to? I am asking you what you mean by that.

DYLAN: Well, cards being marked in advance is someone who knows what someone else is holding, you know, by the way they deal out the deck, by certain cuts on the cards or certain ways of marking them so it would be evident to one person and not to another.

The two men circled around each other for another minute or two before Bob was cross-examined about the rest of that stanza.

ATTORNEY: And there you are saying "be in the palm of some fool's hand"; is that the judge you are referring to?

DYLAN: That would be whoever Satan gave power to.

ATTORNEY: To be the judge?

DYLAN: Well, right here it would be whoever was blind to the truth and was living by his own truth, that would be whoever the fool would be.

ATTORNEY: Whomever testified?

DYLAN: Whoever that fits, whoever—no, no. We are just talking here—not on who testified. I mean—

ATTORNEY: The judge?

DYLAN: No. You couldn't possibly believe that whoever testified would have anyone in the palm of their hand.

That answer was pure Dylan bluff. When Bob walked into the Correctional Institution for Women that December afternoon in 1975 he was convinced he had the situation perfectly under control. Maybe even in the palm of his hand. In theory, it amounted to nothing more than another segment of the Rolling Thunder Revue, and while the gig happened to be a medium-security prison, it was no different than a lot of the other holes they had played. As far as security went, it had been tighter at theaters in New England where paranoia was rampant. There was so much traffic going in and out of the joint, what with the band and the crew and an army of curious journalists, that it wouldn't have surprised anyone if an inmate or two tried to make a break.

As it turned out, Bob should have smuggled himself out in a laundry truck. One look at the place was enough to raise a red flag—a tiny, tiny gym, the smallest audience on the tour made up mostly of black inmates, none of whom had the slightest inkling who Bob Dylan was—nor cared. In fact, a majority of inmates had chosen not to come to the gig. It was visiting day, and they had the option of either participating in a conjugal visit or watching the show. Of those who did make it, probably everyone except Rubin Carter regarded the Rolling Thunder Revue as another dreary institutional talent show on the order of Amateur Night.

Luckily, Roberta Flack had been invited to join the ensemble, otherwise they might have touched off a prison riot. The inmates couldn't relate at all to Joni Mitchell's creamy white pastorales. Two minutes into her set, hoots and catcalls sailed up over the makeshift stage, thawing Joni's icy composure. That tomcat face of hers puckered into a wicked sneer. "We came here to give you love," she lectured them. "If you can't handle it, that's your problem." Rob Stoner remembers: "Talk about wrong moves—that warmed-over Sixties shit was the worst thing she could have said to them. It was like that chick on *Romper Room*—'Do-Bee says: Respect your visitors!' I mean, you could see guys giving each other looks that said, 'Throw that bitch out here and we'll teach her a thing or two about *clouds!*'"

It was Allen Ginsberg, of all people, who recaptured the audience's heart. Instead of walking out on stage dressed in jeans and funky threads, an ingratiating manner and a set full of upbeat, bawdy tunes, Allen tumbled out there in a boxy brown suit and wide tie as if he'd stopped off on his way to the bank. The inmates took one look at this soft, doughy, nerdish-looking gink and flashed—"fresh meat for the barbecue." Imagine the chill he sent down their spines when, after a moment of adjustment, he opened his mouth and bellowed the name of the poem he was going to recite: "Kiss Ass!" Why, the place went wild with shrieks and whistles, those big black mothers slapping each other on the shoulders and stomping their feet. Allen grinned sheepishly, then began:

Kissass is the Part of Peace
America will have to
Kissass Mother Earth
Whites will have to Kissass
Blacks, for Peace and
Pleasure,
Only Pathway to Peace,
Kissass.

Talk about a hard act to follow! When Joan Baez took the stage, there was some serious misgivings emanating from the prison gallery. One of the reporters cased the scene and thought, "Joan sings 'Mary Hamilton' and, Quaker or not, she's gonna have to fight her way out of here." No doubt other members of the press had the same impression of Joan, for you could feel their collective apprehensiveness. They were unaware of her reputation for doing unexpected and self-effacing sets. And they underestimated her savvy. Joan Baez, the white goddess of folk music, took one look at her audience and ripped through a no-nonsense version of "Land of 1000 Dances." *Aw-riiiight!* She milked that number for all it was worth, boogeying across the stage and straddling the mike like Tina Turner. She wriggled and writhed and twitched and jerked her trim body in time to the thumping bass beat. Then, after working the crowd into a groove, she yanked an inmate on stage and danced the Bump with him. There was instant delirium in that tiny guy, and Joan walked off to a rousing, seriously horny ovation.

As the applause reached a crescendo, Bob's confidence visibly melted away. "He was definitely nervous," Rob Stoner recalls. "You could spot it as soon as he strapped on his guitar. He was more uncommunicative than usual, he refused to make eye contact with any of us, he stayed off by himself and lacked that 'I-am-the-bandleader/this-is-my-show' attitude that had been so evident at the rest of the gigs we had done."

Bob recognized at once that this wasn't his crowd. Even the fact that he'd spoken out for Hurricane Carter cut no mustard with them. The inmates could relate to a guy like Johnny Cash because he'd done time in the can and was considered one of them. But Bob Dylan was a complete mystery.

Bob tried his best to connect with them. He opened with "Blowin' in the Wind"—a nice gesture of social consciousness, and, who knows, maybe they'd even heard Stevie Wonder's version of it. But in the middle of the second verse, at a point where audiences usually glowed with respect, the inmates got fed up. They didn't want to hear about walking down roads like a man when they had another twenty years to face behind bars. They knew the answer, my friend, and it wasn't blowin' in no wind. Fuck this shit! It was request time as far as the inmates were concerned. "Hey! hey! Y'all know 'Dancin' the Night Away'?" a voice yelled out in the middle of "Blowin' in the Wind." "You boys know 'It's Yo' Thing'?" "Hey, man, do 'Nothin' from Nothin'!" "Yeah!—do that one! Do '*Shaaaaaft*'!"

What a scream! The band was in stitches, but poor Bob hadn't the sense to break off early and turn the whole thing into a gag. Unfortunately everything went downhill from there. He fumffered through a final abbreviated chorus and barreled into "Hurricane." That held them for a few minutes, and after a futile attempt at "Knockin' on Heaven's Door," he bolted from the stage.

A group of prison officials intercepted Bob as he made his escape. "This was such a good thing you did coming out here and blah, blah, blah," they gushed. Bob mumbled his usual "Oh, yeah, sure—I'll be back," but you could bet it would have to be in cuffs and chains.

28

Rolling Blunder

Officially, the Rolling Thunder Revue concluded with a December 8th benefit at New York's Madison Square Garden. "The Night of the Hurricane," as it was called, proved a fitting climax to one of the most triumphant, if not the most innovative, tours in the history of pop music. The audience was studded with celebrities and politicians. The stage spilled over with stars. The music was truly spectacular, with Bob contributing twenty-one emotion-filled songs in a supremely sturdy voice. Only an appearance by Muhammed Ali threatened to drag the evening down to the level of cheap parody that was typical of such charity events.

The Champ, dressed in a black polyester leisure suit, was trundled on stage halfway through the first act to deliver an impassioned appeal on behalf of Rubin Carter. It was staged as a poignant gesture—from one boxer to another, the whole black-brother-facing-the-fight-of-his-life bit—until Ali turned it into one of his moronic shuck and jives. After speaking to Rubin via a live telephone hookup, Ali introduced one of his business cronies from Tennessee as "the next President of the United States." Out popped a slick white politician who looked like he'd been sent over from Central Casting, a fried-chicken franchiser named John Jay Hooker Jr., who'd been shuttling Ali around the country in his private jet. Roundly booed by a disillusioned post-

Watergate audience that was sick of political grandstanding, Hooker couldn't get a word of his peace-and-justice pitch in. Nor could Ali regain control of the crowd. The booing continued unabated as he fought to introduce a number of other political hacks, until the Champ was finally driven from the stage.

Nevertheless, the Garden gig ended on an emotionally upbeat note. Word was passed backstage that Rubin Carter had succeeded in getting a new trial date and would be released from prison before Christmas. The astounding news came from no less a source than Carter himself, who had telephoned Bob during the show's half-hour intermission. "Bob was ecstatic," recalls one of his band members. "He grabbed me around the shoulders and said, 'Hey, man—we really accomplished something. This is what it's all about!'" Promising Rubin he'd make the dramatic announcement from the stage of Madison Square Garden, Bob said good-bye and tuned up for the show's second act.

It wasn't until he was practically under the lights again that Bob learned the story was a figment of Rubin Carter's imagination. A concert official had called New Jersey Governor Brenden Byrne's office to confirm the report and was told it sounded like a desperate publicity stunt. There wasn't an ounce of truth to it. When Bob heard the news, he was profoundly disappointed. He had spent a year attempting to convince people that Carter had been framed and was really a man of his word. At that very moment, there were twenty-two thousand people waiting to hear Bob sing about how the Hurricane "was falsely tried." What had led him to that forensic conclusion? Why, *Rubin*, of course. He believed Rubin when the boxer looked him in the eye and swore he was innocent. He *still* believed Rubin; nevertheless he sang the protest song that night with considerably less conviction than on some of the other shows along the tour.

Even in the aftermath of this fiasco, Bob managed a convincing game face. The post-concert party at the Garden's Felt Forum (where, a year earlier, he appeared at the Chile benefit) was his moment to savor the triumph. The handpicked crowd of performers, technicians, and friends watched with fascination as a flushed Bob Dylan, holding Sara's hand, worked the cavernous room, personally thanking everyone there for his or her part in making the tour an unqualified financial and critical success. The band, in particular, marveled that their notoriously tight boss had added a bonus to their paychecks. Bob told them the Rolling Thunder Revue had turned an unexpected profit, and he'd decided to cut them in for a slice of the pie. Wasn't that a lovely gesture? An early week's pay? Initially, that's what everybody thought, but once the meaning of it sank in, some of the musicians began to fume.

"It was his way of letting us know we'd been *fired!*" says a disgruntled accompanist who operated under the delusion of perpetual employment. "You know, from the show that was supposed to run forever! The one he promised us would provide us with jobs for as long as we wanted. Bob never led us to believe anything other than that would happen. And like most of us, I thought, 'Wow, man, I'll do this until I get the gold watch.' But that night, as we pocketed our bonuses it finally dawned on us that we were unemployed."

In retrospect, that might have been a blessing in disguise, but by mid-January Bob was homesick for the road. The band was rounded up and instructed to report to Los Angeles, where it was to begin rehearsals for yet another benefit concert to stoke Rubin Carter's legal war chest. Bob was charged up about doing another big show that could have an impact on the outcome of Carter's trial. He trotted out all the superlatives in describing their upcoming gig. It was going to be bigger, more spectacular, flashier, and more star-studded than anything the Rolling Thunder Revue had ever attempted. To drive home his point, he even revealed the location of the extravaganza—the seventy-thousand-seat Astrodome in Houston, Texas.

Bob's decision to play the Astrodome was either the most courageous gambit of his career or a supreme blunder. Designed originally as an indoor baseball stadium, the Astrodome was the ultimate concert facility—a daunting eight city blocks long, four wide, with a seating plan that required closed-circuit video screens to provide the audience with a decent view of the stage. As comedian Albert Brooks used to say of it: "You're better off just flying over the state and collecting money." Intimacy wasn't one of its strong points. And the acoustics were a performer's nightmare. In fact, there weren't any. Sound caromed off the inside of the domed shell like a ballistic missile test, so that nothing could be heard with any distinction, only a thunderous roar. As such, it was suited to the kind of decibel warfare practiced by heavy-metal bands, but even a local favorite like Z.Z. Top had difficulty filling so many seats. The Rolling Thunder

Revue, an act that prided itself on playing in small, intimate settings, had struggled to sell out the tiny Palace Theatre in Waterbury, Connecticut; at more than twenty-three times its size, the Astrodome was a fool's paradise.

Like Texas, everything on this date was destined to be bigger and grander, beginning with the rehearsal. It was held at the gigantic S.I.R. soundstage in Hollywood and resembled an open casting call for a major motion picture. All sorts of new faces turned up to audition for the Revue—Ringo Starr, Sonny Bono, Dennis Hopper, Carlos Santana, Stephen Stills, Sally Kirkland. The guys from the Band, all of whom had moved out to Zuma Beach, put in an appearance. As did forty or fifty of L.A.'s rock 'n roll elite who patrolled the back of the room with their shades on, casually checking out the scene and waiting for the right moment to leap onto the stage.

No one seemed to be more at home in this element than Bob Dylan. He appeared tan and relaxed, his perpetually unhealthy features resuscitated by the sun-washed California climate. Even his manner had changed from that of the brooding, self-contained songwriter to an animated, accessible guy who never tired of rehearsing new songs. The couple of weeks' layoff had definitely recharged his batteries and, once more, roused his generosity.

Within two days of the band's arrival he sent the entire Revue to Nudie's Rodeo Tower in North Hollywood with the understanding that they could order a complete suit of stage clothes. "And have it billed to me!" Bob insisted, like a doting uncle. It was a magnanimous offer, considering they ran up a bill of around fifty thousand dollars that afternoon.

Bob was unpredictable by nature, but with money he was as chancy as a roll of the dice. For instance, before his world tour in 1978, Bob was so preoccupied with his divorce that he entrusted the band's entire rehearsal to his bass player, Rob Stoner. The setup was similar to the way Nelson Riddle worked with an orchestra so that Frank Sinatra could simply just show up at the last minute and sing. To express his appreciation, Bob decided to reward Stoner with a gift. "I'm gonna buy you a car," Bob promised him. "Just tell me what kind you want and it's yours."

Stoner was thunderstruck by the gesture. He might have expected as much if his boss were someone like Elvis who doled out cars like they were cheap wristwatches, but from Bob Dylan—it was completely out of character. As such, Stoner resolved not to take advantage of the situation. Instead of hitting him for a Ferrari or a Lamborghini like his friends urged, he settled on a restored '65 Mustang convertible that he'd seen in a custom car shop near the rehearsal studio. It was a modest little roadster that certainly wasn't out of Bob's price range. "So I told him about it," Stoner says. "Bob nodded ambiguously, and that was the last I ever heard about the car."

Nevertheless, Bob was behaving like a sugar daddy in preparation for the Astrodome show. The musicians were decked out in their spectacularly vulgar Nudie outfits, the rehearsal buffets rivaled four-star feasts, room tabs at the Sunset Marquis were unlimited.

The supply of drugs that inspirited the second Rolling Thunder Revue was unlimited, too. The L.A. music scene was notorious for being a twenty-four-hour pharmacy. Out there, rock and dope went together like a burger and fries. All the gang were at home with their "connect," and the endless string of backyard parties made it easier to score than in New York, where your source conducted business like a psychotic arbitrager on some crowded dance floor. There was always plenty of blow around the Rolling Thunder Revue, but the tour had managed to steer clear of the heavy junk scene. Now, however, smack began sifting into the picture, and the appetite of several players grew voracious and more sophisticated.

Bob snorted an occasional line or two of cocaine to get himself up before and after a show, but for the most part he was absorbed in what was shaping up to be his greatest adventure on the Revue. The arrangements for Houston demanded all of his attention and a clear head. Somehow he had to make room on stage for Ringo Starr, as well as Rick Danko. Kinky Friedman, a bizarre country singer who wore silk cowboy shirts imprinted with menorahs, replaced Jack Elliott as the Revue's authentic Jewish troubadour and needed time to acquaint himself with the routine. Then there was Stevie Wonder and his entire band. And Isaac Hayes and *his band!* The cozy little show had been blown way out of proportion. It was an embarrassment of riches and had at last begun to resemble the carnival Bob originally envisioned, only more surrealistic.

Even the band was temporarily blinded by the grandeur. For months, the guys had been content to open the second half of the show with a medley of Byrds hits built around Roger McGuinn's signature vocals. It was frankly nostalgic and even a little maudlin. But it gave them a chance to cut loose with an interlude of rock favorites that never failed to charm the audience. That had satisfied them as long as the Revue stuck to its low-profile manifesto. Now, however, they smelled a "commercial opportunity" and wanted to capitalize on it by featuring themselves as a new "supergroup"—Thunderbyrd. With a little imagination you could already see the album cover. And hear the ad copy: *"A marriage of rock's legendary masters—the Byrds and Bob Dylan's Rolling Thunder Revue...."* No doubt an act with that pedigree would make the labels drool. Except that Bob wouldn't hear of it. There were already too many bands on the tour, he argued. It was beginning to feel like the St. Patrick's Day parade.

It wasn't until they left for Houston that Bob got a real look at how unwieldy things had gotten. His entourage had swollen to over a hundred people. Perpetuating one of Hollywood's old-line institutions—freeloading—scores of semifamous movie stars, entertainment leeches, and other four-flushers had talked their way onto the Revue's chartered plane. Then, as soon as they landed in Houston, other faces started turning up at the hotel.

One was Stephen Stills, who announced that he intended to play the Astrodome as a member of the Rolling Thunder Revue, and he had brought along his own road crew, equipment team, and band. Bob got one look at Stills's paraphernalia and nearly had a coronary. Literally a fortress of Marshall stacks, the granddaddy of earsplitting amplifiers, had been dumped backstage, on the arena's loading platform. Hadn't anybody hipped Stills to the Revue's policy of using only small amps? Bob wanted to know. In fact, someone had, but Stills didn't give a shit. A gluttonous drug abuser, he was coked-up and in an extremely sinister mood fraught with such violent overtones that, instead of insisting he comply, the equipment man wisely backed off.

The threats, however, bounced impotently off Bob. He refused to have his own band upstaged by a column of deafening amps. Before the afternoon sound check, he grabbed Rob Stoner and ordered him to deliver an ultimatum to Stills. "Tell him if he wants to come on and do an acoustic set, that's cool. If he wants to use our band, that's cool, too. But I won't have those big amps on stage," he said.

The ever-obedient serf, Stoner flew off directly to Stills's hotel room and found the beefy guitar virtuoso in a rage. "He was snorting coke from the biggest coke-shaker I'd ever seen," Stoner recalls. "Just dumping it out, leaving more on the table than a respectable coke-user consumes in a week. I saw immediately that he was beyond reason. He was wired up and belligerent and implied that all sorts of bad things might happen to us if he didn't get his way. In fact, he insisted his band would play whether or not we approved, and if Bob Dylan didn't like it he could go fuck himself."

Stills just held out until Bob relented, and he played an intrusive, unusually boisterous set that for all its hostility was ideally suited to the Astrodome's cosmic scale. The rest of the show, however, was a disaster. For one thing, Bob had seriously misjudged his popularity in the South. Texas was a heavy-metal bastion, and local rock fans didn't give a hoot about a bunch of overaged hippies singing folk music for an imprisoned boxer. They weren't interested in Bob Dylan. Or Stevie Wonder, for that matter.

Despite an aggressive last-minute publicity drive, which stooped to radio giveaways, only thirty-five thousand people showed up for the concert. Considering the capacity of the Astrodome, the turnout was catastrophic. It meant that an area one-and-a-half times the size of Madison Square Garden was deserted. From the stage, the emptiness was palpable. There were acres of dark barren space in the audience, and at the conclusion of each song the performers could actually pinpoint black holes from which no response emanated.

The more conspicuous it became, the more it rattled Bob. His pace was thrown off; the singing was ragged. There was none of that quirky thrust to his delivery which usually roused a comatose audience. After struggling to locate himself, groping for the special combination of music and moves that would fire up the crowd, he simply shut down. Riding his guitar aimlessly across the stage, Bob gave off appreciable vibes of alienation, an almost ominous indifference, like an exhausted old hack who performed the same melodies night after night at a hotel bar.

That night, nothing went right for the newly reunited Rolling Thunder Revue. To begin with, the musicians had entrusted the job of tuning their instruments to one of Stephen Stills's technicians, but when Bob and the band plugged in, there was complete chaos. The instruments were in tune—just not to each other. Sabotaged! The show was shaky, the audience grew bored and restless, and to top it off Stevie Wonder refused Bob's invitation to join him on stage for a duet of their respective hit, "Blowin' in the Wind." Bob was visibly unhinged by the whole mess.

The evening's biggest loser, as luck would have it, was its intended beneficiary—Rubin Carter. Had the concert proved successful, the boxer stood to gain roughly three hundred thousand dollars toward his appeal. But production expenses spiraled, ticket sales were dreadful, and the show itself was a bust. As it turned out, the hapless promoters were unable to raise even a nickel from the proceeds. Except for a ten-thousand dollar contribution from the Astrodome itself, the concert was not so much a hurricane as a financial washout.

After Houston, most of the troupe believed their idyllic enterprise had met its unfortunate end. The critics delivered the inevitable obituary buried bluntly within their reviews. The best of the notices were scathing; the others descended to the level of crude put-downs and slams that were often hurled by low-level flak. But the message was ultimately the same. The show, they agreed, appeared to have run its course. Its magical spirit was moldering. No member of the tour dared pronounce the Rolling Thunder Revue dead, but you can be sure they all had reached similar conclusions as they prepared to creep out of dismal Texas. The hospitality suite at the hotel was somber as a morgue. There was none of the mischievous high jinks or whacked-out revelry that usually followed a performance. None of the cocky bravado that went with elite membership in the Revue. The prevailing mood was closer to resignation. "Bob'd have to be crazy to want to do this again," one musician sighed, summing up the general outlook.

Craziness, however, is a subjective diagnosis. Some people lose touch with reality and wind up muttering to themselves in the street. Some lapse into uncontrollable rage. Still others pour billions into a dream like the Strategic Defense Initiative. Be that as it may, Bob Dylan decided to persevere with the Rolling Thunder Revue. Come April 1976, the gang was summoned to the unlikely crossroads of Clearwater, Florida, for what they were told was yet another go-round.

Bob showed up in an astonishingly upbeat mood. He was dying to play and interrupted a jam session–in–progress to break in his chops. The result was an unprecedented burst of music—three hours of nonstop rock 'n roll oldies, then all his stuff from *Highway 61*, which saw

Bob flit from the piano to lead guitar and even to a stint on the drums. He was all over the place, singing and harmonizing with joyful abandon. Smiling from ear to ear. According to several eyewitnesses, it was the best Dylan music they'd ever heard.

If tour personnel had been skeptical of this newest Rolling Thunder reunion, their fears soon disappeared. Their leader was in top form, a whole slew of dates had fallen neatly into place, and to everyone's amazement a TV special was booked to feature the ensemble in a typical "intimate" setting. Says Rob Stoner, "All of us figured Bob was trying to vindicate himself for that Houston disaster. He wanted to do it one more time and to get it right. So we were real optimistic—until the bad news hit."

Late that afternoon, Bob was called away and informed that Phil Ochs was dead. Depressed and destitute, Ochs had hung himself at his sister's house in Far Rockaway, New York, only days after learning he wasn't being invited to join the latest touring company of the Rolling Thunder Revue. Friends and relatives contend Phil lobbied furiously for a chance to fill Jack Elliott's spot on the tour and deluded himself into believing he had won it. Some even swear that Bob promised him the gig, although that is highly unlikely. By that time, Phil was a very nasty drunk and completely unreliable. He could never have survived the road in his condition. Paranoid delusions consumed him, leading him to provoke dark, abusive arguments with people who loved and supported him. "Phil had gotten crazier and crazier," laments his longtime associate Arthur Gorson. "Everything he did at the end was based on madness and illusion and falsehood, and a lot of it stemmed from the phantom competition he imagined with Bob. Oddly enough, he counted on Bob, his nemesis, to bail him out of the worst jam of his life and was very hurt when it failed to materialize."

Bob took the news of Ochs's death very badly. Perhaps excessively so. He and Phil had never been particularly close. In fact, they did things to each other designed to repel a normal productive friendship. Take Phil's treasured photograph, for instance. In it, he's perched grandly on a tombstone inscribed with the name ZIMMERMAN, a satisfied grin creasing his boyish face. That one really broke up the guys on MacDougal Street. And he continuously needled Bob in the press, questioning his political commitment. Bob, for his part, treated

Ochs like the Village idiot. He made no secret of the fact he held Phil's music in low esteem. It was naive pop journalism put to sloppy, sentimental melodies. As far as Bob cared, Phil was stuck somewhere back in the dopey Sixties.

But deep down Phil was still . . . Phil. There was something unavoidably amusing, though difficult, about him. He was like one of those boyhood chums you outgrow but still looked forward to seeing every once in a while. And now, with Phil's death, Bob surely felt part of his own past slip away. Perhaps it was that happy-go-lucky portion of his life he pined for in a song like "Bob Dylan's Dream," when he longed for nothin' but talkin' and a-jokin' and singin' with his friends. Or maybe it reminded him of the last time he saw Phil—at a sixty-first birthday party for Mike Porco—when he staggered on stage at Folk City, beyond drunkenness, and astounded Bob and the crowd by singing three traditional folk songs and a breathtaking version of "Lay Down Your Weary Tune," a parting tribute to his friend.

In some small way Bob must have blamed himself for Phil's final desperate act. It must have haunted him afterward that he might have been able to cheat fate by bringing Phil on the road. But those were illusory consequences arising from the tragedy. Says Arthur Gorson, "Bob's only crime was that Phil considered him a *fine artist.* That was all Phil ever wanted from life—to be taken seriously as a songwriter—and unfortunately Bob Dylan served as a constant reminder of how far he was from ever achieving his goal."

In Clearwater, Bob canceled rehearsal and went into seclusion. No one was sure what had happened to him. The first few days he wasn't seen at all. Then, at night, he'd be spotted prowling around the grounds by himself. Or hanging out by the pool at dawn. Or sitting despondently in a car, his head down in contemplation. Anyone who approached him and attempted to strike up a conversation was rudely ignored. The band was forced to rehearse without him, going over songs the musicians assumed he would perform in the keys in which he usually performed them. But with Bob you couldn't be sure of anything. And with the TV special almost upon them, the band was laying bets against its ever coming off at all.

Once Bob returned, everything went rapidly downhill. He began drinking more, and not the cheap French wine or aperitifs he'd favored for the last twenty years. Bob had graduated to bourbon, the breakfast of champions. Bourbon, it was said, worked faster on people who were desperate to forget, and Bob began to run up his intake at an alarming pace. He began walking around clutching a fifth of Jack Daniels, which he'd polish off in a day. Day after day. The deteriorating effect it had on him confounded the other performers. Drunk and belligerent was hard enough to handle, but Bob got drunk and *cosmic.* He talked in circles, like a senile philosopher. Or he'd grab the band and put it through a grueling two-hour rehearsal of *only one song,* the way he did with "Simple Twist of Fate," over and over again, reminding anyone who groaned that he was being paid to play anything Bob damn well pleased for as long as it pleased him.

Once they actually got out on the road, there were long periods of time during which Bob refused to talk to anyone in the band. For gigs at a time! It seemed like he was intentionally trying to divide them, trying to foment a climate of paranoia and negativity that spilled over into his act. On stage, he'd shoot dirty looks at individual musicians or throw them deliberate curves in mid-show. For instance, he'd start strumming the chords to "Maggie's Farm," the band would kick in behind him... only to discover that Bob had switched to "Highway 61"! If anyone pointed out the unexpected change, Bob snarled: "Well, it goes like *this* now. Understand?" Bullshit answers. It frustrated the rest of the group. They felt as if he were deliberately trying to make them look bad—or to drag them down along with him.

It didn't take a psychiatrist to realize that Bob was behaving like a person on the verge of a serious breakdown. Nearly everyone who came into contact with him came away with the same impression. Bob was more unpredictable that ever. His moods were erratic and fitful. Like a child, he seemed unable to concentrate on any one subject for more than a few minutes at a time. You couldn't talk to him about anything.

Even more disturbing was Bob's lack of someone in whom he could confide. Someone he trusted and depended on to help him unload all the pressure that mounted up on the road. Usually that role fell to someone like Bobby Neuwirth or Rob Stoner, but Bob had already cut himself off from those guys. Joan, too, felt increasingly alienated from him and eventually devoted all her spare time to her young son, who had recently joined her on the tour. Bob rejected all other offers of friendship. Instead, he surrounded himself with a bunch of weirdos who catered to his eccentricities as if he were a simpleminded king. The astrologer he hired to compile everyone's chart turned out to be a real pain in the ass. A performer would be rehearsing a new bit, trying to get a tricky rhythm down, while this "nutcase" pestered him for the exact time of his birth. Another woman joined the Revue for no purpose other than to hang a tapestry on Bob's dressing room wall before each show. Watching this happen to someone like Bob Dylan was unspeakably sad. Jacques Levy, who held a degree in clinical psychology, warned several members of the Rolling Thunder troupe that Bob's behavior pattern spelled trouble ahead.

No one, however, was aware of the enormous pressures that had been multiplying around him for some time. For one thing, Bob's marriage was hanging on by a slender thread. Sara had stayed home in California, but that didn't preclude her from receiving almost daily bulletins from the road. She had her spies, and they were only too happy to fill her in on all the action—especially the action her husband was getting in the arms of his hot little girlfriend. Of course she knew he was fucking around—wives have a way of sensing those things without being told. But he could have been more discreet about it. That would have at least spared her the indignity of having to turn up unannounced in order to confront that little worm.

Those were always miserable scenes. Sara would suddenly appear, sending a ripple of panic through the Revue ranks. Occasionally Bob would be off with his girlfriend, and he had to literally get her out one door as Sara was coming in the other one. But mostly there'd be ugly confrontations in a parking lot or outside one of the motels or behind the paper-thin walls of someone's room. He'd give her that angry look of his that would stop a bus, but it had absolutely no effect on his wife. Sara knew how to deal with that I-am-the-star business, and you could tell just by looking at her that she was bored with it. Her face was a mask of cool detachment, an expression worn by someone who was wise enough to accept the inevitable and to recognize that the end was near.

The box office also proved a source of constant tension in Bob's life. Despite the enormous success of *Desire* and the fact that he had never been hotter, the tour was bombing on the road. Tallahassee, Gainesville, Pensacola, Hattiesburg, Corpus Christi, Fort Worth—those cities weren't Bob Dylan strongholds. They were boogie-band towns. Audiences there wanted to drink beer and be blown out of their seat by high-voltage pyrotechnics. They wanted the Allman Brothers, not some cornball folkie revue! Barry Imhoff, the promoter, had relied on the same kind of popularity Bob enjoyed in New England to carry him through the South and the Midwest, but it hadn't materialized. To make matters worse, the tour's itinerary followed on the heels of Paul McCartney's "Wings Over America" tour by a week-and-a-half, so by the time the Rolling Thunder Revue got to town, the kids had already spent half their concert allowance on the competition.

On May 8, 1976, when they returned to Houston, it was clear that some emergency help was needed to fill the hall. Ticket sales had been so sluggish at previous Texas shows that scattered dates were canceled to avoid embarrassment, but in Houston they had an old score to settle. The scene of the previous Hurricane fiasco, it was essential they prove the critics wrong with a knockout show. This time, they booked a more realistic arena, the 10,700-seat Hofheinz Pavilion, for a pair of back-to-back concerts. Advance tickets, however, were still way off the mark, requiring the two shows to become one, but even that failed to do the trick. Competition from a pair of John Denver shows and a sold-out Johnny Winter/Weather Report concert stalled the intended comeback, so it was high time to bring in the heavy artillery. Whom do you rely on in Texas to ensure a sellout? Only one man—Willie Nelson.

If Willie Nelson was the solution, the problem was his manager, Neil Reshen, one of the most notorious ballbusters in the history of the rock music business. Reshen was reluctant to put up his cash cow to rescue the ailing Rolling Thunder Revue. He wanted insurance, and in response Columbia Records offered to underwrite an album featuring Bob and Willie on the order of Barbra and Barry, but Reshen refused. There was only one thing that interested him—money. According to an interview Reshen gave *Rolling Stone* in June 1976, he said, "CBS [then] called up and offered in excess of $10,000 as payment to ensure Bob Dylan sold the date. We played."

They also brought along their own trouble free of charge. Just before showtime, two plainclothes U.S. marshals showed up outside Willie's dressing room with a subpoena. "Bam! Bam! Bam! Open up, Mr. Nelson." Those of the Rolling Thunder gang who were hanging around outside ran for cover. Says Rob Stoner, "We were all pretty uptight about it. There was a lot of real flagrant coke-sniffing going on and we were certain they were going to bust Willie then and there." As it turned out, he was only served with an order to appear before a Dallas grand jury that was conducting a probe into heroin and cocaine trafficking. *Whew!*—that had been a close shave, but Reshen performed some fancy footwork, and the U.S. agents left happily, each pocketing his personalized Willie Nelson autograph to take home and show the kids.

After that, there was nothing left to do but to play.

29

Irreconcilable Differences

After the Rolling Thunder Revue played its final chord, Bob Dylan returned home to face the music. The tour had destroyed whatever remained of his original relationship with Sara, the separation serving not so much to provide a remedy as it did to establish detente. Now, without distance to cushion the squabbling, hostilities between them heated up anew, although in Bob's case his inscrutable slow burn exacerbated the situation. An eidolon, he became the archetypal Enemy in Our Midst—guarded, cryptic, and menacing. His arsenal of passive-aggressive weaponry proved indefensible. Sara was certainly no match for him. According to close friends of the Dylans, Bob had become as elusive around the house as he was on stage; Sara was treated no differently than a rejected fan who was ignored or glared at or was berated into leaving him alone. She was effectively locked out of Bob's life, yet still forced to deal with him both as the man who shared her house and as the father of her children. Because he also happened to be her sole provider, she was really no better off than a prisoner—an emotional prisoner—with Bob as her sadistic warden.

Though Bob's behavior toward Sara was reprehensible, it wasn't out of character. It's perfectly clear that he was acting on a familiar instinct. Bob was a man who provoked situations by antagonism and manipulation. He wasn't the type to look someone in the eye and say exactly what was on his mind. That was too confrontational, too painful. Bob preferred you intuit his unhappiness and do something about it, preferably without requiring his involvement, like when Joan Baez bailed out of the *Don't Look Back* tour. If that didn't solve things or you were simply too thick to catch on, he sent out little signals to prompt a reaction. Usually they took the form of brooding silences or unprovoked flashes of anger designed to get your attention. A stroke of that had worked rather nicely on the Rolling Thunder band. But in extreme situations he reached into his old bag of tricks for a fail-safe device—*mind-fucking,* that old Sixties spark plug. Sowing the seeds of paranoia was always one of Bob's most reliable expedients. He had a real knack for it—bombarding his targets with powerful delusions until they became so flustered by it they actually believed *they* were crazy. Joan was victimized by that one, too. And Suze Rotolo—her whole family was juggled into the dark abyss of that little game.

But making someone paranoid required cooperation. He or she had to be weaker and more insecure than Bob was, or the strategy collapsed. Ordinarily Sara was a cool customer where Bob was concerned. More mature and less susceptible than his former lovers, she was immune to his malicious intrigues. All of which leads one to conclude that Bob was incredibly determined to undermine her morale by tightening the emotional screws. How else would he have driven her to divorce him?

If we are to believe the details spelled out in a five-page affidavit she filed on March 1, 1977, in Santa Monica Superior Court, Sara was punished by Bob's unrelenting cruelty. The scenes she claimed he initiated were so grotesque they might have been directed by Brian De Palma. "He began to act in a bizarre and frightening manner, causing me to be terrified of him," Sara contended. "He would come in and out of the house at all hours, often bursting into my room, where he would stand and gaze at me in silence and refuse to leave." She charged that he hit her in the face and subjected her to a torrent of physical abuse, including "violent outbursts and temper tantrums." And perhaps too self-servingly, she claimed he shrank from his responsibilities as a father. "During the time he and I were married, he expressed little or no interest in our children," Sara attested. "He refused to even come near the hospital when all but the last of our children was born. Once, because he wanted to *finish a chess game.*"

Naturally, she exploited Bob's profession. A songwriter, a rock 'n roll star!—that looked just peachy in court. Rock stars were arrested all the time for disturbing the peace. And for drugs. Sara alleged Bob was too busy making films, playing concerts, taking art lessons, and concentrating on other distractions to help her raise the children. But the clincher was a scene Sara recounted with incriminating detail.

Early on the morning of February 22nd, she awoke in the bedroom of their recently completed Malibu pad and shuffled down to breakfast. A light breeze was blowing in off the ocean. Sunlight poured through the windows and the overhead skylight, bathing the sparsely decorated interior with warm, golden hues. As she made her way toward the kitchen, Sara could hear that breakfast was already in progress. Bob and the kids had obviously gotten up before her and, from the sound of things, were already at the table. That wasn't anything unusual. Sara often slept later than her family and relied on their wherewithal to start the day without her. But as she pushed through the door to the kitchen she discovered Bob sitting at the table surrounded by the children *and another woman!* He had brought one of his girlfriends into the house, a woman named Malka, who had been on the fringe of his life for a few weeks. The sight of them sitting together was so shocking to Sara that it took a couple of seconds for the picture to snap into sharp focus: Bob... the kids... *Malka*.... She should have grabbed the nearest frying pan and whacked his freewheelin' fanny off the fucking chair. But Bob quickly dismissed her. Four days later, according to Sara's complaint, he ordered her to leave home and to take the children with her so he could live there with Malka.

By March 1st, Sara could bear the humiliation no longer. She filed for divorce, seeking permanent custody of the children, child support, spousal support, and court-supervised disposition of their community property, which included real estate and Bob's holdings in publishing companies, recordings, copyrights, and song royalties. To help her gain a speedy settlement, Sara retained Beverly Hills legal shark Marvin M. Mitchelson, Counsel to the Stars, whose fame would later flourish as the father of *palimony*. Mitchelson was an acknowledged killer as far as California divorce proceedings went. He routinely asked for everything and settled for nothing less. As it already stood, Sara wanted half of everything Bob owned, which amounted to a ridiculously large sum of money. Maybe in the ten- to twenty-million-dollar range. To make matters worse, Bob had recently been swindled out of seventy-eight thousand dollars in a Ponzi-type investment scheme and was feeling the pinch, but—hey!—it was only money. Another album or two, a foreign concert tour, he could make it all back in no time. And Mitchelson or not, his lawyers assured him, no figure was beyond compromise. They'd eventually arrive at a sensible settlement.

The only thing standing in their way was the children. Like the pragmatic King Solomon, Sara refused to see them divided between self-interested parents. That wouldn't serve their youthful needs. No, she wanted *total* custody. She demanded it, in fact. Let their two-timing father fend for himself. If he wanted children so badly, let Malka have them! Let *her* see what it was like raising five kids while their father was off gallivanting around the globe singing and sitting around coffeehouses with the boys until dawn. See if she can put up with that shit for twelve years.

Just as negotiations for a settlement were beginning, the kids ran away from Sara. They turned up at their father's place and moved into the empty bedrooms. Sure, they could stay, he told them. In fact, nothing had to change. They could still go to their school in Beverly Hills, just like normal, and to guarantee they had sufficient privacy, he assigned a pair of bodyguards to shadow them. Just in case. It was a good thing he did, too. A few days later, after Sara returned from a trip to Hawaii, she showed up at school accompanied by three men. She came to retrieve the kids, she explained to a teacher named Rex Burke. Suspicious at once, Burke returned to the classroom and asked Jesse, the Dylans' eldest child, if his mother was expected. Nothing doing, Jesse replied, refusing to leave with Sara. A scuffle broke out, and in the confusion Sara reportedly choked Burke and struck him squarely in the chest. (Sara was later fined one hundred twenty-five dollars and given a suspended ten-day sentence for disrupting the classroom. Additionally, the judge placed her on six-months' unsupervised probation. The misdemeanor charge for choking and hitting Burke was subsequently dismissed.)

Sara was eventually granted custody of the children and reached agreement with Bob on a huge settlement estimated at around twelve million. The fringe benefit, she insisted, was her freedom. And not just from Bob, but from the whole sordid scene. Rock 'n roll wasn't Sara's essence. Not the hanging-out, not the music, and certainly not the life-style. For over a decade she'd lived like a Nantucket whaler's wife, waiting at home while her husband spent extended months on the road, plying his trade in the rather salty tradition of a buccaneer. Even when Bob returned, he was strangely distant, often taking days, or even weeks, to unwind. That wasn't Sara's notion of an ideal marriage. At thirty-four, she was still young, vital, and beautiful enough to start over again, pursuing a normal existence with a real man instead of a living legend.

Bob, on the other hand, was caught in the vise grip of troublesome projects. For one, geologists reported that the three-million-dollar refurbished Malibu home he retained in the divorce settlement was slipping into the ocean. Then, Folkways Records released a piece of crap entitled *Bob Dylan vs. A. J. Weberman,* on which the pesty Dylanologist misled record-buyers into believing Bob performed on the disc. He had as many as three legitimate albums of his own under way—one in the U.S. and two in Japan. A grueling concert schedule, nicknamed "The Alimony Tour," was being planned. And perhaps the trickiest, most punishing undertaking of Bob's career, his film chronicle of the Rolling Thunder Revue—*Renaldo & Clara.*

Making the movie had been child's play. Bob counted on it to cement the relationship with his new touring family and to satisfy his lifelong obsession with film. Unlike in the past, money wasn't going to be a prohibitive factor. He had plenty of bread to underwrite the enterprise and decent connections as far as assembling a professional crew went. Mel Howard was recruited to oversee the production chores, and a couple of other accredited filmmakers named David Meyers and Larry Johnson were also added to the on-line staff: one as a camera operator and the other as sound man. Bob had even conned playwright Sam Shepard into contributing a screenplay, which was later abandoned as the tour provided its own loose scenario for individual scenes. And out of loyalty, Bob entrusted principal photography to the same old hack he always got involved with, Howard Alk.

The way Bob originally planned it, *Renaldo & Clara* wouldn't require the work of fancy actors. He had a built-in cast to draw on from the Rolling Thunder Revue. Everyone on the tour, from the musicians to the advance men, was prepared to play one or several roles. Ronee Blakely, who was no stranger to the camera having segued from her debut in Robert Altman's *Nashville,* provided a semblance of experience. Bob had done his share of film work. Joan and Neuwirth were naturals. And guys like Allen Ginsberg could always be counted on to ham it up at the expense of any merit or value.

So they set to work, filming short, entirely improvised scenes that Bob planned to knit together later, along with musical footage from the tour. The cast did little cryptic bits in New York. They performed a pseudo-mystical ceremony at Jack Kerouac's gravesight in Lowell, Massachusetts, another on the beach at Newport, Rhode Island, conducted by a Cherokee medicine man named Chief Rolling Thunder, as well as hundreds of smarmy vignettes, put-ons really, with setups designed to make people look idiotic and gullible and to let the lowly viewers know exactly how unhip they were compared to the privileged cast (or, maybe *caste*).

Then the movie lapsed into Bob's idea of a Bergmanesque art film. Scenes unfolded in which no one is quite who he or she seems. Identities shuffled, overlapped, and collided. Bob plays Renaldo, a poet in whiteface who talks in long, maundering exchanges, but Ronnie Hawkins appears as "Bob Dylan." Sara plays Clara—not necessarily Renaldo's wife—in the shadow of Ronee Blakely's "Mrs. Dylan," and both women bear an uncanny resemblance to Joan Baez, who, in turn, appears as herself, as a whore, and as the mysterious Woman in White who is eventually traded for a horse. *Rolling Stone,* which analyzed the picture, concluded, "This is meant to work at the level of Freud, but it is a lot closer to fraud."

Four camera crews had worked simultaneously on *Renaldo & Clara,* and when it was over they had shot a staggering one hundred hours of film. The result was hundreds of thousands of feet of celluloid nonsense in which the color varied from shot to shot, frames were mismatched, and the tone of voices pitched and moaned like the soundtrack of *Marat/Sade.* Said *New Yorker* critic Pauline Kael, "It's what Louis and Marie Antoinette might have done at Versailles if only they'd had the cameras." Cutting it to resemble a coherent narrative presented Bob with an almost hopeless task.

Bob worked through the end of 1977 trying to provide the film with a definite point of view. Hours of playacting, hours of singing, it took some kind of alchemy—one of *Renaldo & Clara*'s recurring themes—to splice the random footage together into an intelligible rough cut. The result of all this labor—two dozen reels of film that stretched into a final three-hour-and-fifty-two minute version (at the cost of over 1.2 million dollars)—was a commercial washout. It was a mystery in the most problematic sense—nearly four hours of incomprehensible double-talk that one newspaper headlined "a tiring bore." A lot of the cast and crew disassociated themselves from it, but with Bob the best defense was a good offense. He scoffed at the terrible reviews, insisting the movie was too personal, too witty for the critics. How could they judge it fairly if they weren't hip to its subtleties? Didn't they realize that absolute art was illusory? Comparing the movie to a cubist painting, Bob declared, "Maybe there are only two or three people in the universe who are going to understand what it's about." Still, at that he had probably overestimated by two. Audiences were stupefied by the image of Allen Ginsberg being shaved, by Bobby Neuwirth cavorting as someone called the Masked Tortilla, and by the panorama of freaks, wiseguys, and sylphs parading by the camera mysteriously carrying long-stem roses. James Walcott, writing in the *Village Voice,* said it sank so many reputations "It's like watching the defeat of the Spanish Armada."

Word of the film's troubles spread faster than an outbreak of the flu. To salvage his investment, Bob launched an all-out media blitz. Paul Wasserman, a slick L.A. press agent, was hired to shop Bob around to a number of the national magazines—*Rolling Stone, Newsweek, Time, Us, People, The New York Times, Esquire, Playboy,* and *New Times.* The deal was an interview with the chronically reclusive superstar in exchange for a cover story. Wasserman convinced Bob that with a few well-placed covers he could rekindle the Dylan mystique and resurrect *Renaldo & Clara.* However, *Time* saw the movie and passed. *Newsweek* wasn't interested. *Esquire, Us,* and *People* rejected the terms. *New Times* put him on the cover, albeit with a memo superimposed over his photograph that read "Dear Mr. Dylan, Here's the cover we promised you—The Editors," then featured him in a story about overkill and hype. Only *Rolling Stone* caved in to Wasserman's extortion, awarding Bob not only the cover, but the right to edit the transcript of his interview!

As the year progressed, Bob's credibility became a hotly debated issue. *Renaldo & Clara* was a spectacular embarrassment at its four-hour length, and a two-hour version edited for overseas distribution was simply a shorter mess. (Both disappeared after only a few weeks at theaters.) *Hard Rain,* the soundtrack album of a television concert, drew criticism not only for the musical retreads it offered and its lack of inspiring performances, but also for the shameless manner in which it was dumped on the market. *Live at Budakan,* a two-record "greatest hits" package issued on the heels of his Japan tour, appeared to be yet another smokescreen to replenish his depleted fortunes.

Each new piece of "product" raised the speculation that Bob Dylan was in a creative rut. For the first time, the fans began to question his relevance. Maybe Bob's career had run its course, they speculated. Or maybe he had reached a point where he was so locked into a format established by his legend that it was impossible for him to evolve or be absorbed by the new wave of trend and talent to emerge in the late 1970s. That assessment had its merit. Even the ridiculously loyal *Rolling Stone,* in reporting on Bob's upcoming new studio album, insinuated it contained "a typical slow Dylan tune and a typical upbeat Dylan tune." Judging by the course of events, Bob Dylan was on the verge of becoming a has-been.

Certainly Bob was sensitive to that tragic possibility. He worked assiduously to prop up his sagging reputation, but there was only so much he could do. He had to keep moving forward, he had to update that prehistoric Sixties image, but it would have been suicide for him suddenly to assume a totally new identity. He'd always followed his own instinct. He'd blazed his own trails. "If you try to be anyone but yourself you will fail," he told *Playboy* as late as March 1978. Anyway, his fans wouldn't buy a blatantly show-biz image. No, there had to be some middle ground for him to plow where he wouldn't risk losing the respect of his audience or type himself as a relic of the past.

Surprisingly enough, the answer lay in his own backyard. His record company, Columbia, provided an excellent window on rock 'n roll artists like himself who were able to "cross over" to broader audiences as their careers began to wane. Johnny Cash, James Taylor, and Billy Joel had all shed their punk identities in favor of a more universal appeal without sacrificing their fans. And Neil Diamond! Columbia regarded him as one of the label's most important stars. They treated him like royalty, even put up billboards on Sunset Boulevard that Bob had to look at every time he drove out to see a friend in the Hills. That really raised his dander. He listed twenty-one albums in Columbia's current catalogue, and they'd never honored him like that. Not that he'd ever wanted it before, but they could have at least asked.

Neil Diamond—that guy was all over the place in Los Angeles. He was a big star there. His shows at the Universal Amphitheatre were regarded as major events; he got standing ovations at the Grammys, a fat Hollywood contract in his pocket, offers to appear at the White House. His reputation and his price kept skyrocketing. What was it this guy had going for him that knocked audiences out the way he did?

Bob decided to see for himself. Earlier in the year, he'd stopped off in Las Vegas to catch Neil Diamond's show, and what he saw astounded him. Diamond wasn't simply another singer-songwriter in concert; he was an *entertainer*. He had a professional act built to showcase his songs without compromising any of their punch. And his personal style cut right through the flash of Vegas with power and confidence.

As Bob sat hidden in the stylishly dressed audience, it became apparent that Neil Diamond and he had more than a record company in common. They were around the same age and build. Both men had started out among New York's tune vendors, working with acoustic guitars and writing songs that became famous in the hands of more commercial groups—Bob with Peter, Paul & Mary; Diamond with the Monkees. A couple of Jewish boys who rose to conquer the stage. But as Bob looked on, he no doubt realized that Diamond's audience consisted largely of people who at one time in their lives had been *his* fans. No longer activists or angry young rebels, the "over-thirties" professional, suburban crowd craved a more stagy brand of entertainment when they went out to see a show. Not in an arena filled with screaming teenagers, but in a setting conducive to their adult lifestyles. Bob could never play the Flamingo or the MGM Grand like Neil Diamond, but he could do the next best thing—cut Diamond's multifaceted act to fit the Bob Dylan show and make it sparkle.

Several weeks later, Bob launched the experiment by signing an exclusive contract with Jerry Weintraub's Management III. Not only did Weintraub represent Neil Diamond; he also handled show-biz institutions like Frank Sinatra, John Denver, and Elvis Presley. Logically, Bob saw himself as a member of that performing aristocracy, and no doubt in signing with Weintraub he elected to franchise his act out to the kind of establishment houses known to promote The Big Show.

Weintraub very shrewdly chose the Universal Amphitheatre, the site of Neil Diamond's spectacular success, to launch Bob's reemergence as a major American concert attraction. It would offer Bob the ideal audience—twenty-five hundred upscale concertgoers used to *celebrity* shows—in a beautiful atmospheric setting right off the Hollywood Freeway. What's more, though a small house, it gave the impression of spaciousness befitting an arena ten times its size and allowed a performer to work "large" and uninhibited in front of an intimate crowd.

Bob opened a week-long engagement there on June 1, 1978, and as expected, the first show catered to a typical first-night audience. The seats were packed with Hollywood stars, West Coast music dignitaries and their secretaries, and the New York rock press who were flown in to record each glittering moment of Bob's performance. By showtime, the sun had set on the Pacific. The house lights dimmed, and when they came up again, the spots revealed a nine-piece backup band that began vamping a hot instrumental overture. Almost celestially, a gospel trio—three black women in hooker threads—belted out the response, "Oh, it's a-hard" over and over behind a couple of bars of "Hard Rain." Then, without any announcement, Bob bounded on stage in *a black studded pants suit* and watusied toward the mike. The crowd gasped in an odd fanfare of recognition and disbelief, followed by a rhapsodic ovation. Bob, meanwhile, planted himself center stage, kicked out his electric guitar, and launched into an animated rendition of the Tampa Red blues standard "Love Her with a Feeling." The audience cooed in ecstasy.

What followed, however, was one of the most puzzling transformations in rock music history. At once, Bob performed a cross section of his hits that should have lifted the crowd to a level of near-pandemonium. Instead, they were rudely stunned into silence. His first medley—"Mr. Tambourine Man," "Shelter from the Storm," "Love Minus Zero/No Limit," and "Tangled Up in Blue"—bore little, if any, similarity to the original versions. The completely overhauled arrangements were totally unsuited to his lyrics and tripped up the audience like carefully camouflaged land mines. Then, on "Ballad of a Thin Man," Bob snatched the microphone from its stand and strolled out around the apron of the stage, kneeling to shake hands with the audience!

After intermission, Bob reappeared in a fetching jumpsuit trussed tightly around his skinny frame and open to his navel, with white sequined thunderbolts flashing resplendently down his flanks. "Like to say hello to Richard Manuel and *Raquel Welch* out there tonight," he echoed à la Sammy Davis Jr., and segued into each song with embarrassing Vegas-style patter: "Here's a song I recorded with the Band!" he snapped before "Going, Going, Gone," or: "As Jerry Garcia says, 'I must be checking on down the line.'" As one critic pointed out, "All I Really Want to Do" was sung to the tune of "The 59th Street Bridge Song (Feelin' Groovy)," and on "Like a Rolling Stone" Bob left the climactic notes of each verse to the backup singers.

The West Coast fans reacted politely as though they were sitting through a videotaping of the *Sonny & Cher Show.* But by the time the tour reached New York, the press was ready to unload. *Rolling Stone,* noting Bob's debt to Neil Diamond, headlined the question: "Dylan Going Vegas?" And *Time,* reviewing the Garden show alongside a rave for Neil Young, concluded, "He lets the songs rip like some Bleecker Street parody of a Vegas lounge lizard. In concert, with billowing shirt, plunging neckline and a crooner's microphone calisthenics, Dylan works his way through his standard repertory and sometimes looks as if he is auditioning for *The Gong Show.*"

As if this weren't bad enough, Bob's new album, *Street Legal,* released to correspond with the tour, was creamed by most critics. Griel Marcus, writing in *Rolling Stone,* was eloquently vicious: "Most of the stuff here is dead air... he's never sounded so utterly fake... intolerably smug... an imitation of caring that couldn't fool a stuffed dog." Dave Marsh jumped on the bandwagon with a similar slam in *Stone,* concluding, "Not only does *Street Legal* reveal that Dylan is Elvis Presley's legitimate successor as Clown Prince of Rock 'n Roll, it also prevents us from ever taking him seriously again." The attacks were so pitiless and extreme that Jann Wenner, publisher of *Rolling Stone,* printed a weasly apology to Bob by re-reviewing the album himself, this time favorably, in a follow-up issue.

Wenner's eagerness to stroke Bob was emblematic of *Rolling Stone*'s precipitate decline. No longer the counterculture's watchdog, the magazine catered shamelessly to its benefactors—the rock establishment, which provided *Stone* with monthly news items and cover stories, and the advertisers. In that regard, alienating an ally like Bob was considered editorial suicide. Dylan's face splashed across the cover still guaranteed a good newsstand sale. And the perennial "Bob Dylan Interview" was a Wenner favorite. *Ròlling Stone*'s new motto might have been: "You don't bite the hand that feeds you."

Shaken by the hypercritical reaction, Bob took off for Europe where he played nineteen generally well-received shows. His fans overseas were more willing to accept the tinkering he'd done with their cherished anthems, acknowledging a performer's obligation to refresh his material every few years. "He steam-rollered legend and nostalgia out of existence by powerful rearranged versions of his best known songs," observed the *Evening Standard* following a gala opening at Earl's Court. "He turned his London concert into a triumph last night by combining his old fervent passion with a surprise element of show business polish."

Bob's offstage life during his London engagement, however, was anything but triumphant. He was still reeling from the setbacks, still licking his wounds. Friends who encountered him found Bob pensive and depressed. He looked terrible, haggard, as if he hadn't had a good night's sleep in months. His eyes seemed lifeless, their whites marbled by chronic redness. His skin had turned a colicky basement-gray. If you didn't know who he was you might have mistaken him for one of the weirdos who hung out around Picadilly Circus waiting for something to happen.

Even his hair-trigger wit, that sweet-and-sour ragging he perfected, had been replaced by bitterness. Now, Bob would get very hostile. He no longer played friends off on one another or provoked quarrels or even put people on. No, when Bob got hostile, he became philosophical. He'd corner an easy mark and unload all the repressed anger he'd been carrying around in a long-winded convoluted rap. He got down into the deepest depths of his psyche and articulated what he found there. It wasn't necessary for him to come off cool or witty anymore. Hey—he was Bob Dylan! Magazines had always hounded him for interviews; reporters interpreted his lyrics for clues to his mind. So he'd decided to talk. And talk. And talk.

One interview, in particular, wound up splashed across the pages of the *London Evening News* in as sensational a manner as any government scandal the British fed upon. Responding to a reporter's question about his less-than-ordinary life-style, Bob yapped back, "I could be happy pounding metal all day, going home to a big fat wife and eating a meal, and you know, going to bed." In the past, Bob could have gotten off a line like that any day of the week without raising so much as an eyebrow. But he was in no mood to let it rest. After expounding his personal philosophy on marriage, he narrowed the subject to what he felt was the single-most deterrent to happy relationships: women.

"Women are sentimental," he pontificated. "They get into that romantic thing more easily. But I see that as a prelude. Women use romance and passion to sweeten you up, and a man is no more than victim of that passion. You give me a woman who can cook and sew, and I'll take that over passion any day of the week." Bull's-eye! That was the kind of loose talk the gossip columnists pounced on, especially from an alleged wife-beater. The next day, all the news services picked up the story—"Bob Dylan . . . fat woman . . . cook and sew. . . ." It was splashed across every newspaper on the Continent.

As for the intensity of Bob's feelings, the extremity of his remarks—think of his most romantic lyrics, those incredible songs he'd written about Sara! Think of all those images he evoked that revealed how much she meant to him. He was no longer married to Sara, but it was obvious he was having difficulty divorcing himself from her. "I cut the whole experience right off," he insisted to Los Angeles columnist Bob Hilburn, but the long-term effect was poignantly clear.

On top of that he was demoralized and disturbed by what he considered to be the critics' plot to destroy him. Bob expressed strong doubts that the lousy press that *Street Legal* and *Renaldo & Clara* received had anything to do with their contents. As he saw it, the reviews were inconsequential. Nothing could persuade Bob that the record and movie weren't up to his usual standards. Rather, the media were out to "get" him in order to counteract the Dylan myth they'd helped to create in the Sixties. The raves from the European press fueled Bob's paranoia more than ever. Now he was feeling embattled, like he was struggling to maintain his integrity.

Most entertainers under such strain would have pulled up stakes and quit. They might have disappeared for a couple of years or retired, or, in the saddest of cases, OD'd. For Bob Dylan it was easier to hit the road. Despite all the turmoil in his life, the anguish, the denials, the self-loathing, he committed himself to the road as a way to deflect, and even disavow, his true feelings. After nineteen shows on the Continent, he returned home to start a punishing *sixty-five-city* tour! He crisscrossed North America, affording each local newspaper the opportunity to interview him and rehash the stories about "heartbreaks and failures."

"Bob was undoubtedly at the lowest point of his life," observes a friend who traveled with the *Street Legal* entourage. "He was drinking heavily, just slugging down one brandy after the next. His moods were more inconsistent than usual. It seemed to me like he was trying to blot everything out." Some of the band members worried that if Bob didn't find something new to live for, some vital inspiration, he might go off the deep end.

That was the prognosis on December 16, 1978, as the tour limped to a fitful end. Grim stares reflected the exhaustion behind their eyes as the tour members straggled through stuffy LAX toward the caravan of cars and taxis waiting outside. Though they were physically beat, they were buoyed by the prospect of returning home after four months on the road, and their faces were flush with expectation. Only Bob among them looked ashen, listless, out of it. He seemed to have sunk even further into that dark hole from where everything appeared impenetrable and hopeless. From that perspective, these homecomings were harrowing affairs. He would watch while the last remnants of his temporary "family" rushed off to their lovers, wives, and children, and, in effect, experienced all over again the most painful repercussion of his divorce—splitting up. It was an unfortunate irony that the man who so eloquently articulated longing and desire in a song like "Tomorrow Is a Long Time" should return to an empty house. Unlike so many tours before, his own true love wasn't waiting, nor could he hear her heart softly pounding, nor feel her lying by him. So it should come as no great shock that when he crossed the threshold of his abandoned Malibu estate, Bob Dylan rushed into the arms of the Lord.

30

At Play in the Fields of the Lord

With the release of *Slow Train Coming* in the summer of 1979, Bob's dramatic conversion to Christianity was complete, although it was really only the culmination of a process that had begun during the waning hours of the Rolling Thunder Revue.

The gloom that had surrounded Bob attracted the attention of his guitar player, T-Bone Burnett, whose built-in radar detected the blips of his boss's emotional crisis like an early-warning device. A lanky, raven-eyed Texan whose main function on stage was to inject spontaneous bits of humor into the show (for instance, during the nightly performance of "Chestnut Mare," when Roger McGuinn reached the line "I'm gonna get that horse," Burnett would lasso him), T-Bone moonlighted in the service of the Lord. He was an early disciple of born-again fundamentalism, the type of guy who loved to party and get crazy just like anyone else—up to a certain point. Then, as if some excess had tripped a spiritual circuit-breaker, his personality was driven by a different current and suddenly T-Bone possessed all the spooky religious rhetoric of a Christian missionary. He was very earnest about his born-again experience and babbled rapturously about the Word of God, righteousness, and the blessing of salvation. Rob Stoner credits T-Bone with Bob's religious recruitment, although his influence was anything but Svengali-like or irresistible. The steady, low-pressure manner in which T-Bone described things like his "inner light" was persuasive enough, and Bob, vulnerable and open-minded, swallowed the bait like a prize fish.

Once he was hooked, Bob experienced divine revelations and other supernatural phenomena that furnished proof, or at the very least provided a rationalization, that the essence of God was somewhere within him. The turning point was an awe-inspiring incident that occurred in late 1978, "a vision and feeling" as Bob described it, during which the room he was in supposedly moved. He felt a transcendental presence enter the room, a heavenly and infinite power that was trying to communicate with him. Bob reported other, less spectacular visions that he had, but none that so strongly confirmed the calling. It was a moment fraught with enormous significance. He described it in detail to his girlfriend, an L.A. actress named Mary Alice Artes, and the way she interpreted it, Bob had probably experienced a spiritual visit from Jesus.

Jesus—it was as if a little light went on in Bob's head, a divine flash, a spiritual connection. The thought had never occurred to him, but after a couple of minutes he decided it wasn't all that preposterous. He'd heard a lot of people say the same thing recently, people who were involved in the spiritual renaissance sweeping the country. A lot of them were people just like him, children of the Sixties who'd turned their back on God and conducted their spiritual search through the ministries of psychedelic drugs and the free-love movement. But that faith, the hippie faith, had failed, and after slogging through the decadence of the early Seventies, these same people had found something new to believe in.

But... *Jesus?* Jesus was a concept for the gentiles. He was their Son of God, their Messiah. He walked on water and raised bodies from the dead. Jews weren't supposed to believe all that hocus-pocus. Bob's own great-grandfather, B.H., would have suffered apoplexy had he known one of his descendants even entertained such curiosity. In B.H.'s home, Jesus was the god of ignorant Rangers who made fun of him and blasphemed his religion. As such, the name Jesus never sat well in a Zimmerman's mouth. *Jesus!*—here Bob was not only acknowledging His name, but actually accepting the possibility of a Christly visit.

Mary Alice herself was a hard-core convert to born-again Christianity.

She had recently "rededicated her life to the Lord" as a result of some intensive fundamentalist proselytizing, and suggested that Bob check out the Bible school she'd attended. Dylan was understandably reluctant. Discussions about Jesus were one thing, but actually *studying* Him?—*converting?* That was too drastic a step for even an old folk prophet like Bob Dylan. But Mary Alice, like most Jesus freaks, wasn't easily deterred. She contacted Ken Gulliksen, a pastor at the devoutly chic Vineyard Fellowship in West Los Angeles, who dispatched two of his smoothest, most articulate proselytizers to deliver the canon to Bob.

The next morning, Larry Myers and Paul Edmond turned up on Bob's doorstep for the purpose of "ministering" to his doubts. Imagine if you will what transpired at that religious rap session. The customary procedure for ministering to nonbelievers involves some prior detective work in order to determine the subject's susceptibility or particular need. In Bob's case, he had experienced a supernatural presence that wasn't immediately discernible. Supernatural presences? No problem! They just happened to retain the leading authority on unexplainable religious phenomena—the *Bible.* Fundamentalists interpreted the Bible the way A. J. Weberman interpreted Bob Dylan's songs. Any passage could be construed to support their dogma or even to explain a mysterious vision like the one Bob had experienced. The trick was to get that Bible open and keep whacking away at it, hurling scriptures like an evangelical knuckleballer, until a potential convert submitted to the Lord.

No sooner did Myers and Edmond get their feet in Bob's door than a Bible was produced and opened to the Book of Romans. Bob listened attentively as they explained how the Holy Spirit inspired man's faith and guided him along the path to salvation. Though naturally skeptical, Bob remained open-minded, receptive, an unreluctant participant. That day they took him through the standard indoctrination. Speaking in soothing, almost hypnotic tones, they initiated prolonged discussions about all the self-doubts Bob had been wrestling with as well as his ongoing quest for spiritual peace. Then, after he appeared comfortable and eager to hear more, they eased him into the underlying bulwark of fundamentalism—man as sinner. Maundering through passage after passage of demonstrative scripture designed to illustrate man's compulsion to sin, they assured him that Jesus was ready to become his personal sin-bearer. All Bob had to do was to ask Him for help. Each of his questions was buttressed by more scriptural testimony, more incontrovertible evidence, until, at the end of the day, Bob announced he was ready to receive the Lord.

Myers and Edmond spelled out the initial step he'd have to take if he was serious about being redeemed: a three-month crash course in Bible study. It was a prerequisite to any meaningful relationship with God, they assured him. There was no shorter route to the Lord. You can imagine the effect that had on their disciple. A lifelong autodidact, Bob's attention span wasn't programmed for formal instruction. He'd never even managed to stick with piano lessons, let alone college! Why, it took everything he had just to concentrate on a game of chess. How did they expect him to dedicate three months to the Bible? Especially when he was due back on the road.

That Bible study business had all but put the kibosh on Bob's flirtation with Christianity. But a week later, his faith was literally reawakened by still another mystical phenomenon. He had been in a deep sleep, having turned in late the night before, and suddenly sat bolt upright in bed. Rubbing his grainy eyes, he glanced at the clock on a nearby nightstand. Something must have gone wrong with the power; according to the dial it was only 7 a.m. He *couldn't* have been asleep for that short a period. Yet on further inspection he discovered it was indeed the accurate time. Hmmm—that was strange. Then, the next thing Bob knew, he was in the car, driving to the Vineyard Fellowship, as if being pulled there by some strange hypnotic force. "I couldn't believe I was there," he told a reporter in 1980, as they replayed the experience for the *Los Angeles Times*.

Nevertheless, Bob enrolled in the Vineyard's School of Discipleship, arriving at the ministry every day, five days a week, for a period of three-and-a-half months. "He was faithful there every day, learning the Word, growing in the Lord," says Pastor Gulliksen, who often received Bob personally in his casual parish. Other times, Bob joined the rest of the flock in the classroom adjunct, studying the life of Jesus, principles of discipleship, the sermon on the Mount, what it means to be a believer, how to grow, how to share—the daily workshops were steeped in doctrinal, as well as philosophical, theology, and were designed to help restructure one's sinful life-style.

Bob, as we know, was no saint. An acknowledged recidivist, he felt himself capable of sinking to the lowliest depths. And to make matters worse, he was an international pop star. The church regarded entertainers as notorious transgressors—seducers, drug addicts, opportunists, adulterers, blasphemers, narcissists, alcoholics, gluttons, egotists, corrupters of little girls—there was no limit to their licentious behavior. In most cases, the Lord looked unfavorably upon show business and cheap commercialism. Strict fundamentalists, like Jimmy Swaggert, forbade their congregations to listen to rock 'n roll and damned its standard-bearers from their pulpits. So in a purely Christianlike sense, Gulliksen and the Vineyard Fellowship found themselves in a bit of a predicament with their celebrated convert. They couldn't ask Bob Dylan to renounce his career and everything he'd stood for; on the other hand, it was unlikely they could accept Brother Bob's public persona the way it was.

The alternative, of course, was a fully reborn and reconditioned Bob Dylan—a new, improved model, whose additional features included redemption, faith, reverence, Christian charity, and the exaltation of the Lord's name. In Bob Dylan, the fundamentalists had a powerful new communicator, a personality of extraordinary proportions who could potentially preach the gospel and attract more people to their born-again philosophy than was ever before thought possible. Nor was it lost on Gulliksen that Bob had at one time been branded the "messiah" of his generation. "We strongly encouraged him that he had a platform that no one else had and in that position he should continue," says Gulliksen. "We told him to be open to God's leading if he felt he should do something else."

By May 1970, Bob had been baptized, and he immediately recorded a heavily symbolic, fundamentalist album of songs entitled *Slow Train Coming.* Dylan fans were shocked and bewildered by this newest transformation. They had dealt with his conversion to rock 'n roll and the brief encounter with country music; they'd even survived his two creative droughts in the early 1970s. But those crucifixes on the back and front covers of the new album were more than any fan could be expected to tolerate. They were scarifying images to a major portion of his audience, and the music inside was a complete anomaly.

Slow Train Coming was by no means an experimental brush with Christianity. Track after track crepitated with Bible-thumping and inspirational verse. The opening cut, "Gotta Serve Somebody," was rife with religious allegory. "Gonna Change My Way of Thinking" rips with a hell-and-damnation litany concerning a woman who walks in the "spirit of the Lord." "When You Gonna Wake Up" is an evangelistic rocker depicting Bob's prophecy of Armageddon. And "I Believe in You" stands as a reaffirmation of his faith in a new Savior. The final, moody spiritual, "When He Returns," was originally written to showcase the female gospel trio—Carolyn Dennis, Regina Havis, and Helena Springs—who sang backup on the album, but after Bob prepared a demo for them to rehearse with, he decided his performance was too good to ignore and recorded the song himself. So much for charity.

Slow Train was received skeptically, if not with disdain, by most of Dylan's secular audience. Long-standing fans were repulsed by the preachy, born-again choruses and holy rock 'n rolling. Rock critic Griel Marcus accused Bob of using Christianity to pump up a badly deflated career and to polish his tarnished mystique after a divorce in which he was accused of wife-beating, as did other critical voices. Only Jann Wenner, *Rolling Stone*'s indefatigable publisher, defended the album and sang its praise as "one of the finest records Dylan has ever made. In time," Wenner contended, "it is possible that it might even be considered his greatest."

Wenner's analysis was as ridiculously biased and extreme as those which had condemned *Slow Train Coming;* however, the album *was* unjustifiably maligned. Regardless of its message, *Slow Train* crackles with a vibrancy heretofore missing on Bob Dylan albums, owing to the record's brilliant production. In the past, his performances were essentially unproduced. Oh, there was always some person sitting behind the control panel who answered to the title and turned off the lights, but that person was about as creative or effective as a trained pony. Bob's producers were corporate watchdogs, empowered by record-company accountants to monitor the sessions' balance sheets. No producer ever made a significant impact on a Bob Dylan record.

Enter Jerry Wexler, whose reputation as a superb studio technician and role player was unparalleled in the rock music business. At Atlantic Records, Wexler had produced watershed recordings for the Drifters, Ray Charles, Aretha Franklin, Solomon Burke, Dusty Springfield, and Wilson Pickett. Moreover, his signature helped to create "the Atlantic Sound," which Wexler himself defined as "a mystique we generated... our own particular brand of clean funk which we knew how to create using our feeling and knowledge of blues, jazz, and old race records." Wexler produced *Slow Train Coming* in Muscle Shoals, Alabama, his old stomping ground and the scene of so many of his extraordinary sessions with Wilson Pickett. Using an ensemble of first-rate session men, he insisted on inventive arrangements, instruments that actually played in tune, and overdubs to mask the clams—all of which were entirely new approaches for Bob. As a result, the album has a clean, crisp sound and richly textured vocals that remain unsurpassed in Bob's miscellany of most creaky performances.

Slow Train Coming racked up huge sales, thanks in no small part to an expanded audience of born-again Christians who cheered his conversion. For many, it was the first Dylan album they'd ever bought and proved to be yet another hearty revelation in their continuing spiritual odyssey. Buoyed by the message but baffled by that voice, they gradually became converts to the Dylan myth and, in no time, produced a run on his catalogue that caused Columbia Records to give thanks. Now not only did they want to hear him, they wanted to see him and to *pray* with him as well.

By November 1979, the new show was ready for the road. Bob decided to open his tour with an unprecedented fourteen shows at the Fox Warfield Theatre, one of those old, run-down movie palaces, in San Francisco. The Bay City had always been fertile Dylan country; the audiences were hip. Bill Graham had agreed to produce the run—no doubt fans assumed it'd be like one of the city's legendary Grateful Dead marathons. "Fourteen shows, man—outta sight! Let's go to 'em all!" Boy, were they in for a rude surprise.

The first show was an eye-opener for the twenty-two hundred hardcore Dylan fans who jammed into the theater. They sat for nearly half an hour in frenzied expectation waiting for the show to start. Then, when the lights finally went down, they let out a sustained burst of nearly hysterical screams and shouts. But when the lights came up again, in place of Bob Dylan stood a female gospel trio dressed in garish gold lamé jackets and stretch pants. Without introduction, they launched into a hand-clappin', foot-stompin' piano number, hailing Jesus, and testifying loud and long, in the manner of a Southern Baptist revival show.

After the second song, the audience began to come out of its shock. "We want Dylan!" someone shouted over the rhythmic seesawing of the piano. "Yeah!" another voice echoed in the darkness, "*—rock 'n* *roll!*" But the gospel chants and supplications stretched on for another twenty-five minutes. Once Bob took the stage, the audience wanted to hear the hits—but *fast*. Instead, what they got was ninety minutes of devotional songs, one after the next—"Gotta Serve Somebody," "I Believe in You," "When You Gonna Wake Up," "When He Returns," "Man Gave Names to All the Animals," "Slow Train," "Solid Rock," "Saved," "Blessed Is the Name." After the finale, "Pressing On," Bob spoke his first words: "That's the show for tonight. I hope you've been uplifted." Then he disappeared, carried off stage by a volley of boos and catcalls.

Uplifted? In San Francisco? That wasn't exactly your typical God-fearing audience he'd appealed to. They wanted music, they wanted Dylan, and that meant "Like a Rolling Stone," "Just Like a Woman," and "All along the Watchtower." In the way of spirituals they might have settled for "I Shall Be Released," but the show Bob performed—the show he had hoped would promote feelings of thanksgiving and brotherhood—produced outright hostility. The fans felt ripped off and deceived.

The local papers echoed their negative reactions. The *San Francisco Examiner,* in a front-page review of the show, proclaimed "Born-Again Dylan Bombs." And the *Chronicle* responded: "Bob Dylan's God-Awful Gospel." Some fans who held tickets for the remaining shows attempted to sell them at substantial discounts. Others read the reviews with heavyhearted curiosity and determined to stand by their old mentor.

One of them was Bob's old friend Maria Muldaur, who had moved to nearby Mill Valley and was enjoying her own professional rebirth of sorts. "I read those reviews and started to cry," recalls Maria, who understood and empathized with Bob's spiritual reawakening. Maria herself had recently been "saved" from a chronic drinking problem and cocaine dependency. Then, following her daughter's near-fatal car accident, she was delivered into the arms of Jesus Christ. "So I wrote Bob a letter telling him about everything that had happened to me," Maria says. "I basically reminded him of that night at Newport when the fans booed and turned against him—when they couldn't understand what he was doing. I just wanted him to know that his songs had reached me and changed my life, and I thanked him for helping me remember there was a God to turn to and to set me on another course."

The very next day Maria got a frantic call from her answering service. "Bob Dylan's been calling you!" the operator said. He left a message for her to meet him backstage after any of the Warfield concerts and to bring as many friends as she liked. "Are you sure it was Bob Dylan?" asked Maria, who remembered the surly, aloof, antagonistic guy she'd known in Woodstock.

If this version of Bob was a revelation, then the subsequent show she attended was a shock. "People were standing up, worshipping, rocking back and forth," Maria recalls, "while others were hooting and screaming, 'C'mon—enough of this God shit! We want rock 'n roll!' There was bedlam in that theater." Backstage, she was startled by a visible change in Bob. "I was used to seeing him with his leg twitching and the people around him uncomfortable about how he was treating them, and that was *gone.* Here he was just as calm and peaceful as anyone could be—Bob Dylan, wearing a little gold cross on a chain around his neck, a smile plastered on his face. He jumped up and just hugged me. It felt solid as a rock and full of love. There was a light force in that hug."

Bob was delighted to see Maria. He'd known her since the early days in the Village, when they were both putting together folk music acts. Then, in Woodstock, they'd been neighbors, and Bob recalled many an afternoon when Maria and Sara sat on his front porch with their babies, Jenny and Jesse, on each mother's lap. "He said he really wanted to talk to me and asked me if he could come by my place on his day off."

Two days later, on November 5, 1979, Bob, as promised, rolled up to Maria's house in Marin County. It was rainy and miserable, so they sat in her kitchen and discussed the subject that had, after all these years, reunited them again: Jesus Christ, their Lord and Savior. "He was still calm and relaxed," Maria says, "but there was an urgency to his visit. It was as if he wanted me to know certain things. He wanted to help save me. I think he sensed that I was still on the fence about my spiritual commitment and wanted to provide me with some encouragement. But when I asked him what I do next, he replied: 'Read the Bible.' That really disappointed me. I hated all that heavy stuff, all the 'thees' and the 'thys' and the 'thous,' but he insisted, saying, 'I promise you—read it every day and the Word of God will reveal itself to you.'" Then he proceeded to explain the fundamentalist theory of *raima,* in which the essence of the spirit supposedly jumps off the page of the Bible and implants itself in one's heart beyond verbal understanding. Bob felt he had already reached that exhilaratingly naked plain of spirituality and assured Maria that she would join him there if she faithfully read the Bible every day and prayed.

Maria derived strength from the absolute trust Bob exhibited in his faith. It was part of her whole attraction to the born-again movement—the blind faith, the mad enthusiasm which cast a spell over people, the total commitment. But there was another, dark side to Bob's faith, an almost nihilistic inclination, that frightened her.

Bob had become fascinated with the Book of Revelations, a bizarre, mystogogical addendum to the New Testament, in whose scriptures lie the prophecies of Armageddon. "He was convinced that everything currently happening in the Middle East was a sign of what Revelations called 'the end times,'" Maria recalls. According to the Bible, good and evil would fight the ultimate war on on the plain of Megiddo. Well, Bob did a little investigation, with the help of an atlas, and figured out that the biblical location was dead-center of Ayatollah Khomeini's mayhem. "I'm telling you, Maria, it's happening right now," he told her.

Bob hit her with the whole hell-and-damnation spiel. He went on and on about how Satan and the devil would set up the Antichrist to reign over earth, how it would be Satan's last great reign, and we were all doomed to eternal suffering. The whole thing was giving Maria the creeps. "You mean to tell me you believe all this stuff?" she asked him.

"Every word of it," Bob assured her. "Satan's real, Maria. You'll see. Everything I told you is already happening."

By January 1980, he was preaching a cosmic cataclysm in his concerts. Sandwiching songs between emotional tirades, he was funneling the unease of an audience troubled over events in Iran and Afghanistan into righteous finger-pointing. Paranoia had returned to Bob's discipline, cloaked in the guise of holy prophecy. And disdain. He was aggravated that his audience still clamored for the old songs. In Albuquerque, he battled fans all night who cried out for "Rolling Stone." Then, in Tempe, after one of the rock dicks shouted "Rock 'n roll!" Bob stopped a song and sneered, "You want rock 'n roll—go see Queen."

The infidels didn't concern him. He wasn't going to heed their pleas or do their sinful bidding. If anything, his shows grew more sacred and evangelical, his demeanor more solemn. Offstage, too, he tried to live in the plain and simple manner befitting a subject of the Lord. The Malibu mansion remained home for Bob, but when he was in L.A., he spent most of his time at a one-bedroom pad he rented in Brentwood, a nondescript, modest apartment with a piano in the living room and little else in the way of luxuries.

It was there he took Maria Muldaur to hear a rough tape of *Saved* in the summer of 1980. "He had just finished recording it and was incredibly excited," she recalls, "so we went back there to hear it again." On the way home, Bob stopped off to pick up some bread, cheese, and wine. Maria watched greedily as he came out of the liquor store carrying an expensive French burgundy. She was having a problem with alcohol again, especially during her gigs when she depended on more than a couple drinks to see her through the show, and the bottle of wine looked increasingly inviting. When they got to Bob's Brentwood hideaway, Maria put out the bread and cheese, uncorked the wine, and pulled out two crystal glasses from the bar.

"No, no, no," Bob admonished her, "I don't want it." He moved away from the glasses as if they were contaminated.

Maria squinted her confusion. "What are you talking about? You love wine."

"Not anymore," Bob said. "The Lord delivered me from drinking about six weeks ago. He just lifted any desire."

"Gee, I wish he'd do that for me," Maria said, drinking her wine, then Bob's. Then she looked at him and felt a profound sadness. Her mind drifted back to the first time Bob had returned from Europe, in 1963. They were both sitting at the bar in Gerdes Folk City, and Bob lectured her about all the pleasures he'd discovered while overseas, one of which included drinking wine. "You gotta try it, Maria," he told her then. "Everybody in Italy drinks white wine—it's really great stuff!" That had been one of those magical moments in the Village. Now here we are, she thought, both nearing forty, divorced, running from city to city, hotel to hotel, and the poor guy can't even enjoy a glass of wine. "Look at the successes we've become, huh Bobby?"

Small wonder that he had tunneled so far into his Christianity. Bob was looking for quick answers to some extremely disturbing questions. "Look at the junkies and the winos and the troubled people," he lamented to Robert Hilburn in a 1980 interview. "It's all a sickness which can be healed in an instant." For Bob, however, it was a self-fulfilling prophecy. He had fallen so far and lost so much of himself in the process, that there was a desperate desire for him to go back to the beginning, to be reborn, to reinvent himself one more time.

Bob had always assumed a curious identity for the stage. There is a long tradition in show business that permits a performer to adopt an ethnic identity not necessarily his own, and Bob took advantage of that more than most. First, he embodied Little Richard's black gospel performance, and then he was an Okie or a hillbilly, both of which were fundamentally Christian in spirit. But folksingers themselves weren't in the least like Christians. There wasn't a shred of Christianity in Woody Guthrie's music. Those hobo-type singers, those proletarian singers, were godless; they were humanitarian rather than religious—which left Bob with a difficult dual stage role to portray. He oscillated between stage Christian and stage agnostic, discovering ultimately that once you've taken off your identity and put on a mask, you can *change* masks. You can go from one mask to another with little difficulty.

It took almost two years before Bob was comfortable enough to remove his born-again mask. The earliest sign was at a concert at the Stanley Theatre in Pittsburgh, on May 16, 1980. He had just finished playing thirteen of his most religious songs before breaking into a familiar refrain: the first eight bars of "Lay, Lady, Lay." The audience went wild, applauding and whistling like the heathens they undoubtedly were. It had been the first of "the hits" he'd played in a long time. But just as quickly as he'd started it, he stopped. "Unh-unh-unh," Bob teased into the mike. "Not tonight!" Then he rebounded into "In the Garden."

It was another six months before he dared to test a mixed bag of songs before his audience. Ironically, the place was the Fox Warfield Theatre in San Francisco, the scene of his earlier startling transformation. He'd scheduled a series of twelve concerts there, beginning on November 9th, and word was in the air that Bob had decided to moderate his position with a few old tunes. As such, the shows sold out within a few days of their announcement.

The opening-night crowd, however, grew alarmed as the show unfolded. They were expecting the "old Dylan," their rebel-hero, but were bombarded with more of the rock gospel. Willie Smith backed the girls on piano, as they mugged through half an hour's worth of "hallelujahs" and "praise the Lord's," with Bob nowhere in sight. When he finally took the stage, it was the same old tune: "Gotta Serve Somebody" and "I Believe in You."

The crowd's restlessness became palpable. The old seats began to creak as the fans shifted with collective frustration. A mild buzz wafted through the orchestra. Nervous glances were exchanged and wristwatches consulted in a mass wave of impatience. Then a note rang out and pandemonium exploded throughout the theater. He was doing it! He was playing "Like a Rolling Stone"! The fans jumped to their feet and began to sing with him at the top of their lungs, screaming each time when they got to: "Didn't—*yewwwwwww!*" Bob was right: pray and your prayers would be answered. The fans hadn't given up hope, and he was singing to them again. "Didn't—*yewwwwwww!*" he growled, and they responded with another thunderous burst of approval.

That night he mixed in a few favorite oldies: "Rolling Stone," "Girl from the North Country," "Just Like a Woman," "Señor," and the encore—"Blowin' in the Wind." The next night he added "Simple Twist of Fate" and "It's All Over Now, Baby Blue." By the end of the tour, in Portland, Oregon, he'd played just about all the songs he was known for: "Mr. Tambourine Man," "All along the Watchtower," "Hard Rain," "To Ramona," "Just Like Tom Thumb's Blues," "Don't Think Twice."

Again Maria Muldaur visited with him and noticed another change in Bob. "He was very restless, distracted," she recalls. At an Italian Thanksgiving dinner she made for Bob and the musicians, he couldn't stay seated at the table. While everyone ate, thanked God for His bounty, and celebrated the holiday, Bob sat on the front porch, smoking cigarettes and staring into space. His mind was on fire, and Maria could see he was on some different plain. "It was as if he wanted to get back to work," she says. "Back in touch with music and with the past."

When he finally came inside, he whispered to Maria: "Hey, doesn't Michael Bloomfield live out here?" Sure, Maria told him. "And Bob Johnston, too? Do you have their numbers?"

Johnston, his old producer, was delighted to hear from Bob and insisted he come right over. Bloomfield's phone number was busy, so he and Maria hopped into the car and spent a half hour at Johnston's house, reminiscing and talking about music. Bob tried Bloomfield's number several more times, but with no better luck. "C'mon," Maria said, "I'll run you over there."

Maria was actually leery about hooking Bob up with Mike Bloomfield. She had just heard a strange story about Bloomfield and another rock performer—a drunken, wild, unsavory episode involving guns and underaged girls—that had made the rounds of Bay City musicians. She also knew that in his attempt to stay off dope, Bloomfield had discovered another distraction: alcohol. All these years, he never drank; suddenly he had a bottle in his hand all the time. And to make matters worse, he was a sloppy drunk—loud, vulgar, all hands. In Bob's present state, that was the last thing Maria thought he needed.

It was pouring when they pulled up in front of Mike Bloomfield's place. Several band members waited in the car as Bob and Maria trudged up the steep driveway toward the little suburban house. The lights were on, and as Bob peeked in the window, he could see the television throwing off a pattern of dark and light shadows. Maria knocked, and within seconds Mike Bloomfield stood behind the screen door in his bedroom slippers, looking tan and healthy, and sipping from a container of grapefruit juice. "Michael, *open up!*" Maria said, "I've got a surprise for you."

Bloomfield saw Bob and almost tore through the screen. It had been years since the two men had last seen each other, and now they hugged and clapped each other on the back like a couple of long, lost camp buddies. They visited for a half-hour to the video drone of *Godfather II,* which Mike had been watching, before Bob got up to go. Mike faced him squarely. "So I hear you're a Christian now," he snickered. "Oy gevalt!" Bob took the kidding good-naturedly. "Listen pal, wait here a minute, I've got something I want to give you."

Bloomfield disappeared into another room, and when he returned, he was carrying a Bible wrapped in an ornately engraved silver cover. "Here," he extended it to Bob. "I want you to have it. My grandmother gave it to me. It's been in the family for over a hundred years, but Lord knows, I'll never read it." Bob seemed almost embarrassed to take it, but Michael insisted. "Put it to good use, *boychick,*" he grinned and pushed his friends out the door.

Bob was incredibly touched by his friend's gesture, and as they drove away, Maria watched him turning it over and over in his lap. It was the Old Testament, an important book from Bob's past, from an important old friend. "I felt as if I'd just witnessed a rite of passage," Maria says now. "That Bible was like a gentle nudge in a new direction, a push off the shallow end of a pool maybe Bob had been contemplating jumping into for some time. I knew the times were a-changin' and I was waiting to see where it led him next."

Maria pursued that personal odyssey the following spring, when she stopped in Los Angeles on the way home from a show. Bob was at Main Street studios, recording what would be the final album in his religious trilogy, the brilliant *Shot of Love,* when Maria arrived unannounced. "I went upstairs where they were rehearsing," she recalls, "looking forward to saying hello to the old gang. It had been some time since we'd last seen each other, but I felt as if we'd become a close-knit family that met for reunions every once in awhile." Instead of the big welcome she expected, however, Maria was kept waiting on a sofa for what seemed like an inordinately long time. "Finally I saw his face at the little window," she says. "He looked right at me and *right through me.* Then he whispered something to a friend and ignored me, which was a message, I guess, so I took off."

Put yourself in the place of someone who had known Bob all those years and tried to keep up with the conflicting messages he sent out. All those embraces and rebuffs, the smiles and the "looks," the eagerness and the rejection—you attempt to ride the highs and lows as long as it is humanly possible. But after a while, you just give up trying.

Maria went back to San Francisco feeling like she'd lost one of her best friends, just as others before her—and after her—had felt when they had been dismissed from the entourage with similar blunt shrift. Joan Baez, John Bucklen, Bobby Neuwirth, Rob Stoner, Echo, Suze, Sara. . . .

That summer, Bob had reconnected with his old college flame Judy Rubin, who was a registered nurse now living in Minneapolis. They'd seen each other on and off for a few years, and now Bob was callingwith some urgent message at eight o'clock in the morning, just as Judy was about to rush off to work. He had to see her, he said, and they made plans to get together later at her house.

That night, Bob arrived and made small talk with Judy and her boyfriend. They talked about each other's kids, the old gang, how great Minneapolis looked. "Then," recalls Judy, "he got into his religion rap. He told me that he had found a better way. Worse, lightning would strike me because I *hadn't* found the way. At first, I didn't know what he was talking about. Then it dawned on me that he meant I was divorced and living in sin with a man. *That hypocrite!*

"I was furious, but he refused to let up. He attacked me, attacked Judaism, he called me a fallen woman and said he felt sorry for me. *Sorry!* Well, I knew about all his escapades and exactly who and what he was, so I kicked him out. I pushed him out the door and said, 'Don't you ever come back here again.'"

Thus began a period for Bob of hard work and extreme isolation. Following a short European tour, he withdrew to the house in Malibu, where he wrote the songs for the 1984 album, *Infidels.* Less spontaneous, less ecclesiastical, *Infidels* signaled a drastic change in Bob's ideology. The fundamentalist ethic was nowhere in evidence, nor was the trusty gospel trio from his Christian trilogy. The songs were elegant, romantic, political—and spun of the old Dylan imagery. And his voice—*that voice!*—sounded richer and stronger than it had in years.

Part of the album's texture could be attributed to its production. *Infidels* materialized under the whip hand of Dire Straits guitarist Mark Knopfler, who coaxed a meticulous, albeit loose and unforced, performance out of Bob. Clearly, *Infidels* wasn't punched out overnight, like so many of Bob's previous albums. "I decided to take my time, like other people do," he says, in answer to the obvious comparisons with his twenty-seven predecessors. For a change, he paid niggling attention to the album's sound, its *feel.* He allowed reverb to be added to his vocals and tons of EQ to clean up the sound in order to make the album more competitive in the present cutthroat market. He even used Sly Dunbar and Robbie Shakespeare, two of rock music's most overused session men, to provide an agonizingly familiar commercial beat.

In all, *Infidels* stunned Dylan fans and critics alike, who had already been drafting Bob's professional obituary. Once again, he mined a musical gem to remind people of his capacity for innovation. And to attract new and younger audiences who wanted something more from their music than the vapid technorock of the Eighties, cranked out by ersatz rockers like Phil Collins, John Mellencamp, and George Michael. *Infidels* pricked the thin-skinned Yuppie cortex with insights into greed, false prophets, hypocrisy, superpatriotism, corrupt unions, and American imperialism—controversial issues that required a real reaction from listeners. And from the media.

Suddenly, Bob Dylan was page-one news again. As a "protest singer," he provided terrific copy. He'd become a voice of the Eighties, a new-age oracle resurrected from the graveyard of the pop fossils of the Sixties. Predictably, magazines and newspapers rushed to announce that Bob Dylan was indeed *back.* Even Columbia Records got behind *Infidels,* promoting Bob as if he were one of the label's top attractions, which, from time to time, the company claimed he was. However, it was no secret around Black Rock that Bob Dylan wasn't a "priority push." For years the record company had sloughed him off as an "adult contemporary artist" with a fair-to-moderate sales outlook, and, as such, he received the same promotional effort as, say, Johnny Mathis or Jerry Vale, which is to say, not very much. Bob himself blamed Columbia for the dismal performance of *Shot of Love* and *Saved.* But now Columbia was loading its big guns to give Dylan a blast of publicity that warranted four-star attention. The record company even dusted off the old catalogue, hastily removed the "Nice Price—$3.99" stickers from his early albums, whisked them out of the cutout bins, and laid back as they rang up impressive sales.

The issue dogging Bob's modern-day reputation, however, has been one of consistency. Since the release of *Blonde on Blonde* in 1966, his recording peaks have been interspersed with interminable lows, during which he issued such clinkers as *Self-Portrait, Dylan, Pat Garrett & Billy the Kid, Hard Rain, Live at Budakan,* and any number of marginal records to stem the demand for new product. Despite all the accolades lavished upon him, Bob Dylan is conceivably the king of greatest-hits packages, issuing (before *Infidels*) as many as six "oldies" collections. Now, on the heels of his latest success, Bob put out still another Dylan omnibus, this one entitled *Real Live,* and one which ultimately disappointed everyone concerned.

Disguised as a chronicle of his 1984 tour, *Real Live* served up bland, lukewarm helpings of old standbys like "Masters of War," "Girl from the North Country," "Tombstone Blues"—songs that had little relevance or connection to an audience teething on the newest, the latest, the freshest, the fastest, and the most ultramodern of trends. His fans didn't want to hear "Highway 61 Revisited" or "Tangled Up in Blue" for the umpteenth time. "Maggie's Farm" alone had been on four previous albums! They wanted *nouvelle cuisine,* not leftovers. With a chance to bring himself into the Eighties, Bob retreated into the past and stranded old and new fans alike who hoped *Infidels* was a barometer by which they could predict his future course.

No such luck. In fact, *Empire Burlesque,* Bob's mid-1985 studio effort, sailed off in yet another haphazard direction. Muddied by a splashy and obtrusive rhythm section that boasted name-musicians Ron Wood, Mick Taylor, Jim Keltner, Sly Dunbar, and Robbie Shakespeare, not to mention a jarring horn section, and mixed convulsively by disco dancemaster Arthur Baker, the album wasn't so much a mess as a morass of incompatible styles. The songs failed to connect their listeners to the kind of gut emotions wrenched up by earlier Dylan truisms. For example, "Trust Yourself," a paranoid lament about the dearth of integrity in relationships, was certainly Eighties in tone but too depressing. Ironically, it was reminiscent of John Lennon's send-up of "You Gotta Serve Somebody," which he recorded as "You Gotta Serve Yourself." "Trust Yourself" deadpanned an identical statement—if you don't serve yourself, asshole, nobody else will—but it was a message that nobody particularly wanted to hear.

With *Empire Burlesque* word began to circulate that Bob Dylan was asleep at the wheel. He wasn't driving anymore. Perhaps rock 'n roll had finally eluded even his flexible grasp. Or maybe he'd outgrown it. He was still insisting, "I just write 'em as they come, you know?" But he hadn't produced anything important. He seemed to be drifting from sound to sound, not so much exploring each one as he was searching for a comfortable groove. But clearly he hadn't found one that pleased his fans. *Empire Burlesque* drew a salvo of mixed reviews. *Time* viewed it as "a tentative kind of triumph," while the *Village Voice* branded it "CLUNK NOT FUNK" and, as far as recent Bob Dylan albums went, declared it "one more dead battery."

Columbia Records, hoping to salvage what loomed as a potentially marooned audience, proposed a familiar enough solution—another Dylan compilation. But not just another greatest-hits record, the company wanted this one to be a spectacular retrospective, the kind of boxed-set collection usually reserved for composers who have been dead for at least ten or twenty years. A marketing phenomenon. Actually, *Biograph,* as it was called, had been in the works for some time. Columbia's vaults laden with literally miles of unreleased Dylan tracks, the label had tried on numerous occasions to talk Bob into letting it release a series of records that provided an accurate self-portrait of the artist and his vagabond styles. In the past Bob had demurred; however, he finally gave the project his blessing, with no stipulation other than he be allowed to approve the albums' final sequence.

Biograph appeared in November 1985, a massive five-record set that took fans and the record industry by complete surprise. Released during the Christmas rush, when album sales are perhaps at their most competitive, *Biograph* was a retail sensation. The novelty of a boxed set attracted even the most disinterested record-buyer's attention, and what lay inside was a revelation. Fifty-three songs, mastered digitally and accompanied by annotated notes, were evidence of one of the most prolific and seminal influences in show business and served as a vintage sampling of the modern American songbook. Hearing them remastered and in one package like that was an extraordinary experience. It was startling to realize that one man had written so many moving and quintessential songs. And they sounded so fresh and timeless, demanding an audience again and again. The competition paled by comparison.

Still, *Biograph* provided no quite cure for Bob's professional malaise. He was still moving from one style to another, with the mien of a once-important boxer groping for the right punch combination. He staggered through a succession of nonproductive sessions with bands like X, the Eurythmics, the Cruzados (with whom he appeared on *Late Night with David Letterman*) and half a dozen other lightweights who were eager to play with the legendary Dylan. Finally his bid for attention was no more than a glancing blow, an unfortunate little album entitled *Knocked out Loaded,* released in 1986, featuring an oddball cast of collaborators that included Tom Petty, Kris Kristofferson, Sam Shepard, a mawkish children's choir, and, incomprehensibly, pop-lyricist Carole Bayer Sager. The album was an instant stiff. Not even a world tour with Tom Petty & The Heartbreakers generated enough interest in it to boost it onto the charts. Airplay was virtually nonexistent. Critics dismissed it with a yawn.

That year, Bob's occasional stabs at show business were equally eccentric—and, for the most part, inconsequential. The first was a trivial, thrown-together theatrical fiasco entitled *Bob Dylan, Words & Music,* which premiered in San Francisco during the fall of 1986. Not about Bob, but rather what certain schlocko entrepreneurs assumed the public believed Bob was about, the show starred Bob Miles, a hapless Dylan imitator who, oddly enough, had been a caretaker at Bob and Sara's Woodstock estate during the late 1960s and had made his living ever since mimicking his reclusive boss. In what could have only been a momentary mental lapse, Bob actually sanctioned the show, modeled after the grotesque Beatles-ripoff, *Beatlemania;* however, it closed quickly owing to horrendous reviews.

Next, he composed three songs for the soundtrack to a B-movie called *Band of the Hand,* directed by the man responsible for TV's *Miami Vice.* Another movie role followed—*Hearts of Fire*—in which Bob starred as an aging rocker who falls in love with a young star. It was judged unsuitable for the American film market, however, and remains scuttled in the can. Bob rebounded with another slipshod album, *Down in the Groove,* which got minimal airplay and even less publicity.

In light of these miscues, it would be easy to write off Bob Dylan as a rock 'n roll has-been. Nearing fifty, distanced by the obstacles of age and experience, it becomes difficult for an entertainer to remain either influential or indisposable to a predominantly youth-oriented culture. Bob Dylan no longer speaks for or to teenagers, nor does his music transfigure the current pop form. The language of his lyrics is dated by its wisdom. His abstractions belie the instant gratification of a fast-food–MTV–*USA Today*–type life-style. His sex appeal is a memory of middle-aged women. His concerts reflect the past instead of prefiguring the future. "Bob Dylan is *history!*" exclaimed a scalper hawking Prince tickets outside a recent gig Bob played with Tom Petty.

Still, the modern history of Bob's poetry and music is essential to the world we live in. "What makes the poet the potent figure he is, or was, or ought to be," wrote Wallace Stevens, "is that he creates the world to which we turn incessantly and without knowing it and that he gives to life the supreme fictions without which we are able to conceive of it." Bob Dylan's songs present an individual point of view that has defined the look and language of popular culture. He created a musical standard against which everything that evolves must be measured. And a body of music that lifts our hearts, reminding us of all the passion and desire and frustration and sacrifice and pity and pride which mold our lives.

Epilogue

Jerusalem, Israel
September 7, 1987

By midnight, or at least by dawn after the bars had closed, the final word had been written. The stories had been filed, and the Israeli press corps, that great stone-faced bunch with those smashing tans and clumps of downy chest hair, were in a snit.Of course, that wasn't anything new. It came with the territory—that vast wasteland which often required them to sit through hours of screechy cello, piccolo, coronet, clavichord, or contrabassoon recitals in another of the country's air-conditioned bunkers. But this snit was more a tempest. It was a devil of an ill wind they breathed, and its inspiration was sparked by a single word: *Dylan!*

Ah, yes, Bob Dylan. The name that had touched off a night of endless vodka tonics. Dylan had dropped a bombshell on them. He'd handed them the classic critic's nightmare: How to pan a national hero and live to tell about it. There were but a few options at their disposal, the first, of course, being truth—"he stank." That'd be a tough pill for Israelis to swallow. As would a big lie: polite praise, without actually saying anything about the performance. Or perhaps, just perhaps, they could get away with not reviewing the show at all, ignoring it, as *The Times* does those chainsaw massacre movies. Hmmmmmmmmmmmm—no, that wouldn't do either. The fans wouldn't buy it and the vodka tonics wouldn't make the problem go away, and by dawn, in their Absolut hazes, the Israeli critics circle seemed as baffled as before.

By the time the morning editions hit the stands, however, their position was unanimously clear. "Robert Zimmerman, your time has passed!" blared the newspaper *Maariv*. "We got the legend when it was already shattered!" echoed the daily *Hadashot*. The mass circulation *Yedioth Aharonoth* decried, "You mocked the best audience you ever had. For an hour you sang the same monotonous song." Israeli rock star Shalom Hanoch wrote: "I lost patience after four or five songs. I expected more substance, more contact. It was as if he wasn't there." Others used words like "boring," "withdrawn," "flat," "tired," and "arrogant" to describe Dylan's stage presence. Oh, it was a merry old gang that wrote those columns, and by noon the country was embroiled in still another Middle East dispute.

How could Bob Dylan show his face in Jerusalem, the City of Gold, after such scathing notices? "Maybe he'll cancel," speculated Yael, a doe-eyed Israeli student, as she uncovered a picnic basket about a hundred feet from the outdoor stage. "He might be better off, after the other night."

"Agghhh! That was Tel Aviv," said her friend. "This is Yerushaliem!"

And indeed, the comparison was everywhere in evidence. No arena or fenced-in facility, Sultan's Pool, as the concert area was known, lay inside a natural rock formation, just in front of ancient Jerusalem. To the right, the wall of the old city, where the Temple had stood, glistened in the evening sun. Centuries-old houses adjoined the periphery, and a gaggle of hunchbacked women leaned out of the windows, waving at the young crowd.

The Tel Aviv fans had been an aggregate not unlike one you'd expect to see on King's Highway in Brooklyn. But in Jerusalem, the smaller audience of nine thousand appeared more urban and sophisticated. It was a very good-looking group of concertgoers that tromped into the amphitheater that evening, with their one-and-a-half-shekel red rental cushions and homemade breads. Before the concert, they seemed subdued, even a bit hostile, as the stagecrew skittered about, making final adjustments. Everyone had read the reviews and expected the worst. "Dylan's finished, as far as we're concerned," declared a bearded *aliyah,* who had first seen Bob in concert with Joan Baez, back in 1964. "We're here, but, you know, we're a country that goes to funerals, too."

Almost in emphasis, the sun dropped like a shot. The sky grew coal black, and the temperature, which had wavered between eighty-five and ninety degrees, plummeted to an ominous sixty-five. At first, the darkness spread out like an eerie opaque veil; then the moon sailed into range—a huge, clear globe. A cluster of brilliant stars appeared behind it, and the audience applauded as the stagelights dimmed.

"This is Roger McGuinn!" an unseen announcer blared, and the ex-Byrd performed an engaging twenty-minute set. Tom Petty and the Heartbreakers followed, with forty-five minutes of upbeat rock 'n roll, and then, just after ten o'clock, Dylan appeared.

The crowd stood to applaud as Bob ambled out on stage. If Tel Aviv had been fresh in everyone's mind, the slate was wiped clean as the ovation dragged on for several minutes. Finally, with a nod to the band, Bob began, and with a song his fans had been waiting twenty-five years to hear him play live—"The Times They Are A-Changin'." Again applause thundered through the centuries-old ruins, before the tempo abruptly changed. Something was wrong with the guitar! The band continued to play, as Bob grabbed an electric guitar from some unseen stagehand, strummed it twice, and then began the song anew—with a completely different melody and phrasing!

From that moment on, he was incredible. He spit out the words to thirteen quintessential Dylan songs, and the crowd was with him every breath of the way. "Like a Rolling Stone," "Rainy Day Women," "Ballad of a Thin Man," "You've Got to Serve Somebody"—Bob's eyes burned like lasers as he threw himself into each successive performance. By "Shot of Love" the place really rocked, the audience clapping away in time to the thumping bass progression.

"Shot of love—*ooooooo yeah!*—I need a—*oooooooo yeah!* . . ."

Yael was on her feet now, along with the rest of the crowd. Her friend was dancing with a stranger, a barefoot, balding guy, doing a quasi-folk/quasi-shuffle dance that, in some offbeat way, assimilated the ages. "I need a—*ooooooooo yeah!* . . ." Others had already given themselves up wholly to the music, even the huffiest critics, and suddenly the nightscape was an epochal blur. It was Newport, Forest Hills, the Garden, Tel Aviv, all the musical battlegrounds where Dylan had fended off timid arbiters. The music stopped momentarily, the audience howled, and Yael's voice sliced through the din of approval. "Too much!" she screamed. "He's too much, too much, too much, too much. . . ."

Notes

Chapter 1

Page

9 "After all, anybody is as . . .": From "An American and France," by Gertrude Stein, 1936

10 "Pockets of civilization . . .": Interview with Patricia Mestek, Hibbing Historical Society, May 2, 1985.

10 Von Ahlen: "He had come as a hopeful immigrant from Kirkboitzen, Hanover, Germany, where he was born on December 14, 1856, as Frank Dietrich Von Ahlen." *Hibbing, The Man and the Village,* by Samuel J. Guello, Hibbing Historical Society, 1957.

11 "their self-imposed segregation": Interview with Greg Rochester, May 4, 1985.

11 "Dylan would later claim . . .": *Hibbing High Times,* October 18, 1978.

12 "Mr. Dylan is vague . . .": "Bob Dylan: A Distinctive Folk Stylist," by Robert Shelton, *New York Times,* September 29, 1961.

12 B.H. and Lyba Edelstein: Details from the early family life of the Zimmermans were related by Max Edelstein, Bob's uncle.

12 "If you were unlucky enough . . .": Interview with Linda Fidler Wendell, February 2, 1985.

12 "My grandfather was a man . . .": Interview with Melvin Bennett Rutstein, May 29, 1985.

13 "To that end, B.H. spent . . .": Information supplied by Ethel Edelstein Crystal, May 29, 1985.

13 The Edelstein family theater business: Culled from the interviews with Ethel Crystal, Sylvia Goldberg, Charles Edelstein, and Melvin Bennett Rutstein.

13 "Florence was the distaff . . .": Interviews with Sylvia Edelstein Goldberg and Ethel Crystal.

Page

13 Florence Stone: Details about her childhood provided by Max Edelstein and Ethyl Crystal.

14 Abe Zimmerman's birth: Statistics courtesy of the County Clerk, Department of Birth Records, Duluth, Minnesota.

14 "a rambunctious little boy . . .": Interview with Marion Zimmerman Kenner, June 3, 1985.

14 "Abe had an uncanny way . . .": Interview with Robert Karon, June 11, 1985.

15 "He took it very hard . . .": Interview with Ben Overman, June 3, 1985.

15 "You could name the few Jewish families . . .": Wendell.

16 "Beatty could take control . . .": Interview with Barbara Edelstein Fisher, January 26, 1985.

16 Abe and Beatty's wedding: Ceremony performed by Rabbi B. Gusse. Details provided by Ethel Edelstein Crystal.

17 Bob's birth: Details provided in an interview with Mr. and Mrs. George Berman, June 3, 1985.

Chapter 2

18 "Companies with national identities . . .": Interview with Judy Crane, St. Louis County Historical Association, June 11, 1985.

18 the Zimmerman's move to Hibbing: "Abe had seen the handwriting on the wall," George Berman said in an interview, June 3, 1985.

19 "Maurice was a refrigeration engineer . . .": Interview with Ben Orlando, May 3, 1985.

19 "The World's Largest Open Pit": Interview with Linda Fidler Wendell, February 2, 1985.

19 "The landscape was an environmentalist's . . .": Interview with Jeff Syme, *Hibbing Star and Tribune,* June 2, 1985.

20 "Back in Hibbing, the Zimmerman family . . .": *Hibbing City Directory,* 1947–1948, Hibbing Public Library.

20 "Built in 1939 . . .": City Assessor's Office, Hibbing, Minnesota.

20 "During that time, he stuck pretty close . . .": Interview with Leroy Hoikkala, June, 3, 1985. He recalled, "Bob spent a lot of time at home by himself, listening to music. I thought he was kind of trapped because he didn't hang out with a crowd."

20 Hank Williams: "A Tennessee farmer once asked Hank [Williams], 'Hank, how do you make all those songs?' 'You've had to surveyed a lot of farm land over the backside of a mule to be a good country singer.'": From liner notes to *24 of Hank Williams Greatest Hits,* by Jerry Rivers, Polygram Records.

20 "Bobby was just a very ordinary kid . . .": Interview with Barbara Edelstein Fisher, January 26, 1985.

21 Bob's bedroom: Details provided by Leroy Hoikkala and John Bucklen over the course of several interviews.

21 "In fact, wealth . . .": Wendell.

Page

22 "You can have some amazing hallucinogenic experiences . . .": "Bob Dylan: The Playboy Interview," by Ron Rosenbaum, *Playboy,* November 1978.

22 "Bobby was obsessed with talking to this guy . . .": Interview with Echo Helstrom Fernandez, March 2, 1985.

23 "Hellraisers": Interview with Greg Rochester.

23 "When the train rolled through town . . .": Dylan interviewed by journalist Ken Hughes, Sydney, Australia, April 1, 1978, *Rock Express.*

24 "In lieu of the twenty-five cent admission . . .": Fernandez.

25 James Dean: "We really mourned James Dean. When he died, we talked about death a lot. He was everything we wanted to be—very independent—so we identified completely with him." Hoikkala.

26 "Bobby made a beeline for Feldman's . . .": Hoikkala.

27 Bob's grades and IQ score: Interview with various administrators at Hibbing Sr. High School, May 3, 1985.

28 "Last seat back there . . .": Interview with Charles Miller, May 4, 1985.

28 "You've got to hear what they're playing . . .": Interview with John Bucklen, April 3, 1985.

Chapter 3

29 Bob's rock 'n roll: "Bob's love of rock really disturbed the Rangers." Interview with John Bucklen, April 12, 1985.

30 Bob's discovery of rock 'n roll: "When Bob heard rock 'n roll, he couldn't believe it—it blew him away. It was if something just socked him in the mouth." Bucklen.

31 "Every night at ten o'clock . . .": Bucklen.

31 "In reality, Page was the same . . .": Interview with Frank "Gatemouth" Page, August 6, 1985.

31 Ray "Groovy Boy" Bartlett: "He was a certified nut, and his show was wild—really wild." Page.

32 Page's rap: "I couldn't copy Bartlett, I couldn't imitate that crazy black accent he used, so I affected a kind of relaxed black southern brogue that was 'cool' and jivey instead of 'crazy.' . . ." Page.

33 "Bobby was an instant convert": "Bob never missed Page's show. He loved the music that was played and the whole feel of the south right there in his bedroom. . . .": Bucklen.

33 R&B's influence on Dylan: "Late at night, I used to listen to Muddy Waters, John Lee Hooker, Jimmy Reed and Howlin' Wolf blastin' in from Shreveport. . . . I used to stay up til two, three o'clock in the morning. Listened to all those songs, then tried to figure them out." "The Rolling Stone Interview: Bob Dylan," by Curt Loder, *Rolling Stone,* June 21, 1984, p. 18.

34 "Stan's Shoeshine Parlor . . .": Stan Lewis remembers, "It was a tiny crackerbox of a place built on cinder blocks, right next to a popcorn stand. Once I started selling R&B records, I began pulling KKK stickers off the door as regularly as the sun comes up." Interview, August 5, 1985.

34 "Suzy-Q": This song was recorded in Frank Page's studio at KWKH. Says Page, "The radio station had the best facilities in Shreveport, and Stan sat in on guitar."

Page

35 "The kids who regularly . . . ": John Bucklen recalls, "That's where we got all of our records from. Crippa's didn't have them, and Bob couldn't wait until he got to Minneapolis, so he ordered 'em by mail."

35 *No-Name Jive's* demographics: "The show reached all the way to Nebraska and the Dakotas. KCIJ broadcast it out of Texas and Mexico where the show was helmed by Wolfman Jack and Tommy Sands." Lewis.

36 "Each morning Stan trundled off . . . ": Says Lewis, "We had to pack each shipment with extreme care since the records were basically 78s, so each day I took stacks of cartons to the post office by myself."

36 Stan's mail-order business: "Before I knew it, I began selling 6,000 to 8,000 copies of each record, with orders pouring in from all over the country." Lewis.

36 "His shipments to Hibbing . . . ": "I was stunned the show got all the way to a place like Hibbing and wondered what a person like that thought of the music . . . " Lewis.

Chapter 4

37 Bob's piano odyssey: "Bob used to sit at the piano picking out the tunes we'd heard on *No-Name Jive*. . . . " Interview with John Bucklen, April 12, 1985.

38 Country & western: "We all listened to country & western music. It was all around us, and, hell, it took nothing to sing those songs. . . . " Interview with Leroy Hoikkala, May 3, 1985.

39 "None of us had ever heard . . . ": Interview with Larry Fabbro, January 30, 1985.

39 "The group jammed . . . ": Says Larry Fabbro, "We were very loud. It was hard to tell if we were any good."

39 College Capers: Fabbro.

41 "The general impression we had . . . ": Interview with Sanford Margolies, May 19, 1985.

42 *Blackboard Jungle*: "The movie had been to town and was probably responsible for introducing the kids in Hibbing to rock 'n roll"; Fabbro. Also, Leroy Hoikkala remembers, "Bob and I saw it at the State Theatre, and afterward he just kept saying, 'Wow!'"

43 John Bucklen: "They were inseparable, Bob and John. Bob was a hero to him, the greatest thing that ever came his way, and John followed him around like a little puppy. Bob could talk him into anything." Interview with Echo Helstrom Fernandez, March 2, 1985.

44 Melrad's: "We'd walk there almost every afternoon and, over a cup of coffee, play the jukebox: 'Donna' and 'Angel Baby' and Bob's favorite, 'La Bamba.' Only Bob and I hung out there—it was 'our' place." Bucklen.

44 Gene Vincent: "We'd always listen to music and pantomime to records. One day, we bought ourselves two blue caps at Feldman's, put on 'Be Bop A-Lula' and pretended we were on stage. . . . " Bucklen.

45 Bobby's ostracism: "He was a loner, all right, and people thought he was weird, but as I remember it Bob really didn't care if he was accepted by the majority or not." Interview with Monte Edwardson, March 19, 1985.

46 Jim Dandy: Bob listened to the deejay on WHLB in Virginia, Minnesota; Interview with Dave Mosenphin, WHLB. "Bob said, 'Hey, Leroy—there's this colored deejay in Virginia. We gotta go meet him.'" Hoikkala.

Page

47 Jim Reese and his house: Details provided by the friends who accompanied Bob there: John Bucklen, Echo Helstrom, and Leroy Hoikkala.

48 "It was like sitting in a bar. . . .": Fernandez.

49 The Golden Chords: "I remember *exactly* how we decided to start a band. Bob met us as we were leaving Feldman's. . . ." Hoikkala.

50 "He wrote a thing called 'Big Black Train' that we used to do. At the time I couldn't believe one of us could just *write* a song." Edwardson.

50 Jacket Jamboree: Details provided by Leroy Hoikkala, Monte Edwardson, and John Bucklen.

51 "I had always known him . . .": Interview with William Law, April 3, 1985.

51 "John Bucklen, cowering . . .": "I remember sitting in the balcony, feeling real embarrassed, as he did 'Jenny, Jenny.' At the time I thought: this guy's so far out. But I admired him for his fortitude." Bucklen.

52 B. J. "Bonnie" Rolfzen: From *Positively Main Street,* by Toby Thompson, Coward, McCann & Geoghegan, New York, 1971, p. 50.

52 Charles Miller: "The teachers felt they couldn't permit that type of stuff on stage. They compared it to when Elvis Presley rolled his hips, and it caused the same kind of response." Interview, May 5, 1985.

52 "His classmates were shocked": Monte Edwardson recalls, "The other kids were bewildered and kind of stunned. We got a lot of ribbing in school because of it. Bob was probably the easier one to tease; he took it more seriously than we did."

52 Sundays at Collier's: "Collier's became *our* place. Those hot Sunday afternoons we'd just take over the upstairs and play until enough kids stopped by that the place would be jammed." Hoikkala.

53 Bob's conversion to guitar: "When he began playing with me and Leroy, I taught him a few chords on the guitar and before long he performed with it more than the piano." Interview with Monte Edwardson, November 29, 1985.

54 "First I bought a Nick Manoloff book . . . and I had a Silvertone guitar from Sears": "The Rolling Stone Interview: Bob Dylan," by Curt Loder, *Rolling Stone,* June 21, 1984, p. 18.

54 Silvertone guitar: Leroy Hoikkala claims Bob bought his first guitar at B&D Music, across from the Lybba Theatre, and John Bucklen substantiates that, saying: "We both had Silvertones we bought for around $22 apiece at a music store on First Avenue near the Lybba."

54 "He'd run all over town . . .": Fernandez.

54 "He tried to pattern himself . . .": "We tried to copy our guitar playing after Scotty Moore. We listened to the early Presley stuff—"Mystery Train" and "That's All Right, Mama—that good, basic country sound.": Bucklen.

55 Mr. Hautela: "He didn't understand what we were trying to do with rock 'n roll, but Bob and I loved talking to him. He was strange, so I guess we felt like we were all outcasts in Hibbing." Bucklen.

55 Bobby's twitch: Interview with Hibbing psychologist Greg Rochester, May 5, 1985.

Chapter Five

Page

57 Bob's first crush: "Every day he'd call and tell me how wild he was about Barb. He'd say, 'Guess what?' And I'd go: 'Yeah, I know, you love Barb." Interview with John Bucklen, April 3, 1985.

58 "She had an ingenue's name . . .": Echo's brother and sister were born fourteen months apart; she was born fourteen months later—hence: Echo. Her middle name was a result of her mother's discovery of a perfect star that had formed in the ice-rimed hospital window when she was born. Interview with Martha Helstrom, February 19, 1985.

58 "a real outlandish creature": "A friend of mine told me I looked like a cross between Marilyn Monroe and Brigitte Bardot—the epitome of femininity and sexiness—and that was all I needed to know." Interview with Echo Helstrom Fernandez, March 3, 1985.

58 "Everybody thought they were a joke . . .": Interview with Linda Fidler Wendell, February 2, 1985.

59 "a perverse attraction . . .": Echo says, "He seems to be really at home with poor people. He used to come over and talk to my mother a lot. She made him feel comfortable." Fernandez.

59 Echo's family: "My dad was crazy, like an old hillbilly. The kind of guy who'd run out of the house in long underwear and with boots on, carrying a shotgun, to chase away guys who were interested in me." Fernandez.

60 Zimmerman Electric and Furniture: A detailed reminiscence of the business and complexion of the community was provided by Ben Orlando in an interview, May 3, 1985.

62 Bobby and Abe: "It was an unspoken rule—you didn't talk about his dad. I even remember John Bucklen telling me not to mention Abe in front of Bobby." Fernandez.

62 Bobby's Harley: "His dad sure didn't like the whole idea of a motorcycle. He often told me he wished Bobby didn't ride it, but it didn't seem to make much of a difference. Bobby usually won out where things like that were concerned." Orlando.

63 "a smart Ranger . . .": Interview with Patricia Mestek, May 2, 1985.

63 Bobby Vee: "He let that one go on for a long time. I never knew if he was putting me on, and as I got to know him better I realized he stretched the truth to entertain people." Bucklen.

64 Crippa's: "We'd go in there, take stacks of records and spend the day listening to them"; interview with Leroy Hoikkala, May 3, 1985. "Bob would go into Crippa's and purposely ask for stuff they didn't have. It made him feel like he knew something special and they didn't." Bucklen.

64 Bob, John, and Leroy: "People didn't understand us. They called us hoods because we rode motorcycles, but the three of us spent a lot of time together—we were very independent—and respected each other's privacy. Often, we'd walk around for hours and just not talk. It wasn't necessary because we knew what was on each others' minds." Hoikkala.

65 "It didn't matter that he was laughed at . . .": John Bucklen recalls, "The laughter didn't seem to bother him. He knew what he wanted to do and he did it. If people didn't go for it, he didn't care."

65 Winter Frolic talent contest: Information and anecdotes provided by Leroy Hoikkala, Monte Edwardson, and John Bucklen, as well as an encounter of the event in the *Hibbing Star and Tribune,* February 14, 1958.

Page

65 "Three leading pastimes...": "This is directly related to the long winters and the lack of stimulation in the region." Interview with Greg Rochester, May 4, 1985.

67 "During the summer months...": Echo says, "We sat in my yard, on the steps, on the swings, in the car—every place. And the talk was always me, Bob, and John going to Hollywood or Nashville and becoming stars."

67 Dial-in: "He drove over in a blue Ford, hopped out and said, 'I've finally found a name....'" Fernandez.

68 junior prom: "Bobby really wanted to go. I wore a blue-green pastel dress; he wore a pale blue suit. We were sure all the kids were gonna laugh at us. It was a warm night and, afterwards, we fell asleep in the car." Fernandez.

Chapter 6

70 a twit: "He wasn't taken seriously. Everyone felt he was just a kid from Hibbing who probably couldn't put two sentences together if his life depended on it." Interview with Lorna Sullivan, December 10, 1984.

71 "By day he'd be Bob Zimmerman...": "He'd sneak away from the fraternity house at night to play the guitar, sometimes crawling through the upper lattice of his locked door so we wouldn't know he was gone." Interview with Richard Rocklin, January 8, 1986.

72 "The first Sammy to befriend...": "I knew at once he wasn't being very truthful, nevertheless he seemed like a nice kid." Interview with Wayne Freeman, September 13, 1985.

73 "he was 'an anomaly...'" Rocklin.

74 "Bobby felt even more alienated...": "He was always kind of out in left field someplace and because of that the other kids wanted nothing to do with him. They tried to talk me out of seeing him." Interview with Judy Rubin Shaffer, January 26, 1986.

74 Camp Hertzl: "Bobby always had only one friend there who he'd hang around with for the entire summer. He was a little skinny kid and never left the bunk without a harmonica jammed in his back pocket." Interview with Karen Tessler Katz, January 11, 1986.

74 Judy Rubin: Culled from interviews with Karen Katz, Richard Rocklin, Judy Shaffer, and others.

74 "We pretended to be good sports...": Rocklin.

76 Romantic socialism: *Gates of Eden: American Culture in the Sixties,* by Morris Dickstein, Basic Books, New York, 1971, p. 21.

76 The Young Intelligentsia: From a collection of Mills' essays called *Power, Politics and People,* by Irving Lewis Horowitz, Oxford University Press, New York, 1963.

76 Dinkytown's hangouts: "It was a wonderful playground, if you took advantage of all it had to offer...." Interview with Stanley Gottleib, January 29, 1986.

78 "Bob Dylan, with his electric guitar...": "We were still both rock 'n rollers at heart. When the folk crowd had emptied out of the Scholar, Bobby and I used to sit at the piano there and play rock 'n roll—but first he swore me to secrecy, because it wasn't cool to play that kind of music anymore." Interview with Paul Davies, December 12, 1984.

Page

79 "Lead singers would always come in . . .": "The Rolling Stone Interview: Bob Dylan," by Curt Loder, *Rolling Stone,* June 21, 1984, p. 18.

82 "Echo, to his amazement, had gotten married . . .": Interview with Echo Helstrom Fernandez, March 3, 1985.

82 Judy's black velveteen dress: "It was gorgeous—black slacks and matching top—one of the prettiest outfits I'd ever seen. But my mother made me send it right back." Shaffer.

84 "He wasn't any good . . .": "He came into the Scholar one night and said, 'I'm a folksinger. Mind if I play here?'" Interview with David Lee, December 10, 1984.

84 "Dylan appealed to the college girls . . .": Davies.

85 "As a guitarist, I would look at . . .": "It was clear to me that he only knew two chords, and for a while some of us thought he had a muscular disability the way he strummed." Interview with Dave Matheny, December 11, 1984.

85 Dylan and Matheny: "Matheny was really pissed at him. Dylan kept right on playing from the audience for about an hour. . . ." Interview with John Koerner, December 10, 1984.

86 Dylan's sticky fingers: "He took things that belonged to his friends. There were a lot of apartments where the rule was not to leave Dylan alone in a room." Gottleib.

86 "We were all getting by on money from home . . .": Interview with Hugh Brown, December 11, 1984.

87 "His ambition naturally pissed off . . .": "Bob was fighting a very hard fight, playing a scene which already had two accomplished guitarists [John Koerner and Dave Ray]." Gottleib.

87 "Hell, he'd marry her . . .": Says Judy Shaffer, "I just wasn't in love with him. My parents didn't like him, neither did a lot of my friends, and there were too many things, including drugs, that separated us." Shaffer.

88 "Without Judy, there was a gargantuan hole . . .": "We spent hours in the Varsity Cafe mourning Judy. Despite the fact she was so straight, they had talked about marriage, but in the end Bobby was really married to his guitar." Davies.

89 The lyric to "Love Bug," copyright © 1962 by NINA MUSIC (BMI), by John Koerner, is reprinted by permission of the publisher.

90 "He became a terror on stage . . .": "He would tell the audience to shut up. Sometimes they did, sometimes they didn't. Most of us were offended by it. We felt Dylan was putting on airs he didn't deserve, and I guess he got the message that he wasn't going to get very far staying in Minneapolis." Gottleib.

90 Gretel Hoffman: "That was a wonderful time for Bob and me. We did nothing but soak up all the city's culture and talk about books and music." Interview with Gretel Hoffman Pelto, April 8, 1985.

91 "His crash pad . . .": "We were beating the landlady out of rent. Dylan was taking wheat germ pills to make his fingers stronger and he dumped them on the way out, believing the landlady was gonna think he was a dope addict." Koerner.

94 "Dylan didn't know nothing . . .": "He was a quick learner. He realized there was a lot out there, and he listened carefully." Interview with David Whitaker, April 25, 1985.

95 *Bound for Glory*: "It was the first book I ever saw him read"; Whitaker. "I had borrowed the book from Harry Weber, then Dylan borrowed it from me. He didn't want to give it up; he sat in the Scholar and cut pages from it." Interview with Hugh Brown, December 10, 1984.

Page

95 Woody Guthrie: Biographical information from *Woody Guthrie: A Life,* by Joe Klein, Knopf, New York, 1980.

96 Woody's music: "He became immediately fluent in the Guthrie songbook"; Brown. "One day he ran over and said 'Hey, I want you to hear this—my first Guthrie song,' and just sat down and rattled off 'Tom Joad,' all twenty minutes of it." Whitaker.

96 David and Gretel's marriage: "He was very upset, and it wasn't until then I realized how much of the potential of our relationship hadn't been realized." Pelto.

Chapter 7

101 Sugie's and the Satire: Interview with Walter Conley, May 5, 1985.

103 "The Satire's audiences responded indifferently . . .": "Nobody was crazy about his singing. People were kind of turned off by Bob. They were looking for a more commercial sound, while he was into the harp around his neck, the beat-up old guitar and true folk roots." Conley.

107 missing records: Interviews with Dave Hamil, May 11, 1985, and Conley.

108 more missing records: "My first suspect was Dylan. . . ." *No Direction Home,* by Robert Shelton, Morrow, New York, 1986, p. 73.

Chapter 8

113 "Like his previous pilgrimages . . .": Before arriving in New York, Bob stopped off in Chicago and Minneapolis, where he spent a few weeks with David and Gretel Whitaker. He talked excitedly about his upcoming trip to New York. "He had this idea of a quest—that he was going to find Guthrie. He also said he was going to be a success as a singer. He was extremely confident and said, 'I'll make it—you'll see.'" Interview with Gretel Hoffman Pelto, April 8, 1985.

113 "Most people thought the trip . . .": "When he told us he was going to New York, we thought he was crazy. We said, 'You can't make it *here;* how the fuck are you gonna make it there?' We thought he'd be back in a few weeks." Interview with Stanley Gottleib, January 29, 1986.

114 "Aside from folksinger Jack Elliott . . .": "On September 17, [Woody] grew concerned because Marjorie—who'd been visiting regularly (as had Jack Elliot, but practically none of his other alleged friends). . . ." *Woody Guthrie: A Life,* by Joe Klein, Knopf, New York, 1980.

114 "It was all he wanted to talk about . . ." Interview with Mark Spoelstra, March 11, 1985.

115 Café Bazaar: "Dylan conceived this whole spoof right on the spot. His whole face and attitude changed as he went at it." Interview with Mark Spoelstra, July 21, 1986.

120 "This strident *popularization* . . .": From the liner notes for *The Folk Box,* Elektra Records.

120 "The Village coffeehouses still featured . . .": "Dave Van Ronk always used to ask me why my generation had to get dressed up to sing." Interview with Cynthia Gooding, January 21, 1985.

Page

120 "abandoned laundromats, pizza parlors . . .": "The Gaslight had been an old cellar used for miscellaneous storage that hadn't seen the light of day since Prohibition, and then it was as a speakeasy called the Vagabondi." Interview with John Mitchell, February 16, 1985.

120 Von Emsen: Interview with Dave Van Ronk, February 14, 1986.

121 baskethouses: "We'd play baskethouses practically every day. That was the only money we were making, and Dylan went over very well with that crowd." Spoelstra, March 11, 1985.

123 Gil Turner's review: "Bob Dylan—A New Voice Singing New Songs," by Gil Turner, *Sing Out!*, Vol. 12, No. 4, October–November 1962.

123 "The New York Dylan . . .": "When he came back from New York and played at Kaufman Union on campus, I couldn't believe it: he sounded like an Okie. You could hardly understand what he was saying. I was disgusted." Interview with Paul Davies, December 12, 1984.

123 "with all the husk and bark . . .": "Bob Dylan: A Distinctive Folk-Song Stylist," by Robert Shelton, *New York Times*, September 29, 1961, p. 31.

124 "Some, like Van Ronk and Paxton . . .": "The first night we heard Bob, Van Ronk and I were *very* impressed. We turned to each other and said, 'This guy's good—very good. Let's find out who he is.'" Interview with Tom Paxton, December 22, 1984.

124 Eric Darling: "Eric really hated Dylan. He couldn't stand to be in the same room as Bob, and used to tell me, 'I hate that son of a bitch!'" Interview with Mark Spoelstra, June 21, 1986.

124 Arthur Gorson: "Bob was an attention-grabber. At a party on Sheridan Square, I remember him taking his guitar out on a window ledge and everybody thinking he was gonna jump. But he just sat there for an hour scaring the shit out of us and getting all the attention in the world—a real pose-master." Interview with Arthur Gorson, March 1, 1985.

126 Bob's chess prowess: "It was murder playing against Bobby, because there was always so much more going on than just the game." Van Ronk.

128 Music parties: "That's where we really learned how to perform. There was a real nucleus of singers, poets, and artists who all just happened to be drawn to New York, as though some muse had called us together." Spoelstra.

Chapter 9

133 "Bob continued to visit his hero . . .": Bob visited Woody weekly, taking friends along whenever they expressed interest. Barry Kornfeld, a regular on the Street, made the trip several times. "Woody was in such terrible shape that I could hardly understand him, but Bob could and he had to virtually translate for me. He reacted very positively to Bob and Bob, for his part, was very sincere. He'd sing songs for Woody and ask how they were treating him. One time, we even gave Woody a pack of cigarettes, and after opening them up, the first thing he did was to walk up and down the hall, giving all the other patients cigarettes"; Interview with Barry Kornfeld, December 26, 1984. Bob also invited Gretel Whitaker's sister to accompany him to Greystone. "There were about six or seven of us. Bob was very cavalier about it; he didn't prepare us for what to expect, but for someone who'd never seen Woody before it was a shocking experience. He was very bad off. Bob was very kind to Woody—gentle and caring. They talked to each other for over an hour. It didn't matter that we were there or not; we were more or less witnesses. I was incredibly uncomfortable, very disturbed." Interview with Melanie Margolis, May 19, 1985.

Page

133 The Room: Interview with Tom Paxton, December 22, 1984.

134 Bob's chess-club song: "It was a powerful experience for me. Bob had taken the folk format and driven it a light-year into the future. I remember thinking, 'This guy is incredible—what a mind!'" Interview with Noel Stookey, April 2, 1985.

135 "Talkin' Bear Mountain": "After that, I instinctively knew that he had it together and that he would be able to take any idea and capture the essence of it." Stookey.

136 Bob and Sid Gleason: Interview, February 23, 1985.

137 "Before noon, Sid Gleason would help...": *Woody Guthrie: A Life,* by Joe Klein, Knopf, New York, 1980, pp. 426–427.

137 "Due to his celebrity status, Pete Seeger...": "Pete Seeger is a nice guy, but when he came out here he insisted on being the center of attention. The trouble with Pete is, he's always 'on.' So Bobby had to sit in the corner and listen while Pete sang. I suppose he took what he wanted from Pete, but that's the way it always was for both of them." Sid Gleason.

140 Peter, Paul & Mary: Mary's spot had earlier been offered to Carolyn Hester, who turned it down. Grossman had also propositioned an old pal from Chicago, folksinger Bob Gibson, but he was finally rejected as undependable. Interviews with Carolyn Hester, February 27, 1985, and Bob Gibson, December 23, 1984.

Chapter 10

143 Mike Porco: "Mike Porco didn't know from nothing. A good guy, but he's probably the first one to admit he didn't know the first thing about folk music. Mike was a bartender, and that was about it." Interview with Tom Paxton, December 22, 1984.

145 Bob's wardrobe for the Folk City debut: Sid Gleason also claims she loaned Bob a pair of Woody's shoes and that he only walked on the sides of them, not wanting to wear out the soles. Interview, February 23, 1985.

146 "After his Folk City run...": "He was stung that I... had been so busy listening to Hooker and interviewing him that I never heard his own sets." *No Direction Home,* by Robert Shelton, Morrow, New York, 1986, p. 96.

146 Terri Thal shopped Bob's tape: "One night at the Gaslight, Victor Maimudes engineered an audition tape that Bobby made for me when I managed him. It included Dave [Van Ronk] and Bobby singing 'Car, Car,' 'Talkin' Bear Mountain,' 'Pretty Peggy-O,' and a few others, but nobody was interested." Interview with Terri Thal, January 22, 1985.

146 "Tom Paxton dragged Bob...": "Before we left, Bobby and I walked uptown to Central Park and we started writing a talking blues as we walked along: 'Want to be a mugger, tell you what to do/ Join a mugger's union and you pay your mugger's dues....'" Paxton.

146 Dinkytown: "When he came back to visit, Bob told us he saw Woody and played for him, and I remember him saying, 'Woody likes my stuff.' Interview with David Whitaker, April 25, 1985.

146 "Mississippi Fred McDowell...": "[Bob's] personality was changing, and he got very energized to making it, very ambitious. He used to watch other performers and say, 'I got a whole lot more of what it takes. I should be playing here, not him.'" Interview with Mark Spoelstra, July 21, 1986.

Page

147 "Attitude and mystery . . .": "He wanted to create this ramblin', gamblin' image. But when the *Little Sandy Review* broke the story of Dylan being Zimmerman, all of us on the Street read it with great relish. We'd look at each other, say the magic word—Zimmerman—and just start laughing." Interview with Barry Kornfeld, December 26, 1984.

147 Chopped liver/tuna fish: Kornfeld.

147 "Mark Spoelstra quickly tired . . .": "I couldn't deal with the attitude and the lies anymore. There was a lot of crap flying about him playing for Bobby Vee and Little Richard. And then he told me he played behind Jerry Lee Lewis, too." Interview with Mark Spoelstra, March 11, 1985.

148 Bob and girls: "He had a lot of nerve with girls. More than I did. Chasing them, coming onto them, not being intimidated—man, Dylan was remarkable." Spoelstra.

149 Averill: "She was a fine lady and Bob and she lived together for a while." Spoelstra.

149 "For living quarters . . .": "He always needed a floor or a couch to sleep on, he never had any money, but one of us always came through in those 'difficult' times." Kornfeld.

150 Sue Zuckerman: Interview with Sue Zuckerman Green, April 14, 1985.

150 Riverside Church concert: Details provided through interviews with Susan Rotolo, Carla Rotolo, and Peter Karman. "Bob Dylan of Gallup, New Mexico, played the guitar and harmonica simultaneously, and with real gusto." "Riverside Radio Broadcasts All-Day Folk Music Program," by Pete Karman, *New York Mirror,* August 6, 1961.

150 "After the show . . .": "I left Dylan and Carla off together, so I had the feeling that he and Carla, who was older and more sophisticated, had hit it off and would eventually get it together." Interview with Peter Karman, January 3, 1985.

151 "Why don't you come by Gerdes . . .": Interview with Susan Rotolo, January 4, 1985.

152 "funny and clownlike . . .": "It was a charming role, but entirely different from other times." Susan Rotolo.

154 "How did Suze's mother greet . . .": "At first I didn't mind. But he told me so many lies right away, and while my daughters and their friends didn't seem to notice, they were stories that were highly suspect and beyond belief to an older woman." Interview with Mary Rotolo, December 28, 1984.

154 Mary at Gerdes: "He was playing with Dave Van Ronk, whose music I liked very much, but I didn't care for Bobby's music. I met him that same evening, but I didn't really understand anything he said." Mary Rotolo.

154 "Who is this guy? . . .": "You could smell him a mile away. And his teeth were green. He was very unhygienic." Interview with Mary Rotolo, November 26, 1986.

154 Bob's lies: "They were preposterous—beyond belief. So that I was leery from Day One." Mary Rotolo. "I remember her reaction [to Bob's stories] was: 'Oh Christ!— what a number!' I believed him, but I don't think for very long." Susan Rotolo.

156 "I saw a Negro musician . . .": Shelton, p. 151.

156 Big Joe Williams: Interview with Dave Van Ronk, February 14, 1986.

157 "He Was a Friend of Mine": Dylan recorded the song for his first album, although it wasn't included in the final sequence. In his book, Robert Shelton incorrectly says Bob adapted it

Page

"from a song he learned from a Chicago street singer, Blind Arvella Gray"—information he no doubt got from Bob.

157 Club 47: Interviews with Ric Von Schmidt, December 28, 1984; and Robert L. Jones, May 21, 1985.

158 Richard Fariña: "Dick was Mr. Mystery. You could never tell how much of what he said was the truth, how much he was making up on the spot, and how much he made up a few blocks down the road." Von Schmidt.

158 "compelled him to pack a .38-calibre revolver...": "He was always carrying a .38 around. He thought the Protestants were going to bump him off." *Baby, Let Me Follow You Down,* by Eric Von Schmidt and Jim Rooney, Anchor, New York, 1979, p. 89.

160 John Hammond signs Carolyn Hester: "I wanted to continue signing folksingers. I passed on Joan Baez, whom I heard at the Newport Folk Festival, because she was asking a great deal of money while still a relatively unknown artist.... I decided to look further." *John Hammond on Record,* by John Hammond, with Irving Townsend, Summit, New York, 1977, pp. 349–351.

161 "looked so unhealthy": "He was so bleached out, white, pale. His fingernails were very long and his hair was scruffier than most people wore it. I thought, 'This guy looks almost transparent, like a fish out of water.'" Interview with Carolyn Hester, February 27, 1985.

Chapter 11

164 "Ac-cen-chew-ate...": "I used to carry Bobby around as a kid and he would sing 'Accentuate the positive/ eliminate the negative.' It was his favorite song and it made everyone smile when he sang it." Interview with Robert Karon, June 11, 1985.

164 "He could rot in a joint like Gerdes...": "A lot of performers stopped working there because Porco paid so little to the performers. The ones who stayed on there never rose above the tide." Interview with Dave Van Ronk, February 14, 1986.

164 Robert Shelton: "He was one of the gang, always around. Drank with us—in fact, he drank like a fish. Very eccentric. I first dragged him into Gerdes to hear Bobby, who,at first, he thought, was a mystery, then—boom! He went nuts for him." Interview with Carla Rotolo, April 5, 1985.

165 second Gerdes show: "He stood in front of my mirror all afternoon, trying on clothes, jiggling, adjusting." Interview with Carla Rotolo, October 2, 1986.

165 "Robert Shelton was blown away": "I looked at him a few times during the show, and his eyes were wide open. He was mesmerized by Bobby." Interview with Carla Rotolo, January 3, 1987.

167 Shelton's review: "We knew the review was coming out. Shelton told Bob. Not that he came right out and told us what was in it, but he played with Bob, implying it was special. That night, we bought the *Times* together. Bob bought a stack of copies, then we ran back to where my mother was staying and reread it a million times." Interview with Susan Rotolo, January 8, 1987.

167 "There is no doubt that he is bursting...": "Bob Dylan: A Distinctive Folk-Song Artist," by Robert Shelton, New York Times, September 29, 1961, p. 31.

167 "He's so aware of the impression...": Interview with Susan Rotolo, January 4, 1985.

Page

169 "Hammond couldn't have shown less interest...": "He rushed me through that session. John just wanted to get things down and move on." Interview with Carolyn Hester, February 27, 1985.

169 "Hammond had pulled Bob aside...": Interview with John Hammond Sr., February 2, 1985.

170 Mitch Miller: "Mitch issued this ridiculous fiat that Columbia would never go into the rock 'n roll business." Interview with David Kapralik, February 21, 1985.

170 Hammond signs Dylan: "Hammond was one of those dynamite talent scouts you couldn't ignore, so when he said, 'Dave I gotta take you to Gerdes to see someone tonight,' I went." Kapralik.

171 Bob's recording ability: "To me, he was ridiculous." Hammond.

171 Bob's record contract: "It came as a surprise to all of us. Of all the people on the Street who tried to get contracts, he was the only one who got picked up by Columbia. He handled it in a very low-key way, as if he was almost embarrassed by it"; interview with Carla Rotolo, January 19, 1987. "I remember that, on the outside, everybody was very excited for him. But a lot of them thought, 'Great!—now what about an album for me?'" Interview with Dave Van Ronk, December 28, 1986.

173 material on Bob's first album: "He would come up with all kinds of stuff, maybe do it once or twice and drop it. You knew the album was going to be a grab-bag of stuff, because that's what he [performed]." Van Ronk.

174 "Song to Woody": "His 'Song to Woody' was really the first sign we had that this was a major songwriter. It also signaled that Bobby had not yet acquired enough material to do his first record, and had he held out a while longer, he would have put out a stunner." Van Ronk.

175 "House of the Rising Sun": "That was the only argument between Bobby and Dave that I can remember, but it was a killer." Interview with Terri Thal, January 22, 1985.

176 Dylan and Grossman: "Anybody with a lick of sense was on to Albert. You had to be an oaf to fall for him, and socially Bobby was an oaf." Interview with Dave Van Ronk, November 9, 1986.

176 Al Grossman's favorite ploy: "He pulled that one on me over and over again." Interview with a confidential source, December 28, 1984.

177 "Bob had heard all the stories...": "Dylan cornered me one night at Folk City and asked, 'Whaddya think of Al Grossman? He wants me to work with him.' And I told him the truth: I didn't like Al Grossman. I was burned by him, as were others, but if any manager could make a guy successful, he could." Interview with Manny Greenhill, November 11, 1985.

178 Gate of Horn: Details provided by Samuel Freifeld, Bob Gibson, Les Brown, and several confidential sources.

178 University of Chicago: "Al and I graduated from Roosevelt University but it didn't have the cachet that U. of C. had so he substituted schools in conversation because he was ashamed." Interview with Les Brown, March 3, 1985. Additional source: Joan Curry, University of Chicago Alumni Association.

178 Grossman and the Chicago Housing Authority: "Al had gotten into some trouble with the Chicago Housing Authority—they had fired him. He couldn't get a job very easily after

Page

that. He seemed very depressed, he had a lot of problems with women, and so we decided to set up a nightclub." Les Brown.

178 Deerborne Homes: Interview with Robert Murphy, April 2, 1985.

179 "The greatest folksinger in the world": "It took me only two songs to think that Al was out of his mind with Dylan." Interview with Sam Freifeld, April 27, 1985.

180 "The Dylan mystique": "It was the first time I'd heard anyone refer to any of us lowly folksingers in a professional, Hollywood-like manner." Interview with Noel Stookey, April 2, 1985.

180 "He concluded the press was useless...": "Albert used to talk a lot about how useless the press was, how they were morons who could be duped by anyone smart enough to put them on. We were instructed not to play ball with anyone dumb enough to call himself a reporter." Interview with a confidential source, February 1, 1985.

181 paranoia: "Albert had basically drummed that paranoia into him—about how everyone was out to use him, how he should be wary of people, don't talk about anything. It completely changed Bobby, and after that it was difficult for anyone to get close to him." Interview with a confidential source, April 24, 1985.

181 Hammond's folly: "Aside from Hammond, the rest of the company regarded the Dylan album indulgently. He wasn't exactly the contemporary sound we were looking for"; Kapralik. Hammond knew Kapralik wasn't going to help: "David didn't have any ears. He was a shoe salesman." Hammond.

182 Goddard Leiberson: "Goddard had a relationship with Paley that was unique—he and Babe were very close friends. And just as I had relied on him to use that clout in signing Pete Seeger [after Seeger was blacklisted], he went to bat for Dylan, too." Hammond.

182 The album cover: Interview with Susan Rotolo, January 4, 1985.

182 Shelton's liner notes: "The *Times* music department had an unwritten code that members should have nothing to do with the production of recordings that they might review." *No Direction Home,* by Robert Shelton, Morrow, New York, 1986, p. 124.

182 the first album released: "Bob was very depressed after that. It had taken so long for it to be released that he was no longer doing that material. He was embarrassed by it and the whole experience must have been a diminishing one for his self-esteem." Interview with Dave Van Ronk, January 26, 1984.

183 "considered Bob too esoteric": "Outside Hammond and a few others, most people at Columbia thought [Dylan] was a freak, at best a 'different performer.'" *Clive: Inside the Record Business,* by Clive Davis, with James Willwerth, Morrow, New York, 1974, pp. 49–50.

183 "Over my dead body!": "The last thing I wanted to be responsible for was dealing the death blow to the great John Hammond. I figured, 'Let him have Dylan. They'll both disappear together.' Shows you how much I knew." Kapralik.

Chapter 12

184 "capable of earning $50,000...": *No Direction Home,* by Robert Shelton, Morrow, New York, 1986, p. 143.

Page

184 Bob regarded the first album with distaste: "By the time the album was released, he was embarrassed, regarding it as early work left in a bottom desk drawer . . . and that he wished he could have done this or that over again"; Shelton, p. 117. Mark Spoelstra presents a strikingly different account: "When the record came out, I remember going to his apartment and he played cut after cut for me. He pointed out every harmonica flourish and extended phrasing. Played it over and over—maybe three or four times—and I thought, 'Jesus Christ, what a fucking ego!'" Interview, March 11, 1985.

185 "Use what you see . . .": Woody Guthrie's letter to Allan Lomax, September 19, 1940.

186 Suze's letter to Sue Zuckerman: Dated December 7, 1961, it began: "I am miserable, so be prepared for a long, depressed letter which better be answered or I'll consider suicide. Hah! Hah!" Interview with Sue Zuckerman Green, April 14, 1985.

186 Bob and Suze's apartment: "We talked for a long time about moving in together, but people—the older people on the Street—told Bob, 'Be careful, she's not legal.' So we had to wait until I was eighteen." Interview with Susan Rotolo, June 1, 1988.

188 Dylan and Yarrow: "He and Yarrow were showing off for each other, and together they were putting me in my place. The topic was Big Bucks, and I was duly impressed." Interview with Mark Spoelstra, July 21, 1986.

189 Spoelstra: "He was always complaining that he had to suck hind tittie. He was a good performer, but we all got sick and tired of his whining." Interview with Dave Van Ronk, January 26, 1984.

189 Professional jealousies: "Once Bob became prolific and the songs improved, the pressure was on everybody to start writing. They not only wanted to write great stuff, but also grab the big record contract and the rented limo." Van Ronk.

191 Mikki Isaacson: "I took one look at Bob's face and could tell he was embarrassed the way she was pouring it on." Spoelstra.

192 "Ballad of Donald White": "I once clearly saw Bob get inspired by something and write a song right on the spot. It was at West 4th Street, we were all watching television. There was a show on about a black man who was driven, by poverty and despair, into blindly lashing out. I think he had killed his wife and children. Anyway, he was being interviewed, and even before the show had ended, Bobby jumped up, ran over to his desk in the corner of the room, and started writing." Green.

192 "Blowin' in the Wind" and Gil Turner: David Cohen, who claimed to be with Bob when he wrote the song, told this version of the story in *Bringing It All Back Home,* by Robbie Wolliver, Pantheon, New York, 1987, pp. 83–84. Suze Rotolo also remembers him returning home from Gerdes saying that people were excited by it. Interview, January 4, 1985.

196 "Greenwich Village had become a dreadful place . . .": Suze Rotolo's letter to Sue Zuckerman.

196 "told her 'not to look so good' . . .": "I remember Bob telling her to put on plain-looking clothes, things that weren't as fancy as something she would have ordinarily worn, so as not to outshine him." Interview with Carla Rotolo, February 5, 1987.

196 "Suze was clearly depressed . . .": "Things went from sunny days or normal days to gray days, continually gray." Susan Rotolo. Also Green.

196 Mary detested the relationship: "[Mary and I] both agreed it was a terrible relationship. Mary was more than encouraging Suze to go to Italy." Interview with Peter Karman, January 3, 1985.

Page

198 "I want Suze!": "He was a jerky kid, and then again, so was Suze. And Mrs. Rotolo—she was a tough broad. She never even tried to hide her contempt for Bobby. She didn't like him from the get-go. If Bobby and Suze had been allowed to work things out for themselves it would have probably come down to the same thing, but it would have been a helluva lot less painful for everybody involved." Interview with Dave Van Ronk, November 9, 1986.

198 Drugs: "Dylan was definitely into drugs then—pot and peyote—and it turned me off"; Spoelstra. "Bob was one of the first guys I knew who had drugs. In fact, he was the first person to turn me on. We were in his West 4th Street apartment and he pulled out an envelope full of grass. We smoked about a half-joint until we heard footsteps outside on the stairs. Bob got so paranoid he just popped the rest of the joint in the toilet and flushed the rest away." Interview with John Herald, December 22, 1984.

199 "stretching the folk idiom": "To people like Ewan McColl and the New Lost City Ramblers, there was a limit which you just did not go beyond. When I saw what Bob had done with folk songs, I instinctively knew the boundaries had become obsolete." Interview with Noel Stookey, April 2, 1985.

200 "Elvis's 'I'm a-so lonely'": "Heartbreak Hotel," by Tommy Durden, Mae Axton, and Elvis Presley.

200 "the stuff he was doing was so transparent . . . ": Interview with Lillian Bailey, January 15, 1985.

200 "Several folksingers complained . . . ": "We all felt kind of queasy about it because Bob could have treated Paul fairly. Instead he just ignored it. He acted as if the melody was totally original." Interview with Barry Kornfeld, December 26, 1984. "Before Dylan came along, every folksinger performed 'Who's Gonna Buy Your Chickens' as well as 'No More Ribbon Saw,' which he just took verbatim for 'Blowin' in the Wind.'" Interview with Cynthia Gooding, January 21, 1985.

200 "I really dig 'Who's Gonna Buy . . . '": Kornfeld.

200 "Clayton himself had copped it . . . ": Cynthia Gooding, who performed both versions, points out the similarities, as does Kornfeld and Van Ronk. Kornfeld says Clayton cheerfully admitted lifting the melody from "Chickens."

200 "Fair enough—Bob'll probably do . . . ": Interview with Dave Van Ronk, February 14, 1986.

201 "If you can't rewrite copyright": Kornfeld.

201 "Clayton scuffling": Clayton made a small royalty from the hit record "Gotta Travel On," whose lyric ("Done stayed around, done played around, this old town too long . . . ") was immensely familiar, but it wasn't enough to pay his bills. "I, for one, was very pissed off that Bobby was toying with Clayton. It was a very slimy way of operating." Van Ronk, November 9, 1986.

202 Dylan's contract dispute: Letter from *John Hammond on Record,* by John Hammond, with Irving Townsend, Summit, New York, 1977, p. 355.

202 "stench of Albert Grossman": "I knew Grossman was behind it from the start. Bob would never have come up with this nonsense on his own. He was basically a good kid. Besides, Bobby had signed his contract before taking on Grossman as a manager. If and when the album earned back its advance, Grossman didn't stand to earn a cent of royalties on it, so this was his little scheme." Interview with John Hammond, February 2, 1985. Clive Davis

Page

contends it was perpetrated to get Bob a better deal elsewhere. *Clive: Inside the Record Business*, by Clive Davis, with James Willwerth, Morrow, New York, 1974, pp. 49–50. "My vague recollection is that Albert had a better offer from Warner Bros., where he had Peter, Paul & Mary." Interview with Dave Van Ronk, December 28, 1986.

202 getting Bob to disavow the letter: Davis, p. 50.

202 "Bobby, unless you repudiate this...": Hammond interview.

202 "Another version takes place...": In this version, Hammond metes out punishment by requiring Bob to add two option periods onto his contract. *John Hammond on Record,* p. 356.

202 Leeds Music: Interview with John Hammond, February 2, 1985.

203 "Grossman was making a name for himself...": Interviews with confidential sources.

203 Artie Mogull: Hammond Interview. The story is also repeated, albeit in a somewhat more businesslike manner, in Shelton's book.

204 "one-punch fight talk...": Interview with a confidential source. Grossman's Chicago attorney, Sam Freifeld, reports advising Albert, "Do unto others as they'd do unto you—only do it first." He also advised him: "If you threaten to shoot, then shoot." Interview with Samuel Freifeld, April 27, 1985.

204 "Hard Rain": "I told Bob it was kind of wasted as a poem. Maybe he should try to set a tune to it. For all I know, it was his intention all along to set it to music. You never knew with Bob." Interview with Tom Paxton, December 22, 1984.

205 "Hard Rain": "It was the first blatantly symbolistic thing that any of us had written. I was blown away by it." Interview with Dave Van Ronk, December 28, 1986.

205 "it made him want to go home and write more...": "There's no doubt in my mind that Bobby loved that response and used it to sustain his enthusiasm during that period." Van Ronk.

205 Suze's letter to Carla: Interview with Carla Rotolo, April 23, 1987.

205 Bob's letters to Suze: The letters he sent her were all what she called "come home letters," and she says they made her realize his defenses were down. Interview with Susan Rotolo, April 24, 1985.

Chapter 13

207 *The Madhouse on Castle Street*: Broadcast on January 13, 1963, Bob played "an anarchic young student who wrote songs." He was trouble from the start, showing up late for rehearsals and rewriting his lines. This eventually limited him to a single line of dialogue: "Well, I don't know, I'll have to go home and think about it." BBC files; and *No Direction Home,* by Robert Shelton, Morrow, New York, 1986, p. 224.

207 Bob's beeline for Italy: Suze knew he was en route (Bob called her from London), and split for home before Bob arrived. Interviews with Odetta, February 13, 1985, and Susan Rotolo, June 1, 1988.

208 "no longer with Carolyn Hester...": Fariña had obtained a Mexican divorce. A few days later, he was secretly married to Joan Baez's fourteen-year-old sister, Mimi. *Baby, Let Me Follow You Down,* by Eric Von Schmidt and Jim Rooney, Anchor, New York, 1979, p. 118.

Page

208 Dylan, Fariña, and Von Schmidt in London: "Underneath all the bullshit, Dylan and Fariña actually liked each other a lot. When we got to smoking dope they'd get into a heavy rap and I'd feel like I was missing the point half the time. They were on a real close wavelength." Interview with Eric Von Schmidt, December 28, 1984.

210 "Bob Dylan's Dream": "We played at some folk song club one night and heard . . . Martin Carthy do a folk song called "The Franklin." . . . Dylan got Martin to show him all the chords and put the melody right in that amazing head of his. Next record he puts out, there it is. 'As I was riding on a western train . . .'" *Baby, Let Me Follow You Down,* pp. 115–16.

210 recording in London: *Dick Fariña and Eric Von Schmidt,* Folklore (F-LEUT 7), recorded January 14 and 15, 1963.

210 "musicians played on their friends' albums . . .": "He made a big thing out of not being able to use his name on the record." Von Schmidt.

210 "true fortuneteller of my soul": from *11 Outlined Epitaphs,* by Bob Dylan, copyright 1964 by Special Rider Music.

211 "Eve McKenzie: Interview with Susan Rotolo, April 24, 1985.

211 "Their relationship had become public": When Suze came back from Italy, she says people were jumping all over her, talking about how Bob was singing songs to her from the stage. Everyone had a painful story to tell her, asking "What did you do to that guy?" Susan Rotolo.

212 Bob's second album: Sessions for *Freewheelin'* took place on April 4, October 26, November 14, and December 6, 1962.

212 "Blowin' in the Wind": "I'm lucky I got that song on tape." Interview with John Hammond.

212 Bob and Hammond's studio troubles: Suze Rotolo recalls that, as time wore on, Hammond's production technique upset Bob, and that he was very dissatisfied.

212 "John, sitting in the control room . . .": "Albert and I felt that Bob should have been stopped and things should have been started over for musical reasons." Interview with John Court, February 21, 1985.

213 "he banished the managers . . .": "I kicked them out of the studio. I said, 'Listen, I don't need your advice. Get the hell out of here. You're interfering with a producer and his relationship with the artist.'" Hammond.

213 "Grossman took up the grievance": Kapralik contends the split was exacerbated by Hammond's unwillingness to allow Bob to use rock 'n roll musicians as accompaniment, "Bob was hearing sounds on other artists' records and was no longer content to be his own back-up. John is a purist. He didn't want to add instrumentation." Interview with David Kapralik, February 21, 1985.

213 Tom Wilson: "Perhaps it was inverse racist thinking on my part, but I felt Bob Dylan would champion Tom." Kapralik.

214 *Ed Sullivan Show* interview: "He'd obviously played 'John Birch' at the meeting, but no one picked up on the lyric or its political significance." Interview with Bob Precht, November 3, 1986.

215 "*Ed Sullivan!*—you sold out!": "Johnny and I figured Bob was right—he'd eventually be able to pull his weight. Only we didn't give him the satisfaction of knowing how we felt." Interview with Janet Reynolds Kerr, January 15, 1985.

Page

215 "the Dylan legend": "'Bullshit,' Dylan almost screamed. 'I sing that or I sing nothing.' And he stalked off"; *Bob Dylan,* by Anthony Scaduto, Grosset & Dunlap, New York, 1971, p. 140. "Sullivan and Precht were annoyed, Grossman irate, Dylan furious.... He stomped out of the studio and crashed around the Village that night in a blazing, raging temper, cursing 'those bastards!'" Shelton, p. 166.

215 "It's your network...": News article by Bob Williams, *New York Post,* May 14, 1963.

216 "He simply didn't mean anything...": "After all, it wasn't as if we'd brought in the Beatles. He had no name and was a rather obscure person. From our point of view, he was lucky to be on the show." Precht.

216 Columbia's exclusion of "John Birch": "He was very angry.... I kept apologizing and defending myself, saying I was a liberal Democrat, and so on." *Clive: Inside the Record Business,* by Clive Davis, with James Willwerth, Morrow, New York, 1974, p. 49.

217 "'a young giant'": "Bob Dylan Sings His Compositions," by Robert Shelton, *The New York Times,* April 13, 1983.

217 "a joke on the Street": It became painfully obvious over the next couple of years that, as a guitarist, the man simply could not cut it. But what Bobby had was a marvelous sense of timing"; Interview with Dave Van Ronk, December 28, 1986. "He can hardly play the guitar at all, and on those numbers in which Bruce Langhorne substitutes for him on the instrument, the difference is immeasurable." "A New Folk Star in Residence," by Joe Goldberg, *HiFi/Stereo Review,* November 1963.

219 Monterey Folk Festival: "The crowd hadn't seen anyone like Dylan before. They didn't know what to make of him." Interview with Jac Holtzman, February 28, 1985.

220 Bob hit on Mimi: "We both met Bob that evening. He asked me to go to a party with him, and my big sister said I couldn't." Interview with Mimi Fariña, April 1, 1985.

220 Greenhill plays Dylan for Baez: In late 1962, Bob recorded about thirty songs at Columbia Studios—informal renditions on either the piano or guitar—which Whitmark sent out in the hope of attracting cover versions. Two more demo sessions occurred following the release of *Freewheelin'* to update his catalogue with "Mr. Tambourine Man," "Percy's Song," "The Times They Are A-Changin'," and "Mama, You've Been On My Mind."

220 "Joanie was even more impressed...": "He was expressing things Joan wanted to express." Interview with Manny Greenhill, December 28, 1984.

221 "He called Suze every day...": Susan Rotolo.

222 Baez and Dylan: "I wanted to take care of him and have him sing... I mean, brush his hair and brush his teeth and get him on stage." Scaduto, p. 146.

Chapter 14

224 "The Young Generation": Norman Podhoretz, reprinted in *Doings and Undoings,* New York, Farrar, Straus, 1964.

225 "It is beginning to appear that Dylan's music...": "A New Folk Star in Residence," by Joe Goldberg, *HiFi/Stereo Review,* November 1963.

225 "so unerringly crystalizes...": *High Fidelity,* November 1963.

Page

225 "A Folknik Hero": "Bob Dylan, 22, a Folknik Hero," *Variety,* September 4, 1963.

225 registration rally: "He'd written all those socially conscious songs. I thought it only proper that Bob should touch and feel and smell what this movement was all about." Interview with Theodore Bikel, January 19, 1985.

226 "The atmosphere would be tense": Suze Rotolo recalls that Bob was scared. He was worried that he might be shot at and that nobody knew him in Mississippi. Interview with Susan Rotolo, June 7, 1987.

226 "Everybody wanted to make a claim on him." Susan Rotolo.

226 "Mr. and Mrs. Dylan": Suze Rotolo claims they weren't supposed to stay together unless they were married. Interview, April 24, 1985.

227 Bob's performance at the convention: "It was fun to shock these people, shock the bigwigs. He felt like he had this power to get his point across." Susan Rotolo.

227 Leiberson's dinner invitation: "It was wonderful in those days to be able to say 'no!' to authority. It was also very funny"; Susan Rotolo. "At first we thought it was very funny." Interview with Carla Rotolo, October 2, 1986.

227 "Carla had a big fucking mouth": "I had become The Enemy in Puerto Rico. Goddard Leiberson was being gracious, but Bobby was so nervous around him that he wound up being rude. Then, in the hotel room, the Truth Attacks started—he told me the truth about myself as only he had the vision to see it. He could be very brutal and very cruel." Carla Rotolo.

228 Bob on JFK: "A World of His Own," by Jack A. Smith, *National Guardian,* August 22, 1963.

230 Spoelstra and Joan Baez: "I remembered that night vividly all those years later, she was so amazing." Interview with Spoelstra, March 11, 1985.

230 "a torrid relationship...": Suze Rotolo says Joan came to Newport with Kim Chappell, so she had no suspicion about Bob and Joan.

231 "Folk music is just a bunch of fat people": "The Crackin', Shakin', Breakin' Sounds," by Nat Hentoff, *New Yorker,* October 24, 1964.

232 "Suze was no longer in the audience": Interview with Eric Von Schmidt, December 28, 1984, and interview with a confidential source.

232 Suze's suicide attempt: "Bob was very frightened. I guess I was the first person he called; he didn't know what to do. But by the time I got there, Suze was okay." Carla Rotolo. Additional information provided by Terri Thal and Van Ronk.

232 Bob joins Baez in concert: "...when they heard my songs, they were just flabbergasted." *No Direction Home,* by Robert Shelton, Morrow, New York, 1986, p. 188.

233 disgruntled Baez fans: Letters to the Hollywood Bowl Association—both dated October 13, 1963—provided by Manny Greenhill.

233 Suze's abortion: "I remember her lying on the bed and me running back and forth with towels and cold things to try and stop the bleeding. And *Bob just sat there!*" Carla Rotolo. Additional information provided by Sue Zuckerman Green, Van Ronk, Kornfeld, and a confidential source.

Page

234 Tom Wilson: "Out of ignorance, more than anything, he'd say 'Okay,' and go back to a magazine or making dates on the phone. Literally not paying attention. I was in shock watching this." Interview with Paul Rothchild, March 1, 1985.

237 Beatty at Carnegie Hall: Details provided by Richard Rocklin, January 8, 1986.

237 the Carnegie Hall program: "We knew him as this curly-haired little boy who had a Bar Mitzvah and did none of the things he claimed he did." Rocklin.

237 Bob ducks his family at Carnegie Hall: "It was as if he didn't at all want to be recognized by us. Or say a word to us. We weren't good for his image." Rocklin.

238 *Newsweek* article: November 4, 1963.

238 Shelton criticizes *Newsweek*: "I accused *Newsweek* of its own journalistic standards in running a 'hatchet job' that more fittingly belonged to *Confidential.* I called Andrew Svedberg's interview with me rankly incompetent. . . . I sent copies [of my letter to *Newsweek*] to fifteen writers, editors, and music-world leaders." Shelton, p. 194.

239 "Blowin' in the Wind": Lorre Wyatt alleged he had written a song called "Freedom Is Blowing in the Wind" long before he'd seen Dylan's version. Later, however, Wyatt wrote an article for *New Times* admitting the entire incident was a hoax. "The Story Behind the 'Blowin' in the Wind' Story," by Lorre Wyatt, *New Times,* February 1974.

239 "The blues is a pair of pants . . .": *The Brown (University) Daily Herald,* article by Stuart Crump.

239 "I don't remember being one": "The Bare Hungry Sniffin' Truth," by Marty Lackman, *In Magazine.*

239 Tom Paine Award dinner: Interview with Edith Tiger, March 27, 1985.

240 "He was stoned": Suze Rotolo says she knew Bob was stoned when he left the apartment. Interview, April 24, 1985.

241 Dylan's speech: Courtesy of the Emergency Civil Liberties Committee.

242 "they feared a repercussion . . .": "They expected the FBI to barge in and say we were responsible for killing John Kennedy. It was a very traumatic moment." Tiger.

243 An embarrassed hush . . .": "Here he was berating an audience that had bucked the blacklist. A serious mistake on Dylan's part. He came up to my office a few days later and was very uncomfortable." Interview with Harold Leventhal, November 30, 1984.

244 "A Message": Courtesy of the Emergency Civil Liberties Committee.

245 *New Yorker* interview: "I just can't make it with any organization. I fell into a trap once—last December—when I agreed to accept the Tom Paine Award from the Emergency Civil Liberties Committee. . . . As soon as I got there I felt uptight. . . . Here were these people who'd been involved with the left in the thirties, and now they were supporting civil-rights drives. That's groovy, but they also had minks and jewels, and it was like they were giving money out of guilt." Hentoff.

Chapter 15

247 "Christmas had been an utter disaster": "Now my mother and her husband were the enemy. I was there—I was the enemy, too. Bob didn't want to be there, so he was in enemy territory. It was God-awful." Interview with Carla Rotolo, October 2, 1986.

Page

249 "Restless Farewell": "Of course songs like 'Restless Farewell' I've written just to fill up an album." Bob Dylan in "Dylan Is Back," by Hubert Saal, *Newsweek,* February 26, 1968.

249 Bob's letter to *Broadside*: "A Letter from Bob Dylan," *Broadside,* No. 38, January 20, 1964, courtesy of Gordon Freisen and Sis Cunningham.

250 "You fuckin' Baez, man?": Interview with Peter Karman, January 3, 1985.

251 "the passenger list . . . ": Justifying his journey to Robert Shelton, Bob admitted, "I'm lucky. Not because I make a lot of bread, but because I can be around groovy people." *No Direction Home,* by Robert Shelton, Morrow, New York, 1986, p. 240.

251 Paul Clayton: Interview with Barry Kornfeld, December 26, 1984. Interview with Steve Wilson, December 1, 1986.

252 "Paul was madly in love . . . ": Kornfeld.

252 "Carla tried to talk . . . ": Carla Rotolo.

252 *Quest*: The show was broadcast March 10, 1964. Bob performed "The Times They Are A-Changin'," "Hard Rain," "Talkin' World War III Blues," "Hattie Carroll," "Girl from the North Country," and the only version of "Restless Farewell" he ever sang live until the summer of 1987.

253 the striking miners: "He endorsed it reluctantly. This was so he could do something privately, without getting involved as a spokesperson." Interview with Susan Rotolo, July 22, 1987.

254 "Bob was very pissed-off . . . ": Karman.

254 Sandburg: Karman.

256 Shelton's analysis of "Chimes of Freedom": Shelton, p. 220.

256 "A Romantic, Blakean childhood . . . ": Shelton quotes a Dylanologist whose observations are couched in pseudo-intellectual mumbo-jumbo. Shelton, p. 220.

257 Bob's androgyny: "There was one night I really thought Dylan was into me sexually. We came back to this pad late one night, found there was only one bed, and Bob made it clear that if we crashed in the same bed there would be something sexual." Interview with Mark Spoelstra, January 2, 1987.

258 "Karman constantly challenged Bob": "I thought he was full of shit and used every opportunity to try to call his bluff." Karman.

259 Dylan in Carmel: Interview with Mimi Fariña, October 25, 1985.

260 *The Steve Allen Show*: Videotape of Bob's appearance provided courtesy of Steve Allen and Meadowlark Productions.

264 "Ballad in Plain D" night: "Suze was telling him to leave—'Get out! Go away!'—while Bob was screaming at her. . . . She began to scream and then fell to the floor"; Interview with Carla Rotolo, January 5, 1987. "[Clayton and I] walked in and there was Carla practically foaming at the mouth, Dylan practically foaming at the mouth, and Suze sitting in bed, literally in shock. Suze had just sort of tuned out. Bob and Carla were still going at it—they were both totally incoherent." Kornfeld.

266 Dylan inscription: Courtesy of Susan Rotolo.

Chapter 16

Page

269 Dylan-Baez tour: "Contrary to the prevailing notion, they barely filled some of the concert halls. There weren't people clamoring for seats. It was successful, but far short of being overwhelming, which is what many of us expected." Interview with Manny Greenhill, December 28, 1984.

270 Grossman and Greenhill: "Al suggested we do it together, and I said no. I just could not trust him, so I was stuck with it." Greenhill.

271 "admitted attempting to duplicate": "There was one thing I tried to do which wasn't a good idea for me. I tried to write another 'Mr. Tambourine Man.' It's the only song I tried to write 'another one.' But after enough going at it, it just began bothering me, so I dropped it." "Conversations with Bob Dylan," by John Cohen and Happy Traum, *Sing Out!*, October–November 1968.

273 LSD: "There's no doubt in my mind that turning Bob on made a whole other area of poetry possible. It was where any poets starts: exploration of self." Interview with Paul Rothchild, April 1, 1985.

275 Bob's cruel parodies: Interview with Mimi Fariña, October 25, 1985.

277 Bob meets Sara: "Sara met Bob in the Village, while he was still living on West 4th Street. He was so oblique, but Sara understood all that." Interview with Greg Shucker, June 4, 1985.

277 The Barlow School: Information provided in an interview with Jeri Hertzenberg, January 3, 1986, and by a confidential source.

278 "Mr. Tambourine Man": "Sara and I had lunch, but afterwards she had to get back to transcribe the scribbles he'd made on a yellow piece of paper, entitled 'Mr. Tambourine Man.' She told me Bob was asleep, so she swiped the paper and read the words to me." Shucker.

280 Dylan, Neuwirth, and Pennebaker: "The two of them were baiting me. There was some testing going on that was part of the essential process." Interview with D. A. Pennebaker, June 13, 1985.

280 "out conning the world . . .": "From the very first meeting with Dylan I got something special. I saw the most incredible spiritual ascendancy I'd ever seen, except maybe for John Kennedy." Pennebaker.

282 Heathrow: "Bob Dylan got the full star treatment at London Airport on Monday night. . . ." "Screams for Dylan," by Max Jones and Ray Coleman, *Melody Maker*, May 1, 1965.

285 press conference: "Monosyllabic, weary-eyed, the American folksinger Bob Dylan appeared in London yesterday to start his tour of eight concerts up and down the country." "Overcoming Dylan," *Guardian*, April 24, 1965.

285 "It is hard to believe . . .": From an article in *The Sun*, by Mike Nevard, April 24, 1965.

286 at Leicester: "Only one aside by Dylan caused hilarious uproar." "A Beatle-Size Fever without the Screams," by Ray Coleman, *Melody Maker*, May 8, 1965; "I didn't mean to put the guy [Donovan] down in my songs. I just did it for a joke, that's all." Jones and Coleman.

286 "Silent audiences . . .": From a news article by Ray Coleman, *Melody Maker*, May 22, 1965.

Page

287 Dylan on Baez: "She came with me, man, and I don't owe her nothing.... There is no place for her in my music.... she don't fit into my music." *No Direction Home,* by Robert Shelton, Morrow, New York, 1986, p. 220.

287 Baez and the gypsies: Pennebaker.

288 The Beatles: Lennon said, "Paul got [Dylan's records] off whoever they belonged to, and for the rest of our three weeks in Paris we didn't stop playing them." *Melody Maker,* May 22, 1965.

288 "Bob's 'ego equal'...": "John had told [Al] Aronowitz he wanted to meet Dylan, but 'only on his own terms' when John had become his 'ego equal.'" *The Love You Make,* by Peter Brown and Steven Gaines, McGraw-Hill, New York, 1983, p. 155.

289 "BRING ME BOB DYLAN!": Interview with Albert Goldman, January 3, 1986.

289 Bob at the Lennons': "The Savoy officials warned him that he would have to dress if he wanted to eat in their restaurant.... Lennon, hearing of this, invited Bob to dine with him and Cynthia." Nevard.

289 "We Beatle-fied it...": "I could have made 'I'm a Loser' even more Dylanish if I tried." *Melody Maker.*

290 "The room is full of millionaires...": Pennebaker.

290 Dylan meets Donovan: "I was amazed by how gently Dylan treated him." Pennebaker.

292 "Joanie never had a chance...": Mimi Fariña.

293 John Bucklen: "We went to a party that night. I had a bottle of Vodka and asked him if he wanted a drink, and he said, 'I can't drink that hard stuff, only red wine.' I asked, 'Why?' And he said, 'Because I had this heroin habit and it messed up my stomach.' At the time I remember thinking: Is this just another one of Bob's stories or what?" Interview with John Bucklen, April 3, 1985.

293 Dylan takes on *Time*: Pennebaker.

295 Bucklen sees Dylan perform: "Watching Bob perform was a shock for me. After every verse of 'With God on Our Side' people cheered. It was like a dream." Bucklen.

Chapter 17

297 *Highway 61 Revisited*: "That's the sound I've always heard.... It was the sound of the streets. It still is. I symbolically hear that sound wherever I am.... It's the sound of the street with the sunrays, the sun shining down at a particular time, on a particular type of building. A particular type of people walking on a particular type of street. It's an outdoor sound that drifts even into open windows that you can hear." "The Playboy Interview: Bob Dylan," by Ron Rosenbaum, *Playboy,* March 1978, p. 69.

298 recording "Like a Rolling Stone": "It's amazing. It sounds like it's so together. That was back in the days when we used to do...oh, man, six, eight, ten tunes a session." "The Rolling Stone Interview: Bob Dylan," by Curt Loder, *Rolling Stone,* June 21, 1984, p. 23.

298 Al Kooper: "In a flash I was on Tom Wilson, telling him that I had a great part for the song and *please* (oh God) could I have a shot at it." *Backstage Passes,* by Al Kooper, with Ben Edmonds, Stein & Day, New York, 1977, p. 55.

Page

299 Neuwirth called Rothchild: Rothchild said, "The only thing I kept saying was 'Bob, this is a smash. This is a huge smash hit record.' And I remember feelings of envy." Interview, April 1, 1985.

301 blues workshop at Newport: Interview with Eric Von Schmidt, December 28, 1984.

301 Elektra's *Folk Sampler*: Interviews with Jac Holtzman, February 28, 1985, and Paul Rothchild.

302 Grossman vs. Lomax: "I was cheering. I said, 'Kick that ass, Albert'"; "Dylan Goes Electric," by Michael Bloomfield, *The Sixties,* Rolling Stone Press, New York, 1977, p. 150.

302 "It was a gas, man. Everybody loved it. There were a lot of folk notables there watching the melee with great, *great* joy"; Von Schmidt. "It was a perfect confrontation whose symbolism was lost on none of us." Rothchild.

303 "I'm going to take over...": Interview with Paul Butterfield, June 16, 1985.

303 backstage at Newport: Details provided by Paul Rothchild, Theodore Bikel, Harold Leventhal, and several confidential sources.

305 "Bob had been holed up...": Details provided by several musicians and friends. Similarly told in Shelton. Also, "He spent the whole day in the sound truck, with his bodyguard and Bobby Neuwirth, getting high and fermenting his brain." Bloomfield.

306 Yarrow restrains Seeger: "Peter Yarrow appeared out of nowhere and stood his ground. Yarrow—a little guy among all these not-so-little guys. He was magnificent." Rothchild.

306 out front at Newport: Interview with Maria Muldaur, December 29, 1984.

307 Bob returns to the stage: "[Yarrow] was up there pleading for about ten minutes, and then in the back room he said, 'Oh, Bob, go out and do one of your old numbers. Come on, Bob, you don't want to let your fans down....' Dylan should have just given them the finger and said, 'Hey, this is what I do. It's all over now, Baby Blue.'" Bloomfield, p. 152.

308 "They wanted to hear protest songs...": "I couldn't go on being the lone folkie out there, you know, strumming 'Blowin' in the Wind' for three hours every night." Rosenbaum, p. 69.

308 the party: Details provided in interviews with Eric Von Schmidt, Paul Rothchild, and Maria Muldaur.

Chapter 18

311 Silber and Nelson: "What's Happening," by Irwin Silber and Paul Nelson, *Sing Out!*, Vol. 15, No. 5, November 1965, pp. 5–8.

311 Izzy Young: "Bob Dylan has become a pawn in his own game. He has ceased his Quest for the Universal Sound and has settled for a liaison with the music trade's Top Forty Hit Parade." "Frets and Frails," by Israel G. Young, *Sing Out!,* Vol. 15, No. 5, November 1965, pp. 114–115.

312 Don West: "Not that I think Phil [Ochs] is a phony as I thought Dylan was from the beginning...but [at least] he takes a bath and I like him personally." "Topical Songs and Folksinging," *Sing Out!,* Vol. 15, No. 4, September 1965, pp. 9–10.

Page

312 Ewan McColl blasts Dylan, "Topical Songs and Folksinging."

312 "It's sad to see Ewan McColl . . .": "His attack on Bob Dylan is not only sour and bilious; it is also pathetically ill-informed, critically understudied, and—surprise, surprise—full of political naivety [sic]." *Melody Maker,* September 25, 1965.

313 Paul Simon: "I do agree with the point about Dylan's poetry being punk and old-hat. I think it is just rehashed [Allen] Ginsberg." Quoted in "Just Who Does Ewan McColl Think He Is?", *Melody Maker,* October 2, 1965.

313 "Joan Baez [SQUARE]": "Rock 'n Roll: The Sound of the Sixties," *Time,* May 21, 1965.

313 the "New Sound": ". . . folk rock was the NEW SOUND, the latest mutation in the biology of the big beat." "The Folk and the Rock," *Newsweek,* September 20, 1965, pp. 88–89.

314 Rothchild converts McGuinn: Interview with Paul Rothchild, April 1, 1985.

314 "his first number-one charted hit": *Billboard,* June 5, 1965.

315 "Eve of Destruction": "I gave Phil Sloan a pair of boots and a hat and a copy of the Dylan album, and a week later he came back with ten songs, including 'Eve of Destruction.' It was a natural feel for him—he's a great mimic." Interview with Lou Adler, by Richard Williams, *Melody Maker,* February 5, 1972, p. 25.

316 message songs: "People will be able to come and hear more messages then they've ever heard before in their life." "The Playboy Interview: Bob Dylan," by Nat Hentoff, *Playboy,* March 1966.

316 "just going through the motions": "I was doing fine, you know, singing and playing my guitar. . . . I was getting very bored with that. I was thinking of quitting. Out front it was a sure thing. I knew what the audience was gonna do, how they would react. It was very automatic." "The Bob Dylan Interview," by Nora Ephron and Susan Edmiston, reprinted in *Bob Dylan: A Retrospective,* by Craig McGregor, Morrow, New York, 1972.

316 Forest Hills: Details provided in interviews with Harvey Brooks, October 30, 1986, and Sari Becker, November 2, 1984.

317 "I know what to expect . . .": "I didn't know what to expect when we walked out there because we knew from Newport that people were freaked when he played with Butterfield. Dylan and I talked about it before the show. . . ." Brooks. "It's going to be some kind of carnival, and I want you all to know that up front." Dylan quoted in *Backstage Passes,* by Al Kooper, with Ben Edmonds, Stein & Day, New York, 1977, pp. 64–65.

318 Robbie and Levin: Background culled from *Mystery Train,* by Greil Marcus, Dutton, New York, 1975, pp. 43–74; and *No Direction Home,* by Robert Shelton, Morrow, New York, 1986, pp. 314–319.

319 "That night, he was in command": "Dylan didn't flinch. He just bullied his way straight through the hour-plus set." Kooper, pp. 64–65.

322 Dylan and Neuwirth as hip photographers: "I told Bobby that was about one of the stupidest stunts I'd ever seen him pull. He acted like a six-year-old." Interview with Dave Van Ronk, December 28, 1986.

322 The Kettle: "If Dylan got drunk enough he'd select a target from among the assembled singer/songwriters, and then pick him apart like a cat toying with a wounded mouse." Kooper, p. 62. And details provided by Van Ronk, Rothchild, Paxton, Gorson, and others.

Page

323 Eric Andersen: Gorson, March 1, 1985.

323 "You can make a fortune": "I was disgusted. I was furious with him. It was an idiotic way to treat his friends." Interview with Dave Van Ronk, November 9, 1986.

Chapter 19

326 Bob's press reviews: "Let's Face the Awful Truth: Dylan's Gone Commercial," by Antony Ferry, *Toronto Daily Star,* November 15, 1965; and "Bob Dylan Fires Vocal Guns Here," by Glenn C. Pullen, *Cleveland Plain Dealer,* November 13, 1965.

326 "a reporter in Austin . . .": "The Austin Interview," by Craig McGregor, *Bob Dylan: A Retrospective,* Morrow, New York, 1972, pp. 162–163.

327 Getting married: "'If it happens, it happens,' Bob said quite artlessly." "Bob Dylan Talking," by Joseph Haas, *Panorama, Chicago Daily News,* November 27, 1965.

327 Van Ronk meets Sara: "That was my sole meeting with Mrs. Dylan." Interview with Dave Van Ronk, November 9, 1986.

327 "I don't have any family": from "Well, What Have We Here," by Jules Siegel, *Saturday Evening Post,* July 30, 1966.

327 "When I want money": from "The Bob Dylan Interview," by Nora Ephron and Susan Edmiston, in McGregor.

327 "Philosophy can't give me anything . . .": Haas.

328 "I wouldn't advise anybody to use drugs . . .": Hentoff, *Playboy,* March 1966.

331 Bobby Neuwirth: Details provided by Von Schmidt, Muldaur, Fariña, Brice Marden, and Terri Blum.

333 Brian Jones: Interview with Janet Reynolds Kerr, January 15, 1985, and two confidential sources.

333 Dylan and Neuwirth at Albert's: Interview with a confidential source, February 1, 1985.

334 artificial stimulants: Interviews with D.A. Pennebaker, Bob Johnston, and several confidential sources.

335 Bob Johnston takes over: "If they're the artist, they should be allowed to either succeed or fuck-up on their own." Interview with Bob Johnston, March 25, 1987.

336 "Who are we recording with today?": "I honestly had never heard of him. I had no idea who we were working with." Interview with Kenny Buttrey, March 27, 1987.

336 "Actually, McCoy knew about Bob": "At the time, I knew of Bob Dylan, that he had a bit of a folk following. But he was not a big artist. Especially, not in Nashville, where he was practically an unknown." Interview with Charlie McCoy, April 4, 1985.

337 "Sad-Eyed Lady of the Lowlands": Elsewhere, Bob claims to have written the song in a night-long session at the Chelsea Hotel, but it is clear, from eyewitness accounts, that he finished it at Columbia Studios in Nashville.

338 Kooper and Robertson arrive: "We were expecting the worst—you know, these big-shot New York musicians who fly in and act like they know everything—but they turned out to be great." Buttrey.

Page

341 "the whole session seemed like a childish joke...": Buttrey.

341 "In all, *Blonde on Blonde* took...": "The closest I ever got to the sound I hear in my mind was on individual bands in the *Blonde on Blonde* album. It's that thin, that wild mercury sound. It's metallic and bright gold, with whatever that conjures up. That's my particular sound." "The Playboy Interview: Bob Dylan," by Ron Rosenbaum, *Playboy,* March 1978, p. 69.

343 Wilfred Mellers analysis: "Although ['Rainy Day Women #12 & 35'] is a joke number, the joke itself may have profound implications." *A Darker Side of Pale: A Backdrop to Bob Dylan,* by Wilfred Mellers, Oxford University Press, New York, 1984, pp. 144–145.

343 Bill King: *Bob Dylan: The Artist in the Marketplace* (unpublished thesis).

344 "I'm sick of giving creeps money...": *No Direction Home,* by Robert Shelton, Morrow, New York, 1986, p. 343.

344 Ralph J. Gleason, an early Dylan partisan: Shelton, p. 385.

344 "In between there were psychedelics": "There was so much drug-taking going on, we could have opened our own pharmacy." Interview with a confidential source, April 29, 1985.

344 heroin: Van Ronk.

345 Suze and Bob discuss drugs: Interview with Susan Rotolo, April 24, 1985, and a confidential source.

Chapter 20

348 "Bob has me buffaloed": "Electric Dylan Turns to Banality," by William Littler, *Vancouver Sun,* March 28, 1966.

349 "Australia is not a very nice place...": "The composer of 'Blowin' in the Wind' lost no time shooting a cold breeze...." *Time,* April 24, 1966.

349 "blaring headlines...": "In print they all attacked him. A PHONY! A CHARLATAN!" Introduction to *Bob Dylan: A Retrospective,* by Craig McGregor, Morrow, New York, 1972, p. 5.

350 "He could turn on you...": "I wasn't against drugs, per se—and if other people worked off them, who was I to judge—but I didn't necessarily want to make a film about drugs." Interview with D. A. Pennebaker, August 19, 1987.

353 "The guy was possessed": Interview with a confidential source, June 23, 1987.

354 "Oh, man—what a drag": "The lean and wiry Bob Dylan, hair longer and more unruly than ever, left behind 2,500 frustrated fans." *Disc,* May 13, 1966.

354 "It was the climax of mutual contempt...": From an article by Vincent Doyle, *Melody Maker,* May 13, 1966.

355 Pennebaker's eyewitness account: "That night I could hardly stay up." Pennebaker.

357 "monotone inanities": "For some fifteen minutes photographers exposed innumerable rolls of film at Dylan looking bored, slumped on a window sill. Finally, he removed his dark glasses... but somehow managed to look exactly the same." From "Dylan's Press Deception," by Keith Altham, *New Musical Express,* May 13, 1966.

Page

358 "Joan Baez was an accident": Quotes taken from detailed accounts of the press conference in *Melody Maker, Disc,* and *NME*—all May 13, 1966.

358 "A little diversion to keep Bob amused . . . ": "Man," [Bobby Neuwirth] extolled, "Dylan just wanted us to come along and record a press reception so we could hear how ridiculous and infantile all reporters are." Altham, p. 2.

359 "Like anyone else, he smoked": "John always told me that he didn't get into heavy drugs until Toronto, in '67." Pennebaker and Albert Goldman.

363 treatment of Geno: Pennebaker and a confidential source.

364 "It means nothing!": *Melody Maker,* June 4, 1966.

365 TILT! TILT! TILT!: "I was straining pretty hard and couldn't have gone on living that way much longer. The fact that I made it through what I did is pretty miraculous." "The Playboy Interview: Bob Dylan," by Ron Rosenbaum, *Playboy,* March 1978.

366 Bob meets the Stones: "It was the week before Dylan had his famous motorcycle accident." Interview with Brice Marden, July 2, 1986.

Chapter 21

371 "hadn't suffered any brain damage . . . ": "When Nasatir heard about the deal, he immediately got himself a limo and went to Woodstock to see if Dylan had any brain damage." Interview with Jerry Schoenbaum, March 20, 1985.

373 the Walter Cronkite decision: "Finally, I decided that the company just couldn't afford to match [MGM's] offer." *Clive: Inside the Record Business,* by Clive Davis, with James Willwerth, Morrow, New York, 1974, p. 54.

373 a loss leader: "I was trying to build a company at MGM and felt that if I could get Dylan and break even on it, I would create an environment which would bring other artists to the label." Interview with Mort Nasatir, May 28, 1985.

374 Janis Joplin: Grossman offered me a three-year deal for Janis Joplin for $400,000, but Nasatir took an automatic pass." Schoenbaum.

376 "We're going to sit on it": "It wasn't the way the record industry ran, but it was the way MGM ran and was therefore the way I had to work." Nasatir.

377 "the Dylan name will be worth shit": Nasatir.

377 "Columbia had as many as twenty albums . . . ": "Allen went around telling everybody they had twenty albums. . . . " Nasatir.

379 a private detective: "It was told to me through a third party at MGM. It could have come from [Allen] Klein. Nobody knew why he went there, but it was said he went there for treatment. The implication was, any guy who drives once a week to this particular place was obviously very sick mentally and physically . . . so I hired a private detective"; Nasatir. Also Schoenbaum.

380 MGM sends recording crew to Woodstock: "They weren't called *The Basement Tapes* yet. They were just some things Al [Grossman] said were recorded to give me a feel for what he was doing and what he had in mind." Nasatir.

Page

380 "I Got You, Babe": Tiny Tim also appeared on another track.

380 Bob's deal for no advance money: "[Albert Grossman] came to my office with . . . David Braun, and said, 'Look, we've had an outstanding deal with MGM (I *knew*), but Bob is having second thoughts . . . so I want to propose something unorthodox which is acceptable to Bob and myself if you'll agree. Bob will require no guaranty if you'll ask for no minimum product." Davis, p. 56.

380 MGM gets opportunity to rescind Dylan's deal: "Al called me and said, 'Do you want out? CBS is really fighting hard and we don't have a signed contract with MGM. What do you want me to do?'" Nasatir.

Chapter 22

383 Abe visits Pennebaker: "He talked a lot about Bob, but he always referred to him as Mr. Dylan." Interview with D. A. Pennebaker, June 13, 1985.

384 "the film too unrevealing . . .": "But it is Bob Dylan that we came to see, and it is ultimately frustrating to discern so little of the man beneath the bushy hair, the dark glasses and the leather jacket. Even in what appears to be candid shots, the performer's public face is turned to the camera." "The Screen: Bob Dylan and Company," by Donal J. Henahan, *New York Times,* September 7, 1967.

384 Richard Goldstein: "His flagrant *mysterioso*—even if it is sincere—evokes hungry demands for at least a penetrating glimpse of the oracle-star." "Dylan: We Trust What He Tells Us," by Richard Goldstein, *New York Times,* October 22, 1967.

385 Ralph Gleason's article: "The Children's Crusade," by Ralph J. Gleason, *Ramparts,* March 1966.

387 Dr. Ed Thaler: Interview with Ethel Romm, November 26, 1987.

388 "Bob listened raptly as Tim performed . . .": "Dylan looked at me. His eyes were wide open. He was *intense.*" Interview with Tiny Tim, December 11, 1987.

389 Bob Johnston: "Sara and Joey did all the talking. Bob and I watched the fire without exchanging a single word." Interview with Bob Johnston, March 25, 1987.

389 "We just put it down . . .": "The playback in the control room turned out to be the final mix. Whatever we played was *it.*" Interview with Kenny Buttrey, March 27, 1987.

390 "Who else but Bob Dylan . . .": "For an album to be released amidst *Sgt. Pepper, Their Satanic Majesties Request, Strange Days,* and *After Bathing at Baxters,* somebody must have had a lot of confidence in what he was doing." "John Wesley Harding," by Jon Landau, *Crawdaddy,* 1968.

390 "reading the Bible": "In his Woodstock study, Dylan had a huge Bible opened on a raised wooden bookstand." *No Direction Home,* by Robert Shelton, Morrow, New York, 1986, p. 445.

390 *Time*'s review: "Basic Dylan," *Time,* January 12, 1968, p. 50.

391 Guthrie tribute: In addition to Bob Dylan, the January 20, 1968, concert featured Judy Collins, Jack Elliot, Arlo Guthrie, Richie Havens, Odetta, Tom Paxton, and Pete Seeger, and was narrated by actors Will Geer and Robert Ryan, two of Woody's old Lefty pals

Page

from Hollywood. Bob sang "Grand Coulee Dam," "Mrs. Roosevelt," and "I Ain't Got No Home," accompanied by The Band.

392 Bob's voice: Buttrey.

393 bongos, cowbells: "My original plan was to combine their ideas *out of spite,* to show them how bad it was going to sound. To this day, it's probably the tastiest, if not my personal favorite drum part of all time." Buttrey.

394 "crap hit the fan": "Dylan just said to me: 'Hey, man, you're not gonna let those people do anything to my record, are you?' And I said, 'Certainly not.' So I locked it up in a vault and that was it. Luckily, Davis didn't lean on me, but the people under him made it clear I'd never work for CBS again." Johnston.

395 "Dylan, the satisfied man . . .": From a review in *Billboard,* by Ed Ochs, July 12, 1969.

396 Abe's funeral: "When his father passed away, he was so stoned out of his mind at the funeral. He stayed in his limousine and wouldn't talk to anybody." Interview with Judy Rubin Shaffer, January 26, 1986; and a confidential source.

396 kaddish: "I told him, 'You're responsible for kaddish for him every year as long as you're alive—just like I was for my father.' He promised me he would do that." Interview with Max Edelstein, March 10, 1985.

396 Bob looks for a home in Nashville: "He was going to buy a house in Nashville and I took him around to see some places, but he was in such an uncommunicative mood that at the end of the deal the real estate agent pulled me aside and asked, 'Hey, man, is that guy deaf and dumb?'" Johnston.

396 Bob alluded to tour: "[The English] are the most loyal fans I have and that was one of the reasons to . . . come to England to make my comeback. . . ." From an interview in *The London Daily Sketch,* by Chris White, August 16, 1969.

Chapter 23

397 "It was a real strange session": "I'd listened to what he'd done and figured it was only a work tape." McCoy.

398 "*he wasn't even in town!*": "I was put off by the [*Self-Portrait*] session, and don't think I ever listened to the finished album." Interview with Kenny Buttrey, March 27, 1987.

399 "friends, Bob Dylan is back . . .": "Calling his latest outing *New Morning* may very well be his way of saying, 'I'm back.'" "New Morning," by Ed Ward, *Rolling Stone,* November 26, 1970.

399 Gleason's review: "Come on, Bob! We need you. That's the truth, man, we really do. Come out, Bob, come out!" "Perspectives: We've Got Dylan Back Again," by Ralph J. Gleason, *Rolling Stone,* November 26, 1970, p. 19.

400 leaving Woodstock: Woodstock "had become a joke. . . ." *No Direction Home,* by Robert Shelton, Morrow, New York, 1986, p. 433.

400 A. J. Weberman: *Dylan: A Retrospective,* by Craig McGregor, Morrow, New York, 1972.

400 Toby Thompson in Hibbing: *Positively Main Street: An Unorthodox View of Bob Dylan,* by Toby Thompson, Coward, McCann & Geohegan, New York, 1970.

Page

401 ". . . A. B. Fall went to jail . . .": "I've been one of the speculators [as to why he chose the name for the album]." "John Wesley Harding *is* Bob Dylan," by Gordon Freisen, *Broadside* No. 93, July/August 1968, p. 6.

401 "Weberman was convinced Bob spoke directly to him": In 1985, Echo Helstrom Fernandez told the author: "Everyone tells me that *Blonde on Blonde* is about me. You know [points to her platinum-tinted hair-do] 'blonde on blonde.' And 'blonde on blonde' is an *echo* of the word. So they must be right." Interview, March 3, 1985.

405 Joe Schick: Schick recalled, "Dylan and I broke out laughing because we were both wearing the same hat." Interview, August 14, 1986.

406 "That Lucky Old Sun": Fifteen years later, Bob included the song in his tour with Tom Petty and the Heartbreakers, often opening with it or saving it for the encore.

406 Lennon goes to Paris: "As it turned out, Lennon never could have followed Dylan's performance and couldn't cope with having the spotlight stolen away from him." Interview with Albert Goldman, May 12, 1986.

407 Bob and the J.D.L.: "For a year or more, Dylan has been 'getting into this ethnic Jewish thing,' says his friend and annotator, A. J. Weberman." *Time,* May 31, 1971, p. 47.

407 *Pat Garrett*: "Bob Dylan has once again broken the mold, only this time with the least acceptable method available to him, an album neither exceptional, nor truly different, but merely awful." "Dylan Redefines Himself: Merely Awful," by Jon Landau, *Rolling Stone,* August 30, 1973.

408 Malibu: "I always told him, 'Someday you'll all move out here. Mark my words.'" Interview with Jac Holtzman, February 28, 1985.

408 "That's news to me": Interview with a confidential source, October 2, 1986.

409 Chicago behaves like prima donnas: Clive Davis described the group's demands as "utterly gluttonous." Says Davis, "Frequently they wanted the kitchen sink—and then some." *Clive: Inside the Record Business*, by Clive Davis, with James Willwerth, Morrow, New York, 1974, pp. 118–119.

410 The *Dylan* album: "[These songs] were just not to be used. I thought it was well understood." *Knockin' on Dylan's Door,* by the editors of *Rolling Stone*, Pocket Books, New York, 1974, p. 45.

411 *Planet Waves*: The title was provided by Allen Ginsberg's collection of poetry, *Planet News.*

411 "Forever Young": "We did five versions of it. Two of them are on the album, another one is acoustic." Interview with Rob Fraboni, October 2, 1986.

Chapter 24

418 "Who the hell wants to see Bob Dylan": "Can't think of anything I'd want to see less. He should be left in the archives of rock." From "Highway '66 Revisited," by Ray Coleman, *Melody Maker,* February 23, 1974.

419 "Fans expected flash": "When Dylan and the Band decided to go on tour, they worried at first that their brand of music wasn't enough to impress a new audience of people used to seeing the theatrics of 'decadent' rock stars like Alice Cooper or David Bowie." "Dylan—Rolling Again," by Maureen Orth, *Newsweek,* January 14, 1974, pp. 46–49.

Page

420 ". . . definitely not nostalgia": "Dylan: Once Again, It's Alright Ma," by David DeVoss, *Time,* January 21, 1974.

421 "I'm only involved in communication . . . ": *On the Road with Bob Dylan,* by Larry Sloman, Bantam, New York, 1975, p. 50.

421 ". . . blase professionalism.": "The Band with Bob Dylan: It's Right on the Dot," by Ben Fong-Torres, *Knockin' on Dylan's Door,* Pocket Books, New York, 1974, p. 50.

421 Bob's "rehearsals": Interview with Rob Fraboni, October 2, 1986.

423 Graham turned it into a TOUR: "Originally, I wanted to play small halls, but I was just talked out of that." Fong-Torres, p. 50.

426 "I'm real nervous . . . " Coleman.

429 groupies: "They came up with the greatest system to weed out the groupies. . . ." Fraboni.

430 "an ultra-Zionist": "Super-Dylanologist A. J. Weberman, who became famous by going through Dylan's garbage cans for relics of Saint Bob, now thinks the tour smells suspiciously like a Zionist plot." Orth.

430 Mimi Fariña: Interview with Mimi Fariña, April 1, 1985.

431 Mimi's letter: *San Francisco Chronicle,* February 15, 1974.

Chapter 25

432 "I'm gonna pull this thing off . . . ": "He was totally wasted, but managed to get out 'We're doing this show. Everyone's gonna help us, and we'll make an incredible statement about what's going on in Chile." Interview with Faris Bouhafa, February 14, 1985.

433 "two weeks before the gig . . . ": "Man, were we in trouble. We had to find someone to help us sell tickets—*anyone.*" Bouhafa.

434 Phil thrown out of Bob's limo: *No Direction Home,* by Robert Shelton, Morrow, New York, 1986, p. 331.

437 Dylan and Hopper: Shelton, p. 416.

437 Van Ronk and Bouhafa: "Man, we went down to the Iron Horse and got smashed. We just drank and told stories." Interview with Dave Van Ronk, November 9, 1986.

438 Delsener, Dylan, and Ochs: "Bob was really hot for the idea. Phil had gotten him excited about playing small places, little clubs, and giving the money away." Ron Delsener in *Death of a Rebel,* by Marc Eliot, Doubleday, New York, p. 237.

438 "*Planet Waves* sold a meager . . . ": "That's fantastic for Bob. His influence and importance have always been greater than his sales and he's naive to think otherwise." David Geffen quoted in "Dylan Back to Columbia," by Judith Sims, *Rolling Stone,* September 12, 1974, p. 18.

439 Bob sells *Before the Flood* on TV: "Bob now strongly wanted to do something unorthodox—sell the tour album himself through a saturation mail-order campaign on television. . . . I was very negative. It seemed—at best—undignified to have Dylan huckstered on a crash television campaign." *Clive: Inside the Record Business,* by Clive Davis, with James Willwerth, Morrow, New York, 1974, p. 71.

Page

441 "I trusted him...": "[Dylan] said, 'I don't want to sign a contract, will you take my word on it?' I thought, Bob Dylan, the guy who wrote 'Blowin' in the Wind' and 'The Times They Are A-Changin'"—I trusted him. And he fucked me." *Bob Dylan: An Illustrated History,* by Michael Gross, Elm Tree Books, London, 1978, p. 117.

441 Eric Weissberg: "I bumped into Phil Ramone on the street and he was in a tricky situation." Interview with Eric Weissberg, December 21, 1987.

443 David Zimmerman: "He'd had a hell of a time shaking off the specter of being Bob Dylan's brother." Interview with Kevin Odegard, February 16, 1988.

443 lyrics written on message slips: Odegard.

445 "Four of the songs...": Interview with Paul Martinson, February 15, 1988.

446 "*Stone* pulled out all the stops..." "Blood on the Tracks"—two reviews under this title—"Back Inside the Rain," by Jonathan Cott; and "After the Flood," by Jon Landau, both *Rolling Stone,* March 13, 1975, pp. 43–51.

447 "Peppermint Twist": "When compared to people who are thought (usually mistakenly so, in my view) to make their records in the same natural, unproduced style in which [Dylan] has made his, I find him wanting"; Landau.

447 Landau's review no doubt led to Bob's comment, "Oh, Landau, man. He's got his head up his ass.... He's into rock 'n roll, man, the way it was in the '50s." *On the Road with Bob Dylan,* by Larry Sloman, Bantam, New York, 1975, p. 50.

447 Hilburn's comments: "Top Critics Track Dylan," *Rolling Stone,* March 13, 1975.

Chapter 26

449 "Sara couldn't talk rock 'n roll": "Sara was one of those kind of wives who create a little world for their husbands without really understanding what they do." Interview with Maria Muldaur, February 11, 1985.

449 "run out of patience": "Bob told me that Sara'd finally had enough and threw him out." Interview with a confidential source, April 3, 1985.

450 "Bleecker and MacDougal": "The neighborhood has been overrun by aging Sixties acid casualties, panhandling for a pint of Wild Irish Rose with which to wash down their methadone tabs." "Dylan: Freewheelin' Through the Village," by Lucian K. Truscott IV, *Rolling Stone,* August 28, 1975, p. 10.

451 "Bob told me how much he missed his family—it was killing him and he didn't try to hide it." Interview with a confidential source, April 3, 1985.

453 Bob meets Patti Smith: "I told Dylan, 'You've got to see Patti Smith.' Because, to me, Patti was sort of his alter-ego. He'd never heard of her, but he said, 'Yeah, maybe I'll show up.'" Faris Bouhafa, February 14, 1985.

453 Scarlet Rivera: "Bob Dylan Spotted Scarlet Rivera on the Street, the Rest Is History," by Jim Jerome, *People,* February 23, 1976, pp. 53–54. "They drove aimlessly now, down Second Avenue, heading toward the East Village, when Dylan spotted this woman with hair down to her waist, carrying a violin...[Scarlet] told me later that she thought I was a prostitute and Bob was my pimp and we were trying to get her into the ring." *On the Road with Bob Dylan,* by Larry Sloman, Bantam, New York, p. 104.

Page

455 "The guy really seems lost": Interview with Madeline Beckman, April 5, 1985.

459 "I'd rather have Patti than McGuinn": "He just didn't seem to have that much respect for McGuinn. He felt he could have anybody, so if it came down to it, he'd rather have Patti Smith than McGuinn." Bouhafa.

459 birth of Rolling Thunder: "I remember the first time I heard Bob talk about that concept." Muldaur.

460 "Levon Helm and Rick Danko remembered...": Interview with a confidential source, November 11, 1984.

460 The *Desire* session: "That first night had to be the most bizarre gathering of musicians ever under one roof." Interview with Rob Stoner, February 3, 1985.

462 "Gee, Rockin' Rob...": Stoner.

462 Eric Clapton: "It was very hard to keep up with [Dylan]. He wasn't sure what he wanted. He was really looking, racing from song to song. I had to get out in the fresh air 'cause it was just madness in there." "The Rolling Stone Interview: Eric Clapton," *Rolling Stone,* November 20, 1975, p. 11.

464 Emmylou Harris: "She was going nuts, man. She was trying hard to keep up with him, but with Bob that's impossible and Emmylou was really upset." Stoner.

466 Recording "Sara": "He'd apparently just written it and wanted to surprise her. This is like a peace treaty or something. He was trying to reach her, to reconcile." Bouhafa.

467 the Gallo family: Bouhafa; and a confidential source.

467 reaction at CBS: "You've got to understand, to the gang at Columbia, Dylan was shit. They acted as if they were stuck with him." Bouhafa. "Dylan was an afterthought at the label": Interview with Sam Hood, November 21, 1984.

468 Neuwirth returns: Bouhafa, and a confidential source.

469 Neuwirth ghosts Dylan songs: "Neuwirth told me how he'd written lots of Bob's best lines, and I remember nights when they huddled, writing together." Interview with D. A. Pennebaker, August 19, 1987.

472 Jack Elliot: "Jack used to watch Dylan perform and say, 'He does me better than I do.'" Interview with Dave Van Ronk, November 9, 1986.

472 Patti Smith bows out: "I had to give her credit—that was a tough decision and a real missed opportunity." Stoner.

474 Bob visits Baez at her hotel: Interview with Mimi Fariña, April 1, 1985.

475 Imhoff: "Imhoff became the scapegoat for everything that went wrong during the tour. I was surprised Bob trusted something like the Revue to Barry because he'd made such a disaster of the George Harrison tour. That was the first thing he'd done on his own, and word was out that he needed more experience." Stoner.

Chapter 27

480 hit singles: "He was always after me about his inability to have hit records." Interview with Rob Stoner, February 3, 1985.

Page

481 bus trip to New England: "We felt like the Soldiers of Rock 'n Roll, rolling toward the battlefront. There was entertainment on the bus, everybody singing, watching videotapes, listening to new groups, working on songs." Stoner.

482 Roger McGuinn on his "old lady": *On the Road with Bob Dylan,* by Larry Sloman, Bantam, New York, p. 104.

484 Ronee Blakely: "Actually, she posed the only real problem on the tour, making a spectacle of herself, getting stoned on pills and passing out in the middle of the dressing-room floor—anti-social behavior like that. Other than that, she hogged the spotlight each chance she got." Stoner.

485 Sal Angatti: "I called Sal and said, 'Hi, it's Faris—I've got some great news for you.'" Interview with Faris Bouhafa, February 14, 1985.

490 Singing harmony with Bob: Stoner.

492 Sloman: "Word filtered back to me that Sloman was walking Bob's dog. . . . The stories he filed were pure fluff, and when I learned he'd given Bob editorial control of his quotes, I fired him." Interview with Chet Flippo, August 16, 1987. "Sloman's position on the tour was very tenuous. It started out that he was just an annoyance, but Bob had this underlying sense of mischief toward him. There was this constant cat-and-mouse game everynight where Sloman was the pawn being used by Dylan to let everyone know who's boss." Stoner. "[Sloman] calls *Rolling Stone* for some additional expense money and gets the word from Flippo. It is no longer desirable in their eyes . . . to keep the reporter on the road." Sloman, p. 204. "*Rolling Stone* just cut me off . . . because I wouldn't write that bureaucratic bullshit." Sloman, p. 207. "One of [Sloman's] duties was to take care of Dylan's not-so-housebroken puppy beagle." Sloman, p. 219.

492 "*Stone* was righteously miffed . . .": "Dylan Tour Snowballs: 'It's Not a Nightclub Show.'" *Rolling Stone,* December 18, 1975, p. 9.

492 "All right, I want some fuckin' money . . ." "Dylan Tour Snowballs."

493 "'Hurricane' had already peaked . . .": *The Billboard Book of Top 40 Hits,* by Joel Whitburn, Billboard Publications Inc., New York, 1983.

494 deposition: Provided by a confidential source.

495 Rolling Thunder goes to jail: Details provided by Stoner; from a tape-recording of the event; by two confidential sources; and by "Knockin' on Hurricane's Door," by Les Ledbetter, *Rolling Stone,* January 15, 1976, p. 11.

Chapter 28

499 Ali at the Garden: Interview with Rob Stoner, February 3, 1985, and the following printed accounts: "Ali babbled about how great Carter is and joked about how he had never heard of Bob Dylan. . . . Then Ali . . . trotted out a middle-aged man whom he introduced as 'a next president of the United States'"; from "Hurricane's Night: Thunder in the Garden," by Chet Flippo, *Rolling Stone,* January 15, 1976, pp. 10–11. "Muhamad [sic] Ali spoke briefly and cheerfully, commending the predominantly white crowd and saying it had 'the connections and the complexion to get the protection' for Mr. Carter"; "Dylan Returns to Garden with Rolling Thunder Review [sic] in Benefit for Carter," by John Rockwell, *New York Times,* December 9, 1975. "One moment was especially bizarre. With Muhammad

Page

Ali on stage, Rubin Carter was hooked up by amplified telephone. . . . he had to wait until Ali completed his act, fulfilled his due quota of fables and boasts"; "Night of the Aging Children," by Nik Cohn, *New York,* December 22, 1975, p. 65.

500 "Bob was ecstatic . . . ": Stoner.

502 Hollywood rehearsal: Details provided by two confidential sources.

503 "an embarrassment of riches . . . ": "Originally the Revue was supposed to have a circus motif. We were talking about getting unicyclists and midgets and things like that to come onstage before we play, but eventually that idea was dropped." Stoner.

504 Stephen Stills: Information provided by Stoner and several confidential sources.

505 "Sabotage!": "We knew what had happened. That bastard had sabotaged our equipment." Stoner.

506 "the evening's biggest loser": "Except for a $10,000 donation to the Rubin Carter defense fund from the Astrodome itself, no money was made for the Freedom For All, Forever Corporation." "Hurricane II a Financial Washout," by Merrill Shindler, *Rolling Stone,* March 11, 1976.

507 Phil Ochs's death: "Phil suffered from the humiliation he felt at his behavior and the way he abused people who loved him. Unfortunately, he was powerless to do anything about it. After Dylan left town, Phil went into seclusion and finally took his life."Interviews with Arthur Gorson, March 1, 1985, and Sonny Ochs and Michael Ochs, March 2, 1985.

510 "Sara would suddenly appear . . . ": Interview with a confidential source, March 13, 1986.

511 Willie Nelson bails out Rolling Thunder: "Willie Nelson's manager, Neil Reshen, claimed his act was added to the bill to boost ticket sales." "Thunder Deep in the Heart of Texas," by Joe Nick Patoski, *Rolling Stone,* June 17, 1976, p. 10.

511 Willie and the law: Stoner, and Patoski, "Nelson Subpoenaed in Texas Drug Probe," *Rolling Stone,* June 17, 1976, p. 10.

Chapter 29

514 "elusive around the house": Interview with a confidential source, January 29, 1988.

514 the divorce complaint: from a court document entitled "Declaration of Sara Dylan," provided by a confidential source.

516 Bob swindled out of $78,000: "Gulling the Beautiful People," *Time,* July 8, 1975, p. 45.

516 Sara accosted the teacher: "Mrs. Dylan, 38, of Beverly Hills, entered a guilty plea Tuesday to the charge of disrupting a classroom. . . . ": "People," *San Jose Mercury,* September 14, 1978.

518 "This is meant to work . . . ": "Ballad in Plain Dull," by Dave Marsh, *Rolling Stone,* March 9, 1978, p. 31.

518 "It's what Louis and Marie Antoinette . . . ": "The Current Cinema: The Calvary Gig," by Pauline Kael, *New Yorker,* February 13, 1978, pp. 107–111.

519 "a tiring bore": "Bob Dylan's 'Renaldo' Is a Tiring Bore," *New York Post,* February 3, 1978.

Page

519 hiring Wasserman: "Wasserman told a somewhat surprised Dylan that with a few cover stories and interviews in the right places, the people out there, their interest in his mystique rekindled, would flock to the theatres." "Renaldo and Wasso," by Joel Kotkin, *New Times,* February 2, 1978, p. 44.

519 "loyal *Rolling Stone*...": "It's very rock & roll with some rhythm & blues and a typical slow Dylan tune and a typical upbeat Dylan tune." "Bob Dylan Is Still Rolling," by Delores Ziebarth, *Rolling Stone,* June 29, 1978, p. 9.

520 "If you try to be anyone but yourself...": "If you are not true to your own heart, you will fail. Then again, there's no success like failure." "The Playboy Interview: Bob Dylan," by Ron Rosenbaum, *Playboy,* March 1978, p. 74.

522 "As one critic pointed out...": "There is no other way to explain satisfactorily such perverse arrangements...." "The Main Event," by Ira Kaplan, *Soho Weekly News,* October 5, 1978, p. 8.

523 "Dylan going Vegas?": "He could take this show to Vegas and not change one note." "Dylan Going Vegas?" by Cameron Crowe, *Rolling Stone,* July 13, 1978, p. 10.

523 "*The Gong Show*": "Instead of making the music an intimate form of expression, Dylan seems to be estranged from himself, too." "Dylan and Young on the Road," by Jay Cocks, *Time,* November 6, 1978.

523 Dave Marsh: "And Dylan now squanders his talent as only Elvis could." "Knockin' on Heaven's Door," by Dave Marsh, *Rolling Stone,* August 30, 1978, p. 30.

523 Wenner's apology: "The review of *Street Legal*... in many ways, seemed based on a weird hostility and bitterness.... Marcus's and Marsh's articles were ad hominum attacks.... As a whole this LP is his most comprehensive comment about our current state since *Blonde on Blonde.*" "Dylan and the Stones in the Seventies," by Jann S. Wenner, *Rolling Stone,* September 21, 1978.

524 "He turned his London concert...": "Word of Protest," by James Johnson, *Evening Standard,* June 16, 1978.

525 "I cut the whole experience right off": "Bob Dylan Opens Up on Bob Dylan," by Robert Hilburn, *Los Angeles Times,* May 28, 1978, p. 67.

525 "the media was out to 'get' him": "I think I know what happened. In the 60s, *Time, Newsweek*—all those magazines—started calling me the 'father of the revolution,' 'the folk-rock king' and all that stuff. That's what created this mythical Bob Dylan thing. So, now, the magazines must figure they made a mistake back then and they've gotta take it down some." Hilburn, p. 67.

Chapter 30

527 "Rob Stoner credits T-Bone...": "T-Bone, who was a born-again Christian, sensed this guy was really ripe for recruitment and moved right in there." Interview with Rob Stoner, February 3, 1985.

528 "B.H. would have suffered apoplexy...": Kopple Hallock, the Hibbing tailor who clothed Bob before each school year, said, "I know his great grandfather, Mr. Edelstein, would flip over in his grave if he heard the news"; "Dylan and Jesus: The Scratching of Heads in Hibbing," *Minneapolis Tribune,* December 7, 1979, p. 4C. And "B.H. would have killed

Page

him! As it was, Bob was a family disgrace." Interview with a confidential source, March 3, 1985.

529 Bob receives the Lord: "And so Larry Myers and Paul Edmond . . . ministered to him. He responded by saying Yes, he did in fact want Christ in his life and he prayed that day and received the Lord." "Dylan—By His Pastor," *Buzz,* November, 1980.

529 Fundamentalists: provided in a series of interviews with Pastor Dennis Duncan, Calvary Temple, April 27–29, 1988.

530 "How did they expect him to dedicate three months . . .": "At first I said, 'There's no way I can devote three months to this. I've got to be back on the road soon.'" "Bob Dylan Opens Up on Bob Dylan," by Robert Hilburn, *Los Angeles Times,* May 28, 1978, p. 67.

530 "I couldn't believe I was there": Hilburn.

532 Wenner's review: "Bob Dylan in Our Times: The Slow Train Is Coming," by Jann S. Wenner, *Rolling Stone,* September 20, 1979, p. 94.

532 "the Atlantic Sound . . .": *The Making of Superstars,* by Bob Spitz, Doubleday & Co., New York, 1978, p. 259.

535 "Backstage, she was startled . . .": Interview with Maria Muldaur, February 11, 1985. "Spring 1980—I was still drinking, having a problem with it at gigs. I'd start the evening sober and get more and more looped as the evening went on. Hung over the next day, just enough time to pull it together by showtime, then I'd start the whole cycle over again. My life, at the time, was a complete mess."

542 "I just write 'em as they come": "The Rolling Stone Interview: Bob Dylan," "Bob Dylan: The Rolling Stone Interview," by Curt Loder, *Rolling Stone,* June 21, 1984, p. 23.

544 *Empire Burlesque*: ". . . a record of survival and a tentative kind of triumph. Maybe Bob Dylan got a little lost, but he never left the field"; "Here's What's Happening, Mr. Jones," by Jay Cocks, *Time,* June 10, 1985, p. 84. "But here it is, *Empire Burlesque* (Columbia), one more dead battery . . ."; "Bob Dylan: Comeback Time Again," by Griel Marcus, *Village Voice,* August 13, 1985, p. 63.

Discography

Compiled by Jeff Friedman

This discography is intended to present, in chronological order, all known recordings by Bob Dylan, including officially released albums, singles, and videos, as well as recordings that are circulating among private collectors.

Only professionally shot videos are included, unless there is no other source for the entry. The discography also includes Bob Dylan's appearances as a guest on other artists' recordings, with his contributions noted.

Because of the scarcity of concert tapes prior to 1974, full lists of songs performed are given. Since his return to live performing in 1974, Dylan's tour schedule has been extensive; for this reason, only the itineraries of each tour are listed.

What is not included are rumors, either of Dylan supposedly appearing on other artists' recordings or of some tape that might exist in somebody's closet. Simply put, if a recording is circulating among collectors, it is listed here.

Released Dylan albums appear in ***bold italics.*** Single releases are only listed if a song did not appear on an album at the time of its release.

Sincere and heartfelt thanks to Christian Behrens, Mitchell Blank, The Finos, Michael Krogsgaard, Paul Loeber, Bill Pagel, Jacques van Son, and most of all C. Parker—without whom . . .

If anyone knows of any recordings that are not listed here, regardless of how incidental they might seem, please contact Jeff Friedman, P.O.B. 1595, Old Chelsea Station, New York, NY 10113–0935.

Symbols Used:

(V) = Video as well as audio, unless otherwise noted.
(INC) = Incomplete recording.
(*) = Undiscovered show. Recording of this show is not known to exist. This symbol is only used on tours after 1974.
(SC) = Soundcheck recording—recorded prior to show.

(Fall '60) Minneapolis, Minnesota
Red Rosy Bush/Johnny, I Hardly Knew You/Jesus Christ/Streets of Glory/K.C. Moan/Mule Skinner Blues/I'm a Gambler/Talkin' Columbia *(one verse)*/Talkin' Merchant Marine/Talkin' Hugh Brown/Talkin' Lobbyist

(2–3/61) East Orange, New Jersey—home of Bob and Sid Gleason
San Francisco Bay Blues/Jesus Met the Woman at the Well/Gypsy Davey/Pastures of Plenty/Trail of the Buffalo/Jesse James/Sweetheart Remember Me

(5/61) Minneapolis, Minnesota
Ramblin' Round/Death Don't Have No Mercy/It's Hard to Be Blind/This Train/Harp Blues/Talkin' Fisherman/Pastures of Plenty/This Land Is Your Land/Two Trains/Wild Mountain Thyme/Howja Do/Car, Car/Don't You Push Me Down/Come See/I Want My Milk/San Francisco Bay Blues/Long Time A-Growin'/Devilish Mary/Railroad Bill/Will the Circle Be Unbroken/Man of Constant Sorrow/Pretty Polly/Railroad Boy (Little Willie)/Times Ain't What They Used to Be/Why'd You Cut My Hair

(5/6/61) Branford, Connecticut—Indian Neck Folk Festival, Montowese Hotel
Talkin' Columbia/Slipknot/Talkin' Fisherman

(6/61) GUEST ARTIST— *Midnight Special,* Harry Belafonte, RCA LSP-2449 (released 3/62)
Midnight Special *(on harmonica)*

(c. '61) New York, New York—Cynthia Gooding's apartment
Ballad of Donald White/When I Left Wichita/Acne-Teenager in Love/Rocks and Gravel/Long Time Man *(fragment)*

(c. '61) (INC) New York, New York—Folk City
Ranger's Command/San Francisco Bay Blues/The Great Divide

(7/29/61) New York, New York—Riverside Church, "Saturday Afternoon of Folk Music," Live broadcast over WRVR-FM
Handsome Molly/Naomi Wise/Poor Lazarus/Mean Old Southern Railroad *(on harmonica, with Danny Kalb)*/Acne *(with Ramblin' Jack Elliott)*

(9/61) New York, New York—The Gaslight
Man on the Street/He Was a Friend of Mine/Talkin' Bear Mountain Picnic Massacre Blues/Song to Woody/Pretty Polly/Car, Car *(with Dave Van Ronk)*

(9/29/61) GUEST ARTIST—*Carolyn Hester,* Columbia CS-8596/CL-1796 (mono) (released '62)
I'll Fly Away/Swing and Turn Jubilee/Come Back Baby *(on harmonica)*

(10/21/61) GUEST ARTIST—*Victoria Spivey, Big Joe Williams, Lonnie Johnson:* Volume 1, Spivey LP-1004 (released 11/64)
Sitting on Top of the World/Wichita

Volume 2, Spivey LP-1014 (released 7/72)
Big Joe, Dylan, and Victoria/It's Dangerous *(on harmonica and vocals)*

(11/4/61) (INC) New York, New York—Carnegie Chapter Hall
Pretty Peggy-O/In the Pines/Gospel Plow/1913 Massacre/Backwater Blues/Long Time A-Growin'/Fixin' to Die

(11/20, 22/61) *Bob Dylan*—Columbia CS-8579/CL-1779 (mono) (released 3/62)
You're No Good/Talkin' New York/In My Time of Dyin'/Man of Constant Sorrow/Fixin' to Die/Pretty Peggy-O/Highway 51/Baby, Let Me Follow You Down/House of the Rising Sun/Freight Train Blues/Song to Woody/See That My Grave Is Kept Clean

(11/23/61) New York, New York—home of Eve and Mac MacKenzie
Hard Times in N.Y. Town/Lonesome Whistle Blues/Worried Blues/Baby, Let Me Follow You Down/San Francisco Bay Blues/You're No Good/House of the Rising Sun/Bells of Rhymney/Highway 51/This Land Is Your Land/See That My Grave Is Kept Clean/Ballad of Donald White/A Hard Rain's A-Gonna Fall

(12/61) Minneapolis, Minnesota
Candy Man/Baby Please Don't Go/Hard Times in N.Y. Town/Stealin'/Poor Lazarus/I Ain't Got No Home/It's Hard to Be Blind/Dink's Song/Man of Constant Sorrow/The East Orange Story/Naomi Wise/Wade in the Water/I Was Young When I Left Home/In the Evening/Baby, Let Me Follow You Down/Sally Gal/Gospel Plow/Long John/Cocaine/See That My Grave Is Kept Clean/Ramblin' Round/VD Blues/VD Waltz/VD City/VD Gunner's Blues/Black Cross

(late '61/early '62) New York, New York—Leeds Music demos
He Was a Friend of Mine/Man on the Street/Hard Times in N.Y. Town/Man on the Street/Talkin' Bear Mountain Picnic Massacre Blues/Standing on the Highway/Poor Boy Blues/Ballad for a Friend/Ramblin', Gamblin' Willie

(late '61) New York, New York—the Billy James interview

(3/62) New York, New York—"Broadside Show," WBAI-FM
Ballad of Donald White/The Death of Emmett Till

Both songs, above, on "Broadside Reunion," Folkways Records, FR-5315 (released late '72)
Blowin' in the Wind

(c. '62) New York, New York—possibly off a radio broadcast
Honey, Just Allow Me One More Chance/Talkin' New York—Talkin' Folklore Center/Corrina, Corrina/Deep Ellum Blues/Blowin' in the Wind

(6/62) Montreal, Canada—Finjan Club
Hiram Hubbard/Blowin' in the Wind/Solid Road (Rocks & Gravel)/Quit Your Lowdown Ways/He Was a Friend of Mine/

Let Me Die in My Footsteps/Two Trains/Ramblin' on My Mind/Muleskinner Blues/The Death of Emmett Till/Stealin'

(c. 62) (INC) Minneapolis, Minnesota—recorded by Tony Glover
Tomorrow Is a Long Time

(1962–64) New York, New York—M. Witmark & Sons demos
Guess I'm Doin' Fine/Only a Hobo/The Death of Emmett Till/Blowin' in the Wind/All over You/Bob Dylan's Dream/Quit Your Lowdown Ways/Ain't Gonna Grieve/Baby, I'm in the Mood for You/Talkin' John Birch Paranoid Blues/Bob Dylan's Blues/John Brown/Ballad of Hollis Brown/Long Ago, Far Away/Long Time Gone/Girl from the North Country/Boots of Spanish Leather/Tomorrow Is a Long Time/Hero Blues/Let Me Die in My Footsteps/I Shall Be Free/A Hard Rain's A-Gonna Fall/Seven Curses/Farewell/Don't Think Twice, It's Alright/Oxford Town/Baby, Let Me Follow You Down/Bound to Lose, Bound to Win/Whatcha Gonna Do/Gypsy Lou/Paths of Victory/I'd Hate to Be You on That Dreadful Day/Walkin' down the Line/Masters of War/When the Ship Comes In/The Times They Are A-Changin'/I'll Keep It with Mine/Mama, You've Been on My Mind/Mr. Tambourine Man/Mama, You've Been on My Mind

(7/62–4/63) *The Freewheelin' Bob Dylan*—Columbia CS-8786/CL-1986 (mono) (released 5/63)
Blowin' in the Wind/Girl from the North Country/Masters of War/Down the Highway/Bob Dylan's Blues/A Hard Rain's A-Gonna Fall/Don't Think Twice, It's Alright/Bob Dylan's Dream/Oxford Town/Talkin' World War III Blues/Corrina, Corrina/Honey, Just Allow Me One More Chance/I Shall Be Free

Note: Early promo discs contained:
Let Me Die in My Footsteps/Solid Rock/Ramblin', Gamblin' Willie/Talkin' John Birch Paranoid Blues

They were replaced by:
Girl from the North Country/Masters of War/Bob Dylan's Dream/Talkin' World War III Blues

(7/62–4/63) New York, New York—Columbia Studios
Baby I'm in the Mood for You/Quit Your Lowdown Ways/Worried Blues/Going Down to New Orleans/Corrina, Corrina/The Death of Emmett Till/Lonesome Whistle Blues/Solid Road (Rocks & Gravel)/Talkin' Hava Negeilan Blues/Baby, Please Don't Go/Milk Cow Blues *(two takes)*/Talkin' Bear Mountain Picnic Massacre Blues/When I Left Wichita *(two takes)*

(c. '62) New York, New York—miscellaneous Columbia Records reference acetates
Mixed Up Confusion/Kingsport Blues/Whatcha Gonna Do/Sally Gal

(9/22/62) New York, New York—Carnegie Hall, "Hoot"
Sally Gal/Highway 51/Talkin' John Birch Paranoid Blues/Ballad of Hollis Brown/A Hard Rain's A-Gonna Fall

(late '62) New York, New York—Gaslight

Barbara Allen/A Hard Rain's A-Gonna Fall/Don't Think Twice/Black Cross/No More Auction Block/Moonshine Blues/Solid Road (Rocks & Gravel)/Motherless Child/Handsome Molly/John Brown/Ballad of Hollis Brown/I Got a Kindhearted Woman/See That My Grave Is Kept Clean/Ain't No More Cane on the Brazos/Cocaine/The Cuckoo Is a Pretty Bird/Goin' Down to Texas

(10/62) New York, New York—*Broadside* magazine

I'd Hate to Be You on That Dreadful Day *(released on* "Broadside Reunion," *Folkways Records* FR-5315)/Oxford Town/Paths of Victory/Walkin' down the Line

(10/62) New York, New York—"The Billy Faier Show," WBAI-FM

Baby, Let Me Follow You Down/Talkin' John Birch Paranoid Blues/The Death of Emmett Till/Make Me a Pallet on Your Floor

(late '62) New York, New York—"World of Folk Music," Oscar Brand broadcast over WNBC-AM

Girl from the North Country/Only a Hobo

(11/14/62) SINGLE RELEASE—Columbia Col 4-42656/CBS-2476 (released 11/62)

Mixed Up Confusion/Corrina, Corrina

Note: Additional take of "Mixed Up Confusion" was released on "Masterpieces" in Japan and Australia, CBS/Sony YBPB-3 1-57AP-875-7 (released 3/78).

(with Bruce Langhorne—G, Howie Collins—G, Leonard Gaskin—B, Herb Lovelle—D)

(c. late '62) Unknown live club recording

Ramblin' Round/Freight Train Blues/Walls of Red Wing *(partial)*

(late '62) London, England—"Madhouse on Castle Street," BBC-TV broadcast (1/13/63)

Blowin' in the Wind/Swan on the Lake

(1/14, 15/63) GUEST ARTIST—*Dick Fariña & Eric Von Schmidt,* Folklore Records F-LEUT-7 (released '64), London, England, Dobell's Record Shop

Glory, Glory/You Can Always Tell/Xmas Island/Cocaine/London Waltz/Overseas Stomp *(on harmonica and vocals as Blind Boy Grunt, with Dick Fariña—G and V, Eric Von Schmidt—G and V, Ethan Signer—V)*

(1/63) New York, New York—home of Gil Turner, with Happy Traum

Lonesome River Forge/Grasshoppers on My Pillow/Bob Dylan's Dream/Farewell/All Over You/Masters of War/Keep Your Hands Off Her/Honey Babe/Back to Romance/Stealin'

(1/63) New York, New York—*Broadside* magazine offices (released on "Broadside Reunion," Folkways Records FR-5315 late '72)
I Shall Be Free/Train A-Travelin'/Cuban Missile Crisis

(1/19/63) New York, New York—*Broadside* magazine offices
Farewell *(with Gil Turner)*

(1/24/63) New York, New York—*Broadside* magazine offices
Masters of War/Ye Playboys and Ye Playgirls

(early '63) *Broadside Ballads,* BR-5301 (released 9/63)
John Brown/Only a Hobo/Talkin' Devil/Let Me Die in My Footsteps *(with Happy Traum, as Blind Boy Grunt)*

(2–3/63) New York, New York—"The Skip Weshner Show," WBAI-FM
Tomorrow Is a Long Time/Masters of War/Bob Dylan's Blues

(4/12/63) New York, New York—home of Eve and Mac MacKenzie
Times Ain't What They Used to Be/Long Time Gone/Only a Hobo/House of the Rising Sun

(4/12/63) (INC) New York, New York—Town Hall
Ramblin' Round/Bob Dylan's Dream/Tomorrow Is a Long Time *(released on KG-31120)***/Bob Dylan's New Orleans Rag/Masters of War/Walls of Red Wing/Hero Blues/Who Killed Davy Moore/With God on Our Side/All Over You**

('63) *Bob Dylan in Concert* (unreleased album)
Last Thoughts on Woody Guthrie/Lay Down Your Weary Tune/Dusty Old Fairgrounds/John Brown/When the Ship Comes In/Who Killed Davy Moore?/Percy's Song/Bob Dylan's New Orleans Rag/Seven Curses
Note: LP was given the catalogue number Col-CS-9102/CL-2302 (mono).

(4–5/63) Chicago, Illinois—The Bear
Honey, Just Allow Me One More Chance/Talkin' John Birch Paranoid Blues/Bob Dylan's Dream/Hollis Brown/Talkin' World War III Blues/A Hard Rain's A-Gonna Fall/With God on Our Side

(5/63) Chicago, Illinois—"Studs Terkel's Wax Museum," broadcast over WFMT
Farewell/A Hard Rain's A-Gonna Fall/Bob Dylan's Dream/Boots of Spanish Leather/John Brown/Who Killed Davy Moore?/Blowin' in the Wind

(c. '63) (INC) Minneapolis, Minnesota—recorded by Tony Glover
Ballad of Hollis Brown/Girl from the North Country/Boots of Spanish Leather/Eternal Circle/Hero Blues

(7/6/63) (V) Greenwood, Mississippi—voter-registration rally
Only a Pawn in Their Game *(two verses* **in "Don't Look Back")**

(7/26–28/63) Newport, Rhode Island—Newport Folk Festival (released on Vanguard VSD-79144 and VRS-9144 in '64)
With God on Our Side/Ye Playboys and Ye Playgirls *(released on Vanguard VSD-79148 and VRS-9148 in '64)* **Blowin' in the Wind/We Shall Overcome** *(on chorus)*

(8/63) New York, New York—"Songs of Freedom," WNEW-TV broadcast (8/26/63)
Blowin' in the Wind/Only a Pawn in Their Game

(8/17/63) Forest Hills, New York—Forest Hills Tennis Stadium, Joan Baez concert
Troubled and I Don't Know Why/Blowin' in the Wind *(partial)*

(8/28/63) Washington, D.C.—civil-rights march
Only a Pawn in Their Game *(two verses released on Broadside Records BR-5592, '64)*/**Hold On** *(on chorus)*

(8–10/63) *The Times They Are A-Changin'*—Columbia CS-8905/CL-2105 (mono) (released 1/64)
The Times They Are A-Changin'/Ballad of Hollis Brown/With God on Our Side/ One Too Many Mornings/North Country Blues/Only a Pawn in Their Game/Boots of Spanish Leather/When the Ship Comes In/Lonesome Death of Hattie Carroll/Restless Farewell

(late '63) New York, New York—Columbia Studios
Eternal Circle/Paths of Victory/The Cough Song/I'll Keep It with Mine/California/Percy's Song/Walls of Red Wing/Only a Hobo/Moonshine Blues/Lay Down Your Weary Tune/Eternal Circle/Seven Curses/Percy's Song

('64) (V) London, England—"Tonight," BBC-TV, probably not recorded in London
With God on Our Side *(partial)*

(2/1/64) (V) Toronto, Canada—"Quest," CBC-TV (broadcast 3/10/64)
The Times They Are A-Changin'/Talkin' World War III Blues/Lonesome Death of Hattie Carroll/Girl from the North Country/A Hard Rain's A-Gonna Fall/Restless Farewell

(2/25/64) New York, New York—"The Steve Allen Show," syndicated TV show
Lonesome Death of Hattie Carroll

('64) GUEST ARTIST—*Ramblin' Jack Elliot,* Vanguard VSD-79151 (released 6/64)
Will the Circle Be Unbroken *(on harmonica as Tedham Porterhouse)*

('64) GUEST ARTIST—*The Blues Project,* Elektra EKS-7264/EKL-264 (mono), recorded at Mastertone Studios, New York, New York (released 6/64)
Downtown Blues *(on piano as Bob Landy)*

(6/9/64) *Another Side of Bob Dylan*—Columbia CS-8993/CL-2193 (mono) (released 8/64)
All I Really Want to Do/Black Crow Blues/Spanish Harlem Incident/Chimes of Freedom/I Shall Be Free #10/To Ramona/ Motorpsycho Nightmare/My Back Pages/I Don't Believe You/ Ballad in Plain D/It Ain't Me Babe

('64) New York, New York—Columbia Studios
Bob Dylan's New Orleans Rag/Denise/Bob Dylan's New Orleans Rag/That's Alright Mama/East Laredo Blues/Farewell

(c. '64) New York, New York—Misc. Columbia Records reference acetates
Hero Blues/That's Alright Mama/ I'll Keep It with Mine *(instrumental)*

(8/8/64) Forest Hills, New York—guest at Joan Baez concert
Mama, You've Been on My Mind/It Ain't Me Babe/With God on Our Side

('64) Philadelphia, Pennsylvania—Town Hall
The Times They Are A-Changin'/Girl from the North Country/ Who Killed Davy Moore?/Talkin' John Birch Paranoid Blues/ To Ramona/Ballad of Hollis Brown/Chimes of Freedom/I Don't Believe You/It's Alright Ma/Mr. Tambourine Man/ Talkin' World War III Blues/A Hard Rain's A-Gonna Fall/ Don't Think Twice, It's Alright/Only a Pawn in Their Game/ With God on Our Side/It Ain't Me Babe/Lonesome Death of Hattie Carroll/All I Really Want to Do

(10/31/64) New York, New York—Philharmonic Hall
The Times They Are A-Changin'/Spanish Harlem Incident/ Talkin' John Birch Paranoid Blues/To Ramona/Who Killed Davy Moore?/Gates of Eden/If You Gotta Go, Go Now/It's Alright Ma/I Don't Believe You/Mr. Tambourine Man/A Hard Rain's A-Gonna Fall/Talkin' World War III Blues/Don't Think Twice, It's Alright/Lonesome Death of Hattie Carroll/Mama, You've Been on My Mind/Silver Dagger *(on harmonica with Joan Baez)*/With God on our Side *(w/Joan Baez)*/It Ain't Me Babe *(with Joan Baez)*/All I Really Want to Do

(11/25/64) (INC) San José, California—San José Auditorium
The Times They Are A-Changin'/Talkin' John Birch Paranoid Blues/To Ramona/Gates of Eden/If You Gotta Go, Go Now/ It's Alright Ma/Mr. Tambourine Man/A Hard Rain's A-Gonna Fall/Talkin' World War III Blues/Don't Think Twice It's Alright

(11–12/64) (INC) Berkeley or San José, California
Gates of Eden/If You Gotta Go, Go Now/It's Alright Ma/ Talkin' World War III Blues/Don't Think Twice It's Alright/ Mama, You've Been on My Mind

(12/64) Long Beach, California—the Bob Blackmar interview

(1/14, 15/65) *Bringing It All Back Home*—**Columbia Col CS-9128/ CL-2328 (mono) (released 3/65)**

Subterranean Homesick Blues/She Belongs to Me/Maggie's Farm/Love Minus Zero; No Limit/Outlaw Blues/On the Road Again/Bob Dylan's 115th Dream/Mr. Tambourine Man/Gates of Eden/It's Alright Ma/It's All Over Now, Baby Blue ***(with Bruce Langhorne—G, Al Gorgoni—G, Kenny Rankin—G, John Hammond, Jr.—G, Paul Griffin—P, Frank Owens—P, Joseph Macho, Jr.—B, Lillian E. Lee—B, John Sebastian—B, John Boone—B, Bobby Gregg—D)***

('65) New York, New York—Columbia Studios

It's All Over Now, Baby Blue/She Belongs to Me/Love Minus Zero; No Limit

(2/17/65) New York, New York—"The Les Crane Show," broadcast live over WABC-TV

It's All Over Now, Baby Blue/It's Alright Ma ***(with Bruce Langhorne—G)***

(4/65) Santa Monica, California—Santa Monica Civic Auditorium

To Ramona/Gates of Eden/If You Gotta Go, Go Now/It's Alright Ma/Love Minus Zero; No Limit/Mr. Tambourine Man/Don't Think Twice, It's Alright/With God on Our Side/She Belongs to Me/It Ain't Me Babe/Lonesome Death of Hattie Carroll/All I Really Want to Do/It's All Over Now, Baby Blue

(4/30/65) (INC) Sheffield, England—City Hall

The Times They Are A-Changin'/To Ramona/Gates of Eden/If You Gotta Go, Go Now/It's Alright Ma/Love Minus Zero; No Limit

(5/7/65) Manchester, England—Free Trade Hall

The Times They Are A-Changin'/To Ramona/Gates of Eden/If You Gotta Go, Go Now/It's Alright Ma/Love Minus Zero; No Limit/Mr. Tambourine Man/Talkin' World War III Blues/Don't Think Twice, It's Alright/With God on Our Side/She Belongs to Me/It Ain't Me Babe/Lonesome Death of Hattie Carroll/All I Really Want to Do/It's All Over Now, Baby Blue

(5/10/65) London, England—Royal Albert Hall

The Times They Are A-Changin'/To Ramona/Gates of Eden/If You Gotta Go, Go Now/Mr. Tambourine Man/Talkin' World War III Blues/Don't Think Twice It's Alright/With God on Our Side/Lonesome Death of Hattie Carroll/All I Really Want to Do/Love Minus Zero; No Limit/It's All Over Now, Baby Blue/It's Alright Ma

(c. 5/65) (V) Miscellaneous in concert

To Ramona ***(portion broadcast 10/10/85 on "20/20" over ABC-TV)*** **(V)**

(5/12/65) London, England—Levy's Studio, recorded message for CBS sales convention

If You Gotta Go, Go Now

(6/8/65) London, England—BBC-TV Studios (broadcast 6/19/65)
Ballad of Hollis Brown/It Ain't Me Babe/Gates of Eden/If You Gotta Go, Go Now/Lonesome Death of Hattie Carroll/Mr. Tambourine Man *(broadcast 6/26/65)*
Love Minus Zero; No Limit/One Too Many Mornings/Boots of Spanish Leather/It's Alright Ma/She Belongs to Me/It's All Over Now, Baby Blue

(4–6/65) (V) *Don't Look Back*—tour film, directed by D. A. Pennebaker (released 5/17/67; later released on Paramount Home Video, #2382, 8/86)

(4–6/65) (V) SONG VIDEO—(from *Don't Look Back,* released 1/86; used as promotion for "Biograph")
Subterranean Homesick Blues

(1965) London, England—BBC Studios, Jack DeManio interview

(1965) SINGLE RELEASE—CBS CBS-2921 (Dutch pressing only)
If You Gotta Go, Go Now
Note: Alternate take has surfaced.

(7/25/65) Newport, Rhode Island—Newport Folk Festival
Maggie's Farm/Like a Rolling Stone/It Takes a Lot to Laugh *(above with Al Kooper—O/with Mike Bloomfield—G/Barry Goldberg—P/Jerome Arnold—B/Sam Lay—D)*/**All I Really Want to Do** *(from workshop)*/**It's All Over Now, Baby Blue/Mr. Tambourine Man**

(7/25/65) (V) *Festival*—film, directed by Murray Lerner (released 1966); Dylan portions recorded at Newport Folk Festival, Newport, Rhode Island
All I Really Want to Do *(from workshop)*/**Maggie's Farm/Mr. Tambourine Man**

(7/29/65) SINGLE RELEASE—Columbia Col 4-43389 (released 9/65; also released on Columbia KCS-9463 and KCL-2663)
Positively 4th Street *(with Mike Bloomfield—G/Paul Griffin—P/Al Kooper—O/Harvey Brooks—B/Bobby Gregg—D)*

('65) SINGLE RELEASE
Can You Please Crawl Out Your Window?
Note: This version labeled "Positively 4th Street" and accidentally released that way (9/65).

(6–8/65) ***Highway 61 Revisited*—Columbia CS-9189/CL-2389 (mono) (released 9/65)**
Like a Rolling Stone/Tombstone Blues/It Takes a Lot to Laugh, It Takes a Train to Cry/From a Buick 6/Ballad of a Thin Man/Queen Jane Approximately/Highway 61 Revisited/Just Like Tom Thumb's Blues/Desolation Row
Note: From a Buick 6—alternate take found on stereo disks with 1-A added to matrix number and on Japanese pressings; Can You Please Crawl Out Your Window?—demo; Desolation Row—alternate take found on *Highway 61* master tape, which also contains snippets before and after songs from LP.

('65) New York, New York—Columbia Studios
Sitting on a Barbed Wire Fence/It Takes a Lot to Laugh/ Visions of Johanna/She's Your Lover Now/Sitting on a Barbed Wire Fence *(latter three found on acetates)*

(8/28/65) Forest Hills, New York—Forest Hills Tennis Stadium
She Belongs to Me/To Ramona/Gates of Eden/Love Minus Zero; No Limit/Desolation Row/It's All Over Now, Baby Blue/ Mr. Tambourine Man/Tombstone Blues/I Don't Believe You/ From a Buick 6/Just Like Tom Thumb's Blues/Maggie's Farm/ It Ain't Me Babe/Ballad of a Thin Man/Like a Rolling Stone *(with Al Kooper—K/Harvey Brooks—B/Robbie Robertson—G/ Levon Helm—D)*

(c. '65) (V) New York, New York—film footage, probably shot by Andy Warhol used in the documentary *The Velvet Underground* (broadcast 1986, "The South Bank Show," LWT, London, England).
Note: There is no audio—just a brief moment of film.

(10/65) New York, New York—Columbia Studios, with The Band
Can You Please Crawl Out Your Window?/I Wanna Be Your Lover/Number One/Visions of Johanna/She's Your Lover Now

(10/65) Detroit, Michigan—Allen Stone interview, WDTM Radio

(11/30/65) SINGLE RELEASE—Columbia 4-43477, CBS 201900 (released 12/65)
Can You Please Crawl Out Your Window?

(12/3/65) (V) San Francisco, California—press conference, filmed by KQED-TV, hosted by Ralph J. Gleason

(12/65) (V) Los Angeles, California—press conference.
Note: Only a portion of this has surfaced on video; the audio is complete.

(1–3/66) ***Blonde on Blonde*—Columbia C2S-841/C2L-41 (mono) (released 6/66; recorded in Nashville, Tennessee)**
Rainy Day Women Nos. 12 and 35/Pledging My Time/Visions of Johanna/One of Us Must Know (Sooner or Later)/I Want You/Stuck Inside of Mobile with the Memphis Blues Again/ Leopard-Skin Pillbox Hat/Just Like a Woman/Most Likely You Go Your Way/Temporary Like Achilles/Absolutely Sweet Marie/Fourth Time Around/Obviously Five Believers/Sad-eyed Lady of the Lowlands

('66) New York, New York—"The Bob Fass Show," WBAI-FM, interview and phone calls

(c. '66) Nat Hentoff interview—for *Playboy* magazine
Note: This was not the interview that was published.

(2/5/66) (INC) White Plains, New York—Westchester County Center
She Belongs to Me/To Ramona/Visions of Johanna/It's All Over Now, Baby Blue/Desolation Row/Love Minus Zero; No

Limit/Mr. Tambourine Man/Tell Me, Momma/I Don't Believe You

(2/6/66) (INC) Pittsburgh, Pennsylvania—Syria Mosque
She Belongs to Me/To Ramona/Visions of Johanna/It's All Over Now, Baby Blue/Desolation Row/Love Minus Zero; No Limit/Mr. Tambourine Man/Positively 4th Street/Like a Rolling Stone

(2/20/66) Montreal, Quebec—Place des Arts, Martin Bronstein interview

(2/26/66) (INC) Hempstead, New York—Island Garden
She Belongs to Me/Fourth Time Around/Visions of Johanna/It's All Over Now, Baby Blue/Desolation Row/Love Minus Zero; No Limit/Mr. Tambourine Man/Tell Me, Momma/I Don't Believe You/Baby, Let Me Follow You Down/Just Like Tom Thumb's Blues/Leopard-Skin Pillbox Hat/One Too Many Mornings

(4/66) Adelaide, Australia—press conference

(4/20/66) (INC) Melbourne, Australia—Festival Hall
She Belongs to Me/Fourth Time Around/Visions of Johanna/It's All Over Now, Baby Blue/Desolation Row/Just Like a Woman/Baby, Let Me Follow You Down/Just Like Tom Thumb's Blues/Tell Me, Momma

(4/66) Melbourne, Australia—Stan Profe interview, broadcast 4/66 over Radio 3V2, Melbourne

(4/66) (V) Stockholm, Sweden—arrival at airport

(4/28/66) Solna, Sweden—Hotel Flamingo, press conference

(4/29/66) Stockholm, Sweden—flashes of interview

(4/29/66) (INC) Stockholm, Sweden
She Belongs to Me/Fourth Time Around/Visions of Johanna/It's All Over Now, Baby Blue/Desolation Row/I Don't Believe You/Baby, Let Me Follow You Down/Just Like Tom Thumb's Blues/Leopard-Skin Pillbox Hat/One Too Many Mornings/Ballad of a Thin Man

(5/5/66) (INC) Dublin, Ireland—Adelphi Theatre
Visions of Johanna/Fourth Time Around/It's All Over Now, Baby Blue/Desolation Row/Just Like a Woman/Mr. Tambourine Man

(5/10/66) Bristol, England—Colston Hall
She Belongs to Me/Fourth Time Around/Visions of Johanna/It's All Over Now, Baby Blue/Desolation Row/Just Like a Woman/Mr. Tambourine Man/Tell Me, Momma/I Don't Believe You/Baby, Let Me Follow You Down/Just Like Tom Thumb's Blues/Leopard-Skin Pillbox Hat/One Too Many Mornings/Ballad of a Thin Man/Like a Rolling Stone

('66) Miscellaneous in concert
Tell Me, Momma ***(found on Big Ben Music acetate)***

(5/14/66) SINGLE RELEASE—Columbia 4/43683, CBS 202258 (released 6/66)
Just Like Tom Thumb's Blues ***(recorded live, Liverpool, England, Odeon Cinema)***
Note: This is the flip side of "I Want You"

(5/17/66) (INC) Manchester, England—Free Trade Hall
Ballad of a Thin Man/Just Like Tom Thumb's Blues ***(partial)***
Note: Above two probably from soundcheck before show.
She Belongs to Me/Fourth Time Around/Visions of Johanna/It's All Over Now, Baby Blue/Desolation Row ***(partial)*****/Tell Me, Momma/I Don't Believe You/Baby, Let Me Follow You Down/Just Like Tom Thumb's Blues/Leopard-Skin Pillbox Hat/One Too Many Mornings/Ballad of a Thin Man/Like a Rolling Stone**

(5/20/66) Edinburgh, Scotland—ABC Cinema
She Belongs to Me/Fourth Time Around/Visions of Johanna/It's All Over Now, Baby Blue/Desolation Row/Just Like a Woman/Tell Me, Momma/Mr. Tambourine Man/Tell Me, Momma/I Don't Believe You/Baby, Let Me Follow You Down/Just Like Tom Thumb's Blues/Leopard-Skin Pillbox Hat/One Too Many Mornings/Ballad of a Thin Man/Like a Rolling Stone

(5/23/66) Paris, France—George V Hotel, press conference

(5/26/66) (INC) London, England—Royal Albert Hall
She Belongs to Me/Fourth Time Around/Visions of Johanna/One Too Many Mornings/Ballad of a Thin Man
Note: "Visions of Johanna" released on C5X-38830.

(5/27/66) (INC) London, England—Royal Albert Hall
She Belongs to Me/Fourth Time Around/Visions of Johanna/It's All Over Now, Baby Blue/Desolation Row/Just Like a Woman/Mr. Tambourine Man
Note: "It's All Over Now, Baby Blue" released on C5X-38830.

(Summer '66) (V) *Eat the Document*—film directed by Bob Dylan and Howard Alk from 1966 European tour plus outtake from film with John Lennon
Ballad of a Thin Man ***(partial)***

(c. '66) (V) "It Was Twenty Years Ago Today"—Granada TV, Beatles documentary: "Ballad of a Thin Man (probably from *Eat the Document,* color footage). Black-and-white film clip (very brief footage not previously seen)

('67) ***Bob Dylan's Greatest Hits*****—Columbia KCS-9463/KCL-2663 (mono) (released 4/67)**
Rainy Day Women Nos. 12 and 35/Blowin' in the Wind/The Times They Are A-Changin'/It Ain't Me Babe/Like a Rolling

Stone/Mr. Tambourine Man/Subterranean Homesick Blues/I Want You/Positively 4th Street/Just Like a Woman

(6–10/67) *The Basement Tapes*—West Saugerties, New York, Columbia C2-33682 (released 7/75)

Odds & Ends/Million Dollar Bash/Goin' to Acapulco/Lo and Behold!/Clothes Line Saga/Apple Suckling Tree/Please, Mrs. Henry/Tears of Rage/Too Much of Nothing/Yea! Heavy and a Bottle of Bread/Down in the Flood/Tiny Montgomery/You Ain't Goin' Nowhere/Nothing Was Delivered/Open the Door, Homer/This Wheel's on Fire

Note: Only the songs in which Dylan appears are listed.

(6–10/67) Additional and alternate takes

I Shall Be Released/Nothing Was Delivered/Open the Door, Homer/Clothes Line Saga *(false start only)*/Tears of Rage/ Mighty Quinn/Apple Suckling Tree/Sign on the Cross/Don't Ya Tell Henry/Lock Your Door *(partial)*/Baby, Won't You Be My Baby/Try Me Little Girl/I Can't Make It Alone/Don't You Try Me Now/He's Young but Daily Growing/Bonnie Ship the Diamond/The Hills of Mexico/Down on Me *(partial)*/One for the Road/I'm Alright/One Single River/People Get Ready/I Don't Hurt Anymore/Stones That You Throw/One Man's Loss/Guitars/All You Have to Do Is Dream *(two takes)*/ Instrumental/Instrumental/Instrumental/Instrumental/Baby Ain't That Fine/A Night without Sleep/A Fool Such As I/ Gonna Get You Now

(10/17, 11/6, and 29/67) *John Wesley Harding*—Columbia CS-9604/CL-2804 (mono) recorded in Nashville, Tennessee (released 12/67)

John Wesley Harding/As I Went Out One Morning/I Dreamed I Saw St. Augustine/All along the Watchtower/Ballad of Frankie Lee and Judas Priest/Drifter's Escape/Dear Landlord/I Am a Lonesome Hobo/I Pity the Poor Immigrant/The Wicked Messenger/Down along the Cove/I'll Be Your Baby Tonight

(1/20/68) New York, New York—Carnegie Hall, Woody Guthrie Memorial Concert, with The Band (then known as The Hawks)

Grand Coulee Dam/Dear Mrs. Roosevelt/I Ain't Got No Home/This Train *(with the entire cast)*

Note: All songs except "This Train" released 3/72 on Columbia KC-31171.

(early '68) (V) "Johnny Cash, the Man and His Music"—WNET television broadcast, New York, New York

Girl from the North Country *(on Columbia CS-9825)*/One Too Many Mornings *(also released on* The Other Side of Nashville, *MGM/UA Home Video, MV600351, 1983)*

(2/13, 14, and 17/69) *Nashville Skyline*—Columbia KCS-9825, recorded in Nashville, Tennessee (released 5/69)

Girl from the North Country/Nashville Skyline/To Be Alone with You/I Threw It All Away/Peggy Day/Lay Lady Lay/One

More Night/Tell Me That It Isn't True/Country Pie/Tonight, I'll Be Staying Here

(2/17–18/69) New York, New York—Columbia Studios, with Johnny Cash and his band

One Too Many Mornings/Mountain Dew/I Still Miss Someone/Careless Love/Matchbox/That's Alright Mama/Big River/I Walk the Line/You Are My Sunshine/Ring of Fire/I Guess Things Happen That Way/Just a Closer Walk with Thee/Blue Yodel #1/Blue Yodel #4

(5/1/69) (V) Nashville, Tennessee—"The Johnny Cash Show" from the Grand Ole Opry, ABC-TV, broadcast 6/7/69

I Threw It All Away/Living the Blues/Girl from the North Country

('69) New York, New York—Columbia Studios

Folsom Prison Blues/Ring of Fire

(8/31/69) Isle of Wight, England—Isle of Wight Festival, with The Band

She Belongs to Me/I Threw It All Away/Maggie's Farm/Wild Mountain Thyme/It Ain't Me Babe/To Ramona/Mr. Tambourine Man/I Dreamed I Saw St. Augustine/Lay Lady Lay/Highway 61/One Too Many Mornings/I Pity the Poor Immigrant/Like a Rolling Stone/I'll Be Your Baby Tonight/Quinn the Eskimo/Minstrel Boy/Rainy Day Women Nos. 12 and 35

Note: The following songs were released on Columbia C2X-30050: She Belongs to Me/Like a Rolling Stone/Mighty Quinn/Minstrel Boy

(V) Isle of Wight, England—Isle of Wight Festival, with The Band

Miscellaneous news film footage with no sound has surfaced.

(late '69) Nashville, Tennessee—Columbia Studios

Song to Woody/Mama, You've Been on My Mind/Instrumental/Yesterday/Just Like Tom Thumb's Blues/I Met Him on a Sunday/Instrumental/One Too Many Mornings

(3/70) *Self-Portrait*—Columbia C2S-30050, recorded in Nashville, Tennessee, Columbia Studios (released 6/70)

All The Tired Horses/Alberta #1/I Forgot More Than You'll Ever Know/Days of 49/Early Morning Rain/In Search of Little Sadie/Let It Be Me/Little Sadie/Woogie Boogie/Belle Isle/Living the Blues/Like a Rolling Stone/Copper Kettle/Gotta Travel On/Blue Moon/The Boxer/Mighty Quinn/Take Me As I Am/Take a Message to Mary/It Hurts Me Too/Minstrel Boy/She Belongs to Me/Wigwam/Alberta #2

('70) *Dylan*—Columbia PC-32747, recorded in New York, New York, and Nashville, Tennessee, Columbia Studios (released 12/73)

Lily of the West/I Can't Help Falling in Love/Sarah Jane/The Ballad of Ira Hayes/Mr. Bojangles/Mary Ann/Big Yellow Taxi/A Fool Such As I/Spanish Is the Loving Tongue

(5/70) Woodstock, New York

Everytime Somebody Comes to Town/I'd Have You Anytime *(both with George Harrison)*

(6–7/70) *New Morning*—Columbia KC-30290, recorded in New York, New York, Columbia Studios (released 10/70)

If Not for You/Day of the Locusts/Time Passes Slowly/Went to See the Gypsy/Winterlude/If Dogs Run Free/New Morning/Sign on the Window/One More Weekend/The Man in Me/Three Angels/Father of Night

(c. '70) Probable outtake from *New Morning*

Working on a Guru

(late '70) (V) Carmel, New York—Earl Scruggs documentary, WNET-TV, New York, New York

East Virginia Blues/Nashville Skyline Rag

Note: "N.S. Rag" released on Columbia C-30584 (1971). Broadcast (1/10 and 17/71).

(1/9/71) New York, New York—phone conversation with A. J. Weberman, portions of which were released on Folkways FB 5322 as "Bob Dylan vs. A. J. Weberman" in 1977. Album was withdrawn because of threat of legal action.

(3/16/71) SINGLE RELEASE—Columbia 4-45400 (released 6/71)

Watching the River Flow *(also released on KG-31120, 11/71; with Leon Russell—P, Jesse Ed Davis—G, Don Preston—G, Carl Radle—B, Jim Keltner—D)*/Spanish Is the Loving Tongue *(also released on CBS-Sony 57AP-875-7, 9/78; Dylan on piano and vocal solo)*

(8/1/71) New York, New York—Madison Square Garden, the Concert for Bangladesh,

Afternoon Show: A Hard Rain's A-Gonna Fall/Blowin' in the Wind/It Takes a Lot to Laugh/Love Minus Zero; No Limit/Just Like a Woman

(8/1/71) (V) *Evening Show:* A Hard Rain's A-Gonna Fall/It Takes a Lot to Laugh/Blowin' in the Wind/Mr. Tambourine Man/Just Like a Woman

Evening show only: (released 12/71, Apple STCX-3385)

Note: Except for "Mr. Tambourine Man," all released theatrically in the film *The Concert for Bangladesh* (3/72) and on Thorn-EMI home video #TVE 2379.

(9/24/71) New York, New York—Columbia KG-31120, recorded in Blue Rock Studios, (released 11/71)

When I Paint My Masterpiece *(with Leon Russell—P, Jesse Ed Davis—G, Don Preston—G, Carl Radle—B, Jim Keltner—D)*

(10/71) New York, New York—Columbia KG-31120, recorded in Columbia Studios (released 11/71)

I Shall Be Released/You Ain't Goin' Nowhere/Crash on the Levee (Down in the Flood)/You Ain't Goin' Nowhere *(alternate take)*

Bob Dylan's Greatest Hits Vol. 2—Columbia KG-31120 (released 11/71)

Watching the River Flow/Don't Think Twice/Lay Lady Lay/Stuck Inside of Mobile/I'll Be Your Baby Tonight/All I Really Want to Do/My Back Pages/Maggie's Farm/Tonight, I'll Be Staying Here/She Belongs to Me/All along the Watchtower/Quinn the Eskimo/Just Like Tom Thumb's Blues/A Hard Rain's A-Gonna Fall/If Not for You/It's All Over Now, Baby Blue/Tomorrow Is a Long Time/When I Paint My Masterpiece/I Shall Be Released/You Ain't Goin' Nowhere/Down in the Flood

(11/4/71) SINGLE RELEASE—Columbia 4-45516/CBS 7688, recorded in Columbia Studios, New York, New York (released 11/71)

George Jackson *(acoustic version)*/George Jackson *(big-band version) (with Ken Buttrey—D, Dan Keith—pedal-steel G, Joshie Armstead—V, Rose Hicks—V)*

(fall '71) (INC) "Freetime"—WNET-TV

Allen Ginsberg and Friends *(Dylan on guitar)*

(11/9–17/71) GUEST ARTIST—*First Blues,* Allen Ginsberg, John Hammond W2X-37673, recorded at Record Plant Recording Studios, New York, New York (released late '82)

Vomit Express/Going to San Diego/Jimmy Berman *(also released on* Disconnected, *Giorno Poetry Systems Records CP5-003, 1974)*

Outtakes:

On My Soul Shalom/Nurse's Song/Many Loves/Parhuspato Rayan/September on Jessore Road/*(one verse released on Flexidisc in* Sing Out *Magazine, vol. 21, no. 2 [1972])*/The Tyger *(Dylan—G, V)*

(9/72) GUEST ARTIST—*Somebody Else's Troubles,* Steve Goodman, Buddah BDS-5121, Bell Sound Studio, New York, New York (released '73)

Somebody Else's Troubles *(Dylan—P and V as Robert Milkwood Thomas)*/Election Year Rag *(released in '73 as single, BDA-326/BDS-5665-2)*

(10/72) GUEST ARTIST—*Doug Sahm and Band,* Atlantic SD-7524, Atlantic Sound Studio, New York, New York (released 12/72)

San Antone/Wallflower/Blues Stay Away from Me/Me and Paul *(Dylan—V, harmonica, G, O)*

(c. 10/72) Columbia reference acetate
Wallflower

(c. '72) GUEST ARTIST—*Roger McGuinn,* Columbia KC-31946, Los Angeles, California (released 12/72)
I'm So Restless *(Dylan—harmonica)*

(1–2/73) ***Pat Garrett and Billy the Kid,*** soundtrack, Columbia KC-32460, Mexico City, Mexico (1/73), Los Angeles, California (2–3/73) (released 5/73)
Main Title Theme (Billy)/Cantina Theme (Workin' for the Law)/Billy 1/Bunkhouse Theme/River Theme/Turkey Chase/Knockin' on Heaven's Door/Final Theme/Billy 4/Billy 7

(1–2/73) (V) *Pat Garrett and Billy the Kid*—film, directed by Sam Peckinpah (released 5/73 theatrically; released on MGM/UA home video, #MV600159)
Note: Re-cut version was released in 1988 and broadcast on cable television. Sound track differs slightly from original version.

(1/73) Mexico City, Mexico—**Pat Garrett and Billy the Kid** outtakes, CBS Discos Studios
Billy *(instrumental, very brief)***/Billy** *(very brief)***/Billy** *(with harmonica only)***/Billy/Billy 4** *(same as LP)***/Turkey** *(instrumental and vocal chorus, very brief)***/Turkey** *(instrumental with harmonica)***/Turkey** *(instrumental with harmonica)***/Turkey #2 and Tom Turkey (Billy)/Billy Surrenders** *(instrumental)***/Cantina Theme** *(with vocal)***/Cantina Theme** *(with vocal)***/Cantina Theme** *(with vocal)***/Goodbye Holly/Peco's Blues** *(instrumental)***/Peco's Blues** *(instrumental)***/Billy** *(with two false starts)*

(2/73) Burbank, California—*Pat Garrett and Billy the Kid* outtakes, Burbank Studios
Knockin' on Heaven's Door/Sweet Amarillo/Knockin' on Heaven's Door *(just chorus portion in movie)***/Final Theme** *(portion in movie and LP)***/Hey Momma Rock Me/Billy/Billy/Instrumental/Instrumental** *(blues progression)***/Ride, Ride, Ride**

(early '73) GUEST ARTIST—*Chronicles,* Booker T and Priscilla, A&M ST-4413, Malibu, California (released '73)
The Crippled Crow *(Dylan—harmonica)*

(7–8/73) GUEST ARTIST—*Barry Goldberg,* Atco SD-7040, Muscle Shoals, Alabama (released '73)
Stormy Weather Cowboy/It's Not the Spotlight/Silver Moon/Minstrel Show/Big City Woman *(Dylan—V, P; producer)*

(11/5, 6, 9/73) ***Planet Waves***—Asylum 7E-1003, Los Angeles, California, Village Recorders (released 1/74)
On a Night Like This/Going, Going, Gone/Tough Mama/Hazel/Something There Is about You/Forever Young/Forever Young/Dirge/You Angel You/Never Say Goodbye/Wedding Song
Note: Album was reissued in 4/82 by Columbia as #PC-37637.

('74) **Tour**—USA and Canada, with The Band: Robbie Robertson—G, Rick Danko—B, Richard Manuel—P, Garth Hudson—K, Levon Helm—D

JAN
3 Chicago, Illinois: Chicago Stadium
4 Chicago, Illinois: Chicago Stadium
6 Philadelphia, Pennsylvania (afternoon): The Spectrum
6 Philadelphia, Pennsylvania (evening): The Spectrum
7 Philadelphia, Pennsylvania: The Spectrum
9 Toronto, Ontario: Maple Leaf Gardens
10 Toronto, Ontario: Maple Leaf Gardens
11 Montreal, Quebec: The Forum
12 Montreal, Quebec: The Forum
14 Boston, Massachusetts (afternoon): Boston Garden
14 Boston, Massachusetts (evening): Boston Garden
15 Largo, Maryland: Capitol Centre
16 Largo, Maryland: Capitol Centre
17 Charlotte, North Carolina: The Coliseum
19 Hollywood, Florida (afternoon): Sportatorium
19 Hollywood, Florida (evening): Sportatorium
21 Atlanta, Georgia: The Omni
22 Atlanta, Georgia: The Omni
23 Memphis, Tennessee: Mid-South Coliseum
25 Forth Worth, Texas: Tarrant County Convention Center
26 Houston, Texas (afternoon): Hofheinz Pavilion
26 Houston, Texas (evening): Hofheinz Pavilion
28 Uniondale, New York: Nassau Coliseum
29 Uniondale, New York: Nassau Coliseum
30 New York, New York: Madison Square Garden
31 New York, New York (afternoon): Madison Square Garden
31 New York, New York: Madison Square Garden

FEB
2 Ann Arbor, Michigan: University of Michigan, Chrysler Arena
3 Bloomington, Indiana: University of Indiana, Assembly Hall
4 St. Louis, Missouri (afternoon): St. Louis Arena
4 St. Louis, Missouri (evening): St. Louis Arena
6 Denver, Colorado (afternoon): Denver Coliseum
6 Denver, Colorado (evening): Denver Coliseum
9 Seattle, Washington (afternoon): Seattle Coliseum
9 Seattle, Washington (evening): Seattle Coliseum
11 Oakland, California (afternoon): Oakland Coliseum
11 Oakland, California (evening): Oakland Coliseum
13 Inglewood, California: The Forum
14 Inglewood, California (afternoon): The Forum
14 Inglewood, California (evening): The Forum

(1–2/74) ***Before the Flood***—Asylum AB-201 (released 6/74)

Most Likely You Go Your Way/Lay Lady Lay/Rainy Day Women Nos. 12 and 35/Knockin' on Heaven's Door/It Ain't Me Babe/Ballad of a Thin Man/Don't Think Twice, It's Alright/Just Like a Woman/It's Alright Ma/All along the Watchtower/Highway 61/Like a Rolling Stone/Blowin' in the Wind

Note: "Most Likely You Go Your Way," "It Ain't Me Babe," "Don't Think Twice, It's Alright," "Just Like a Woman," "It's Alright Ma," "Highway 61," from 2/14/74 (evening); "Lay Lady Lay," "Rainy Day Women Nos. 12 and 35," "Like a Rolling Stone" from 2/13/74;

"Ballad of a Thin Man," "All along the Watchtower" from 2/14/74 (afternoon); "Knockin' on Heaven's Door" from 1/30/74. Additional from master tape: "Hollis Brown" from 1/31/74 (afternoon); "Highway 61" from 2/9/74 (evening).

(5/9/74) New York, New York—Madison Square Garden, Chilean benefit

Deportees *(with Arlo Guthrie)*/**North Country Blues/Spanish Is the Loving Tongue/Blowin' in the Wind** *(with ensemble)*

(9, 12/74) *Blood on the Tracks*—Columbia PC-33235 (released 1/75)

Tangled Up in Blue/Simple Twist of Fate/You're a Big Girl Now/Idiot Wind/You're Gonna Make Me Lonesome When You Go/Meet Me in the Morning/Lily, Rosemary and the Jack of Hearts/If You See Her, Say Hello/Shelter from the Storm/ Buckets of Rain

Note: "Simple Twist of Fate," "You're a Big Girl Now," "You're Gonna Make Me Lonesome When You Go," "Meet Me in the Morning," "Shelter from the Storm," "Buckets of Rain" all recorded 9/74 in New York at A&R Studios; with Tony Brown—B, Buddy Cage—Pedal Steel, Paul Griffin—D, Barry Kornfeld—G, Eric Weissberg and Deliverance. All others recorded 12/74 in Minneapolis at Sound 80; with Chris Weber—Twelve-string G, Kevin Odegard—G, Greg Imhoffer—K, Bill Peterson—B, Bill Berg—D.

(9/74) OUTTAKES—found on original promo disks

Tangled Up in Blue/You're a Big Girl Now/Idiot Wind/Lily, Rosemary and the Jack of Hearts/If You See Her, Say Hello *(above recorded in New York at A&R Studios)*

(3/10/75) Los Angeles, California—Mary Travers interview, syndicated radio broadcast (4/20/75)

(3/23/75) San Francisco, California—Kezar Stadium, SNACK Benefit, broadcast live over K101-FM

Are You Ready for the Country/Ain't That a Lotta Love/ Looking for a Love/Loving You/I Want You/The Weight/ Helpless/Knockin' on Heaven's Door/Will the Circle Be Unbroken *(on vocals, harmonica, guitar and piano; with Neil Young—G and V, Ben Keith—Pedal Steel, Tim Drummond—B, Rick Danko—B, Garth Hudson—K, Levon Helm—D)*

Note: Dylan sang into a dead microphone.

(7/3/75) New York, New York—The Other End

Pretty Boy Floyd/How Long/Abandoned Love *(on vocals and guitar with Jack Elliott)*

(summer '75) New York, New York—home of Bob Dylan

Message Song *(telephone-answering-machine message)*

('75) GUEST ARTIST—*Comin' Back for More,* David Blue, Asylum 7E-1403

Who Love (If Not You Love) *(on harmonica)*

(7–10/75) *Desire*—Columbia PC-33893 (released 1/76)

Hurricane/Isis/Mozambique/One More Cup of Coffee/Oh,

Sister/Joey/Romance in Durango/Black Diamond Bay/Sara

Outtakes:

Hurricane/Seven Days/Romance in Durango *(unedited version, found on quadrophonic disks)*

(7–10/75) SINGLE RELEASE—Columbia 3-10454 (released 11/76)

Rita May *(flip side of "Stuck Inside of Mobile," from PC-33893)*

(9/10/75) (V) Chicago, Illinois—"The World of John Hammond," WTTW-TV (broadcast 12/13/75)

Hurricane/Oh, Sister/Simple Twist of Fate *(with Rob Stoner—B, Scarlett Rivera—V, Howie Wyeth—D)*

(10/75) GUEST ARTIST—*Songs for the New Depression,* Bette Midler, Atlantic SD-18155, recorded in New York at Secret Sound Studios (released 1/76)

Buckets of Rain

Note: Alternate take has also surfaced.

(75–76) **Tour**—"Rolling Thunder Revue," with Joan Baez—V and G, Ronee Blakely—V, Bobby Neuwirth—G and V, Rob Stoner—B, Scarlett Rivera—Violin, T-Bone Burnett—G and V, Roger McGuinn—G and V, Steven Soles—G and V, Mick Ronson—G, David Mansfield—Violin/Dobro/Pedal Steel/and Mandolin, Howie Wyeth—D, Luther Rix—D, Robbie Robertson—G (12/8/75), Kinky Friedman—V (1/25/76), Ringo Starr—D (1/25/76)

OCT

(INC) 30 Plymouth, Massachusetts: Memorial Auditorium
31 Plymouth, Massachusetts: Memorial Auditorium

NOV

(*) 1 North Dartmouth, Massachusetts: Southeastern Massachusetts University
(*) 2 Lowell, Massachusetts: Lowell Technical University
4 Providence, Rhode Island (afternoon): Civic Center
4 Providence, Rhode Island (evening): Civic Center
6 Springfield, Massachusetts (afternoon): Civic Center
(INC) 6 Springfield, Massachusetts (evening): Civic Center
(INC) 8 Burlington, Vermont: University of Vermont, Patrick Gymansium
(INC) 9 Durham, New Hampshire: University of New Hampshire
11 Westbury, Connecticut: Palace Theatre
13 New Haven, Connecticut (afternoon): Coliseum
13 New Haven, Connecticut (evening): Coliseum
(*) 15 Niagara Falls, New York (afternoon): Convention Center
15 Niagara Falls, New York (evening): Convention Center
17 Rochester, New York (afternoon): War Memorial Coliseum
17 Rochester, New York (evening): War Memorial Coliseum
19 Worcester, Massachusetts: Civic Auditorium
20 Cambridge, Massachusetts: Harvard Square Theatre
21 Boston, Massachusetts (afternoon): Music Hall
21 Boston, Massachusetts (evening): Music Hall
22 Waltham, Massachusetts: Shapiro Gym, Brandeis University
24 Hartford, Connecticut: Civic Center
(*) 26 Augusta, Maine: Civic Center

27 Bangor, Maine: Municipal Auditorium
(INC) 29 Quebec City, Quebec: Coliseum
DEC 1 Toronto, Ontario: Maple Leaf Gardens
2 Toronto, Ontario: Maple Leaf Gardens
4 Montreal, Quebec: The Forum
8 New York, New York: Madison Square Garden, "Night of the Hurricane"
JAN 25 Houston, Texas: Houston Astrodome, "Hurricane II"

(10–12/75) (V) *Renaldo & Clara*—film, directed by Bob Dylan (released 1/78)

(10–12/75) (V) SONG VIDEO
Tangled Up in Blue *(directed by Bob Dylan, taken from* **Renaldo and Clara,** *released 1/86, used as promotion for "Biograph")*

(10–12/75) 12″ EP RELEASE—Columbia AS-422 (released 2/78); "4 Songs from *Renaldo and Clara*" (promo release only)
People Get Ready/Never Let Me Go/Isis/It Ain't Me Babe
Note: "Isis" officially released (4/84) as the flip side of Columbia single 38-04425.

(12/7/75) (V) (INC) Clinton, New Jersey—Clinton State Prison, with the Rolling Thunder Revue; two local TV news broadcasts (ABC and CBS)
Blowin' in the Wind *(partial);* **Hurricane** *(partial)*

(4/76) GUEST ARTIST—*No Reason To Cry,* Eric Clapton, RSO Polydor 1-3004, recorded in Los Angeles, California, at Shangri-La Studios (released 9/76)
Sign Language *(on vocals)*

('76) **Tour**—"Rolling Thunder Revue," with Joan Baez—G and V, Bobby Neuwirth—G and V, Rob Stoner—B, Scarlett Rivera—Violin, T-Bone Burnett—G and V, Roger McGuinn—G and V, Steven Soles—G and V, Mick Ronson—G, David Mansfield—Violin/Dobro/Pedal Steel/ and Mandolin, Howie Wyeth—D, Gary Burke—D
APRIL 18 Lakeland, Florida: Civic Center
20 St. Petersburg, Florida: Bay Front Civic Center
21 Tampa, Florida: Curtis Nixon Convention Center
22 Clearwater, Florida (afternoon): Belleview Biltmore Hotel
(INC) 22 Clearwater, Florida (evening): Belleview Biltmore Hotel
23 Orlando, Florida: Sports Stadium
25 Gainesville, Florida: University of Florida
(INC) 27 Tallahassee, Florida: Florida State University
28 Pensacola, Florida: University of West Florida
29 Mobile, Alabama (afternoon): Municipal Auditorium, Expo Hall
29 Mobile, Alabama (evening): Municipal Auditorium, Expo Hall
MAY 1 Hattiesburg, Mississippi: Reid Green Coliseum
(*) 3 New Orleans, Louisiana (afternoon): The Warehouse
3 New Orleans, Louisiana (evening): The Warehouse
(INC) 4 Baton Rouge, Louisiana: Louisiana State University Assembly Center

8 Houston, Texas: Hofheinz Pavilion
(*) 10 Corpus Christi, Texas: Memorial Coliseum
(INC) 11 San Antonio, Texas: Municipal Auditorium
(*) 12 Austin, Texas: Municipal Auditorium
(*) 15 Gatesville, Texas: State School for Boys
16 Fort Worth, Texas: Tarrant County Convention Center
18 Oklahoma City, Oklahoma: State Fair Arena
(INC) 19 Wichita, Kansas: Henry Levitt Arena
23 Fort Collins, Colorado: Hughs Stadium
(*) 24 Salt Lake City, Utah: The Salt Palace

(4/76) Clearwater, Florida—Belleview Biltmore Hotel, rehearsal

Just Like Tom Thumb's Blues/Rainin' in My Heart/Lay Lady Lay/One More Cup of Coffee/It Takes a Lot to Laugh/Hollis Brown/Hold Me/Mozambique/Idiot Wind/One More Cup of Coffee/Shelter from the Storm/Just Like Tom Thumb's Blues/Isis/Rita May/I Threw It All Away

(4/22/76) (V) Clearwater, Florida—Belleview Biltmore Hotel, NBC-TV Special (never broadcast)

Mr. Tambourine Man/The Times They Are A-Changin'/Blowin' in the Wind/I Dreamed I Saw St. Augustine/Diamonds and Rust/When I Paint My Masterpiece/Like a Rolling Stone/Isis/Just Like a Woman/Knockin' on Heaven's Door/Lay Lady Lay

(5/23/76) (V) Fort Collins, Colorado—Hughs Stadium, "Hard Rain," NBC-TV (broadcast 9/14/76)

A Hard Rain's A-Gonna Fall/Blowin' in the Wind/Deportees/I Pity the Poor Immigrant/Shelter from the Storm/Maggie's Farm/One Too Many Mornings/Mozambique/Idiot Wind/Knockin' on Heaven's Door

(5/16–23/76) *Hard Rain*—Columbia PC-34349 (released 9/76)

Maggie's Farm/One Too Many Mornings/Stuck Inside of Mobile/Oh, Sister/Lay Lady Lay/Shelter from the Storm/You're a Big Girl Now/I Threw It All Away/Idiot Wind

Note: "Stuck Inside of Mobile," "Oh, Sister," "Lay Lady Lay," "I Threw It All Away" from 5/16/76; "Maggie's Farm," "One Too Many Mornings," "Shelter from the Storm," "You're a Big Girl Now," "Idiot Wind" from 5/23/76.

(11/25/76) (V) San Francisco, California—Winterland Palace, "The Last Waltz" (band concert)

Baby, Let Me Follow You Down/Hazel/I Don't Believe You/Forever Young/Baby, Let Me Follow You Down/I Shall Be Released *(with entire cast)*

Note: All songs, except "Hazel," released on Warner Bros. 3WS-3146 (4/78) and theatrically released in a film directed by Martin Scorsese (film released 4/78, CBS/FOX Home Video #4567).

(c. 1/77) GUEST ARTIST—*Death of a Ladies Man,* Leonard Cohen, Warner Bros. BS-3125 (released '77)

Don't Go Home with Your Hard On *(on vocals)*

Note: Recorded in Los Angeles, California studios. Dylan is credited on vocals but cannot be heard.

(12/30/77) Santa Monica, California—Rundown Studios, rehearsal
It's All Over Now, Baby Blue/Blowin' in the Wind/Maggie's Farm/Like a Rolling Stone/The Man in Me/To Ramona/Most Likely You Go Your Way/Simple Twist of Fate/Leopard-Skin Pillbox Hat/If Not for You/I Threw It All Away/I'll Be Your Baby

(early '78) Santa Monica, California—Ron Rosenbaum interview for *Playboy* magazine (published 3/78); tape is parts 12 and 13 of 13.

(1/27/78) Santa Monica, California—Rundown Studios, rehearsal
All I Really Want to Do/Absolutely Sweet Marie/Tomorrow Is a Long Time/All I Really Want To Do/The Times They Are A-Changin'/Woke Up This Morning/Shelter from the Storm

(1/30/78) Santa Monica, California—Rundown Studios, rehearsal
I'll Be Your Baby Tonight/The Times They Are A-Changin'/If You See Her, Say Hello/The Man in Me/I Don't Believe You/Tomorrow Is a Long Time/You're a Big Girl Now/Knockin' on Heaven's Door/It's Alright Ma/Forever Young

(1/78) Santa Monica, California—Rundown Studios, rehearsal
Repossession Blues/Sooner or Later/Girl from the North Country

(1/78) Santa Monica, California—Rundown Studios, rehearsal
You're Gonna Make Me Lonesome When You Go/Simple Twist of Fate/Going, Going, Gone

(1–2/78) Santa Monica, California—Rundown Studios, rehearsal
I Think We'd Better Talk This Over/Coming from the Heart/I Threw It All Away/Maggie's Farm/Ballad of a Thin Man/Simple Twist of Fate/To Ramona/If You See Her, Say Hello/I Don't Believe You

('78) **Tour**—Far East and Australia, with Billy Cross—G, Rob Stoner—B, Alan Pasqua—K, David Mansfield—Violin and Mandolin, Steven Soles—G and BV, Steven Douglas—Horns, Bobbye Hall—Perc, Ian Wallace—D, Debbie Dye—BV, Helena Springs—BV, Jo Ann Harris—BV

FEB
20 Tokyo, Japan: Nippon Budokan Hall
21 Tokyo, Japan: Nippon Budokan Hall
23 Tokyo, Japan: Nippon Budokan Hall
24 Osaka, Japan: Matsushita Denki Taiikukon
(INC) 25 Osaka, Japan: Matsushita Denki Taiikukon
26 Osaka, Japan: Matsushita Denki Taiikukon
28 Tokyo, Japan: Nippon Budokan Hall

MARCH
1 Tokyo, Japan: Nippon Budokan Hall
2 Tokyo, Japan: Nippon Budokan Hall
3 Tokyo, Japan: Nippon Budokan Hall
4 Tokyo, Japan: Nippon Budokan Hall
9 Auckland, New Zealand: Western Springs Stadium
12 Brisbane, Australia: Festival Hall

13 Brisbane, Australia: Festival Hall
(INC) 14 Brisbane, Australia: Festival Hall
(INC) 15 Brisbane, Australia: Festival Hall
Note: An incomplete soundboard of a show has surfaced; it is purported to be 3/15.
18 Adelaide, Australia: Westlakes Stadium
(INC) 20 Melbourne, Australia: Myer Music Bowl
21 Melbourne, Australia: Myer Music Bowl
22 Melbourne, Australia: Myer Music Bowl
(*) 25 Perth, Australia: Entertainment Center
(*) 27 Perth, Australia: Entertainment Center
(*) 28 Perth, Australia: Entertainment Center
Note: An incomplete Perth show has surfaced; it is unknown which Perth show it actually is.
APRIL 1 Sydney, Australia: Sportsground

(2–3/78) (V) Japanese TV—press conference, Honeda International Airport (2/19/78); snippets of performances

(2/28, 3/1/78) *At Budokan*—CBS Sony 40 AP-1100-1 (released 11/78 Japan), Columbia PC2-36067 (released 5/79 USA)

Mr. Tambourine Man/Shelter from the Storm/Love Minus Zero; No Limit/Ballad of a Thin Man/Don't Think Twice, It's Alright/Maggie's Farm/One More Cup of Coffee/Like a Rolling Stone/I Shall Be Released/Is Your Love in Vain?/Going, Going, Gone/Blowin' in the Wind/Just Like a Woman/Oh, Sister/Simple Twist of Fate/All Along the Watchtower/I Want You/All I Really Want to Do/Knockin' on Heaven's Door/It's Alright Ma/Forever Young/The Times They Are A-Changin'

Note: All songs recorded 3/1/78 except "Shelter from the Storm," "Love Minus Zero; No Limit," "Don't Think Twice," "Simple Twist of Fate," "It's Alright Ma," "Forever Young," "The Times They Are A-Changin' " (recorded 2/28/78)

(4/1/78) Sydney, Australia—Karen Hughes interview

('78) Julie Orange interview

(4/78) *Street Legal*—Columbia JC-35453 (released 6/78)

Changing of the Guards/New Pony/No Time to Think/Baby, Please Stop Crying/Is Your Love in Vain?/Señor/True Love Tends to Forget/We Better Talk This Over/Where Are You Tonight?

('78) Tour (continued)—USA and Europe, with Jerry Scheff—B, Billy Cross—G, Alan Pasqua—K, Ian Wallace—D, Steven Soles—G, Steven Douglas—Horns, David Mansfield—Violin/Mandolin/Pedal Steel, Bobbye Hall—Perc, Carolyn Dennis—BV, Jo Ann Harris—BV, Helena Springs—BV

JUNE 1–7 Los Angeles, California: Universal Amphitheatre
15 London, England: Earl's Court
16 London, England: Earl's Court
17 London, England: Earl's Court
18 London, England: Earl's Court

19 London, England: Earl's Court
20 London, England: Earl's Court
23 Rotterdam, the Netherlands: Feijenoord Stadium
26 Dortmund, West Germany: Westfallenhalle
27 Dortmund, West Germany: Westfallenhalle
29 West Berlin, West Germany: Deutschlandhalle

JULY
1 Nuremburg, West Germany: Zeppelinfeld
(SC) 3 Paris, France: Pavillon de Paris
(SC) 4 Paris, France: Pavillon de Paris
(SC) 5 Paris, France: Pavillon de Paris
(SC) 6 Paris, France: Pavillon de Paris
(SC) 8 Paris, France: Pavillon de Paris
11 Göteborg, Sweden: Scandinavium Hockey Stadium
(SC) 12 Göteborg, Sweden: Scandinavium Hockey Stadium
15 Hampshire, England: Blackbushe Aerodrome

(7/10/78) (V) Copenhagen, Denmark—Kastrup Airport, Mette Fugl interview, TV (broadcast 7/12/78)

(7/11/78) (V) Göteburg, Sweden—Stuttgart Airport, TV broadcast, brief interview

('78) **Tour (continued)**—USA and Canada, with Jerry Scheff—B, Billy Cross—G, Alan Pasqua—K, Ian Wallace—D, Steven Soles—G, Steven Douglas—Horns, Bobbye Hall—Perc, David Mansfield—Violin/Mandolin/Pedal Steel, Carolyn Dennis—BV, Jo Ann Harris—BV, Helena Springs—BV

SEPT
15 Augusta, Maine: Civic Center
16 Portland, Maine: Cumberland Civic Center
(SC) 17 New Haven, Connecticut: Veterans Memorial Coliseum
19 Montreal, Quebec: The Forum
20 Boston, Massachusetts: Boston Garden
(SC) 22 Syracuse, New York: War Memorial Auditorium
(INC) 23 Rochester, New York: War Memorial Auditorium
24 Binghampton, New York: Broome County Arena
26 Springfield, Massachusetts: Civic Center
27 Uniondale, New York: Nassau Coliseum
29 New York, New York: Madison Square Garden
30 New York, New York: Madison Square Garden

OCT
3 Norfolk, Virginia: Scope Arena
4 Baltimore, Maryland: Civic Center
5 Largo, Maryland: Capitol Centre
6 Philadelphia, Pennsylvania: The Spectrum
7 Providence, Rhode Island: Civic Center
9 Buffalo, New York: Memorial Auditorium
12 Toronto, Ontario: Maple Leaf Gardens
13 Detroit, Michigan: Olympia Stadium
14 Terre Haute, Indiana: The Holman Center
15 Cincinnati, Ohio: Riverfront Coliseum
17 Chicago, Illinois: Chicago Stadium
18 Chicago, Illinois: Chicago Stadium
20 Cleveland, Ohio: Richfield Coliseum
21 Toledo, Ohio: Centennial Arena
22 Dayton, Ohio: University of Ohio Arena

(*) 24 Louisville, Kentucky: Freedom Hall
25 Indianapolis, Indiana: Market Square Arena
27 Kalamazoo, Michigan: Wings Stadium
(SC) 28 Carbondale, Illinois: Illinois State University Arena
(SC) 29 St. Louis, Missouri: Checkerdome
31 St. Paul, Minnesota: Civic Center
(11/78) 1 Madison, Wisconsin: Dane Coliseum
3 Kansas City, Missouri: Kemper Arena
(SC) 4 Omaha, Nebraska: Civic Auditorium
(*) 6 Denver, Colorado: McNichols Arena
9 Portland, Oregon: Memorial Coliseum
10 Seattle, Washington: Edmundson Pavillion
11 Vancouver, British Columbia: Pacific Northwest Exhibition Hall
13 Oakland, California: Oakland Coliseum
14 Oakland, California: Oakland Coliseum
15 Inglewood, California: The Forum
(INC) 17 San Diego, California: Sports Arena
(SC) 18 Tempe, Arizona: Arizona State Activity Center
19 Tuscon, Arizona: McKale Center
21 El Paso, Texas: Special Events Arena
23 Norman, Oklahoma: Lloyd Noble Center
24 Ft. Worth, Texas: Tarrent County Convention Center
25 Austin, Texas: Special Events Arena
(INC) 26 Houston, Texas: The Summit
28 Jackson, Mississippi: Coliseum
29 Baton Rouge, Louisiana: LSU University Arena
DEC 1 Memphis, Tennessee: Mid-South Coliseum
(SC) 2 Nashville, Tennessee: Municipal Auditorium
3 Birmingham, Alabama: Jefferson Civic Center
5 Mobile, Alabama: Municipal Auditorium
7 Greensboro, North Carolina: Coliseum
8 Savannah, Georgia: Civic Center
9 Columbia, South Carolina: Coliseum
10 Charlotte, North Carolina: Coliseum
12 Atlanta, Georgia: The Omni
13 Jacksonville, Florida: Coliseum
15 Lakeland, Florida: Civic Center
16 Hollywood, Florida: Sportatorium

(9/15/78) Augusta, Maine—Senator Motel, Matt Damsker interview

(9/15, 16/78) (V) ABC-TV Network News Report—Bob Brown reporting, including footage from Augusta, Maine (9/15/78), Portland, Maine (9/16/78), *Renaldo & Clara* (broadcast 9/30/78)

(9/15, 16, 29/78) (V) Miscellaneous concert footage—shot for ABC-TV, Bob Brown report (never broadcast)
Love Minus Zero/Rolling Stone/Changing of the Guards *(Augusta, Maine, 9/15/78);* **Blowin' in the Wind** *(Portland, Maine, 9/16/78);* **It's Alright Ma/Forever Young** *(New York, New York, 9/29/78)*

(9/22/78) Syracuse, New York—War Memorial Auditorium, Mark Roland interview

(12/2/78) (V) Nashville, Tennessee—Municipal Auditorium
Mr. Tambourine Man/Masters of War/Changing of the Guards *(from RIA-TV, Rome, Italy)*

(12/12/78) Atlanta, Georgia—Interview with Lynne Allen and Tony Paris

(5/79) *Slow Train Coming*—**Columbia FC-36120, Sheffield, Alabama, Muscle Shoals Sound Studios (released 8/79)**
Gotta Serve Somebody/Precious Angel/I Believe in You/Slow Train/Gonna Change My Way of Thinking/Do Right to Me Baby/Do unto Others/Man Gave Names to All the Animals/When He Returns

(5/79) SINGLE RELEASE—Columbia 1-11072 (released 9/79)
Trouble in Mind *(flip side of "Gotta Serve Somebody" and from "Slow Train" sessions)*
Note: Same take with extra verse has surfaced.

(10/20/79) (V) New York, New York—"Saturday Night Live," NBC-TV, broadcast live
Gotta Serve Somebody/I Believe in You/When You Gonna Wake Up (*with* Fred Tackett—G, Spooner Oldham—K, Terry Young—K, Tim Drummond—B, Jim Keltner—D, Helena Springs—BV, Regina Havis—BV, Mona Lisa Young—BV

('79) **Tour**—USA, with Fred Tackett—G, Tim Drummond—B, Jim Keltner—D, Spooner Oldham—K, Terry Young—K, Helena Springs—BV, Regina Havis—BV, Mona Lisa Young—BV

NOV
1 San Francisco, California: Fox-Warfield Theatre
2 San Francisco, California: Fox-Warfield Theatre
3 San Francisco, California: Fox-Warfield Theatre
4 San Francisco, California: Fox-Warfield Theatre
6 San Francisco, California: Fox-Warfield Theatre
7 San Francisco, California: Fox-Warfield Theatre
8 San Francisco, California: Fox-Warfield Theatre
9 San Francisco, California: Fox-Warfield Theatre
10 San Francisco, California: Fox-Warfield Theatre
11 San Francisco, California: Fox-Warfield Theatre
13 San Francisco, California: Fox-Warfield Theatre
14 San Francisco, California: Fox-Warfield Theatre
15 San Francisco, California: Fox-Warfield Theatre
16 San Francisco, California: Fox-Warfield Theatre
18 Santa Monica, California: Civic Auditorium
19 Santa Monica, California: Civic Auditorium
20 Santa Monica, California: Civic Auditorium
21 Santa Monica, California: Civic Auditorium
25 Tempe, Arizona: Gammage Center
26 Tempe, Arizona: Gammage Center
27 San Diego, California: Golden Hall
28 San Diego, California: Golden Hall

DEC (SC)
4 Albuquerque, New Mexico: Convention Center
5 Albuquerque, New Mexico: Convention Center

8 Tuscon, Arizona: Community Center
9 Tuscon, Arizona: Community Center

(12/7/79) Tuscon, Arizona—Bruce Heiman interview, KMEX, Tuscon, Arizona (broadcast 12/8/79)

('80) **Tour**—USA, with Fred Tackett—G, Tim Drummond—B, Jim Keltner—D, Spooner Oldham—K, Terry Young—K, Carolyn Dennis—BV, Regina Peebles—BV, Mona Lisa Young—BV

JAN (*) 11 Portland, Oregon: Paramount Theatre
(*) 12 Portland, Oregon: Paramount Theatre
13 Seattle, Washington: Paramount Theatre
14 Seattle, Washington: Paramount Theatre
(*) 15 Seattle, Washington: Paramount Theatre
16 Portland, Oregon: Paramount Theatre
(*) 17 Spokane, Washington: Rainbow Opera House
(*) 18 Spokane, Washington: Rainbow Opera House
21 Denver, Colorado: Music Hall
(INC) 22 Denver, Colorado: Music Hall
23 Denver, Colorado: Music Hall
25 Omaha, Nebraska: Orpheum Theatre
26 Omaha, Nebraska: Orpheum Theatre
27 Kansas City, Missouri: Uptown Theatre
28 Kansas City, Missouri: Uptown Theatre
29 Kansas City, Missouri: Uptown Theatre
31 Memphis, Tennessee: Orpheum Theatre
FEB 1 Memphis, Tennessee: Orpheum Theatre
2 Birmingham, Alabama: Jefferson Civic Center
3 Birmingham, Alabama: Jefferson Civic Center
5 Knoxville, Tennessee: Civic Auditorium
6 Knoxville, Tennessee: Civic Auditorium
8 Charleston, West Virginia: Municipal Auditorium
9 Charleston, West Virginia: Municipal Auditorium

(2/80) ***Saved*—Columbia FC-36553, Sheffield, Alabama, Muscle Shoals Sound Studios (released 6/80)**

A Satisfied Mind/Saved/Covenant Woman/What Can I Do for You?/Solid Rock/Pressin' On/In the Garden/Saving Grace/Are You Ready?

(2/27/80) (V) Los Angeles, California—Biltmore Hotel, 22nd Annual Grammy Awards

Gotta Serve Somebody *(plus award-acceptance speech)*

('80) GUEST ARTIST—*So You Wanna Go Back to Egypt,* Keith Green, Pretty Good Records (PGR-1) (released '80 via mail order only)

Pledge My Head to Heaven *(on harmonica)*

('80) **Tour (continued)**—Canada and USA, with Fred Tackett–G, Tim Drummond—B, Jim Keltner—D, Spooner Oldham—K, Terry Young—K, Clydie King—BV, Gwen Evans—BV, Mona Lisa Young—BV, Mary Elizabeth Bridget—BV

APRIL (SC) 17 Toronto, Ontario: Massey Hall
18 Toronto, Ontario: Massey Hall
19 Toronto, Ontario: Massey Hall
20 Toronto, Ontario: Massey Hall
(SC) 22 Montreal, Quebec: Theatre St. Denis
23 Montreal, Quebec: Theatre St. Denis
24 Montreal, Quebec: Theatre St. Denis
25 Montreal, Quebec: Theatre St. Denis
27 Albany, New York: Palace Theatre
28 Albany, New York: Palace Theatre
30 Buffalo, New York: Kleinhans Music Hall
(5/80) MAY 1 Buffalo, New York: Kleinhans Music Hall
2 Worcester, Massachusetts: Worcester Auditorium
3 Worcester, Massachusetts: Worcester Auditorium
4 Syracuse, New York: Landmark Hall
5 Syracuse, New York: Landmark Hall
7 Hartford, Connecticut: Bushnell Memorial Theatre
8 Hartford, Connecticut: Bushnell Memorial Theatre
9 Portland, Maine: City Hall
(*) 10 Portland, Maine: City Hall
11 Providence, Rhode Island: Ocean State Performing Arts Center
(*) 12 Providence, Rhode Island: Ocean State Performing Arts Center
(*) 14 Pittsburgh, Pennsylvania: Stanley Theatre
15 Pittsburgh, Pennsylvania: Stanley Theatre
16 Pittsburgh, Pennsylvania: Stanley Theatre
17 Akron, Ohio: Civic Theatre
18 Akron, Ohio: Civic Theatre
20 Columbus, Ohio: Veterans Memorial Auditorium
21 Dayton, Ohio: Memorial Hall

(5/15/80) Pittsburgh, Pennsylvania—Hilton Hotel, Pat Crosby interview, KDKA-TV

(10/80) Santa Monica, California—Rundown Studios

Blowin' in the Wind/Gotta Serve Somebody/Mr. Tambourine Man/Slow Train

Note: The versions of these songs are available only as snippets that were broadcast in an ad for the upcoming tour. The ads were handled by Bill Graham.

('80) **Tour (continued)**—USA, "A Musical Retrospective," with Fred Tackett—G, Tim Drummond—B, Jim Keltner—D, Willie Smith—K, Clydie King—BV, Carolyn Dennis—BV, Regina McCreary—BV

NOV 9 San Francisco, California: Fox-Warfield Theatre
10 San Francisco, California: Fox-Warfield Theatre
11 San Francisco, California: Fox-Warfield Theatre
12 San Francisco, California: Fox-Warfield Theatre
13 San Francisco, California: Fox-Warfield Theatre
15 San Francisco, California: Fox-Warfield Theatre
16 San Francisco, California: Fox-Warfield Theatre
17 San Francisco, California: Fox-Warfield Theatre
18 San Francisco, California: Fox-Warfield Theatre
(SC) 19 San Francisco, California: Fox-Warfield Theatre
21 San Francisco, California: Fox-Warfield Theatre

22 San Francisco, California: Fox-Warfield Theatre
24 Tuscon, Arizona: Community Center
26 San Diego, California: Golden Hall
29 Seattle, Washington: Paramount Theatre
30 Seattle, Washington: Paramount Theatre
DEC 2 Salem, Oregon: Armory
3 Portland, Oregon: Paramount Theatre
4 Portland, Oregon: Paramount Theatre

(11/18/80) San Francisco, California—Fox-Warfield Theatre, Paul Vincent interview, KMEL-FM (broadcast 11/19/80)

(11/21/80) San Diego, California—Ernest Bladden interview via telephone, KPRI-FM (broadcast 11/25/80)

(5/81) *Shot of Love*—Columbia TC-37496 (released 8/81)

Shot of Love/Heart of Mine/Property of Jesus/Lenny Bruce/ Watered-Down Love/The Groom's Still Waiting at the Altar/ Dead Man, Dead Man/In the Summertime/Trouble/Every Grain of Sand

Note: "The Groom's Still Waiting at the Altar" was not on original pressing but was added to later pressings.

(5/81) OUTTAKES

Watered-Down Love ***(same as album with extra verse)*****/Heart of Mine/Yonder Comes Sin/I Need a Woman/Angelina/Mystery Train**

Note: Acetates contain extra snippets and continuation of songs with no fadeouts. Some mixes are different as well.

(5/81) SINGLE RELEASE—CBS A-1406 (released 8/81)

Let It Be Me

Note: This was the flip side of "Heart of Mine" and released only in Europe.

(5/81) SINGLE RELEASE—Columbia 18-02510 (released 9/81)

The Groom's Still Waiting at the Altar

Note: This was the flip side of "Heart of Mine" and released only in the United States. It was added to later pressings of Columbia TC-37496.

('81) Tour—USA, with Fred Tackett—G, Steve Ripley—G, Tim Drummond—B, Willie Smith—K, Jim Keltner—D, Clydie King—BV, Regina Havis—BV, Carolyn Dennis—BV, Madelyn Quebec—BV

JUNE 10 Elgin, Illinois: Poplar Creek Music Theatre
(SC) 11 Clarkston, Michigan: Pine Knob Music Theatre
(SC) 12 Clarkston, Michigan: Pine Knob Music Theatre
(SC) 14 Columbia, Maryland: Merriweather Post Pavilion

(6/15/81) London, England—Tim Blackmore interview, Capitol Radio

Note: This was a telephone interview. Dylan was in the United States; Blackmore was in London.

(6/20/81) London, England—"Rock On," Paul Gambaccini interview, Radio 1

Note: This was a telephone interview. Dylan was in the United States; Gambaccini was in London.

(6/21/81) Toulouse, France—Yves Bigot interview, Europe Radio 1 (broadcast 6/22 and 23/81)

(7/2/81) London, England—Dave Herman interview (broadcast WNEW-FM, New York, New York, 7/27/81; later released on Columbia Promo AS-1259)

(7/13/81) Travemunde, West Germany—Kurhaushotel, press conference

('81) **Tour (continued)**—Europe, with Fred Tackett—G, Steve Ripley—G, Tim Drummond—B, Willie Smith—K, Jim Keltner—D, Clydie King—BV, Regina Havis—BV, Carolyn Dennis—BV, Madelyn Quebec—BV

JUNE
21 Toulouse, France: Stade Municipal des Minimes
23 Paris, France: Stade Yves-du-Manoir
26 London, England: Earl's Court
27 London, England: Earl's Court
28 London, England: Earl's Court
29 London, England: Earl's Court
30 London, England: Earl's Court

JULY
1 London, England: Earl's Court
4 Birmingham, England: National Exhibition Centre
5 Birmingham, England: National Exhibition Centre
8 Stockholm, Sweden: Johanneshovs Isstadium
9 Oslo, Norway: Drammenhallen
10 Oslo, Norway: Drammenhallen
12 Copenhagen, Denmark: Brondbyhallen
14 Bad Segeberg, West Germany: Freilicut Theatre
15 Bad Segeberg, West Germany: Freilicut Theatre
17 Loreley, West Germany: Freilichtbuhne
18 Mannheim, West Germany: Eisstadion
19 Munich, West Germany: Olympiahalle
20 Munich, West Germany: Olympiahalle
21 Vienna, Austria: Stadthalle
23 Basel, Switzerland: St. Jacobshalle Sporthalle
25 Avignon, France: Palace des Sports

(7/22/81) (V) Vienna, Austria—Andreas Forst interview, on a street (broadcast ORF-TV, Channel 2, Austria, 1/8/82)

('81) **Tour (continued)**—USA and Canada, with Al Kooper—K, Fred Tackett—G, Steve Ripley—G, Tim Drummond—B, Jim Keltner—D, Clydie King—BV, Madeline Quebec—BV, Regina McCrary—BV

OCT
16 Milwaukee, Wisconsin: The Mecca Auditorium
17 Milwaukee, Wisconsin: The Mecca Auditorium
18 Madison, Wisconsin: Dane County Coliseum
19 Merriville, Indiana: Holiday Star Theatre
21 Boston, Massachusetts: The Orpheum
(SC) 23 Philadelphia, Pennsylvania: The Spectrum

24 College Park, Pennsylvania: Pennsylvania State University
25 Bethlehem, Pennsylvania: Lehigh University
27 East Rutherford, New Jersey: Brendan Byrne Arena
29 Toronto, Ontario: Maple Leaf Gardens
30 Montreal, Quebec: The Forum
31 Kitchener, Ontario: Arena
NOV 2 Ottawa, Ontario: Civic Center
4 Cincinnati, Ohio: Music Hall
5 Cincinnati, Ohio: Music Hall
6 West Lafayette, Indiana: Elliott Music Hall, Perdue University
7 Ann Arbor, Michigan: Hill Auditorium
8 Ann Arbor, Michigan: Hill Auditorium
10 New Orleans, Louisiana: Saenger Theatre
11 New Orleans, Louisiana: Saenger Theatre
12 Houston, Texas: The Summit
14 Nashville, Tennessee: Municipal Auditorium
15 Atlanta, Georgia: Fox Theatre
16 Atlanta, Georgia: Fox Theatre
19 Miami, Florida: Sunrise Musical Theatre
20 Miami, Florida: Sunrise Musical Theatre
21 Lakeland, Florida: Civic Center

(c. 10–11/81) (V) Promotional films—live recordings
Heart of Mine/Shot of Love
Note: Portions have been shown by MTV, ABC-TV, etc.

(11/10/81) SINGLE RELEASE—Columbia 38T-73062 (released 10/89)
Dead Man, Dead Man
Note: Live track from New Orleans, Louisiana, at Saenger Theatre. Flip side of "Everything Is Broken" (cassette single).

(2/23/82) Santa Monica, California—Rundown Studios, Allen Ginsberg recordings, with Allen Ginsberg—V and Harmonium, Peter Orlovsky—V, David Mansfield—G/P/Dobro/and Mandolin, Jim Keltner—D, Steven Taylor—G/B/and Organ
Meditation Rock/Airplane Blues/Airplane Blues/Capitol Air *(Allen Ginsberg—V)*/Feeding Them Raspberries to Grow *(Peter Orlovsky—V, Dylan—Bass G)*

(3/15/82) (V) New York, New York—Hilton Hotel, Songwriters Hall of Fame Dinner, acceptance speech and comments.
Note: Portions were broadcast on WABC-TV, New York, New York, and "Good Morning, America," ABC-TV network.

(6/6/82) (V) Pasadena, California—Rose Bowl, "Peace Sunday"
With God on Our Side/Pirate Looks at Forty/Blowin' in the Wind/*(with Joan Baez)*

(2/16/83) New York, New York—Lone Star Cafe
Your Cheatin' Heart/Doin' the Hand Jive/Blues, Stay Away from Me/Ain't No More Cane/Goin' Down *(on G and V; with Levon Helm, and Rick Danko as a guest during late show of their performance)*

(c. 8/83) OUTTAKES—from *INFIDELS*

When the Night Comes Fallin' from the Sky/This Was My Love/Sweetheart Like You

Note: Many takes, false starts, etc. Above were definitely recorded before the finished album.

(8/83) *Infidels*—Columbia QC-38819 (released 11/83)

Jokerman/Sweetheart Like You/Neighborhood Bully/License to Kill/Man of Peace/Union Sundown/I and I/Don't Fall Apart on Me Tonight

(c. '83) (V) Promotional films—shot by the Maysle Brothers during recording sessions for *Infidels* and never released. Audio track is the same as album

License to Kill/Don't Fall Apart on Me Tonight

(c. '83) (V) SONG VIDEO—directed by Mark Robinson, released late '83 as promotion for *Infidels*

Sweetheart Like You

(2/10/84) (V) SONG VIDEO—directed by George Lois and Jerry Cotts, released 3/27/84 as promotion for *Infidels*

Jokerman

(8/83) OUTTAKES—from *Infidels*

Jokerman/Don't Fall Apart on Me Tonight/Man of Peace/Blind Willie McTell/Sweetheart Like You/Clean-Cut Kid/Julius and Ethel/Death Is Not the End *(later released on Columbia OC-40957)*/Foot of Pride/Someone's Got a Hold of My Heart/Lord, Protect My Child/Union Sundown/Tell Me/Blind Willie McTell

(8/83) SINGLE RELEASE—CBS A-3916 (released 10/83)

Angels Flying Too Close to the Ground

Note: This was the flip side of "Union Sundown" and was released only in Europe.

(2/28/84) (V) Los Angeles, California—Shrine Auditorium, 26th Annual Grammy Awards, presentation for Best Song with Stevie Wonder

(3/22/84) (V) New York, New York—"Late Night with David Letterman," NBC-TV, rehearsals before show

I Once Knew a Man/Jokerman/License to Kill/Treat Her Right/Instrumental

(3/22/84) (V) New York, New York—"Late Night with David Letterman," NBC-TV

Don't Start Me Talkin'/License to Kill/Jokerman

Note: Show was recorded about 5:00 P.M. and broadcast later that evening.

(3/27/84) (V) New York, New York—Farkas Studios Limited, Hart Perry interview with John Hammond, "American Masters," WNET-TV (broadcast 8/20/90)

Note: Interview was shot same day as filming for "Jokerman" song video.

(5/23/84) Los Angeles, California—Beverly Theatre, rehearsals

Maggie's Farm/All Along the Watchtower/Just Like a Woman/When You Gonna Wake Up?/Shelter from the Storm/Watered Down Love/Masters of War/Jokerman/Simple Twist of Fate/Man of Peace/I and I/It's All Over Now, Baby Blue/Ballad of a Thin Man/Heart of Mine/Highway 61/(?)/Leopard-Skin Pillbox Hat/It's All Over Now, Baby Blue/(?)/You Were Always on My Mind/Every Grain of Sand/Girl from the North Country

(5/27 or 28/84) Verona, Italy—rehearsals (date and place probable)

Instrumental/Brief Harmonica Instrumental/Harmonica and Instrumental/Vocal—sings off microphone/Instrumental/Miscellaneous Instrumentals/Vocal/Miscellaneous Instrumentals/Almost Done/Almost Done/Almost Done/Miscellaneous Instrumentals/Enough Is Enough/Miscellaneous Instrumentals/Dirty Lies/Why Do I Have to Choose?/To Each His Own/Instrumental/Jokerman/All Along the Watchtower/Just Like a Woman/Highway 61/I and I/Girl from the North Country *(incomplete)*/Shelter from the Storm/Shelter from the Storm/License to Kill/Ballad of a Thin Man/When You Gonna Wake Up?/To Ramona

('84) Tour—Europe, with Mick Taylor—G, Greg Sutton—B, Ian McLagen—K, Colin Allen—D, Carlos Santana—G (on encores)

MAY
28 Verona, Italy: Arena di Verona
31 Hamburg, West Germany: St. Pauli Stadion

JUNE
2 Basel, Switzerland: St. Jacobstadion
3 Munich, West Germany: Olympiastadion
4 Rotterdam, The Netherlands: Sportpaleis
6 Rotterdam, The Netherlands: Sportpaleis
7 Brussels, Belgium: Schaerbeek Stadion
9 Göteburg, Sweden: Ullevi Stadium
10 Copenhagen, Denmark: Idreats Parken
11 Offenbach, West Germany: Stadion Bieberer Berg
13 West Berlin, West Germany: Waldbühne
14 Vienna, Austria: Stadthalle
16 Cologne, West Germany: Mungersdorfer Stadion
17 Nice, France: Stade de L'Ouest
19 Rome, Italy: Palaeur
20 Rome, Italy: Palaeur
21 Rome, Italy: Palaeur
24 Milan, Italy: San Siro Stadion
26 Madrid, Spain: Estadio del Rayo Vallecano
28 Barcelona, Spain: Minestadio C.F.
30 Nantes, France: Stade Marcel Saupin

JULY
1 Paris, France: Parc de Sceaux
3 Grenoble, France: Halle Alpexpo
5 Newcastle, England: St. James Park
7 London, England: Wembley Stadium
8 Dublin, Ireland: Slane Castle

(12/84) *Real Live*—Columbia PC-39944 (released 12/84)
Highway 61 Revisited/Maggie's Farm/I and I/License to Kill/It Ain't Me Babe/Tangled Up in Blue/Masters of War/Ballad of a Thin Man/Girl from the North Country/Tombstone Blues
Note: "License to Kill," "Tombstone Blues" from 7/5/84; "Highway 61 Revisited," "Maggie's Farm," "It Ain't Me Babe," "Tangled Up in Blue," "Masters of War," "Ballad of a Thin Man" from 7/7/84; "I and I," "Girl from the North Country" from 7/8/84

(5/28, 29/84) (V) Italian TV coverage of tour—broadcast by RAI-TV
Blowin' in the Wind *(6/19/84)***/The Times They Are A-Changin** *(6/28/84)***/Press Conference** *(5/29/84)***/Blowin' in the Wind** *(5/28/84)*

(5/29/84) Sirmione, Italy—press conference

(5/31/84) Hamburg, West Germany—press conference

(6/17/84) (V) Nice, France—Stade de L'Ouest, French TV report, interview and performance footage
Blowin' in the Wind/Mr. Tambourine Man/Heart of Mine *(from '81 promo film)***/Don't Think Twice**

(6/28/84) (V) Barcelona, Spain—Minestadio C.F., "Estoc de Pop," Spanish TV report, TV-3
Like a Rolling Stone/Mr. Tambourine Man/Don't Think Twice/Blowin' in the Wind

(7/7/84) (V) Wembley Stadium London, England—Martha Quinn interview and some performance footage, partial broadcast over MTV

(c. 7/84) (V) *Clancy Bros. & Tommy Makem*—documentary film, probably filmed in Dublin, Ireland, broadcast over WNET-TV, New York; comments on the Clancy Brothers

(late '84) New York, New York—"Dylan on Dylan," interview with Artie Mogul and Bert Kleinman, Westwood One Syndicated Radio Show (broadcast 11/18/84)

(1/28/85) GUEST ARTIST—Hollywood, California, A&M Studios
We Are the World
Note: Released on Columbia USA-40043 (LP), US 7-04839 (45), and US 2-05179 (12")

(V) SONG VIDEO—"We Are the World," directed by Tom Trbovich, released 3/85 as promotion for record release; audio track is the same as record release

(V) "The Story behind the Song"—documentary on recording session, HBO TV (broadcast 4/85); includes footage of Dylan before and during recording

(V) Local TV-reports broadcast (1/29/85) showing footage of recording session

OUTTAKES—from beginning to end of Dylan's takes of his portion of the song; audio only

(early '85) *Empire Burlesque*—Columbia FC-40110 (released 6/85)

Tight Connection to My Heart/Seeing the Real You at Last/I'll Remember You/Clean-Cut Kid/Never Gonna Be the Same Again/Trust Yourself/Emotionally Yours/When the Night Comes Falling from the Sky/Something's Burning, Baby/Dark Eyes

(V) SONG VIDEO—"Tight Connection to My Heart," directed by Paul Schrader, released 5/85 as promotion for *Empire Burlesque*

(V) SONG VIDEO—"When the Night Comes Falling from the Sky," directed by Dave Stewart, released 9/85 as promotion for *Empire Burlesque*

(V) SONG VIDEO—"Emotionally Yours," directed by Dave Stewart, released 9/85 as promotion for *Empire Burlesque*

(early '85) OUTTAKES

Is It Worth It?/Instrumental/Yes Sir, No Sir/Was It Magic?/You're a Child to Me/Wind Blowing on the Water/All the Way Home/My Oriental Home *(inst.)*/On Borrowed Time/I Want You to Know I Love You/On a Rocking Boat/It's Dangerous to Me *(inst.)*/More to This Than Meets the Eye *(inst.)*/Straw Hat *(inst.)*/Gonna Love Her Anyway *(inst.)* / Instrumental Calypso/Wait and See/Walking on Eggs *(inst.)*/ Well Water *(inst.)*/All the Way *(inst.)*/Almost Persuaded *(inst.)*/ Tune after Almost Persuaded *(inst.)*

(early '85) ADDITIONAL OUTTAKES

Drifting Too Far from Shore/Instrumental/Who Loves You More/Instrumental/Go Away Little Boy/Something's Burning Baby/Danville Girl/Clean-Cut Kid/The Real You at Last/Something Is Burning/Trust Yourself/Waiting to Get Beat/Straight A's in Love/The Very Thought of You

(6/17/85) New York, New York—"Rockline," Bob Coburn syndicated radio interview (broadcast live over WNEW-FM); program made up of listeners phoning in questions and Dylan answering them

(early 7/85) New York, New York (probably)—rehearsals for "Live Aid," with Ron Wood and Keith Richards

Ballad of Hollis Brown/Ballad of Hollis Brown/Girl from the North Country/Trouble *(cut)*/Blowin' in the Wind

(7/13/85) (V) Philadelphia, Pennsylvania—JFK Stadium, "Live Aid," broadcast live worldwide, with Keith Richards—G, Ron Wood—G

Hollis Brown/When the Ship Comes In/Blowin' in the Wind/We Are the World *(with entire cast)*

Note: Dylan walks off stage in the middle of "We Are the World."

(8/22/85) Hollywood, California—Gymnasium of First Methodist Church, audio track of film shoot for promo video of "When the Night Comes Falling from the Sky"

(c. summer '85) GUEST ARTIST—*Language Barrier,* Sly & Robbie, Island ILPS-9831 (released 8/85)
No Name on the Bullet *(on harmonica)*

(c. summer '85) GUEST ARTIST—*Sun City,* Artists Against Apartheid, Manhattan ST-53019 (LP) and V-56013 (12") (released 12/85)
Sun City *(on vocals)*

(V) SONG VIDEO—"Sun City," directed by Steve Van Zandt, released 10/85; Dylan makes a brief appearance; Audio track is same as record release

(9/19/85) (V) Malibu, California—home of Bob Dylan, Bob Brown interview
Note: This is the complete version of what was broadcast on "20/20."

(9/19/85) (V) Los Angeles, California—rehearsals for "Farm Aid," with Tom Petty and The Heartbreakers
I Got a Woman/Baby, What You Want Me to Do/Shake/I'll Remember You/Forever Young/Louie, Louie/And Then He Kissed Me/Instrumental/Lucky Old Sun/Forever Young *(partial, with footage of Dylan and the girls sitting and smoking)*

(summer '85) (V) "20/20"—ABC-TV weekly network show, includes Bob Brown interview (9/19/85), footage from rehearsals for "Farm Aid" (9/19/85), footage from "Farm Aid" (9/22/85) (broadcast 10/10/85)

(9/21/85) Champaign, Illinois—Memorial Stadium, "Farm Aid," soundcheck
Trust Yourself/Lucky Old Sun/Maggie's Farm/I Like It Like That

(9/22/85) (V) Champaign, Illinois—Memorial Stadium, "Farm Aid," with Tom Petty and The Heartbreakers and Willie Nelson—G (on "Trust Yourself," "Lucky Old Sun," "Maggie's Farm"); broadcast live over the Nashville Network (cable)
Clean-Cut Kid/Shake/I'll Remember You/Trust Yourself/Lucky Old Sun/Maggie's Farm
Note: No video for "Clean-Cut Kid," "Shake," "Lucky Old Sun." Footage shot by ABC-TV for "20/20" broadcast has additional scenes backstage prior to show and scene after show; this was not aired. ABC-TV performance footage is cut up and incomplete.

(9/29/85) (V) Los Angeles, California—Charles M. Young interview, portions broadcast over MTV

(11/14/85) (V) New York, New York—Whitney Museum, party for release of *Biograph* album; film snippets are from local TV-reports, "Entertainment Tonight," and MTV

(11/26/85) (V) London, England—The Church, "Whistle Test" rehearsals with Dave Stewart and band and Andy Kershaw interview (TV broadcast over Channel 4)

Biograph—Columbia C5X-38830 (released 11/85)

Lay Lady Lay/Baby Let Me Follow You Down/If Not for You/I'll Be Your Baby Tonight/*I'll Keep It with Mine*/The Times They Are A-Changin'/Blowin' in the Wind/Masters of War/Lonesome Death of Hattie Carroll/*Percy's Song*/Mixed Up Confusion/Tombstone Blues/The Groom's Still Waiting at the Altar/Most Likely/Like a Rolling Stone/*Lay Down Your Weary Tune*/Subterranean Homesick Blues/*I Don't Believe You*/*Visions of Johanna*/Every Grain of Sand/*Quinn the Eskimo*/Mr. Tambourine Man/Dear Landlord/It Ain't Me Babe/You Angel You/Million Dollar Bash/To Ramona/*You're a Big Girl Now*/*Abandoned Love*/Tangled Up in Blue/*It's All Over Now, Baby Blue*/Please, Crawl Out Your Window/Positively 4th Street/*Isis*/*Jet Pilot*/*Caribbean Wind*/*Up to Me*/*Baby I'm in the Mood for You*/*I Wanna Be Your Lover*/I Want You/*Heart of Mine*/On a Night Like This/Just Like a Woman/*Romance in Durango*/Señor/Gotta Serve Somebody/I Believe in You/Time Passes Slowly/I Shall Be Released/Knockin' on Heaven's Door/All Along the Watchtower/Solid Rock/*Forever Young*

Note: Songs in *italics* were previously unreleased. *Biograph* master tape contains snippets of songs cut off the actual release: "Abandoned Love" (extra introduction)/"I Don't Believe You" (extra introduction)/"Jet Pilot" (extra introduction and ending)/"I'll Keep It with Mine" (extra introduction)/"Visions of Johanna" (extra introduction and ending)/"If You Gotta Go, Go Now" (outtake—see summer '65).

(1/20/86) (V) Washington, D.C.—John F. Kennedy Center for Performing Arts, "Tribute to Martin Luther King, Jr."

Song of Hope *(with Stevie Wonder)*/I Shall Be Released/Blowin' in the Wind *(with Stevie Wonder and Peter, Paul and Mary)*/Happy Birthday, Martin *(with entire cast)*

Note: Audio only for "Song of Hope." Video portion was broadcast over ABC-TV a few hours after the event.

(c. 1/86) (V) American Music Awards—congratulation speech to Willie Nelson, supplied tape to TV show, ABC-TV (broadcast 1/27/86)

(c. 1/86) (V) Los Angeles, California—George Negus interview for "60 Minutes," Australian TV, includes interview, footage from "Don't Look Back," Australian soundcheck, airport arrival in Wellington, New Zealand (broadcast 2/10/86)

('86) **Tour**—Far East, with Tom Petty and The Heartbreakers, Tom Petty—G and V, Mike Campbell—G, Howie Epstein—B and Mandolin, Benmont Tench—K, Stan

Lynch—D, Madeline Quebec—BV, Queen Esther Marrow—BV, Elisecia Wright—BV, Debra Byrd—BV

FEB 5 Wellington, New Zealand: Sportsground
7 Auckland, New Zealand: Mt. Smart
10 Sydney, Australia: Entertainment Center
11 Sydney, Australia: Entertainment Center
12 Sydney, Australia: Entertainment Center
13 Sydney, Australia: Entertainment Center
15 Adelaide, Australia: Memorial Drive
(*) 17 Perth, Australia: Entertainment Center
(*) 18 Perth, Australia: Entertainment Center
20 Melbourne, Australia: Kooyong Tennis Stadium
21 Melbourne, Australia: Kooyong Tennis Stadium
22 Melbourne, Australia: Kooyong Tennis Stadium
24 Sydney, Australia: Entertainment Center
25 Sydney, Australia: Entertainment Center
MARCH (*) 1 Brisbane, Australia: Lang Park
5 Tokyo, Japan: Nippon Budokan Hall
6 Osaka, Japan: Castle Hall
8 Nagoya, Japan: Nagoya Gymnasium
10 Tokyo, Japan: Nippon Budokan Hall

(2/6/86) Wellington, New Zealand—Hotel bar, jam with Tom Petty and Stevie Nicks

(2/10/86) Sydney, Australia—studio of Brett Whiteley, press conference for Australian tour with Tom Petty and The Heartbreakers

(2/19/86) Melbourne, Australia—Sports and Entertainment Center, guest appearance at a Dire Straits concert
All Along the Watchtower/Leopard-Skin Pillbox Hat/License to Kill/Knockin' on Heaven's Door *(on guitar, harmonica, and vocal)*

(2/22/86) (V) Melbourne, Australia—Maurice Parker interview for "State Affair," Australian TV, includes interview and song, "Like a Rolling Stone" (2/22/86) (broadcast 2/24/86 over TWT-TV)

(2/24, 25/86) (V) "Hard to Handle" Sydney, Australia—directed by Gillian Armstrong (originally broadcast over HBO Cable TV, 6/20/86; later released on home video by CBS-FOX #3502, 10/86)
In the Garden/Just Like a Woman/Like a Rolling Stone/It's Alright Ma/Girl from the North Country/Lenny Bruce/When the Night Comes Falling/Ballad of a Thin Man/I'll Remember You/Knockin' on Heaven's Door
Note: All songs from 2/24/86 except "Like a Rolling Stone," "It's Alright Ma," "Lenny Bruce," "Knockin' on Heaven's Door," which are from 2/25/86.

(2/86) SINGLE RELEASE—MCA 23633 (released 4/86)
Band of the Hand

Note: Recorded in Sydney, Australia, with Tom Petty and The Heartbreakers.

(V) SONG VIDEO—"Band of the Hand," directed by Paul Michael Stewart, released 3/86; Dylan does not appear in the video, and the audio track is the same as the single release

(3/10/86) Tokyo, Japan—Budokan, interview (partial broadcast 4/86 over MTV)

(4/1/86) (V) Beverly Hills, California—Chason's Restaurant, ASCAP Awards Dinner, portions broadcast 4/2/86 over "Entertainment Tonight," syndicated TV show; footage shows Dylan accepting award and responding to questions

(4/10/86) (V) Los Angeles, California—Westwood One Radio Network offices, press conference with Tom Petty and The Heartbreakers; video is partial, audio is complete

(5/21/86) Los Angeles, California—telephone interview with Bob Fass, Robert Knight, and Steve Ben Israel (broadcast live over WBAI-FM, New York, New York)

Note: Dylan was in Los Angeles, the others in New York.

(6/7/86) Inglewood, California—The Forum, Amnesty International Concert, with Tom Petty and The Heartbreakers

Band of the Hand/License to Kill/Shake a Hand

(c. '86) *Knocked Out Loaded*—Columbia DC-40439 (released 6/86)

You Wanna Ramble/And They Killed Him/Driftin' Too Far from Shore/Precious Memories/Maybe Someday/Brownsville Girl/Got My Mind Made Up/Under Your Spell

(c. '86) GUEST ARTIST—*Kingdom Blow,* Curtis Blow, Mercury 830-215-1 (released 10/86)

Street Rock *(on vocals)*

Note: Dylan's vocals (on tape) were delivered to Greene St. Recording Studios, New York, where they were mixed onto the final track by engineer Roddy Hui.

('86) **Tour (continued)**—USA and Canada, "True Confessions," with Tom Petty and The Heartbreakers, Tom Petty—G and V, Mike Campbell—G, Howie Epstein—B and Mandolin, Benmont Tench—K, Stan Lynch—D, Madeline Quebec—V, Queen Esther Marrow—V, Carolyn Dennis—V

JUNE
9 San Diego, California: Sports Arena
11 Reno, Nevada: Lawlor Events Center
12 Sacramento, California: California Expo Amphitheatre
13 Berkeley, California: Greek Theatre

14 Berkeley, California: Greek Theatre
16 Costa Mesa, California: Pacific Amphitheatre
17 Costa Mesa, California: Pacific Amphitheatre
18 Phoenix, Arizona: Veteran's Memorial Coliseum
20 Houston, Texas: Southern Star Amphitheatre
21 Austin, Texas: Special Events Center
22 Dallas, Texas: Reunion Arena
24 Indianapolis, Indiana: Market Square Arena
26 Minneapolis, Minnesota: H.H.H. Metrodome
27 East Troy, Wisconsin: Alpine Valley
29 Elgin, Illinois: Poplar Creek Music Theatre
30 Detroit, Michigan: Pine Knob Music Theatre
JULY 1 Detroit, Michigan: Pine Knob Music Theatre
2 Akron, Ohio: Rubber Bowl
4 Buffalo, New York: Rich Stadium
6 Washington, D.C.: Robert F. Kennedy Stadium
7 Washington, D.C.: Robert F. Kennedy Stadium
8 Mansfield, Massachusetts: Great Woods Amphitheatre
9 Mansfield, Massachusetts: Great Woods Amphitheatre
11 Hartford, Connecticut: Civic Center
13 Saratoga Springs, New York: Saratoga Performing Arts Center
15 New York, New York: Madison Square Garden
16 New York, New York: Madison Square Garden
17 New York, New York: Madison Square Garden
(SC) 19 Philadelphia, Pennsylvania: The Spectrum
20 Philadelphia, Pennsylvania: The Spectrum
21 East Rutherford, New Jersey: Brendan Byrne Arena
22 Mansfield, Massachusetts: Great Woods Amphitheatre
24 Bonner Springs, Kansas: Sandstone Amphitheatre
(INC) 26 Red Rocks, Colorado: Red Rocks Amphitheatre
27 Red Rocks, Colorado: Red Rocks Amphitheatre
29 Portland, Oregon: Civic Auditorium
31 Tacoma, Washington: The Tacomadome
AUG 1 Vancouver, British Columbia: B.C. Place
3 Inglewood, California: The Forum
5 Mountainview, California: Shoreline Amphitheatre
(SC) 6 Paso Robles, California: Mid-State Fair Grounds

(7/2/86) Akron, Ohio—Rubber Bowl, with the Grateful Dead

Little Red Rooster/Don't Think Twice/It's Alright/It's All Over Now, Baby Blue *(on guitar and vocals)*

Note: Dylan appeared during Grateful Dead set of this show, in which they shared billing.

(7/4/86) Buffalo, New York—Rich Stadium
(V)

So Long, Good Luck, and Goodbye/Positively 4th Street/Clean-Cut Kid/Emotionally Yours/Trust Yourself/We Had It All/Masters of War/To Ramona/One Too Many Mornings/A Hard Rain's A-Gonna Fall/I've Forgotten More/Band of the Hand/When the Night Comes Falling from the Sky/Lonesome Town/Ballad of a Thin Man/Rainy Day Women Nos. 12 and 35/The Real You at Last/Borderline

Note: Show was partially broadcast over VH1-Cable Network for Farm Aid II; remaining songs were picked up from satellite feed.

(7/6/86) (V) Washington, D.C.—Robert F. Kennedy Stadium, local TV news report (never broadcast)
Positively 4th Street/Clean-Cut Kid

(7/7/86) Washington, D.C.—Robert F. Kennedy Stadium, with the Grateful Dead
It's All Over Now, Baby Blue/Desolation Row *(on guitar and vocals)*
Note: Dylan appeared during Grateful Dead set of this show, in which they shared billing.

(7/10/86) Providence, Rhode Island—Marriott Hotel Lounge
You Win Again/King Bee/Let the Good Times Roll/Earth Angel/Goodnight Sweetheart *(all with hotel-lounge band)*

(7/15/86) (V) New York, New York—Madison Square Garden, WABC-TV local news report
Clean-Cut Kid *(partial)*

(7/24, 25/86 and 7/31/86) Superstar Concert Series—Westwood One Radio (broadcast 8/30/86)
Positively 4th Street/All Along the Watchtower/Masters of War/I'll Remember You/I've Forgotten More/Just Like a Woman/Blowin' in the Wind/Lucky Old Sun/Like a Rolling Stone/Knockin' on Heaven's Door
Note: (1) The following songs were added to the Japanese and European radio broadcasts: "It Ain't Me Babe," "When the Night Comes Falling from the Sky," "Girl from the North Country." (2) "Positively 4th Street," "Masters of War," "I'll Remember You," "I've Forgotten More," "Just Like a Woman," "Lucky Old Sun," "When the Night Comes Falling from the Sky," "Girl from the North Country" from 2/24/86; "Blowin' in the Wind," "Like a Rolling Stone," "Knockin' on Heaven's Door" from 2/25/86; "All Along the Watchtower," "It Ain't Me Babe" from 7/31/86.

(8/6/86) (V) Paso Robles, California—Mid-State Fair Grounds, "Entertainment Tonight," syndicated TV report
Brownsville Girl *(chorus only)*

(c. 8/86) (V) "Ian and Sylvia"—TV show, short speech to Ian and Sylvia (broadcast over Canadian TV 9/86)

(c. 8/86) (V) New York, New York—"L'Chaim! To Life!," Chabad Lubavitch Telethon, Manhattan Cable TV (broadcast 9/14/86)
Thank God *(with Tom Petty and The Heartbreakers)*
Note: Also includes a pledge appeal from Dylan who is on the set of *Hearts of Fire.*

(8/17/86) London, England—National Film Theatre, *Hearts of Fire* press conference

(V) London, England—snippets from a press conference over BBC and Channel 4

(8/10/86) (V) London, England—"Omnibus," TV special broadcast over BBC 1, London (9/18/87). Includes "With God on Our Side" from "Tonight," BBC-TV (1964); arrival at Rhoose Airport, South Wales, England (9/86); press conference (8/17/86); film shoots, Bristol (9/86); London (9/86); Surrey (9/86); Toronto (10/86); interview with Christopher Sykes (10/86); street scene in Hamilton (10/86)

(9/19/86) Bristol, England—Colston Hall, *Hearts of Fire* film shoot

(10/10/86) Hamilton, Ontario—General Electric warehouse, *Hearts of Fire* film shoot

(8–10/86) (V) *Hearts of Fire*—film, directed by Richard Marquand (theatrically released London, England, 10/87; U.S. release on Warner home video, 4/90)

(8–10/86) ***Hearts of Fire***—soundtrack, Columbia SC-40870 (released 10/87)
The Usual/Night after Night/I Had a Dream about You, Baby

(11/10/86) (V) Toronto, Ontario—Royal York Hotel, Juno Award Ceremony, presents award to Gordon Lightfoot

(2/19/87) (V) West Hollywood, California—Palamino, with Taj Mahal—G and V, Jesse Ed Davis—G, George Harrison—G and V, John Fogerty–G and V, and Dylan—G and V, Taj Mahal's band
Matchbox/Lucille/In the Midnight Hour/Honey Don't/Blue Suede Shoes/Watching the River Flow/Proud Mary/Johnny B Goode/Willie and the Hand Jive/Peggy Sue/Dizzy Miss Lizzy/Twist and Shout

(3/11/87) (V) Brooklyn, New York—Brooklyn Academy of Music Opera House, "The Gershwin Gala" (broadcast over PBS-TV 7/87)
Soon
Note: Local TV news reports broadcast 3/12/87 were shot at the rehearsal.

(4/20/87) Los Angeles, California—Los Angeles Sports Arena, guest appearance at a U2 concert
I Shall Be Released/Knockin' on Heaven's Door *(Dylan—G and V)*

(c. 4/87) GUEST ARTIST—*Sentimental Hygiene,* Warren Zevon, Virgin 7-90603-1 (released 6/87)
The Factory (Dylan—*harmonica*)

(c. 4/87) (V) Los Angeles, California—"The La Bamba Revue," MTV Special, interview in moving car (broadcast 7/23/87)

(4–5/87) Hollywood, California—Sunset Studios, "Woody Guthrie Special," BBC Radio 2 (broadcast 9/30, 10/14, and 10/21/87)

(4–5/87) *Down in the Groove*—Columbia OC 40957 (released 6/88)

Let's Stick Together/When Did You Leave Heaven?/Sally Sue Brown/Death Is Not the End *(recorded 1983)*/Had a Dream About You, Baby/Ugliest Girl in the World/Silvio/Ninety Miles an Hour/Shenandoah/Rank Strangers to Me

(4–5/87) OUTTAKES

Got Love If You Want It/Important Words

(c. 4/87) San Rafael, California—Club Front, rehearsals with the Grateful Dead

The Times They Are A-Changin'/When I Paint My Masterpiece/Man of Peace/I'll Be Your Baby Tonight/Ballad of Ira Hayes/I Want You/Ballad of a Thin Man/Stuck Inside of Mobile/Dead Man, Dead Man/Queen Jane Approximately/Boy in the Bubble/(?)/In the Summertime/Man of Peace/Union Sundown/It's All Over Now, Baby Blue/Joey/If Not for You *(instrumental)*/If Not For You/Slow Train/Tomorrow Is a Long Time/Ballad of Frankie Lee and Judas Priest/John Brown/I'll Be Your Baby Tonight/Don't Keep Me Waiting Too Long/Stealin'/I Want You/Oh Boy!/Tangled Up in Blue/Walkin' Down the Line/Simple Twist of Fate/Gotta Serve Somebody/Change My Way of Thinking/Maggie's Farm/Chimes of Freedom/All I Really Want to Do/John Brown/Heart of Mine/Rollin' in My Sweet Baby's Arms/John Brown/Heart of Mine/Pledging My Time/Señor/The Wicked Messenger/Watching the River Flow

('87) Tour—USA, with the Grateful Dead, Jerry Garcia—G/Pedal Steel/V, Bob Weir—G and V, Phil Lesh—B, Brent Mydland—K and V, Mickey Hart—D, Bill Kreutzmann—D

(7/87)
4 Foxboro, Massachusetts: Sullivan Stadium
10 Philadelphia, Pennsylvania: JFK Stadium
12 E. Rutherford, New Jersey: Giants Stadium
19 Eugene, Oregon: Autzen Stadium
24 Oakland, California: Oakland Stadium
26 Anaheim, California: Anaheim Stadium

(7/4/87) (V) Foxboro, Massachusetts—Sullivan Stadium, in-house video shoot of show with the Grateful Dead

The Times They Are A-Changin'/Man of Peace/I'll Be Your Baby Tonight/John Brown/I Want You/Ballad of a Thin Man/Stuck Inside of Mobile/Queen Jane Approximately/Chimes of Freedom/Slow Train/Joey

(7/12/87) (V) East Rutherford, New Jersey—Giants Stadium, in-house video shoot of show with the Grateful Dead

Stuck Inside of Mobile/Tomorrow Is a Long Time/Highway 61/It's All Over Now, Baby Blue/Ballad of a Thin Man/John Brown/The Wicked Messenger/Queen Jane Approximately/Chimes of Freedom/Joey/All Along the Watchtower *(partial)*

(7/4, 19, 24, and 26/87) *Dylan and the Dead*—Columbia CK-45056 (released 1/89)

Slow Train/I Want You/Gotta Serve Somebody/Queen Jane Approximately/Joey/All Along the Watchtower/Knockin' on Heaven's Door/

Note: "Slow Train," "Joey" from 7/4/87; "Queen Jane Approximately" from 7/19/87; "I Want You" from 7/24/87; "Gotta Serve," "Watchtower,"/"Heaven's Door" from 7/26/87.

('87) **Tour (continued)**—Israel and Europe, "Temples in Flames," with Tom Petty and The Heartbreakers, Queen Esther Marrow—BV, Madeline Quebec—BV, Louise Bethune—BV

SEPT 5 Tel Aviv, Israel: Hayarkon Park
7 Jerusalem, Israel: Sultan's Pool
10 Basel, Switzerland: Sporthalle St. Jacob
12 Modena, Italy: Aera Ex-Autodromo
13 Torino, Italy: Falasport
15 Dortmund, West Germany: Westfallenhalle
16 Nuremburg, West Germany: Franken Hall
17 East Berlin, East Germany: Treptower Festwiese
19 Rotterdam, The Netherlands: Sportpalais Ahoy
20 Hannover, West Germany: Messehalle 20
21 Copenhagen, Denmark: Valby Hallen
23 Helsinki, Finland: Jaahalli
25 Göteberg, Sweden: Scandinavium
26 Stockholm, Sweden: Johanneshovs Isstadion
28 Frankfurt, West Germany: Festhalle
29 Stuttgart, West Germany: Hans-Martin-Schleyer Halle
30 Munich, West Germany: Olympiahalle
1 Verona, Italy: Arena Di Verona
3 Rome, Italy: Palaeur
4 Milan, Italy: Arena Civica
5 Locarno, Switzerland: Piazza Grande
7 Paris, France: P.O.P.B. Bercy
8 Brussels, Belgium: Vorst National
10 Birmingham, England: National Exhibition Center
11 Birmingham, England: National Exhibition Center
12 Birmingham, England: National Exhibition Center
15 London, England: Wembley Arena
16 London, England: Wembley Arena
17 London, England: Wembley Arena

(9/17/87) (V) East Berlin, East Germany—Treptower Festwiese, broadcast over WNEW-TV, New York, New York

Blowin' in the Wind ***(partial)***

(1/20/88) (V) New York, New York—The Waldorf-Astoria Grand Ballroom, Third Annual Rock 'n' Roll Hall of Fame Dinner, induction speech by Bruce Springsteen and acceptance

Twist and Shout/All Along the Watchtower/I Saw Her Standing There/Stand by Me/Stop, in The Name of Love/ Whole Lotta Shakin' Goin' On/Hound Dog/Barbara Ann/Born

on the Bayou/Like a Rolling Stone/Satisfaction ***(on guitar and vocals)***

(c. 3–4/88) *Traveling Wilburys Vol. 1*—Warner Brothers–Wilbury 925796 (released 10/88)

Handle with Care/Dirty World/Rattled/Last Night/Not Alone Anymore/Congratulations/Heading for the Light/Margarita/Tweeter and the Monkey Man/End of the Line ***(as Lucky Wilbury)***

OUTTAKES

Last Night ***(Petty vocal same as album, but sings whole song)***/**Congratulations** ***(Dylan vocal same as album)***/**Dirty World** ***(Dylan vocal different)***/**Rattled** ***(Lynne vocal different)***/**Heading for the Light** ***(instrumental)***/**End of the Line** ***(all vocals different)***/**Handle with Care** ***(all vocals same as album)***

Note: All outtakes are different mixes/basic tracks and contain extra snippets.

(V) SONG VIDEO—"Handle with Care," directed by Willy Smax, released 10/88 as promotion for *Traveling Wilburys Vol. 1*

(V) SONG VIDEO—"End of the Line," directed by Willy Smax, released 1/89 as promotion for *Traveling Wilburys Vol. 1*

(V) PROMOTIONAL FILM—B & W film with audio track the same as *Traveling Wilburys Vol. 1* album, but with a lot of footage of Dylan previously not seen; film shown at NARM record convention in New Orleans, Louisiana 3/89

(c. 5/88) GUEST ARTIST—*Rattle & Hum,* U2, Island 7-91003 (released 10/88)

Hawkmoon 269 ***(Dylan—Hammond Organ, A&M Studios, Los Angeles, California)***/**Love Rescue Me** ***(Dylan—BV, Sun Studios, Memphis, Tennessee)***

(5/29/88) New York, New York—Lone Star Cafe, Levon Helm concert, late show

The Weight/Nadine ***(Dylan—G and V as a surprise guest)***

('88) **Tour**—USA and Canada, with G. E. Smith—G, Kenny Aaronson—B, Christopher Parker—D

JUNE
7 Concord, California: Concord Pavilion
9 Sacramento, California: Cal Expo
10 Berkeley, California: Greek Theatre
11 Mountainview, California: Shoreline Amphitheatre
13 Park City, Utah: Park West
15 Denver, Colorado: Fiddler's Green Amphitheatre
17 St. Louis, Missouri: The Muny-Forest Park
18 East Troy, Wisconsin: Alpine Valley
21 Cuyahoga Falls, Ohio: Blossom Music Centre
22 Cincinnati, Ohio: River Bend Music Centre
24 Holmdel, New Jersey: Garden State Arts Center

	25 Holmdel, New Jersey: Garden State Arts Center
	26 Saratoga Springs, New York: Saratoga Performing Arts Center
	28 Canandaigua, New York: Finger Lakes Performing Arts Center
	30 Jones Beach, New York: Music Theatre
JULY	1 Jones Beach, New York: Music Theatre
	2 Mansfield, Massachusetts: Great Woods Amphitheatre
	3 Old Orchard Beach, Maine: The Ballpark
	6 Philadelphia, Pennsylvania: Mann Music Center
	8 Montreal, Quebec: The Forum
	9 Ottawa, Ontario: Civic Center
	11 Hamilton, Ontario: Copps Coliseum
	13 Charlevoix, Michigan: The Castle
	14 Hoffman Estates, Illinois: Poplar Creek Music Theatre
	15 Indianapolis, Indiana: State Fairgrounds
	17 Rochester, Michigan: Meadowbrook
	18 Rochester, Michigan: Meadowbrook
	20 Columbia, Maryland: Merriweather Post Pavilion
	22 Nashville, Tennessee: Starwood Amphitheatre
	24 Atlanta, Georgia: Chastain Park Amphitheatre
	25 Atlanta, Georgia: Chastain Park Amphitheatre
	26 Memphis, Tennessee: Mud Island
	28 Dallas, Texas: Starplex
	30 Mesa, Arizona: Mesa Amphitheatre
	31 Costa Mesa, California: Pacific Amphitheatre
AUG	2 Los Angeles, California: Greek Theatre
	3 Los Angeles, California: Greek Theatre
	4 Los Angeles, California: Greek Theatre
	6 Carlsbad, California: Sammis Pavilion
	7 Santa Barbara, California: County Bowl
	19 Portland, Oregon: Civic Auditorium
	20 George, Washington: Champs de Brionne
	21 Vancouver, British Columbia: PNE Pacific Coliseum
	23 Calgary, Alberta: Olympic Saddledome
	24 Edmondton, Alberta: Northlands Coliseum
	27 Winnipeg, Manitoba: Winnipeg Arena
	29 Toronto, Ontario: Exhibition Stadium
	31 Syracuse, New York: State Fairgrounds
SEPT	2 Middletown, New York: Orange County Fair
	3 Manchester, New Hampshire: The River
	4 Bristol, Connecticut: Lake Compounce Festival Park
	7 Essex Junction, Vermont: Champlain Valley Fairgrounds
	8 Binghamton, New York: Broome County Arena
	10 Stanhope, New Jersey: Waterloo Village
	11 Fairfax, Virginia: George Madison University
	13 Pittsburgh, Pennsylvania: Civic Arena
	15 Chapel Hill, North Carolina: Dean E. Smith Center, University of North Carolina
	16 Columbia, South Carolina: Coliseum, University of South Carolina
	17 Charlotte, North Carolina: New Charlotte Coliseum
	18 Knoxville, Tennessee: University of Tennessee
	19 Charlottesville, Virginia: University Hall, University of Virginia
	22 Tampa, Florida: University of Southern Florida
	23 Miami, Florida: Miami Arena
	24 Gainsville, Florida: O'Connell Center, University of Florida
	25 New Orleans, Louisiana: Audubon Zoo

OCT (SC) 13 Upper Darby, Pennsylvania: Tower Theatre
14 Upper Darby, Pennsylvania: Tower Theatre
16 New York, New York: Radio City Music Hall
17 New York, New York: Radio City Music Hall
18 New York, New York: Radio City Music Hall
19 New York, New York: Radio City Music Hall

(c. late '88) GUEST ARTIST—"Folkways—A Vision Shared," Columbia 44034 (released 8/88)
Pretty Boy Floyd *(solo performance on guitar, harmonica, vocal)*

(12/4/88) (V) Oakland, California—Oakland Coliseum, "A Bridge School Benefit," with G. E. Smith—Acoustic Guitar
San Francisco Bay Blues/Pretty Boy Floyd/With God on Our Side/Girl from the North Country/Gates of Eden/Forever Young

(12/19/88) (V) Las Vegas, Nevada—Caesar's Palace, Sugar Ray Leonard versus Donny LaLonde boxing match, broadcast live over HBO Cable. Dylan can be seen sitting ringside

(2/12/89) (V) Inglewood, California—The Forum, Grateful Dead Concert, second set and encore
Iko, Iko/Monkey and the Engineer/Alabama Getaway/Dire Wolf/Cassidy/Stuck Inside of Mobile/Not Fade Away/Knockin' on Heaven's Door *(Dylan—G and V as a surprise guest)*
Note: Audience video is included because of the unusual nature of this entry. Audio tape is an SB recording.

(c. 3–4/89) *Oh Mercy*—Columbia 45281, New Orleans, Louisiana, Studio on the Move (released 9/89)
Political World/Where Teardrops Fall/Everything Is Broken/Ring Them Bells/Man in the Long Black Coat/Most of the Time/What Good Am I?/Disease of Conceit/What Was It You Wanted?/Shooting Star

(V) SONG VIDEO—"Political World," directed by John Mellencamp, released 12/89 as promotion for *Oh Mercy,* shot 11/89 in Bloomington, Indiana, at the R & T Building of Indiana University

(V) SONG VIDEO—"Most of the Time," directed by Tony Curtis (Jesse Dylan), live performance shot at the Record Plant at Culver City Studios, Hollywood, California, released as promotion for *Oh Mercy,*

(3/16/90) Hollywood, California—the Record Plant, Culver City Studios
Most of the Time
Note: This is a different take of the above song video; released as CD promo only, Columbia CSK-73326. Musicians on these two tracks are David Lindley—G, Terry Jackson—B, Kenny Aaronoff—D.

('89) **Tour—Europe, USA and Canada—Tony Garnier replaces Aaronson on bass except for 5/27, 5/28, 5/30, 6/4, 6/6, 6/7, 6/8, and 7/23 (second electric set only).**

MAY
27 Andrarum, Sweden: Christine Hof Slott
28 Stockholm, Sweden: Globe Arena
30 Helsinki, Finland: Jaahalli

JUNE
3 Dublin, Ireland: RDS Simmonscourt
4 Dublin, Ireland: RDS Simmonscourt
6 Glasgow, Scotland: Scottish Exhibition Centre
7 Birmingham, England: National Exhibition Centre
8 London, England: Wembley Arena
10 The Hague, The Netherlands: Statenhal
11 Brussels, Belgium: Forest National
13 Frejus, France: Arenes Romaines
15 Madrid, Spain: Palaces Deportes Comunidad
16 Barcelona, Spain: Palacio Municipal de' Sports
17 San Sebastian, Spain: Velodromo Anoeta
19 Milan, Italy: Palatrussadi
20 Rome, Italy: Palazza della Civilia e Lavoro
21 Cava dei Tirreni, Italy: Stadio Comunale S.L.
22 Livorno, Italy: Stadio Comunale
(INC) 24 Istanbul, Turkey: Acikhava Tiyatrosu
26 Patras, Greece: Patras National Stadium
28 Athens, Greece: Pahathinaikos Stadium

JULY
1 Peoria, Illinois: Civic Center Arena
2 Hoffman Estates, Illinois: Poplar Creek Amphitheatre
3 Milwaukee, Wisconsin: Marcus Amphitheatre
5 Rochester, Michigan: Meadowbrook Music Festival
6 Rochester, Michigan: Meadowbrook Music Festival
8 Nobleville, Indiana: Deer Creek Music Center
9 Cuyahoga Falls, Ohio: Blossom Music Center
11 Harrisburg, Pennsylvania: Riverside Stadium
12 Allentown, Pennsylvania: Allentown Fairgrounds
13 Mansfield, Massachusetts: Great Woods Amphitheatre
15 Old Orchard Beach, Maine: Seashore Performing Arts Center
16 Bristol, Connecticut: Lake Compounce Festival Park
17 Stanhope, New Jersey: Waterloo Village-Field
19 Columbia, Maryland: Merriweather Post Pavillion
20 Atlantic City, New Jersey: Bally's Grandstand
21 Holmdel, New Jersey: Garden State Arts Centre
23 Wantaugh, New York: Jones Beach Music Theatre
25 Canandaigua, New York: Finger Lakes Performing Arts Center
26 Saratoga Springs, New York: Saratoga Performing Arts Center
28 Pittsburgh, Pennsylvania: Civic Arena
29 Toronto, Ontario: Kingswood Music Theatre
30 Ottawa, Ontario: Civic Centre
31 Joliette, Quebec: L'Amphithéâtre

AUG
3 St. Paul, Minnesota: Riverfest
4 Madison, Wisconsin: Dane County Coliseum
5 Grand Rapids, Michigan: Walsh Auditorium
6 Columbus, Ohio: Cooper Stadium
8 Toledo, Ohio: University of Toledo
9 St. Louis, Missouri: The Muny-Forest Park
10 Cincinnati, Ohio: Riverbend
12 Doswell, Virginia: Kings Dominion Amusement Park

13 Charlotte, North Carolina: Carowinds Amusement Park
15 Atlanta, Georgia: Chastain Park
16 Atlanta, Georgia: Chastain Park
18 Louisville, Kentucky: Freedom Hall
19 Springfield, Illinois: State Fairgrounds
20 Nashville, Tennessee: Starwood Amphitheatre
22 Bonner Springs, Kansas: Sandstone Amphitheatre
23 Oklahoma City, Oklahoma: Zoo Amphitheatre
25 New Orleans, Louisiana: Lakefront Arena, University of New Orleans
26 Houston, Texas: Summit
27 Dallas, Texas: Starplex
29 Las Cruces, New Mexico: Pan American
31 Englewood, Colorado: Fiddler's Green

SEPT 1 Park City, Utah: Park West
3 Berkeley, California: Greek Theatre
5 Santa Barbara, California: County Bowl
6 San Diego, California: Starlight Bowl
8 Costa Mesa, California: Pacific Amphitheatre
9 Los Angeles, California: Greek Theatre
10 Los Angeles, California: Greek Theatre

(9/24/89) Los Angeles, California—KCET Studios, Chabad Lubavitch Telethon (broadcast live via cable TV), with Peter Himmelman—G and V, Harry Dean Stanton—G and V

Yiddish Song/Spanish Song/Hava Negeilah *(Dylan—flute, recorder, harmonica, vocal)*

(9/25/89) Malibu, California—guest house at home of Bob Dylan, Dan Neer and DeWitt Nelson interview, broadcast nationally in "Up Close," syndicated radio show; CDs distributed to stations, CD #8923/MediaAmerica Radio/Neer Perfect Productions

(10/10/89) New York, New York—outside of Beacon Theatre, autograph signing, a fan and Dylan

('89) **Tour (continued)**—USA, with G. E. Smith—G, Tony Garnier—B, Christopher Parker—D

OCT (SC) 10 New York, New York: Beacon Theatre
11 New York, New York: Beacon Theatre
(SC) 12 New York, New York: Beacon Theatre
(SC) 13 New York, New York: Beacon Theatre
(SC) 15 Upper Darby, Pennsylvania: Tower Theatre
16 Upper Darby, Pennsylvania: Tower Theatre
17 Washington, D.C.: Constitution Hall
18 Washington, D.C.: Constitution Hall
20 Poughkeepsie, New York: Mid-Hudson Civic Centre
21 Kingston, Rhode Island: Keaney Gymnasium, University of Rhode Island
23 Boston, Massachusetts: Opera House
24 Boston, Massachusetts: Opera House
25 Boston, Massachusetts: Opera House
27 Troy, New York: RPI Fieldhouse
29 Ithaca, New York: Ben Light Gymnasium, Ithaca College

31 Chicago, Illinois: Arie Crown Theatre
NOV 1 Ann Arbor, Michigan: Hill Auditorium
2 Cleveland, Ohio: State Theatre, Playhouse Square
4 Indiana, Pennsylvania: Fisher Auditorium, University of Pennsylvania
6 Blacksburg, Virginia: Cassel Coliseum
(INC) 7 Norfolk, Virginia: Chrysler Hall, Scope Center
8 Durham, North Carolina: Cameron Indoor Stadium, Duke University
10 Atlanta, Georgia: The Fox
12 Miami, Florida: Sunrise Musical Theatre
13 Miami, Florida: Sunrise Musical Theatre
14 Tampa, Florida: Tampa Bay Performing Arts Centre
15 Tampa, Florida: Tampa Bay Performing Arts Centre

(11/20/89) GUEST ARTIST—*Flashback,* motion-picture soundtrack album, WTG Records (Columbia) NK-46042, Bellmont Mall Recording Studios, Bloomington, Indiana (released 12/89)
People Get Ready

(1/3/90) *Under the Red Sky*—Columbia 46794 (released 9/90)
Wiggle, Wiggle/Under the Red Sky/Unbelievable/Born in Time/TV Talking Song/10,000 Men/2 × 2/God Knows/Handy, Dandy/Cat's in the Well

(c. early '90) (V) SONG VIDEO—"Unbelievable," directed by Paris Barclay, Filmed 6/90; released 9/90 as promotion for *Under the Red Sky*

('90) Tour—USA, Brazil, Europe, and Canada, with G. E. Smith—G, Tony Garnier—B, Christopher Parker—D
JAN 12 New Haven, Connecticut: Toad's Place
14 College Park, Pennsylvania: Penn State University
15 Princeton, New Jersey: McCarter Theatre, Princeton University
(*) 18 São Paulo, Brazil: Estadio Cicero Pompeu de Toledo
25 Rio de Janeiro, Brazil: Sambodromo
29 Paris, France: Grande Rex
30 Paris, France: Grande Rex
31 Paris, France: Grande Rex
FEB 1 Paris, France: Grande Rex
3 London, England: Hammersmith Odeon
4 London, England: Hammersmith Odeon
5 London, England: Hammersmith Odeon
6 London, England: Hammersmith Odeon
7 London, England: Hammersmith Odeon
8 London, England: Hammersmith Odeon

(1/25/90) (V) Rio de Janeiro, Brazil—Sambodromo, five songs shot and broadcast by Brazilian TV have surfaced.

(1/29/90) (V) Paris, France—Palais Royale, Dylan named Commander of Order of Arts and Letters; presentation by Jack Lang

(2/24/90) (V) Los Angeles, California—Universal Amphitheatre, "Tribute to Roy Orbison," (broadcast over the Showtime Cable TV Network); with Roger McGuinn—12-string G and V, Chris Hillman—B and V, David Crosby—G and V, John Jorgenson—G, Steve Duncan—D

Mr. Tambourine Man (the Byrds—V and G)/He Was a Friend of Mine (The Byrds—G)/Only the Lonely/*(with entire ensemble, Dylan—G)*

Note: "He Was a Friend of Mine," audio only; "Mr. Tambourine Man," released 11/90, Columbia/Legacy 46773.

(c. 4/90) SINGLE RELEASE—with Traveling Wilburys, Warner Brothers–Wilbury W9773 (released in England 7/90; also released in USA, Warner Brothers LP-9-26280-2, 8/90)

Nobody's Child

Note: Released for charity, "In Aid of the Romanian Angel Appeal."

(c. 5–7/90) *Traveling Wilburys Vol. 3*—Warner Brothers–Wilbury 9-26324-2 (released 10/90)

She's My Baby/Inside Out/If You Belonged to Me/The Devil's Been Busy/7 Deadly Sins/Poor House/Where Were You Last Night?/Cool Dry Place/New Blue Moon/You Took My Breath Away/Wilbury Twist *(as Boo Wilbury)*

ROUGH MIXES AND OUTTAKES

You Took My Breath Away *(outtake)*/If You Belonged to Me *(same)*/Poor House *(same)*/She's My Baby *(outtake)*/The Devil's Been Busy *(same)*/Inside Out *(same)*/Where Were You Last Night? *(same)*/Go Away, Let Me Be *(outtake)*/Wilbury Twist *(same)*/7 Deadly Sins *(same)*/New Blue Moon *(same)*/Cool Dry Place *(same)*/Runaway *(almost same as CD single but slightly longer and additional harmonica solo)*/Maxine *(outtake)*

Note: Songs marked *"(same)"* are early mixes of album cuts but contain some additional vocals and snippits.

(c. 5–7/90) (V) SONG VIDEO—"She's My Baby," directed by Willy Smax, released 11/90 as promotion for *Traveling Wilburys Vol. 3*.

(V) SONG VIDEO—"Inside Out," directed by Willy Smax, released 11/90 as promotion for *Traveling Wilburys Vol. 3*

(V) SONG VIDEO—"Wilbury Twist," directed by Willy Smax, released 11/90 as promotion for *Traveling Wilburys Vol. 3*

(c. 4/90) SINGLE RELEASE—with Traveling Wilburys, Warner Brothers–Wilbury W9523 (UK release only 11/90)

New Blue Moon *(instrumental)*/Runaway

Note: Additional non-LP tracks on CD single of "She's My Baby."

('90) **Tour (continued)**—Canada, USA, and Europe—with G. E. Smith—G, Tony Garnier—B, Christopher Parker—D. (For acoustic set, Garnier played stand-up bass and Parker played drums with brushes)

MAY
29 Montreal, Quebec: Sportif Centre, Université de Montréal
30 Kingston, Ontario: Kingston Memorial Centre

JUNE
1 Ottawa, Ontario: National Arts Centre

Note: Charlie Rock Show immediately following 6/1/90.

2 Ottawa, Ontario: National Arts Centre
4 London, Ontario: Alumni Hall
5 Toronto, Ontario: O'Keefe Centre
6 Toronto, Ontario: O'Keefe Centre
7 Toronto, Ontario: O'Keefe Centre
9 East Troy, Wisconsin: Alpine Valley
10 Davenport, Iowa: Adler Theater
12 La Crosse, Wisconsin: Civic Center
13 Sioux Falls, South Dakota: Arena
14 Fargo, North Dakota: Memorial Auditorium
15 Bismark, North Dakota: Civic Center
17 Winnipeg, Manitoba: Manitoba Centennial Centre
18 Winnipeg, Manitoba: Manitoba Centennial Centre
27 Reykjavik, Iceland: Laugardalsholl
29 Roskilde, Denmark: Orange Stage, Roskilde Festival
30 Kalvola, Norway: Kalvola Festival

JULY
1 Turku, Finland: Ruissulo Camping, Åbo Festival
3 Hamburg, West Germany: Stadtpark
5 West Berlin, West Germany: International Congress Centrum
7 Tourhout, Belgium: Tourhout Festival
8 Werchter, Belgium: Werchter Festival
9 Montreux, Switzerland: Casino de Montreux

Note: G. E. Smith remained on the tour at this point but was not on stage for every song. New guitarists were auditioned live. They were John Stahaley (8/12/15), Steve Bruton (8/19–29), Miles Joseph (8/31–9/4), Steve Ripley (9/5–9), Cesar Diaz (9/11–12).

AUG
12 Edmonton, Manitoba: Jubilee Auditorium
13 Edmonton, Manitoba: Jubilee Auditorium
15 Calgary, Alberta: Jubilee Auditorium
16 Calgary, Alberta: Jubilee Auditorium
18 George, Washington: Champs de Brionne
19 Victoria, British Columbia: Memorial Arena
20 Vancouver, British Columbia: Coliseum
21 Portland, Oregon: Schnitzer Hall
24 Pueblo, Colorado: State Fair Grounds
26 Des Moines, Iowa: State Fair Grounds
27 Merrillville, Indiana: Holiday Star
28 Merrillville, Indiana: Holiday Star
29 St. Paul, Minnesota: State Fair Grounds
31 Lincoln, Nebraska: Bob Devaney Sports Center

SEP
1 Lampe, Missouri: Swiss Villa
2 Hannibal, Missouri: Riverfront Amphitheatre
4 Tulsa, Oklahoma: Riverpark Amphitheatre
(*) 5 Oklahoma City, Oklahoma: Civic Center
6 Dallas, Texas: Fairpark Music Hall
8 San Antonio, Texas: Sunken Garden Theatre

9 Austin, Texas: Palmer Auditorium
11 Santa Fe, New Mexico: Pablo Soleri Amphitheatre
12 Mesa, Arizona: Mesa Amphitheatre
Note: G. E. Smith remained on the tour through 10/18/90. Cesar Diaz remained on guitar; Steve Bruton played mandolin on the acoustic songs 10/11/90, and guitar on the acoustic encore 10/12/90; John Stahaley rejoined the tour on guitar beginning 10/15/90.

OCT
11 Brookville, New York: C. W. Post College, Tilles Center
12 Springfield, Massachusetts: Paramount Theatre
13 West Point, New York: Eisenhower Hall Theatre
15 New York, New York: Beacon Theatre
16 New York, New York: Beacon Theatre
17 New York, New York: Beacon Theatre
18 New York, New York: Beacon Theatre
19 New York, New York: Beacon Theatre
21 Richmond, Virginia: Mosque Theatre
22 Pittsburgh, Pennsylvania: Syria Mosque
23 Charleston, West Virginia: Municipal Auditorium
25 Oxford, Massachusetts: Tad Smith Coliseum
26 Tuscaloosa, Alabama: University of Alabama
27 Nashville, Tennessee: Vanderbilt University
28 Athens, Georgia: Coliseum, University of Georgia
30 Boone, North Carolina: Appalachian State College
31 Charlotte, North Carolina: Ovens Auditorium

NOV
2 Lexington, Kentucky: University of Kentucky
3 Carbondale, Illinois: S.I.U. Arena
4 St. Louis, Missouri: The Fox
6 De Kalb, Illinois: Chick Evans Fieldhouse
8 Iowa City, Iowa: Carver Hawkeye Arena
9 Chicago, Illinois: Chicago Theatre
10 Milwaukee, Wisconsin: Riverside Theatre
12 East Lansing, Michigan: Michigan State University
13 Dayton, Ohio: University of Dayton Arena
14 Normal, Illinois: Braden Auditorium
16 Columbus, Ohio: Palace Theatre
17 Cleveland, Ohio: Music Hall
18 Detroit, Michigan: Fox Theatre

('91) **Tour**—Europe and USA—with Johnny Jackson—G, Cesar Diaz—G, Tony Garnier—B, Ian Wallace—D

JAN
28 Zurich, Switzerland: Hallenstadion
30 Brussels, Belgium: Forest National
31 Utrecht, Holland: Vreden Muziek Center

FEB
2 Glasgow, Scotland: SECC
3 Glasgow, Scotland: SECC
5 Dublin, Ireland: The Point Depot
6 Belfast, Ireland: Dundonald Ice Bowl
8 London, England: Hammersmith Odeon
9 London, England: Hammersmith Odeon
10 London, England: Hammersmith Odeon
12 London, England: Hammersmith Odeon
13 London, England: Hammersmith Odeon
15 London, England: Hammersmith Odeon
16 London, England: Hammersmith Odeon

(2/20/91) New York, New York—Radio City Music Hall, 33rd
(V) Annual Grammy Awards, broadcast live over WCBS-TV Network; presentation by Jack Nicholson of Lifetime Achievement Award and acceptance; musicians same band as 1991 tour

Masters of War

('91) Tour (continued)—USA and Mexico

21 Williamsport, Pennsylvania: Capitol Theatre
22 Owings Mills, Maryland: Painter's Mill Theatre
FEB (*) 25 Guadalajara, Mexico: Institudo de Cultural Cabaña
(*) 27 Guadalajara, Mexico: Institudo de Cultural Cabaña
MAR (*) 1 Mexico City: Palacio de Sports
(*) 2 Mexico City: Palacio de Sports

(3/91) *The Bootleg Series—Volumes I, II, and III*—Columbia 47382 (released 3/91)

Hard Times in NY Town/He Was a Friend of Mine/Man on the Street/No More Auction Block/House Carpenter/Talkin' Bear Mountain Picnic Blues/Let Me Die in My Footsteps/Ramblin' Gamblin' Willie/Talkin' Hava Negeilah Blues/Quit Your Low Down Ways/Worried Blues/Kingsport Town/Walkin' Down the Line/Walls of Red Wing/Paths of Victory/Talkin' John Birch Paranoid Blues/Who Killed Davey Moore?/Only a Hobo/Moonshine/When the Ship Comes In/The Times They Are A-Changin'/Last Thoughts on Woody Guthrie/Seven Curses/Eternal Circle/Suze (The Cough Song)/Mama, You've Been on My Mind/Farewell, Angelina/Subterranean Homesick Blues/If You Gotta Go, Go Now/Sitting on a Barbed Wire Fence/Like a Rolling Stone/It Takes a Lot to Laugh/I'll Keep It with Mine/She's Your Lover Now/I Shall Be Released/Santa Fe/If Not for You/Wallflower/Nobody 'Cept You/Tangled Up in Blue/Call Letter Blues/Idiot Wind/If You See Her, Say Hello/Golden Loom/Catfish/Seven Days/Ye Shall Be Changed/Every Grain of Sand/You Changed My Life/Need a Woman/Angelina/Someone's Got Ahold of My Heart/Tell Me/Lord Protect My Child/Foot of Pride/Blind Willie McTell/When the Night Comes Falling from the Sky/Series of Dreams

Note: All tracks were previously unreleased.

(V) SONG VIDEO—"Series of Dreams," released 3/91 as promotion for *The Bootleg Series, Vols. I, II, and III*

Index